The

PRACTICAL COGITATOR

The
PRACTICAL
COGITATOR

The Thinker's Anthology

Selected and Edited by
CHARLES P. CURTIS, JR.
FERRIS GREENSLET

Third Edition · Revised and Enlarged
With an Introduction by John H. Finley, Jr.

Decorations by
Edwin Earle

Houghton Mifflin Company Boston

Library of Congress Catalog Card Number: 62-11481

ISBN 0-395-34635-5 pbk.

Printed in the United States of America

Q 10 9 8 7 6 5

For the use of selections from copyrighted material, the editors are indebted to the following publishers and copyright proprietors:

APPLETON-CENTURY-CROFTS, INC.: *Abraham Lincoln*, Herndon and Week. *Life and Letters of Thomas H. Huxley*, Leonard Huxley.

ATLANTIC MONTHLY: "The American Loneliness," Thornton Wilder (by special permission of the author). "Toward an American Language," Thornton Wilder (by special permission of the author).

BASIL BLACKWELL AND MOTT, LTD.: *History in a Changing World*, Geoffrey Barraclough; copyright by Basil Blackwell, Great Britain; courtesy of the American publishers, University of Oklahoma Press.

BEACON PRESS: *The New Society*, Edward Carr.

BRYN MAWR COLLEGE: *Commencement Address, June 2, 1927*, Judge Learned Hand.

CAMBRIDGE UNIVERSITY PRESS: *The Sources of Eddington's Philosophy* (Eighth Arthur Stanley Eddington Memorial Lecture), Herbert Dingle.

CHATTO AND WINDUS, LTD.: *The Seventeenth Century Background*, Basil Willey; published jointly with Columbia University Press.

CLARENDON PRESS, THE: *Making, Knowing and Judging*, W. H. Auden.

COLUMBIA UNIVERSITY PRESS: *The World of the Four Freedoms*, Sumner Welles.

DODD, MEAD AND COMPANY: *Heretics*, G. K. Chesterton.

DOUBLEDAY AND COMPANY, INC.: *Man, the Social Creator*, Henry Demarest Lloyd. *Religion and Freedom of Thought*, Perry Miller, Robert L. Calhoun, Nathan M. Pusey and Reinhold Niebuhr; copyright 1954 by Union Theological Seminary; reprinted by permission of Doubleday and Company, Inc. *The New Freedom*, Woodrow Wilson.

DUTTON, E. P., AND COMPANY, INC.: *Memories of My Life*, Francis Galton. *Cobb of "The World": A Leader in Liberalism*, John L. Heaton. *The Grammar of Science*, Karl Pearson. *First the Blade*, Candace Thurber Stevenson; copyright 1952 by E. P. Dutton and Company, Inc.; reprinted by permission of the publisher.

FABER AND FABER, LTD.: *Selected Poems of Marianne Moore* with Introduction by T. S. Eliot.

FARRAR, STRAUS AND CUDAHY, INC.: *A Piece of My Mind*, Edmund Wilson.

FAWCETT, FREDERICK J.: *Selected Poems* of William Vaughn Moody, Robert Morse Lovett, ed.

FORTUNE MAGAZINE: October 1941: "Where Do We Go From Here?", Geoffrey Crowther; courtesy of Fortune Magazine. June 1955: "Can We Survive Technology," John von Neumann; courtesy of Fortune Magazine.

GEORGE ALLEN AND UNWIN, LTD.: *Human Society in Ethics and Politics*, Bertrand Russell; courtesy also of Simon and Schuster, Inc.

HARCOURT, BRACE AND WORLD, INC.: *The Just and the Unjust*, James Gould Cozzens. *The Last Adam*, James Gould Cozzens. *95 Poems*, E. E. Cummings; © 1958 by E. E. Cummings; reprinted by permission of Harcourt, Brace & World, Inc. *Four Quartets*, T. S. Eliot; copyright 1943 by T. S. Eliot; reprinted by permission of Harcourt, Brace and World, Inc. *Collected Legal Papers*, Oliver Wendell Holmes. *The General Theory of Employment Interest and Money*, John Maynard Keynes. *Religion and the Rise of Capitalism*, R. H. Tawney. *The Art of Thought*, Graham Welles.

HARPER AND ROW: *Texts and Pretexts*, Aldous Huxley. *T.V.A.: Democracy on the March*, David Lilienthal. *An International Economy*, Gunnar Myrdal. *The Mind in the Making*, James Harvey Robinson. *Lord Juggler*, Roberta Swartz. *One Man's Meat*, E. B. White. *The Fox of Peapack*, E. B. White. *The Ides of March*, Thornton Wilder (by special permission of the author).

HARVARD BUSINESS REVIEW: November 1951: "Basic Elements of a Free, Dynamic Society—Part I," Paul G. Hoffman, Chester I. Barnard, Erwin D. Canham, Russell W. Davenport, Peter F. Drucker, Lewis Galantiere, Harry D. Gideonse, Frank Tannenbaum, Walter H. Wheeler, Jr.

HARVARD UNIVERSITY PRESS: *Totalitarianism*, Carl J. Friedrich, ed. *Holmes-Pollock Letters*, Col. Mark Howe, ed. *Conflicts of Principle*, A. Lawrence Lowell. *The Care of the Patient*, Francis W. Peabody. *Collected Papers*, Charles Sanders Peirce. *History of Science*, George Sarton. *Poétique Musicale*, Igor Stravinski. *Leadership in a Free Society*, T. N. Whitehead.

HENDERSON, LAWRENCE J.: *Lectures in Sociology, the Study of Man*, Paper in *Transactions of the Association of American Physicians, 1936*, Lawrence Henderson.

HOLT, RINEHART AND WINSTON, INC.: *1 x 1*, copyright 1944 by E. E. Cummings. *The Complete Poems of Robert Frost*; "A Masque of Reason"; copyright 1945 by Holt, Rinehart and Winston, Inc.; reprinted by permission of Holt, Rinehart and Winston, Inc.; courtesy also of Jonathan Cape, Ltd. *Fire and Ice*, Robert Frost. *Psychology*, William James. *Talks to Teachers*, William James.

HORIZON PRESS, INC.: *Essays in Biography*, John Maynard Keynes; reprinted by permission of the Publisher, Horizon Press, Inc.

HOUGHTON MIFFLIN COMPANY: *The Education of Henry Adams*, Henry Adams. *Mont-Saint-Michel*, Henry Adams. *Youth and Life*, Randolph S. Bourne. *The Works of Thoreau*, Henry Seidel Canby, ed. *John Jay Chapman and His Letters*, John Jay Chapman (M. A. DeWolfe Howe, ed.). *The Easy Chair*, Bernard DeVoto. *The Big Money*, John Dos Passos. *The Dance of Life*, Havelock Ellis. *Greek Imperialism*, William S. Ferguson. *A History of Europe*, H. A. L. Fisher. *The Corsican*, R. M. Johnston, ed. *The Autobiography of Montaigne*, Marvin Lowenthal. *The Road to Xanadu*, John L. Lowes. *A Time to Act*, A. MacLeish. *The Endless Adventure*, F. S. Oliver. *Youth's Companion Anthology*, Lovell Thompson. *The Human Use of Human Beings: Cybernetics and Society*, Norbert Wiener.

HOWE, COL. MARK: Unpublished letter of Oliver Wendell Holmes, Jr.

KNOPF, ALFRED A., INC.: *A History of Medicine*, Arturo Castiglioni, M.D. *The Spirit of Liberty*, Judge Learned Hand; reprinted by permission of Alfred A. Knopf, Inc.; copyright 1952 by Alfred A. Knopf, Inc. *The Decline of the West*, Oswald Spengler.

LAWRENCE COLLEGE: *Commencement Address, May 24, 1942*, Lloyd Garrison.

LISTENER, THE, (B.B.C.): August 16, 1956, George C. Homans; reprinted with permission of the publisher from *Sentiments and Activities* by George C. Homans; copyright © 1962 by The Free Press of Glencoe, a division of The Macmillan Company.

LITTLE, BROWN AND COMPANY: *Minority Report*, Bernard DeVoto. *The Poems of Emily Dickinson*. *Letters*, William James. *The Good Society*, Walter Lippman. *Jesuits in America*, Francis Parkman. *As I Remember Him*, Hans Zinnser. *Rats, Lice and History*, Hans Zinnser.

LONGMANS, GREEN AND COMPANY, INC.: *Foundations of Belief*, A. J. Balfour. *The Meaning of Truth*, William James. *Memories and Studies*, William James. *Philosophy of William James*, William James. *The Will to Believe*, William James. *History of England*, G. M. Trevelyan.

MACMILLAN COMPANY, THE: *The Study of History*, Lord Acton. *The Degradation of the Democratic Dogma*, Henry Adams. *The Logic of Modern Physics*, P. W. Bridgman. *Nature and Sources of the Law*, John C. Gray. *Epilegomena to the Study of Greek Religion*, J. E. Harrison. *W. B. Yeats*, Joseph Howes. *The Method of Freedom*, Walter Lippmann. *Preface to Morals*, Walter Lippman. *What a University President Has Learned*, A. Lawrence Lowell. "Poetry," Marianne Moore; reprinted with the permission of The Macmillan Company from *Collected Poems*; copyright 1935 by Marianne Moore. *The University and the Modern World*, S. Nash. *Time the Refreshing River*, Joseph Needham. *Confessio Medici*, Stephen Paget. *The Tragic Sense of Life*,

Miguel de Unamuno. *The Great Society*, Graham Wallas. *The Changing West*, William Allen White. *Adventures of Ideas*, A. N. Whitehead. *Science and the Modern World*, A. N. Whitehead. *Symbolism*, A. N. Whitehead. *Philosophical Investigations*, Ludwig Wittgenstein; courtesy also of Basil Blackwell and Mott, Ltd. "All Things Can Tempt Me," W. B. Yeats; reprinted with the permission of the publisher from *Collected Poems*; copyright 1912 by The Macmillan Company, copyright 1940 by Bertha Georgie Yeats. "Two Songs from a Play," by W. B. Yeats; reprinted with the permission of the publisher from *Collected Poems*; copyright 1928 by The Macmillan Company, copyright 1956 by Bertha Georgie Yeats. "Under Ben Bulben," W. B. Yeats; reprinted with the permission of The Macmillan Company from *Collected Poems*; copyright 1940 by Bertha Georgie Yeats.

MASSACHUSETTS BAR ASSOCIATION: *Proceedings of 250th Birthday of the Supreme Judicial Court of Massachusetts, November 1942*, address by Judge Learned Hand.

METHUEN AND COMPANY: *Existentialism and Humanism*, Jean-Paul Sartre (Philip Mairet, trans.); courtesy also of Les Editions Nagel, Paris.

NEW ENGLAND MUSEUM OF NATURAL HISTORY BULLETIN: April, 1931: *What Is Natural History?* W. M. Wheeler.

NORTON, W. W., AND COMPANY, INC.: *Experience and Nature*, John Dewey. *The Skeptical Biologist*, Joseph Needham. *Duino Elegies*, Rainer Maria Rilke. *Where Did You Go? Out. What Did You Do? Nothing.*, by Robert Paul Smith; copyirght © 1957 by Robert Paul Smith.

OPPENHEIMER, ROBERT J.: *The Open Mind*; all rights reserved; © 1955 by J. Robert Oppenheimer; reprinted by permission of Simon and Schuster, Inc.

OVERBROOK PRESS, THE: *Address* (before the Elizabethan Club, May, 1941), Judge Learned Hand.

OXFORD UNIVERSITY PRESS: *Historical Inevitability*, Isaiah Berlin. *Life of Sir William Osler*, Harvey Cushing. *Oxford Book of Greek Verse in Translation*, T. F. Higham and C. M. Bowra. *The Integrity of Music*, Donald F. Tovey. *A Musician Talks*, Donald F. Tovey. *An Historian's Approach to Religion*, Arnold J. Toynbee. *A Study of History*, Arnold J. Toynbee.

PANTHEON BOOKS, INC.: *Zen in the Art of Archery*, Eugen Herrigel; reprinted by permission of Pantheon Books; copyright 1953 by Pantheon Books, Inc.

PARTISAN REVIEW: "Religion and the Intellectuals," Paul Tillich; reprinted by permission of Partisan Review.

PRICE, LUCIEN: *The Will to Create*.

PUTNAM'S, G. P., SONS: *Law: Its Origin, Growth, and Function*, James C. Carter.

RANDOM HOUSE, INC.: *Storm*, George Stewart. *The Wisdom of China and India*, Lin Yutang.

READER'S DIGEST, THE: Quotations from Charles Beard.

REPORTER MAGAZINE COMPANY, THE: "Mr. Myrdal Brings Utilitarianism Up to Date," Walt and Elspeth Rostow; © 1956 by The Reporter Magazine Company.

SATURDAY REVIEW: February 1, 1958: "Money Is Not Enough," Claude M. Fuess.

SCIENTIFIC AMERICAN: September, 1950: "The Age of Science: 1900–1950," Robert Oppenheimer.

SCRIBNER'S, CHARLES, SONS: *Character and Opinion in the United States*, George Santayana. *Theory of Business Enterprise*, Thorstein Veblen. *English Composition*, Barrett Wendell.

TILLICH, PAUL: *Man's Right to Knowledge*.

TIMES PUBLISHING COMPANY, THE, LTD.: "Freedom of the Shelves," by Rebecca West. © The Times Publishing Company Limited, 1958; all rights reserved; reprinted by permission from *The Times Literary Supplement* of August 15, 1958. "The Shakespeare Paradox: Universal Stage of the Man from Stratford," John Dover Wilson; © The Times Publishing Company Limited, 1957; all rights reserved; reprinted by permission from *The Times Literary Supplement* of September 2, 1957.

UNIVERSITY OF CHICAGO PRESS: *The Astonished Muse*, Reuel Denney; copyright 1957 by the University of Chicago. *Medical Care for the American People*, Walter H. Hamilton. *Speculative Instruments*, I. A. Richards; copyright 1955 by the University of Chicago; courtesy also of Routledge and Kegan Paul, Ltd.

VIKING PRESS, THE, INC.: *The Letters of Sacco and Vanzetti*, Marion Denman Frankfurter and Gardner Jackson, eds. *Like a Bulwark*, Marianne Moore.

WHEELOCK, JOHN HALL: T. S. Eliot as quoted by John Hall Wheelock; *The American Scholar*, 1957.

WHITE, E. B.: *The Wild Flag;* copyright 1946 by E. B. White, from an editorial first published in *The New Yorker*.

YALE UNIVERSITY PRESS: *The Heavenly City of Eighteenth Century Philosophers*, Carl L. Becker. *New Liberties From Old*, Carl L. Becker. *The Public and its Government*, Felix Frankfurter.

Publishers' Note

WHEN Charles Curtis began discussing this book in the offices of Houghton Mifflin Company, the nation was just beginning to feel the weight of its first peacetime draft. In the earlier war Curtis had commanded a destroyer on Atlantic convoy. He knew about the waiting, the boredom, and the stagnation of war, as well as about its dangers; and he had begun to think that though there was little one could do about the dangers, a lot might be done about the stagnation and the idle-mindedness. He suggested a book of quotations. It was to be a long book, printed in small type on thin paper, so that it might fit into the pocket of a soldier's tunic. This book was to be more than compact in format; it was to be highly concentrated in content as well. He wanted to select out of his enormous reading — he used to read Homer in the original Greek as a commuter's pastime — essential passages on the great themes of life. He already had a stout black notebook crammed with favorites. Here were paragraphs subtle and intricate in reasoning, boundless as it seemed in implication and application, often blindingly true and as often unrepentantly irritating. He wanted this book to have thought for a day, or a week, on every page. He wanted to edit an anthology that even a long war might not exhaust, that could seem new with every reading, with every new experience, with each enlargement of a man's mind and spirit.

To the publishers this looked like a big undertaking. It was, however, at once agreed that this was no book for a committee. It was a book to be dyed with the colors of one or two brilliant, penetrating, and restless minds. Though many suggestions were made by the editorial staff and though the search for appropriate passages became a sort of office game, not many were accepted by the compilers, who firmly, but not always politely, showed their would-be collaborators back to their desks.

The miraculous partnership between Charles Curtis and Ferris Greenslet that was the result of that first discussion in the publishers' office is described in the introduction to this edition of the work. However, the compilation *was* a large undertaking. You cannot pack the thought of the ages into one volume overnight. You cannot expect to provide thought for a decade in much less than a decade of thought. *The Practical Cogitator* was never read on the battlefields of Normandy or on the transports that carried men to Guadalcanal and Leyte. It was first published as the Battle of the Bulge began. It *was* read in Korea.

However, the remarkable thing about the book to the publishers, who were not used to making their publications as slow-reading as possible, was its immediate success with the general public. Some 30,000 copies were sold in the first season. For example, soon after publication a member of the editorial staff found himself in a bookstore in a small western town. While he waited for the attention of the clerk, a huge, roughly dressed man, carrying the gear of a prospector, entered the store. He was in a hurry and asked over the heads of others for a copy of *The Practical Cogitator*. As he strode to the dusty street, brandishing his purchase, he fixed one fellow customer with a stern though flashing eye and said, "Thar's GOLD in that book, GOLD." The editor unhesitatingly agreed.

Since publication in 1945 almost 100,000 copies of *The Practical Cogitator* have been distributed. On the publishers' list the book is ranked with the modern classics and with some of the great works on which it draws, for, in fact, it is hardly an anthology at all. So original was it in both idea and execution, so individual were the minds that constructed it, that though there is no original writing in the book the whole has an individuality of character and a noble singleness of purpose that separates it from its individual parts and makes it not so much greater as wholly different from them.

However, after the big bang on the White Sands Proving Ground, man was given a new problem; hitherto, the Sorcerer's Apprentice had never been armed with the power to destroy all thought for ever. The absoluteness of the destruction now within man's reach gave him not merely a bigger terror but an altogether different terror. He had dreamed and feared that God might destroy the world; he had not thought of doing it himself. In his heart he had trusted God as any child must trust even an avenging parent. He must believe that he will rise disciplined and purified from the ashes of punishment. Yet, though man may so trust his God and though he may be God's instrument, it does not follow that in his heart he equally trusts himself. After 1945 philosophy had a new dimension. The publishers asked the compilers not exactly to add to the *Cogitator,* though certainly not to subtract or eliminate; they asked them to survey again the whole world of thought with the mid-century view so different from all that had gone before. Even as late as the Thirties it was possible to hope that the First Great War would be the last. By this mid-century it seemed rather sure that the Second Great War would be at least the next to last.

The work was done. A new, stout, black notebook, in fact a bag of them, traveled in and out of the office. The old joyous argument began again, but the final processes of winnowing and ordering were not complete when death interfered.

Nothing has been added to the work of the compilers; nothing has been changed, but omissions have been made. What was left to the publishers was admittedly still too heavy a tome to fit into the "soldier's tunic." After they had completed their work, they asked John Finley, friend and son-in-law of one of the editors, friend and brother classicist of the other, to review what they had done and to add an introductory note on the nature of the book and on the partnership of its creators. To the publishers it now seems that the gift of miraculousness, which has always been a part of the *Cogitator,* has not departed. Without stretching his texts in any way Mr. Finley has used the compilers' own writings to describe their two natures and the friendship they shared — the alliance that is the little miracle of *The Practical Cogitator.*

Introduction to the Third Edition

PARTNERSHIP, though among the firmest facts of life, is among the most mysterious because beyond ordinary calculation. The phoebe who nests on your back porch does not ask your permission, nor had you built the ledge over the window for her benefit. She arrives, and you like the house and the spring better for her company. Or, on a mightier plane, "How did the close alliance between Churchill and the Prof. come about?" asks Sir Roy Harrod [1] in his memoir of F. A. Lindemann, who was to become Lord Cherwell.

> In later days it was taken for granted as a long-established fact and sustained by Churchill's loyalty to his old familiar friend. But it must have had a beginning. Why had the friendship started in the first instance? I would suggest that it can only be that Churchill, and F. E. Smith along with him, spotted in the Prof. a brain of original and outstanding quality. F. E. and Churchill were already in the front rank of politics during the 'twenties. They had met, or had opportunities for meeting, all the distinguished people. One new professor, one new scientist, even one new scientist alleged to be of exceptional promise, could in itself mean nothing to them. The Prof. at that time was already beginning to be something of a social luminary. But there was nothing in that for them; on the whole they only met social luminaries . . . One can hardly escape the conclusion that what these two men, severally and together, saw in him can only have been his innate quality of mind. That is not to be measured simply by the position that he had then obtained in his own university, or in his own subject of physics . . . It was something in the quality of his mind that made anything he had to say worth listening to, on the kind of topics that they themselves were interested in talking over.

[1] R. F. Harrod, *The Prof.* (London: Macmillan, 1959), pp. 8–15.

Harrod goes on to describe Lord Cherwell's comparative obtuseness to important sides of Churchill: his humor, his oratory, the dramatic side of his leadership. Then, after the highest estimate of Churchill's intellectual gifts and after placing him above Gladstone in grasp of detail and above Burke in political theory, he concludes:

> Thus I believe that the long intimacy of Churchill and the Prof. rested on the firm basis of an appreciation by each of the intellectual qualities of the other. No doubt there are also factors of temperament, which govern the possibilities of friendship. Intellectual affinity is important if the friendship is to be durable.

The partnership of Charles Curtis and Ferris Greenslet in the present book was of this unforeseen and initially improbable kind. As a Boston lawyer, Curtis had Houghton Mifflin Company among his clients; Greenslet was the literary editor of Houghton Mifflin. They were cast together and, being readers and given to remembering and talking about what they read, presumably at first discovered simply the pleasure of like-mindedness. Aristotle defined pleasure as a joyous tone accompanying right function, but this tone does not simply accompany; it can also guide and beckon. It is a blandishment of nature, like that of a dog who dances ahead looking back over his shoulder when he wants you to take a walk. The two men's separate reading unpremeditatedly converged through conversation toward partnership.

Curtis took the first step. Since he joined his reading to a vivid mind and both to the habit of making excerpts, he had acquired a collection of passages, which he brought to Greenslet for criticism and enlargement. Then appeared the other side of collaboration, which is a matter not merely of like-mindedness but of different-mindedness. If Pope's maxim "compose with fury but correct with phlegm" did not fully apply to the two partners, since each had his enthusiasms, it applied nevertheless. Curtis was the out-reacher, the man of leaping recognition and response; Greenslet had a mind as wide but cooler, was the appraiser of finish, the admirer of phrase. Both respected the world, in the sense that they sought enlivening company in the present and past and had regard for men who had left a mark; neither was philosophical, in the sense of preferring ideas as such, divorced from men. But their path toward mature judgment had been different: Curtis's from a patrician at-homeness in institutions and sense of responsibility for them which, by his sheer intellectual momentum, carried him beyond any given institution to its greater function and setting; Greenslet's from a youthful enchantment with nature and literature (he once wrote on the Grail legend and on Pater) which verged in his maturity toward connoisseurship. The one was of the mold of Bacon or Hand, the other of Saintsbury or Berenson. Add to Curtis's sense of institutions his sparkling sympathies; add to Greenslet's wide taste his native deftness; add to both their love of the play and color of the world; and you have predestined, if unforeseeing, collaborators.

A famous speech of the *Iliad,* spoken to Helen and Priam as they look out over the battlefield from the Trojan wall, describes Menelaus and Odysseus, and if the lines hardly apply to Greenslet as Menelaus, they fit Curtis as Odysseus.

> Years ago brilliant Odysseus came here with warlike Menelaus on an errand about you. I lodged and entertained them in my house and learned their cast of nature and firm thoughts. When they met among the gathered Trojans and the two stood, Menelaus was shoulders taller, but Odysseus was the finer when they sat. Now when they began to spin their words and thoughts before all, Menelaus spoke fluently, not at length but very clearly. He was not given to long or random talk and was, besides, the younger. But when Odysseus, that man of many ideas, leapt up, he would first wait staring at the ground; he moved his staff neither back nor forward but held it stiff, like an idiot. You would have thought him irritated or vacuous. But then as the great voice came from his chest and words like the snows of winter, no living mortal could vie with Odysseus. We forgot our surprise at our first sight of him.

One may half disregard, in thinking of Curtis, the lines on Odysseus' silence as he gathered thoughts (he was evidently a sure-footed man), though even here there is something of Curtis, who paused and slightly stumbled over words as he gathered flight or would pound his leg and make favoring ejaculations as another was ending and he about to begin. But his physical type was that of Odysseus: the square build, the strong chest, the fine voice, the noble head, and (Homer might have added) the short arms, the blunt, expressive fingers, the alert stance. This was a man born to command, by act and idea. Such coalescence of the mind and character in action seemed to him in fact the final spring of a man's effectiveness.

> Your best is done as a matter of course [he wrote in *It's Your Law*], when you scarcely know that you are exerting yourself, when you are least conscious of the effort . . . This, I think, is the explanation of Holmes's paradox that only by our best efforts do we attain the inevitable. Our efforts pile up so high a head behind what we are doing that it becomes inevitable that we should do it . . . I suggest that what I am trying to say is the cooperation of the whole of you, and that the efficacy of what I have called the matter of course, resides in the fact that the whole of you is bent to the task . . . When a man is fully conscious of what he is doing, there is too little of him left to do it. You can put the whole of yourself to work only when part of you is not watching you.

The law, as meeting ground of act and idea, of shaping past and emergent present, marvelously suited him. Its active side first immersed him, in his practice, as the youngest Fellow of Harvard College, as author of the Massachusetts Fair Employment Act, but his *Introduction to Pareto* and lively part in the founding of the Society of Fellows at Harvard showed the temper of his action. He turned with time to the less immediate — in his *Lions under the Throne* (on the Supreme Court), *It's Your Law,* and *Law as Large as Life* (on Natural Law) — though the living breath of institutions was in these books too, and he returned intensely to the present in his *The Oppenheimer Case.* It was characteristic of him to write relatively briefly on many subjects rather than at length on a few; he resembled a wood fire, not a coal fire. There was something of the meteor about him; he animated and illuminated the slow starlike movements of history, of which he was himself at the same time a glowing part. "When he [the advocate] goes to interview a witness as well as when he goes to the law library, he goes to get something. He will waste a lot of time if he goes with an open mind." Only the totally fair-minded, the totally engaged, man could say just that. It is corollary to the further statement, "It is not that you do not make an effort, but most of the effort is long past. You have been making it for a long time now. Almost, what you are doing now as a matter of course, you find it impossible not to do." Are these the words of an active or of an intellectual man? Of a man, in any case, in his greatest and most engaged years.

Greenslet had been the precocious child, a reader from before he could remember, but conversant with the country near his native Lake George almost as early as with books; then the young literary man at Columbia, contributor to the *Nation,* and presently assistant editor of the *Atlantic;* then, with a certain wrench, the fosterer at Houghton Mifflin of other men's work (he persuaded Henry Adams to publish the *Autobiography*) rather than the creator of his own; was often, meanwhile, in England, fishing when he was not reading or encouraging authors; through all this time kept augmenting the detailed store of biographical and historical knowledge (astonishing in a busy man) that early showed in his *Joseph Glanville* and *James Russell Lowell,* later and most variously in his *The Lowells and their Seven Worlds.* Then emerged the remembered Greenslet. What he said in his autobiography, *Under the Bridge,* of Montaigne described himself:

> In whatever language I read him, he seems the perfect pattern of the reasonable man: as full of respect for others as for himself, with humility as well as pride of intellect, gay in manner, serious of heart, yet never forgetful of duty. He took for his guide, as he says, "the ways of the world and the experience of the senses."

Add another passage, on England.

> I see her from the sea almost in the round: her busy ports, Liverpool, Bristol, Fishguard, Falmouth, Plymouth, Southampton, Portsmouth, Newhaven, Folkestone, Dover, Tilbury . . . I see the hills tramped over under misty suns and unwetting rains, Exmoor, Dartmoor, the Cotswolds, the Downs, the Moors of Yorkshire . . . I walk the murky streets of London and Edinburgh, the gardens and lawns of Oxford and Cambridge, the crescents and quadrants of Bath . . . I found them a friendly, free-spoken race, with no nonsense about them, recalling Montesquieu's affirmation, "No people have true common sense but those who are born in England." They wore comfortable clothes. It has been said that the Frenchman invented the ruffle, the Englishman invented the shirt. If, through their history, they have never known when they were beaten, neither have they seemed to me, however blue their noses, to know when they were cold . . . What other dictionary of national biography is so rich in varied talent, or, from a thousand years of history and thirty thousand names from Abbadie to Zuylestein, brings together so many men one would like to have known?

Fond as he was of England, one need not overstate his feeling; what is more notable in this passage is his accuracy. He remembered people, places, landscapes, and streams as he remembered books and lines of verse, detailedly. He liked, so to speak, the exact sunlight and clear ripples and pools of life; but though he saw the mystery of the pools, he preferred not to dwell on it, rather to fix his mind on the well-cast line that lured from the shadowy underwater. Is exactitude a form of bravery, a stance of mind that shuns the impenetrable in favor of the word and act so right as to hint at the impenetrable while skirting it? He had a completeness of attention analogous to Curtis's, different as their worlds were.

One returns then to the mystery of collaboration, which may be even stranger than the mystery of excellence. In achieving something excellent, a man is with his own thoughts, wresting shape out of half-disorder (like the phoebe nesting on the porch); in collaboration, two minds cross, each initially private and asking generosity if they are to come together. The result, when successful, is moving and curiously reassuring; it suggests the difference between Odysseus and the Ancient Mariner, the difference between getting back and not quite getting back from private voyages.

JOHN H. FINLEY, JR.

Preface to the First Edition
(1945)

To BEGIN WITH, this anthology is for the thinker, and not for the feeler, primarily for the extrovert thinker. Needless to say, it runs over into some of his introverted and intuitive margins.

The editors laid down certain rules:

Nothing that is probably already too familiar or too accessible.

Nothing purely inspirational, nothing sentimental. And yet nothing cynical. Nobility of thought keeps on the crown of the road, out of the gutters.

Nothing that is not worth re-reading. Some things that can be chewed over almost indefinitely. Pieces that are tough enough, juicy enough to chew. Some that are scarcely worth reading only once.

As between the ancient and the modern, the modern. When we have used the ancient, it is because we know of nothing better since.

The form in which the piece is written to make no odds. Treatise, textbook, letter, novel, speech, verse, anything is given equal welcome. As to verse, none for its own sake, none simply because it was beautiful. Verse has been treated simply as another, more elegant, more memorable, form of speech.

C. P. C., Jr., is responsible for most of the translations. Some of them are faithful after their own fashion. If apologies are due, they are here tendered, to the author.

For reasons of space, no more of the context than necessary. Not even enough. Worse than that, some things are cut without warning.

There is no attempt at complete exposition. The extracts provide pegs, stout and well driven in, on which you can hang your own further thoughts.

These pegs for further thought have been put more or less into line. The juxtapositions are deliberate, not to say, as we believe, sometimes artful. If you will read the pieces in order, so much the better, but random reading is never really wrong. Not that the sequence is always logical. Sometimes the sequence is a bit puzzling. Sometimes, we like to think, apocalyptic.

We have tried to build a dry wall. If the reader finds that one of the stones has fallen out into the field, let him only take care not to stumble over it. The only cement is a few comments, from which the editors, looking over the reader's shoulder, could not refrain.

The book is broken up into sections. They have been arranged in this way:

> Man in Search of Himself
> He Solicits His Past
> He Turns to Nature
> And Scrutinizes Her
> And Himself
> He Lives with His Fellows
> They Better Their Condition
> They Must Have Peace, Security, and Liberty
> And Justice
> He Seeks Solace and Beauty
> And Friendship and Love
> And Even Something More
> He Takes Better Aim

This anthology has been set on the firm basis of personal choice. Many good things have been omitted, from prejudice and from ignorance, but sometimes the editors can plead lack of space. They will be disappointed if they do not get reproaches for omissions as well as suggestions of substitutions.

Does any reader suggest that we have drawn too heavily on some few, Holmes, James, Whitehead, etc.? It is not for us to act as if talent were spread more evenly than it is. It is not for us to be more egalitarian than the uneven bounty of nature. And time has not yet done sorting out the moderns. So we have had to do it, unless you'd sooner we had played safe by scattering.

This book has been called, after Bowditch's *Practical Navigator,* "The Practical Cogitator." At any rate, it should be a sort of cerebral Coast Pilot, a compilation of what those who have been down this way before report to those who might otherwise have to pick their course through these channels and into these harbors with nothing but the lead line.

And with that the editors make their bows, to the readers and then, each to the other.

C. P. C., Jr.
F. G.

> Ferris, this fumbling through other minds
> Has made me thirsty. Tell me where one finds
> A place where you and I can sit,
> And slake the dust of other peoples' wit.
>
> Charlie, I know a tavern not too distant
> Where we can sit and talk o'er wine consistent
> With our own thoughts; and while we're drinking
> We will atone for all vicarious thinking.

Preface to the Second Edition
(1950)

IN RESPONSE to numerous inquiries and requests, the editors have added to the present printing a section of references to sources. And the editors also yielded to the lure of making some comments and of adding a few more quotations.

Contents

MAN IN SEARCH OF HIMSELF

*Man Thinking; him Nature solicits
with all her placid, all her monitory
pictures; him the past instructs; him
the future invites. Is not indeed every
man a student, and do not all things
exist for the student's behoof? And,
finally, is not the true scholar the only
true master? But the old oracle said,
"All things have two handles: beware
of the wrong one."*

EMERSON

O. W. HOLMES, JR. 1841–1935

Any two philosophers can tell each other all they know in two hours.

JOHN ADAMS TO THOMAS JEFFERSON 1812

I am weary of contemplating nations from the lowest and most beastly degradations of human life to the highest refinement of civilization. I am weary of philosophers, theologians, politicians, and historians. They are immense masses of absurdities, vices, and lies. Montesquieu had sense enough to say, in jest, that all our knowledge might be comprehended in twelve pages in duodecimo; and I believe him in earnest. I could express my faith in shorter terms. He who loves the workman and his work, and does what he can to preserve and improve it, shall be accepted of him.

JEAN DE LA BRUYÈRE 1645–1696

Where a book raises your spirit, and inspires you with noble and courageous feelings, seek for no other rule to judge the event by; it is good and made by a good workman.

GOETHE 1749–1832

Man lernt nichts kennen als was man liebt.
A man doesn't learn to understand anything unless he loves it.

THOREAU 1817–1862

The only way to speak the truth is to speak lovingly.

O. W. HOLMES, JR., TO POLLOCK 1920

I dare say that I have worked off my fundamental formula on you that the chief end of man is to frame general propositions and that no general proposition is worth a damn.

Am I?

UNAMUNO 1864–1936

The defect of Descartes' Discourse on Method lies in his resolution to begin by emptying himself of himself, of Descartes, of the real man, the man of flesh and bone, the man who does not want to die, in order that he might be a mere thinker — that is, an abstraction. But the real man returned and thrust himself into his philosophy.

Cogito ergo sum . . . but the *ego* implicit in this enthymeme, *ego cogito, ergo ego sum,* is an unreal — that is, an ideal — *ego* or I, and its *sum,* its existence, something unreal also. "I think, therefore I am," can only mean "I think, therefore I am a thinker." This being of the "I am," which is deduced from "I think," is merely a knowing. This being is knowledge, but not life. And the primary reality is not what I think, but what I live, for those also live who do not think. Although this living may not be a real living. God! What contradictions when we seek to join in wedlock life and reason!

The truth is *sum, ergo cogito* — I am, therefore I think, although not everything that is thinks. Is not conscious thinking above all consciousness of being? Is pure thought possible, without consciousness of self, without personality? Can there exist pure knowledge without feeling, without that species of materiality which feeling lends to it? Do we not perhaps feel thought, and do we not feel ourselves in the act of knowing and willing?

This passage from Unamuno is marked in Hans Zinsser's copy of *The Tragic Sense of Life*.

Am I Thinking?

JAMES HARVEY ROBINSON   1863–1936

The truest and most profound observations on Intelligence have in the past been made by the poets and, in recent times, by story-writers. They have been keen observers and recorders and reckoned freely with the emotions and sentiments. Most philosophers, on the other hand, have exhibited a grotesque ignorance of man's life and have built up systems that are elaborate and imposing, but quite unrelated to actual human affairs. They have almost consistently neglected the actual process of thought and have set the mind off as something apart to be studied by itself. But no such mind, exempt from bodily processes, animal impulses, savage traditions, infantile impressions, conventional reactions, and traditional knowledge, ever existed, even in the case of the most abstract of metaphysicians. Kant entitled his great work *A Critique of Pure Reason*. But to the modern student of mind pure reason seems as mythical as the pure gold, transparent as glass, with which the celestial city is paved.

We do not think enough about thinking, and much of our confusion is the result of current illusions in regard to it. Let us forget for the moment any impressions we may have derived from the philosophers, and see what seems to happen in ourselves. The first thing that we notice is that our thought moves with such incredible rapidity that it is almost impossible to arrest any specimen of it long enough to have a look at it. When we are offered a penny for our thoughts, we always find that we have recently had so many things in mind that we can easily make a selection which will not compromise us too nakedly. On inspection we shall find that even if we are not downright ashamed of a great part of our spontaneous thinking, it is far too intimate, personal, ignoble, or trivial to permit us to reveal more than a small part of it. I believe this must be true of everyone. We do not, of course, know what goes on in other people's heads. They tell us very little and we tell them very little. The spigot of speech, rarely fully opened, could never emit more than driblets of the ever-renewed hogshead of thought — *noch grösser wie's Heidelberger Fass*. We find it hard to believe that other people's thoughts are as silly as our own, but they probably are.

We all appear to ourselves to be thinking all the time during our waking hours, and most of us are aware that we go on thinking while we are asleep, even more foolishly than when awake. When uninterrupted by some practical issue we are engaged in what is now known as a reverie. This is our spontaneous and favorite kind of thinking. We allow our ideas to take their own course and this course is determined by our hopes and fears, our spontaneous desires, their fulfillment or frustration; by our likes and dislikes, our loves and hates and resentments. There is nothing else anything like so interesting to ourselves as ourselves. All thought that is not more or less laboriously controlled and directed will inevitably circle about the beloved Ego. It is amusing and pathetic to observe this tendency in ourselves and in others. We learn politely and generously to overlook this truth, but if we dare to think of it, it blazes forth like the noontide sun.

We sometimes find ourselves changing our minds without any resistance or heavy emotion, but if we are told that we are wrong we resent the imputation and harden our hearts. We are incredibly heedless in the formation of our beliefs, but find ourselves filled with an illicit passion for them when anyone proposes to rob us of their companionship. It is obviously not the ideas themselves that are dear to us, but our self-esteem, which is threatened. We are by nature stubbornly pledged to defend our own from attack, whether it be our person, our family, our property, or our opinion. A United States Senator once remarked to a friend of mine that God Almighty could not make him change his mind on our Latin-America policy. We may surrender, but rarely confess ourselves vanquished. In the Intellectual world at least peace is without victory.

Few of us take the pains to study the origin of our cherished convictions; indeed, we have a natural repugnance to so doing. We like to continue to believe what we have been accustomed to accept as true, and the resentment aroused when doubt is cast upon any of our assumptions leads us to seek every manner of excuse for clinging to them. The result is that most of our so-called reasoning consists in finding arguments for going on believing as we already do.

PASCAL   1623–1662

M. de Roannez said: "Reasons come to me afterwards, but at first a thing pleases or shocks me without my knowing the reason, and yet it shocks me for that reason which I only discover afterwards." But I believe, not that it shocked him for the reasons which were found afterwards, but that these reasons were only found because it shocks him.

A Rosy Sanctuary will I dress
With the wreath'd trellis of a working brain

KEATS TO HIS FRIEND REYNOLDS   1818

I had an idea that a Man might pass a very pleasant life in this manner — Let him on a certain day read a certain page of full Poesy or distilled Prose, and let him wander with it, and muse upon it, and reflect from it, and bring home to it, and prophesy upon it, and dream upon it: until it becomes stale — But when will it do so? Never — When Man has arrived at a certain ripeness in intellect any one grand and spiritual passage serves him as a starting-post towards all "the two-and-thirty Palaces." Now it appears to me that almost any Man may like the spider spin from his own inwards his own airy Citadel — the points of leaves and twigs on which the spider begins her work are few, and she fills the air with a beautiful circuiting. Man should be content with as few points to tip with the fine Web of his Soul, and weave a tapestry empyrean — full of symbols for his spiritual eye, of softness for his spiritual touch, of space for his wandering, of distinctness for his luxury.

Thought Moves out into the World

FREUD   1856–1939

We have long observed that every neurosis has the result, and therefore probably the purpose, of forcing the patient out of real life, of alienating him from actuality. The neurotic turns away from reality because he finds it unbearable — either the whole or parts of it. The most extreme type of this alienation from reality is shown in certain cases of hallucinatory psychosis which aim at denying the existence of the particular event that occasioned the outbreak of insanity. But actually every neurotic does the same with some fragment of reality. And now we are confronted with the task of investigating the development of the relation of the neurotic and of mankind in general to reality.

In the psychology which is founded on psycho-analysis we have accustomed ourselves to take as our starting-point the unconscious mental processes, with the peculiarities of which we have become acquainted through analysis. These we consider to be the older, primary processes, the residues of a phase of development in which they were the only kind of mental processes. The sovereign tendency obeyed by these primary processes is easy of recognition; it is called the pleasure-pain principle, or more shortly the pleasure-principle. These processes strive towards gaining pleasure; from any operation which might arouse unpleasantness ("pain") mental activity draws back (repression). Our nocturnal dreams, our waking tendency to shut our painful impressions, are remnants of the supremacy of this principle and proofs of its power.

This attempt at satisfaction was abandoned only in consequence of the absence of the expected gratification, because of the disappointment experienced. Instead, the mental apparatus had to decide to form a conception of the real circumstances in the outer world and to exert itself to alter them. A new principle of mental functioning was thus introduced; what was conceived of was no longer that which was pleasant, but that which was real, even if it should be unpleasant.

The increased significance of external reality heightened the significance of the sense-organs directed towards the outer world, and of the consciousness attached to them; the latter now learned to comprehend the qualities of sense in addition to the qualities of pleasure and "pain" which hitherto had alone been of interest to it. A special function was instituted which had periodically to search the outer world in order that its data might be already familiar if an urgent inner need should arise; this function was attention. Its activity meets the sense-impressions halfway, instead of awaiting their appearance. At the same time there was probably introduced a system of notation, whose task was to deposit the results of this periodical activity of consciousness — a part of that which we call memory.

In place of repression, there developed an impartial passing of judgment, which had to decide whether a particular idea was true or false, that is, was in agreement with reality or not; decision was determined by comparison with the memory-traces of reality.

With the introduction of the reality-principle one mode of thought-activity was split off; it was kept free from reality-testing and remained subordinated to the pleasure-principle alone. Just as a nation whose wealth rests on the exploitation of its land yet reserves certain territory to be preserved in its original state and protected from cultural alterations, e.g. Yellowstone Park. This is the act of phantasy-making, which begins already in the games of children, and later, continued as daydreaming, abandons its dependence on real objects.

As the pleasure-ego can do nothing but wish, work towards gaining pleasure and avoiding "pain," so the reality-ego need do nothing but strive for what is useful and guard itself against damage. The superiority of the reality-ego over the pleasure-ego is aptly expressed by Bernard Shaw in these words: "To be able to choose the line of greatest advantage instead of yielding in the direction of least resistance." Actually, the substitution of the reality-principle for the pleasure-principle denotes no dethronement of the pleasure-principle, but only a safeguarding of it. A momentary pleasure, uncertain in its results, is given up, but only in order to gain in the new way an assured pleasure coming later. The doctrine of reward in a future life for the — voluntary or enforced — renunciation of earthly lusts is nothing but a mythical projection of this revolution in the mind. In logical pursuit of this prototype, religions have been able to effect absolute promise of compensation in a future life; they have not, however, achieved a conquest of the pleasure-principle in this way. It is science which comes nearest to succeeding in this conquest; science, however, also offers intellectual pleasure during its work and promises practical gain at the end.

THE DISCIPLINE OF THOUGHT

Thought, dealing as it must with the outside world of reality, has tried to fit itself for the struggle.

The Test of Thought

GRAHAM WALLAS   1858–1932

It is a historical fact that human thinking has been enormously improved by the invention of logical rules in the past. Aristotle's formal syllogistic scheme seems to us now so poor and clumsy that any insistence upon it is a hindrance rather than a furtherance to Thought, But that is because we have already absorbed its main results into the words and implications of our ordinary speech. How could we think to any effect about the complexities of modern life if we had no words like "principle" and "instance" or "proof" and "disproof"? The repetition of such formulas as "All A is B" wearies us now, but they stood at one time for a passionate new conviction that nature is uniform, and that the same conditions might always be trusted to produce the same results. To understand what the invention of the syllogism gave to mankind we must compare it with that world of thought which it helped to supersede, the incalculable divinities, the contradictory maxims and proverbs, the disconnected fragments of observation and experience which make the apparatus of the primitive mind. Bacon's *Organon* itself, and even the Four Methods of Experimental Enquiry in Mill's *Logic*, seem inadequate and almost irrelevant to a modern man of science, simply because he takes the need of testing hypotheses by experiment for granted.

HERACLITUS   500 B.C.

The waking have one and the same world, the sleeping turn aside each into a world of his own.

Franciscus de Verulamio sic cogitavit

BACON   1561–1626

Man, being the servant and interpreter of nature, can do and understand so much and so much only as he has observed in fact or in thought of the course of nature: beyond this he neither knows anything nor can do anything.

Human knowledge and human power meet in one; for where the cause is not known the effect cannot be produced. Nature to be commanded must be obeyed; and that which in contemplation is the cause is in operation the rule.

The subtlety of nature is greater many times over than the subtlety of the senses and understanding; so that all those pretty meditations, speculations, and controversies in which men indulge are really quite mad, only there is no one detached enough to observe it.

The conclusions of human reason as ordinarily applied to nature, I call for the sake of distinction Anticipations of Nature (as a thing rash or premature). That reason which is elicited from facts by a just and methodical process, I call Interpretation of Nature.

Though all the wits of all the ages should meet together and combine and transmit their labors, yet will no great progress ever be made in science by means of anticipations; because radical errors in the first concoction of the mind are not to be cured by the excellence of functions and remedies subsequent.

This must be plainly avowed: no judgment can be rightly formed either of my method or of the discoveries to which it leads, by means of anticipations (that is to say, of the reasoning which is now in use); since I cannot be called on to abide by the sentence of a tribunal which is itself on trial.

One method of delivery alone remains to us; which is

simply this: we must lead men to the particulars themselves, and their series and order; while men on their
side must force themselves for a while to lay their notions by and begin to familiarize themselves with facts.

The idols and false notions which now possess the human understanding have taken deep root therein. Not
only do they so beset men's minds that truth can hardly
find entrance, but even after its entrance, they will again,
in the very insaturation of the sciences, meet and trouble
us, unless men being forewarned fortify themselves as
far as may be against them.

There are four idols which beset men's minds. To
these for distinction's sake I have assigned names. I call
the first Idols of the Tribe; the second, Idols of the Cave;
the third, Idols of the Market-Place; the fourth, Idols of
the Theatre.

The Idols of the Tribe are founded in human nature
itself, and in the very tribe or race of men. For it is a
false assertion that the sense of man is the measure of
things. On the contrary, all perceptions, as well of the
sense as of the mind, accord to the measure of the individual, not to the measure of the universe. And the human understanding is like an irregular mirror, which
distorts and discolors the nature of things by mingling its
own nature with it.

The Idols of the Cave are the idols of the individual
man. For everyone, besides the errors common to human nature in general, has a cave or den of his own,
which refracts and discolors the light of nature; owing
to his own proper and peculiar nature or to his education and conversation with others; or to the reading of
books, and the authority of those whom he esteems and
admires; or to the differences of impressions, in a mind
preoccupied and predisposed or on a mind indifferent
and settled; or the like. So that the spirit of man, however it is disposed to different individuals, is a thing variable and full of perturbation, and governed as it were by
chance. Whence it was well observed by Heraclitus that
men look for sciences in their own little worlds, and not
in the great and common world.

There are also idols formed by the intercourse and association of men with each other, which I call Idols of the Market-Place, on account of the commerce and consort of men there. For it is by discourse that men associate; and words are imposed according to the apprehension of the vulgar. And therefore the ill and unfit choice of words wonderfully obsesses the understanding. Nor do the definitions or explanations, wherewith in some things learned men are wont to guard and defend themselves, by any means set the matter right. But words plainly force and overrule the understanding, and throw all into confusion, and lead men away into innumerable and inane controversies and fancies.

Lastly, there are idols which have immigrated into men's minds from the various dogmas of philosophies, and also from perverse laws of logic. These I call Idols of the Theatre; because in my judgment all the received systems are but so many stage-plays, representing worlds of their own creation after an unreal and scenic fashion. Nor is it only of the systems now in vogue, or only of the ancient sects and philosophies that I speak; for many more plays of the same kind may yet be composed and in like artificial manner set forth; seeing that errors the most widely different have nevertheless causes for the most part alike. Neither again do I mean this only of entire systems, but also of many principles and axioms in science, which by tradition, credulity, and negligence have come to be received.

But of these several kinds of idols I must speak more largely and exactly, that the understanding may be duly cautioned.

The human understanding, owing to its own peculiar nature, easily supposes more order and regularity in things than it finds. And though there be many singular things in nature, yet it devises for them parallels and analogies and relatives which do not exist. Hence the fiction that all celestial bodies move in perfect circles. And so on of other dreams.

The human understanding when it has once adopted

an opinion, either as being the received opinion or as being agreeable to itself, draws all things else to support and agree with it. And though there be a greater number and weight of instances to be found on the other side, yet these it either neglects and despises, or else by some distinction sets aside, and rejects; in order that by this great and pernicious predetermination the authority of its former conclusions may remain inviolate. And therefore it was a good answer that was made by the man who was shown hanging in a temple a picture of those who had paid their vows as having escaped shipwreck. They would have him say whether he did not now acknowledge the power of the gods — "Aye," asked he again, "but where are they painted that were drowned after their vows?"

The same reasoning applies to almost all superstition, whether in astrology, dreams, omens, divine judgments, or the like; wherein men, having a delight in such vanities, mark the events where they are fulfilled, but where they fail, though this happens much oftener, neglect and pass them by. But with far more subtlety does this mischief insinuate itself into philosophy and the sciences; in which the first conclusion colors and brings into conformity with itself all that comes after, though far sounder and better. Besides, independently of that delight and vanity which I have described, it is the peculiar and perpetual error of the human intellect to be more moved and excited by affirmatives than by negatives; whereas it ought properly to hold itself indifferently disposed towards both alike. Indeed in the establishment of any true axiom, the negative instance is the more forcible.

The human understanding is moved by those things most which strike and enter the mind simultaneously and suddenly, and so fill the imagination. Then it feigns and supposes all other things to be somehow, though it cannot see how, similar to those few things by which it is obsessed. But for that going to and fro to remote and heterogeneous instances, by which axioms are tried as in the fire, the intellect is altogether slow and unfit, unless it be forced thereto by severe laws and overruling authority.

The human understanding is unquiet; it cannot stop or rest, and still presses onward, but in vain. Therefore it is that we cannot conceive of any end or limit to the world; but always as of necessity it occurs to us that there is something beyond. The like subtlety arises touching the infinite divisibility of lines, from the same inability of thought to stop. But this inability interferes more mischievously in the discovery of causes. For although the most general principles in nature ought to be held absolute, as they are discovered, and not to be referred to a cause, nevertheless the human understanding, unable to rest, still seeks something prior in the order of nature. And then it is that in struggling towards that which is further off, it falls back upon that which is more nigh at hand, namely, on final causes. Clearly they relate to the nature of man rather than to the nature of the universe, and from this source have strangely defiled philosophy. But he is no less an unskilled and shallow philosopher who seeks causes of that which is most general than he who in things subordinate and subaltern omits to do so.

The human understanding is no dry light, but receives an infusion from the will and affections; whence proceed sciences which may be called "sciences as one would." For what a man had rather were true, that he more readily believes. Therefore he rejects difficult things from impatience of research; sober things, because they narrow hope; the deeper things of nature, from superstition; the light of experience, from arrogance and pride, lest his mind should seem to be occupied with things mean and transitory; things not commonly believed, out of deference to the opinion of the vulgar. Numberless in short are the ways, and sometimes imperceptible, in which the affections color and infect the understanding.

But by far the greatest hindrance and aberration of the human understanding proceeds from the dullness, incompetency, and deceptions of the senses; so that things which strike the sense outweigh things which do not immediately strike it, though they be more important.

There is one principal and as it were radical distinction between different minds, in respect of philosophy and the sciences; which is this: that some minds are stronger and apter to mark the differences of things, others to mark their resemblances. The steady and acute mind can fix its contemplations and dwell and fasten on the subtlest distinctions; the lofty and discursive mind recognizes and puts together the finest and most general resemblances. Both kinds, however, easily err in excess, by catching the one at gradations, the other at shadows.

There are found some minds given to an admiration of antiquity, others to a love and appetite for novelty; but few so duly tempered that they can hold the mean, neither carping at what has been well laid down by the ancients, nor despising what is well introduced by the moderns.

And generally let every student of nature take this as a rule — that whatever his mind seizes and dwells upon with peculiar satisfaction is to be held in suspicion, and that so much the more care is to be taken in dealing with such questions to keep the understanding even and clear.

But the Idols of the Market-Place are the most troublesome of all: idols which have crept into the understanding through their alliances with words and names. For men believe that their reason governs words. But words turn and twist the understanding. This it is that has rendered philosophy and the sciences sophistical and inactive. Words are mostly cut to the common fashion and draw the distinctions which are most obvious to the common understanding. Whenever an understanding of greater acuteness or more diligent observation would alter those lines to suit the true distinctions of nature, words complain.

Hence it is that great and solemn discussions of learned men end oftentimes in disputes about words and names; with which, according to the use and wisdom of the mathematicians, it would be more prudent to begin, and so by means of definitions reduce them to order.

Yet even definitions cannot cure this evil in dealing with natural and material things, since the definitions themselves consist of words, and those words beget others. So it is necessary to recur to particular instances, and those in due series and order.

Bacon's Idols are too well known for any comment but Bacon's own. The *Novum Organum* was published in Latin in 1620, a scant twenty years after *Hamlet* was produced. Just as Hamlet was in a way the first modern man, so the *Novum Organum* was the modern scientific creed. James the First said it struck him like the Peace of God which passeth all understanding. The Latin head is Bacon's own. The translation is Headlam's, made for Spedding and improved by the editors.

A. N. WHITEHEAD   1861–1947

The greatest invention of the nineteenth century was the invention of the method of invention. A new method entered into life. In order to understand our epoch, we can neglect all the details of change, such as railways, telegraphs, radios, spinning machines, synthetic dyes. We must concentrate on the method itself; that is the real novelty, which has broken up the foundations of the old civilisation. The prophecy of Francis Bacon has now been fulfilled; and man, who at times dreamt of himself as a little lower than the angels, has submitted to become the servant and the minister of nature. It still remains to be seen whether the same actor can play both parts.

WHAT ARE HYPOTHESES?

"It must be remembered," said Vaihinger, "that the object of the world of ideas as a whole is not the portrayal of reality — this would be an utterly impossible task — but rather to provide us with an instrument for finding our way about in this world more easily."

Dogmas, Hypotheses, and Fictions

HAVELOCK ELLIS   1859–1939

The problem which Vaihinger set out to solve was this: How comes it about that with consciously false ideas we yet reach conclusions that are in harmony with Nature and appeal to us as Truth? That we do so is obvious, especially in the "exact" branches of science. In mathematics it is notorious that we start from absurdities to reach a realm of law, and our whole conception of the nature of the world is based on a foundation which we believe to have no existence. For even the most sober scientific investigator in science, the most thoroughgoing Positivist, cannot dispense with fiction; he must at least make use of categories, and they are already fictions, analogical fictions, or labels, which give us the same pleasure as children receive when they are told the "name" of a thing. Fiction is, indeed, an indispensable supplement to logic, or even a part of it; whether we are working inductively or deductively, both ways hang closely together with fiction; and axioms, though they seek to be primary verities, are more akin to fiction. If we had realised the nature of axioms, the doctrine of Einstein, which sweeps away axioms so familiar to us that they seem obvious truths, and substitutes others which seem absurd because they are unfamiliar, might not have been so bewildering.

Vaihinger is throughout careful to distinguish fiction alike from hypothesis and dogma. He regards the distinction as, methodologically, highly important, though not always easy to make. The "dogma" is put forward as an absolute and unquestionable truth; the "hypothesis" is a possible or probable truth, such as Darwin's doctrine of descent; the "fiction" is impossible, but it enables us to reach what for us is relatively truth, and, above all, while hypothesis simply contributes to knowledge, fiction thus used becomes a guide to practical action and indispensable to what we feel to be progress. Thus the mighty and civilizing structure of Roman law was built up by the aid of what the Romans themselves recognized as fictions, while in the different and more flexible system of English laws a constant inspiration to action has been furnished by the supposed privileges gained by Magna Carta, though we now recognize them as fictitious. Many of our ideas tend to go through the three stages of Dogma, Hypothesis, and Fiction, sometimes in that order and sometimes in the reverse order. Hypothesis especially presents a state of labile stability which is unpleasant to the mind, so it tends to become either dogma or fiction. The ideas of Christianity, beginning as dogmas, have passed through all three stages in the minds of thinkers during recent centuries: the myths of Plato, beginning as fiction, not only passed through the three stages, but then passed back again, being now again regarded as fiction. The scientifically valuable fiction is a child of modern times, but we have already emerged from the period when the use of fiction was confined to the exact sciences.

Thus we find fiction fruitfully flourishing in the biological and social sciences and even in the highest spheres of human spiritual activity. The Linnaean and similar classificatory systems are fictions, even though put forward as hypotheses, having their value simply as pictures, as forms of representation, but leading to contradictions and liable to be replaced by other systems which present more helpful pictures. There are still people who disdain Adam Smith's "economic man," as though proceeding from a purely selfish view of life, although Buckle, forestalling Vaihinger, long ago explained that Smith was deliberately making use of a "valid artifice," separating facts that he knew to be in nature inseparable — he based his moral theory on a totally different kind of man — because so he could reach results approximately true to the observed phenomena. Bentham also adopted a fiction for his own system, though believing it to be an hypothesis, and Mill criticised it as being "geometrical"; the criticism is correct, comments Vaihinger, but the method was not thereby invalidated, for in complicated fields no other method can be fruitfully used.

The same law holds when we approach our highest and most sacred conceptions. It was recognised by enlightened philosophers and theologians before Vaihinger that the difference between body and soul is not different from that between matter and force — a provisional and useful distinction — that light and darkness, life and death, are abstractions, necessary, indeed, but in their application to reality always to be used with precaution. On the threshold of the moral world we meet the idea of Freedom. "One of the weightiest conceptions man has ever formed," once a dogma, in course of time an hypothesis, now in the eyes of many a fiction; yet we can not do without it, even although we may be firmly convinced that our acts are determined by laws that cannot be broken. Many other great conceptions have tended to follow the same course. God, the Soul, Immortality, the Moral World-Order. The critical hearers understand what is meant when these great words are used, and if the uncritical misunderstand, that, adds Vaihinger, may sometimes be also useful. For these things are Ideals, and all Ideals are, logically speaking, fictions. As Science leads to the Imaginary, so Life leads to the Impossible; without them we cannot reach the heights we are born to scale. "Taken literally, however, our most valuable conceptions are worthless."

Vaihinger's doctrine of the "as if" is not immune from criticism on more than one side, and it is fairly obvious that, however sound the general principle, particular "fictions" may alter their status, and have even done so since the book was written. Moreover, the doctrine is not always quite congruous with itself. Nor can it be said that Vaihinger ever really answered the question with which he set out. In philosophy, however, it is not the attainment of the goal that matters, it is the things that are met with by the way. And Vaihinger's philosophy is not only of interest because it presents so clearly and vigorously a prevailing tendency in modern thought. Rightly understood, it supplies a fortifying influence to those who may have seen their cherished spiritual edifice, whatever it may be, fall around them and are tempted to a mood of disillusionment. We make our own world; when we have made it awry, we can remake it, approximately truer, though it cannot be absolutely true, to the facts. It will never be finally made; we are always stretching forth to larger and better fictions which answer more truly to our growing knowledge and experience. Even when we walk, it is only by a series of regulated errors, Vaihinger well points out, a perpetual succession of falls to one side and the other side. Our whole progress through life is of the same nature; all thinking is a regulated error. For we cannot, as Vaihinger insists, choose our errors at random or in accordance with what happens to please us; such fictions are only too likely to turn into deadening dogmas; the old *vis dormitiva* is the type of them, mere husks that are of no vital use and help us not at all. There are good fictions and bad fictions, just as there are good poets and bad poets. It is in the choice and regulation of our errors, in our readiness to accept ever-closer approximations to the unattainable reality, that we think rightly and live rightly. We triumph in so far as we succeed in that regulation. "A lost battle," Foch, quoting De Maistre, lays down in his *Principes de Guerre,* "is a battle one thinks one has lost"; the battle is won by the fiction that it is won. It is so also in the battle of life, in the whole art of living. Freud regards dreaming as fiction that helps us to sleep; thinking we may regard as fiction that helps us to live. Man lives by imagination.

This is from Havelock Ellis's account of Vaihinger, a German professor of philosophy who wrote his *Philosophy of the As If* in 1876, but dared not publish it till 1911. Ellis introduced it in England in his *Dance of Life,* from which this is taken and where you can most easily get an account of Vaihinger.

MAKING OUR IDEAS CLEAR

Our thoughts need cutting edges.

CHARLES S. PEIRCE   1839–1914

The very first lesson that we have a right to demand that
logic shall teach us is, how to make our ideas clear; and a
most important one it is, depreciated only by minds who
stand in need of it. To know what we think, to be masters of our own meaning, will make a solid foundation
for great and weighty thought. It is most easily learned
by those whose ideas are meagre and restricted; and far
happier they than such as wallow helplessly in a
rich mud of conceptions. A nation, it is true, may, in the
course of generations, overcome the disadvantage of an
excessive wealth of language and its natural concomitant,
a vast, unfathomable deep of ideas. We may see it in
history, slowly perfecting its literary forms, sloughing at
length its metaphysics, and, by virtue of the untirable patience which is often a compensation, attaining great excellence in every branch of mental acquirement. The
page of history is not yet unrolled which is to tell
us whether such a people will or will not in the long run
prevail over one whose ideas (like the words of their
language) are few, but which possesses a wonderful mastery over those which it has. For an individual, however, there can be no question that a few clear ideas are
worth more than many confused ones. A young man
would hardly be persuaded to sacrifice the greater part
of his thoughts to save the rest; and the muddled head
is the least apt to see the necessity of such a sacrifice.

Him we can usually only commiserate, as a person with a congenital defect. Time will help him, but intellectual maturity with regard to clearness comes rather late, an unfortunate arrangement of Nature, inasmuch as clearness is of less use to a man settled in life, whose errors have in great measure had their effect, than it would be to one whose path lies before him. It is terrible to see how a single unclear idea, a single formula without meaning lurking in a young man's head, will sometimes act like an obstruction of inert matter in an artery, hindering the nutrition of the brain, and condemning its victim to pine away in the fullness of his intellectual vigor and in the midst of intellectual plenty. Many a man has cherished for years as his hobby some vague shadow of an idea, too meaningless to be positively false; he has, nevertheless, passionately loved it, has made it his companion by day and by night, and has given to it his strength and his life, leaving all other occupations for its sake, and in short has lived with it and for it, until it has become, as it were, flesh of his flesh and bone of his bone; and then he was waked up some bright morning to find it gone, clean vanished away like the beautiful Melusina of the fable, and the essence of his life gone with it. I have myself known such a man; and who can tell how many histories of circle-squarers, metaphysicians, astrologers, and what-not, may not be told in the old German story?

In this process we observe two sorts of elements of consciousness, the distinction between which may best be made clear by means of an illustration. In a piece of music there are the separate notes, and there is the air. A single tone may be prolonged for an hour or a day, and it exists as perfectly in each second of that time as in the whole taken together; so that, as long as it is sounding, it might be present to a sense from which everything in the past was as completely absent as the future itself. But it is different with the air, the performance of which occupies a certain time, during the portions of which only portions of it are played. It consists in an orderliness in the succession of sounds which strike the ear at different times; and to perceive it there must be some continuity of consciousness which makes the events of a lapse of time present to us. We certainly only perceive the air by hearing the separate notes; yet we cannot be said to directly hear it, for we hear only what is present at the instant, and an orderliness of succession cannot exist in an instant. These two sorts of objects, what we are *immediately* conscious of and what we are *mediately* conscious of, are found in all consciousness. Some elements (the sensations) are completely present at every instant so long as they last, while others (like thought) are actions having beginning, middle, and end, and consist in a congruence in the succession of sensations which flow through the mind. They cannot be immediately present to us, but must cover some portion of the past or future. Thought is a thread of melody running through the succession of our sensations.

We may add that just as a piece of music may be written in parts, each part having its own air, so various systems of relationship of succession subsist together between the same sensations. These different systems are distinguished by having different motives, ideas, or functions. Thought is only one such system, for its sole motive, idea, and function is to produce belief, and whatever does not concern that purpose belongs to some other system of relations. The action of thinking may incidentally have other results; it may serve to amuse us, for example, and among *dilettanti* it is not rare to find those who have so perverted thought to the purposes of pleasure that it seems to vex them to think that the questions upon which they delight to exercise it may ever get finally settled; and a positive discovery which takes a favorite subject out of the arena of literary debate is met with ill-concealed dislike. This disposition is the very debauchery of thought. But the soul and meaning of thought, abstracted from the other elements which accompany it, though it may be voluntarily thwarted, can never be made to direct itself toward anything but the production of belief. Thought in action has for its only possible motive the attainment of thought at rest; and whatever does not refer to belief is no part of the thought itself.

And what, then, is belief? It is the demi-cadence which closes a musical phrase in the symphony of our intellectual life. We have seen that it has just three properties: First, it is something that we are aware of; second, it appeases the irritation of doubt; and, third, it involves the establishment in our nature of a rule of action, or, say for short, a habit. As it appeases the irritation of doubt which is the motive for thinking, thought relaxes, and comes to rest for a moment when belief is reached. But, since belief is a rule for action, the application of which involves further doubt and further thought, at the same time that it is a stopping-place, it is also a new starting-place for thought. That is why I have permitted myself to call it thought at rest, although thought is essentially an action. The final upshot of thinking is the exercise of volition, and of this thought no longer forms a part; but belief is only a stadium of mental action, an effect upon our nature due to thought, which will influence future thinking.

We shall be perfectly safe so long as we reflect that the whole function of thought is to produce habits of action; and that whatever there is connected with a thought, but irrelevant to its purpose, is an accretion to it, but no part of it. If there be a unity among our sensations which has no reference to how we shall act on a given occasion, as when we listen to a piece of music, why do we not call that thinking? To develop its meaning, we have, therefore, simply to determine what habits it produces, for what a thing means is simply what habits it involves. Now, the identity of a habit depends on how it might lead us to act, not merely under such circumstances as are likely to arise, but under such as might possibly occur, no matter how improbable they may be. What the habit is depends on when and how it causes us to act. As for the *how*, every purpose of action is to produce some sensible result. Thus, we come down to what is tangible and practical, as the root of every real distinction of thought, no matter how subtle it may be; and there is no distinction of meaning so fine as to consist of anything but a possible difference of practice.

It appears, then, that the rule for attaining the third grade of clearness of apprehension is as follows: Consider what effects, which might conceivably have practical bearings, we conceive the object of our conception to have. Then, our conception of these effects is the whole of our conception of the object.

The *Popular Science Monthly* in 1878 published this in an article called "How to Make Our Ideas Clear." Twenty years later, William James christened this way of thinking Pragmatism.

WHAT IS TRUTH?

Stay a moment for some answers.

Pragmatism

WILLIAM JAMES   1842–1910

The pragmatic rule is that the meaning of a concept may always be found, if not in some sensible particular which it directly designates, then in some particular difference in the course of human experience which its being true will make. Test every concept by the question, "What sensible difference to anybody will its truth make?" and you are in the best possible position for understanding what it means and for discussing its importance. If, questioning whether a certain concept be true or false, you can think of absolutely nothing that would practically differ in the two cases, you may assume that the alternative is meaningless and that your concept is no distinct idea. If two concepts lead you to infer the same particular consequence, then you may assume that they embody the same meaning under different names.

The pivotal part of my book named *Pragmatism* is its account of the relation called "truth" which may obtain between an idea (opinion, belief, statement, or what-not) and its object. "Truth," I there say, "is a property of certain of our ideas. It means their agreement, as falsity means their disagreement, with reality. Pragmatists and intellectualists both accept this definition as a matter of course.

"Where our ideas [do] not copy definitely their object, what does agreement with that object mean? . . . Pragmatism asks its usual question. 'Grant an idea or belief to be true,' it says, 'what concrete difference will its being true make in anyone's actual life? What experiences [may] be different from those which would obtain if the belief were false? How will the truth be realized? What, in short, is the truth's cash-value in experiential terms?' The moment pragmatism asks this question, it sees the answer. True ideas are those that we can assimilate, validate, corroborate, and verify. False ideas are those that we cannot. That is the practical difference it makes to us to have true ideas; that therefore is the meaning of truth, for it is all that truth is known as.

"The truth of an idea is not a stagnant property inherent in it. Truth happens to an idea. It becomes true, is made true by events. Its verity is in fact an event, a process, the process namely of its verifying itself, its verification. Its validity is the process of its validation.[1]

"To agree in the widest sense with a reality can only mean to be guided either straight up to it or into its surroundings, or to be put into such working touch with it as to handle either it or something connected with it better than if we disagreed. Better either intellectually or practically. . . . Any idea that helps us to deal, whether practically or intellectually, with either the reality or its belongings, that doesn't entangle our progress in frustrations, that fits, in fact, and adapts our life to the reality's whole setting, will agree sufficiently to meet the requirement. It will be true of that reality.

"The true, to put it very briefly, is only the expedient in the way of our thinking, just as the right is only the expedient in the way of our behaving. Expedient in almost any fashion, and expedient in the long run and on the whole, of course; for what meets expediently all the experience in sight won't necessarily meet all further

---

[1] But "verifiability," I add, "is as good as verification. For one truth-process completed, there are a million in our lives that function in [the] state of nascency. They lead us towards direct verification; lead us into the surroundings of the object they envisage; and then, if everything runs on harmoniously, we are so sure that verification is possible that we omit it, and are usually justified by all that happens."

experiences equally satisfactorily. Experience, as we know, has ways of boiling over, and making us correct our present formulas."

This account of truth, following upon the similar ones given by Messrs. Dewey and Schiller, has occasioned the liveliest discussion. Few critics have defended it, most of them have scouted it. It seems evident that the subject is a hard one to understand, under its apparent simplicity; and evident also, I think, that the definitive settlement of it will mark a turning-point in the history of epistemology and consequently in that of general philosophy.

LEONARDO DA VINCI   1452–1519

Iron rusts from disuse, stagnant water loses its purity and in cold weather becomes frozen; even so does inaction sap the vigors of the mind.

BACON   1561–1626

If we begin with certainties, we shall end in doubts; but if we begin with doubts, and are patient in them, we shall end in certainties.

Can't Helps

O. W. HOLMES, JR.   1841–1935

I used to say, when I was young, that truth was the majority vote of that nation that could lick all others. Certainly we may expect that the received opinion about the present war will depend a good deal upon which side wins (I hope with all my soul it will be mine), and I think that the statement was correct in so far as it implied that our test of truth is a reference to either a present or an imagined future majority in favor of our view. If, as I have suggested elsewhere, the truth may be defined as the system of my (intellectual) limitations, which gives it objectivity, is the fact that I find my fellow man to a greater or less extent (never wholly) subject to the same *Can't Helps*. If I think that I am sitting at a table, I find that the other persons present agree with me; so if I say that the sum of the angles of a triangle is equal to two right angles. If I am in a minority of one. they send for a doctor or lock me up; and I am so far able to transcend the to me convincing testimony of my senses or my reason as to recognize that if I am alone probably something is wrong with my works.

FREUD   1856–1939

The conceptions I have summarized here I first put forward only tentatively, but in the course of time they have won such a hold over me that I can no longer think in any other way.

CONFUCIUS   551–479 B.C.

It is man that makes truth great, not truth that makes man great.

OLIVER CROMWELL   1599–1658

My brethren, by the bowels of Christ I beseech you, bethink you that you may be mistaken.

A. N. WHITEHEAD   1861–1947

It requires a very unusual mind to undertake the analysis of the obvious.

Henry Adams Opens Every Door

HENRY ADAMS   1838–1918

Psychology was to him a new study, and a dark corner of education. As he lay on Wenlock Edge, with the sheep nibbling the grass close about him as they or their betters had nibbled the grass — or whatever there was to nibble — in the Silurian kingdom of Pteraspis, he seemed to have fallen on an evolution far more wonderful than that of fishes. He did not like it; he could not account for it; and he determined to stop it. Never since the days of his *Limulus* ancestry had any of his ascendants thought thus. Their modes of thought might be many, but their thought was one. Out of his millions of millions of ancestors, back to the Cambrian mollusks, every one had probably lived and died in the illusion of Truths which did not amuse him, and which had never changed. Henry Adams was the first in an infinite series to discover and admit to himself that he really did not care whether truth was, or was not, true. He did not even care that it should be proved true, unless the process were new and amusing. He was a Darwinian for fun.

From the beginning of history, this attitude had been branded as criminal — worse than crime — sacrilege! Society punished it ferociously and justly, in self-defence. Mr. Adams, the father, looked on it as moral weakness; it annoyed him; but it did not annoy him nearly so much as it annoyed his son, who had no need to learn from Hamlet the fatal effect of the pale cast of thought on enterprises great or small. He had no notion of letting the currents of his action be turned awry by this form of conscience. To him the current of his time was to be his current, lead where it might. He put psychology under lock and key; he insisted on maintaining his absolute standards; on aiming at ultimate Unity. The mania for handling all the sides of every question, looking into every window, and opening every door, was, as Blue-beard judiciously pointed out to his wives, fatal to their practical usefulness in society.

Truth Is Not Certitude

O. W. HOLMES, JR.   1841–1935

Certitude is not the test of certainty. We have been cock-sure of many things that were not so. If I may quote my-self again, property, friendship, and truth have a common root in time. One cannot be wrenched from the rocky crevices into which one has grown for many years without feeling that one is attacked in one's life. What we most love and revere generally is determined by early associations. I love granite rocks and barberry bushes, no doubt because with them were my earliest joys that reach back through the past eternity of my life. But while one's experience thus makes certain preferences dogmatic for oneself, recognition of how they came to be so leaves one able to see that others, poor souls, may be equally dogmatic about something else. And this again means scepticism. Not that one's belief or love does not remain. Not that we would not fight and die for it if important — we all, whether we know it or not, are fighting to make the kind of a world that we should like — but that we have learned to recognize that others will fight and die to make a different world, with equal sincerity or belief. Deep-seated preferences cannot be argued about — you cannot argue a man into liking a glass of beer — and therefore, when differences are sufficiently far-reaching, we try to kill the other man rather than let him have his way. But that is perfectly consistent with admitting that, so far as appears, his grounds are just as good as ours.

FREUD   1856–1939

Illusions commend themselves to us because they save us pain and allow us to enjoy pleasure instead. We must therefore accept it without complaint when they sometimes collide with a bit of reality against which they are dashed to pieces.

A. N. WHITEHEAD   1861–1947

If you have had your attention directed to the novelties in thought in your own lifetime, you will have observed that almost all really new ideas have a certain aspect of foolishness when they are first produced, and almost any idea which jogs you out of your current abstractions may be better than nothing.

PERCY W. BRIDGMAN   1882–1961

There is no adequate defense, except stupidity, against the impact of a new idea.

CAN WE BE SURE OF WHAT WE MEAN?

One way is a ruthless purge of sentiment. We can do that by thinking only in terms of operations.

The Purge of Sentiment

PERCY W. BRIDGMAN   1882–1961

To find the length of an object, we have to perform certain physical operations. The concept of length is therefore fixed when the operations by which length is measured are fixed: that is, the concept of length involves as much as and nothing more than the set of operations by which length is determined. In general, we mean by any concept nothing more than a set of operations; the concept is synonymous with the corresponding set of operations.

A consequence of the operational character of our concepts is that it is quite possible, nay even disquietingly easy, to invent expressions or to ask questions that are meaningless. It constitutes a great advance in our critical attitude toward nature to realize that a great many of the questions that we uncritically ask are without meaning. If a specific question has meaning, it must be possible to find operations by which an answer may be given to it. It will be found in many cases that the operations cannot exist, and the question therefore has no meaning.

To state that a certain question about nature is meaningless is to make a significant statement about nature itself, because the fundamental operations are determined by nature, and to state that nature cannot be described in terms of certain operations is a significant statement.

It must be recognized, however, that there is a sense

in which no serious question is entirely without meaning, because doubtless the questioner had in mind some intention in asking the question. But to give meaning in this sense to a question, one must inquire into the meaning of the concepts as used by the questioner, and it will often be found that these concepts can be defined only in terms of fictitious properties so that the meaning to be ascribed to the question in this way has no connection with reality. I believe that it will enable us to make more significant and interesting statements, and therefore will be more useful, to adopt exclusively the operational view, and so admit the possibility of questions entirely without meaning.

This matter of meaningless questions is a very subtle thing which may poison much more of our thought than that dealing with purely physical phenomena. I believe that many of the questions asked about social and philosophical subjects will be found to be meaningless when examined from the point of view of operations. It would doubtless conduce greatly to clarity of thought if the operational mode of thinking were adopted in all fields of inquiry as well as in the physical. Just as in the physical domain, so in other domains, one is making a significant statement about his subject in stating that a certain question is meaningless.

To adopt the operational point of view involves much more than a mere restriction of the sense in which we understand "concept," but means a far-reaching change in all our habits of thought, in that we shall no longer permit ourselves to use as tools in our thinking concepts of which we cannot give an adequate account in terms of operations. In some respects thinking becomes simpler, because certain old generalizations and idealizations become incapable of use; for instance, many of the speculations of the early natural philosophers become simply unreadable. In other respects, however, thinking becomes much more difficult, because the operational implications of a concept are often very involved. For example, it is most difficult to grasp adequately all that is contained in the apparently simple concept of "time," and requires the continual correction of mental tendencies which we have long unquestioningly accepted.

Not only will operational thinking reform the social art of conversation, but all our social relations will be liable to reform. Let anyone examine in operational terms any popular present-day discussion of religious or moral questions to realize the magnitude of the reformation awaiting us. Wherever we temporize or compromise in applying our theories of conduct to practical life we may suspect a failure of operational thinking.

Later Bridgman proposed replacing the word "meaningless" by "footless."

Operational Thinking Is a Ruthless Process

EMILY DICKINSON   1830–1886

> *Surgeons must be very careful*
> *When they take the knife!*
> *Underneath their fine incisions*
> *Stirs the culprit, — Life!*

Apply it, for example, to a discussion of poetry by T. S. Eliot, here arguing with I. A. Richards:

T. S. ELIOT   1888–

And I confess to considerable difficulty in analysing my own feelings, a difficulty which makes me hesitate to accept Mr. Richards's theory of "pseudo-statements." On reading the line which he uses,

> *Beauty is truth, truth beauty . . .*

I am at first inclined to agree with him, because this statement of equivalence means nothing to me. But on rereading the whole Ode, this line strikes me as a serious blemish on a beautiful poem; and the reason must be either that I fail to understand it, or that it is a statement which is untrue. And I suppose that Keats meant something by it, however remote his truth and his beauty may have been from these words in ordinary use. And I am sure that he would have repudiated any explanation of the line which called it a pseudo-statement. On the other hand the line I have often quoted from Shakespeare,

> *Ripeness is all,*

or the line I have quoted of Dante,

> *la sua voluntade è nostra pace,*

strikes very differently on my ear. I observe that the propositions in these words are very different in kind, not only from that of Keats, but from each other. The statement of Keats seems to me meaningless: or perhaps, the fact that it is grammatically meaningless conceals another meaning from me. The statement of Shakespeare seems to me to have profound emotional meaning, with, at least, no literal fallacy. And the statement of Dante seems to me *literally true.*

The Shakespeare line is from *Lear,* Act V. In *Hamlet* it is "The readiness is all."

As to Beauty and Truth, EMILY DICKINSON *said:*

> I died for beauty, but was scarce
> Adjusted in the tomb,
> When one who died for truth was lain
> In an adjoining room.
>
> He questioned softly why I failed?
> "For beauty," I replied.
> "And I for truth — the two are one;
> We brethren are," he said.
>
> And so, as kinsmen met a-night,
> We talked between the rooms,
> Until the moss had reached our lips,
> And covered up our names.

But Must We Be So Ruthless?

HERBERT DINGLE   1890–

If I like tomatoes and you do not, it is idle to discuss whether that is because we both experience the same physical tastes but value them differently, or because we have a common standard of valuation but experience different physical tastes. The alternatives are only verbally different, because there is no conceivable means of deciding between them. In just the same way, it is idle to discuss whether God is in the room and only one man is conscious of his presence, or whether God is not in the room but one man is deluded into thinking that he is. Only the individual can answer that question in an intelligible way, and therefore no criterion of existence which can be generally accepted is possible. We may therefore amend our former remark by saying that common experiences, which are those amenable to Science, are experiences of which we can agree on a definition in terms of external existences;[1] individual experiences are those with respect to which we can reach no such agreement.

It is for this reason that attempts to define such postulates as Beauty, Goodness, Humor, and the like, have always failed; we have almost as many definitions as we have persons capable of expressing their individual experiences. It is inevitably so, and arguments as to whether such-and-such a statement on these matters is truer than others are vain babblings, because there is no means of ensuring that the disputants are talking about the same things. There is no meaning in asking whether a certain situation is "funny" or not, because the question implies a common standard of "funniness" which does not exist. The situation may be funny to some and tragic to others, and the question, Which is right? is meaningless.

Why do we thus divide these individual experiences so arbitrarily into an external cause and a sensitive percipient? The emotion of humor is not accepted merely as an emotion; it is called "seeing the joke," as if there were an objective joke and a faculty for seeing it. Similarly, the aesthetic experience is an "appreciation of beauty," and the religious experience a "vision of God."

[1] This, of course, implies no answer to the metaphysical question whether there are external existences or not.

Why is this so? The question is really one for the anthropologist or the psychologist or the philologist to deal with, but, speaking without expert knowledge, I would suggest that the attempt to objectify all our experiences may have been suggested by the proven value for practical ends of the objectifying of common experiences. From the days of animism onwards the practice has been universal. In the Middle Ages it was abused, as we have seen, by the assumption of occult qualities, and in modern Science it survives in the formulation of hypotheses.

Galileo said that of two hypotheses the simpler was the better. Not the logically simpler, CHARLES S. PEIRCE (1839–1914) *said:*

It was not until long experience forced me to realize that subsequent discoveries were every time showing I had been wrong, while those who understood the maxim as Galileo had done, early unlocked the secret, that the scales fell from my eyes and my mind awoke to the broad and flaming daylight that it is the simpler hypothesis in the sense of the more facile and natural, the one that instinct suggests that must be preferred; for the reason that, unless man have a natural bent in accordance with nature's, he has no chance of understanding nature at all.

SIMPLICITY AND ABSTRACTION

*Simplicity — which is not so simple;
and the Abstract — which is not the
Concrete.*

A. N. WHITEHEAD   **1861–1947**

Seek simplicity, and distrust it.

HENRI POINCARÉ   **1854–1912**

In Science we are led to act as though a simple law, when other things were equal, must be more probable than a complicated law. Half a century ago one frankly confessed it, and proclaimed that Nature loves simplicity. She has since given us too often the lie. Today this tendency is no longer avowed, and only as much of it is preserved as is indispensable so that science shall not become impossible.

The Fallacy of Misplaced Concreteness

A. N. WHITEHEAD   **1861–1947**

Of course, substance and quality are the most natural ideas for the human mind. It is the way in which we think of things, and without these ways of thinking we could not get our ideas straight for daily use. There is no doubt about this. The only question is, How concretely are we thinking when we consider nature under these conceptions? My point will be, that we are presenting ourselves with simplified editions of immediate matters of fact. When we examine the primary elements of these simplified editions, we shall find that they are in truth only to be justified as being elaborate logical constructions of a high degree of abstraction. Of course, as a point of individual psychology, we get at the idea by the rough-and-ready method of suppressing what appear to be irrelevant details. But when we attempt to justify this suppression of irrelevance, we find that, though there are entities left corresponding to the entities we talk about, yet these entities are of a high degree of abstraction.

Locke, writing with a knowledge of Newtonian dynamics, places mass among the primary qualities of bodies. In short, he elaborates a theory of primary and secondary qualities in accordance with the state of physical science at the close of the seventeenth century. The primary qualities are the essential qualities of substances whose spatio-temporal relationships constitute nature. The orderliness of these relationships constitutes the order of nature. The occurrences of nature are in some way apprehended by minds, which are associated with living bodies. Primarily, the mental apprehension is aroused by the occurrences in certain parts of the correlated body, the occurrences in the brain, for instance. But the mind in apprehending also experiences sensations which, properly speaking, are qualities of the mind alone. These sensations are projected by the mind so as to clothe appropriate bodies in external nature. Thus, the bodies are perceived as with qualities which in reality do not belong to them, qualities which in fact are purely the offspring of the mind. Thus nature gets credit which should in truth be reserved for ourselves: the rose for its scent: the nightingale for his song: and the sun for his radiance. The poets are entirely mistaken. They should address their lyrics to themselves, and should turn them into odes of self-congratulation on the excellency of the human mind. Nature is a dull affair, soundless, scentless, colorless; merely the hurrying of material, endlessly, meaninglessly.

However you disguise it, this is the practical outcome of the characteristic scientific philosophy which closed the seventeenth century.

In the first place, we must note its astounding efficiency

as a system of concepts for the organization of scientific research. In this respect, it is fully worthy of the genius of the century which produced it. It has held its own as the guiding principle of scientific studies ever since. It is still reigning. Every university in the world organizes itself in accordance with it. No alternative system of organizing the pursuit of scientific truth has been suggested. It is not only reigning, but it is without a rival.

And yet — it is quite unbelievable. This conception of the universe is surely framed in terms of high abstractions, and the paradox only arises because we have mistaken our abstraction for concrete realities.

The advantage of confining attention to a definite group of abstractions is that you confine your thoughts to clear-cut definite things, with clear-cut definite relations. Accordingly, if you have a logical head, you can deduce a variety of conclusions respecting the relationships between these abstract entities. Furthermore, if the abstractions are well-founded — that is to say, if they do not abstract from everything that is important in experience — the scientific thought which confines itself to these abstractions will arrive at a variety of important truths relating to our experience of nature. We all know those clear-cut trenchant intellects, immovably encased in a hard shell of abstractions. They hold you to their abstractions by the sheer grip of personality.

The disadvantage of exclusive attention to a group of abstractions, however well-founded, is that, by the nature of the case, you have abstracted from the remainder of things. In so far as the excluded things are important in your experience, your modes of thought are not fitted to deal with them. You cannot think without abstractions; accordingly, it is of the utmost importance to be vigilant in critically revising your *modes* of abstraction. It is here that philosophy finds its niche as essential to the healthy progress of society. It is the critic of abstractions. A civilization which cannot burst through its current abstractions is doomed to sterility after a very limited period of progress. An active school of philosophy is quite as important for the locomotion of ideas as is an active school of railway engineers for the locomotion of fuel.

L. J. HENDERSON   1878-1942

When we possess adequate knowledge of a system in which n factors are involved and have arrived at a description of this system in terms of the n factors, so that their interactions are also described, it is possible to reason successfully concerning changes in the state of the system in so far as these n factors alone are concerned, to a given approximation, in the process that is being studied. But when a further factor is also involved, our reasoning can never be trusted and is in general illusory. It is perhaps partly for this reason that anatomists, physiologists, and pathologists do not practice medicine, and this is probably the principal source of the familiar attitude of suspicion toward the laboratory sciences that may be seen among experienced clinicians. When men reason deductively about the complex affairs of everyday life, they nearly always leave out something, or rather many things, both things they forget and things they don't know. More often than not their conclusions are therefore unsound. This is what Whitehead calls "the fallacy of misplaced concreteness." I am not sure that it can be appreciated by anyone who has not experienced the difficult task of putting together the pieces obtained by analytical studies and thus building up an adequate description of a system in which many factors interact. Experience alone can teach most people the immense complexity of interactions between many factors, and the mathematical solution of such problems seems to be the only means of clearly conceiving the nature of such phenomena.

PARETO   1848-1923

It was a happy circumstance for the beginning of astronomy that in Kepler's time the observations of Mars were not too exact. If they had been, Kepler would not have discovered that the curve described by the planet was an ellipse and he would have failed to discover the law of planetary motion. It was also fortunate that he chose to study the motion of Mars rather than the motion of the Moon, whose perturbations are much greater.

What was then due to good chance the method of successive approximations ought to do now. There are always those who complain that the scientific theories of economics or of sociology neglect certain details. That is their merit. We are first to get a general idea of a phenomenon, neglecting the details, considering them as perturbations; then to take in these details, first the more important and successively the less important.

Give me a good fruitful error any time, full of seeds, bursting with its own corrections. You can keep your sterile truth for yourself.

But If You Treat Life Abstractly —

WILLIAM JAMES   1842–1910

You reach the Mephistophelian point of view as well as the point of view of justice by treating cases as if they belonged rigorously to abstract classes. Pure rationalism, complete immunity from prejudice, consists in refusing to see that the case before one is absolutely unique. It is always possible to treat the country of one's nativity, the house of one's fathers, the bed in which one's mother died, nay, the mother herself if need be, on a naked equality with all other specimens of so many respective genera. It shows the world in a clear frosty light from which all fuliginous mists of affection, all swamp-lights of sentimentality, are absent. Straight and immediate action becomes easy then — witness a Napoleon's or a Frederick's career. But the question always remains, "Are not the mists and vapors *worth* retaining?" The illogical refusal to treat certain concretes by the mere law of their genus has made the drama of human history. The obstinate insisting that tweedledum is *not* tweedledee is the bone and marrow of life. Look at the Jews and the Scots, with their miserable factions and sectarian disputes, their loyalties and patriotisms and exclusions

— their annals now become a classic heritage, because men of genius took part and sang in them. A thing is important if any one *think* it important. The process of history consists in certain folks becoming possessed of the mania that certain special things are important infinitely, whilst other folks cannot agree in the belief. The Shah of Persia refused to be taken to the Derby Day, saying, "It is already known to me that one horse can run faster than another." He made the question "*which* horse?" immaterial. Any question can be made immaterial by subsuming all its answers under a common head. Imagine what college ball-games and races would be if the teams were to forget the absolute distinctness of Harvard from Yale and think of both as One in the higher genus College. The sovereign road to indifference, whether to evils or to goods, lies in the thought of the higher genus. "When we have meat before us," says Marcus Aurelius, seeking indifference to *that* kind of good, "we must receive the impression that this is the dead body of a fish, and this is the dead body of a bird or of a pig; and again that this Falernian is only a little grape-juice, and this purple robe some sheep's wool dyed with the blood of a shell-fish. Such, then, are these impressions, and they reach the things themselves and penetrate them, and we see what kind of things they are. Just in the same way ought we to act through life, and where there are things which appear most worthy of our approbation, we ought to lay them bare and look at their worthlessness and strip them of all the words by which they are exalted."

JOHN DEWEY   1859–1952

The importance of the intellectual transition from concrete to abstract is generally recognized. But it is often misconceived. It is not infrequently regarded as if it signified simply the selection by discriminative attention of some one quality or relation from a total object already sensibly present or present in memory. In fact, it marks a change in dimensions. Things are concrete to us in the degree in which they are either means directly used or are ends directly appropriated and enjoyed. Mathematical ideas were "concrete" when they were employed exclusively for building bins for grain or measuring land, selling goods, or aiding a pilot in guiding his ship. They became abstract when they were freed from connection with any particular existential application and use. This happened when operations made possible by symbols were performed exclusively with reference to facilitating and directing other operations also symbolic in nature. It is one kind of thing, a concrete one, to measure the area of a triangle so as to measure a piece of land, and another kind — an abstract one — to measure it simply as a means of measuring other areas symbolically designated. The latter type of operation makes possible a system of conceptions related together *as* conceptions.

WHITEHEAD *is not content with such a dusty answer:*
Abstraction expresses nature's mode of interaction and is not merely mental. When it abstracts, thought is merely conforming to nature — or rather, it is exhibiting itself as an element in nature. Synthesis and analysis require each other. Such a conception is paradoxical if you will persist in thinking of the actual world as a collection of passive actual substances with their private characters or qualities. In that case, it must be nonsense to ask, how one such substance can form a component in the make-up of another such substance. So long as this conception is retained, the difficulty is not relieved by calling each actual substance an event, or a pattern, or an occasion. The difficulty, which arises for such a conception, is to explain how the substances can be actually together in a sense derivative from that in which each individual substance is actual. But the conception of the world here adopted is that of functional activity. By that I mean that every actual thing is something by reason of its activity; whereby its nature consists in its relevance to other things, and its individuality consists in its synthesis of other things so far as they are relevant to it.

THE TECHNIQUE OF THOUGHT

There is a technique, a knack, for thinking, just as there is for doing other things. You are not wholly at the mercy of your thoughts, any more than they are you. They are a machine you can learn to operate.

EMERSON   **1872**

Look sharply after your thoughts. They come unlooked for, like a new bird seen on your trees, and, if you turn to your usual task, disappear; and you shall never find that perception again; never, I say — but perhaps years, ages, and I know not what events and worlds may lie between you and its return!

BARRETT WENDELL   **1855–1921**

My method of clearing my ideas is by no means the only one. I have known people who could do it best by talking; by putting somebody else in a comfortable chair and making him listen to their efforts to discover what they really think. I have known others who could really do best by sitting still and pondering in apparent idleness; others who could do best by walking alone in the open air; others, by stating to themselves the problems they wish to solve, and then going about all manner of business, trusting from experience, to something they call unconscious cerebration. Each man, I take it, must find his own method; at different times each man may find different methods the best.

The Art of Thought

GRAHAM WALLAS   **1858–1932**

Helmholtz, for instance, the great German physicist, speaking in 1891 at a banquet on his seventieth birthday, described the way in which his most important new thoughts had come to him. He said that after previous investigation of the problem "in all directions . . . happy ideas come unexpectedly without effort, like an inspiration. So far as I am concerned, they have never come to me when my mind was fatigued, or when I was at my working table. . . . They came particularly readily during the slow ascent of wooded hills on a sunny day."

Helmholtz here gives us three stages in the formation of a new thought. The first in time I shall call Preparation, the stage during which the problem was "investigated . . . in all directions"; the second is the stage during which he was not consciously thinking about the problem, which I shall call Incubation; the third, consisting of the appearance of the "happy idea" together with the psychological events which immediately preceded and accompanied that appearance, I shall call Illumination.

And I shall add a fourth stage, of Verification, which Helmholtz does not here mention. Henri Poincaré, for instance, in the book *Science and Method,* describes in vivid detail the successive stages of two of his great mathematical discoveries. Both of them came to him after a period of Incubation (due in one case to his military service as a reservist, and in the other case to a journey), during which no conscious mathematical thinking was done, but, as Poincaré believed, much unconscious mental exploration took place. In both cases Incubation was preceded by a Preparation stage of hard, conscious, systematic, and fruitless analysis of the problem. In both cases the final idea came to him "with the same characteristics of conciseness, suddenness, and immediate certainty." Each was followed by a period of Verification, in which both the validity of the idea was tested, and the idea itself was reduced to exact form. "It never happens," says Poincaré, in his description of the Verification stage, "that unconscious work supplies ready-made the result of a lengthy calculation in which we have only to apply fixed rules. . . . All that we can hope from these inspirations, which are the fruit of unconscious work, is to obtain points of departure or such calculations. As for the calculations themselves, they must be made in the second period of conscious work which follows the inspiration, and in which the results of the inspiration are verified and the consequences deduced. The rules of these calculations are strict and complicated; they demand discipline, attention, will, and consequently, consciousness."

In the daily stream of thought these four different stages constantly overlap each other as we explore different problems. An economist reading a Blue Book, a physiologist watching an experiment, or a business man going through his morning's letters, may at the same time be "incubating" on a problem which he proposed to himself a few days ago, be accumulating knowledge in "preparation" for a second problem, and be "verifying" his conclusions on a third problem. Even in exploring the same problem, the mind may be unconsciously incubating on one aspect of it, while it is consciously employed in preparing for or verifying another aspect. And it must always be remembered that much very important thinking, done for instance by a poet exploring his own memories, or by a man trying to see clearly his emotional relation to his country or his party, resembles musical composition in that the stages leading to success are not very easily fitted into a "problem and solution" scheme. Yet, even when success in thought means the creation of something felt to be beautiful and true rather than the solution of a prescribed problem, the four stages of Preparation, Incubation, Illumination, and the Verification of the final result can generally be distinguished from each other.

If we accept this analysis, we are in a position to ask to what degree, and by what means, we can bring conscious effort, and the habits which arise from conscious effort, to bear upon each of the four stages. Preparation includes the whole process of intellectual education. Men have known for thousands of years that conscious effort and its resulting habits can be used to improve the

thought-processes of young persons, and have formulated
for that purpose an elaborate art of education. The "educated" man can, in consequence, "put his mind on" to
a chosen subject, and "turn his mind off" in a way which
is impossible to an uneducated man. The educated man
has also acquired, by the effort of observation and mem-
orizing, a body of remembered facts and words which
gives him a wider range in the final moment of association, as well as a number of those habitual tracks of
association which constitute "thought-systems" like
"French policy" or "scholastic philosophy" or "biological
evolution," and which present themselves as units in the
process of thought.

The educated man has, again, learnt, and can, in the
Preparation stage, voluntarily or habitually follow out,
rules as to the order in which he shall direct his attention to the successive elements in a problem. Hobbes referred to this fact when in the *Leviathan* he described
"regulated thought" and contrasted it with that "wild
ranging of the mind" which occurs when the thought-
process is undirected. Regulated thought is, he says, a
"seeking." "Sometimes," for instance, "a man seeks what
he has lost. . . . Sometimes a man knows a place deter-
minate, within the compass whereof he is to seek; and
then his thoughts run over all the parts thereof, in the
same manner as one would sweep a room to find a jewel;
or as a spaniel ranges the field, till he finds a scent; or as
a man should run over the alphabet, to start a rhyme."
A spaniel with the brain of an educated human being
could not, by a direct effort of will, scent a partridge in
a distant part of the field. But he could so "quarter" the
field by a preliminary voluntary arrangement that the
less-voluntary process of smelling would be given every
chance of successfully taking place.

There remain the second and third stages, Incubation
and Illumination. The Incubation stage covers two different things, of which the first is the negative fact that
during Incubation we do not voluntarily or consciously
think on a particular problem, and the second is the positive fact that a series of unconscious and involuntary (or

foreconscious and forevoluntary) mental events may take place during that period. It is the first fact about Incubation which I shall now discuss, leaving the second fact — of subconscious thought during Incubation, and the relation of such thought to Illumination — to be more fully discussed in connection with the Illumination stage. Voluntary abstention from conscious thought on any particular problem may, itself, take two forms: the period of abstention may be spent either in conscious mental work on other problems, or in a relaxation from all conscious mental work. The first kind of Incubation economizes time, and is therefore often the better. We can often get more result in the same time by beginning several problems in succession, and voluntarily leaving them unfinished while we turn to others, than by finishing our work on each problem at one sitting. A well-known academic psychologist, for instance, who was also a preacher, told me that he found by experience that his Sunday sermon was much better if he posed the problem on Monday, than if he did so later in the week, although he might give the same number of hours of conscious work to it in each case. It seems to be a tradition among practicing barristers to put off any consideration of each brief to the latest possible moment before they have to deal with it, and to forget the whole matter as rapidly as possible after dealing with it. This fact may help to explain a certain want of depth which has often been noticed in the typical lawyer-statesman, and which may be due to his conscious thought not being sufficiently extended and enriched by subconscious thought.

But, in the case of the more difficult forms of creative thought, the making, for instance, of a scientific discovery, or the writing of a poem or play, or the formulation of an important political decision, it is desirable not only that there should be an interval free from conscious thought on the particular problem concerned, but also that that interval should be so spent that nothing should interfere with the free working of the unconscious or partially conscious processes of the mind. In those cases, the stage of Incubation should include a large amount of actual mental relaxation. It would, indeed, be interesting to examine, from that point of view, the biographies of a couple of hundred original thinkers and writers. A. R. Wallace, for instance, hit upon the theory of evolution by natural selection in his berth during an attack of malarial fever at sea; and Darwin was compelled by ill-health to spend the greater part of his waking hours in physical and mental relaxation. Sometimes a thinker has been able to get a sufficiency of relaxation owing to a disposition to idleness, against which he has vainly struggled. More often, perhaps, what he has thought to be idleness, is really that urgent craving for intense and uninterrupted day-dreaming which Anthony Trollope describes in his account of his boyhood.

One effect of such a comparative biographical study might be the formulation of a few rules as to the relation between original intellectual work and the virtue of industry. There are thousands of idle "geniuses" who require to learn that, without a degree of industry in Preparation and Verification, of which many of them have no conception, no great intellectual work can be done, and that the habit of procrastination may be even more disastrous to a professional thinker than it is to a man of business. And yet a thinker of good health and naturally fertile mind may have to be told that mere industry is for him, as it was for Trollope in his later years, the worst temptation of the devil.

Mental relaxation during the Incubation stage may of course include, and sometimes requires, a certain amount of physical exercise. I have already quoted Helmholtz's reference to "the ascent of wooded hills on a sunny day." A. Carrel, the great New York physiologist, is said to receive all his really important thoughts while quietly walking during the summer vacation in his native Brittany. Jastrow says that "thinkers have at all times resorted to the restful inspiration of a walk in the woods or a stroll over hill and dale." When I once discussed this fact with an athletic Cambridge friend, he expressed his gratitude for any evidence which would prove that it was the duty of all intellectual workers to spend their vacations in Alpine climbing. Alpine climbing has undoubtedly much to give both to health and to imagination, but it would be an interesting quantitative problem whether Goethe, while riding a mule over the Gemmi Pass, and Wordsworth, while walking over the Simplon, were in a more or in a less fruitful condition of Incubation than are a modern Alpine Club party ascending with hands and feet and rope and ice-axe, the Finster-Aarhorn.

But perhaps the most dangerous substitute for bodily and mental relaxation during the stage of Incubation is neither violent exercise nor routine administration, but the habit of industrious passive reading. Schopenhauer wrote that "to put away one's own original thoughts in order to take up a book is the sin against the Holy Ghost." During the century from 1760 to 1860, many of the best brains in England were prevented from acting with full efficiency by the way in which the Greek and Latin classics were then read. It is true that Shelley's imagination was stung into activity by Plato and Aeschylus, and that Keats won a new vision of life from Chapman's translation of Homer; but even the ablest of those who then accepted the educational ideals of Harrow and Eton and Oxford and Cambridge did not approach the classical writers with Shelley's or Keats' hunger in their souls. They plodded through Horace and Sophocles and Virgil and Demosthenes with a mild conscious aesthetic feeling, and with a stronger and less conscious feeling of social, intellectual, and moral superiority; anyone who was in the habit of reading the classics with his feet on the fender must certainly, they felt, be not only a gentleman and a scholar but also a good man.

THOUGHT AND ACTION

We cannot think first and act afterwards. From the moment of birth we are immersed in action, and can only fitfully guide it by taking thought.

A. N. WHITEHEAD

If we put together all that we have learned from anthropology and ethnology about primitive men and primitive society, we perceive that the first task of life is to live. Men begin with acts, not with thoughts.

W. G. SUMNER

Action the Source of Thought

JOHN JAY CHAPMAN   1862–1933

The generous youths who came to manhood between 1820 and 1830, while this deadly era was maturing, seem to have undergone a revulsion against the world almost before touching it; at least two of them suffered, revolted, and condemned, while still boys sitting on benches in school, and came forth advancing upon this old society like gladiators. The activity of William Lloyd Garrison, the man of action, preceded by several years that of Emerson, who is his prophet. Both of them were parts of one revolution. One of Emerson's articles of faith was that a man's thoughts spring from his actions rather than his actions from his thoughts, and possibly the same thing holds good for society at large. Perhaps all truths, whether moral or economic, must be worked out in real life before they are discovered by the student, and it was therefore necessary that Garrison should be evolved earlier than Emerson.

"Logic! Good gracious! What rubbish!" exclaimed E. M. Forster's Old Lady. "How can I tell what I think till I see what I say?"

Speak Before You Think

JOHN J. CHAPMAN TO HENRY JAMES   1926

There are lots of people who can't think seriously without injuring their minds. Their minds were not meant for this use, and so the more they think the feebler they grow.

The cure is simple.

Speak out opinions before you think — and before the other fellow speaks. Thus you will give your mind some chance of forming them in a natural way — unconsciously. Accustom yourself to not knowing what your opinions are till you have blurted them out, and thus find what they are. That's what talk is for — and it doesn't prevent the careful summarizing of ideas upon occasion when this is in order. Your valued father went the limit in the expression of things in writing in this improvised way, for he never knew quite what was in his mind — as he told me himself — till he wrote; and it was by this course that he made his most telling cracks: for it is only in the poetic element that truth is told. For truth to be truth must be new.

If one is dealing with such simple matters as making an engine — adding a cog to it — or finding a microbe — you may reason and ratiocinate to good ends. But if you're dealing with human nature in any form, you go broke if you reason — you're an ass to reason — you must put the thing off your mind and allow the probabilities to occur to you — and never be sure then.

O. W. HOLMES, JR.   1905

General propositions do not decide concrete cases. The decision will depend on a judgment or intuition more subtle than any articulate major premise.

What Philosophy Has to Offer

CHARLES S. PEIRCE   1839–1914

There are sciences, of course, many of whose results are almost immediately applicable to human life, such as physiology and chemistry. But the true scientific investigator completely loses sight of the utility of what he is about. It never enters his mind. Do you think that the physiologist who cuts up a dog reflects, while doing so, that he may be saving a human life? Nonsense. If he did, it would spoil him for a scientific man; and then the vivisection would become a crime. However, in physiology and in chemistry, the man whose brain is occupied with utilities, though he will not do much for science, may do a great deal for human life. But in philosophy, touching as it does upon matters which are, and ought to be, sacred to us, the investigator who does not stand aloof from all intent to make practical applications will not only obstruct the advance of the pure science, but, what is infinitely worse, he will endanger his own moral integrity and that of his readers.

In my opinion, the present infantile condition of philosophy — for as long as earnest and industrious students of it are able to come to agreement upon scarce a single principle, I do not see how it can be considered as otherwise than in its infancy — is due to the fact that during this century it has chiefly been pursued by men who have not been nurtured in dissecting-rooms and other laboratories, and who consequently have not been animated by the true scientific *Eros*;[1] but who have on the contrary come from theological seminaries, and have consequently been inflamed with a desire to amend the lives of themselves and others, a spirit no doubt more important than the love of science, for men in average situations, but radically unfitting them for the task of scientific investigation. And it is precisely because of this utterly unsettled and uncertain condition of philosophy at present that I regard any practical applications of it to religion and conduct as exceedingly dangerous. I have not one word to say against the philosophy of religion or of ethics in general or in particular. I only say that for the present it is all far too dubious to warrant risking any human life upon it. I do not say that philosophical science should not ultimately influence religion and morality; I only say that it should be allowed to do so only with secular slowness and the most conservative caution.

Now I may be utterly wrong in all this, and I do not

---

[1] *Eros* is a direct reference to Plato's *Symposium*, where it is hard to say that it doesn't mean God. *The Editors.*

propose to argue the question. I do not ask you to go with me. But to avoid any possible misapprehension, I am bound honestly to declare that I do not hold forth the slightest promise that I have any philosophical wares to offer you which will make you either better men or more successful men.

If we fall into the error of believing that vitally important questions are to be decided by reasoning, the only hope of salvation lies in formal logic, which demonstrates in the clearest manner that reasoning itself testifies to its own ultimate subordination to sentiment. It is like a Pope who should declare *ex cathedra* and call upon all the faithful to implicitly believe on pain of damnation by the power of the keys that he was *not* the supreme authority.

Sentimentality

G. K. CHESTERTON   1874–1936

The chief of all, of course, is that miserable fear of being sentimental, which is the meanest of all the modern terrors — meaner even than the terror which produces hygiene. Everywhere the robust and uproarious humour has come from the men who were capable, not merely of sentimentalism, but a very silly sentimentalism. There has been no humour so robust or uproarious as that of the sentimentalist Steele or the sentimentalist Sterne or the sentimentalist Dickens. These creatures who wept like women were the creatures who laughed like men. It is true that the humour of Micawber is good literature and that the pathos of Little Nell is bad. But the kind of man who had the courage to write so badly in the one case is the kind of man who would have the courage to write so well in the other.

T. H. HUXLEY   1825–1895

The world is neither wise nor just, but it makes up for its folly and injustice by being damnably sentimental.

INTELLIGENCE AND CONDUCT

I come from the Town of Stupidity; it lieth about four degrees beyond the City of Destruction.

BUNYAN

It seems to me that the whole scheme of salvation depends on having a required modicum of intelligence. People are born fools and damned for not being wiser. I often say over to myself the verse, "O God, be merciful to me a fool," the fallacy of which to my mind (you won't agree with me) is in the "me," that it looks on man as a little God over against the universe, instead of as a cosmic ganglion, a momentary intersection of what humanly speaking we call streams of energy, such as gives white light at one point and the power of making syllogisms at another, but always an inseverable part of the unimaginable, in which we live and move and have our being, no more needing its mercy than my little toe needs mine. It would be well if the intelligent classes could forget the word sin and think less of being good. We learn how to behave as lawyers, soldiers, merchants, or what not by being them. Life, not the parson, teaches conduct.

The player on the other side is hidden from us. We know that his play is always fair, just, and patient. But also we know, to our cost, that he never overlooks a mistake, or makes the smallest allowance for ignorance. To the man who plays well, the highest stakes are paid, with that sort of overflowing generosity with which the strong shows delight in strength. And one who plays ill is check-mated — without haste, but without remorse.

VOLTAIRE 1694–1778
And whoever begins by being a dupe ends by becoming a scoundrel.

HOW TO COMPOSE YOUR LIFE

Pursue, keep up with, circle round and round your life, as a dog does his master's chaise. Do what you love. Know your own bone; gnaw at it, bury it, unearth it, and gnaw it still.

THOREAU

MONTAIGNE 1533–1592

If you have known how to compose your life, you have accomplished a great deal more than the man who knows how to compose a book. Have you been able to take your stride? You have done more than the man who has taken cities and empires.

The great and glorious masterpiece of man is to live to the point. All other things — to reign, to hoard, to build — are, at most, but inconsiderate props and appendages.

The truly wise man must be as intelligent and expert in the use of natural pleasures as in all the other functions of life. So the sages live, gently yielding to the laws of our human lot, to Venus and to Bacchus. Relaxation and versatility, it seems to me, go best with a strong and noble mind, and do it singular honor. There is nothing more notable in Socrates than that he found time, when he was an old man, to learn music and dancing, and thought it time well spent.

MACHIAVELLI 1469–1527

Here I am on the farm; and, since those last experiences of mine, the number of days that I have spent in Florence does not amount to twenty, all told. I have spent my time since then in fowling — thrushes — with my own hand, rising before daylight. I have been setting birdlime and going along with a bundle of cages on my back, for all the world like Geta when he came from the harbour with Amphitryon's books. I have been catching at least two thrushes a day, and sometimes as many as seven. In this way I occupied myself for the whole of September. After that, this sport came to an end (to my regret, in spite of its being odd and not worth caring about); and I will now tell you what my life has been since then.

I rise with the sun, and go my ways to my wood, which I am having cut. I stay there two hours inspecting the previous day's work and passing the time with the wood-cutters, who always have some trouble on hand, with their neighbors if not among themselves. About that wood I have a thousand tales to tell of the things that have happened to me.

After leaving the wood, I go off to a spring, and from there to a fowling-place of mine, with a book stowed away: a Dante or a Petrarch or one of these minor poets: say, Tibulus or Ovid or the like. I read those tales of lovers' passions and call to mind my own and indulge myself a little in such reminiscences. Then I transfer my quarters to the roadside inn, talk with the passersby, ask them the news of their villages, hear all kinds of things and note the various tastes and diverse fantasies of Mankind. Then comes the hour for dinner, when I eat, with my household, of such viands as this poor farm of mine and this tiny property can afford me. So soon as I have eaten, I return to the inn; and, here, most days, I find the inn-keeper, a butcher, a miller, and two kiln-tenders. With this company I amuse myself to day's end playing cards — source of a thousand disputes and a thousand bouts of mutual abuse. Most times the stakes are a farthing; and, for all that, our shouts can be heard from San Casciano. Thus, amid these trifles in which I am enveloped, I drag my brain out of the mildew in which it moulders and purge out the malignity of my fortune — content to let Fate trample on me in this way, if only to see whether she won't become ashamed of herself.

When the evening comes, I return to the house, and go into my study; and at the door I take off my country clothes, all caked with mud and slime, and put on court dress; and, when I am thus decently re-clad, I enter into the ancient mansions of the men of ancient days. And there I am received by my hosts with all loving-kindness, and I feast myself on that food which alone is my true nourishment, and which I was born for. And here I am not abashed to speak with these ancients and to question them on the reasons for their actions. And they, in their humanity, deign to answer me. And so, for four hours long, I feel no *gêne*, I forget every worry, I have no fear of poverty, I am not appalled by the thought of death: I sink my identity in that of my ancient mentors. And since Dante says that there can be no science without some retention of that which Thought has once comprehended, I have made notes of the mental capital that I have acquired from their conversation, and have composed an essay *De Principatibus,* in which I try to penetrate as deep as I can into the theory of the subject — discussing what Sovereignty is, what varieties of it there are, how these are acquired, and how they are maintained, and through what causes they are lost. And if ever any conceit of mine has pleased you, you should not be displeased by this, while a sovereign — and especially one newly installed — should find it acceptable. Accordingly, I am dedicating it to His Magnificence Giuliano [de' Medici]. Filippo Casavecchia has seen it and will be able to regale you with the substance of the thing and with the arguments I have had with him — though all the time I am enriching it and re-polishing it.

ERASMUS   1466–1536

Avoid late and unseasonable Studies, for they murder Wit, and are very prejudicial to Health. The Muses love the Morning, and that is a fit Time for Study. After you have din'd, either divert yourself at some Exercise, or take a Walk, and discourse merrily, and Study between whiles. As for Diet, eat only as much as shall be sufficient to preserve Health, and not as much or more than the Appetite may crave. Before Supper, take a little Walk, and do the same after Supper. A little before you go to sleep read something that is exquisite, and worth remembering; and contemplate upon it till you fall asleep; and when you awake in the Morning, call yourself to an Account for it.

LEONARDO DA VINCI   1452–1519

Small rooms or dwellings set the mind in the right path, large ones cause it to go astray.

JANE AUSTEN   1775–1817

"I hope everyone had a pleasant evening," said Mr. Woodhouse, in his quiet way. "I had. Once I felt the fire rather too much; but then I moved back my chair a little and it did not disturb me."

WALTER BAGEHOT   1826–1877

Pascal said that most of the evils of life arose from "man's being unable to sit still in a room"; and though I do not go that length, it is certain that we should have been a far wiser race than we are if we had been readier to sit quiet — we should have known much better the way in which it was best to act when we came to act. The rise of physical science, the first great body of practical truth provable to all men, exemplifies this in the plainest way. If it had not been for quiet people, who sat still and studied the sections of the cone, if other quiet people had not sat still and studied the theory of infinitesimals, or other quiet people had not sat still and worked out the doctrine of chances, the most "dreamy moonshine," as the purely practical mind would consider, of all human pursuits; if "idle star-gazers" had not watched long and carefully the motions of the heavenly bodies — our modern astronomy would have been impossible, and without our astronomy "our ships, our colonies, our seamen," all which makes modern life could not have existed. Ages of sedentary, quiet, thinking people were required before that noisy existence began, and without those pale preliminary students it never could have been brought into being. And nine-tenths of modern science is in this respect the same: it is the produce of men whom their contemporaries thought dreamers — who were laughed at for caring for what did not concern them — who, as the proverb went, "walked into a well from looking at the stars" — who were believed to be useless, if anyone could be such. And the conclusion is plain that if there had been more such people, if the world had not laughed at those there were, if rather it had encouraged them, there would have been a great accumulation of proved science ages before there was. It was the irritable activity, the "wish to be doing something," that prevented it. Most men inherited a nature too eager and too restless to be quiet and find out things; and even worse — with their idle clamor they "disturbed the brooding hen"; they would not let those be quiet who wished to be so, and out of whose calm thought much good might have come forth.

JOHN SELDEN   1584–1654

Ceremony keeps up all things. 'Tis like a penny glass to a rich spirit, or some excellent water. Without it the water were spilt, the spirit lost.

THOMAS LOVE PEACOCK   1785–1866

Names are changed more readily than doctrines, and doctrines more readily than ceremonies.

"I find it won't do," the Duchess of Argyle said, dying. "Desire the Duke to leave the room."

Confucius

LOWES DICKINSON   1862–1932

Confucianism, it is sometimes said, is not a religion at all; and if by religion be meant a set of dogmatic propositions dealing with a supernatural world radically distinct from our own, the statement is, no doubt, strictly true. It was, in fact, one of the objects of Confucius to discourage preoccupation with the supernatural, and the true disciple endeavors in this respect to follow in his master's footsteps. "Beware of religion," a Mandarin says, meaning "beware of superstition"; and in this sense, but in this sense only, Confucianism is irreligious. Again, it is said that Confucianism is merely an ethical system; and this, too, is true, in so far as its whole aim and purport is to direct and inspire right conduct. But, on the other hand — and this is the point I wish to make — it is not merely a teaching, but a life. The principles it enjoins are those which are actually embodied in the structure of our society, so that they are inculcated not merely by written and spoken word, but by the whole habit of everyday experience.

This is from *Letters from a Chinese Official,* published as if they came from a genuine Chinese and everyone at first accepted them as such.

ALDOUS HUXLEY   1894–

Nowhere except in China has the gentleman's code assumed the proportions of a great religion, nowhere else has the codifier, the original arch-gentleman and scholar, been regarded as a religious leader. Confucius was no solitary, and his mind was so excessively matter-of-fact that he seems not to have preoccupied himself in the least with gods or other worlds, only with man's behavior in this.

CONFUCIUS   551–479 B.C.

The superior man understands what is right; the inferior man understands what will sell.

The superior man loves his soul; the inferior man loves his property. The superior man always remembers how he was punished for his mistakes; the inferior man always remembers what presents he got.

The superior man is liberal toward others' opinions, but does not completely agree with them; the inferior man completely agrees with others' opinions, but is not liberal toward them.

The superior man is firm, but does not fight; he mixes easily with others, but does not form cliques.

The superior man blames himself; the inferior man blames others.

The superior man is always candid and at ease with himself or others; the inferior man is always worried about something.

A man who has committed a mistake and doesn't correct it is committing another mistake.

Baron Wen Chi said that he always thought three times before he acted. When Confucius heard this, he remarked, "To think twice is quite enough."

Tsekung asked Confucius, "What would you say if all the people of the village like a person?" "That is not enough," replied Confucius. "What would you say if all the people of the village dislike a person?" "That is not enough," said Confucius. "It is better when the good people of the village like him, and the bad people of the village dislike him."

The people who live extravagantly are apt to be snobbish (or conceited), and the people who live simply are apt to be vulgar. I prefer the vulgar people to the snobs.

Tsekung asked, "Does the superior man also have certain things that he hates?" "Yes, there are things that the superior man hates," said Confucius. "He hates those who like to criticize people or reveal their weaknesses. He hates those who, in the position of inferiors, like to malign or spread rumors about those in authority. He hates those who are chivalrous and headstrong but are not restrained by propriety. He hates those who are sure of themselves and are narrow-minded." "But what do you hate?" asked Sze. "I hate those who like to spy on others and think they are very clever. I hate those who think they are brave when they are merely unruly. And I hate the wily persons who pretend to be honest gentlemen."

Tsekung asked about government, and Confucius replied: "People must have sufficient to eat; there must be a sufficient army; and there must be confidence of the people in the ruler." "If you are forced to give up one of these three objectives, what would you go without first?" asked Tsekung. Confucius said, "I would go without the army first." "And if you were forced to go without one of the two remaining factors, what would you rather go without?" asked Tsekung again. "I would rather go without sufficient food for the people. There have always been deaths in every generation since man lived, but a nation cannot exist without confidence in its ruler."

I know now why the moral life is not practical. The wise mistake moral law for something higher than what it really is; and the foolish do not know enough what moral law really is. I know now why the moral law is not understood. The noble natures want to live too high, high above their moral ordinary self; and ignoble natures do not live high enough, i.e., not up to their moral ordinary true self. There is no one who does not eat and drink. But few there are who really know flavor.

KOHELETH   5TH, 4TH, OR 3D CENTURY B.C.

What gain has a man of all his toil,
Which he toils under the sun?
Generation comes and generation goes,
But the earth remains forever.
The sun rises and the sun sets,
And to his rising place he returns.
Around to the south and circling to the north,
Around and around goes the wind,
And on its circuits the wind returns.

All streams flow into the sea,
But the sea is not full.
To the place whither the streams flow,
From there they flow back again.
Everything is wearied,
Beyond human utterance,
Beyond sight and hearing.
What has been is that which shall be;
And what has happened is that which shall happen,
So that there is nothing new under the sun.

Therefore, it seems to me the thing that is good and proper is to eat, drink, and to have a good time with all one's toil under the sun during the span of life which God has allotted to one, for that is his portion. Every man to whom God has given riches and possessions and who has also the power to enjoy it and to take his portion and to be happy in his toil — this is a gift of God. For he should remember that life is short and that God approves of joy.

I have seen all kinds of things in my life of vanity. Here is a righteous man who perishes by his righteousness, and there is a wicked man rounding out his life in his wickedness. Therefore, be not overrighteous and be not overwise — why ruin thyself? But do not be overwicked and do not be a fool — why die before thy time? It is good to take hold of this and not to refrain from that. There is no man on earth so righteous that he always does the right thing and never sins.

> *And again, I experienced under the sun that*
> *The race is not to the swift,*
> *Nor the battle to the strong;*
> *Wise men lack an income,*
> *Prophets do not possess riches,*
> *And the learned lack wealth,*
> *But time and chance overtake them all.*

Furthermore, man does not know his time. As fish are caught in a net, and as birds are trapped, so the children of men are entrapped at an unlucky moment, when evil comes suddenly upon them.

This I experienced under the sun, and it seemed a great evil to me.

There was a small town with few inhabitants, and a great king came and surrounded it and built great bulwarks against it. And there was in the town a man of humble birth but wise, and he saved the town through his wisdom, but no one took notice of that man of humble birth. And I reflected that wisdom nevertheless is

better than strength, even when the wisdom of the man
of humble birth is despised and his words be not heeded.

As thou knowest not the way of the spirit
into the bones in a pregnant womb,
so thou dost not know the work of God who makes all things.
In the morning sow thy seed,
and till evening let not thy hand rest,
For thou knowest not which will succeed, this or that,
or whether both alike shall be good.

This is Morris Jastrow's translation, not the Authorized Version, and it is made from the original text of Ecclesiastes restored, and stripped, he says, of later additions by pious commentators whose aim was to offset the unorthodox character of the original book.

Manner and Manners

LORD CHESTERFIELD TO HIS SON   1694–1773

I acquainted you in a former letter, that I had brought a bill into the House of Lords for correcting and reforming our present calendar, which is the Julian; and for adopting the Gregorian. I will now give you a more particular account of that affair; from which reflections will naturally occur to you, that I hope may be useful, and which I fear you have not made. It was notorious, that the Julian calendar was erroneous, and had overcharged the solar year with eleven days. Pope Gregory the Thirteenth corrected this error; his reformed calendar was immediately received by all the Catholic Powers in Europe, and afterwards adopted by all the Protestant ones, except Russia, Sweden, and England. It was not, in my opinion, very honourable for England to remain in a gross and avowed error, especially in such company; the inconveniency of it was likewise felt by all those who had foreign correspondences, whether political or mercantile. I determined, therefore, to attempt the reformation; I consulted the best lawyers and the most skilful astronomers, and we cooked up a bill for that purpose. But then my difficulty began: I was to bring in this bill, which was necessarily composed of law jargon and astronomical calculations, to both which I am an utter stranger. However, it was absolutely necessary to make the House of Lords think that I knew something of the matter; and also to make them believe that they knew something of it themselves, which they do not. For my own part, I could just as soon have talked Celtic or Sclavonian to them, as astronomy, and they would have understood me full as well: so I resolved to do better than speak to the purpose, and to please instead of informing them. I gave them, therefore, only an historical account of calendars, from the Egyptian down to the Gregorian, amusing them now and then with little episodes; but I was particularly attentive to the choice of my words, to the harmony and roundness of my periods, to my elocution, to my action. This succeeded, and ever will succeed; they thought I informed, because I pleased them; and many of them said, that I had made the whole very clear to them; when, God knows, I had not even attempted it. Lord Macclesfield, who had the greatest share in forming the bill, and who is one of the greatest mathematicians and astronomers in Europe, spoke afterwards with infinite knowledge, and all the clearness that so intricate a matter would admit of; but as his words, his periods and his utterance, were not near so good as mine, the preference was most unanimously, though most unjustly, given to me.

Practical Advice from the Greatest of Theorists

NEWTON   1642–1727

On the 18th of May, 1669, Isaac Newton wrote to his young friend Mr. Aston:

Trinity College, Cambridge
May 18, 1669.

Sir, —

Since in your letter you give mee so much liberty of spending my judgment about what may be to your advantage in travelling, I shall do it more freely than perhaps otherwise would have been decent. First then, I will lay down some general rules, most of which, I believe, you have considered already; but, if any of them be new to you, they may excuse the rest; if none at all, yet is my punishment more in writing than yours in reading. When you come to any fresh company — 1. Observe their humours. 2. Suit your own carriage thereto, by which insinuation you will make their converse more free and open. 3. Let your discourse be more in querys and doubtings than peremptory assertions or disputings, it being the designe of travellers to learn, not to teach. Besides, it will persuade your acquaintance that you have the greater esteem of them, and soe make them more ready to communicate what they know to you; whereas, nothing sooner occasions disrespect and quarrels than peremptorinesse. You will find little or no advantage in seeming wiser, or much more ignorant, than your company. 4. Seldom discommend anything, though never so bad, or do it but moderately, lest you bee unexpectedly forced to an unhansom retraction. It is safer to commend anything more than it deserves; for commendations meet not soe often with oppositions, or at least, are not usually so ill-resented by men that think otherwise, as discommendations; and you will insinuate into men's favour by nothing sooner than seeming to approve and commend what they like; but beware of doing it by a comparison. 5. If you be affronted, it is better, in a forraine country, to pass it by in silence, and with a jest, though with some dishonour, than to endeavour revenge; for, in the first case, your credit's ne'er the worse when you return to England, or come into other company that have not heard of the quarrel. But, in the second case, you may beare the marks of the quarrel while you live, if you out-live it at all. But, if you find yourself unavoidably engaged, 'tis best, I think, if you can command your passion and language, to keep them pretty eavenly at some certain moderate pitch, not much hightning them to exasperate your adversary or provoke his friends, nor letting them grow over much dejected to make him insult. In a word, if

you can keep reason above passion, that and watchful-
nesse will be your best defendants. To which purpose
you may consider that, though such excuses as this — He
provok't mee so much I could not forbear — may pass
among friends, yet amongst strangers they are insignificant, and only argue a traveller's weaknesse. To these
I may add some general heads for inquiries or observations, such as at present I can think on. As — 1. To observe the policys, wealth, and state affairs of nations, so
far as a solitary traveller may conveniently doe. Their
impositions upon all sorts of people, trades, or commoditys, that are remarkable. 3. Their laws and customs; how far they differ from ours. 4. Their trades and
arts; wherein they excel or come short of us in England.
5. Such fortifications as you shall meet with; their fashion, strength, and advantages for defence, and other such
military affairs as are considerable. 6. The power and
respect belonging to their degrees of nobility or maj-
istracy. 7. It will not be time mispent to make a
catalogue of the names and excellencys of those men that
are most wise, learned, or esteemed in any nation. 8. Observe the mechanisme and manner of guiding ships. 9.
Observe the products of nature in several places, especially in mines, with the circumstances of mining, and of
extracting metals or minerals out of their oare, and of
refining them; and if you meet with any transmutations
out of their own species into another, as out of iron into
copper, out of any metal into quicksilver, out of one salt
into another, or into an insipid body, etc., those above all
will be worth your noting, being the most luciferous,
and many times luciferous experiments too in philosophy.
10. The prices of diets and other things. 11. And the
staple commoditys of places.

These generals, such as at present I could think of, if
they will serve for nothing else, yet they may assist you
in drawing up a model to regulate your travels by. . . .
You may inform yourself whether the Dutch have any
tricks to keep their ships from being all worm-eaten in
their voyages to the Indies. Whether pendulum clocks do
any service in finding out the longitude, etc. I am very

weary, and shall not stay to part with a long compliment, only I wish you a good journey, and God be with you.

Is. NEWTON.

Pavlov's Bequest to the Academic Youth of Soviet Russia

Written just before his death, at the age of eighty-seven years, on February 27, 1936.

What can I wish to the youth of my country who devote themselves to science?

Firstly, gradualness. About this most important condition of fruitful scientific work I never can speak without emotion. Gradualness, gradualness and gradualness. From the very beginning of your work, school yourselves to severe gradualness in the accumulation of knowledge.

Learn the ABC of science before you try to ascend to its summit. Never begin the subsequent without mastering the preceding. Never attempt to screen an insufficiency of knowledge even by the most audacious surmise and hypothesis. Howsoever this soap-bubble will rejoice your eyes by its play, it inevitably will burst and you will have nothing except shame.

School yourselves to demureness and patience. Learn to inure yourselves to drudgery in science. Learn, compare, collect the facts!

Perfect as is the wing of a bird, it never could raise the bird up without resting on air. Facts are the air of a scientist. Without them you never can fly. Without them your "theories" are vain efforts.

But learning, experimenting, observing, try not to stay on the surface of the facts. Do not become the archivists of facts. Try to penetrate to the secret of their occurrence, persistently search for the laws which govern them.

Secondly, modesty. Never think that you already know all. However highly you are appraised, always have the courage to say of yourself — I am ignorant.

Do not allow haughtiness to take you in possession.

Due to that you will be obstinate where it is necessary to agree, you will refuse useful advice and friendly help, you will lose the standard of objectiveness.

Thirdly, passion. Remember that science demands from a man all his life. If you had two lives that would be not enough for you. Be passionate in your work and your searchings.

MME. DU DEFFAND TO HORACE WALPOLE   1697–1780

Come, come, it's only the passions that make you think.

WILLIAM JAMES   1868

I have been growing lately to feel that a great mistake of my past life — which has been prejudicial to my education, and by telling me which, and by making me understand it some years ago, someone might have conferred a great benefit on me — is an impatience of *results.* Inexperience of life is the cause of it, and I imagine it is generally an American characteristic. I think you suffer from it. Results should not be too voluntarily aimed at or too busily thought of. They are *sure* to float up of their own accord, from a long enough daily work at a given matter; and I think the work as a mere occupation ought to be the primary interest with us.

WILLIAM OSLER TO HIS STUDENTS   1849–1919

As to your method of work, I have a single bit of advice, which I give with the earnest conviction of its paramount influence in any success which may have attended my efforts in life — Take no thought for the morrow. Live neither in the past nor in the future, but let each day's work absorb your entire energies, and satisfy your widest ambition. That was a singular but very wise answer which Cromwell gave to Bellevire — "No one rises so high as he who knows not whither he is going," and there is much truth in it. The student who is worrying about his future, anxious over the examinations, doubting his fitness for the profession, is certain not to do so well as the man who cares for nothing but the matter in hand, and who knows not whither he is going!

GOETHE   1749–1832

> *Mein Kind, ich hab' es klug gemacht:*
> *Ich habe nie ueber das Denken gedacht.*

> *My boy, I'll say that I've been clever:*
> *I think, but think of thinking never.*

Ruskin said of Turner, the painter, that he did right only when he ceased to reflect, was powerful only when he made no effort, and successful only when he had taken no aim.

However, EMERSON *said that*

[the Greeks] cut the Pentelican marble as if it were snow, and their perfect works in architecture and sculpture seemed things of course, not more difficult than the completion of a new ship at the Medford yards, or new mills at Lowell. These things are in course, may be taken for granted.

The Substance of Laughter

OSLER TO SOME DOCTORS: 1848–1919

I cavilled at Bergson's conclusion — that like sea-froth the substance of laughter is scanty and the after-taste bitter. It is not always so. Joubert is right. There is a form that springs from the heart, heard every day in the merry voice of childhood, the expression of a laughter-loving spirit that defies analysis by the philosopher, which has nothing rigid or mechanical in it, and is totally without social significance. Bubbling spontaneously from the artless heart of child or man, without egoism and full of feeling, laughter is the music of life. After his magical survey of the world in the *Anatomy of Melancholy,* Burton could not well decide, *fleat Heraclitus an rideat Democritus,* whether to weep with the one or laugh with the other, and at the end of the day this is often the mental attitude of the doctor; but once with ears attuned to the music of which I speak, he is ever on the side of the great Abderite, and there is the happy possibility that, like Lionel in, I think, one of Shelley's poems, he may keep himself young with laughter.

HOBBES   1588–1679

Sudden glory is the passion which maketh those grimaces called laughter.

PLATO   427–347 B.C.

When you swear, swear seriously and solemnly, but at the same time with a smile, for a smile is the twin sister of seriousness.

This comes from his Sixth Epistle, near the end. Some solemn scholars have said that it is not Plato's at all, one of them partly because he thought it wrong to smile when you took an oath. Better scholars, Jaeger, Meyer, and Wilamowitz, assure us that it is genuine. Of course it is.

The Strangest Lightness

WILLIAM JAMES   1842–1910

I am often confronted by the necessity of standing by one of my empirical selves and relinquishing the rest. Not that I would not, if I could, be both handsome and fat and well-dressed, and a great athlete, and make a million a year, be a wit, a *bon-vivant,* a lady-killer, as well as a philosopher; a philanthropist, statesman, warrior, and African explorer, as well as a "tone-poet" and saint. But the thing is simply impossible. The millionaire's work would run counter to the saint's; the *bon-vivant* and the philanthropist would trip each other up; the philosopher and the lady-killer could not well keep house in the same tenement of clay. Such different characters may conceivably at the outset of life be alike *possible* to a man. But to make any one of them actual, the rest must more or less be suppressed. So the seeker of his truest, strongest, deepest self must review the list carefully, and pick out the one on which to stake his salvation. All other selves thereupon become unreal, but the fortunes of this self are real. Its failures are real failures, its triumphs real triumphs, carrying shame and gladness with them. This is as strong an example as there is of that selective industry of the mind on which I insisted some pages back. Our thought, incessantly deciding, among many things of a kind, which ones for it shall be realities, here chooses one of many possible selves or characters, and forthwith reckons it no shame to fail in any of those not adopted expressly as its own.

I, who for the time have staked my all on being a psychologist, am mortified if others know much more psychology than I. But I am contented to wallow in the grossest ignorance of Greek. My deficiencies there give me no sense of personal humiliation at all. Had I "pretensions" to be a linguist, it would have been just the reverse. So we have the paradox of a man shamed to death because he is only the second pugilist or the second oarsman in the world. That he is able to beat the whole population of the globe minus one is nothing; he has "pitted" himself to beat that one; and as long as he doesn't do that nothing else counts. He is to his own regard as if he were not, indeed he *is* not.

Yonder puny fellow, however, whom everyone can beat, suffers no chagrin about it, for he has long ago abandoned the attempt to "carry that line," as the merchants say, of self at all. With no attempt there can be no failure; with no failure no humiliation. So our self-feeling in this world depends entirely on what we *back* ourselves to be and do. It is determined by the ratio of our actualities to our supposed potentialities; a fraction of which our pretensions are the denominator and the numerator our success: thus,

$$\text{Self-esteem} = \frac{\text{Success}}{\text{Pretensions}}$$

Such a fraction may be increased as well by diminishing the denominator as by increasing the numerator.[1] To

[1] Cf. Carlyle: *Sartor Resartus*, "The Everlasting Yea." "I tell thee, blockhead, it all comes of thy vanity; of what thou fanciest those same deserts of thine to be. Fancy that thou deservest to be hanged (as is most likely), thou wilt feel it happiness to be only shot: fancy that thou deservest to be hanged in a hair halter, it will be a lux-

give up pretensions is as blessed a relief as to get them gratified; and where disappointment is incessant and the struggle unending, this is what men will always do. The history of evangelical theology, with its conviction of sin, its self-despair, and its abandonment of salvation by works, is the deepest of possible examples, but we meet others in every walk of life. There is the strangest lightness about the heart when one's nothingness in a particular line is once accepted in good faith.

G. K. CHESTERTON   1874–1936

The Sentimentalist, roughly speaking, is the man who wants to eat his cake and have it. He has no sense of honor about ideas; he will not see that one must pay for an idea as for anything else. He will have them all at once in one wild intellectual harem, no matter how much they quarrel and contradict each other.

LÉON BLUM   1872–

Life does not give itself to one who tries to keep all its advantages at once. I have often thought that morality may perhaps consist solely in the courage of making a choice.

---

ury to die in hemp. . . . What act of legislature was there that *thou* shouldst be happy? A little while ago thou hadst no right to *be* at all," etc., etc.

THE MOTIVES OF MEN

Why do we do what we do?

For a Beard on the Cosmos?

O. W. HOLMES, JR., TO POLLOCK   1910

I don't see why a man should despair because he doesn't
see a beard on his Cosmos. If he believes that he is inside
of it, not it inside of him, he knows that consciousness,
purpose, significance, and ideals are among its possibilities, and if he surmises *in vacuo* that those are all
finite expressions inadequate to the unimaginable, I see
no more ground for despair than when a Catholic says
that he does not know the thoughts and purposes of God.
It is a fallacy, I think, to look to any theory for motives
— we get our motives from our spontaneity — and the
business of Philosophy is to show that we are not fools
for doing what we want to do.

For Conscience' Sake?

MARK TWAIN   1835–1910

Conscience says to me, "What has poor Miss Watson done
to you, that you could see her nigger go off right under
your eyes and never say one single word? What did that
poor old woman do to you, that you could treat her so
mean? Why, she tried to learn you your book, she tried
to learn you your manners, she tried to be good to you
every way she knowed how. *That's* what she done."

I got to feeling so mean and so miserable I most wished
I was dead. I fidgeted up and down the raft, abusing myself to myself, and Jim was fidgeting up and down past

me. We neither of us could keep still. Every time he danced around and says, "Dah's Cairo!" it went through me like a shot, and I thought if it was Cairo I reckoned I would die of miserableness.

Jim talked out loud all the time while I was talking to myself. He was saying how the first thing he would do when he got to a free State he would go to saving up money and never spend a single cent, and when he got enough he would buy his wife, which was owned on a farm close to where Miss Watson lived; and then they would both work to buy the two children, and if their master wouldn't sell them, they'd get an Ab'litionist to go and steal them.

It most froze me to hear such talk. He wouldn't ever dared to talk such talk in his life before. Just see what a difference it made in him the minute he judged he was about free. It was according to the old saying: "Give a nigger an inch and he'll take an ell." Thinks I, this is what comes of my not thinking. Here was this nigger which I had as good as helped to run away, coming right out flat-footed and saying he would steal his children — children that belonged to a man I didn't even know; a man that hadn't ever done me no harm.

I was sorry to hear Jim say that, it was such a lowering of him. My conscience got to stirring me up hotter than ever, until at last I says to it: "Let up on me — it ain't too late, yet — I'll paddle ashore at the first light and tell." I felt easy, and happy and light as a feather, right off. All my troubles was gone. I went to looking out sharp for a light, and sort of singing to myself. By-and-by one showed. Jim sings out:

"We's safe, Huck, we's safe! Jump up and crack yo' heels, dat's de good ole Cairo at las', I jis knows it!"

I says:

"I'll take the canoe and go see, Jim. It mightn't be, you know."

He jumped and got the canoe ready, and put his old coat in the bottom for me to sit on, and give me the paddle; and as I shoved off, he says:

"Pooty soon I'll be a-shout'n for joy, en I'll say, it's

all on accounts o' Huck; I's a free man, en I couldn't ever ben free ef it hadn' been for Huck; Huck done it. Jim won't ever forgit you, Huck; you's de bes' fren' Jim's ever had; en you's de *only* fren' ole Jim's got now."

I was paddling off, all in a sweat to tell on him; but when he says this, it seemed to kind of take the tuck all out of me. I went along slow, then, and I warn't right down certain whether I was glad I started or whether I warn't. When I was fifty yards off, Jim says:

"Dah you goes, de ole true Huck; de on'y white gen'l'man dat ever kep' his promise to ole Jim!"

Well, I just felt sick. But I says, I *got* to do it — I can't get *out* of it. Right then, along comes a skiff with two men in it, with guns, and they stopped and I stopped. One of them says:

"What's that, yonder?"

"A piece of a raft," I says.

"Do you belong on it?"

"Yes, sir."

"Any men on it?"

"Only one, sir."

"Well, there's five niggers run off tonight, up yonder above the head of the bend. Is your man white or black?"

I didn't answer up prompt. I tried to, but the words wouldn't come. I tried, for a second or two, to brace up and out with it, but I warn't man enough — hadn't the spunk of a rabbit. I see I was weakening; so I just give up trying, and up and says:

"He's white."

For Morality's Sake?

CHARLES S. PEIRCE   1839–1914

Somewhat allied to the philosophy of religion is the science of ethics. It is equally useless. Now books of casuistry, indeed, using the word "casuistry" not in any technical sense, but merely to signify discussions of what ought to be done in various difficult situations, might be made at once extremely entertaining and positively useful. But casuistry is just what the ordinary treatises upon ethics do not touch, at least not seriously. They chiefly occupy themselves with reasoning out the basis of morality and other questions secondary to that. Now what's the *use* of prying into the philosophical basis of morality? We all know what morality is: it is behaving as you were brought up to behave; that is, to think you ought to be punished for not behaving. But to believe in thinking as you have been brought up to think defines *conservatism*. It needs no reasoning to perceive that morality is conservatism. But conservatism again means, as you will surely agree, not trusting to one's reasoning powers. To be a moral man is to obey the traditional maxims of your community without hesitation or discussion. Hence, ethics, which is reasoning out an explanation of morality, is — I will not say immoral, that would be going too far — composed of the very substance of immorality.

Ethics, then, even if not a positively dangerous study, as it sometimes proves, is as useless a science as can be conceived. But it must be said, in favor of ethical writers, that they are commonly free from the nauseating custom of boasting of the utility of their science.

As long as ethics is recognized as not being a matter of vital importance or in any way touching the student's conscience, it is, to a normal and healthy mind, a civilizing and valuable study — somewhat more so than the theory of whist, much more so than the question of the landing of Columbus, which things are insignificant not at all because they are useless, nor even because they are little in themselves, but simply and solely because they are detached from the great continuum of ideas.

Service?

LEARNED HAND   1872–1961

But for one reason or another, which we must leave to the psychologists if they can ever find out, you and I know that children take joy in making mud pies and block houses, that men like to set out in a whole-sail breeze, to put a horse over a troublesome jump, to play a good game of tennis, to do anything which calls for skill and self-control. These are only temporary and occasional performances; happily similar satisfactions do not stop there. May I borrow from my personal experience? A judge's life, like every other, has in it much of drudgery, senseless bickerings, stupid obstinacies, captious pettifogging, all disguising and obstructing the only sane purpose which can justify the whole endeavor. These take an inordinate part of his time; they harass and befog the unhappy wretch, and at times almost drive him from that bench where like any other workman he must do his work. If that were all, his life would be mere misery, and he a distracted arbiter between irreconcilable extremes. But there is something else that makes it — anyway to those curious creatures who persist in it — a delectable calling. For when the case is all in, and the turmoil stops, and after he is left alone, things begin to take form. From his pen or in his head, slowly or swiftly as his capacities admit, out of the murk the pattern emerges, his pattern, the expression of what he has seen and what he has therefore made, the impress of his self upon the not-self, upon the hitherto formless material of which he was once but a part and over which he has now become the master. That is a pleasure which nobody who has felt it will be likely to underrate.

I speak but as I know, and yet I know beyond what I speak. For all of us are alike human creatures, and whether it be in building a house, or in planning a dinner, or in drawing a will, or in establishing a business, or in excavating an ancient city, or in rearing a family, or in writing a play, or in observing an epidemic, or in splitting up an atom, or in learning the nature of space, or even in divining the structure of this giddy universe, in all chosen jobs the craftsman must be at work, and the craftsman, as Stevenson says, gets his hire as he goes. Even this obdurate and recalcitrant world is perhaps in the end no more than a complicated series of formulae which we impose upon the flux. If so, we are throughout its builders, unconscious but always at work. In part, at any rate, we consciously compose; and as we do, a happy fortuity gives us the sense of our own actuality, an escape from the effort to escape, a contentment that the mere stream of consciousness cannot bring, a direction, a solace, a power, and a philosophy.

Observe, I suggest no sense of service. More cant, I fancy, is poured out to youthful ears in the name of serving mankind than would fill the tally of those papers on which Panurge passed his momentous judgment some three hundred years ago. I can remember for myself the droning on that score I had to listen to, when I was of your years, the hopeless sense that I ought to abandon all that made this iridescent world so brave a show, and become a drudge in some distasteful pursuit to assist a mankind, not visibly affected by similar endeavors. If it be selfishness to work on the job one likes, because one likes it and for no other end, let us accept the odium.

EMERSON   1863

Take egotism out, and you would castrate the benefactors. Luther, Mirabeau, Napoleon, John Adams, Andrew Jackson.

For Success?

PAVLOV   1849–1936

All my life I have loved and still love both intellectual and manual work, and the second perhaps even more than the first. Especially have I felt satisfaction when into the latter I have been able to carry some good problem, thus uniting head and hands. Upon this same road you are travelling. With all my heart I wish that you may advance far along this path, the only path that secures happiness for man.

EMERSON   1867

Success in your work, the finding a better method, the better understanding that insures the better performing is hat and coat, is food and wine, is fire and horse and health and holiday. At least, I find that any success in my work has the effect on my spirits of all these.

O. W. HOLMES, JR.   1841–1935

The reward of the general is not a bigger tent, but command.

For Credit?

A. LAWRENCE LOWELL   1856–1943

Much of the success of the administrator in carrying out a program depends upon how far it is his sole object overshadowing everything else, or how far he is thinking of himself; for this last is an obstruction that has caused many a good man to stumble and a good cause to fall. The two aims are inconsistent, often enough for us to state as a general rule that one cannot both do things and get the credit for them.

EPICTETUS *is said to have said:*

Bid a singer in a chorus, Know Thyself; and will he not turn for the knowledge to the others, his fellows in the chorus, and to his harmony with them?

Just Gliding?

EMERSON   1834

Went yesterday to Cambridge and spent most of the day at Mount Auburn; got my luncheon at Fresh Pond, and went back again to the woods. After much wandering and seeing many things, four snakes gliding up and down a hollow for no purpose that I could see — not to eat, not for love, but only gliding.

O. W. HOLMES, JR.   1841–1935

Who does not feel that Nansen's account of his search for the Pole rather loses than gains in ideal satisfaction by the pretense of a few trifling acquisitions for science?

Holmes used to say he liked to think that Nansen tried to go to the Pole simply because he wanted to stand on the top and feel the earth turn round under him.

L. J. HENDERSON   1878–1942

But weightier still are the contentment which comes from
work well done, the sense of the value of science for its
own sake, insatiable curiosity, and, above all, the pleasure
of masterly performance and of the chase. These are the
effective forces which move the scientist. The first condition for the progress of science is to bring them into
play.

BERTRAND RUSSELL   1872–

Skilled work, of no matter what kind, is only done well
by those who take a certain pleasure in it, quite apart
from its utility, either to themselves in earning a living,
or to the world through its outcome.

PASCAL   1623–1662

When we do not know the truth of a thing, it is good that
there should exist a common error which determines
the mind of man, as, for example, the moon, to which is
attributed the change of seasons, the progress of diseases,
etc. For the chief malady of man is a restless curiosity
about things which he cannot understand; and it is not
so bad for him to be in error as to be curious to no purpose.

HENRI POINCARÉ   1854–1912

The scientist does not study nature because it is useful.
He studies it because he delights in it, and he delights in
it because it is beautiful.

F. W. MAITLAND   1850–1906

The hunger and thirst for knowledge, the keen delight
in the chase, the good-humored willingness to admit
that the scent was false, the eager desire to get on with
the work, the cheerful resolution to go back and begin
again, the broad good sense, the unaffected modesty, the
imperturbable temper, the gratitude for any little help
that was given — all these will remain in my memory,
though I cannot paint them for others.

Don't Be Cynical

JAMES GOULD COZZENS   1903–

"Don't be cynical," Judge Coates said. "A cynic is just a man who found out when he was about ten that there wasn't any Santa Claus, and he's still upset. Yes, there'll be more wars; and soon, I don't doubt. There always have been. There'll be deaths and disappointments and failures. When they come, you meet them. Nobody promises you a good time or an easy time. I don't know who it was who said when we think of the past we regret and when we think of the future we fear. And with reason. But no bets are off. There is the present to think of, and as long as you live there always will be. In the present, every day is a miracle. The world gets up in the morning and is fed and goes to work, and in the evening it comes home and is fed again and perhaps has a little amusement and goes to sleep. To make that possible, so much has to be done by so many people that, on the face of it, it is impossible. Well, every day we do it; and every day, come hell, come high water, we're going to have to go on doing it as well as we can."

"So it seems," said Abner.

"Yes, so it seems," said Judge Coates, "and so it is, and so it will be! And that's where you come in. That's all we want of you."

Abner said, "What do you want of me?"

"We just want you to do the impossible," Judge Coates said.

Faith

O. W. HOLMES, JR.   1884

To fight out a war, you must believe something and want something with all your might. So must you do to carry anything else to an end worth reaching. More than that, you must be willing to commit yourself to a course, perhaps a long and hard one, without being able to foresee exactly where you will come out.

1895

Who of us could endure a world, although cut up into five-acre lots and having no man upon it who was not well fed and well housed, without the divine folly of honor, without the senseless passion for knowledge outreaching the flaming bounds of the possible, without ideals the essence of which is that they never can be achieved? I do not know what is true. I do not know the meaning of the universe. But in the midst of doubt, in the collapse of creeds, there is one thing I do not doubt, that no man who lives in the same world with most of us can doubt, and that is that the faith is true and adorable which leads a soldier to throw away his life in obedience to a blindly accepted duty, in a cause which he little understands, in a plan of campaign of which he has no notion, under tactics of which he does not see the use.

Adam

JAMES GOULD COZZENS   1903–

In the kitchen George Bull sat back, quiet as the room. Janet could just see him, sidelong through the pantry door. Firelight shone across the solid slope of his cheek, making a shadow up from the arrogant hedge of eyebrow. He watched the flames with that bold, calm stareaway, his blue eyes steady. Now he moved, rousing himself, stretching his big legs, grunting in the comfortable heat. Casual, but sonorous and effortlessly true, she could hear him humming to himself.

There was an immortality about him, she thought; her regard fixed and critical. Something unkillable. Something here when the first men walked erect; here now. The last man would twitch with it when the earth expired. A good greedy vitality, surely the very vitality of the world and the flesh, it survived all blunders and injuries, all attacks and misfortunes, never quite fed full. She shook her head a little, the smile half-derisive in contemptuous affection. Her lips parted enough to say: "The old bastard!"

THE POWER AND THE SPIRIT OF MAN

How deep is the well and what is the source of the spring of Life?

The Depth of the Well

WILLIAM JAMES   1842–1910

(1) What are the limits of human faculty in various directions?

(2) By what diversity of means, in the differing types of human beings, may the faculties be stimulated to their best results?

Read in one way, these two questions sound both trivial and familiar: there is a sense in which we have all asked them ever since we were born. Yet as a methodical programme of scientific inquiry, I doubt whether they have ever been seriously taken up. If answered fully, almost the whole of mental science and of the science of conduct would find a place under them. I propose, in what follows, to press them on the reader's attention in an informal way.

The first point to agree upon in this enterprise is that as a rule men habitually use only a small part of the powers which they actually possess and which they might use under appropriate conditions.

Everyone is familiar with the phenomenon of feeling more or less alive on different days. Everyone knows on any given day that there are energies slumbering in him which the incitements of the day do not call forth, but which he might display if these were greater. Most of us feel as if a sort of cloud weighed upon us, keeping us below our highest notch of clearness in discernment, sureness in reasoning, or firmness in deciding. Compared with what we ought to be, we are only half awake. Our fires are damped, our drafts are checked. We are making use of only a small part of our possible mental and physical resources.

Stating the thing broadly, the human individual thus lives usually far within his limits; he possesses powers of various sorts which he habitually fails to use. He energizes below his maximum, and he behaves below his optimum. In elementary faculty, in co-ordination, in power of inhibition and control, in every conceivable way, his life is contracted like the field of vision of an hysteric subject — but with less excuse, for the poor hysteric is diseased, while in the rest of us it is only an inveterate habit — the habit of inferiority to our full self — that is bad.

Then the practical question ensues: to what do the better men owe their escape? and, In the fluctuations which all men feel in their own degree of energizing, to what are the improvements due, when they occur?

In general terms the answer is plain: Either some unusual stimulus fills them with emotional excitement, or some unusual idea of necessity induces them to make an extra effort of will. Excitements, ideas, and efforts, in a word, are what carry us over the dam.

We find that the stimuli that carry us over the usually effective dam are most often the classic emotional ones, love, anger, crowd-contagion, or despair. Despair lames most people, but it wakes others fully up. Every siege or shipwreck or polar expedition brings out some hero who keeps the whole company in heart.

A new position of responsibility will usually show a man to be a far stronger creature than was supposed. Cromwell's and Grant's careers are the stock examples of how war will wake a man up. I owe to Professor C. E. Norton, my colleague, the permission to print part of a private letter from Colonel Baird-Smith written shortly after the six weeks' siege of Delhi, in 1857, for the victorious issue of which that excellent officer was chiefly to be thanked. He writes as follows:

". . . My poor wife had some reason to think that war

and disease between them had left very little of a husband to take under nursing when she got him again. An attack of camp-scurvy had filled my mouth with sores, shaken every joint in my body, and covered me all over with sores and livid spots, so that I was marvellously unlovely to look upon. A smart knock on the ankle-joint from the splinter of a shell that burst in my face, in itself a mere bagatelle of a wound, had been of necessity neglected under the pressing and incessant calls upon me, and had grown worse and worse till the whole foot below the ankle became a black mass and seemed to threaten mortification. I insisted, however, on being allowed to use it till the place was taken, mortification or no; and though the pain was sometimes horrible, I carried my point and kept up to the last. On the day after the assault I had an unlucky fall on some bad ground, and it was an open question for a day or two whether I hadn't broken my arm at the elbow. Fortunately it turned out to be only a severe sprain, but I am still conscious of the wrench it gave me. To crown the whole pleasant catalogue, I was worn to a shadow by a constant diarrhoea, and consumed as much opium as would have done credit to my father-in-law [Thomas De Quincey]. However, thank God, I have a good share of Tapleyism in me and come out strong under difficulties. I think I may confidently say that no man ever saw me out of heart, or ever heard one croaking word from me even when our prospects were gloomiest. We were sadly scourged by the cholera, and it was almost appalling to me to find that out of twenty-seven officers present, I could only muster fifteen for the operations of the attack. However, it was done, and after it was done came the collapse. Don't be horrified when I tell you that for the whole of the actual siege, and in truth for some little time before, I almost lived on brandy. Appetite for food I had none, but I forced myself to eat just sufficient to sustain life, and I had an incessant craving for brandy as the strongest stimulant I could get. Strange to say, I was quite unconscious of its affecting me in the slightest degree. The excitement of the work was so great that no lesser one seemed to have any chance against it, and I certainly never found my intellect clearer or my nerves stronger in my life."

Colonel Baird-Smith, needing to draw on altogether extraordinary stores of energy, found that brandy and opium were ways of throwing them into gear.

Such cases are humanly typical. We are all to some degree oppressed, unfree. We don't come to our own. It is there, but we don't get at it. The threshold must be made to shift. Then many of us find that an eccentric activity — a "spree," say — relieves. There is no doubt that to some men sprees and excesses of almost any kind are medicinal, temporarily at any rate, in spite of what the moralists and doctors say.

But when the normal tasks and stimulations of life don't put a man's deeper levels of energy on tap, and he requires distinctly deleterious excitements, his constitution verges on the abnormal. The normal opener of deeper and deeper levels of energy is the will.

The Source of the Spring

WILLIAM JAMES *quotes* TOLSTOY   1828–1910

But the great understander of these mysterious ebbs and flows is Tolstoy. They throb all through his novels. In his *War and Peace,* the hero, Peter, is supposed to be the richest man in the Russian Empire. During the French invasion he is taken prisoner and dragged through much of the retreat. Cold, vermin, hunger, and every form of misery assail him, the result being a revelation to him of the real scale of life's values. "Here only, and for the first time, he appreciated, because he was deprived of it, the happiness of eating when he was hungry, of drinking when he was thirsty, of sleeping when he was sleepy, and of talking when he felt the desire to exchange some words. . . . Later in life he always recurred with joy to this month of captivity, and never failed to speak with enthusiasm of the powerful and ineffaceable sensations, and especially of the moral calm which he had experienced at this epoch. When at daybreak, on the morrow of his imprisonment, he saw [I abridge here Tolstoy's description] the mountains with their wooded slopes disappearing in the grayish mist; when he felt the cool breeze caress him; when he saw the light drive away the vapors, and the sun rise majestically behind the clouds and cupolas, and the crosses, the dew, the distance, the river, sparkle in the splendid, cheerful rays — his heart overflowed with emotion. This emotion kept continually with him and increased a hundred-fold as the difficulties of his situation grew graver. . . . He learnt that man is meant for happiness and that this happiness is in him, in the satisfaction of the daily needs of existence, and that unhappiness is the fatal result, not of our need but of our abundance. . . . When calm reigned in the camp, and the embers paled and little by little went out, the full moon had reached the zenith. The woods and the fields roundabout lay clearly visible; and, beyond the inundation of light which filled them, the view plunged into the limitless horizon. Then Peter cast his eyes upon the firmament, filled at that hour with myriads of stars. 'All that is mine,' he thought. 'All that is in me, is me! And that is what they think they have taken prisoner! That is what they have shut up in a cabin!' So he smiled and turned in to sleep among his comrades."

The occasion and the experience, then, are nothing. It all depends on the capacity of the soul to be grasped, to have its life-currents absorbed by what is given. "Crossing a bare common," says Emerson, "in snow puddled, at twilight, under a clouded sky, without having in my thoughts any occurrence of special good fortune, I have enjoyed a perfect exhilaration. I am glad to the brink of fear."

THOREAU   1817–1862

Sometimes, when I compare myself with other men, it seems as if I were more favored by the gods than they, beyond any deserts that I am conscious of — as if I had a warrant and surety at their hands which my fellows have not, and were especially guided and guarded. I do not flatter myself, but if it be possible they flatter me. I have never felt lonesome, or in the least oppressed by a sense of solitude, but once, and that was a few weeks after I came to the woods, when, for an hour, I doubted if the near neighborhood of man was not essential to a serene and healthy life. To be alone was something unpleasant. But I was at the same time conscious of a slight insanity in my mood, and seemed to foresee my recovery. In the midst of a gentle rain, while these thoughts prevailed, I was suddenly sensible of such sweet and beneficent society in Nature, in the very pattering of the drops, and in every sound and sight around my house, an infinite and unaccountable friendliness all at once like an atmosphere sustaining me, as made the fancied advantages of human neighborhood insignificant, and I have never thought of them since. Every little pine needle expanded and swelled with sympathy, and befriended me. I was so distinctly made aware of the presence of something kindred to me, even in scenes which we are accustomed to call wild and dreary, and also that the nearest of blood to me and humanest was not a person nor a villager, that I thought no place could ever be strange to me again.

WILLIAM JAMES *quotes* R. L. STEVENSON   1850–1894

Wherever a process of life communicates an eagerness to him who lives it, there the life becomes genuinely significant. Sometimes the eagerness is more knit up with the motor activities, sometimes with the perceptions, sometimes with the imagination, sometimes with reflective thought. But, wherever it is found, there is the zest, the tingle, the excitement of reality; and there is "importance" in the only real and positive sense in which importance ever anywhere can be.

Robert Louis Stevenson has illustrated this by a case, drawn from the sphere of the imagination, in an essay which I really think deserves to become immortal, both for the truth of its matter and the excellence of its form.

"Toward the end of September," Stevenson writes, "when school-time was drawing near, and the nights were already black, we would begin to sally from our respective villas, each equipped with a tin bull's-eye lantern. We wore them buckled to the waist upon a cricket belt, and over them, such was the rigor of the game, a buttoned top-coat. They smelled noisomely of blistered tin. They never burned aright, though they would always burn our fingers. Their use was naught, the pleasure of them merely fanciful, and yet a boy with a bull's-eye under his top-coat asked for nothing more. The fishermen used lanterns about their boats, and it was from them, I suppose, that we had got the hint; but theirs were not bull's-eyes, nor did we ever play at being fishermen. The police carried them at their belts, and we had plainly copied them in that; yet we did not pretend to be policemen. Burglars, indeed, we may have had some haunting thought of; and we had certainly an eye to past ages when lanterns were more common, and to certain story-books in which we had found them to figure very largely. But take it for all in all, the pleasure of the thing was substantive; and to be a boy with a bull's-eye under his top-coat was good enough for us.

"When two of these asses met, there would be an anxious 'Have you got your lantern?' and a gratified 'Yes!' That was the shibboleth, and very needful, too; for, as it was the rule to keep our glory contained, none could recognize a lantern-bearer unless (like the polecat) by the smell. Four or five would sometimes climb into the belly of a ten-man lugger, with nothing but the thwarts above them — for the cabin was usually locked — or chose out some hollow of the links where the wind might whistle overhead. Then the coats would be unbuttoned, and the bull's-eyes discovered; and under the chequering glimmer, under the huge, windy hall of the night, and cheered by a rich steam of toasting tinware, these fortunate young gentlemen would crouch together in the cold sand of the links, or on the scaly bilges of the fishing-boat, and delight them with inappropriate talk. Woe is me that I cannot give some specimens! . . . But the talk was but a condiment, and these gatherings themselves only accidents in the career of the lantern-bearer. The essence of this bliss was to walk by yourself in the black night, the slide shut, the top-coat buttoned, not a ray escaping, whether to conduct your footsteps or to make your glory public — a mere pillar of darkness in the dark; and all the while, deep down in the privacy of your fool's heart, to know you had a bull's-eye at your belt, and to exult and sing over the knowledge.

". . . There is one fable that touches very near the quick of life — the fable of the monk who passed into the woods, heard a bird break into song, hearkened for a trill or two, and found himself at his return a stranger at his convent gates; for he had been absent fifty years, and of all his comrades there survived but one to recognize him. It is not only in the woods that this enchanter carols, though perhaps he is native there. He sings in the most doleful places. The miser hears him and chuckles, and his days are moments. With no more apparatus than an evil-smelling lantern, I have evoked him on the naked links. All life that is not merely mechanical is spun out of two strands — seeking for that bird and hearing him. And it is just this that makes life so hard to value, and the delight of each so incommunicable. And it is just a knowledge of this, and a remembrance of those fortunate hours in which the bird has sung to us, that fills us with such wonder when we turn to the pages of the realist.

"For, to repeat, the ground of a man's joy is often hard to hit. It may hinge at times upon a mere accessory, like the lantern; it may reside in the mysterious inwards of psychology. . . . It has so little bond with externals . . . that it may even touch them not, and the man's true life, for which he consents to live, lie together in the field of fancy. . . . In such a case the poetry runs underground. The observer (poor soul, with his documents!) is all abroad. For to look at the man is but to court deception. We shall see the trunk from which he draws his nourishment; but he himself is above and abroad in the green dome of foliage, hummed through by winds and nested in by nightingales. And the true realism were that of the poets, to climb after him like a squirrel, and catch some glimpse of the heaven in which he lives. And the true realism, always and everywhere, is that of the poets: to find out where joy resides, and give it a voice far beyond singing.

"For to miss the joy is to miss all. In the joy of the actors lies the sense of any action. That is the explanation, that the excuse. To one who has not the secret of the lanterns the scene upon the links is meaningless. And hence the haunting and truly spectral unreality of realistic books. . . . In each we miss the personal poetry, the enchanted atmosphere, that rainbow work of fancy that clothes what is naked and seems to ennoble what is base; in each, life falls dead like dough instead of soaring away like a balloon into the colors of the sunset; each is true, each inconceivable; for no man lives in the external truth among salts and acids, but in the warm, phantasmagoric chamber of his brain, with the painted windows and the storied wall."

PART II

HE SOLICITS HIS PAST

History is simply a piece of paper covered with print; the main thing is still to make history, not to write it.

BISMARCK

*Anybody can make history; only **a** great man can write it.*

OSCAR WILDE

The Poetry of History

G. M. TREVELYAN   1876–1956

The appeal of History to us all is in the last analysis poetic. But the poetry of History does not consist of imagination roaming at large, but of imagination pursuing
the fact and fastening upon it. That which compels the
historian to "scorn delights and live laborious days" is
the ardor of his own curiosity to know what really happened long ago in that land of mystery which we call the
past. To peer into that magic mirror and see fresh figures there every day is a burning desire that consumes
and satisfies him all his life, that carries him each morning, eager as a lover, to the library and muniment room.
It haunts him like a passion of almost terrible potency,
because it is poetic. The dead were and are not. Their
place knows them no more and is ours today. Yet they
were once as real as we, and we shall tomorrow be shadows like them. In men's first astonishment over that un-
changing mystery lay the origins of poetry, philosophy,
and religion. From it, too, is derived in more modern
times this peculiar call of the spirit, the type of intellectual curiosity that we name the historical sense. Unlike
most forms of imaginative life it cannot be satisfied save
by facts. In the realm of History, the moment we have
reason to think that we are being given fiction instead
of fact, be the fiction ever so brilliant, our interest col-
lapses like a pricked balloon. To hold our interest you
must tell us something we believe to be true about the

men who once walked the earth. It is the fact about the past that is poetic; just because it really happened, it gathers round it all the inscrutable mystery of life and death and time. Let the science and research of the historian find the fact, and let his imagination and art make clear its significance.

ARISTOTLE   384–322 B.C.

Poetry is finer and more philosophical than history, for poetry expresses the universal, and history only the particular.

The Role of the Particular

J. ROBERT OPPENHEIMER   1953

We have been impressed, and I must say I never stop being impressed, by the great sweep of general order in which particulars are recognized as united. You know the examples: electricity and light, the quantum theory and the theory of valence, places where things that appeared to be separate, and each having its own order, appear as illustrations of a more general order. And one may say, I suppose, that science is a search for regularity and order in those domains of experience which have proven accessible to it.

I am not sure that the effect of the impressive victory of man's mind in this enterprise has not been to make us a little obtuse to the role of the contingent and the particular in life. It is true that many particulars can be understood and subsumed by a general order. But it is probably no less a great truth that elements of abstractly irreconcilable general orders can be subsumed by a particular. And this notion might be more useful to our friends who study man and his life than an insistence on following the lines which in natural science have been so overwhelmingly successful.

Unprejudiced History

LANFREY   1828–1877

It is no longer possible today for a historian to be national in any strict sense. His patriotism is simply love of the truth. He is not a man of any particular race or of any particular country. He is a citizen of all countries and he speaks in the name of all civilization.

GEOFFREY BARRACLOUGH   1957

The only difference between the narrator of contemporary affairs and the ordinary historian is that moral judgments about the present provoke fiercer reactions and have more immediately practical implications than moral judgments about the past.

ARNOLD S. NASH

A historian on the American side of the Atlantic received a fitting rebuke to his implied assumption that to be outside a particular tradition made an unbiased view of controversial questions possible. In conducting the oral examination of a Mormon student who was submitting a Ph.D. thesis on a particular period of Mormon history, the historian asked the student if he, being a Mormon, considered himself sufficiently unprejudiced to write a thesis of Mormon history. The somewhat daring student appositely remarked, "Yes, if you, not a Mormon, consider yourself unprejudiced enough to examine it."

This implicit assumption that the rationalist can transcend all bias and achieve an impartial perspective is not limited to his dicta on religion. He feels the same way about politics. Thus he has no difficulty in rejecting the Nazi or the Marxist philosophy in the name of Reason. He fails to see that it is in the name of Reason as he understands it. To those who maintain that there is no common rational ground on which the democrat and the Nazi can resolve their theoretical differences he replies, with W. T. Stace, that "in that case, our preference for democracy, we shall have to admit, is in the end nothing but an irrational prejudice." This reply rests upon a completely mistaken understanding of the function of Reason in human thought and life. Each system, whether Nazi, or Marxist, or liberal, or rationalist, or Protestant, or Catholic, or Hindu, has its own view of Reason. Reason, therefore, is not a neutral principle which can be appealed to in favor of one rather than another of the competing systems. An illuminating parallel is that of language. It is impossible to describe a language except in terms of a particular language, for there is no language which is a "neutral."

Points on What Curve?

WILLIAM S. FERGUSON   1875–1954

History is, of course, a science, but not one of the common type. Unlike the ordinary scientist, the scientific historian has to practice, not self-suppression, but self-expansion. He must become conscious, so far as that is possible, of the prejudices and special interests of his own age, and, divested of them, he must migrate into a strange land in order to bring back thence a report that is at once an unbiased account of what he has seen and a story that is comprehensible to his fellow-citizens, or, at least, to his fellow-historians. He dare not treat the past as one in spirit with the present, or as resolvable into precisely the same factors. He must be alive to the existence of many different pasts leading to the present in no predeterminable succession, much less progression. The points must make a line, but the line may be of any conceivable curve.

What Is an Explanation?

BASIL WILLEY *on the seventeenth century*   1934

I wish first to enquire, briefly, what is "explanation?"

   Dictionary definitions will not help us much here. "To explain," we learn, means to "make clear," to "render intelligible." But wherein consists the clarity, the intelligibility? The clarity of an explanation seems to depend upon the degree of satisfaction that it affords. An explanation "explains" best when it meets some need of our nature, some deep-seated demand for assurance. "Explanation" may perhaps be roughly defined as a restatement of something — event, theory, doctrine, etc. — in terms of the current interests and assumptions. It satisfies, as explanation, because it appeals to that particular set of assumptions, as superseding those of a past age or of a former state of mind. Thus it is necessary, if an explanation is to seem satisfactory, that its terms should seem ultimate, incapable of further analysis. Directly we allow ourselves to ask "What, after all, does this explanation amount to?" We have really demanded an explanation of the explanation, that is to say, we have seen that the terms of the first explanation are not ultimate, but can be analyzed into other terms — which perhaps for the moment do seem to us to be ultimate. Thus, for example, we may choose to accept a psychological explanation of a metaphysical proposition, or we may prefer a metaphysical explanation of a psychological proposition. All depends upon our presuppositions, which in turn depend upon our training, whereby we have come to regard (or to feel) one set of terms as ultimate, the other not. An explanation commands our assent with immediate authority, when it presupposes the "reality," the "truth," of what seems to us most real, most true. One cannot, therefore, define "explanation" absolutely; one can only say that it is a statement which satisfies the demands of a particular time or place.

A general demand for restatement or explanation seems to have arisen from time to time, perhaps never more vehemently than in the period we are considering. Such a demand presumably indicates a disharmony between traditional explanations and current needs. It does not necessarily imply the "falsehood" of the older statement; it may merely mean that men now wish to live and to act according to a different formula. This is especially evident in our period whenever a "scientific" explanation replaces a theological one. For example, the spots on the moon's surface might be due, theologically, to the fact that it was God's will they should be there; scientifically they might be "explained" as the craters of extinct volcanoes. The newer explanation may be said, not so much to contain "more" truth than the older, as to supply the *kind* of truth which was now demanded. An event was "explained" — and this, of course, may be said as much of our own time as of the seventeenth century — when its history had been traced and described. A comet, for example, or an eclipse, was explained when instead of being a disastrous omen which "with fear of change perplexes monarchs" it could be shown to be the "necessary" result of a demonstrable chain of causes. No one, it need hardly be said, wishes to deny that this explanation had and still has a more "satisfying" quality than the one it superseded. But why was it more satisfying? It was more satisfying, we may suppose, because now, instead of the kind of "truth" which is consistent with authoritative teaching, men began to desire the kind which would enable them to measure, to weigh and to control the things around them; they desired, in Bacon's words, "to extend more widely the limits of the power and greatness of man." Interest was now directed to the *how,* the manner of causation, not its *why,* its final cause. For a scientific type of explanation to be satisfying, for it to convince us with a sense of its necessary truth, we must be in the condition of needing and desiring that type of explanation and no other.

HENRY ADAMS *summed up his theory
of history this way:*   1838–1918

No one who has watched the course of history during the last generation can have felt doubt of its tendency. Those of us who read Buckle's first volume when it appeared in 1857, and almost immediately afterwards, in 1859, read the *Origin of Species* and felt the violent impulse which Darwin gave to the study of natural laws, never doubted that historians would follow until they had exhausted every possible hypothesis to create a science of history. Year after year passed, and little progress has been made. Perhaps the mass of students are more skeptical now than they were thirty years ago of the possibility that such a science can be created. Yet almost every successful historian has been busy with it, adding here a new analysis, a new generalization there; a clear and definite connection where before the rupture of idea was absolute; and, above all, extending the field of study until it shall include all races, all countries, and all times. Like other branches of science, history is now encumbered and hampered by its own mass, but its tendency is always the same, and cannot be other than what it is. That the effort to make history a science may fail is possible, and perhaps probable; but that it should cease, unless for reasons that would cause all science to cease, is not within the range of experience. Historians will not, and even if they would they cannot, abandon the attempt. Science itself would admit its own failure if it admitted that man, the most important of all its subjects, could not be brought within its range.

You may be sure that four out of five serious students of history who are living today have, in the course of their work, felt that they stood on the brink of a great generalization that would reduce all history under a law as clear as the laws which govern the material world. As the great writers of our time have touched one by one the separate fragments of admitted law by which society betrays its character as a subject for science, not one of them can have failed to feel an instant's hope that he might find the secret which would transform these odds and ends of philosophy into one self-evident, harmonious, and complete system. He has seemed to have it, as the Spanish say, in his inkstand. Scores of times he must have dropped his pen to think how one short step, one sudden inspiration, would show all human knowledge; how, in these thickset forests of history, one corner turned, one faint trail struck, would bring him on the highroad of science. Every professor who has tried to teach the doubtful facts which we now call history must have felt that sooner or later he or another would put order in the chaos and bring light into darkness. Not so much genius or favor was needed as patience and good luck. The law was certainly there, and as certainly was in places actually visible, to be touched and handled as though it were a law of chemistry or physics. No teacher with a spark of imagination or with an idea of scientific method can have helped dreaming of the immortality

that would be achieved by the man who should successfully apply Darwin's method to the facts of human history.

Those of us who have had occasion to keep abreast of
the rapid progress which has been made in history during the last fifty years must be convinced that the same
rate of progress during another half-century would necessarily raise history to the rank of a science. Our only
doubt is whether the same rate can possibly be maintained. If not, our situation is simple. In that case, we
shall remain more or less where we are. But we have
reached a point where we ought to face the possibility of
a great and perhaps a sudden change in the importance
of our profession. We cannot help asking ourselves what
would happen if some new Darwin were to demonstrate
the laws of historical evolution.

I admit that the mere idea of such an event fills my
mind with anxiety. When I remember the astonishing
influence exerted by a mere theorist like Rousseau; by a
reasoner like Adam Smith; by a philosopher, beyond contact with material interests, like Darwin, I cannot imagine the limits of the shock that might follow the establishment of a fixed science of history. Hitherto our profession has been encouraged, or, at all events, tolerated,
by governments and by society as an amusing or instructive and, at any rate, a safe and harmless branch of inquiry. But what will be the attitude of government or of
society toward any conceivable science of history? We
know what followed Rousseau; what industrial and political struggles have resulted from the teachings of Adam
Smith; what a revolution and what vehement opposition has been and still is caused by the ideas of Darwin.
Can we imagine any science of history that would not be
vastly more violent in its effects than the dissensions
roused by any one or by all three of these great men?

I ask myself, What shape can be given to any science of
history that will not shake to its foundations some pro-
digious interest? The world is made up of a few immense forces, each with an organization that corresponds
with its strength. The church stands first; and at the out-

set we must assume that the church will not and cannot accept any science of history, because science, by its definition, must exclude the idea of a personal and active providence. The state stands next; and the hostility of the state would be assured toward any system or science that might not strengthen its arm. Property is growing more and more timid and looks with extreme jealousy on any new idea that may weaken vested rights. Labor is growing more and more self-confident and looks with contempt on all theories that do not support its own. Yet we cannot conceive of a science of history that would not, directly or indirectly, affect all these vast social forces.

Any science assumes a necessary sequence of cause and effect, a force resulting in motion which cannot be other than what it is. Any science of history must be absolute, like other sciences, and must fix with mathematical certainty the path which human society has got to follow. That path can hardly lead toward the interests of all the great social organizations. We cannot conceive that it should help at the same time the church and the state, property and communism, capital and poverty, science and religion, trade and art. Whatever may be its orbit, it must, at least for a time, point away from some of these forces toward others which are regarded as hostile. Conceivably, it might lead off in eccentric lines away from them all, but by no power of our imagination can we conceive that it should lead toward them all.

If it pointed to a socialistic triumph, it would place us in an attitude of hostility toward existing institutions. Even supposing that our universities would permit their professors in this country to announce the scientific certainty of communistic triumphs, could Europe be equally liberal? Would property, on which the universities depend, allow such freedom of instruction? Would the state suffer its foundation to be destroyed? Would society as now constituted tolerate the open assertion of a necessity which should affirm its approaching overthrow?

If, on the other hand, the new science required us to announce that the present evils of the world — its huge armaments, its vast accumulations of capital, its advancing materialism, and declining arts — were to be continued, exaggerated, over another thousand years, no one would listen to us with satisfaction. Society would shut its eyes and ears. If we proved the certainty of our results, we should prove it without a sympathetic audience and without good effect. No one except artists and socialists would listen, and the conviction which we should produce on them could lead only to despair and attempts at anarchy in art, in thought, and in society.

If, finally, the science should prove that society must at a given time revert to the church and recover its old foundation of absolute faith in a personal providence and a revealed religion, it commits suicide.

In whatever direction we look we can see no possibility of converting history into a science without bringing it into hostility toward one or more of the most powerful organizations of the era. If the world is to continue moving toward the point which it has so energetically pursued during the last fifty years, it will destroy the hopes of the vast organizations of labor. If it is to change its course and become communistic, it places us in direct hostility to the entire fabric of our social and political system. If it goes on, we must preach despair. If it goes back, it must deny and repudiate science. If it goes forward, round a circle which leads through communism, we must declare ourselves hostile to the property that pays us and the institutions we are bound in duty to support.

A science cannot be played with. If an hypothesis is advanced that obviously brings into a direct sequence of cause and effect all the phenomena of human history, we must accept it, and if we accept, we must teach it. The mere fact that it overthrows social organizations cannot affect our attitude. The rest of society can reject or ignore, but we must follow the new light no matter where it leads. Only about two hundred and fifty years ago the common sense of mankind, supported by the authority of revealed religion, affirmed an undoubted and self-evident fact that the sun moved round the earth. Galileo suddenly asserted and proved that the earth moved round the sun. You know what followed, and the famous *"E pur si muove."* Even if we, like Galileo, should be obliged by the religious or secular authority to recant and repudiate our science, we should still have to say, as he did in secret if not in public, *"E pur si muove."*

Those of us who have reached or passed middle age need not trouble ourselves very much about the future. We have seen one or two great revolutions in thought and we have had enough. We are not likely to accept any new theory that shall threaten to disturb our repose. We should reject at once, and probably by a large majority, a hypothetical science that must obviously be incapable of proof. We should take the same attitude that our fathers took toward the theories and hypotheses of Darwin. We may meantime reply to such conundrums by the formula that has smoothed our path in life over many disasters and cataclysms: "Perhaps the crisis will never occur; and even if it does occur, we shall probably be dead." To us who have already gone as far as we set out to go, this answer is good and sufficient, but those who are to be the professors and historians of the future have got duties and responsibilities of a heavier kind than we older ones ever have had to carry. They cannot afford to deal with such a question in such a spirit. They would have to rejoin in Heine's words:

> *Also fragen wir beständig,*
> *Bis man uns mit einer Handvoll*
> *Erde endlich stopft die Mäuler,*
> *Aber ist das eine Antwort?*

This was Henry Adams's presidential address to the American Historical Association in 1894, written *in absentia* as a letter from Mexico.

And BROOKS ADAMS, *his brother, this way:*   1848–1927

Thought is one of the manifestations of human energy, and among the earlier and simpler phases of thought, two stand conspicuous — Fear and Greed. Fear, which, by stimulating the imagination, creates a belief in an

invisible world, and ultimately develops a priesthood;
and Greed, which dissipates energy in war and trade.

Probably the velocity of the social movement of any
community is proportionate to its energy and mass, and
its centralization is proportionate to its velocity; therefore, as human movement is accelerated, societies centralize. In the earlier stages of concentration, fear appears to be the channel through which energy finds the
readiest outlet; accordingly, in primitive and scattered
communities, the imagination is vivid, and the mental
types produced are religious, military, artistic. As consolidation advances, fear yields to greed, and the economic organism tends to supersede the emotional martial.

Whenever a race is so richly endowed with the
energetic material that it does not expend all its energy
in the daily struggle for life, the surplus may be stored
in the shape of wealth and this stock of stored energy
may be transferred from community to community,
either by conquest or by superiority in economic competition.

However large may be the store of energy accumulated
by conquest, a race must, sooner or later, reach the limit
of its martial energy, when it must enter on the phase
of economic competition. But, as the economic organism
radically differs from the emotional martial, the effect
of economic competition has been, perhaps invariably, to
dissipate the energy amassed by war.

When surplus energy has accumulated in such bulk as
to preponderate over productive energy, it becomes the
controlling social force. Thenceforward, capital is auto-
cratic, and energy vents itself through those organisms
best fitted to give expression to the power of capital. In
this last stage of consolidation, the economic, and, perhaps, the scientific intellect is propagated, while the imagination fades, and the emotional, the martial, and artistic types of manhood decay. When a social velocity has
been attained at which the waste of energetic material is
so great that the martial and imaginative stocks fail to
reproduce themselves, intensifying competition appears

to generate two extreme economic types — the usurer in his most formidable aspect, and the peasant whose nervous system is best adapted to thrive on scanty nutriment. At length a point must be reached when pressure can go no further, and then, perhaps, one of two results may follow: A stationary period may supervene, which may last until ended by war, by exhaustion, or by both combined, as seems to have been the case with the Eastern Empire; or, as in the Western, disintegration may set in, the civilized population may perish, and reversion may take place to a primitive form of organism.

F. W. MAITLAND   1850–1906

Nowadays we may see the office of historical research as that of explaining, and therefore lightening, the pressure that the past must exercise upon the present, and the present upon the future. Today we study the day before yesterday, in order that yesterday may not paralyse today, and today may not paralyse tomorrow.

JOHN E. E. DALBERY-ACTON   1834–1902

Lord Acton had this to say:

I shall never again enjoy the opportunity of speaking my thoughts to such an audience as this, and on so privileged an occasion a lecturer may well be tempted to bethink himself whether he knows of any neglected truth, any cardinal proposition, that might serve as his selected epigraph, as a last signal, perhaps even as a target. I am not thinking of those shining precepts which are the registered property of every school; that is to say — Learn as much by writing as by reading; be not content with the best book: seek sidelights from the others; have no favorites; keep men and things apart; guard against the prestige of great names; see that your judgments are your own, and do not shrink from disagreement; no trusting without testing; be more severe to ideas than to actions; do not overlook the strength of the bad cause or the weakness of the good; never be surprised by the crumbling of an idol or the disclosure of a skeleton; judge talent at its best and character at its worst; suspect power more than vice, and study problems in preference to periods; for instance: the derivation of Luther, the scientific influence of Bacon, the predecessors of Adam Smith, the mediaeval masters of Rousseau, the consistency of Burke, the identity of the first Whig. Most of this, I suppose, is undisputed, and calls for no enlargement. But the weight of opinion is against me when I exhort you never to debase the moral currency or to lower the standard of rectitude, but to try others by the final maxim that governs your own lives, and to suffer no man and no cause to escape the undying penalty which history has the power to inflict on wrong. The plea in extenuation of guilt and mitigation of punishment is perpetual. At every step we are met by arguments which go to excuse, to palliate, to confound right and wrong, and reduce the just man to the level of the reprobate. The men who plot to baffle and resist us are, first of all, those who made history what it has become. They set up the principle that only a foolish Conservative judges the present time with ideas of the Past; that only a foolish Liberal judges the Past with ideas of the Present.

The mission of that school was to make distant times, and especially the Middle Ages, then most distant of all, intelligible and acceptable to a society issuing from the eighteenth century. There were difficulties in the way; and among others this, that, in the first fervor of the Crusades, the men who took the Cross, after receiving communion, heartily devoted the day to the extermination of Jews. To judge them by a fixed standard, to call them sacrilegious fanatics or furious hypocrites, was to yield a gratuitous victory to Voltaire. It became a rule of policy to praise the spirit when you could not defend the deed. So that we have no common code; our moral notions are always fluid; and you must consider the times, the class from which men sprang, the surrounding influences, the masters in their schools, the preachers in their pulpits, the movement they obscurely obeyed, and so on, until responsibility is merged in numbers, and not a culprit is left for execution. A murderer was no criminal if he followed local custom, if neighbors approved, if he was encouraged by official advisers or prompted by just authority, if he acted for the reason of state or the pure love of religion, or if he sheltered himself behind the complicity of the Law. The depression of morality was flagrant; but the motives were those which have enabled us to contemplate with distressing complacency the secret of unhallowed lives. The code that is greatly modified by time and place will vary according to the cause. The amnesty is an artifice that enables us to make exceptions, to tamper with weights and measures, to deal unequal justice to friends and enemies.

It is associated with that philosophy which Cato attributes to the gods. For we have a theory which justifies Providence by the event, and holds nothing so deserving as success, to which there can be no victory in a bad cause, prescription and duration constitute legitimacy, and whatever exists is right and reasonable; and as God manifests his will by that which He tolerates, we must conform to the divine decree by living to shape the Future after the ratified image of the Past. Another theory, less confidently urged, regards History as our guide, as much by showing errors to evade as examples to pursue. It is suspicious of illusions in success, and, though there may be hope of ultimate triumph for what is true, if not by its own attractions, by the gradual exhaustion of error, it admits no corresponding promise for what is ethically right. It deems the canonization of the historic Past more perilous than ignorance or denial, because it would perpetuate the reign of sin and acknowledge the sovereignty of wrong, and conceives it the part of real greatness to know how to stand and fall alone, stemming, for a lifetime, the contemporary flood.

Whatever a man's notions of these later centuries are, such, in the main, the man himself will be. Under the name of History, they cover the articles of his philosophic, his religious, and his political creed. They give his measure; they denote his character: and, as praise is the shipwreck of historians, his preferences betray him more than his aversions. Modern history touches us so nearly, it is so deep a question of life and death, that we are bound to find our own way through it, and to owe our insight to ourselves. The historians of former ages, unapproachable for us in knowledge and in talent, cannot be our limit. We have the power to be more rigidly impersonal, disinterested, and just than they; and to learn from undisguised and genuine records to look with remorse upon the past, and to the future with assured hope of better things; bearing this in mind, that if we lower our standard in history, we cannot uphold it in Church or State.

Apart from what is technical, method is only the reduplication of common sense, and is best acquired by observing its use by the ablest men in every variety of intellectual employment. Bentham acknowledged that he learnt less from his own profession than from writers like Linnaeus and Cullen; and Brougham advised the student of Law to begin with Dante. Liebig described his *Organic Chemistry* as an application of ideas found in Mill's *Logic,* and a distinguished physician, not to be named lest he should overhear me, read three books to enlarge his medical mind; and they were Gibbon, Grote, and Mill. He goes on to say, "An educated man cannot become so on one study alone, but must be brought under the influence of natural, civil, and moral modes of thought." I quote my colleague's golden words in order to reciprocate them. If men of science owe anything to us, we may learn much from them that is essential. For they can show how to test proof, how to secure fulness and soundness in induction, how to restrain and to employ with safety hypothesis and analogy. It is they who hold the secret of the mysterious property of the mind by which error ministers to truth, and truth slowly but irrevocably prevails. Theirs is the logic of discovery, the demonstration of the advance of knowledge and the development of ideas, which, as the earthly wants and passions of men remain almost unchanged, are the charter of progress, and the vital spark in history. And they often give us invaluable counsel when they attend to their own subjects and address their own people. Remember Darwin, taking note only of those passages that raised difficulties in his way; the French philosopher complaining that his work stood still, because he found no more contradicting facts; Baer, who thinks error treated thoroughly nearly as remunerative as truth, by the discovery of new objections; for, as Sir Robert Ball warns us, it is by considering objections that we often learn. Faraday declares that "in knowledge, that man only is to be condemned and despised who is not in a state of transition." And John Hunter spoke for all of us, when he said: "Never ask me what I have said or what I have written; but if you will ask me what my present opinions are, I will tell you."

GOETHE, *when someone toasted Memory* 1823

After the concert we had supper with the Egloffsteins at Goethe's, who was in a most agreeable humor. When among other toasts one was made to Memory, he broke out suddenly with these words:

"I admit no memory in your sense of the word, which is only a clumsy way of expressing it. Whatever we come on that is great, beautiful, significant, cannot be recollected. It must from the first be evolved from within us, be made and become a part of us, developed into a new and better self, and so, continuously created in us, live and operate as part of us. There is no Past that we can bring back to us by the longing for it, there is only an eternally new Now that builds and creates itself out of the elements of the Past as the Past withdraws. The true desire to bring the Past back to us must always be productive and create something new and something better."

LORD ACTON 1895

A speech of Antigone, a single sentence of Socrates, a few lines that were inscribed on an Indian rock before the Second Punic War, the footsteps of a silent yet prophetic people who dwelt by the Dead Sea, and perished in the fall of Jerusalem, come nearer to our lives than the ancestral wisdom of barbarians who fed their swine on the Hercynian acorns.

Acton here anticipated the cross-word puzzles with his reference to "a few lines." They had nothing to do with the Punic Wars. They were Buddhist inscriptions set up in China by King Asoka.

CHARLES A. BEARD (1874–1948), *asked if he could summarize the lessons of history in a short book, said he could do it in four sentences:*

1. Whom the gods would destroy, they first make mad with power.
2. The mills of God grind slowly, but they grind exceeding small.
3. The bee fertilizes the flower it robs.
4. When it is dark enough, you can see the stars.

The Causal and the Casual

JOHN BUCHAN, LORD TWEEDSMUIR   1875–1940

The historian is wise if, like the Romans of the early Empire, he admits Fortuna and even Sors to a place in his Pantheon, and concedes the eternal presence of the irrational and the inexplicable.

It is a recognition which encourages intellectual humility. I venture to think, too, that our sense of the mystery and variousness of life is enlarged, when we realise that the very great may spring from the very small. How does Edmund Burke put it? — "A common soldier, a child, a girl at the door of an inn, have changed the face of fortune, and almost of Nature." History is full of these momentous trifles — the accident which kills or preserves in life some figure of destiny; the weather on some critical battlefield, like the fog at Lutzen or the snow at Towton; the change of wind which brings two fleets to a decisive action; the severe winter of 1788 which produces the famine of 1789, and thereby perhaps the French Revolution; the birth or the death of a child; a sudden idea which results in some potent invention. Let me give you an instance from the most recent history. The success of Turkish Nationalism under Kemal was due to the complete rout of the Greek armies in 1922 in

Asia Minor. That ill-omened Greek campaign was largely due to the restoration in 1920 of King Constantine, which led to the Western Allies dissociating themselves from Greek policy and leaving Greece to her own devices. King Constantine was recalled as a consequence of a general election when M. Venizelos was defeated, and that election was held because young King Alexander, the protégé of the Allies, died early in the autumn of 1920. The cause of his death was blood-poisoning due to the bite of a pet monkey in the palace gardens. I cannot better Mr. Churchill's comment: "A quarter of a million persons died of that monkey's bite."

To look for such pregnant trifles is an instructive game, very suitable for academic circles in the winter season. But it must be played according to the rules. The business is to find the momentous accident, and obviously the smaller you make the accident, the more you reduce it to its ultimate elements, the more startling will be the disproportion between the vast consequence and the minute cause. The accident must be small, and it must be a true parent of consequences.

But let me offer to you — in the spirit of the game which I have suggested — one or two cases where destiny does seem for one moment to have trembled in the balance.

The first is a November day in London in the year 1612. There is a curious hush in the city. Men and women go about with soft feet and grave faces. People whisper anxiously at street corners; even the noise in the taverns is stilled. The only sound is a melancholy wind howling up the river. Suddenly above the wind rises the tolling of a bell, and at the sound women cover their heads and weep, and men uncover theirs and pray. For it is the Great Bell of Paul's, which tolls only for a royal death. It means that Henry, Prince of Wales, at the age of eighteen is dead. He died of a malignant fever which puzzled the doctors. It was an age of strange diseases, but a prince was jealously guarded against them, and I think he must have caught the infection on one of his visits to Sir Walter Raleigh in the Bloody Tower, when he went to talk of high politics and hear tales of the Indies, and admire the model ship called *The Prince,* which Raleigh and Keymis had made for him. Prisons in those days, even prisons reserved for grandees, were haunts of pestilence, and in some alley of the Tower, in that heavy autumn weather, he may have caught the germ which brought him to his death. A chance breath drew the malignant micro-organism into his body, and he was doomed.

Supposing that breath had not been drawn, and the Prince had lived the full span of life, for there was uncommon tenacity in his stock. So far as we can judge, he resembled his sister, Elizabeth of the Palatine, who was for many years the star to adventurous youth. In no respect did he resemble his brother Charles. He was a *revenant* from the Elizabethan Age, and his chief mentor was Walter Raleigh himself. He was a Protestant enthusiast, to whom Protestantism was identified with patriotism, after the stalwart fashion of Cromwell thirty years later. Not for him any philandering with Spain. He would have gladly warned England as Cromwell did in 1656: "Truly your great enemy is the Spaniard! He is naturally so — by reason of that enmity which is in him against whatsoever is of God." When a French marriage was proposed to him, he told his father that "he was resolved that two religions should not lie in his bed."

Had Henry lived, what might have happened? In European politics he would have made Britain the leader of the struggle against the Counter-Reformation. We cannot assess his abilities in the field, but judging from the respect in which Raleigh held his brains, it is possible that he might have taken the place of Gustavus Adolphus. In any case Britain was a greater power than Sweden, and almost certainly he would have led the Continental Protestants. As for domestic affairs, it is clear that he had that indefinable magnetism which his sister had, and which attracted easily and instantly a universal popularity. He would have been a people's king. More, he would have shared the politics of the vast bulk of his subjects, their uncompromising Protestantism, their nascent imperialism. In ecclesiastical matters he would have found the *via media* which Charles missed. He would not have quarrelled with his Parliaments, for his views were theirs. They would have followed him voluntarily and raised no question of rights against the Crown, because the Crown thought as they did, and one does not question the rights of a willingly accepted leader. The change from the Tudor to the modern monarchy would have been of a very different kind. There would have been no Civil War. Cromwell might have died the first general in Europe and Duke of Huntingdon.

PASCAL   1623–1662

Cromwell was about to ravage all Christendom; the royal family was undone, and his own forever established, save for a little grain of sand which formed in his ureter. Rome herself was trembling under him; but this small piece of gravel having formed there, he is dead, his family cast down, all is peaceful, and the king is restored.

Progress

THOMAS JEFFERSON   1743–1826

Let a philosophic observer commence a journey from the savages of the Rocky Mountains eastwardly towards our seacoast. These he would observe in the earliest stage of association, living under no law but that of nature, subsisting and covering themselves with the flesh and skins of wild beasts. He would next find those on our frontiers in the pastoral state, raising domestic animals to supply the defects of hunting. Then succeed our own semi-barbarous citizens, the pioneers of the advance of civilization, and so in his progress he would meet the gradual shades of improving man until he would reach his, as yet, most improved state in our seaport towns. This, in fact, is equivalent to a survey, in time, of the progress of man from the infancy of creation to the present day.

I have observed this march of civilization advancing from the seacoast, passing over us like a cloud of light, increasing our knowledge and improving our condition, insomuch as that we are at this time more advanced in civilization here than the seaports were when I was a boy. And where this progress will stop no one can say. Barbarism has, in the meantime, been receding before the steady step of amelioration; and will in time, I trust, disappear from the earth.

Is There a Pattern?

H. A. L. FISHER   1865–1940

One intellectual excitement has, however, been denied me. Men wiser and more learned than I have discovered in history a plot, a rhythm, a predetermined pattern. These harmonies are concealed from me. I can see only one emergency following upon another as wave follows upon wave, only one great fact with respect to which, since it is unique, there can be no generalizations, only one safe rule for the historian; that he should recognize in the development of human destinies the play of the contingent and the unforeseen. This is not a doctrine of cynicism and despair. The fact of progress is written plain and large on the page of history; but progress is not a law of nature. The ground gained by one generation may be lost by the next. The thoughts of men may flow into the channels which lead to disaster and barbarism.

ISAIAH BERLIN   1954

Writing some ten years ago in his place of refuge during the German occupation of Northern Italy, Mr. Bernard Berenson set down his thoughts on what he called the "Accidental View of History": "It led me," he declared, "far from the doctrine, lapped up in my youth about the inevitability of events and the Moloch still devouring us today, 'historical inevitability'. I believe less and less in these more than doubtful and certainly dangerous dogmas, which tend to make us accept whatever happens as irresistible and foolhardy to oppose." The great critic's words are particularly timely at a moment when there is, at any rate among philosophers of history, if not among historians, a tendency to return to the ancient view that all that is, is ("objectively viewed") best; that to explain is ("in the last resort") to justify; or that to know all is to forgive all; ringing falsehoods (charitably described as half-truths) which have led to special pleading and, indeed, obfuscation of the issue on a heroic scale.

The notion that history obeys laws, whether natural or supernatural, that every event of human life is an element in a necessary pattern has deep metaphysical origins. Infatuation with the natural sciences feeds this stream, but is not its sole nor, indeed, its principal source. In the first place, there is the teleological outlook whose roots reach back to the beginnings of human thought. It occurs in many versions, but what is common to them all is the belief that men, and all living creatures, and perhaps inanimate things as well, not merely are as they are, but have functions and pursue purposes. These purposes are either imposed upon them by a creator who has made every person and thing to serve each a specific goal; or else these purposes are not, indeed, imposed from outside but are, as it were, internal to their possessors, so that every entity has a "nature" and pursues a specific goal which is "natural" to it, and the measure of its perfection consists in the degree to which it fulfils it. Evil, vice, imperfection, all the various forms of chaos and error, are, on this view, forms of frustration, impeded efforts to reach such goals, failures due either to misfortune which puts obstacles in the path of self-fulfilment, or to misdirected effort to fulfil some goal not "natural" to the entity in question.

In this cosmology the world of men (and, in some versions, the entire universe) is a single all-inclusive hierarchy; so that to explain why each object in it is as, and where, and when it is, and does what it does, is *eo ipso* to say what its goal is, how far it successfully fulfils it, and what are the relations of coordination and subordination between the goals of the various goal-pursuing entities in the harmonious pyramid which they collectively form. If this is a true picture of reality, then historical explanation, like every other form of explanation, must consist, above all, in the attribution of individuals, groups, nations, species, each to its own proper place in the universal pattern. To know the "cosmic" place of a thing or a person is to say what it is and does, and at the same time why it should be and do as it is and does. Hence to be and to have value, to exist and to have a function (and to fulfil it less or more successfully) are one and the same. The pattern, and it alone, brings into being and causes to pass away and confers purpose, that is to say, value and meaning, on all there is. To understand is to perceive patterns. To offer historical explanations is not merely to describe a succession of events, but to make it intelligible. To make intelligible is to reveal the basic pattern; not one of several possible patterns, but the one unique pattern which, by being as it is, fulfils only one particular purpose, and consequently is revealed as fitting in a specifiable fashion within the single, "cosmic", over-all schema which is the goal of the universe, the goal in virtue of which alone it is a universe at all, and not a chaos of unrelated bits and pieces. The more thoroughly the nature of this purpose is understood, and with it the patterns it entails in the various forms of human activity, the more explanatory or illuminating — the "deeper" — the activity of the historian will be. Unless an event, or the character of an individual, or the activity of this or that institution or group or historical personage, is explained as a necessary consequence of its place in the pattern (and the larger, that is, the more comprehensive the schema, the more likely it is to be the true one), no explanation — and therefore no historical account — is being provided. The more inevitable an event or an action or a character can be exhibited as being, the better it has been understood, the profounder the researcher's insight, the nearer we are to the one ultimate truth.

This attitude is profoundly anti-empirical. We attribute purposes to all things and persons not because we have evidence for this hypothesis; for if there were a question of evidence for it, there could in principle be evidence against it; and then some things and events might turn out to have no purpose, and therefore, in the sense used above, be incapable of being fitted into the pattern, that is, of being explained at all; but this cannot be, and is rejected in advance, *a priori.* We are plainly dealing not with an empirical theory but with a metaphysical attitude which takes for granted that to explain a thing, to describe it as it "truly" is, even to define it more than verbally, that is, superficially, is to discover its purpose.

The Rhythm of the Universe

ARNOLD J. TOYNBEE   1889–

The two alternating forces or phases in the rhythm of the Universe which Empedocles calls Love and Hate have also been detected — quite independently of the movement of Hellenic thought — by observers in the Sinic world, who have named them Yin and Yang. The nucleus of the Sinic character which stands for Yin seems to represent dark coiling clouds overshadowing the Sun, while the nucleus of the character which stands for Yang seems to represent the unclouded Sun disk emitting its rays. In the original everyday usage, Yin appears to have signified the side of a mountain or a valley which is in the shadow, and Yang the side which is in the sunshine. Sinic philosophers conceived Yin and Yang as two different kinds of matter. As substances, Yin symbolized water and Yang fire. As phases of the Universe, they symbolized the seasons; and the regular annual alternation of the seasons suggested the Sinic conception of how Yin and Yang are related to one another. Each in turn comes into the ascendant at the other's expense; yet even at the high tide of its expansion it never quite submerges the other, so that, when its tide ebbs, as it always does after reaching high-water mark, there is still a nucleus of the other element left free to expand, as its perpetual rival and partner contracts, until it arrives in due course at the opposite turning point where the whole movement begins all over again.

Of the various symbols in which different observers in different societies have expressed the alternation between a static condition and a dynamic activity in the rhythm of the Universe, Yin and Yang are the most apt, because they convey the measure of the rhythm direct and not through some metaphor derived from psychology or mechanics or mathematics.

We are now in search of the positive factor which, within the last six thousand years, has shaken part of mankind out of the Yin-state which we may call "the Integration of Custom" into a Yang-activity which we may call "the Differentiation of Civilization." There are several alternative directions in which this positive factor may be looked for. It may be sought in some special quality in the human beings who have made this particular transition from Yin to Yang on the twenty-one occasions of which we have knowledge; or it may be sought in some special feature in the environments in which the transition has taken place; or again it may be sought in some interaction between the microcosm and the macrocosm, in some prowess of the race when confronted with some challenge from environment. Let us explore these alternatives one by one. Let us consider first the factor of race, and second the factor of environment, each in and by itself. If neither factor appears capable, in isolation, of generating the momentum for which, *ex hypothesi,* we have to account, then we must find our unknown quantity in some product of the two factors, if we are to find it at all. It may be that, when they interact under certain conditions, they produce effects which do not follow from their action under other conditions either separately or together — as air and petrol vapor, when mixed in a carburetor and introduced into a combustion chamber, produce explosions powerful enough to drive the engine of a motor-car, though the air in the atmosphere and the petrol in the petrol-tank remain inert.

The belief that differences of physical race are immutable is not peculiar to our age or our society. The rhetorical question: "Can the Ethiopian change his skin, or the leopard his spots?" anticipates, in poetic imagery, the modern Western racialist's travesty of the modern Western biologist's proposition that acquired characteristics are not transmissible — and the doctrine is not the more securely established for being formulated in prose. The present vogue of racialism in the West, however, has really little to do with current scientific hypotheses. A prejudice so strong as this cannot be accounted for by a cause so rational. Modern Western racial prejudice is not so much a distortion of Western scientific thought as a pseudo-intellectual reflection of Western race-feeling; and this feeling, as we see it in our time, is a consequence of the expansion of our Western civilization over the face of the earth since the last quarter of the fifteenth century of our era.

This has been a misfortune for mankind, for the Protestant temper and attitude and conduct in regard to race, as in many other vital issues, is inspired largely by the Old Testament; and in matters of race the promptings of this old-fashioned Syriac oracle are very clear and very savage. The "Bible Christian" of European origin and race who has settled among peoples of non-European race overseas has inevitably identified himself with Israel obeying the will of Jehovah and doing the Lord's work by taking possession of the Promised Land, while he has identified the non-Europeans who have crossed his path with the Canaanites whom the Lord has delivered into the hand of his Chosen People to be destroyed or subjugated. Under this inspiration, the English-speaking Protestant settlers in the New World exterminated the North American Indian, as well as the bison, from coast to coast of the continent, whereas the Spanish Catholics only exterminated the Indian in the Caribbean Islands and were content, on the continent, to step into the shoes of the Aztecs and the Incas — sparing the conquered in order to rule them as subject populations, converting their subjects to their own religion, and interbreeding with their converts.

We have next to see whether we can find our unknown quantity in the environments in which the geneses of civilizations have occurred.

The modern Western concept of race, which we have now weighed in the balance and found wanting, was evoked, as we have noticed, by the expansion of our Western society over the world from the close of the fifteenth century of our era onwards. This expansion brought the peoples of the West into intimate contact with peoples of other physique and other culture; the differences, thus empirically observed, between human beings who were living on the surface of the same planet at the same time presented a problem to Western minds; and these minds solved that problem to their own satisfaction by improvising the concept of race from the theological materials at their command. Hellenic minds were confronted with the same problem in consequence of a similar expansion of the Hellenic society, which began towards the close of the eighth century B.C., and they solved the problem — also to their own satisfaction — by working out a theoretical explanation on quite different lines. It is noteworthy that although in Hellenic history this intellectual problem presented itself some four centuries earlier than in our Western history, the Hellenic solution, instead of being the cruder, as might be expected *a priori,* was actually superior to the Western solution in all points. It was more imaginative, more rational, and more humane; and, above all, it was unprejudiced. The self-regarding element which is so general, so prominent, and so ugly a feature in our Western race-theories is conspicuous by its absence here. For, so far from being roused to race-consciousness by contact with human beings who were not as they were, the Hellenes drew an inference which made them more sceptical about Race than they had been before. They explained the manifest differences between themselves and their newly discovered neighbors as being the effects of diverse environments upon a uniform human nature, instead of seeing in them the outward manifestations of a diversity that was somehow intrinsic in human nature itself.

The environment theory of the geneses of civilizations has none of the moral repulsiveness of the race theory, yet intellectually it is no less vulnerable. Both theories attempt to account for the empirically observed diversity in the physical behavior and performance of different fractions of mankind by supposing that this physical diversity is fixedly and permanently correlated, in the relation of effect to cause, with certain elements of diversity, likewise given by empirical observation, in the non-psychical domain of Nature. The race theory finds its differentiating natural cause in the diversity of human physique; the environment theory finds it in the climatic, topographical, and hydrographical conditions in which different human societies live; but this discrepancy between the two theories is not fundamental. They are merely two different attempts to find a solution for the same equation by assigning different values to the same unknown quantity. The structure of the equation which is postulated in the two theories is identical; and neither can stand if the common underlying formula will not bear examination. The essence of the formula is a correlation between two sets of variations; and this correlation must be demonstrated to be fixed and permanent — it must maintain itself in every instance under all conditions — before any theories founded on it can claim the status of scientific laws. Under this test, we have already seen the race theory break down; and we shall now see the environment theory fare no better.

We have now drawn the covert of environment, and we have had the same experience as when we drew the covert of race. We have not found the quarry which we are hunting; but we have fought our way through the thicket and have come out on the other side into open country again. We have seen through the environment theory as we saw through the race theory before. We have seen it for what it is: the hallucination of a wanderer lost in the forest, who has turned and turned again in an ever-narrowing circle till he cannot see the wood for trees. When we struggled clear of the first thicket in our path we found that we had liberated ourselves from the conception of racial powers peculiar to this or that branch of the human family and had attained the conception of an omnipresent power, manifesting itself in the conduct and achievements of all Mankind and all Life, in which we recognize the philosopher's *élan vital* or the mystic's God. Looking back now upon the second thicket from which we have just broken out into the daylight, we shall find that, this time, we have shaken ourselves free from the conception of environmental stimuli, peculiar to this or that climate and area, or this or that human background, or this or that combination of the two. The environment resolves itself into an omnipresent object confronting the omnipresent power which manifests itself in life. We may conceive of this object as an obstacle lying across the path of the *élan vital* or as an adversary challenging a living God to halt or do battle. On either view, we shall have to admit, once again, that we are not here face to face with the immediate object of our research. We have not yet found the positive factor which, within the last six thousand years, has shaken part of mankind out of the Yin-state which we have called "the Integration of Custom" into the Yang-activity which we have called "the Differentiation of Civilization." An object which presents itself perpetually in every part of the field of Life cannot, in and by itself, be the unknown quantity which, in certain times and places, has given an impetus to part of mankind and not to the whole. Our hunt must go on; and, with two coverts drawn, only one possibility remains open. If our unknown quantity is neither race nor environment, neither God nor the Devil, it cannot be a simple quantity, but must be a product of two: some interaction between environment and race, some encounter between the Devil and God. That is the plot of the Book of Job and the plot of Goethe's *Faust*. Is it, perhaps, the plot of life and the plot of history?

In this fresh survey, we shall be concerned with race

and environment once more, but we shall regard them in a new light and shall place a different interpretation upon the phenomena. We shall no longer be on the look-out for some simple cause of the geneses of civilizations which can be demonstrated always and everywhere to produce an identical effect. We shall no longer be surprised if, in the production of civilizations, the same race, or the same environment, appears to be fruitful in one instance and sterile in another. Indeed, we shall not be surprised to find this phenomenon of inconstancy and variability in the effects produced, on different occasions, by one and the same cause, even when that cause is an interaction between the same race and the same environment under the same conditions. However scientifically exact the identity between two or more situations may be, we shall not expect the respective outcomes of these situations to conform with one another in the same degree of exactitude, or even in any degree at all. In fact, we shall no longer make the scientific postulate of the uniformity of nature, which we rightly made so long as we were thinking of our problem in scientific terms as a function of the play of inanimate forces. We shall be prepared now to recognize, *a priori,* that, even if we were exactly acquainted with all the racial, environmental, or other data that are capable of being formulated scientifically, we should not be able to predict the outcome of the interaction between the forces which these data represent, any more than a military expert can predict the outcome of a battle or a campaign from an "inside knowledge" of the dispositions and resources of both the opposing general staffs, or a bridge expert the outcome of a game or a rubber from a similar knowledge of all the cards in every hand.

In both these analogies, "inside knowledge" is not sufficient to enable its possessor to predict results with any exactness or assurance, because it is not the same thing as complete knowledge. There is one thing which must remain an unknown quantity to the best-informed on-looker, because it is beyond the knowledge of the combatants, or the players, themselves; and their ignorance of this quantity makes calculation impossible, because it is the most important term in the equation which the would-be calculator has to solve. This unknown quantity is the reaction of the actors to the ordeal when it actually comes. "Les causes physiques n'agissent que sur les principes cachés qui contribuent à former notre esprit et notre caractère." A general may have an accurate knowledge of his own man-power and munition-power and almost as good a knowledge of his opponent's; he may also have a shrewd idea of his opponent's plans; and, in the light of all this knowledge, he may have laid his own plans to his own best advantage. He cannot, however, foreknow how his opponent, or any of the other men who compose the force under his opponent's command, will behave, in action, when the campaign is opened and the battle joined; he cannot foreknow how his own men will behave; he cannot foreknow how he will behave himself. Yet these psychological momenta, which are inherently impossible to weigh and measure and therefore to estimate scientifically in advance, are the very forces which actually decide the issue when the encounter takes place. The military genius is the general who repeatedly succeeds in divining the unpredictable by guesswork or intuition; and most of the historic military geniuses — commanders of such diverse temperament and outlook as a Cromwell and a Napoleon — have recognized clearly that man-power and munition-power and intelligence and strategy are not the talismans that have brought them their victories. After estimating all the measurable and manageable factors at their full value — insisting that "God is on the side of the big battalions," that "God helps those who help themselves," that you should "trust in God and keep your powder dry" — they have admitted frankly that, when all is said and done, victory cannot be predicted by thought or commanded by will because it comes in the end from a source to which neither thought nor will has access. If they have been religious-minded, they have cried "Thanks be to God which giveth us the victory"; if they have been sceptical-minded, they have ascribed their vic-

tories — in superstitious terms — to the operations of
fortune or to the ascendancy of their personal star; but,
whatever language they have used, they have testified to
the reality of the same experience: the experience that
the outcome of an encounter cannot be predicted and
has no appearance of being predetermined, but arises, in
the likeness of a new creation, out of the encounter itself.

We have now to complete the task which we have set
ourselves in this chapter by considering the phenomenon
of challenges from the human environment; and here we
shall find it convenient to begin our examination with
the "related" civilizations and to consider the "unrelated" civilizations afterwards.

At the genesis of every "related" civilization, a challenge from the human environment is given and taken
ex hypothesi. This challenge is implicit in the relation
itself, which begins with a differentiation and culminates
in a secession. The differentiation takes place within
the bosom of the antecedent civilization when that
civilization begins to lose the creative power through
which, in its period of growth, it has once upon a time
inspired a voluntary allegiance in the hearts of people below its surface or beyond its borders. When this happens,
the ailing civilization pays the penalty for its failure of
vitality by becoming disintegrated into a dominant minority which attempts to find a substitute for its vanishing leadership in a régime of force, and a proletariat (internal and external) which responds to this challenge by
becoming conscious that it has a soul of its own and by
making up its mind to save its soul alive. The dominant
minority's will to repress evokes in the proletariat a will
to secede; and the conflict between these two wills continues while the declining civilization verges to its fall,
until, when it is *in articulo mortis,* the proletariat at
length breaks free from a *ci-devant* spiritual home which
has been transformed first into a prison-house and
finally into a city of destruction. In this conflict between
a proletariat and a dominant minority, as it works itself
out from beginning to end, we can discern one of those
dramatic spiritual encounters which renew the work of

creation by carrying the life of the Universe out of the stagnation of autumn through the pains of winter into the ferment of spring. The secession of the proletariat is the dynamic act, in response to the challenge, through which the change from Yin to Yang is brought about; and, in this dynamic separation between the proletariat and the dominant minority of the antecedent civilization, the "related" civilization is born.

GEOFFREY BARRACLOUGH   1955

What I am suggesting is that we to-day stand on the verge, like the Romans of 100 B.C., of the imperial phase. We can see already the inadequacy of national economies, but clinging to outworn sovereignties, cannot overcome it. We can also see the need for a radical redistribution of purchasing power to provide new life for an economy in which the classical device of exploitation of the external market is played out; but how far will our modern Gracchi, our radicals and reformers, be able to bring about the modification of the social structure without which there can be no enduring increase in the purchasing power of the working classes? We can see, to whatever political party we belong, the inadequacy of inherited political institutions to the tasks of the present; but can the necessary readjustment be made in the face of vested opposition from both right and left?

It is easy, and it is fashionable, to give the answer "Yes." Toynbee ends his *Study of History* with "a message of encouragement for us children of the western civilization, as we drift to-day alone, with none but stricken civilizations around us." "No known law of historical determinism," he says, "compels us to leap out of the intolerable frying-pan of our time of troubles into the slow and steady fire of a universal state, where we shall in due course be reduced to dust and ashes." "The divine spark of creative power is still alive in us, and if we have the grace to kindle it into flame, then the stars in their courses cannot defeat our efforts to attain the goal of human endeavor." It is finely put; but it can be put more concisely in the old, trite saying, "where there's a will there's a way." But the more fundamental question still remains: is there a will? Is "the divine spark of creative power" still alive in us, despite what Toynbee calls "the spiritual inadequacy" of our eighteenth-century Enlightenment? We are much pre-occupied to-day with economic problems; but we must remember, as Toynbee says, that "the economic explanation of the decay of the Ancient World must be rejected completely," because it was simply the outcome of a preceding spiritual decay, because already "society . . . had gone to pieces." And there is another point as well. It is easy to talk of our "will," but (in Spengler's words) "no culture is at liberty to choose the path and conduct" it will follow. Our actions are conditioned by our environment; and it is evident that the broad pattern of the postwar world, much as we may dislike it, has already been set, in part by the inexorable development of American industrial potential between 1939 and 1945, in part by the failure of statesmen of all countries after 1945 to cast off the blighting shadow of supposed national interests and come to grips with realities.

Therefore I find it hard to assimilate the fashionable optimism; but I do not think the alternative is pessimism. On the contrary, I think the crude alternative: "optimism–pessimism," puts the whole issue in a false perspective. Those who see the course of history as "cyclic" are commonly denounced as pessimists, because they are supposed to regard the whole of human destiny as subject to mechanical "laws." In fact, nothing could be more mistaken. If you wish for an analogy to illustrate the position more vividly, then it is not to the laws of mechanics that you should turn, but to the rhythm of human life; and I do not think that any of us are pessimistic because we know that youth will give way to maturity, passion to calm, activity to serenity, because we know that our creative powers will not last, though our intellects may remain untarnished, and because we are conscious that death will ensue.

There is much exaggeration to-day in the depicting

of our crisis. People talk of the "fate of man" being at stake, but it is only the fate of one civilization that is at stake — and only our egocentricity makes us think that the whole of mankind is involved. H. G. Wells's fearful prediction of the supersession of man by a new species of "unclean intrusive monsters" lacks all basis in fact — it is mere fantasy — and however destructive a war conducted with hydrogen-bombs might be, there is no reason to think that it would wipe mankind off the face of the earth. What we can see, if we have eyes to see, is the dim shape of the coming civilization which will supersede our own, just as a Roman with eyes to see might have perceived the shape of things to come when, in 113 B.C., Teutons and Cimbrians moved forward on a broad front and came "over the Alps in a huge migration." But even the sight of our own successors growing up side by side with us, as the empire of Charlemagne grew up side by side with the empire of Rome, which survived in Constantinople, should not dismay. History does not move in cataclysms; Rome in 113 B.C. still had five centuries of existence before it, even in the west; and as we stand on the verge of a new universal state, we shall do well to recall Gibbon's famous judgement that the peoples of Europe were never happier than under the imperial regime of the Antonines.

Hence there is still much to look forward to in western civilization, provided we realize (as Spengler said) that "we are civilized, not Gothic or Rococo people," and provided that we "reckon with the hard cold facts of a late life, to which the parallel is to be found not in Pericles' Athens, but in Caesar's Rome." Of great painting and great music there can, no doubt, no longer be any question; our architectural possibilities have been exhausted for a hundred and fifty years, and we are destined to monster buildings like the Colosseum and the baths of Caraculla. Yet for a sound and vigorous generation that knows its limitations, there is much worth doing to be done. If effort which will go down into the dust seems to us vain and wearisome, if we are only prepared to strive under the illusion of perpetuity, the fault is in us, and not in the world around us; the rose is no less worth growing and tending because it fades tomorrow and withers next week. It is for us to grasp this cardinal fact in relation to ourselves and to our own civilization. "What is important in life," said Goethe, "is life and not the result of life," and if we make that belief our own, we shall see no cause for pessimism in a society which is not governed by a law of progress. On the contrary, the fact — as I hinted earlier — that there is not one single line of development, all deviations from which are cast aside as worthless waste-efforts, adds to the richness of life. For at once "there emerges an astonishing wealth of actual forms," and "in place of that empty figment of one linear history, which can only be kept up by shutting one's eyes to the overwhelming multitude of facts," we see unfolding before us "the drama of a number of mighty cultures," each springing with primitive strength from the soil of different regions; each stamping its material in its own image; each having its own idea, its own passion, its own life, will and feeling, its own death. Here indeed are colors, lights and movements; for each civilization has its own possibilities of self-expression which arise, mature, decay and never return. The pitiful fantasy of an "ageing Mankind," petering out in senile decay, until finally dispatched by a mythical "Superman," is gone; and in its place we have a picture, fresh and exhilarating, of endless formations and transformations, of achievement without end, of waxing and waning. Though our own spring and summer may have passed, we can look forward to a new spring and a new summer, and know, as we move into our September, that — however different — the spring and summer that will assuredly come, will be just as fair and no less inspiring than the last.

HISTORY AS SHE IS WRIT

A short piece by a modern English-man; something by a legal historian; a longer passage in the grand manner by an earl and grandfather of two Queens of England. Then three extracts from American historians, one by a professor of horticulture at Harvard, the others by modern Americans.

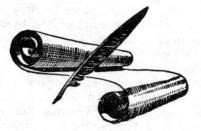

The Golden Hind

G. M. TREVELYAN 1876–1956

Since Magellan had discovered a way round the southern
end of America, the passage had been generally avoided
as too stormy and dangerous for the tiny vessels of the
day. The Spanish ships on the Pacific coast were built
in situ, and communication with the Atlantic went over-
land by the Isthmus of Panama. When therefore Drake
appeared from the south upon the coast of Chile, he
seemed "like a visitation from heaven" to the secure and
lightly armed Spaniards, who had learnt to think of the
Pacific as an inland lake closed to the shipping of the
world. Although he had less than a hundred men in the
Golden Hind, which alone of his tempest-tost squadron
had held right on past the Horn and the Straits of Magellan, it was the easiest part of his task to rob the long
coast-line of its fabulous wealth, and ballast his little
bark with the precious metals. Then he turned home-
wards across the Pacific Ocean, bound for the Cape of
Good Hope.

Such was the importance attached in Spain and England to these proceedings, of which word came to Europe
by Panama, and so loud was the outcry raised by the
Spanish ambassador, that if Drake had failed to return
home safe and rich, the victory at court might have
rested with Cecil's more timid policy, and the victory in
the world-contest might have fallen to Spain and Rome.
Drake had told his companions that if they failed in

their venture "the like would never be attempted again." When the *Golden Hind* grounded on a shoal in the uncharted Molucca Sea and hung for twenty hours on the edge of apparently certain destruction, to glide off safe into deep water at the last moment, vast destinies depended on the relation of a capful of wind and a tropical sandbank to a few planks of English oak.

As Drake entered Plymouth Sound after nearly three years' absence from Europe, his first question to some passing fishermen was whether the Queen were alive and well. Yes, in spite of all her enemies, she was still alive, and well enough to come next year and knight him on board his ship at Deptford. It was the most important knighthood ever conferred by an English sovereign, for it was a direct challenge to Spain and an appeal to the people of England to look to the sea for their strength. In view of this deed, disapproved by her faithful Cecil, who shall say Elizabeth could never act boldly? Her bold decisions are few and can be numbered, but each of them began an epoch.

QUEEN ELIZABETH   1533–1603

As for my own part, I care not for death; for all men are mortal, and though I be a mortal, yet I have as good a courage answerable to my place as ever my father had. I am your anointed Queen. I will never be by violence constrained to do anything. I thank God I am endued with such qualities that if I were turned out of the realm in my petticoat, I were able to live in any place in Christendom.

Etcetera

F. W. MAITLAND   1850–1906

For nearly two hundred and fifty years the solemn style and title of the king or queen of this country ended with the words "and so forth," or in Latin *et caetera*. On the first day of the nineteenth century a change was made. Queen Victoria's grandfather became King of a "United Kingdom" of Great Britain and Ireland. He ceased to be King of France. He also ceased to be "and so forth."

Had this phrase always been meaningless? I venture to suggest that it had its origin in a happy thought, a stroke of genius.

If we look at the book to which we naturally turn when we would study the styles and titles of our English kings, if we look at Sir Thomas Hardy's *Introduction to the Charter Rolls,* we shall observe that the first sovereign who wears an "&c." is Queen Elizabeth. Now let us for a moment place ourselves in the first days of her reign. Shall we not be eager to know what this new queen will call herself, for will not her style be a presage of her policy? No doubt she is by the Grace of God of England, France, and Ireland Queen. No doubt she is Defender of the Faith, though we cannot be sure what faith she will defend. But is that all? Is she or is she not Supreme Head upon earth of the Church of England and Ireland?

The full difficulty of the question which this young lady had to face so soon as she was safely queen may not be justly appreciated by our modern minds. We say, perhaps, that acts of Parliament had bestowed a certain title, and had since been repealed by other acts of Parliament. But to this bald statement we must make two additions. In the first place, one at least of the Henrician statutes had declared that the headship of the Church was annexed to the kingship by a bond stronger and holier than any act of Parliament: to wit, by the very word of God. In the second place, one of the Marian statutes had rushed to the opposite limit. It had in effect declared that Henry's ecclesiastical supremacy had all along been a nullity. It had indeed excused Queen Mary's temporary assumption of a title that was not rightfully hers, and documents in which the obnoxious phrase occurred were not for that reason to be invalid; but it applauded Mary for having seen the error of her ways, and having of her own motion rejected a title which no Parliament could lawfully confer.

It was a difficult problem. On both sides there were men with extreme opinions, who, however, agreed in holding that the solution of the question was not to be found in any earthly statute book. That question had been answered for good and all in one sense or the other by the *ius divinum*, by the word of God. We know that Elizabeth was urged to treat the Marian statutes as void or voidable, because passed by a Parliament whose being was unlawful, since it was summoned by a Queen who had unlawfully abdicated her God-given headship of the Church. This, if in our British and Calvinian way we make too free with the Greek version of Thomas Lüber's name, we may call the opinion of the immoderate Erastians: — what God has joined together man attempts to put asunder "under pain of nullity." At the opposite pole stood a more composite body, for those who would talk of the vanity of all attempts to rob Christ's vicar of his vicariate were being reinforced by strange allies from Geneva, where Calvin had spoken ill of Henricianism. Then between these extremes there was room for many shades of doctrine, and in particular for that which would preach the omnicompetence of Parliament.

Then a happy thought occurs. Let her Highness etceterate herself. This will leave her hands free, and then afterwards she can explain the etceteration as occasion shall require. Suppose that sooner or later she must submit to the Pope, she can still say that she has done no wrong. She can plead that, at least in some of his documents, King Philip, the Catholic King, etceterates himself. There are always, so it might be said, some odds and ends that might conveniently be packed up in "and so forth." What of the Channel Islands, for example? They are not parts of England, and they are hardly parts of France. Besides, even Paul IV would be insaner than we think him, if, when securing so grand a prize as England, he boggled over an "&c." And then, on the other hand, if her Grace finds it advisable, as perhaps it will be, to declare that the Marian statutes are null, she cannot be reproached with having been as bad as her sister, for we shall say that no reasonable man, considering all that has happened, can have doubted that the "&c." signified that portion of King Henry's title and King Edward's title which, for the sake of brevity, was not written in full. Lastly, suppose that the Parliament which is now to be summoned is willing to go great lengths in an Erastian and Protestant direction, no harm will have been done. Indeed, hereafter the Queen's Highness in her exercise of her ecclesiastical supremacy may find it advisable to assert that this supremacy was in being before any Parliament recognised its existence, and therefore is not to be controlled even by the estates of the realm. Therefore let her be "defender of the Faith, and so forth." He who knows what faith is "the" faith will be able to make a good guess touching the import of "and so forth."

The Trial, Death, and Character of King Charles I

EDWARD HYDE, EARL OF CLARENDON   1609–1674

"Ne quid False dicere audeat, ne quid Veri non audeat." Cicero

When He was first brought to Westminster Hall, which was upon the twentieth of January, before their High Court of Justice, he looked upon them, and sate down, without any manifestation of trouble, never stirring his Hat; all the impudent Judges sitting cover'd, and fixing their Eyes upon him, without the least shew of respect. The odious Libel, which they called a Charge and Impeachment, was then read by the Clerk; which, in effect, contain'd, "that he had been admitted King of England, and trusted with a limited power to govern according to Law; and, by his Oath and Office, was obliged to use the power committed to him for the good and benefit of the People; but that he had, out of a wicked design to erect to himself an Illimited and Tyrannical power, and to overthrow the Rights and Liberties of the People, Trayterously levied War against the present Parliament, and the People therein represented." And then it mention'd his first appearance at York with a Guard, then his being at Beverly, then his setting up his Standard at Nottingham, the day of the Month and the Year in which the Battle had been at Edge-hill, and all the other several Battles which had been fought in his presence; "in which," it said, "he had caused and procured many thousands of the free-born People of the Nation to be slain: that after all his Forces had been defeated, and Himself become a Prisoner, he had, in that very year, caused many Insurrections to be made in England, and given a Commission to the Prince his Son to raise a new War against the Parliament; whereby many who were in their Service, and trusted by them, had revolted, broken their Trust, and betook themselves to the Service of the Prince against the Parliament and the People": that he had been the Author and Contriver of the unnatural, cruel, and bloody Wars; and was therein guilty of all the Treasons, Murthers, Rapines, Burnings, and Spoiles, Desolations, Damage, and Mischief to the Nation, which had been committed in the said War, or been occasion'd thereby; and that he was therefore impeached for the said Treasons and Crimes, on the behalf of the People of England, as a Tyrant, Traytor, and Murtherer, and a publick implacable Enemy to the Common-wealth of England. And it was prayed, "that he might be put to Answer to all the particulars, to the end that such an Examination, Trial, and Judgement, might be had thereupon, as should be agreeable to Justice."

Which being read, their President Bradshaw, after he had insolently reprehended the King "for not having shew'd more respect to that High Tribunal," told him, "that the Parliament of England had appointed that Court to try him for the several Treasons, and Misdemeanours, which he had committed against the Kingdom during the evil administration of his Government; and that, upon the Examination thereof, Justice might be done." And, after a great sawciness and impudence of talk, he asked the King, "what Answer he had to make to that Impeachment."

The King, without any alteration in his Countenance by all that insolent provocation, told them, "he would first know of them, by what Authority they presumed by force to bring him before them, and who gave them power to judge of his Actions, for which he was accountable to none but God; though they had been allways such as he need not be ashamed to own them before all the world." He told them, "that He was their King, They his Subjects; who owed him Duty and Obedience: that no Parliament had Authority to call him before them; but that They were not the Parliament, nor had any Authority from the Parliament to sit in that manner: That of all the Persons who sate there, and took upon them to judge him, except those Persons who being Officers of the Army he could not but know whilst he was forced to be amongst them, there were only two faces which he had ever seen before, or whose names were known to him." And, after urging "their Duty, that was due to him, and his Superiority over them," by such lively Reasons, and Arguments, as were not capable of any Answer, he concluded, "that he would not so much betray himself, and his Royal Dignity, as to Answer any thing they objected against him, which were to acknowledge their Authority; though he believ'd that every one of Themselves, as well as the Spectators, did, in their own Consciences, absolve him from all the Material things which were objected against him."

Bradshaw advised him, in a very arrogant manner, "not to deceive himself with an opinion that any thing he had said would do him any good: that the Parliament knew their own Authority, and would not suffer it to be called in question or debated": therefore required him, "to think better of it, against he should be next brought thither, and that he would Answer directly to his Charge; otherwise, he could not be so ignorant, as not to know what Judgement the Law pronounced against those who stood mute, and obstinately refused to plead." So the Guard carried his Majesty back to St. James's; where they treated him as before.

There was an accident happen'd that first day, which may be fit to be remember'd. When all those who were Commissioners had taken their places, and the King was brought in, the first ceremony was, to read their Commission; which was the Ordinance of Parliament for the Trial; and then the Judges were all called, every Man answering to his name as he was called, and the President being first called and making Answer, the next who was called being the General, Lord Fairfax, and no Answer being made, the Officer called him the second time, when there was a voice heard that said, "he had more Wit than to be there"; which put the Court into some disorder, and some body asking, who it was, there was no other Answer but a little murmuring. But, presently, when the Impeachment was read, and that expression used, of "All the good people of England," the same voice in a louder tone, Answer'd, "No, nor the hundredth part of them": upon which, one of the Officers bid the Soldiers give fire into that Box whence those presumptuous words were utter'd. But it was quickly discern'd that it was the General's Wife, the Lady Fairfax, who had utter'd both those sharp sayings; who was presently perswaded or forced to leave the place, to prevent any new disorder. She was of a very noble Extraction, one of the Daughters and Heirs of Horace Lord Vere of Tilbury; who, having been bred in Holland, had not that reverence for the Church of England, as she ought to have had, and so had unhappily concurr'd in her Husband's entring into Rebellion, never imagining what misery it would bring upon the Kingdom; and now abhorr'd the work in hand as much as any Body could do, and did all she could to hinder her Husband from acting any part in it. Nor did he ever sit in that bloody Court, though he was throughout overwitted by Cromwell, and made a property to bring that to pass which could very hardly have been otherwise effected.

As there was in many Persons present at that woful Spectacle a real Duty and Compassion for the King, so there was in others so barbarous and brutal a behaviour towards him, that they called him Tyrant, and Murtherer; and one spit in his face; which his Majesty, without expressing any trouble, wiped off with his Handkerchief. . . .

But it will not be unnecessary to add a short Character of his Person, that Posterity may know the inestimable loss which the Nation then underwent, in being depriv'd of a Prince whose example would have had a greater influence upon the manners, and piety of the Nation, than the most strict Laws can have. To speak first of his private Qualifications as a Man, before the mention of his Princely and Royal Virtues; He was, if ever any, the most worthy of the title of an Honest Man; so great a lover of Justice, that no temptation could dispose him to a wrongful Action, except it was so disguised to him that he believ'd it to be just. He had a tenderness and compassion of Nature, which restrain'd him from ever doing a hard-hearted thing: and therefore he was so apt to grant pardon to Malefactors, that the Judges of the Land represented to him the damage and insecurity to the Publick, that flowed from such his Indulgence. And then he restrain'd himself from pardoning either Murthers, or High-way Robberies, and quickly discern'd the fruits of his severity by a wonderful Reformation of those Enormities. He was very punctual and regular in his Devotions; he was never known to enter upon his Recreations or Sports, though never so early in the Morning, before he had been at Publick Prayers; so that on hunting days his Chaplains were bound to a very early Attendance. He was likewise very strict in observing the hours of his private Cabinet Devotions; and was so severe an exactor of gravity and reverence in all mention of Religion, that he could never endure any light or prophane word, with what sharpness of Wit soever it was cover'd: and though he was well pleased, and delighted with reading Verses made upon any occasion, no Man durst bring before him any thing that was prophane or unclean. That kind of Wit had never any Countenance then. He was so great an Example of Conjugal Affection, that they who did not imitate him in that particular, durst not brag of their Liberty: and he did not only permit, but direct his Bishops, to prosecute those scandalous Vices, in the Ecclesiastical Courts, against Persons of Eminence, and near Relation to his Service.

His Kingly Virtues had some mixture and allay, that hindred them from shining in full Lustre, and from producing those fruits they should have been attended with. He was not in his Nature very bountiful, though he gave very much. This appear'd more after the Duke of Buckingham's death, after which those showres fell very rarely; and he paused too long in giving, which made those to whom he gave, less sensible of the benefit. He kept State to the full, which made his Court very orderly; no Man presuming to be seen in a place where he had no pretence to be. He saw, and observ'd Men long, before he receiv'd them about his Person; and did not love strangers, nor very confident Men. He was a patient hearer of Causes; which he frequently accustom'd himself to at the Council-Board; and judged very well, and was dextrous in the mediating part: so that he often put an end to Causes by perswasion, which the stubbornness of Men's humours made dilatory in Courts of Justice.

He was very fearless in his Person; but, in his riper years, not very Enterprising. He had an excellent understanding, but was not confident enough of it; which made him often times change his own opinion for a worse, and follow the advice of Men that did not judge so well as Himself. This made him more irresolute than the conjuncture of his Affairs would admit: if he had been of a rougher and more imperious Nature, he would have found more respect and duty. And his not applying some severe cures to approaching Evils, proceeded from the Lenity of his Nature, and the tenderness of his Conscience; which, in all cases of blood, made him choose the softer way, and not hearken to severe counsels, how reasonably soever urged. This only restrain'd him from pursuing his advantage in the first Scotish Expedition, when humanly speaking, he might have reduced that Nation to the most entire obedience that could have been wished. But no Man can say he had then many who advised him to it, but the contrary, by a wonderful indisposition all his Council had to the War, or any other fatigue. He was allways a great Lover of the Scotish Nation, having not only been born there, but educated by that People, and besieged by them allways, having few English about him till he was King; and the major number of his Servants being still of that Nation, who he thought could never fail him. And among these, no Man had such an Ascendent over him, by the humblest insinuations, as Duke Hamilton had.

As he excelled in all other Virtues, so in temperance he was so strict, that he abhorr'd all Debauchery to that degree, that, at a great festival solemnity, where he once was, when very many of the Nobility of the English and Scots were entertain'd, being told by one who withdrew from thence, what vast draughts of Wine they drank, and "that there was one Earl, who had drank most of the rest down, and was not himself moved or alter'd," the King said, "that he deserv'd to be hanged"; and that Earl coming shortly after into the room where his Majesty was, in some gayety, to shew how unhurt he was from that Battle, the King sent one to bid him withdraw from his Majesties presence; nor did he in some days after appear before him.

This unparallel'd Murther and Parricide was committed upon the thirtieth of January, in the year, according to the Account used in England, 1648, in the forty and ninth year of his Age, and when he had such excellent health, and so great Vigour of Body, that when his Murtherers caused him to be open'd (which they did; and were some of them present at it with great curiosity) they confessed, and declared, "that no Man had ever all his vital parts so perfect and unhurt; and that he seem'd to be of so admirable a composition and constitution, that he would probably have liv'd as long as nature could subsist." His Body was immediately carried into a room at White-Hall; where he was exposed for many days to the publick view, that all Men might know that he was not alive. And he was then imbalm'd, and put into a Coffin, and so carried to St. James's; where he likewise remain'd several days. They who were qualified to order his Funeral, declar'd, "that he should be buried at Windsor in a decent manner, provided that the whole Expence should not exceed five hundred pounds." The Duke of Richmond, the Marquis of Hertford, the Earls of

Southampton and Lindsey, who had been of his Bed-Chamber, and allways very faithful to him, desired those who govern'd, "that they might have leave to perform the last duty to their dear Master, and to wait upon him to his Grave"; which, after some pauses, they were permitted to do, with this, "that they should not attend the Corps out of the Town; since they resolv'd it should be privately carried to Windsor without Pomp or noise, and then they should have timely notice, that, if they pleased, they might be at his Interment." And accordingly it was committed to four of those Servants, who had been by them appointed to wait upon him during his Imprisonment, that they should convey the Body to Windsor; which they did. And it was, that Night, placed in that Chamber which had usually been his Bed-Chamber: the next Morning, it was carried into the great Hall; where it remain'd till the Lords came; who arriv'd there in the Afternoon, and immediately went to Colonel Whitchcot, the Governour of the Castle, and shew'd the Order they had from the Parliament to be present at the Burial; which he admitted; but when they desired that his Majesty might be Buried according to the form of the Common-Prayer Book, the Bishop of London being present with them to officiate, he positively and roughly refused to consent to it; and said, "it was not Lawful; that the Common-Prayer Book was put down, and he would not suffer it to be used in that Garrison where He Commanded"; nor could all the reasons, perswasions, and entreaties, prevail with him to suffer it. Then they went into the Church, to make choice of a place for burial. But when they enter'd into it, which they had been so well acquainted with, they found it so alter'd and transform'd, all Inscriptions, and those Land-Marks pulled down, by which all Men knew every particular place in That Church, and such a dismal mutation over the whole, that they knew not where they were: nor was there one old Officer that had belonged to it, or knew where our Princes had used to be interr'd. At last there was a Fellow of the Town who undertook to tell them the place, where, he said, "there was a Vault, in which

King Harry the Eighth and Queen Jane Seymour were interr'd." As near that place as could conveniently be, they caused the Grave to be made. There the King's Body was laid without any words, or other Ceremonies than the tears and sighs of the few beholders. Upon the Coffin was a plate of Silver fixt with these words only, King Charles 1648. When the Coffin was put in, the black Velvet Pall that had cover'd it was thrown over it, and then the Earth thrown in; which the Governor stayed to see perfectly done, and then took the Keys of the Church.

CROMWELL   1599–1658

If any man whatsoever hath carried on the design of deposing the King and disinheriting his posterity; or if any man hath yet such a design he should be the greatest traitor and rebel in the world; but, since the Providence of God hath cast this upon us, I cannot but submit to Providence.

BLENCOWE   1640

I tell you we will cut off his head with the crown upon it.

THOMAS CARLYLE   1795–1881

The civil authority, or that part of it which remained faithful to their trust and true to the ends of the covenant, did, in answer to their consciences, turn out a tyrant, in a way which the Christians in aftertimes will mention with honor, and all tyrants in the world look at with fear.

Isaac Jogues, a Jesuit in North America

FRANCIS PARKMAN   1823–1893

Jogues sat in one of the leading canoes. He was born at Orleans in 1607, and was thirty-five years of age. His oval face and the delicate mould of his features indicated a modest, thoughtful, and refined nature. He was constitutionally timid, with a sensitive conscience and great religious susceptibilities. He was a finished scholar, and might have gained a literary reputation; but he had chosen another career, and one for which he seemed but ill fitted.

The twelve canoes had reached the western end of the Lake of St. Peter, where it is filled with innumerable islands. The forest was close on their right, they kept near the shore to avoid the current, and the shallow water before them was covered with a dense growth of tall bulrushes. Suddenly the silence was frightfully broken. The war-whoop rose from among the rushes, mingled with the reports of guns and the whistling of bullets; and several Iroquois canoes, filled with warriors, pushed out from their concealment, and bore down upon Jogues and his companions. The Hurons in the rear were seized with a shameful panic. They leaped ashore; left canoes, baggage, and weapons; and fled into the woods. The French and the Christian Hurons made fight for a time; but when they saw another fleet of canoes approaching from the opposite shores or islands, they lost heart, and those escaped who could. Jogues sprang into the bulrushes, and might have escaped; but when he saw the neophytes in the clutches of the Iroquois, he had no heart to abandon them, but came out from his hiding-place, and gave himself up to the astonished victors. A few of them had remained to guard the prisoners; the rest were chasing the fugitives. Jogues mastered his agony, and began to baptize those of the captive converts who needed baptism.

Their course was southward, up the River Richelieu and Lake Champlain; thence, by way of Lake George, to the Mohawk towns. The pain and fever of their wounds, and the clouds of mosquitoes, which they could not drive off, left the prisoners no peace by day nor sleep by night. On the eighth day, they learned that a large Iroquois war-party, on their way to Canada, were near at hand; and they soon approached their camp, on a small island near the southern end of Lake Champlain. The warriors, two hundred in number, saluted their victorious countrymen with volleys from their guns; then, armed with clubs and thorny sticks, ranged themselves in two lines, between which the captives were compelled to pass up the side of a rocky hill. On the way, they were beaten with such fury, that Jogues, who was last in the line, fell powerless, drenched in blood and half dead. As the chief man among the French captives, he fared the worst. When, at night, the exhausted sufferers tried to rest, the young warriors came to lacerate their wounds and pull out their hair and beards.

In the morning they resumed their journey. And now the lake narrowed to the semblance of a tranquil river. Before them was a woody mountain, close on their right a rocky promontory, and between these flowed a stream, the outlet of Lake George. First of white men, Jogues and his companions gazed on the romantic lake that bears the name, not of its gentle discoverer, but of the dull Hanoverian king. Like a fair Naiad of the wilderness, it slumbered between the guardian mountains that breathe from crag and forest the stern poetry of war. But all then was solitude; and the clang of trumpets, the roar of cannon, and the deadly crack of the rifle had never as yet awakened their angry echoes.

The Iroquois landed at or near the future site of Fort William Henry, left their canoes, and, with their prisoners, began their march for the nearest Mohawk town. The whoops of the victors announced their approach, and the savage hive sent forth its swarms. They thronged the side of the hill, the old and the young, each with a stick, or a slender iron rod, bought from the Dutchmen on the Hudson. They ranged themselves in a double line, reaching upward to the entrance of the town; and through this "narrow road of Paradise," as Jogues calls it, the captives were led in single file. As they passed, they were saluted with yells, screeches, and a tempest of blows. One, heavier than the others, knocked Jogues's breath from his body, and stretched him on the ground; but it was death to lie there, and, regaining his feet, he staggered on with the rest. When they reached the town, the blows ceased, and they were all placed on a scaffold, or high platform, in the middle of the place.

They were allowed a few minutes to recover their breath, undisturbed, except by the hootings and gibes of the mob below. Then a chief called out, "Come, let us caress these Frenchmen!" — and the crowd, knife in hand, began to mount the scaffold. They ordered a Christian Algonquin woman, a prisoner among them, to cut off Jogues's left thumb, which she did. It is needless to specify further the tortures to which they were subjected, all designed to cause the greatest possible suffering without endangering life. At night, they were removed from the scaffold, and placed in one of the houses, each stretched on his back, with his limbs extended, and his ankles and wrists bound fast to stakes driven into the earthen floor. The children now profited by the examples of their parents, and amused themselves by placing live coals and red-hot ashes on the naked bodies of the prisoners, who, bound fast, and covered with wounds and bruises which made every movement a torture, were sometimes unable to shake them off.

In the morning, they were again placed on the scaffold, where, during this and the two following days, they remained exposed to the taunts of the crowd. Then they were led in triumph to the second Mohawk town, and afterwards to the third, suffering at each a repetition of cruelties, the detail of which would be as monotonous as revolting.

Late in the autumn, a party of the Indians set forth on their yearly deer-hunt, and Jogues was ordered to go with them. Shivering and half famished, he followed them through the chill November forest, and shared their wild bivouac in the depths of the wintry desolation. The game they took was devoted to Areskoui, their god, and eaten in his honor. Jogues would not taste the meat offered to a demon; and thus he starved in the midst of plenty. At night, when the kettle was slung, and the savage crew made merry around their fire, he crouched in a corner of the hut, gnawed by hunger, and pierced to the bone with cold. They thought his presence unpropitious to their hunting, and the women especially hated him. His demeanor at once astonished and incensed his masters. He brought them firewood, like a squaw; he did their bidding without a murmur, and patiently bore their abuse; but when they mocked at his God, and laughed at his devotions, their slave assumed an air and tone of authority, and sternly rebuked them.

The Indians at last grew tired of him, and sent him back to the village. Here he remained till the middle of March, baptizing infants and trying to convert adults. He told them of the sun, moon, planets, and stars. They listened with interest; but when from astronomy he passed to theology, he spent his breath in vain.

Jogues had shown no disposition to escape, and great liberty was therefore allowed him. He went from town to town, giving absolution to the Christian captives, and converting and baptizing the heathen. On one occasion, he baptized a woman in the midst of the fire, under pretence of lifting a cup of water to her parched lips. There was no lack of objects for his zeal. A single war-party returned from the Huron country with nearly a hundred prisoners, who were distributed among the Iroquois towns, and the greater part burned. Of the children of the Mohawks and their neighbors, he had baptized, before August, about seventy; insomuch that he began to regard his captivity as a Providential interposition for the saving of souls.

At the end of July, he went with a party of Indians to a fishing-place on the Hudson, about twenty miles below Fort Orange. A canoe soon after went up the river with some of the Iroquois, and he was allowed to go in it. When they reached Rensselaerswyck, the Indians landed to trade with the Dutch, and took Jogues with them.

The center of this rude little settlement was Fort Orange, a miserable structure of logs, standing on a spot now within the limits of the city of Albany. It contained several houses and other buildings; and behind it was a small church, recently erected, and serving as the abode of the pastor, Dominie Megapolensis, known in our day as the writer of an interesting, though short, account of the Mohawks. Some twenty-five or thirty houses, roughly built of boards and roofed with thatch, were scattered at intervals on or near the borders of the Hudson, above and below the fort. Their inhabitants, about a hundred in number, were for the most part rude Dutch farmers, tenants of Van Rensselaer, the patroon, or lord of the manor. They raised wheat, of which they made beer, and oats, with which they fed their numerous horses. They traded, too, with the Indians, who profited greatly by the competition among them, receiving guns, knives, axes, kettles, cloth, and beads, at moderate rates, in exchange for their furs. The Dutch were on excellent terms with their red neighbors, met them in the forest without the least fear, and sometimes intermarried with them. They had known of Jogues's captivity, and, to their great honor, had made efforts for his release, offering for that purpose goods to a considerable value, but without effect.

He and his Indian masters were lodged together in a large building, like a barn, belonging to a Dutch farmer. It was a hundred feet long, and had no partition of any kind. At one end the farmer kept his cattle; at the other he slept with his wife, a Mohawk squaw, and his children, while his Indian guests lay on the floor in the middle. As he is described as one of the principal persons of the colony, it is clear that the civilization of Rensselaerswyck was not high.

In the evening, Jogues, in such a manner as not to excite the suspicion of the Indians, went out to reconnoitre. There was a fence around the house, and, as he was passing it, a large dog belonging to the farmer flew at him, and bit him very severely in the leg. The Dutchman, hearing the noise, came out with a light, led Jogues back into the building, and bandaged his wound. He seemed to have some suspicion of the prisoner's design; for, fearful perhaps that his escape might exasperate the Indians, he made fast the door in such a manner that it could not readily be opened. Jogues now lay down among the Indians, who, rolled in their blankets, were stretched around him. He was fevered with excitement; and the agitation of his mind, joined to the pain of his wound, kept him awake all night. About dawn, while the Indians were still asleep, a laborer in the employ of the farmer came in with a lantern, and Jogues, who spoke no Dutch, gave him to understand by signs that he needed his help and guidance. The man was disposed to aid him, silently led the way out, quieted the dogs, and showed him the path to the river. It was more than half a mile distant, and the way was rough and broken. Jogues was greatly exhausted, and his wounded limb gave him such pain that he walked with the utmost difficulty. When he reached the shore, the day was breaking, and he found, to his dismay, that the ebb of the tide had left the boat high and dry. He shouted to the vessel, but no one heard him. His desperation gave him strength; and, by working the boat to and fro, he pushed it at length, little by little, into the water, entered it, and rowed to the vessel. The Dutch sailors received him kindly, and hid him in the bottom of the hold, placing a large box over the hatchway.

He remained two days, half-stifled, in this foul lurking-place, while the Indians, furious at his escape, ransacked the settlement in vain to find him. They came off to the vessel, and so terrified the officers, that Jogues was sent on shore at night, and led to the fort. Here he was hidden in the garret of a house occupied by a miserly old man, to whose charge he was consigned. Food was sent to him; but, as his host appropriated the larger part to himself, Jogues was nearly starved. There was a compartment of his garret, separated from the rest by a partition of boards. Here the old Dutchman, who, like many others of the settlers, carried on a trade with the Mohawks, kept a quantity of goods for that purpose; and hither he often brought his customers. The boards of the partition had shrunk, leaving wide crevices; and Jogues could plainly see the Indians, as they passed between him and the light. They, on their part, might as easily have seen him, if he had not, when he heard them entering the house, hidden himself behind some barrels in the corner, where he would sometimes remain crouched for hours, in a constrained and painful posture, half suffocated with heat, and afraid to move a limb. His wounded leg began to show dangerous symptoms; but he was relieved by the care of a Dutch surgeon of the fort. The minister, Megapolensis, also visited him, and did all in his power for the comfort of his Catholic brother, with whom he seems to have been well pleased, and whom he calls "a very learned scholar."

When Jogues had remained for six weeks in this hiding-place, his Dutch friends succeeded in satisfying his Indian masters by the payment of a large ransom. A vessel from Manhattan, now New York, soon after brought up an order from the Director-General, Kieft, that he should be sent to him.

The Director-General, with a humanity that was far from usual with him, exchanged Jogues's squalid and savage dress for a suit of Dutch cloth, and gave him passage in a small vessel which was then about to sail. The voyage was rough and tedious; and the passenger slept on deck or on a coil of ropes, suffering greatly from cold, and often drenched by the waves that broke over the vessel's side. At length she reached Falmouth, on the southern coast of England, when all the crew went ashore for a carouse, leaving Jogues alone on board. A boat presently came alongside with a gang of desperadoes, who boarded her, and rifled her of everything valuable, threatened Jogues with a pistol, and robbed him of his hat and coat. He obtained some assistance from the crew of a French ship in the harbor, and, on the day before Christmas, took passage in a small coal vessel for the neighboring coast of Brittany. In the following afternoon he was set on shore a little to the north of Brest, and, seeing a peasant's cottage not far off, he approached it, and asked the way to the nearest church. The peasant and his wife, as the narrative gravely tells us, mistook him, by reason of his modest deportment, for some poor, but pious Irishman, and asked him to share their supper, after finishing his devotions, an invitation which Jogues, half famished as he was, gladly accepted. He reached the church in time for the early mass, and with an unutterable joy knelt before the altar, and renewed the communion of which he had been deprived so long. When he returned to the cottage, the attention of his hosts was at once attracted to his mutilated and distorted hands. They asked with amazement how he could have received such injuries; and when they heard the story of his tortures, their surprise and veneration knew no bounds. Two young girls, their daughters, begged him to accept all they had to give — a handful of sous; while the peasant made known the character of his new guest to his neighbors. A trader from Rennes brought a horse to the door, and offered the use of it to Jogues, to carry him to the Jesuit college in that town. He gratefully accepted it; and, on the morning of the fifth of January, 1644, reached his destination.

He dismounted, and knocked at the door of the college. The porter opened it, and saw a man wearing on his head an old woollen nightcap, and in an attire little better than that of a beggar. Jogues asked to see the Rector; but the porter answered, coldly, that the Rector was busied in the Sacristy. Jogues begged him to say that a man was at the door with news from Canada. The missions of Canada were at this time an object of primal interest to the Jesuits, and above all to the Jesuits of France. A letter from Jogues, written during his captivity, had already reached France, as had also the Jesuit *Relation* of 1643; which contained a long account of his capture; and he had no doubt been an engrossing theme of conversation in every house of the French Jesuits. The Father Rector was putting on his vestments to say mass; but when he heard that a poor man from Canada had asked for him at the door, he postponed the service, and went to meet him. Jogues, without discovering himself, gave him a letter from the Dutch Director-General attesting his character. The Rector, without reading it, began to question him as to the affairs of Canada, and at length asked him if he knew Father Jogues.

"I knew him very well," was the reply.

"The Iroquois have taken him," pursued the Rector. "Is he dead? Have they murdered him?"

"No," answered Jogues; "he is alive and at liberty, and I am he." And he fell on his knees to ask his Superior's blessing.

A priest with any deformity of body is debarred from saying mass. The teeth and knives of the Iroquois had inflicted an injury worse than the torturers imagined, for they had robbed Jogues of the privilege which was the chief consolation of his life; but the Pope, by a special dispensation, restored it to him, and with the opening spring he sailed again for Canada.

The Men Who Did It

BERNARD DEVOTO   1897–1955

They toiled westward on the sun's path, toward the fourth house of the sky, fulfilling a dream which Meriwether Lewis had had in his boyhood, fulfilling an older, more complex dream of Thomas Jefferson's, and by strength and skill and valor they rolled the unknown back before them. The country ahead of them was an untraveled chaos, the boundary of man's knowledge moved with them, they passed and the map was made forever. The day's march lay between walls of the capricious and treacherous wilderness and walls of a capricious and malevolent race of savages; the day's march ended and the walls had been moved farther back.

Past the Little Missouri, past the Rochejaune which they were the first to call the Yellowstone, past the Big Muddy and the Milk River and the Musselshell. On the twenty-sixth of May, Lewis climbed the highest neighboring hill and looking westward saw lines lift and waver above the horizon and sun flash on distant snow — "the object of all our hopes and the reward of all our ambition," the Rocky Mountains. On June 2d they reached a large river coming down from the north and faced a decision on which success or irrevocable failure hinged. For nothing in their data sufficed to tell them which fork was the true Missouri and would lead them to the continental divide. The north fork, which Lewis was to call Maria's, looked far likelier than the other, and even after both had been reconnoitered the whole party except the captains thought that it was the Missouri. The process by which they determined on the other one might serve as a model of scientific analysis and must be granted a high place in the history of thought. The decision made, Lewis hurried up the south fork to be sure, and was sure when he heard the thunder of the great falls, felt the spray borne by the wind for several miles to fall for the first time on white man's cheeks, and finally stood deafened and dazzled above the gorge.

They got the boats round the falls by a gigantic labor, and went on. A cloudburst nearly destroyed them and, not for the last time, Sacajawea owed her life and her child's to William Clark. Navigation would soon be impossible, game began to fail, the summer was shortening and ice formed in the buckets overnight. Whether they would do Thomas Jefferson's will or fail and probably perish on the continental crest depended on their finding the Shoshones at their accustomed hunting ground — on the Shoshones' being friendly — on their having horses to sell. Clark, the more skillful frontiersman, ranged ahead but did not meet them; then Lewis went, and it was he who finally found them, unfriendly, suspicious, disposed to flight or murder. The Shoshones feared that this prodigy, the first white man they had ever seen, might be working some corrupt device of their enemies and might betray them into ambush. Failure of the great adventure now hung by a single thread above the commander's head, but, telling them about the party of white men to the eastward, of the woman of their nation who was with it, of the marvelous black-skinned man, Lewis managed to allay part of their distrust and they turned back with him. They might have killed him, as in fact he thought they would; they might have gone on to overwhelm the party that was toiling on with Clark — and, ominously, came later than Lewis had promised. But they did not. The arrival of Clark proved Lewis's tongue straight, and at once history soared into that purer ether where fiction dare not venture. For Lewis, desiring clearer speech with the chief Cameahwait, who had accompanied him, sent for Sacajawea to interpret.

A moment later she threw her blanket round the chief and was weeping violently. Just below the continental divide, after five years of separation, she had met her own brother, from whose tent she had been ravished. "After some conversation between them she resumed her seat and attempted to interpret for us; but her new situation seemed to overpower her and she was frequently interrupted by her tears."

They now reached the limit of strain and exhaustion. Various of the men, then Clark, and finally Lewis fell ill. They dosed themselves with Rush's pills and pressed on. The cold thin air of the mountains yielded to sweltering heat as they descended, and this too weakened them. "Today he [Lewis] could hardly sit on his horse, while others were obliged to be put on horseback, and some, from extreme weakness and pain, were forced to lie down alongside of the road [trail] for some time!"

But in the mountains circumstance and the impersonal malice of the wilderness had done their utmost, and the expedition now reached navigable water again, the Kooskooskee River. They camped on its bank and while the sick recovered, the well made canoes for the last stage of the appointed labor. Reverting to a water route, they had no more to face than a daily, routine hazard of skill against destruction. Down the Kooskooskee to the Snake they went, and down the Snake till at last they reached the river for which they had set out. Two years and three months before, the Columbia had been just a dead reckoning in Thomas Jefferson's study, just a hole pricked in blank white paper with the point of his dividers. But now, forever, a known line was drawn in ink across that white paper from Jefferson's study in Washington to the great river of the West.

There were dangerous rapids still to pass, and the food failed sometimes, and wood for fires was scarce. The Indians too were different, treacherous, occasionally dangerous; they were greater thieves, having been more in contact with white men, whose pea jackets, hardware, and venereal diseases came up the Columbia along the immemorial trade route. They shot the last rapid of the

Cascades and came on November 2d to tidewater. The journey now added one climactic indignity: as they floated down the river a storm rose and, after crossing the continental divide and breaking a trail across the arid wilderness, they must be seasick. It was the rainy season, too, and they were hardly to be dry again till next spring. The river widened, high winds made the waves furious, at night their camp was nearly washed from under them. Almost at journey's end, they had to stop on November 10th, and for two days gales, thunder, and hailstorms buffeted them. There was a final precarious moment with some anonymous Indians and, on November 14th, Captain Lewis rounded a last point and saw the open sea.

They were too uncomfortable, too waterlogged, too weary, and much too seasoned to rejoice. The journal says, "Ocian in View! O! the joy," and says little more. A camp-site must be found and preparations for the winter must be begun — better to think of such urgent things than of significances that hovered above that stormy promontory. But the continent had been crossed and was no longer unknown. The trail was blazed, the Americans had occupied their country, the Republic had reached its farthest frontier. An idea with which the restless mind of Thomas Jefferson had wrestled through many nights had been given flesh, Meriwether Lewis's dream had come true, and the thing was done. It was November 14, 1805, and the journey of Lewis and Clark to a foreseen but unknown end had reached that end on a rainy Pacific beach. Another, older, more dreambound journey ended too. The passage to India was achieved, and three ships made harbor that had sailed from the port of Palos on Friday, the third of August, 1492, at about eight in the morning.

The Campers at Kitty Hawk

JOHN DOS PASSOS   1896–

On December seventeenth, nineteen hundred and three, Bishop Wright, of the United Brethren, onetime editor

of the *Religious Telescope,* received in his frame house
on Hawthorn Street in Dayton, Ohio, a telegram from
his boys Wilbur and Orville who'd gotten it into their
heads to spend their vacations in a little camp out on the
dunes of the North Carolina coast tinkering with a
homemade glider they'd knocked together themselves.
The telegram read:

> SUCCESS   FOUR FLIGHTS THURSDAY MORNING ALL
> AGAINST TWENTYONE MILE WIND   STARTED FROM
> LEVEL WITH ENGINEPOWER ALONE   AVERAGE
> SPEED THROUGH AIR THIRTYONE MILES   LONGEST
> FIFTYSEVEN SECONDS   INFORM PRESS HOME
> CHRISTMAS

The figures were a little wrong because the telegraph
operator misread Orville's hasty penciled scrawl
    but the fact remains
    that a couple of young bicycle mechanics from Dayton,
Ohio
    Had designed constructed and flown
    for the first time ever a practical airplane.

*After running the motor a few minutes to heat it up I
released the wire that held the machine to the track and
the machine started forward into the wind. Wilbur ran
at the side of the machine holding the wing to balance it
on the track. Unlike the start on the 14th made in a
calm the machine facing a 27 mile wind started very
slowly. . . . Wilbur was able to stay with it until it lifted
from the track after a forty-foot run. One of the lifesav-
ing men snapped the camera for us taking a picture just
as it reached the end of the track and the machine had
risen to a height of about two feet. . . . The course of
the flight up and down was extremely erratic, partly due
to the irregularities of the air, partly to lack of experience in handling this machine. A sudden dart when a
little over a hundred and twenty feet from the point at
which it rose in the air ended the flight. . . . This flight
lasted only 12 seconds, but it was nevertheless the first in
the history of the world in which a machine carrying a*

*man had raised itself by its own power into the air in full
flight, had sailed forward without reduction of speed
and had finally landed at a point as high as that from
which it started.*

A little later in the day the machine was caught in a
gust of wind and turned over and smashed, almost kill-
ing the coastguardsman who tried to hold it down;
    it was too bad
    but the Wright brothers were too happy to care
    they'd proved that the damn thing flew.

*When these points had been definitely established, we
at once packed our goods and returned home knowing
that the age of the flying machine had come at last.*

They were home for Christmas in Dayton, Ohio,
where they'd been born in the seventies of a family who
had been settled west of the Alleghenies since eighteen
fourteen, in Dayton, Ohio, where they'd been to gram-
marschool and highschool and joined their father's
church and played baseball and hockey and worked out
on the parallel bars and the flying swing and sold newspapers and built themselves a printingpress out of odds
and ends from the junk-heap and flown kites and tink-
ered with mechanical contraptions and gone around
town as boys doing odd jobs to turn an honest penny.

The folks claimed it was the bishop's bringing home a
helicopter, a fiftycent mechanical toy made of two fans
worked by elastic bands that was supposed to hover in
the air, that had got his two youngest boys hipped on the
subject of flight
    so that they stayed home instead of marrying the way
the other boys did, and puttered all day about the house
picking up a living with jobprinting,
    bicyclerepair work,
    sitting up late nights reading books on aerodynamics.

Still they were sincere churchmembers, their bicycle
business was prosperous, a man could rely on their word.
They were popular in Dayton.

In those days flyingmachines were the big laugh of all

the crackerbarrel philosophers. Langley's and Chanute's unsuccessful experiments had been jeered down with an I-told-you-so that rang from coast to coast. The Wrights' big problem was to find a place secluded enough to carry on their experiments without being the horselaugh of the countryside. Then they had no money to spend;

they were practical mechanics; when they needed anything they built it themselves.

They hit on Kitty Hawk,
on the great dunes and sandy banks that stretch
south towards Hatteras seaward of Albemarle Sound,
a vast stretch of seabeach
empty except for a coastguard station, a few fishermen's shacks and the swarms of mosquitoes and the ticks and chiggers in the crabgrass behind the dunes
and overhead the gulls and swooping terns, in the evening fishhawks and cranes flapping across the salt-marshes, occasionally eagles
that the Wright brothers followed soaring with their eyes
as Leonardo watched them centuries before
straining his sharp eyes to apprehend
the laws of flight.

Four miles across the loose sand from the scattering of shacks, the Wright brothers built themselves a camp and a shed for their gliders. It was a long way to pack their groceries, their tools, anything they happened to need; in summer it was hot as blazes, the mosquitoes were hell;

but they were alone there
and they'd figured out that the loose sand was as soft as anything they could find to fall in.

There with a glider made of two planes and a tail in which they lay flat on their bellies and controlled the warp of the planes by shimmying their hips, taking off again and again all day from a big dune named Kill Devil Hill,

they learned to fly.

Once they'd managed to hover for a few seconds

and soar ever so slightly on a rising aircurrent
they decided the time had come
to put a motor in their biplane.

Back in the shop in Dayton, Ohio, they built an air-
tunnel, which is their first great contribution to the science of flying, and tried out model planes in it.

They couldn't interest any builders of gasoline en-
gines so they had to build their own motor.

It worked; after that Christmas of nineteen three the
Wright brothers weren't doing it for fun any more; they
gave up their bicycle business, got the use of a big old
cowpasture belonging to the local banker for practice
flights, spent all the time when they weren't working on
their machine in promotion, worrying about patents, in-
fringements, spies, trying to interest government officials,
to make sense out of the smooth involved heartbreaking
remarks of lawyers.

In two years they had a plane that would cover twenty-
four miles at a stretch round and round the cowpasture.

People on the interurban car used to crane their necks
out of the windows when they passed along the edge of
the field, startled by the clattering pop pop of the old
Wright motor and the sight of the white biplane like a
pair of ironing boards one on top of the other chugging
along a good fifty feet in the air. The cows soon got used
to it.

As the flights got longer
the Wright brothers got backers,
engaged in lawsuits,
lay in their beds at night sleepless with the whine of
phantom millions, worse than the mosquitoes at Kitty
Hawk.

In nineteen-seven they went to Paris,
allowed themselves to be togged out in dress suits and
silk hats,
learned to tip waiters
talked with government experts, got used to gold braid

and postponements and vandyke beards and the out-
spread palms of politicos. For amusement
      they played diabolo in the Tuileries gardens.

They gave publicized flights at Fort Myers, where they
had their first fatal crackup, St. Petersburg, Paris, Berlin;
at Pau they were all the rage,
      such an attraction that the hotelkeeper
      wouldn't charge them for their room.
Alfonso of Spain shook hands with them and was pho-
tographed sitting in the machine,
      King Edward watched a flight,
      the Crown Prince insisted on being taken up,
      the rain of medals began.

They were congratulated by the Czar
and the King of Italy and the amateurs of sport, and
the society climbers and the papal titles,
      and decorated by a society for universal peace.

Aeronautics became the sport of the day.
The Wrights don't seem to have been very much impressed by the upholstery and the braid and the gold
medals and the parades of plush horses,
      they remained practical mechanics
      and insisted on doing all their own work themselves,
      even to filling the gasolinetank.
In nineteen eleven they were back on the dunes
      at Kitty Hawk with a new glider.
Orville stayed up in the air for nine and a half minutes, which remained a long time the record for motor-
less flight.
The same year Wilbur died of typhoid fever in Dayton.
In the rush of new names: Farman, Blériot, Curtiss,
Ferber, Esnault-Peltrie, Delagrange;
      in the snorting impact of bombs and the whine and
rattle of shrapnel and the sudden stutter of machineguns
after the motor's been shut off overhead,
      and we flatten into the mud
      and make ourselves small cowering in the corners of
ruined walls,

the Wright brothers passed out of the headlines
but not even the headlines or the bitter smear of news-
print or the choke of smokescreen and gas or chatter of
brokers on the stockmarket or barking of phantom millions or oratory of brasshats laying wreaths on new monuments
can blur the memory
of the chilly December day
two shivering bicycle mechanics from Dayton, Ohio,
first felt their homemade contraption
whittled out of hickory sticks,
gummed together with Arnstein's bicycle cement,
stretched with muslin they'd sewn on their sister's
sewing-machine in their own backyard on Hawthorn
Street in Dayton, Ohio,
soar into the air
above the dunes and the wide beach
at Kitty Hawk.

HISTORY AS SHE IS MADE

By two American Presidents: John Adams tells how George Washington became commander in chief, Woodrow Wilson how war was declared in 1917.

The only good histories are those written by those who had command in the events they describe.

MONTAIGNE

The Choice of Washington

JOHN ADAMS   1735–1826

In the mean time the New England army investing Boston, the New England legislatures, congresses, and conventions, and the whole body of the people, were left without munitions of war, without arms, clothing, pay, or even countenance and encouragement. Every post brought me letters from my friends, Dr. Winthrop, Dr. Cooper, General James Warren, and sometimes from General Ward and his aids, and General Heath and many others, urging in pathetic terms the impossibility of keeping their men together without the assistance of Congress. I was daily urging all these things, but we were embarrassed with more than one difficulty, not only with the party in favor of the petition to the King, and the party who were jealous of independence, but a third party, which was a Southern party against a Northern, and a jealousy against a New England army under the command of a New England General. Whether this jealousy was sincere, or whether it was mere pride and a haughty ambition of furnishing a southern General to command the northern army, (I cannot say); but the intention was very visible to me that Colonel Washington was their object, and so many of our staunchest men were in the plan, that we could carry nothing without conceding to it. Another embarrassment, which was never publicly known, and which was carefully concealed by those who knew it, the Massachusetts and other

New England delegates were divided. Mr. Hancock and Mr. Cushing hung back; Mr. Paine did not come forward, and even Mr. Samuel Adams was irresolute. Mr. Hancock himself had an ambition to be appointed commander-in-chief. Whether he thought an election a compliment due to him, and intended to have the honor of declining it, or whether he would have accepted, I know not. To the compliment he had some pretensions, for, at that time, his exertions, sacrifices, and general merits in the cause of his country had been incomparably greater than those of Colonel Washington. But the delicacy of his health, and his entire want of experience in actual service, though an excellent militia officer, were decisive objections to him in my mind. In canvassing this subject, out of doors, I found too that even among the delegates of Virginia there were difficulties. The apostolical reasonings among themselves, which should be greatest, were not less energetic among the saints of the ancient dominion than they were among us of New England. In several conversations, I found more than one very cool about the appointment of Washington, and particularly Mr. Pendleton was very clear and full against it. Full of anxieties concerning these confusions, and apprehending daily that we should hear very distressing news from Boston, I walked with Mr. Samuel Adams in the State House yard, for a little exercise and fresh air, before the hour of Congress, and there represented to him the various dangers that surrounded us. He agreed to them all, but said, "What shall we do?" I answered him, that he knew I had taken great pains to get our colleagues to agree upon some plan, that we might be unanimous; but he knew that they would pledge themselves to nothing; but I was determined to take a step which should compel them and all the other members of Congress to declare themselves for or against something. "I am determined this morning to make a direct motion that Congress should adopt the army before Boston, and appoint Colonel Washington commander of it." Mr. Adams seemed to think very seriously of it, but said nothing.

Accordingly, when Congress had assembled, I rose in my place, and in as short a speech as the subject would admit, represented the state of the Colonies, the uncertainty in the minds of the people, their great expectation and anxiety, the distresses of the army, the danger of its dissolution, the difficulty of collecting another, and the probability that the British army would take advantage of our delays, march out of Boston, and spread desolation as far as they could go. I concluded with a motion, in form, that Congress would adopt the army at Cambridge, and appoint a General; that though this was not the proper time to nominate a General, yet, as I had reason to believe this was a point of the greatest difficulty, I had no hesitation to declare that I had but one gentleman in my mind for that important command, and that was a gentleman from Virginia who was among us and very well known to all of us, a gentleman whose skill and experience as an officer, whose independent fortune, great talents, and excellent universal character, would command the approbation of all America, and unite the cordial exertions of all the Colonies better than any other person in the Union. Mr. Washington, who happened to sit near the door, as soon as he heard me allude to him, from his usual modesty, darted into the library-room, Mr. Hancock — who was our President which gave me an opportunity to observe his countenance while I was speaking on the state of the Colonies, the army at Cambridge, and the enemy — heard me with visible pleasure; but when I came to describe Washington for the commander, I never remarked a more sudden and striking change of countenance. Mortification and resentment were expressed as forcibly as his face could exhibit them. Mr. Samuel Adams seconded the motion, and that did not soften the President's physiognomy at all. The subject came under debate, and several gentlemen declared themselves against the appointment of Mr. Washington, not on account of any personal objection against him, but because the army were all from New England, had a General of their own, appeared to be satisfied with him, and had proved themselves able to imprison the British army in Boston, which was all they expected or desired at that time. Mr. Pendleton, of Virginia, Mr. Sherman, of Connecticut, were very explicit in declaring this opinion; Mr. Cushing and several others more faintly expressed their opposition, and their fears of discontents in the army and in New England. Mr. Paine expressed a great opinion of General Ward and a strong friendship for him, having been his classmate at college, or at least his contemporary; but gave no opinion upon the question. The subject was postponed to a future day. In the meantime, pains were taken out of doors to obtain a unanimity, and the voices were generally so clearly in favor of Washington, that the dissentient members were persuaded to withdraw their opposition, and Mr. Washington was nominated, I believe by Mr. Thomas Johnson of Maryland, unanimously elected, and the army adopted.

"Disinterested as the being who made him," Thomas Jefferson said, and he was referring to Adams.

The Night Before

MONTAIGNE   1533–1592

I should rather know the truth of the talk he had in his tent with one of his close friends on the eve of the battle than the speech he made the next day to his army, and what he did in his study or in his own room than what he did in public and in the Senate.

JOHN L. HEATON *on Frank I. Cobb of "The World"*
1869–1923

President Wilson had a way of summoning Cobb to Washington. Cobb rarely spoke of these visits to the White House. Since Wilson's death two of Cobb's associates, Maxwell Anderson and Laurence Stallings, have written down their memory of his recollection of one such occasion which is history. Mr. Anderson remembers that something said in disparagement of Clemenceau gave the impetus to the revelation; Mr. Anderson continues:

" 'He was a tricky old bandit,' said Cobb, as the three of us entered his office. 'A tricky old bandit, but he knew the game. He was the most formidable person at Versailles when it came to a pinch. Lloyd George was a child beside him. W. W. knew it, and knew how to meet the old boy, but he was hampered by having ideals of justice and government. Clemenceau used to look at Wilson as if he were a new and disconcerting species. He thought Wilson had the Messiah complex.

" 'He was dead wrong about it, though, and everybody who thinks Wilson didn't know his way about and didn't know what he was in for should have heard what he said about the war before he went in. Old W. W. knew his history. He knew what wars were fought for, and what they do to nations that wage them.

" 'The night before he asked Congress for a declaration of war against Germany he sent for me. I was late getting the message somehow and didn't reach the White House till one o'clock in the morning. "The old man" was waiting for me, sitting in his study with the typewriter on his table, where he used to type his own messages.

" 'I'd never seen him so worn down. He looked as if he hadn't slept, and he said he hadn't. He said he was probably going before Congress the next day to ask for a declaration of war, and he'd never been so uncertain about anything in his life as about that decision. For nights, he said, he'd been lying awake going over the whole situation; over the provocation given by Germany, over the probable feeling in the United States, over the consequences to the settlement and to the world at large if we entered the mêlée.

" 'He tapped some sheets before him and said that he had written a message and expected to go before Congress with it as it stood. He said he couldn't see any alternative, that he had tried every way he knew to avoid war. "I think I know what war means," he said, and he added that if there were any possibility of avoiding war he wanted to try it. "What else can I do?" he asked. "Is there anything else I can do?"

" 'I told him his hand had been forced by Germany, that so far as I could see we couldn't keep out.

" ' "Yes," he said, "but do you know what that means?" He said war would overturn the world we had known; that so long as we remained out there was a preponderance of neutrality, but that if we joined with the Allies the world would be off the peace basis and onto a war basis.

" 'It would mean that we should lose our heads along with the rest and stop weighing right and wrong. It would mean that a majority of people in this hemisphere would go war-mad, quit thinking and devote their energies to destruction. The President said a declaration of war would mean that Germany would be beaten and so badly beaten that there would be a dictated peace, a victorious peace.

" ' "It means," he said, "an attempt to reconstruct a peacetime civilization with war standards, and at the end of the war there will be no bystanders with sufficient power to influence the terms. There won't be any peace standards left to work with. There will be only war standards."

" 'The President said that such a basis was what the Allies thought they wanted, and that they would have their way in the very thing America had hoped against and struggled against. W. W. was uncanny that night. He had the whole panorama in his mind. He went on to say that so far as he knew he had considered every loophole of escape and as fast as they were discovered, Germany deliberately blocked them with some new outrage.

" 'Then he began to talk about the consequences to the United States. He had no illusions about the fashion in which we were likely to fight the war.

" 'He said when a war got going it was just war and there weren't two kinds of it. It required illiberalism at home to reinforce the men at the front. We couldn't fight Germany and maintain the ideals of Government that all thinking men shared. He said we would try it, but it would be too much for us.

" ' "Once lead this people into war," he said, "and

they'll forget there ever was such a thing as tolerance. To fight you must be brutal and ruthless, and the spirit of ruthless brutality will enter into the very fibre of our national life, infecting Congress, the courts, the policeman on the beat, the man in the street." Conformity would be the only virtue, said the President, and every man who refused to conform would have to pay the penalty.

" 'He thought the Constitution would not survive it; that free speech and the right of assembly would go. He said a nation couldn't put its strength into a war and keep its head level; it had never been done.

" ' "If there is any alternative, for God's sake, let's take it," he exclaimed. Well, I couldn't see any, and I told him so.

" 'The President didn't have illusions about how he was going to come out of it, either. He'd rather have done anything else than head a military machine. All his instincts were against it. He foresaw too clearly the probable influence of a declaration of war on his own fortunes; the adulation certain to follow the certain victory, the derision and attack which would come with the deflation of excessive hopes and in the presence of world responsibility. But if he had it to do over again he would take the same course. It was just a choice of evils.' "

And the next day, April 2, 1917, WILSON *said to Congress:*
It is a distressing and oppressive duty, gentlemen of Congress, which I have performed in thus addressing you. There are, it may be, many months of fiery trial and sacrifice ahead of us. It is a fearful thing to lead this great and peaceful people into war, into the most terrible and disastrous of all wars. Civilization itself seems to be in the balance, but right is more precious than peace, and we shall fight for the things which we have always carried nearest our hearts, for democracy, for the right of those who submit to authority to have a voice in their own government, for the rights and liberties of small nations, for the universal dominion of right by such a con-

cert of free peoples as will bring peace and safety to all nations, and make the world itself at last free. To such a task we can dedicate our lives, our fortunes, everything we are, everything we have, with the pride of those who know the day has come when America is privileged to spend her blood and might for the principles that gave her birth, and the happiness and peace which she has treasured. God helping her, she can do no other.

PART
III

HE TURNS TO NATURE

A little madness in the Spring
Is wholesome even for the King,
But God be with the Clown,
Who ponders this tremendous scene —
This whole experiment in green,
As if it were his own!

EMILY DICKINSON

A green thought in a green shade.

ANDREW MARVELL

A poet ought not to pick nature's
pocket: let him borrow, and so bor-
row as to repay by the very act of
borrowing. Examine nature accu-
rately, but write from recollection,
and trust more to your imagination
than to your memory.

S. T. COLERIDGE

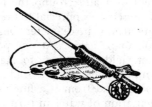

Weather

GEORGE R. STEWART   1895–

In mid-afternoon the front of the Siberian air-mass was pushing slowly across the island-studded ocean which lies east of China and south of Japan. Its cold, heavy air clung close to the surface of the water. Advancing thus as a northeasterly breeze, it forced backward the warmer, lighter air ahead of it, and occasionally pushed beneath this air vigorously enough to cause a shower.

This opposing and retreating air had lain, some days previous, over the tropical ocean near the Philippine Islands. A storm had taken it northeast, shedding rain, clear to the Japanese coast; it had then moved slowly back before the pressure of the cold wave. By this northern foray it had lost its extreme humidity and warmth, and become temperate rather than tropical. Nevertheless it still remained warmer and more moist than the air which had swept down from Siberia.

The advance of the northern air and corresponding retreat of the southern were related, like all movements in the atmosphere, to conditions existing concurrently over the whole earth. The conditions of this particular day were such that the advance was losing its vigor and becoming slower.

An hour before sunset, one section of the front reached a small island — a mere mountain-peak above the ocean. A dead-tired man may stumble over a pebble and fall; but his weariness, rather than the pebble, is the cause. Similarly, a vigorously advancing front would simply have swept over and around the island, but now the obstruction caused an appreciable break, and a hesitant eddy, about a mile in diameter, began to form — weakened — took shape again. At one point the southern air no longer yielded passively to the northern, but actively flowed up its slope, as up a gradual hill. Rising, this air grew cooler, and from it a fine drizzle began to fall. This condensation of water in turn further warmed the air, and caused it to press up the slope more steadily with still further condensation. The process thus became self-perpetuating and self-strengthening.

The movement of this advancing warm air was now a little southwest breeze, where previously all the flow of air had been from the northeast. With this new breeze, air which was still warmer and more moist moved in from the south along the near-by section of the original front, renewing its vigor and causing a little shower. All these new and renewed activities — winds, drizzle, and shower — were now arranged in complex but orderly fashion around a single point.

As from the union of two opposite germ-cells begins a life, so from the contact of northern and southern air had sprung something which before had not been. As a new life, a focus of activity, begins to develop after its kind and grow by what it feeds on, so in the air that complex of forces began to develop and grow strong. A new storm had been born.

Sky

EMERSON   1843

The sky is the daily bread of the eyes.

GUY MURCHIE   1907–

The winds of the airy ocean express the wonder of men of every land and every age. Their names reflect the tongues of history from ancient Cathay to the slang of the United States Army. Consider the dry khamsin of the Arabian desert, reputed to blow sand unceasingly for fifty days; the westerly datoo of the Straits of Gibraltar; the chinook of the dry American plains; the sudden violent williwaw of Alaska and Magellan's Strait; the sirocco of the Sahara; the buran of Russia; the typhoon of the China coast; the zonda and tormento of Argentina; the shamal of Mesopotamia; the gregale of the Ionian Sea; the brickfelder of southern Australia; the harmattan of North Africa; the belat, maloya, imbat, chubasco, bora, tramontana, leste, simoom, galerna, chocolatero, bize, crivetz, etesian, baguio, elephanta, virason, leveche, cordonazo, viuga, mistral, seistan, sonora, ponente, papagayo, kaus, puelche, siffanto, solano, reshabar, purga, and others — hot, cold, dry, or wet — from all the remotest corners of the earth.

If winds are the spirit of the sky's ocean, the clouds are its texture. They are embodied imagination, the sheet music of the heavens, the architecture of moving air. Theirs is easily the most uninhibited dominion of the earth. Nothing in physical shape is too fantastic for them. They can be round as apples or as fine as string, as dense as a jungle, as wispy as a whiff of down, as mild as puddle water or as potent as the belch of a volcano. Some are thunderous anvils formed by violent updrafts from the warm earth. Some are the ragged coattails of storms that have passed. Some are stagnant blankets of warm air resting on cold. Some are mare's tails floating in the chill upper sky. Some are herringbones, sheets, cream puffs, ox-bends, veils, hammerheads, spangled mantillas, sponges, black shrouds.

I have flown over great cloud pastures that seemed to be studded with trees of cotton and flocks of sheep grazing. I have seen clouds in the dawn that looked like a pink Sultan with his pale harem maidens and a yellow slob of eunuch lolling impotent in the background. When thunder was near I've seen sleepy clouds suddenly stand erect, casting their white bedclothes aside, then bulge into titanic genii to the bidding of the gale. In the afternoon I've beheld a quadruple rainbow moving against a stratocumulus layer below. Not an ordinary rainbow that forms an arch, but the special rainbow

called The Glory or Ulloa's Rind, which is known only
to those who fly: a set of complete circles, each inside
the next concentrically. These formed a sort of color
target that sped along the clouds on the opposite side
from the sun with the shadow of the airplane in the
center.

The Problems of Nature Are Insoluble

NAPOLEON   1769–1821

I frightened them pretty well with my invasion of England, didn't I? What was the public talk about it at the
time? Well, you may have joked about it in Paris, but
Pitt wasn't laughing in London. Never was the English
oligarchy in greater peril!

I had made a landing possible; I had the finest army
that ever existed, that of Austerlitz; what more can be
said? In four days I could have reached London; I would
not have entered as a conqueror but as a liberator;
I would have acted the part of William III again, but
with greater generosity. The discipline of my army
would have been perfect; and it would have behaved in
London as it might in Paris. From there I would have
operated from south to north, under the colours of the
Republic, the European regeneration which later I was
on the point of effecting from north to south, under
monarchical forms. The obstacles before which I failed
did not proceed from men but from the elements: in the
south it was the sea destroyed me; and in the north it was
the fire of Moscow and the ice of winter; so there it is,
water, air, fire, all nature and nothing but nature; these
were the opponents of a universal regeneration commanded by Nature herself! The problems of Nature are
insoluble!

Taking the March Winds

FRANCIS DARWIN *about his father*   1848–1925

I used to like to hear him admire the beauty of a flower;
it was a kind of gratitude to the flower itself, and a per-

sonal love for its delicate form and colour. I seem to remember him gently touching a flower he delighted in; it was the same simple admiration that a child might have.

A Happy Excursion

CHUANGTSE   4TH CENTURY B.C.

Chuangtse and Hueitse had strolled onto the bridge over the Hao, when the former observed, "See how the small fish are darting about! That is the happiness of the fish."

"You are not being a fish yourself," said Hueitse, "how can you know the happiness of the fish?"

"And you not being I," retorted Chuangtse, "how can you know that I do not know?"

"If I, not being you, cannot know what you know," urged Hueitse, "it follows that you, not being a fish, cannot know the happiness of the fish."

"Let us go back to your original question," said Chuangtse. "You asked me how I knew the happiness of the fish. Your very question shows that you knew that I knew. I knew it (from my own feelings) on this bridge."

Walden

JAMES H. POWERS   1893–

On the fourth of July, 1845, a century ago this coming week, a thin, shambling, ill-dressed young man at the late end of his twenties tramped in the early morning through the woods near Concord, Massachusetts. At a small clearing on a slope commanding a broad prospect of Walden Pond, which shimmered under pale mists loitering there since the recent daybreak, he halted.

A one-room house, whose frame gleamed yellow still from the axe and saw he had been wielding since March, symbolized the end of his journey. Henry David Thoreau had come home and was entering into his kingdom. Here, during the next two years — until September 7,

1847 — he was to make his residence; and the rolling hills and woodlands cupped around the pond were to be his demesne.

Few outside Concord township knew much of Walden Pond that summer morning. Those who did gave it but the casual heed customary with men who have other, more pressing concerns, to occupy their attention in a rural community. For the business of wresting a living from the earth was then — as now — no child's play. A host of authorities from Hesiod on, to and including the owner of the Hallowell Farm, which Thoreau tried to buy on credit two or three years earlier, had informed him on that point.

But he was indifferent to such aspects of life. "What have I to do with ploughs? I cut another furrow than you see. Where the off ox treads, there it is not, it is farther off; where the nigh ox walks, it will not be, it is nigher still. . . ." Here, in the thicket-besieged clearing above Walden Pond, he had other grist to grind — his own.

Small wonder that such a one should be eyed askance by most of the neighbors, who had watched his unaccountable saunterings as they leaned, horny-handed, on plough handles, their feet ankle deep in the dark rich loam of Concord's alluvial fields, or paused, haying fork in hand, to exchange laconic greetings across rambling, lichen-covered stone walls along the roadside.

With but few exceptions — and these, too, were a puzzle for homespun consideration — to Concord folk this young man was an unaccountable puzzle. Worse: he was suspect as a loafer. Why, if he wasn't, didn't he turn a hand at something more consistently, with his Harvard education to boot?

Concord was thinking of that wood fire he let out of hand some time since through his carelessness — an unforgivable offense to rural proprieties. Concord would continue to be bemused about him three years hence, when he elected to spend a session in jail rather than admit the power and right of the state expressed in a demand bill for his poll tax. How could you weigh and tag such a man?

Concord would continue to be surprised, half a century later, as it gradually became aware of his fame, and pondered the amazing paradox presented by this singular enterprise upon which he was entering now in a hermit haven, built with borrowed tools, standing solitary above Walden Pond. It was enough for Thoreau that all debts of neighborliness were fully acquitted. He owed no obligation. "The owner of the axe," he noted after borrowing it, "as he released his hold on it, said it was the apple of his eye; but I returned it sharper than I received it."

As for the rest, the fame of no dukedom or baronial keep would be more widely spread abroad over the face of the world than his, before he was done with it. In far-away China (whose passivity irked him) *Walden* would one day find translators. War correspondents would become casualties of battle with copies of it in their pockets nearly a hundred years after he began to assemble the material out of which it was woven. Indian revolutionaries would discover in it a path leading straight to collision with the mightiest of empires. And a whole generation of his own fellow countrymen, as the twentieth century consumed itself (and them) in the ravages of a struggle let loose by the primordial war between encroaching statism and creative individuality, would return thoughtfully and, perhaps shamefacedly, to re-explore its pages and weigh the import of its wisdom.

THOREAU   1817–1862

Why should we be in such desperate haste to succeed, and in such desperate enterprises? If a man does not keep pace with his companions, perhaps it is because he hears a different drummer. Let him step to the music which he hears, however measured or far away. It is not important that he should mature as soon as an apple tree or an oak. Shall he turn his spring into summer? If the condition of things which we were made for is not yet, what were any reality which we can substitute? We will not be shipwrecked on a vain reality. Shall we with pains erect a heaven of blue glass over ourselves, though when it is done we shall be sure to gaze still at the true ethereal heaven far above, as if the former were not?

The greater part of what my neighbors call good I believe in my soul to be bad, and if I repent of anything, it is very likely to be my good behavior. What demon possessed me that I behaved so well? You may say the wisest thing you can, old man — you who have lived seventy years, not without honor of a kind — I hear an irresistible voice which invites me away from all that. One generation abandons the enterprises of another like stranded vessels.

I went to the woods because I wished to live deliberately, to front only the essential facts of life, and see if I could not learn what it had to teach, and not, when I came to die, discover that I had not lived. I did not wish to live what was not life, living is so dear; nor did I wish to practise resignation, unless it was quite necessary. I wanted to live deep and suck out all the marrow of life, to live so sturdily and Spartanlike as to put to rout all that was not life, to cut a broad swath and shave close, to drive life into a corner, and reduce it to its lowest terms, and, if it proved to be mean, why, then to get the whole and genuine meanness of it, and publish its meanness to the world; or if it were sublime, to know it by experience, and be able to give a true account of it in my next excursion. For most men, it appears to me, are in a strange uncertainty about it, whether it is of the devil or of God, and have *somewhat hastily* concluded that it is the chief end of man here to "glorify God and enjoy Him forever."

Let us spend one day as deliberately as Nature, and not be thrown off the track by every nutshell and mosquito's wing that falls on the rails. Let us rise early and fast, or break fast, gently and without perturbation; let company come and let company go, let the bells ring and the children cry — determined to make a day of it. Why should we knock under and go with the stream? Let us not be upset and overwhelmed in that terrible rapid and whirl-pool called a dinner, situated in the meridian shallows. Weather this danger and you are safe, for the rest of the way is down hill. With unrelaxed nerves, with morning vigor, sail by it, looking another way, tied to the mast like Ulysses. If the engine whistles, let it whistle till it is hoarse for its pains. If the bell rings, why should we run? We will consider what kind of music they are like. Let us settle ourselves, and work and wedge our feet down-ward through the mud and slush of opinion, and prejudice, and tradition, and delusion, and appearance, that alluvion which covers the globe, through Paris and London, through New York and Boston and Concord, through church and state, through poetry and phi-losophy and religion, till we come to a hard bottom and rocks in place, which we can call *reality,* and say, This is, and no mistake; and then begin, having a *point d'appui,* below freshet and frost and fire, a place where you might found a wall or a state, or set a lamp-post safely, or per-haps a gauge, not a Nilometer, but a Realometer, that future ages might know how deep a freshet of shams and appearances had gathered from time to time. If you stand right fronting and face to face to a fact, you will see the sun glimmer on both its surfaces, as if it were a cimeter, and feel its sweet edge dividing you through the heart and marrow, and so you will happily conclude your mortal career. Be it life or death, we crave only reality. If we are really dying, let us hear the rattle in our throats and feel cold in the extremities; if we are alive, let us go about our business.

Time is but the stream I go a-fishing in. I drink at it; but while I drink, I see the sandy bottom and detect how shallow it is. Its thin current slides away, but eternity remains. I would drink deeper; fish in the sky, whose bottom is pebbly with stars. I cannot count one. I know not the first letter of the alphabet. I have always been regretting that I was not as wise as the day I was born. The intellect is a cleaver; it discerns and rifts its way into the secret of things. I do not wish to be any more busy with my hands than is necessary. My head is hands and feet. I feel all my best faculties concentrated in it. My instinct tells me that my head is an organ for burrowing, as some creatures use their snout and forepaws, and with it I would mine and burrow my way through these hills. I think that the richest vein is somewhere hereabouts; so by the divining rod and thin rising vapors I judge; and here I will begin to mine.

I did not read books the first summer; I hoed beans. Nay, I often did better than this. There were times when I could not afford to sacrifice the bloom of the present moment to any work, whether of the head or hands. I love a broad margin to my life. Sometimes, in a summer morning, having taken my accustomed bath, I sat in my sunny doorway from sunrise till noon, rapt in a reverie, amidst the pines and hickories and sumachs, in undisturbed solitude and stillness, while the birds sang around or flitted noiseless through the house, until by the sun falling in at my west window, or the noise of some traveller's wagon on the distant highway, I was reminded of the lapse of time. I grew in those seasons like corn in the night, and they were far better than any work of the hands would have been. They were not time subtracted from my life, but so much over and above my usual allowance. I realised what the Orientals mean by contemplation and the forsaking of works. For the most part, I minded not how the hours went. The day advanced as if to light some work of mine; it was morning, and lo! now it is evening, and nothing memorable is accomplished. Instead of singing like the birds, I silently smiled at my incessant good fortune. As the sparrow had its trill, sitting on the hickory before my door, so had I my chuckle or suppressed warble which he might hear out of my nest. My days were not days of the week, bearing the stamp of any heathen diety, nor were they minced into hours and fretted by the ticking of a clock; for I lived like the Puri Indians, of whom it is said that "for yesterday, today, and tomorrow they have only one word, and they express the variety of meaning by pointing backward for yesterday, forward for tomorrow, and overhead for the passing day." This was sheer idleness to my fellow-townsmen, no doubt; but if the birds and flowers had tried me by their standard, I should not have been found wanting. A man must find his occasions in himself, it is true. The natural day is very calm, and will hardly reprove his indolence.

I left the woods for as good a reason as I went there. Perhaps it seemed to me that I had several more lives to live, and could not spare any more time for that one. It is remarkable how easily and insensibly we fall into a particular route, and make a beaten track for ourselves. I had not lived there a week before my feet wore a path from my door to the pond-side; and though it is five or six years since I trod it, it is still quite distinct. It is true I fear that others may have fallen into it, and so helped to keep it open. The surface of the earth is soft and impressible by the feet of men; and so with the paths which the mind travels. How worn and dusty, then, must be the highways of the world — how deep the ruts of tradition and conformity! I did not wish to take a cabin passage, but rather to go before the mast and on the deck of the world, for there I could best see the moonlight amid the mountains. I do not wish to go below now.

I learned this, at least, by my experiment: that if one advances confidently in the direction of his dreams, and endeavors to live the life which he has imagined, he will meet with a success unexpected in common hours. He will put some things behind, will pass an invisible boundary; new, universal, and more liberal laws will begin to establish themselves around and within him; or the old laws be expanded, and interpreted in his favor in a more liberal sense and he will live with the license of a higher order of beings. In proportion as he simplifies his life, the laws of the universe will appear less complex, and solitude will not be solitude, nor poverty poverty, nor weakness weakness. If you have built castles in the air, your work need not be lost; that is where they should be. Now put the foundations under them.

Creation

THOREAU   1840

The birds I heard today, which, fortunately, did not come within the scope of my science, sang as freshly as if it had been the first morning of creation.

The Naturalist versus the Biologist

WILLIAM MORTON WHEELER   1865–1937

On reviewing my students and the mature investigators I have known during the past half-century, I find that most of them belong to two extreme types, while the remainder are intermediate or ambiguous composites. These extremes correspond with the romanticist and classicist types respectively, which Ostwald distinguished among physicists and chemists, and also agree very closely with the two general psychological types which Jung calls extraverts and introverts. The more numerous romanticists or extraverts are the naturalists; the classicists or introverts are the biologists in the strict sense. The differences between these two types, which are very probably constitutional or dispositional, will be clear from the following very brief behavioristic diagnosis:

The naturalist is mentally oriented toward and controlled by objective, concrete reality, and probably because his senses, especially those of sight and touch, are highly developed, is powerfully affected by the esthetic appeal of natural objects. He is little interested in and may even be quite blind to abstract or theoretical considerations, and therefore inclined to say with Goethe:

> *Grau, theurer Freund, ist alle Theorie,*
> *Und grün des Lebens goldener Baum.*

He is primarily an observer and fond of outdoor life, a collector, a classifier, a describer, deeply impressed by the overwhelming intricacy of natural phenomena and revelling in their very complexity. He is, therefore, more or less irrational, intuitive, receptive, and passive in his attitude toward natural objects, synthesizing rather than analyzing, a poor mathematician, an amateur in the proper sense of the word. When philosophically inclined, he is apt to be a tough-minded Aristotelian. In his output he is clearly of the romanticist type, publishing copiously and easily, but often without much sense of literary form or proportion.

The biologist *sensu stricto,* on the other hand, is oriented toward and dominated by ideas, and rather terrified or oppressed by the intricate hurly-burly of concrete, sensuous reality and its multiform and multicolored individual manifestations. He often belongs to the motor rather than to the visual type and obtains his esthetic satisfaction from all kinds of analytical procedures and the cold desiccated beauty of logical and mathematical demonstration. His will to power takes the form of experimentation and the controlling of phenomena by capturing them in a net of abstract formulas and laws. He is a denizen of the laboratory. His besetting sin is oversimplification and the tendency to undue isolation of the organisms he studies from their natural environment. As a philosopher he is apt to be a tenderminded Platonist. In his output he is a true classicist. The total volume of his writing is apt to be small, but of high quality.

The naturalist seems to represent the more youthful, the biologist the more mature, type. For this reason a naturalist may develop into something of a biologist, but a biologist never becomes a naturalist. As previously suggested, however, occasional individuals may combine the characteristics of both types. These also differ as students in their attitudes toward their professors. The youthful naturalist is more apt to seek sympathy, encouragement, and information from his teacher; the young biologist, owing to the peculiar orientation of his will to power, is more interested in the professor's bag of tricks, his ability to impart mathematical or laboratory methods. The naturalist never feels really at home in a university environment, probably because university faculties include such a large number of introverts and because he is apt to be a mediocre student in many of the required, standardized subjects of instruction.

If this very hasty diagnosis is correct, we can readily understand why the life sciences are divided between the two types, with the naturalist pre-empting the largely descriptive branches, taxonomy, comparative anatomy, geographical distribution, paleontology, phylogeny, and ecology, and the biologist the more abstruse experimental branches, physiology, embryology, and genetics; and why natural history, though it has lost its old appellation, nevertheless flourishes today much more luxuriantly than it did in the eighteenth and nineteenth centuries, and, owing to the preponderance of extraverts over introverts in the population at large, has many more devotees than it ever had before. Indeed, the sciences which were once called natural history bid fair to have an even greater development in the future. This is foreshadowed by the unmistakable desire for synthesis, a desire to deal with organisms and their behavior as wholes, so clearly manifested in the present organismal orientation of philosophy, psychology, sociology, and even of astronomy, physics, and chemistry. This is obviously a reaction to the intense specialization, analysis, and particularization which have characterized scientific investigation during the past century. Now it is the holistic attitude that has always characterized the naturalist. Even that extremely practical but much-abused science, taxonomy, which would seem to contradict this statement, really supports it, for classification is necessarily always a synthesis as well as an analysis. The same is also true of geographical distribution, paleontology, phylogeny, and ecology, with their background of organic history, or evolution. In these sciences the organism is never fully abstracted from its environment. Such notions as biocaenosis, adaptation, behavior-pattern, configuration, constitution, type, species, and individual, which the naturalist is constantly employing, are not analytical but very complex and synthetic concepts. Their elucidation, which will be largely the work of trained naturalists, will eventually bridge the gap between natural history and biology in the strict sense, between the field and the laboratory investigators.

What was formerly called natural history is the perennial foundation of the biological sciences. It has given rise to all the theoretical branches and will no doubt give rise to others in the future, and all the practical applications of biology have their roots in ecology, which is one of the basic branches of natural history, dealing with the behavior of organisms in relation to one another and to their environment. It formulates most of the basic problems which the experimentalists and biometricians are endeavoring to solve. Its concrete, sensuous, esthetic character will always attract the observer and the thinker, because it attaches itself to the individual organisms, and the individual is always essentially inscrutable and indefinable. The naturalist and the nature-lover will, therefore, always be with us. No matter how far the naturalist may specialize in his study of single groups of organisms or of the faunas and floras of particular regions or geological ages, he is always keenly aware both of the limitations of his specialty and of its relations to the whole realm of living things. Such modesty is not always apparent in the biologist in the strict sense, because he is not engaged in sympathetically exploring the contours of nature, but in determining the extent to which phenomena conform with his experimental, metrical, and therefore highly rational procedure.

KEATS TO BAILEY   1817

The setting sun will always set me to rights — or if a sparrow come before my window, I take part in its existence and pick about the gravel.

EMERSON   1836

Go out of the house to see the moon, and 'tis mere tinsel: it will not please as when its light shines upon your necessary journey.

JOHN DEWEY   1859–1952

Traditional theories have separated life from nature, mind from organic life, and thereby created mysteries. Restore the connection, and the problem of how a mind can know an external world, or even know that there is such a thing, is like the problem of how an animal eats things external to itself; it is the kind of problem that arises only if one assumes that a hibernating bear living off its own stored substance defines the normal procedure, ignoring moreover the question where the bear got its stored material. The problem of how one person knows the existence of other persons is, when the relation of mind and life is genuinely perceived, like the problem of how one animal can associate with other animals, since other is other. A creature generated in a conjunctive union, dependent upon others (as are at least all higher forms) for perpetuation of its being, and carrying in its own structure the organs and marks of its intimate connection with others, will know other creatures if it knows itself. Since both the inanimate and the human environment are involved in the functions of life, it is inevitable, if these functions evolve to the point of thinking and if thinking is naturally serial with biological functions, that it will have as the material of thought, even of its erratic imaginings, the events and connections of this environment. And if the animal succeeds in putting to use any of its thinkings as means of sustaining its functions, those thoughts will have the characters that define knowledge.

PART IV

AND SCRUTINIZES HER

Not meddling with Divinity, Meta-physicks, Moralls, Politicks, Grammar, Rhetorick, or Logick.

ROBERT HOOKE
ABOUT THE ROYAL SOCIETY

The Builders

VANNEVAR BUSH   1959

The process by which the boundaries of knowledge are advanced, and the structure of organized science is built, is a complex process indeed. It corresponds fairly well with the exploitation of a difficult quarry for its building materials and the fitting of these into an edifice; but there are very significant differences. First, the material itself is exceedingly varied, hidden and overlaid with relatively worthless rubble, and the process of uncovering new facts and relationships has some of the attributes of prospecting and exploration rather than of mining or quarrying. Second, the whole effort is highly unorganized. There are no direct orders from architect or quarrymaster. Individuals and small bands proceed about their businesses unimpeded and uncontrolled, digging where they will, working over their material, and tucking it into place in the edifice.

Finally, the edifice itself has a remarkable property, for its form is predestined by the laws of logic and the nature of human reasoning. It is almost as though it had once existed, and its building blocks had then been scattered, hidden, and buried, each with its unique form retained so that it would fit only in its own peculiar position, and with the concomitant limitation that the blocks cannot be found or recognized until the building of the structure has progressed to the point where their position and form reveals itself to the discerning eye of the talented worker in the quarry. Parts of the edifice are being used while construction proceeds, by reason of the applications of science, but other parts are merely admired for their beauty and symmetry, and their possible utility is not in question.

In these circumstances it is not at all strange that the workers sometimes proceed in erratic ways. There are those who are quite content, given a few tools, to dig away unearthing odd blocks, piling them up in the view of fellow workers, and apparently not caring whether they fit anywhere or not. Unfortunately there are also those who watch carefully until some industrious group digs out a particularly ornamental block, whereupon they fit it in place with much gusto and bow to the crowd. Some groups do not dig at all, but spend all their time arguing as to the exact arrangement of a cornice or an abutment. Some spend all their days trying to pull down a block or two that a rival has put in place. Some, indeed, neither dig nor argue, but go along with the crowd, scratch here and there, and enjoy the scenery. Some sit by and give advice, and some just sit.

On the other hand there are those men of rare vision, who can grasp well in advance just the block that is needed for rapid advance on a section of the edifice to be possible, who can tell by some subtle sense where it will be found, and who have an uncanny skill in cleaning away dross and bringing it surely into the light. These are the master workmen. For each of them there can well be many of lesser stature who chip and delve, industriously, but with little grasp of what it is all about, and who nevertheless make the great steps possible.

There are those who can give the structure meaning, who can trace its evolution from early times, and describe the glories that are to be, in ways that inspire those who work and those who enjoy. They bring the inspiration that all is not mere building of monotonous walls, and that there is architecture even though the architect is not seen to guide and order.

There are those who labor to make the utility of the structure real, to cause it to give shelter to the multitude, that they may be better protected, and that they may derive health and well-being because of its presence.

And the edifice is not built by the quarrymen and the masons alone. There are those who bring them food during their labors, and cooling drink when the days are warm, who sing to them and place flowers on the little walls that have grown with the years.

There are also the old men, whose days of vigorous building are done, whose eyes are too dim to see the details of the arch or the needed form of its keystone; but who have built a wall here and there, and lived long in the edifice, who have learned to love it and who have even grasped a suggestion of its ultimate meaning; and who sit in the shade and encourage the young men.

Science as Drama

A. N. WHITEHEAD   1861–1947

The effect of Greek dramatic literature was many-sided so far as concerns the various ways in which it indirectly affected medieval thought. The pilgrim fathers of the scientific imagination as it exists today are the great tragedians of ancient Athens, Aeschylus, Sophocles, Euripides. Their vision of Fate, remorseless and indifferent, urging a tragic incident to its inevitable issue, is the vision possessed by science. Fate in Greek tragedy becomes the order of nature in modern thought. The absorbing interest in the particular heroic incidents, as an example and a verification of the workings of Fate, reappears in our epoch as concentration of interest on the crucial experiments. It was my good fortune to be present at the meeting of the Royal Society in London when the Astronomer Royal for England announced that the photographic plates of the famous eclipse, as measured by his colleagues in Greenwich Observatory, had verified the prediction of Einstein that rays of light are bent as they pass in the neighborhood of the sun. The whole atmosphere of tense interest was exactly that of the Greek drama: we were the chorus commenting on the decree of Destiny as disclosed in the development of a supreme incident. There was dramatic quality in the very staging: the traditional ceremonial, and in the background the picture of Newton to remind us that the greatest of scientific generalizations was now, after more than two centuries, to receive its first modification. Nor was the personal interest wanting: a great adventure in thought had at length come safe to shore.

Let me here remind you that the essence of dramatic tragedy is not unhappiness. It resides in the solemnity of the remorseless working of things. This inevitableness of Destiny can only be illustrated in terms of human life by incidents which in fact involve unhappiness. For it is only by them that the futility of escape can be made evident in the drama. This remorseless inevitableness is what pervades scientific thought. The laws of physics are the decrees of Fate.

The Humility of Science

G. K. CHESTERTON   1874–1936

Men find it extremely difficult to believe that a man who is obviously uprooting mountains and dividing seas, tearing down temples and stretching out hands to the stars, is really a quiet old gentleman who only asks to be allowed to indulge his harmless old hobby and follow his harmless old nose. When a man splits a grain of sand and the universe is turned upside down in consequence, it is difficult to realize that to the man who did it, the splitting of the grain is the great affair, and the capsizing of the cosmos quite a small one. It is hard to enter into the feelings of a man who regards a new heaven and a new earth in the light of a by-product. But undoubtedly it was to this almost eerie innocence of the intellect that the great men of the great scientific period, which now appears to be closing, owed their enormous power and triumph. If they had brought the heavens down like a house of cards, their plea was not even that they had done it on principle; their quite unanswerable plea was that they had done it by accident. Whenever there was in them the least touch of pride in what they had done, there was a good ground for attacking them; but so long as they were wholly humble, they were wholly victorious. There were possible answers to Huxley; there was no answer possible to Darwin. He was convincing because of his unconsciousness; one might almost say because of his dullness. This childlike and prosaic mind is beginning to wane in the world of science. Men of science are beginning to see themselves, as the fine phrase is, in part; they are beginning to be proud of their humility. They are beginning to be aesthetic, like the rest of the world, beginning to spell truth with a capital T, beginning to talk of the creeds they imagine themselves to have destroyed, of the discoveries that their forbears made.

CLAUDE BERNARD   1813–1878

Science increases our power in proportion as it lowers our pride.

CHARLES S. PEIRCE   1839–1914

There is not a single truth of science upon which we ought to bet more than about a million of millions to one.

Nasty, Ugly Little Facts

FRANCIS GALTON   1822–1911

Much has been written, but the last word has not been said, on the rationale of these curious papillary ridges; why in one man and in one finger they form whorls and in another loops. I may mention a characteristic anecdote of Herbert Spencer in connection with this. He asked me to show him my laboratory and to take his prints, which I did. Then I spoke of the failure to discover the origin of these patterns, and how the fingers of unborn children had been dissected to ascertain their earliest stages, and so forth. Spencer remarked that this was beginning in the wrong way; that I ought to consider the purpose the ridges had to fulfil, and to work backwards. Here, he said, it was obvious that the delicate mouths of the sudorific glands required the protection given to them by the ridges on either side of them, and therefrom he elaborated a consistent and ingenious hypothesis at great length.

I replied that his arguments were beautiful and deserved to be true, but it happened that the mouths of the ducts did not run in the valleys between the crests, but along the crests of the ridges themselves. He burst into a good-humored and uproarious laugh, and told me the famous story which I have heard from each of the other two who were present on the occurrence. Huxley was one of them. Spencer, during a pause in conversation at dinner at the Athenaeum, said, "You would little think it, but I once wrote a tragedy." Huxley answered promptly, "I know the catastrophe." Spencer declared it was impossible, for he had never spoken about it before then. Huxley insisted. Spencer asked what it was. Huxley replied, "A beautiful theory, killed by a nasty, ugly little fact."

Galton was the inventor of identification by fingerprints.

EINSTEIN (?)

No amount of experimentation can ever prove me right; a single experiment may at any time prove me wrong.

FRANCIS DARWIN *about his father*   1848–1925

There was one quality of mind which seemed to be of special and extreme advantage in leading him to make discoveries. It was the power of never letting exceptions pass unnoticed. Everybody notices a fact as an exception when it is striking or frequent, but he had a special instinct for arresting an exception. A point apparently slight and unconnected with his present work is passed over by many a man almost unconsciously with some half-considered explanation, which is in fact no explanation. It was just these things that he seized on to make a start from. In a certain sense there is nothing special in this procedure, many discoveries being made by means of it. I only mention it because, as I watched him at work, the value of this power to an experimenter was so strongly impressed upon me.

CHARLES S. PEIRCE   1839–1914

A hypothesis is something which looks as if it might be true and were true, and which is capable of verification or refutation by comparison with facts. The best hypothesis, in the sense of the one most recommending itself to the inquirer, is the one which can be the most readily refuted if it is false. This far outweighs the trifling merit of being likely. For after all, what is a *likely* hypothesis? It is one which falls in with our preconceived ideas. But these may be wrong. Their errors are just what the scientific man is out gunning for more particularly. But if a hypothesis can quickly and easily be cleared away so as to go toward leaving the field free for the main struggle, this is an immense advantage.

God May Be Subtle, but He Isn't Mean

NORBERT WIENER   1950

Albert Einstein's remark is of the greatest significance. *"Der Herr Gott ist raffiniert, aber boshaft ist Er nicht."* "God may be subtle, but he isn't plain mean."

Far from being a cliché, this is a very profound statement concerning the problems of the scientist. To discover the secrets of nature requires a powerful and elaborate technique, but at least we can expect one thing — that as far as inanimate nature goes, any step forward that we may take will not be countered by a change of policy by nature for the deliberate purpose of confusing and frustrating us. There may indeed be certain limitations to this statement as far as living nature is concerned, for the manifestations of hysteria are often made in view of an audience, and with the intention, which is frequently unconscious, of bamboozling that audience. On the other hand, just as we seem to have conquered a germ disease, the germ may mutate and show traits which at least appear to have been developed with the deliberate intention of sending us back to the point where we have started.

These infractuousities of nature, no matter how much they may annoy the practitioner of the life sciences, are fortunately not among the difficulties to be contemplated by the physicist. Nature plays fair and if, after climbing one range of mountains, the physicist sees another on the horizon before him, it has not been deliberately put there to frustrate the effort he has already made.

It may seem superficially that even in the absence of a conscious or purposeful interference by nature, the policy of the research scientist should be to play it safe, and always act so that even a malicious and deceitful nature would not prevent his optimum acquisition and transfer of information. This point of view is unjustified. Communication in general, and scientific research in particular, involve a great deal of effort even if it is useful effort, and the fighting of bogies which are not there wastes effort which ought to be economized. We can not go through our communicative or scientific lives shadowboxing with ghosts. Experience has pretty well convinced the working physicist that any idea of a nature which is not only difficult to interpret but which actively resists interpretation has not been justified as far as his past work is concerned, and therefore, to be an effective scientist, he must be naïve, and even deliberately naïve, in making the assumption that he is dealing with an honest God, and must ask his questions of the world as an honest man.

Thus the naïveté of a scientist, while it is a professional adaptation, is not a professional defect. A man who approaches science with the point of view of an officer of detective police would spend most of his time frustrating tricks that are never going to be played on him, trailing suspects who would be perfectly willing to give an answer to a direct question, and in general playing the fashionable cops-and-robbers game as it is now played within the realm of official and military science. I have not the slightest doubt that the present detective-mindedness of the lords of scientific administration is one of the chief reasons for the barrenness of so much present scientific work.

Science as Sanctity

GEORGE SARTON   1884–1956

Popular resistance has been especially strong against religious reformers and men of science. That saints and scientists should thus be placed in a single category by the opposition of others is far more than a casual occurrence. They have much in common, above all, their other-worldliness. There are but few saints among scientists, as among other men, but truth itself is a goal comparable to sanctity. As the Pythagoreans had already understood it more than twenty-four centuries ago, there is sanctity in pure knowledge, as there is in pure beauty, and the disinterested quest of truth is perhaps the greatest purification.

However, the hostility to saints and to investigators was not altogether of the same kind. Attempts at religious reform aroused popular anger because the inborn conservativeness of man is nowhere stronger than in the field of religion. The religion of his fathers must not be criticized, even if his own profession of it is but an outward show. The most malicious kind of hatred is that which is built upon a theological foundation. On the other hand, the resistance to scientific novelties was due to an intuitive, if unconscious, appreciation of their revolutionary nature. The slightest and the most innocent scientific innovation is but a wedge which is bound to penetrate deeper and deeper and the advance of which will soon be impossible to resist. Conservative people are undoubtedly right in their distrust and hatred of science, for the scientific spirit is the very spirit of innovation and adventure — the most reckless kind of adventure into the unknown. And such is its aggressive strength that its revolutionary activity can neither be restrained nor restricted within its own field. Sooner or later it will go out to conquer other fields and to throw floods of light into all the dark places where superstition and injustice are still rampant. The scientific spirit is the greatest force for construction but also for destruction.

Science as Discovery

HANS ZINSSER   1878–1940

It is an erroneous impression, fostered by sensational popular biography, that scientific discovery is often made by inspiration — a sort of *coup de foudre* — from on high. This is rarely the case. Even Archimedes' sudden inspiration in the bathtub; Newton's experience in the apple orchard; Descartes' geometrical discoveries in his bed; Darwin's flash of lucidity on reading a passage in Malthus; Kekulé's vision of the closed carbon ring which came to him on top of a London bus; and Einstein's brilliant solution of the Michelson puzzle in the patent office in Berne, were not messages out of the blue. They were the final coordinations, by minds of genius, of innumerable accumulated facts and impressions which lesser men could grasp only in their uncorrelated isolation, but which — by them — were seen in entirety and integrated into general principles. The scientist takes off from the manifold observations of predecessors, and shows his intelligence, if any, by his ability to discriminate between the important and the negligible, by selecting here and there the significant stepping-stones that will lead across the difficulties to new understanding. The one who places the last stone and steps across to the *terra firma* of accomplished discovery gets all the credit. Only the initiated know and honor those whose patient integrity and devotion to exact observation have made the last step possible.

HOBBES   1588–1679

Desire to know why, and how, curiosity, which is a lust of the mind, that by a perseverance of delight in the continued and indefatigable generation of knowledge, exceedeth the short vehemence of any carnal pleasure.

Early History of Science

GEORGE SARTON   1884–1956

There is no doubt whatever that our earliest scientific knowledge is of Oriental origin. As to the possible Chinese and Hindu origins, we cannot say much that is definite, but on the contrary with regard to Mesopotamia and Egypt, we are on very solid ground.

For example, as early as the middle of the fourth millennium, the Egyptians were already acquainted with a decimal system of numbers. In an inscription of that time there is reference to 120,000 captives, 400,000 oxen, and 1,422,000 goats, each decimal unit being represented by a special symbol. By the middle of the following millennium, Sumerians had developed a highly technical system of accounting. The astronomical knowledge of these people was equally remarkable. The Egyptian calendar of 365 days was established in 4241. Babylonians accumulated planetary observations for astrological purposes; e.g., elaborate observations of Venus go back to the twentieth century. They compiled lists of stars and were soon able to predict eclipses.

These examples will convince you that a considerable body of systematized knowledge was far anterior to Greek science. In fact this helps to explain what one might call the miracle of Greek civilization. To be sure, no intelligent man could read the *Iliad* and the *Odyssey*, which were the primices of that civilization, without wondering what had made such masterpieces possible. They could not possibly appear like bolts from the blue. Like every glorious beginning, this was not only the prelude of one evolution but the end, the climax, of another. Students of Greek mathematics, of Greek astronomy, and Greek medicine could not help asking themselves similar questions. How could the relative perfection of the Greek scientific treatises be accounted for? The explanation is still very incomplete, but no doubt exists as to the main fact: the Greeks borrowed a large quantity of observations and of crude theories from the Egyptians and the peoples of Mesopotamia.

At any rate, in the present state of our knowledge there is a gap of more than a thousand years between the golden age of Egyptian science and the golden age of Greek science. We are certain that much of the Greek knowledge was borrowed from Eastern sources, but we do not know exactly when or how the borrowing took place.

The spirit of Greek science, which accomplished such wonders within a period of about five centuries, was essentially the Western spirit, whose triumphs are the boast of modern scientists. But we must bear in mind two important qualifications. First that the foundations of that Greek science were wholly Oriental, and however deep the Greek genius it is not certain that it could have built anything comparable to its actual achievements without these foundations. When discussing the fate of a man of genius, we may make many suppositions, but it would be absurd to wonder what would have happened if he had had other parents, for then he would never have been. In the same way we have no right to disregard the Egyptian father and the Mesopotamian mother of the Greek genius. In the second place, while that genius was creating what might be called (in opposition to Egyptian science on one hand and to mediaeval science on the other) the beginning of modern science, another development, equally miraculous, but of an entirely different kind, was taking place in an Oriental country near the easternmost end of the Mediterranean Sea. While Greek philosophers were trying to give a rational explanation of the world and boldly postulated its physical unity, the Hebrew prophets were establishing the moral unity of mankind upon the notion of a single God. These two developments were not parallel but complementary; they were equally momentous but entirely independent; in spite of their spatial proximity, they proceeded for centuries in almost complete ignorance of one another. They did not really come together until the end of ancient times, and their union was finally cemented upon the prostrate bodies of the two civilizations which had given birth to them.

The reader knows how Greece was finally conquered by Rome, and how in the course of time it conquered its conquerors. Yet the old spirit was subdued, and Roman science even at its best was always but a pale imitation of the Greek. The Romans were so afraid of disinterested research, the excess of which had been one of the causes of the Greek corruption, that they went to the other extreme and discouraged any research, the utilitarian value of which was not immediately obvious.

In the meanwhile Jesus Christ had appeared and told the world a new message, a message of love and humility, universal in its scope: Charity does not need knowledge; blessed are the pure in spirit, the pure in heart; on the other hand, knowledge without charity is not only useless but pernicious; it can but lead to pride and damnation. The development of Christianity was a first attempt to bring together the Hebrew and the Greek spirits but as the Roman Christians hardly understood the former and misunderstood the latter thoroughly, the attempt was an utter failure.

We may say that the Greek spirit, that disinterested love of truth which is the very spring of knowledge, was finally smothered by the combination of Roman utilitarianism and Christian sentimentality. Again let us dream for a moment, and wonder what might have happened if the Greeks and the Christians had seen their respective good points instead of seeing only the evil ones. How beautiful if their two types of other-worldliness could have been harmonized! How many miseries mankind would have been spared! But it was not to be. The path of progress is not straight but very crooked; the general direction is clear enough, but only if one considers a very long stretch of it from far off. Before being able to reconcile the love of truth with the love of man, the scientific spirit with the Golden Rule, mankind was obliged to make many strange and cruel experiments.

The contact between ancient Greece and Western Christendom ended by being so precarious that it might have conceivably been broken altogether but for the intervention of another Oriental people, the Arabs. Please note that this was the third great wave of Oriental wisdom, the third time that the creative impulse came from the East. The first initiative — and the most fundamental of all — came from Egypt and Mesopotamia; the second from Israel, and though it influenced science only in an indirect way, it was also of incalculable pregnancy; the third, with which I am going to deal now, came from Arabia and from Persia.

About the year 610 a new prophet appeared at Mecca in Hejaz, Abul-l-Qasim Muhammad of the tribe of Quraysh, who was like a new incarnation of the old Hebrew prophets. At first the people did not pay much attention to him, but after he had abandoned his native town and moved two hundred and fifty-five miles northward to al-Medina, in 622, his success was phenomenal. No prophet was ever more successful. By the time of his death ten years later, he had managed to unite the Arabian tribes and to inspire them with a single-hearted fervor which would enable them later to conquer the world. Damascus was captured in 635, Jerusalem in 637; the conquest of Egypt was completed in 641; that of Persia in the following year; that of Spain somewhat later in 710–12. By this time the Muslims — that is, the Prophet's followers — were ruling a large belt of the world all the way from Central Asia to the Far West.

Under the impulse of these two tremendous forces, Muslim fanaticism and Persian curiosity, and under the guidance of a series of 'Abbasid caliphs who had a passion for knowledge — al-Mansur, Harun al-Rashid, al-Ma'mum — the new civilization developed with incredible speed and efficacy. It was doubly rooted in the past: the Prophet had transmitted to them with very few modifications Semitic monotheism and morality, and their Persian tutors had incited them to drink deeply into the older sources of learning, Sanskrit and Greek. From the Hindus they learned arithmetic, algebra, trigonometry, iatro-chemistry; from the Greeks, logic, geometry, astronomy, and medicine. It did not take them long to realize the immensity of the Greek treasure, and they had no rest until the whole of it (that is, as much as was available to them) was translated into Arabic.

The immense cultural importance of Islam lies in the fact that it brought finally together the two great intellectual streams which had flowed independently in ancient times. Previous attempts, as I have already indicated, had failed. Jews and Greeks had mixed in Alexandria, but in spite of the fact that the former had learned the language of the latter and that one of their learned men, Philon, had made a deep study of both traditions, there had been no real fusion. The Christians had not succeeded any better, because of their single-hearted devotion to the new Gospel, which reduced everything else to futility in their eyes. Now for the first time in the history of the world Semitic religion and Greek knowledge actually combined in the minds of many people. Nor was that integration restricted to a single city or country; the new culture spread like a prairie fire from Baghdad eastward to India, Tranoxsiana, and further still, and westward to the very edge of the world.

The universal extension of that culture caused necessarily many diversities. Muslims were brought closely into touch with all kinds of unbelievers — in the East, Chinese, Mongols, Malays, Hindus; farther west, Magians, Syrians, Greeks, Copts, farther still, Berbers in Africa; Sicilians, Spaniards, and other Franks in southern Europe; Jews, everywhere. These contacts were generally friendly, or at least not unfriendly, for the Muslims treated their *ra'aya* (subjects) with kind and tolerant condescension.

The briefest enumeration of the Arabic contributions to knowledge would be too long to be inserted here, but I must insist on the fact that, though a major part of the activity of Arabic-writing scholars consisted in the translation of Greek works and their assimilation, they did far more than that. They did not simply transmit ancient knowledge, they created a new one. To be sure, none of them attained unto the highest peaks of the Greek genius. No Arabic mathematician can begin to compare with Archimedes or Apollonius. Ibn Sina makes one think of Galen, but no Arabic physician had the wisdom of Hippocrates. However, such comparisons are hardly fair, for a few Greeks had reached almost suddenly extraordinary heights. That is what we call the Greek miracle. But one might speak also, though in a different sense, of an Arabic miracle. The creation of a new civilization of international and encyclopaedic magnitude within less than two centuries is something that we can describe, but not completely explain. This movement, as opposed to the Greek, was perhaps more remarkable for its quantity than for its quality. Yet it was creative; it was the most creative movement of the Middle Ages down to the thirteenth century. The Arabic-writing scientists elaborated algebra (the name is a telltale) and trigonometry on Greco-Hindu foundations; they reconstructed and developed — though, it must be said, very little — Greek geometry; they collected abundant astronomical observations, and their criticisms of the Ptolemaic system, though not always justified, helped to prepare the astronomical reformation of the sixteenth century; they enriched enormously our medical experience; they were the distant originators of modern chemistry; they improved the knowledge of optics and meteorology, the measurement of densities; their geographical investigations extended from one end of the world to the other; they published a number of annals of capital interest, dealing with almost every civilized country outside of Western Christendom; one of their historians, the Berber Ibn Khaldun, expounded a philosophy of history which was by far the most elaborate and the most original of mediaeval times; finally they laid down the principles of Semitic philology.

We may say that from the middle of the eighth century to the end of the eleventh, the Arabic-speaking peoples (including within their ranks, it is true, a number of Jews and Christians) were marching at the head of mankind. Thanks to them Arabic was become not only the sacred language of the Qur'an, the vehicle of God's own thoughts, but the international language of science, the vehicle of human progress. Just as today the shortest way to knowledge for any Oriental, is the mastery of one of the main Occidental languages, even so during these four centuries Arabic was the key, and almost the only key, to the new expanding culture.

Yet by the end of the eleventh century the main task of the Arabic scientists — as far as it concerned the whole world and not only themselves — was already completed, and after that time the relative importance of Muslim culture declined steadily. During the twelfth century its prestige was due even more to its past than to its present achievements, great as these were. In the meanwhile Christians and Jews were feverishly pouring out the Greco-Arabic learning from the Arabic vessels into the Latin and Hebrew ones.

The Christians were far ahead of the Jews in this new stage of transmission, and that for a very simple reason. Down to the eleventh century the philosophic and scientific (as opposed to the purely rabbinical) activities of the Jews were almost exclusively confined to the Muslim world. The Jewish philosophers, grammarians, scientists who lived under the protection of Islam were generally well treated, and some of them — like Hasdai ibn Shaprut in Cordova — attained positions of high authority and became the intellectual as well as the political leaders of their time. These Jews of the Dar al-Islam were bilingual; Hebrew was of course their religious language and probably also their domestic one, but for all philosophic and scientific purposes they thought in Arabic. They had no need of translations. On the contrary, it was much easier for them to read a medical book in Arabic than in Hebrew. Sometimes they would copy Arabic manuscripts in Hebrew script, but even that was not really indispensable; it was more a matter of convenience than of necessity.

On the other hand, as soon as the Latin Christians began to realize the importance of the Arabic literature, as only a few of them could ever hope to master a language as alien to their own and written in such illegible and mystifying script, they longed for translations and did all they could to obtain them. By the end of the eleventh century their longing was partly fulfilled by Constantine the African, aptly called "magister orientis et occidentis"; he was indeed one of the great intermediaries between the East and the West. Constantine translated a large number of Greco-Muslim works from Arabic into Latin at the monastery of Monte Cassino, where he died in 1087. As we might expect, the results of his activity, far from appeasing the hunger of European scholars, stimulated it considerably. It now dawned upon the most advanced of them that the Arabic writings were not simply important but essential, for they contained vast treasures of knowledge, the accumulated learning and experience of the whole past. It is no exaggeration to say that during the twelfth century and down to about the middle of the thirteenth century the foremost activity of Christian scholars was the translation of Arabic treatises into Latin.

At first the Eastern Jews and those of Spain were much better off than the Christians, for the whole of Arabic literature was open to them without effort, but in the twelfth century the scientific life of Judaism began to move from Spain across the Pyrenees, and in the following century it began to decline in its former haunts. By the middle of the thirteenth century, a great many Jews had already been established so long in France, Germany, England, that Arabic had become a foreign language to them. Up to this period the Jews had been generally ahead of the Christians, and far ahead; now for the first time the situation was reversed. Indeed, the Christians had already transferred most of the Arabic knowledge into Latin; the translations from Arabic into Hebrew were naturally far less abundant, and hence the non-Arabic-speaking Jews of western Europe were not only in a position of political inferiority (the Crusades had caused many anti-Semitic persecutions and the Jews of Christendom were everywhere on the defensive), but also — and this was perhaps even more painful — in a position of intellectual inferiority. To be sure, this was soon compensated by the fact that many of them learned

Latin and could then read the Arabic texts in their Latin versions, but even then they did not have any longer an intellectual monopoly against the Christians; they came but second. While the early Jewish physicians had possessed "secrets" of learning which were sealed to their Christian colleagues (this was especially true with regard to eye diseases which were thoroughly investigated in Arabic treatises), the later ones had no such privileges.

During the twelfth century the three civilizations which exerted the deepest influence upon human thought and which had the largest share in the molding of the future, the Jewish, the Christian, and the Muslim, were remarkably well balanced, but that state of equilibrium could not last very long, because it was due to the fact that the Muslims were going down while the two others were going up. By the end of the twelfth century it was already clear (that is, it would have been clear to any outside observer, as it is to ourselves) that the Muslims would soon be out of the race, and that the competition would be restricted to the Christians and the Jews. Now the latter were hopelessly jeopardized by their political servitude and by the jealous intolerance and the utter lack of generosity (to put it mildly) of their rivals. Moreover, for the reason explained above the main sources of knowledge were now less available to them than to their persecutors. This went much deeper than it seems, for when an abundant treasure of knowledge becomes suddenly available to a group of people, it is not only the knowledge itself that matters, but the stimulation following in its wake. The Jews were steadily driven into the background, and in proportion as they were more isolated they tended to increase their isolation by devoting their attention more exclusively to their own Talmudic studies.

Perhaps the main, as well as the least obvious, achievement of the Middle Ages was the creation of the experimental spirit, or more exactly its slow incubation. This was primarily due to Muslims down to the end of the twelfth century, then to Christians. Thus, in this essential respect, East and West co-operated like brothers. However much one may admire Greek science, one must recognize that it was sadly deficient with regard to this (the experimental) point of view which turned out to be the fundamental point of view of modern science. Though their great physicians followed instinctively experimental methods, these methods were never properly appreciated by their philosophers or by the students of nature. A history of the Greek experimental science, outside of medicine, would be exceedingly short. Under the influence of Arabic alchemists and opticians and later of Christian mechanicians and physicists, the experimental spirit grew very slowly. For centuries it remained very weak, comparable to a delicate little plant always in danger of being ruthlessly trampled down by dogmatic theologians and conceited philosophers. The tremendous awakening due to the Western rediscovery of printing and to the exploration of the new world accelerated its development. By the beginning of the sixteenth century, it was already lifting its head up, and we may consider Leonardo da Vinci its first deliberate vindicator. After that its progress became more and more rapid, and by the beginning of the following century, experimental philosophy was admirably explained by another Tuscan, Galileo, the herald of modern science.

Thus, if we take a very broad view of the history of science, we may distinguish in it four main phases. The first is the empirical development of Egyptian and Mesopotamian knowledge. The second is the building of a rational foundation of astounding beauty and strength by the Greeks. The third, and until recently the least known, is the mediaeval period — many centuries of groping. Immense efforts were spent to solve pseudo-problems, chiefly to conciliate the results of Greek philosophy with religious dogmas of various kinds. Such efforts were naturally sterile, as far as their main object was concerned, but they brought into being many incidental results. The main result, as I have just explained, was the incubation of the experimental spirit. Its final emergence marks the transition between the third period and the fourth, which is the period of modern science. Note that out of these four periods the first is entirely Oriental, the third is mostly but not exclusively so; the second and fourth are exclusively Western.

To return to the fourth period — which is still continuing — the final establishment of the experimental philosophy was indeed its main distinction, its standard, and its glory. Not only did the new method open the path to untold and unimaginable discoveries, but it put an end to unprofitable quests and idle discussions; it broke the vicious circles wherein philosophers had been obstinately turning for more than a thousand years. It was simple enough in itself, but could not be understood as long as a series of intellectual prejudices obscured man's vision. It may be summed up as follows: Establish the facts by direct, frequent, and careful observations, and check them repeatedly one against the other; these facts will be your premises. When many variables are related, find out what happens when only one is allowed to vary, the others remaining constant. Multiply such experiments as much as you can, and make them with the utmost precision in your power. Draw your conclusions and express them in mathematical language if possible. Apply all your mathematical resources to the transformation of the equations; confront the new equations thus obtained with reality. That is, see what they mean, which group of facts they represent. Make new experiments on the basis of these new facts, etc., etc.

The Birth of Modern Science

A. N. WHITEHEAD   1861–1947

The way in which the persecution of Galileo has been remembered is a tribute to the quiet commencement of the most intimate change in outlook which the human race had yet encountered. Since a babe was born in a manger, it may be doubted whether so great a thing has happened with so little stir.

Experience? Or Theory?

HERBERT DINGLE *on Eddington's philosophy*   1954

When we examine our procedure in science and state it in the most direct way, we realize that it is simply this. We make observations — pointer-readings, since we are now concerned with physics alone — and represent them by symbols, and we find that they are related with one another in a certain way. We then construct a logical system with postulates so chosen that their implications agree with the relations found to hold between the observations. And that is all. As an aid to progress we try to give the logical system a picturable form, calling its elements the properties of particles or waves or something else that will suggest a way of finding further relations, but that is a means of research, not a discovery, and we freely change the picture as we advance. Everything essential in physics can be described, and all its implications deduced and their significance fully evaluated, in terms of this description.

By contrast, let us now see the same process as conceived by Eddington. We begin, not with what we do but with what we imagine must be "true." Standing remote in the background is the awful Reality of the external world, mysterious, inaccessible. In front is the physical world which presents, but only symbolically, the structure of a part of it. Of this we can attain something called knowledge which, though its name suggests subjectivity, is in effect an objective entity that stands in front of the physical world of which it is a representation. But not a precise representation. It shows us only the probable character of the physical world, and this is what is depicted in the equations of physics. We have still to reach these equations, and before us there is a road called experience. We have for centuries been toiling painfully along this road, and at last we have reached the fundamental equations, so that now we know all that theoretical physics can tell us, namely, the probable character of the structure of part of Reality. But on looking behind we can see that there is another road called reason which also comes out at the same equations. We follow it back, and at the far end we find ourselves again in the land of pure ignorance from which we began our journey. We could therefore have reached the same goal if we had proceeded that way instead of by experience. But we see also that from this point an indefinitely large number of other roads go out. They are all marked reason, and there is nothing in the roads themselves to tell us which one leads to the same destination as the road of experience. There is, however, one way by which we can discover this. If we compare them with the road of experience we see that one, and only one, is parallel to it. If, then, we follow that, we shall get to the equations of physics and so learn the probable state of the symbolical structure of the external world without calling on experience at all. That is the final conclusion that Eddington reached.

When this amazing conception is laid bare, we can only pause before it in mute wonder. How is it possible, we eventually ask, that what is in essence so simple can be twisted into a form so intricate? I do not think an answer can be given on any supposition other than that which I have indicated, that the description had to grant full recognition to both the Victorian external world, from which all life had gone, and the necessary implications of the relativity theory. The practical difficulties of thinking in terms of this labyrinth are obvious enough, but what is of far greater moment is the essentially wrong representation which it gives of the place of experience in science. Instead of showing experience as the origin and centre of interest of the whole effort, it leads us to regard it as merely the lesser of two alternative means towards a greater end. Intent on preserving what it misconceives as the "Truth," it has lost the "Way" and the "Life." Relativity was not so much a revolution in science as a purification; it recalled physics from its traffic with metaphysical notions to its true concern with what we actually observe. By its acknowledgement of the final authority and inviolability of experience it opened the possibility, for the first time in modern history, of granting full licence to science to pursue the rational correlation of experience without danger of conflict with art, religion and other forms of philosophy so long as they also assert nothing that is not grounded in experience. In Eddington's philosophy of science that inestimable clarification is obscured. The essence of the matter is there, but instead of being illuminated it is shrouded in mist.

That is one aspect of the matter, but there is another on which it is more pleasant to dwell. It is easy enough to recognize the enormous burden that Eddington's philosophy must have imposed on its victim, but the incredible fact remains that he not only bore it but used it to reach heights which his contemporaries, for all their advantages of equipment, could not attain. It is not only that he escaped the throes of instinct at strife with reason, of which the Victorian age exhibits so many spectacles, described in Tennyson's *In Memoriam,* Huxley's Romanes Lecture, and countless other records. That struggle he evaded so easily that it is only with an effort that we become aware that it should have involved him in its toils. But the chief marvel is that he could use the dread machinery in which most of us can only become hopelessly entangled to produce a theory which, whatever the ultimate verdict on it may be, is beyond all question a work of the highest genius. It is notoriously dangerous to prophesy unless you know, and in a matter of such difficulty I am very far indeed from knowing, yet I do not hesitate to express the belief that when Eddington's fundamental theory is translated from the terms of his unspeakable philosophy into a language that ordinary mortals can understand, it will be found not only to be a work of outstanding technical skill, but also to contain scientific truths which he alone in his generation had the depth of vision to perceive. It seems a tragedy that a man with such incomparable sight should have been placed at such a point of disadvantage, but let us not fail to recognize that his description of what he saw, though abnormal and in our eyes distorted, was in all probability true. I said that he did not know what he was doing; but I believe that what he did was supremely great.

JOHN MAYNARD KEYNES *says Newton went about it in the same way:*   1883–1946

His experiments were always, I suspect, a means, not of discovering, but always of verifying what he knew already.

Why do I call him a magician? Because he looked on the whole universe and all that is in it *as a riddle,* as a secret which could be read by applying pure thought to certain evidence, certain mystic clues which God had laid about the world to allow a sort of philosopher's treasure hunt to the esoteric brotherhood. He believed that these clues were to be found partly in the evidence of the heavens and in the constitution of elements (and that is what gives the false suggestion of his being an experimental natural philosopher), but also partly in certain papers and traditions handed down by the brethren in an unbroken chain back to the original cryptic revelation in Babylonia. He regarded the universe as a cryptogram set by the Almighty — just as he himself wrapt the discovery of the calculus in a cryptogram when he communicated with Leibnitz. By pure thought, by concentration of mind, the riddle, he believed, would be revealed to the initiate.

He *did* read the riddle of the heavens. And he believed that by the same powers of his introspective imagination he would read the riddle of the Godhead, the riddle of past and future events divinely fore-ordained, the riddle of the elements and their constitution from an original undifferentiated first matter, the riddle of health and of immortality. All would be revealed to him if only he could persevere to the end, uninterrupted, by himself, no interruption for God's sake, no disclosure, no discordant breakings in or criticism, with fear and shrinking as he assailed these half-ordained, half-forbidden things, creeping back into the bosom of the Godhead as into his mother's womb. "Voyaging through strange seas of thought *alone,*" not as Charles

Lamb "a fellow who believed nothing unless it was as clear as the three sides of a triangle."

As Newton Appeared to a Poet

WORDSWORTH   1770–1850

A mind forever
Voyaging through strange seas of thought alone.

As Newton Appeared to Himself

ISAAC NEWTON   1642–1727

I do not know what I may appear to the world; but to myself I seem to have been only like a boy playing on the seashore, and diverting myself in now and then finding of a smoother pebble or a prettier shell than ordinary whilst the great ocean of truth lay all undiscovered before me.

And Darwin to Himself

CHARLES DARWIN   1809–1882

My first notebook was opened in July, 1837. I worked on true Baconian principles, and without any theory collected facts on a wholesale scale, more especially with respect to domesticated productions, by printed enquiries, by conversation with skilful breeders and gardeners, and by extensive reading. When I see the list of books of all kinds which I read and abstracted, including whole series of Journals and Transactions, I am surprised at my industry. I soon perceived that selection was the keystone of man's success in making useful races of animals and plants. But how selections could be applied to organisms living in a state of nature remained for some time a mystery to me.

In October, 1838 — that is, fifteen months after I had begun my systematic enquiry — I happened to read for amusement Malthus on *Population,* and being well prepared to appreciate the struggle for existence which everywhere goes on from long-continued observation of the habits of animals and plants, it at once struck me that under these circumstances favourable variations would tend to be preserved, and unfavourable ones to be destroyed. The result of this would be the formation of new species. Here, then, I had at last got a theory by which to work; but I was so anxious to avoid prejudice that I determined not for some time to write even the briefest sketch of it. In June, 1842, I first allowed myself the satisfaction of writing a very brief abstract of my theory in pencil in 35 pages; and this was enlarged during the summer of 1844 into one of 230 pages, which I had fairly copied out and still possess.

But at that time I overlooked one problem of great importance; and it is astonishing to me, except on the principle of Columbus and his egg, how I could have overlooked it and its solution. This problem is the tendency in organic beings descended from the same stock to diverge in character as they become modified. That they have diverged greatly is obvious from the manner in which species of all kinds can be classed under genera, genera under families, families under sub-orders, and so forth; and I can remember the very spot in the road, whilst in my carriage, when to my joy the solution occurred to me; and this was long after I had come to Down. The solution, as I believe, is that the modified offspring of all dominant and increasing forms tend to become adapted to many and highly diversified places in the economy of nature.

Early in 1856, Lyell advised me to write out my views pretty fully, and I began at once to do so on a scale three or four times as extensive as that which was afterwards followed in my *Origin of Species;* yet it was only an abstract of the materials which I had collected, and I got through about half the work on this scale. But my plans were overthrown, for early in the summer of 1858 Mr. Wallace, who was then in the Malay Archipelago, sent me an essay *On the Tendency of Varieties to depart indefinitely from the Original Type;* and this essay contained exactly the same theory as mine. Mr. Wallace expressed the wish that if I thought well of his essay, I should send it to Lyell for perusal.

The circumstances under which I consented at the request of Lyell and Hooker to allow of an abstract from my manuscript, together with a letter to Asa Gray, dated September 5, 1857, to be published at the same time with Wallace's essay, are given in the *Journal of the Proceedings of the Linnean Society,* 1858, page 45. I was at first very unwilling to consent, as I thought Mr. Wallace might consider my doing so unjustifiable, for I did not then know how generous and noble was his disposition. The extract from my manuscript and the letter to Asa Gray had neither been intended for publication, and were badly written. Mr. Wallace's essay, on the other hand, was admirably expressed and quite clear. Nevertheless, our joint productions excited very little attention, and the only published notice of them which I can remember was by Professor Haughton of Dublin, whose verdict was that all that was new in them was false, and what was true was old. This shows how necessary it is that any new view should be explained at considerable length in order to arouse public attention.

In September, 1858, I set to work by the strong advice of Lyell and Hooker to prepare a volume on the transmutation of species, but was often interrupted by ill-health and short visits to Dr. Lane's delightful hydropathic establishment at Moor Park. I abstracted the manuscript begun on a much larger scale in 1856, and completed the volume on the same reduced scale. It cost me thirteen months and ten days' hard labour. It was published under the title of the *Origin of Species,* in November, 1859.

I have no great quickness of apprehension or wit which is so remarkable in some clever men, for instance, Huxley. I am therefore a poor critic: a paper or book, when first read, generally excites my admiration, and it is only after considerable reflection that I perceive the weak points. My power to follow a long and purely abstract train of thought is very limited; and therefore I could never have succeeded with metaphysics or mathematics. My memory is extensive, yet hazy: it suffices to make me cautious by vaguely telling me that I have observed or read something opposed to the conclusion which I am drawing, or on the other hand in favor of it; and after a time I can generally recollect where to search for my authority. So poor in one sense is my memory that I have never been able to remember for more than a few days a single date or a line of poetry.

Some of my critics have said, "Oh, he is a good observer, but he has no power of reasoning!" I do not think that this can be true, for the *Origin of Species* is one long argument from the beginning to the end, and it has convinced not a few able men. No one could have written it without having some power of reasoning. I have a fair share of invention, and of common sense or judgment, such as every fairly successful lawyer or doctor must have, but not, I believe, in any higher degree.

On the favourable side of the balance, I think that I am superior to the common run of men in noticing things which easily escape attention, and in observing them carefully. My industry has been nearly as great as it could have been in the observation and collection of facts. What is far more important, my love of natural science has been steady and ardent.

This pure love has, however, been much aided by the ambition to be esteemed by my fellow naturalists. From my early youth I have had the strongest desire to understand or explain whatever I observed — that is, to group all facts under some general laws. These causes combined have given me the patience to reflect or ponder for any number of years over any unexplained problem. As far as I can judge, I am not apt to follow blindly the lead of other men. I have steadily endeavored to keep my mind free so as to give up any hypothesis, however much beloved (and I cannot resist forming one on every subject), as soon as facts are shown to be opposed to it. Indeed, I have had no choice but to act in this manner, for with the exception of the Coral Reefs, I cannot remember a single first-formed hypothesis which had not after a time to be given up or greatly modified. This has naturally led me to distrust greatly deductive reasoning in the mixed sciences. On the other hand, I am not very sceptical — a frame of mind which I believe to be injurious to the progress of science. A good deal of scepticism in a scientific man is advisable to avoid much loss of time, but I have met with not a few men, who, I feel sure, have often thus been deterred from experiment or observations which would have proved directly or indirectly serviceable.

Causations and Calculus

HENRY FIELDING *in a chapter heading in "Tom Jones"*   1707–1754

Other grave matters, which those will like best who understand them most.

JOHN DEWEY   1859–1952

Every existence is an event. This fact is nothing at which to repine and nothing to gloat over. It is something to be noted and used. If it is discomfiting when applied to good things, to our friends, possessions, and precious selves, it is consoling also to know that no evil endures forever; that the longest lane turns sometime, and that the memory of loss of nearest and dearest grows dim in time. The eventful character of all existences is no reason for consigning them to the realm of mere appearance any more than it is a reason for idealizing flux into a deity. The important thing is measure, relation, ratio, knowledge of the comparative tempos of change. In mathematics some variables are constants in some problems; so it is in nature and life. The rate of change of some things is so slow, or is so rhythmic, that these changes have all the advantages of stability in dealing with more transitory and irregular happenings — if we know enough. Indeed, if any one thing that concerns us is subject to change, it is fortunate that all other things change. A thing "absolutely" stable and unchangeable would be out of the range of the principle of action and reaction, of resistance and leverage as well as of friction.

Here it would have no applicability, no potentiality of use as measure and control of other events. To designate the slower and the regular rhythmic events structure, and more rapid and irregular ones process, is sound practical sense. It expresses the function of one in respect to the other.

PARETO   1848–1923

In non-mathematical language, the independent variable x in an algebraic equation corresponds to a *cause*. Sometimes that is an admissible translation, sometimes it is not. For *cause*, colloquially speaking, must necessarily come before its effect. Thus, you can consider the price of something as the *effect* and the cost of its production as the *cause*, or you can turn it about and consider the cost of production as *effect* and the selling price to be the *cause*. For in that case there are a series of actions and reactions which permit you to suppose either that the supply of the product precedes the demand or that the demand precedes the supply on the market. In fact, there is a mutual dependence between supply and demand, and this mutual dependence can theoretically be expressed by an equation. You could not, in colloquial language, invert similarly the relation in which you call the freezing of water the cause and the breaking of a pipe its effect, and say that the break *caused* the water to freeze. But, leaving terminology aside, if you are concerned only with the experimental relation between these two facts, isolating them from all others, you could easily deduce the existence of a break in a pipe from the freezing of the water in it and *vice versa*. For, in fact, there is a mutual dependence between the change of temperature which turns the water into ice and the resistance of the pipe containing it. Thermodynamics, thanks to the language of mathematics, expresses this mutual dependence in a rigorous way; colloquial language expresses the same thing, but imperfectly.

Suppose we have two quantities, x and y, in a state of mutual dependence. In mathematical terms, we say that there is an equation between these two variables, and it is unnecessary to say more. But if we speak colloquially, we shall say that x is determined by y, which at once reacts on x, and so y finds itself depending on the new x. You can invert the terms and equally well say that y is determined by x, but that y reacts on x, and so x finds itself also dependent on y. Sometimes this method gives the same results as the mathematical equations; sometimes it does not. So we can substitute the colloquial method only with a good deal of circumspection.

GOETHE   1749–1832

The thinker makes a great mistake when he asks after cause and effect. They both together make up the indivisible phenomenon.

Clerk-Maxwell's Little Demon

KARL PEARSON   1857–1936

A good instance of the *relativity* of natural law is to be found in the so-called *Second Law of Thermodynamics*. This law resumes a wide range of human experience — that is, of sequences observed in *our* sense-impressions — and embraces a great number of conclusions not only bearing on practical life, but upon that dissipation of energy which is even supposed to foreshadow the end of all life. The appreciation of the relativity of natural law is so important that the reader will, I trust, pardon me for citing the entire passage in which Clerk-Maxwell discusses this instance:

"One of the best-established facts in thermodynamics is that it is impossible in a system enclosed in an envelope which permits neither change of volume nor passage of heat, and in which both the temperature and pressure are everywhere the same, to produce any inequality of temperature or of pressure without the expenditure of work. This is the second law of thermodynamics, and it is undoubtedly true so long as we can deal with bodies only in mass, and have no power of perceiving or handling the separate molecules of which they are made up. But if we conceive a being whose faculties are so sharpened that he can follow every molecule in its course, such a being, whose attributes are still as essentially finite as our own, would be able to do what is at present impossible to us. For we have seen that the molecules in a vessel of air at uniform temperature are moving with velocities by no means uniform, though the mean velocity of any great number of them, arbitrarily selected, is almost exactly uniform. Now let us suppose that such a vessel is divided into two portions, *A* and *B,* by a division in which there is a small hole, and that a being, who can see the individual molecules, opens and closes this hole, so as to allow only the swifter molecules to pass from *A* to *B,* and only the slower ones to pass from *B* to *A.* He will thus, without expenditure of work, raise the temperature of *B* and lower that of *A,* in contradiction to the second law of thermodynamics."

To render this passage clear to the lay reader, we have only to add that in this kinetic theory the temperature of a gas depends upon the mean speed of its molecules. Now the second law of thermodynamics resumes with undoubted correctness a wide range of human experience, and is, to that extent, as much a law of nature as that of gravitation. But the kinetic theory of gases, whether it be hypothetical or not, enables us to conceive a demon having a perceptive faculty differing rather in degree than quality from our own, for whom the second law of thermodynamics would not necessarily be a law of nature. Such a conception enables us to grasp how relative what we term nature is to the faculty which perceives it. Scientific law does not, any more than sense-impression, lie in a universe outside and unconditioned by ourselves. Clerk-Maxwell's demon would perceive nature as something totally different from our nature, and to a less extent this is in great probability true for the animal world, and even for man in different stages of growth and civilization. The worlds of the child and of the savage differ widely from that of normal civilized man. One-half of the perceptions which the latter links together in a law of nature may be wanting to the former. Our law of the tides could have no meaning for a blind worm on the shore, for whom the moon had no existence. By the contents and the manner of perception the law of nature is essentially conditioned for each perceptive faculty. To speak, therefore, of the universal validity of a law of nature has only meaning in so far as we refer to a certain type of perceptive faculty, namely, that of a normal human being.

DON MARQUIS' *cockroach, archy*

> *life s too damn funny*
> *for me to explain*

Can Life Cheat Entropy?

JOSEPH NEEDHAM   1900–

The idea that living organisms might be cheats in the game of entropy originated from the conception of the so-called Clerk-Maxwell demon. Clerk-Maxwell, in his expositions of the second law, found it convenient to picture a vessel divided into two compartments which were connected by a hole and a trapdoor which could be opened and shut at will by a "being whose faculties are so sharpened that he can follow every molecule in its course." The demon could thus let through fast molecules but not slow ones, in which case, starting from a uniform temperature, one side would get hot and the other side cold. He could therefore easily, in Kelvin's words, make water run uphill, one end of a poker red-hot and the other ice-cold, and sea water fit to drink. The idea has thus been often put forward that living organisms evade the second law. "Es gibt seine Damonen," cried Driesch, "wir selbst sind sie." But as Clark rightly says, what had really been proved was not that the second law was inapplicable to living matter, but that, if a mind could deal with individual molecules, and if it had suitable frictionless apparatus at its disposal, and if it was desirous of doing so at the moment when an observer happened to be looking, it could decrease entropy. These conditions are never, in practice, fulfilled. So far as we know, living organisms and their minds cannot handle molecules individually. The Maxwellian demon had in fact been endowed in its definition with just the qualities our minds possess of arranging, sorting, and ordering. And our minds do not exist "in a vacuum," created from nothing; they belong to the highest stage in an evolutionary process continuous back to the most primitive single living cells. But the paradox is that in all this arranging, sorting, and ordering which living things perform, there is never any infringement of the second law of thermodynamics.

And Needham cites two fellow scientists:

A. V. Hill (1886–   ) came to the conclusion that it is conceivable that the ultimate minute mechanism, especially of the smallest living cells, may somehow be able to evade the statistical rules which govern larger systems; it may, for example, like Maxwell's demon be able to sort molecules, to use the energy of the more rapidly moving, to employ a unidirectional permeability, and so to avoid the general increase of entropy which appears to be the governing factor in all other material change. Such an evasion, if established, would be of ultimate philosophical, biological, and practical importance; there is no evidence, however, of any value, that it really occurs.

R. S. Lillie (1875–   ) has suggested that the existence of rare disentropic phases in living matter, where infractions of the second law can go on, might account for the subjective persuasion of freedom which all men have and so introduce a kind of free-will into the structure of science itself. He points out that if such intracellular phases may once with reason be postulated, there is no difficulty in imagining their effect on the body as a whole, in view of the extraordinary capacity which the body has of transmitting changes of state from one point in space to another. In this way a voluntary action would arise from an individual escape from the second law in one of the ultramicroscopic intracellular phases in the living being. But is infraction of the second law the same thing as a breakdown of scientific determinism?

It depends on how you define it. Lillie passes by an insensible transition from the latter to the former, but this cannot be justified. Scientific determinism, as it appears in the practice of modern physics, is surely essentially statistical. If in the scientific formulation of things, the individual always escapes, then anything that individual atoms may do in the ultimate recesses of the animal body is metaphysical in the truest and most literal sense of the word.

Lillie himself refers to the expression "physical indeterminism" as a misnomer, and admits that though the laws of the microscopic may not be the same as the laws of the macroscopic, there must be laws of some sort there. And if that is the case, it is difficult to see how on a scientific basis *alone* there can be any spontaneity or freedom. Thus, if we suppose that escape from the second law regularly takes place in the intimate structure of living organisms, it will surely not be escape into freedom, but into the arms of some wider statistical law inevitably brought into existence by the operation of the scientific way of thought. Or, in other words, the inductive method will again assert its supremacy and nothing will escape from all this save what always did escape, namely, individuality. The unique is the only nut that science cannot crack, and freedom implies uniqueness.

Life

HANS ZINSSER   1878–1940

He knows that physicochemical analysis will never give the final clue to life processes; yet he recognizes that "vitalism" and "neovitalism" are little more than a sort of amorphous theology born of a sense of the helplessness of mere "mechanism." So the patient biologist plods along, piling up his empirical observations as honestly as he can — getting what satisfaction he may from the fact that he is helping, by infinite increments, to reduce the scope of vitalistic vagueness to narrower and narrower limits. As Bergson puts it: "A very small element of a

curve is near being a straight line; and the smaller it is
the nearer. . . . So, likewise, 'vitality' is tangent, at any
and every point, to physical and chemical forces. . . . In
reality, however, life is no more made up of physicochemical elements than a curve is composed of straight
lines." The biologist is constantly differentiating the
curve of vitality, quite aware that mankind can approach, but never reach, the "limiting value" of complete comprehension. Moreover, he knows — whenever
he attacks a problem — that before he can advance toward his objective, he must first recede into analysis of
the individual elements that compose the complex systems with which he is occupied.

STEPHEN PAGET   1855–1926

When a man sets to work to study one of the natural
sciences, he provides himself with forms of thought, mental images, which may be called the principles of that
science. The chemist has mental images of atoms com-
bining or separating, under definite laws, with definite
results: the geologist has mental images of an earth
cooled through millions of years from a red-hot haze of
gases to a hard globe, and cracked in the cooling. Other
men of science, the botanist, the bacteriologist, the
physiologist, have mental images of living matter. Is
there any difference, in kind, between the mental images
of chemistry and those of physiology? Surely, there is no
such difference. Matter is none the less matter, though
it be living: and motion is none the less motion, though
it be voluntary.

Dr. Johnson's advice is apt here, that we should clear
our minds of cant. A great deal of cant is talked about
the mystery of life, as if life were somehow more mysterious than the rest of Nature. When a man says that one
fact of Nature is more wonderful than another, he is at
fault. The striking of a match is every bit as wonderful
as the working of a brain: the union of two atoms of hydrogen and one of oxygen in a molecule of water is every
bit as wonderful as the growth of a child. Nature does

not class her works in order of merit; everything is just as easy to her as everything else: she puts her whole mind into all that she does —

> *Lives through all life, extends through all extent,*
> *Spreads undivided, operates unspent —*

perfect at every moment, omnipresent, and, like His Majesty the King, within her dominions supreme. Life is neither more nor less mysterious than the attraction of the magnet, the density of a paving-stone, or the color of a tie: our presence in the midst of Nature's achievements does not affect her estimate of them. She prices her wonderful goods all at the same value, like the stock of a sixpence-halfpenny bazaar, nothing under and nothing over: she makes them all out of the one stuff, constructing with it a grain of sand, a drop of water, a micro-organism, or a nerve-cell, all with equal ease. In brief, all Nature is of the same nature, all her processes are one process, all her facts are one fact, all her acts are one act, and everything material is ultimately identical with everything else. These platitudes, of course, are of a respectable age: they are no more than the doctrine of Thales of Miletus, who lived, if I remember right, six hundred years before our Lord. Arm-in-arm with Thales, I wonder at the mystery of the fabric of my own brain as I wonder at the mystery of the fabric of a pound of butter; and I take it for granted that the forces which animate my tissues are just as natural, that is to say, are just the same, as the forces which animate the tissues of an ape, a frog, an oyster, or a dandelion, and thrill in every grain of sand, and compel two atoms of hydrogen and one of oxygen to clutch each other so close that they are neither hydrogen nor oxygen, nor hydrogen *plus* oxygen, but water.

Hitherto, I have said what I believe to be true. Now, I am going to say what I believe to be false. I pray you, therefore, to give me your most careful attention.

When we strike a match, there is a splutter and a flare, which are the atoms of the match and of the atmosphere performing a new sort of dance. Nothing is added to what was already there; no fresh elements or forces arrive on the gay scene. The atoms are the explosion, and the explosion is the atoms. They hurry up, they change step, they exchange partners: that is all. Before we struck the match, they were dancing, as it were, the second figure of the Lancers; now, they are dancing the third figure, pulling and pushing in that hilarious fashion which is called Kitchen-Lancers: that is all. Even so it is, with consciousness. When something strikes us, there is a splutter and a flare, which are the atoms of our cerebral cells performing, in the crowded ballroom of the brain, a new sort of dance; and that is all. That dance is consciousness, and consciousness is that dance. Consciousness is neither the music which accompanies the dance, nor the reaction which follows the dance: it is the dance, it is atoms in motion. Of course, to dance this particular figure, the atoms must be accustomed to dancing, and there must be enough of them to make up a set, so many ladies and so many gentlemen: and then they can dance till they are tired, and that dance is consciousness. But, we know, it is possible to dance less than sixteen: indeed, a child will dance all alone, without so much as a barrel-organ. Even so it is, with consciousness. In its simplest form, consciousness may be observed even in very humble structures. As, by putting a penny in the slot, we obtain, if the automatic machine be going, a measured projection of chocolate or of scent, or of two foreign bodies called cigarettes, or an electric current, or the exhibition of a moving picture, or the liberation of a balance, so, from the amoeba, if it be going, we get something out, some faint consciousness, a mere glimmer; still, it is the real article, what there is of it. When we stand in the presence of nobler creatures, such as the oyster, we see movements more definitely purposive; and begin to feel fairly sure that the sun of consciousness has risen. We are for a time puzzled, because the oyster has several centres set apart, and far apart, for consciousness; and it is hard to see how an oyster can be conscious in three or four places at once: and this difficulty is not diminished, but rather is increased, when we contemplate the earthworm, which is a sort of common lodging-house of consciousness, with a double row of cubicles right and left all the way up. But, when we come to the frog, we know where we are: for we can see at a glance that the cerebral hemispheres must be conscious of the rest of the frog, and that the rest of the frog cannot be conscious of the cerebral hemispheres. Here, at or about this level of life, we find special organs, brains, so complex that they must of necessity be conscious. But of what are they conscious? Is it of themselves, of their own atomic motion, their own chemical changes? Not a bit of it: they are conscious of sensations, dim pleasures and pains, heat and cold, light and darkness, taste and smell. They feel, they perceive. From this point onward, it is easy to observe the development of consciousness; the brain, as we ascend the scale of life, beginning to divide its experiences into self and not-self. At first, it was conscious: at last, it is self-conscious. Henceforth, it remembers, imagines, thinks, and wills, or thinks that it wills. It reads and writes, pursues the fine arts, invents God, takes an active interest in politics, and, if it be lodged in a male skull, has a vote. Behold, Gentlemen, yourselves: you who are so highly differentiated brains that you can understand anything, even the false doctrine which I have here declared to you. For I no more believe that my brain is self-conscious than I believe that two and two make five.

NIETZSCHE   1844–1900

Man, a hybrid of plant and ghost.

Determinism

CLERK-MAXWELL   1831–1879

It is a metaphysical doctrine that from the same antecedents follow the same consequents. No one can gainsay this. But it is not of much use in a world like this, in which the same antecedents never again concur, and nothing ever happens twice. Indeed, for aught we know, one of the antecedents might be the precise date and place of the event, in which case experience would go for nothing. The metaphysical axiom would be of use only to a being possessed of the knowledge of contingent events, *scientia simplicis intelligentiae* — a degree of knowledge to which mere omniscience of all facts, *scientia visionis*, is but ignorance.

The physical axiom which has a somewhat similar aspect is "That from like antecedents follow like consequents." But here we have passed from sameness to likeness, from absolute accuracy to a more or less rough approximation. There are certain classes of phenomena, as I have said, in which a small error in the data only introduces a small error in the result. Such are, among others, the larger phenomena of the Solar System, and those in which the more elementary laws in Dynamics contribute the greater part of the result. The course of events in these cases is stable.

There are other classes of phenomena which are more complicated, and in which cases of instability may occur, the number of such cases increasing, in an exceedingly rapid manner, as the number of variables increases. Thus, to take a case from a branch of science which comes next to astronomy itself as a manifestation of order: In the refraction of light, the direction of the refracted ray depends on that of the incident ray, so that, in general, if the one direction be slightly altered, the other also will be slightly altered. In doubly refracting media there are two refracting rays, but it is true of each of them that like causes produce like effects. But if the direction of the ray within a biaxal crystal is nearly but not exactly coincident with that of the ray-axis of the crystal, a small change in direction will produce a great change in the direction of the emergent ray. Of course, this arises from a singularity in the properties of the ray-axis, and there are only two ray-axes among the infinite number of possible directions of lines in the crystal; but it is to be expected that in phenomena of higher complexity there will be a far greater number of singularities, near which the axiom about like causes producing like effects ceases to be true. Thus, the conditions under which guncotton explodes are far from being well known; but the aim of chemists is not so much to predict the time at which guncotton will go off of itself, as to find a kind of guncotton which, when placed in certain circumstances, has never yet exploded, and this even when slight irregularities both in the manufacture and in the storage are taken account of by trying numerous and long-continued experiments.

In all such cases there is one common circumstance — the system has a quantity of potential energy, which is capable of being transformed into motion, but which cannot begin to be so transformed till the system has reached a certain configuration, to attain which requires an expenditure of work, which in certain cases may be infinitesimally small, and in general bears no definite proportion to the energy developed in consequence thereof. For example, the rock loosed by frost and balanced on a singular point of the mountain-side, the little spark which kindles the great forest, the little word which sets the world a-fighting, the little scruple which prevents a man from doing his will, the little spore which blights all the potatoes, the little gemmule which makes us philosophers or idiots. Every existence above a certain rank has its singular points: the higher the rank, the more of them. At these points, influences, whose physical magnitude is too small to be taken account of by a finite being, may produce results of the greatest importance. All great results produced by human endeavour depend on taking advantage of these singular states when they occur.

> There is a tide in the affairs of men
> Which, taken at the flood, leads on to fortune.

The man of tact says, "the right word at the right time," and, "a word spoken in due season, how good is it!" The man of no tact is like vinegar upon nitre when he sings his songs to a heavy heart. The ill-timed admonition hardens the heart, and the good resolution, taken when it is sure to be broken, becomes macadamised into pavement for the abyss.

It appears, then, that in our own nature there are more singular points — where prediction, except from absolutely perfect data and guided by the omniscience of contingency, becomes impossible — than there are in any lower organisation. But singular points are by their very nature isolated, and from no appreciable fraction of the continuous course of our existence. Hence predictions of human conduct may be made in many cases. First, with respect to those who have no character at all, especially when considered in crowds, after the statistical method. Second, with respect to individuals of confirmed character, with respect to actions of the kind for which their character is confirmed.

If, therefore, those cultivators of physical science from whom the intelligent public deduce their conception of the physicist, and whose style is recognised as marking with a scientific stamp the doctrines they promulgate, are led in pursuit of the arcana of science to the study of the singularities and instabilities, rather than the continuities and stabilities of things, the promotion of natural knowledge may tend to remove that prejudice in favour of determinism which seems to arise from assuming that the physical science of the future is a mere magnified image of that of the past.

Freedom of Will

HENRY ADAMS   1838–1918

Under any conceivable system the process of getting God and man under the same roof — of bringing two independent energies under the same control — required a painful effort, as science has much cause to know. No doubt, many good Christians and some heretics have been shocked at the *tour de force* by which they felt themselves suddenly seized, bound hand and foot, attached to each other, and dragged into the Church, without consent or consultation. To religious mystics, whose scepticism concerned chiefly themselves and their own existence, Saint Thomas's man seemed hardly worth herding, at so much expense and trouble, into a

Church where he was not eager to go. True religion felt the nearness of God without caring to see the mechanism. Mystics like Saint Bernard, Saint Francis, Saint Bonaventure, or Pascal had a right to make this objection, since they go into the Church, so to speak, by breaking through the windows; but society at large accepted and retains Saint Thomas's man much as Saint Thomas delivered him to the Government; a two-sided being, free or unfree, responsible or irresponsible, an energy or a victim of energy, moved by choice or moved by compulsion, as the interests of society seemed for the moment to need. Certainly Saint Thomas lavished no excess of liberty on the man he created, but still he was more generous than the State has ever been. Saint Thomas asked little from man, and gave much; even as much freedom of will as the State gave or now gives; he added immortality hereafter and eternal happiness under reasonable restraints; his God watched over man's temporal welfare far more anxiously than the State has ever done, and assigned him space in the Church which he never can have in the galleries of Parliament or Congress; more than all this, Saint Thomas and his God placed man in the centre of the universe, and made the sun and the stars for his uses. No statute law ever did as much for man, and no social reform ever will try to do it; yet man bitterly complained that he had not his rights, and even in the Church is still complaining, because Saint Thomas set a limit, more or less vague, to what the man was obstinate in calling his freedom of will.

Understanding Ourselves — Can We?

PERCY W. BRIDGMAN   1958

It is fashionable to stress the differences between the "sciences" and the "humanities." There are, of course, obvious differences, and for certain purposes and in certain contexts it may be desirable to emphasize them, as, for example, in drawing up a curriculum of instruction or in organizing a university faculty into departments. I believe, however, that the differences are more or less superficial; what is common to the sciences and the humanities is far more fundamental and important than the differences. In the first place, both are human enterprises; this gives them a unity which they cannot escape. Furthermore, they are both predominantly intellectual enterprises, even, if I may be permitted to use the term, enterprises of the intelligence. This I would maintain even if we choose to make a concern with values the touchstone of differentiation between the sciences and the humanities. It is often said that science can tell us nothing about values, and that here lies the fundamental distinction between science and the humanities. Perhaps one could by some tour de force set up a definition of science which would forbid it values, but surely one cannot forbid a concern with values to intelligence. Values can be described, analyzed, appraised, and modified, and these are all activities of the intelligence. We cannot act in any situation involving values without engaging in at least some of these activities.

Whether we practice a science or a humanity we cannot avoid exercising our intelligences. It is to some of the consequences of this that I would call your attention. It is, I think, beginning to dawn on us that there is more to this problem of using our minds intelligently than at first strikes the eye. There are techniques of being intelligent. It is not easy to acquire the proper use of the mental tools which we have thoughtlessly inherited or which are implicit in the construction of our brains. Severe effort and long practice are required.

It seems that we are coming to an awareness of the existence and importance of our mental tools from the side of the sciences rather than from the side of the humanities. The reason is not any reflection on the humanities, but is a consequence of human frailty and the fact that the humanities are so much more complex and difficult than the sciences. By far the most important consequence of the conceptual revolution brought about in physics by relativity and quantum theory lies not in such details as that meter sticks shorten when they move or that simultaneous position and momentum have no meaning, but in the insight that we had not been using our minds properly and that it is important to find out how to do so. Although it is no reflection on the humanities that this insight is coming through the comparatively simple situations of physics, I think it *would* be a reflection if this experience of the sciences did not give the humanities pause, or suggest that it is almost inevitable that some modification is necessary in their own conceptual foundations. For would it not be a miracle if an intellectual apparatus which has evolved to cope with the primitive situations of daily life and which has been found to fail when confronted with the comparatively simple needs of modern physics should retain its validity in the incomparably more complex situations presented by human society and the humanities?

The most important intellectual task for the future is to acquire an understanding of the tools, and so to modify our outlook and ideals as to take account of their limitations. This task is not to be accomplished by any "return" to the insights of the past. The insight that there is any problem here at all is devastatingly new in human history. The sciences and the humanities find themselves facing the problem together; it is too difficult and too pressing to permit the luxury of a division of forces. Appreciation of the existence and the nature of the problem is the first step toward the invention of the new methods and outlooks that will be necessary to solve it.

It seems to me that the human race stands on the brink of a major breakthrough. We have advanced to the point where we can put our hand on the hem of the curtain that separates us from an understanding of the nature of our minds. Is it conceivable that we will withdraw our hand and turn back through discouragement and lack of vision?

P A R T
V

AND HIMSELF

An apple a day.

G. K. CHESTERTON   1874–1936

A man can understand astronomy only by being an astronomer; he can understand entomology only by being an entomologist (or, perhaps, an insect); but he can understand a great deal of anthropology merely by being a man. He is himself the animal which he studies. Hence arises the fact which strikes the eye everywhere in the records of ethnology and folklore — the fact that the same frigid and detached spirit which leads to success in the study of astronomy or botany leads to disaster in the study of mythology or human origins. It is necessary to cease to be a man in order to do justice to a microbe; it is not necessary to cease to be a man in order to do justice to men. That same suppression of sympathies, that same waving away of intuitions or guesswork, which make a man preternaturally clever in dealing with the stomach of a spider, will make him preternaturally stupid in dealing with the heart of man.

Half-Healer, Semi-Scientist

ARTURO CASTIGLIONI   1874–1953

The physician of today must be the medical historian of each of his patients, directing particular attention toward discovering the first causes and developments of the illness. In the same way the historian of medicine searches for the origins of the medical thought and pathologic concepts of the past. We can often disclose the evidence which will explain the first causes, and can unveil, in concepts which are accepted as quite modern, thoughts which had already occurred to the great masters of the past, but had remained forgotten, misunderstood, or sterile.

Medicine, and this is one of the most valuable of the teachings of history, cannot remain equal to its great task without preserving for the physician his double character of scientist and worker for the people (demiurge), according to the classic concept. If in the exercise of his art he is guided by his knowledge of the laws of nature, then his technical knowledge, his calm judgment, and his objective reasoning should furnish him with the rules which will determine the application of these natural laws in practice. It is only thus that the clinician can be clinical in the true sense of the word, a far different matter from the mere calculation of figures or the counting of cells, in giving equal consideration to all the endogenous and exogenous factors that can contribute to modify the normal state of health. In the same way the complete industrialization of medicine is fallacious, as are all doctrines founded on the false premise that all individuals are alike. For the same reason the individuality of the physician and his personal aptitudes must be given a free course in changing with the times and with the individuals whom he is called to treat.

We must not forget that the physician above all should keep in mind the welfare of his patient, his constantly changing state, not only in the visible signs of his illness, but also in his state of mind, which must necessarily be an important factor in the success of the treatment. One would be blind not to recognize that before and even after the advent of modern scientific medicine there were great and able healers of the sick who were not men of science, but who had the ability to reassure the patient and thus favourably to influence the course of the illness. It is also obvious that there have been excellent scientists who were very mediocre practitioners.

Thus history teaches us that any division of the science and the art of medicine is necessarily harmful to practice. The physician of today, better realizing the limitations of bacteriological and other technical aids, is experiencing the need of returning to the patient's bedside, from which medicine should never have separated itself. With the extreme swing of the pendulum too much faith has sometimes been placed on the pronouncements of the laboratory when, forgetting the importance of the clinical picture, physicians have based their activities too exclusively on laboratory criteria. For some years now physicians have tended through ignorance of the possibilities and limitations of laboratory methods either to place too much reliance on what came out of the four walls of the laboratory, or not to take advantage of the information that it could properly give. They tended to pay more attention to the evidence of the microscope and of chemical reagents than to the information obtained by their own senses from examination of the patients in the wards of the hospitals.

Today, with a better knowledge of these possibilities and limitations, they tend to scrutinize sagaciously the information received from both sources. Clinical instruction in the Hippocratic sense fortunately never was completely neglected, and voices continued to maintain the necessity of returning to the classical paths, reinforced with the riches of newly acquired knowledge, but with the eye steadfastly fixed on the goal of the patient's welfare. All the marvellous discoveries of recent times cannot remove the physician from his post of honor in detecting morbid phenomena and following the mysterious rhythm of life and death: a post, that is, at the bedside of the patient.

NICARCHUS   1ST OR 2D CENTURY A.D.

Marcus the Physician called yesterday on the marble Zeus. Though marble and though Zeus, the funeral is today.

Hippocrates and the Practice of Medicine

L. J. HENDERSON   1878–1942

In the complex business of living, *both* theory and practice are necessary conditions of understanding, and the method of Hippocrates, the most famous of physicians, is the only method that has ever succeeded widely and generally. The first element of that method is hard, persistent, intelligent, responsible, unremitting labor in the sick-room, not in the library: the complete adaptation of the doctor to his task, an adaptation that is far from being merely intellectual. The second element of that method is accurate observation of things and events, selection, guided by judgment born of familiarity and experience, of the salient and the recurrent phenomena, and their classification and methodical exploitation. The third element of that method is the judicious construction of a theory — not a philosophical theory, nor a grand effort of the imagination, nor a quasi-religious dogma, but a modest pedestrian affair, or perhaps I had better say, a useful walking-stick to help on the way — and the use thereof. All this may be summed up in a word: The physician must have, first, intimate, habitual, intuitive familiarity with things; secondly, systematic knowledge of things; and, thirdly, an effective way of thinking about things.

Experience shows that this is the way to success. It has long been followed in studying sickness, but hardly at all in studying the other experiences of everyday life. The method of this course depends upon the conviction that there is much to be gained by cautiously following the procedure of Hippocrates in the study of the interactions between persons. Let us, therefore, consider more carefully what Hippocrates did and what he did not do.

Hippocrates was in reaction chiefly against three things: first, against the ancient, traditional myths and superstitions which still prevailed among the physicians of his day; secondly, against the recent intrusion of philosophy into medical doctrine; thirdly, against the extravagant system of diagnosis of the Cnidian School, a body of contemporary physicians who seem to have suffered from a familiar form of professional pedantry. Here Hippocrates was opposing a pretentious systematization of knowledge that lacked solid objective foundation; the concealment of ignorance, probably more or less unconsciously, with a show of knowledge.

The so-called genuine works of Hippocrates reveal a method in the exploitation of everyday experience with the lives and deaths of men that can never be too carefully studied. But we must confine ourselves to a few important aspects of the Hippocratic method. In the beginning are the cases. The very first of these is as follows:

"*Case I.* Philiscus lived by the wall. He took to his bed with acute fever on the first day and sweating; night uncomfortable.

"*Second day.* General exacerbation; later a small clyster moved the bowels well. A restful night.

"*Third day.* Early and until midday he appeared to have lost the fever; but towards evening acute fever with sweating; thirst; dry tongue; black urine. An uncomfortable night, without sleep; completely out of his mind.

"*Fourth day.* All symptoms exacerbated; black urine; a more comfortable night, and urine of a better colour.

"*Fifth day.* About midday slight epistaxis of unmixed blood. Urine varied, with scattered, round particles suspended in it, resembling semen; they did not settle. On the application of a suppository the patient passed, with flatulence, scanty excreta. A distressing night, snatches of sleep, irrational talk; extremities everywhere cold, and would not get warm again; black urine; snatches of sleep towards dawn; speechless; cold sweat; extremities livid. About midday on the sixth day the patient died. The breathing throughout, as though he were recollecting to do it, was rare and large. Spleen raised in a round swelling. Cold sweats all the time. The exacerbations on even days."

This case is fairly typical of the collection. The following points are important and should be carefully noted:

(1) It consists of bare observations of bare facts, un-colored by theory or presupposition and condensed to the very limit of possible condensation. These are the practicing physician's data, freed so far as possible from everything that is not a datum. (2) The data are of two kinds. The first kind, contained in the first part, are single observations. The second kind, contained in the second part, are uniformities observed throughout the particular illness of this particular person. (3) The curi-ous form of breathing referred to is the first mention now known of what is called Cheyne-Stokes breathing. Apart from one other reference to the phenomenon in another Hippocratic case, it is the only known reference before the eighteenth century of our era. This is one sign among many that Hippocrates was no casual and no ordinary observer. On the contrary, he was a constant observer with whom observation was a great part of the business of life, a skillful observer whose skill depended upon both native capacity and long practice. Such at least is the interpretation that all current medical experi-ence forces upon us.

The next step is the recognition of a wider kind of uni-formity: the recurrence again and again in different cases, often otherwise very various, of single events or of the uniformity observed within a single case, for example: regularities in the duration of certain fevers, the frequent discharge of fluid through the nose in what we now call diptheria, and in general the prognostic im-portance of a wide range of symptoms. The most famous of all the descriptions of such uniformities is that of the so-called *facies Hippocratica,* the appearance of the face at the point of death in many acute diseases: "Nose sharp, eyes hollow, temples sunken, ears cold and con-tracted with their lobes turned outwards, the skin about the face hard and tense and parched, the color of the face as a whole being yellow or black."

Throughout a great part of his work Hippocrates is thus moving step by step toward the widest generaliza-tions within his reach. In great part he is seeking a nat-ural history of acute disease or at least of those acute diseases that were prevalent among his patients. His success was great, and the whole history of science goes far to support the view that such a methodical procedure is a necessary step in the development of a science that deals with similarly complex and various phenomena.

Beyond this stage there is one even wider generalization that plays an important part in the writings and thought of Hippocrates. This is the principle that came to be known, and is still remembered, as the *vis medicatrix naturae*. For the purposes of sociological study, it is an important principle and we must now examine one or two aspects of it precisely.

Before Hippocrates, about 500 B.C., Alcmaeon of Croton had expressed the opinion that health is an isonomy or harmony (we may say equilibrium) between opposites, sickness a state of monarchy or disequilibrium. Now the widest of all generalizations in the work of Hippocrates is this, that as a rule sick people recover without treatment. The conclusion of Hippocrates was that the state of health is similar to that state defined by Pareto in his treatise on general sociology, *The Mind and Society,* as equilibrium: "a state such that if a small modification different from that which will otherwise occur is impressed upon a system, a reaction will at once appear tending toward the conditions that would have existed if the modification had not been impressed."

Pareto's definition bears the marks of centuries of further work in science and logic. But the Hippocratic analysis comes to much the same thing as Pareto's definition. In both cases there is the underlying theory that equilibrium is an equilibrium of forces, more or less like the equilibrium, for instance, in a box spring; that a small modification leaves the forces substantially intact; and that the forces tend to re-establish the state that would have existed if no modification had occurred, just as a box spring which has been depressed when one lies down on it resumes its original form when one gets up. So last February the people of Louisville, driven away by a flood, returned to their homes when the flood receded; and a few weeks later life was going on with little change. So within a decade the traces of the earthquake and fire in San Francisco could hardly be seen, or the devastation of war along the battlefront in northern France. In such cases the "forces" that tend to produce "the conditions that would have existed if the modification had not been impressed" are what we describe as sentiments and economic interests.

It should now be evident that Hippocrates, probably under the influence of Alcmaeon, made use of his broadest generalization, that sick people usually recover without treatment, in order to construct a conceptual scheme or theory of the nature of sickness. It is herein that he differs from men like Richelieu, Lyautey, Robert Walpole, and Bismarck. He differs from them in that he was both a practitioner and a theorist, while, so far as we know, they were practitioners who made use of no general all-embracing theory or conceptual scheme.

In order to construct a useful conceptual scheme, Hippocrates proceeded to analyze the phenomenon, as he abstractly conceived it, into elements. This analysis and the resulting elaboration of the theory need not detain us. To them we owe the survival of such words as "crisis" and "coction." But the theory, having served its purpose, is obsolete, like Ptolemy's astronomy.

We must, however, note carefully that this obsolete theory, like so many others, once served its purpose well. In particular it was the firm support of the Hippocratic principle of expectant treatment and of the precept "Do no harm," a principle and a precept which still preserve their utility in the practice of medicine and even in government and the affairs of everyday life, and which are too often disregarded by physicians, surgeons, and politicians.

The Hippocratic conceptual scheme suffers from one particular defect that should be carefully noted: it presents a view of the physiological system in a state of equilibrium without giving a satisfactory picture of the constituent parts of the system or of the forces that operate between these parts. We now know that it is convenient and reasonably satisfactory to think of the constituent parts as chemical substances, fluids, cells, tissues, and organs; and of the forces as the force with which theoretical physics and theoretical chemistry are concerned. Such a conception was not available to Hippocrates.

It is not everyone who can become a good diagnostician, like the good physician, of disease and of the private troubles of men, like the skillful lawyer and competent man of affairs, of the complex situations of everyday life and of the purposes that men try to hide. As Aristotle remarked, politicians rarely succeed in communicating their skill to their own sons. In like manner even some of the best medical students turn out to be mediocre internes in a hospital. But the really good hospital interne goes through a change which is perhaps the most remarkable change that can be observed anywhere in our educational system.

More often than not skillful diagnosticians reach a diagnosis before they are aware, or at any rate conscious, of the grounds that justify their decision. If asked to explain the reasons for the diagnosis, they often clearly show by their behavior that they are obliged to think them out, and that to do so is an awkward task. This is true of doctors, of lawyers, and of men of affairs. It is here cited as one mark of a kind of skill, hardly ever learned except by long practice, that is indispensable in the interpretation of what men say.

The probability that a diagnosis is correct is less than the probability that a careful deduction from accurate measurements is correct. But when better ways do not avail, experience shows that the conclusions of the skilled diagnostician may be cautiously used with good results even for scientific purposes. Not less important is the fact that practice in diagnosis is a means of becoming thoroughly familiar with the material in which one works and that skill in diagnosis is an unmistakable sign of that familiarity.

MONTAIGNE   1533–1592

Experience stands on its own dunghill in medicine, and reason yields it place. Medicine has always professed experience to be the touchstone of its operations. Plato was right to say that good doctors themselves ought to have had the diseases they want to cure, and been subject themselves to the misfortunes and circumstances which they have to diagnose. Let them catch the pox if they want to know how to cure it. I'd trust such a doctor.

The Care of the Patient

FRANCIS W. PEABODY   1881–1927

The application of the principles of science to the diagnosis and treatment of disease is only one limited aspect of medical practice. The practice of medicine in its broadest sense includes the whole relationship of the physician with his patient. It is an art, based to an increasing extent on the medical sciences, but comprising much that still remains outside the realm of any science. The art of medicine and the science of medicine are not antagonistic but supplementary to each other. There is no more contradiction between the science of medicine and the art of medicine than between the science of aeronautics and the art of flying.

When a patient enters a hospital, the first thing that commonly happens to him is that he loses his personal identity. He is generally referred to, not as Henry Jones, but as "that case of mitral stenosis in the second bed on the left." There are plenty of reasons why this is so, and the point is, in itself, relatively unimportant; but the trouble is that it leads, more or less directly, to the patient being treated as a case of mitral stenosis, and not as a sick man. The disease is treated, but Henry Jones, lying awake nights while he worries about his wife and children, represents a problem that is much more complex than the pathologic physiology of mitral stenosis, and he is apt to improve very slowly unless a discerning intern discovers why it is that even large doses of digitalis fail to slow his heart rate. Henry happens to have heart disease, but he is not disturbed so much by dyspnea as he is by anxiety for the future, and a talk with an understanding physician who tries to make the situation clear to him, and then gets the social service worker to find a suitable occupation, does more to straighten him out than a book full of drugs and diets. Henry has an excellent example of a certain type of heart disease, and he is glad that all the staff find him interesting, for it makes him feel that they will do the best they can to cure him; but just because he is an interesting case he does not cease to be a human being with very human hopes and fears. Sickness produces an abnormally sensitive emotional state in almost everyone, and in many cases the emotional state repercusses, as it were, on the organic disease. The pneumonia would probably run its course in a week, regardless of treatment, but the experienced physician knows that by quieting the cough, getting the patient to sleep, and giving a bit of encouragement, he can save his patient's strength and lift him through many distressing hours. The institutional eye tends to become focused on the lung, and it forgets that the lung is only one member of the body.

But if teachers and students are inclined to take a limited point of view even toward interesting cases of organic disease, they fall into much more serious error in their attitude toward a large group of patients who do not show objective, organic pathologic conditions, and who are generally spoken of as having "nothing the matter with them." Up to a certain point, as long as they are regarded as diagnostic problems, they command attention; but as soon as the physician has assured himself that they do not have organic disease, he passes them over lightly.

Take the case of a young woman, for instance, who entered the hospital with a history of nausea and discomfort in the upper part of the abdomen after eating. Mrs. Brown had "suffered many things of many physicians." Each of them gave her a tonic and limited her diet. She stopped eating everything that any of her physicians advised her to omit, and is now living on a little milk with a few crackers; but her symptoms persist. The history suggests a possible gastric ulcer or gallstones, and with a proper desire to study the case thoroughly, she is given a test meal, gastric analysis and duodenal intubation, and roetgen-ray examinations are made of the gastro-intestinal tract and gall-bladder. All of these diagnostic methods give negative results; that is, they do not show evidence of any structural change. The case immediately becomes much less interesting than if it had turned out to be a gastric ulcer with atypical symptoms. The visiting physician walks by and says, "Well, there's nothing the matter with her." The clinical clerk says, "I did an awful lot of work on that case and it turned out to be nothing at all." The intern, who wants to clear out the ward so as to make room for some interesting cases, says, "Mrs. Brown, you can send for your clothes and go home tomorrow. There really is nothing the matter with you, and fortunately you have not got any of the serious troubles we suspected. We have used all the most modern and scientific methods and we find that there is no reason why you should not eat anything you want to. I'll give you a tonic to take when you go home." Same story, same colored medicine! Mrs. Brown goes home, somewhat better for her rest in new surroundings, thinking that nurses are kind and physicians are pleasant, but that they do not seem to know much about the sort of medicine that will touch her trouble. She takes up her life and the symptoms return — and then she tries chiropractic, or perhaps Christian Science.

It is rather fashionable to say that the modern physician has become "too scientific." Now, was it too scientific, with all the stomach tubes and blood counts and roentgen-ray examinations? Not at all. Mrs. Brown's symptoms might have been due to a gastric ulcer or to gallstones, and after such a long course it was only proper to use every method that might help to clear the diagnosis. Was it, perhaps, not scientific enough? The popular conception of a scientist as a man who works in a laboratory and who uses instruments of precision is as inaccurate as it is superficial, for a scientist is known, not by his technical processes, but by his intellectual processes; and the essence of the scientific method of thought is that it proceeds in an orderly manner toward the establishment of a truth. Now the chief criticism to be made of the way Mrs. Brown's case was handled is that the staff was contented with a half-truth. The investigation of the patient was decidedly unscientific in that it stopped short of even an attempt to determine the real cause of the symptoms. As soon as organic disease could be excluded, the whole problem was given up, but the symptoms persisted. Speaking candidly, the case was a medical failure in spite of the fact that the patient went home with the assurance that there was "nothing the matter" with her.

EMILY DICKINSON   1830–1886

> *Pain has an element of blank;*
> *It cannot recollect*
> *When it began, or if there were*
> *A day when it was not.*
>
> *It has no future but itself;*
> *Its infinite realms contain*
> *Its past, enlightened to perceive*
> *New periods of pain.*

Telling the Patient the Truth

L. J. HENDERSON   1878–1942

To speak of telling the truth, the whole truth, and noth-but the truth to a patient is absurd. Like absurdity in mathematics, it is absurd simply because it is impossible. I must explain this statement, for all our habits of moralistic thought acquired in early years and derived from the theological and metaphysical traditions of our race interfere with understanding.

Therefore, consider the statement: "This is a carcinoma"; assuming it to be as trustworthy a diagnosis as we ever reach. Now let us look at this statement from a biological standpoint. If you utter it to a patient, it is a stimulus applied to him. This stimulus will produce his response. Need I say that his response will not be chiefly that convenient and misleading metaphysical abstraction called cognition? On the contrary, how much he will understand is uncertain, but if he knows that carcinoma means cancer, it is quite certain that circulatory and respiratory changes and other very intricate changes in the central and peripheral nervous system will follow. He will experience some kind of fear and in most cases a feeling of concern for the economic interests of others. All these and many other elements make up the intricate response of the patient to the stimulus which you have applied by uttering the four words: "This is a carcinoma."

It is certain that you can by no possibility convey to the patient accurate information of this kind independently of the associated affective processes. I suggest, therefore, that if you recognize a duty of "telling the truth to the patient," you can range yourself outside the class of biologists with lawyers and philosophers. The notion that the truth, the whole truth, and nothing but the truth can be conveyed to the patient is a good specimen of that class of fallacies called by Whitehead, "the fallacy of misplaced concreteness." It results from neglecting factors that cannot be excluded from the concrete situation and that are of an order of magnitude and relevancy that make it imperative to consider them. Of course, another fallacy is also often involved, the belief that diagnosis and prognosis are more certain than they are. But that is another question.

At this point there is grave danger that I shall not make my meaning clear. I am not saying that you should always, or in general, or frequently lie to your patients, for I believe that a physician's integrity is a priceless possession. To infer any such conclusion from what I have said would involve a fallacy that I have perhaps sufficiently characterized above. My position is this: that because it is quite impossible in some cases, as I have explained, to tell the truth, the whole truth, and nothing but the truth to the patient, to talk about doing so is simply meaningless. Surely this does not relieve the physician of his moral responsibility. On the contrary, as we more clearly perceive the immense complexity of the phenomena, our appreciation of the difficulty of the task increases and with it our moral responsibility.

MONTAIGNE   1533–1592

Let things work themselves out. The same order of nature that provides for fleas and for moles will provide also for men who have as much patience as fleas and moles to put themselves under its gouvernance. We get nowhere by shouting Gee! and Haw! This is all very well to get hoarse, but it does not get us ahead.

The order of nature is proud and it is pitiless. Our fears, our despairs disgust it, and only keep it from coming to our aid, instead of inviting it. It owes its source to illness as well as to health. Bribes for the one and against the other, it will not take. That is confusion. Follow the order of nature, for God's sake! Follow it! It will lead who follows; and those who will not, it will drag along anyway, and their tempers and their medicines with them. Get a purge for your brain. It will do better for you than for your stomach.

The Place of the Physician in Modern Society

WALTON H. HAMILTON   1881–1958

The organization of medicine is not a thing apart which can be subjected to study in isolation. It is an aspect of a culture whose arrangements are inseparable from the general organization of society.

The ways and means for putting medicine in order must take account of the conditions of life and work among the people whom it must serve. Nor is the organization of medicine a thing which is; it was only yesterday a very different affair; and, whether we assert control or leave it to drift, it will be something different tomorrow. Its reality can, no more than any other institution, be discovered in cross-section; its ills, no more than any other institution, can be successfully diagnosed by a static analysis. It is only as we see how it has come to be that we can appreciate what it is; it is only as we can direct its growth that we can control its future.

A single illustration must suffice to show how a genetic approach serves the end of analysis. The Report refers to the large amount of "free service" given to the indigent as if it were an isolated phenomenon. The practice goes back to the time when the doctor, regarding himself as the servant of the community, gave his services to all in accordance with their needs, and collected fees from each of his patients in accordance with his ability to pay. Thus "charity work" and "the sliding scale" came into existence together; they are complementary aspects of the single institution of the collective provision of the physician's income; if the one imposed upon him an obligation, the other extended to him its correlative right. Each has, by the course of events, been diverted from its original purpose. It may well be true that today "charity work" imposes upon many physicians an unreasonable amount of work for which they are not directly paid; but it is equally true that physicians share with other men the capacity to rationalize their own interests, and that in our modern world the sliding scale is an instrument easily capable of abuse. Above all, it is significant that the connection between the two has been broken, and that the older justifications are no longer relevant. The current problem lies neither in the excessive amount of free work — which for aught we know might well be larger — nor in an exorbitant rate of charges — which in certain income groups might well be much higher. It lies rather in our failure to contrive, as a substitute for the professional principle of earlier days, a scheme for paying the physician which is in accord with the modern conditions under which he has to work. As with so-called free service, so with other problems with which the Report is concerned; an historical account, in the service of analysis, will yield meaning and significance not to be found in a static picture.

And, as it is with the instance, so it is with the whole. An account of how it came into existence will throw the prevailing organization of medicine into clear-cut relief. There can be no personal responsibility for the many unlikeable features of medicine revealed in the Report. No individual, no group, professional or lay, is primarily to blame; for the system — or lack of system — which we know was never designed nor even intended. The elements which make it up were not cut to blueprints nor brought together into a prearranged pattern. Instead, like any other institution — government, church, business, or what not — they grew up quite adventitiously in response to the most immediate and the most diverse necessities. And again, like any other institution, the many parts which hail from many separate ages have come to be crudely fitted together with a sprawling organization. An ancient and honorable craft had become a profession; the profession has lived on into an epoch in which it has had to make its terms with, to employ pecuniary devices from, and to respond to the incentives of, business. And state enterprise, whether or not we approve, has already marked out for itself areas in the ancient domain. In fact, almost every type of control known to society is to be found somewhere within "the medical order." Along each of the seams of this conglomerate pattern a current problem is to be found. Structure has been defined as arrested function; and the problem of problems — which it is the essential task of this Committee to bring into the light — is the adjustment of this far-too-rigid and non-too-responsive organization to the social function which medicine must today be made to perform.

An epitome of the order and disorder which is medicine is to be observed in the plight into which private practice has been driven by the course of unintended events. In this country, up until near the turn of the century, the professional outlook and professional values were dominant. The "family doctor" was an institution; his trade was to him a sacred calling; his ideal imposed upon him the duty to serve all and commanded charity in judging human frailty. The patient attached himself to the physician; his loyalty was of a kind with that given to church or party; the desertion to a fellow practitioner demanded a personal explanation. The physician "built up" a fairly stable practice; he commanded a regular but rather modest income; he knew rather intimately the circumstances of his patients, and tempered his none-too-collectible charges with a studied neglect. In the relations between physician and patient, accounts were kept and money was passed; but, even though individuals might often depart from their ideals, the circumstances of the times and the ethics of the profession kept medicine rather free of commercialism.

If there has been a change, the physician is not primarily to blame. On the contrary, it is a tribute to the profession that the older idealism has exhibited such persistence in an unfavorable environment. The fault — if fault there be — is that the profession has now to be practiced in an industrial world dominated by business. Doctors, like others, must maintain standards of living, give opportunities to their children, and provide security for old age. They must have money incomes, and incomes are to be had by securing and holding patients in rivalry with their fellows. The result is that the pressure from the system within which they must live and work is slowly and insidiously, but rather surely, bringing to the physician a consciousness of his own pecuniary interests, making something more of a business man out of him, and converting the thing once called "private practice" into a system of individual business competition. The institution of medical business enterprise was never developed within the profession; it is an importation from the commercial world, at first tolerated, and then accepted, because there seemed to be no way to avoid it. Its very character is out of harmony with the spirit of the profession.

The incidence of competitive medical enterprise falls heavily upon all the parties concerned. Although "the personal choice of a physician" is an excellent ideal, it does not, under current conditions, work well in practice. An old maxim, long known to every student of social philosophy, calls for a restriction of personal choice when "the consumer is not a proper judge of the quality of the ware." The art of medicine is intricate; the relation of the treatment of the sick to results obtained cannot be appraised by a layman; in medicine, almost more certainly than anywhere else, the patient has not the knowledge requisite for judgment. In almost every city reputable physicians will admit — at least in private — that the competence of their fellows is not in accord with their respective reputations. However free the choice seems to be, it has its practical limit in available knowledge; and that patient usually does best who seeks advice from a professional. Values are treasured long after they have begun to depreciate; and the idea of "free choice" is much too individualistic to be easily surrendered. But its worth is to a large extent fictitious; and the expense and suffering which attends wrong choice and "shopping around" add greatly to the avoidable human costs of medicine.

Nor is the system of individual business enterprise fair to the practitioner. It gives him, if he is skllful or lucky, an opportunity to increase his practice, to extend his services, and to win a fair competence. It grants him a chance — hardly comparable with that of the banker, the business man, or even the lawyer — of winning an estate. But it forces him to practice his profession under the arrangements of an alien trade, to make his services to some extent articles of merchandise, and to respond so far as his standards permit to the acquisitive incentives of business. He cannot do his work in a conscientious way and have his competence appraised and his performance rewarded by colleagues who are competent to judge. Instead income, security, and advancement come to him — if they come at all — as the results of the expansion of a business and through the favor of a laity who do not possess rational standards of judgment. The situation makes it difficult for a physician to earn a living in a business community without yielding to its usages; and the stress and strain to which the code of medical ethics has of late been put indicates the difficulties by which the practitioner is being beset. Nor in an industrial community, in which livings are insecure, incomes are inadequate, and the doctor is almost the last to be paid, is the pressure likely to diminish. A great deal is now being said about "the rewards of private practice" as an urge to "the display of talents." But the case for acquisition as an incentive rests rather upon assertion than upon proof. We cannot know for certain; but I suspect that, aside from the alleviation of suffering, the strongest impulse which moves the physician is the professional motive of winning the esteem of his fellows. And I am inclined to believe that the ordinary physician is an artist who esteems, far more highly than the dubious chance at wealth, a regular and an adequate income, the feeling of security, and freedom to devote himself in an uncompromising way to his calling. The medical profession has, from time out of mind, disclaimed the acquisitive motive. If it is to be true to its high calling, the interests of patients and of physicians alike demand that it be kept out of business.

Here is the heart of the problem of the organization of medicine. A profession has, quite by an historical accident which was not foreseen, fallen into a world of business and is making the adaptation which seems necessary to survival. It has all come about so slowly and so much by stealth that the program of control essential to the maintenance of the integrity of the traditional ideal could not be formulated. As a result the older order of "private practice" is being transformed into a system of competitive enterprise, which no one has consciously willed and which in insidious ways interferes with the great social task which medicine is to perform. In a preindustrial era, medicine in the hands of private practitioners was a "public service." In the modern industrial world business enterprise must be sacrificed, if need be, in order that medicine may remain — or again become — a public service. The older ideals must persist, even at the cost of giving up an instrumentality which has proved valuable. This end is paramount; and I believe it can be attained only by a complete elimination of the aims and the arrangements for profit-making from the practice of the art.

It must, it is hardly necessary to say, comprehend the whole population. A division of labor on a continental scale has bound the fortunes of each of us with the operation of an intricate industrial system and has made us inseparably "members one of another." This interdependence has made the maintenance of the "common health" a public necessity as well as a social duty. If we are to make the most of our human resources, for work and for life, it is necessary that our facilities for health shall be just as available for all who need them as are the schools and the churches. Nor should the matter of a membership in a health service be left to the free choice of the individual. The "reasonable man" of our ancestors, who was prudent and provident and would always seek his own best advantage, now lives only as a fiction. To the myth I should make the concession of a semblance of a choice to mask the fact of compulsion. The matter has some importance; business succeeds rather better than the state in imposing its restraints upon individuals, because its imperatives are disguised as choices. But in essence the opportunity must be compulsory; for men have little capacity to organize in advance the conditions under which they live together; yet, once a new system is established, they easily accommodate their activities to it.

Here Hamilton is dissenting from the report of the majority of the Committee on American Medicine in 1932.

HANS ZINSSER   1878–1940

I remember one dark, rainy day when we buried a Russian doctor. A ragged band of Serbian reservists stood in the mud and played the Russian and Serbian anthems out of tune. The horses on the truck slipped as it was being loaded, and the coffin fell off. When the chanting procession finally disappeared over the hill, I was glad that the rain on my face obscured the tears that I could not hold back. I felt in my heart, then, that I never could or would be an observer, and that, whatever Fate had in store for me, I would always wish to be in the ranks, however humbly or obscurely; and it came upon me suddenly that I was profoundly happy in my profession, in which I would never aspire to administrative power or prominence so long as I could remain close, heart and hands, to the problems of disease.

P A R T
V I

HE LIVES WITH HIS FELLOWS

Profound student of the social life of insects, who has shown that they also can maintain complex communities without the use of reason.

A. LAWRENCE LOWELL, OF WILLIAM
MORTON WHEELER, CONFERRING
UPON HIM THE DEGREE OF DOCTOR
OF SCIENCE, HARVARD, 1930.

Ant-Heaps and Utopias

ARNOLD J. TOYNBEE   1889–

If we enter into the comparison, we shall discern in an
ant-heap and in a beehive, as well as in Plato's *Republic*
or in Mr. Aldous Huxley's *Brave New World* or in Mr.
H. G. Wells's fantasy of a lunar society, the same outstanding features that we have now learnt to recognize in
all the arrested civilizations which we have been studying. The two phenomena of caste and specialization,
and the fatally perfect adaptation of the society to its
particular environment which these two phenomena
bring about between them, are just as characteristic of
the Utopian and the Insect World as they are of the four
actual human societies, just examined, which have suffered arrest. And these resemblances are significant, since
the insect societies and the Utopias are both patently in
a state of arrested development likewise.

The social insects rose to their present social heights,
and came to a permanent standstill at those altitudes,
many millions of years before *Homo sapiens* began to
emerge above the mean level of the rank and file of the
Vertebrate Order. And as for the Utopias, they are static
not only as a matter of fact but *ex hypothesi*. For these
fictitious descriptions of imaginary human societies that
have never existed are really programmes of action mas-
querading in the disguise of descriptive sociology; and
the action which they are intended to evoke is the "peg-
ging," at a certain social level, of an actual society which

has broken down and has entered upon a decline that must end in a fall unless the downward movement can be artificially arrested. To arrest a downward movement is the utmost to which a Utopia can aspire, since Utopias seldom begin to be written in any society until after its members have lost the expectation and ambition of making further progress and have been cowed by adversity into being content if they can succeed in holding the ground which has been won for them by their fathers. Hence, in almost all Utopias — with the noteworthy exception of that work of English genius which has given this whole genre of literature its modern Western name — an invincibly stable equilibrium is the supreme social aim to which all other social values are subordinated and, if need be, sacrificed.

A. N. WHITEHEAD   1861–1947

A rock is nothing else than a society of molecules, indulging in every species of activity open to molecules. I draw attention to this lowly form of society in order to dispel the notion that social life is a peculiarity of the higher organisms. The contrary is the case. So far as survival value is concerned, a piece of rock, with its past history of some eight hundred millions of years, far outstrips the short span attained by any nation. The emergence of life is better conceived as a bid for freedom on the part of organisms, a bid for a certain independence of individuality with self-interests and activities not to be construed purely in terms of environmental obligations. The immediate effect of this emergence of sensitive individuality has been to reduce the term of life for societies from hundreds of millions of years to hundreds of years, or even to scores of years.

My main thesis is that a social system is kept together by the blind force of instinctive actions, and of instinctive emotions clustered around habits and prejudices. It is therefore not true that any advance in the scale of culture inevitably tends to the preservation of society. On the whole, the contrary is more often the case, and any survey of nature confirms this conclusion. A new element in life renders in many ways the operation of the old instincts unsuitable. But unexpressed instincts are unanalysed and blindly felt. Disruptive forces, introduced by a higher level of existence, are then warring in the dark against an invisible enemy. There is no foothold for the intervention of "rational consideration" — to use Henry Osborn Taylor's admirable phrase. The symbolic expression of instinctive forces drags them out into the open: it differentiates them and delineates them. There is then opportunity for reason to effect, with comparative speed, what otherwise must be left to the slow operation of the centuries amid ruin and reconstruction. Mankind misses its opportunities, and its failures are a fair target for ironic criticism. But the fact that reason too often fails does not give fair ground for the hysterical conclusion that it never succeeds. Reason can be compared to the force of gravitation, the weakest of all natural forces, but in the end the creator of suns and of stellar systems: — those great societies of the Universe. Symbolic expression first preserves society by adding emotion to instinct, and secondly it affords a foothold for reason by its delineation of the particular instinct which it expresses. This doctrine of the disruptive tendency due to novelties, even those involving a rise to finer levels, is illustrated by the effect of Christianity on the stability of the Roman Empire. It is also illustrated by the three revolutions which secured liberty and equality for the world — namely, the English revolutionary period of the seventeenth century, the American Revolution, and the French Revolution. England barely escaped a disruption of its social system; America was never in any such danger; France, where the entrance of novelty was most intense, did for a time experience this collapse. Edmund Burke, the Whig statesman of the eighteenth century, was the philosopher who was the approving prophet of the two earlier revolutions, and the denunciatory prophet of the French Revolution. A man of genius and a statesman, who has immediately observed two revolutions, and has meditated deeply on a third, deserves to be heard when he speaks on the forces which bind and disrupt societies.

Burke surveys the standing miracle of the existence of an organized society, culminating in the smooth unified action of the state. Such a society may consist of millions of individuals, each with its individual character, its individual aims, and its individual selfishness. He asks what is the force which leads this throng of separate units to co-operate in the maintenance of an organized state, in which each individual has his part to play — political, economic, and aesthetic. He contrasts the complexity of the functionings of a civilized society with the sheer diversities of its individual citizens considered as a mere group or crowd. His answer to the riddle is that the magnetic force is "prejudice," or in other words, "use and wont." Here he anticipates the whole modern theory of "herd psychology," and at the same time deserts the fundamental doctrine of the Whig Party, as formed in the seventeenth century and sanctioned by Locke. This conventional Whig doctrine was that the state derived its origin from an "original contract" whereby the mere crowd voluntarily organised itself into a society. Such a doctrine seeks the origin of the state in a baseless historical fiction. Burke was well ahead of his time in drawing attention to the importance of precedence as a political force. Unfortunately, in the excitement of the moment, Burke construed the importance of precedence as implying the negation of progressive reform.

Now, when we examine how a society bends its individual members to function in conformity with its needs, we discover that one important operative agency is our vast system of inherited symbolism. There is an intricate expressed symbolism of language and of act, which is spread throughout the community, and which evokes fluctuating apprehension of the basis of common purposes. The particular direction of individual action is directly correlated to the particular sharply defined symbols presented to him at the moment. The response of action to symbol may be so direct as to cut out any effective reference to the ultimate thing symbolized. This elimination of meaning is termed reflex action. Sometimes there does intervene some effective reference to the meaning of the symbol. But this meaning is not recalled with the particularity and definiteness which would yield any rational enlightenment as to the specific action required to secure the final end. The meaning is vague but insistent. Its insistence plays the part of hypnotizing the individual to complete the specific action associated with the symbol. In the whole transaction, the elements which are clear-cut and definite are the specific symbols and the actions which should issue from the symbols. But in themselves the symbols are barren facts whose direct associative force would be insufficient to procure automatic conformity. There is not sufficient repetition, or sufficient similarity of diverse occasions, to secure mere automatic obedience. But in fact the symbol evokes loyalties to vaguely conceived notions, fundamental for our spiritual natures. The result is that our natures are stirred to suspend all antagonistic impulses, so that the symbol procures its required response in action. Thus the social symbolism has a double meaning. It means pragmatically the direction of individuals to specific actions; and it also means theoretically the vague ultimate reasons with their emotional accompaniments, whereby the symbols acquire their power to organize the miscellaneous crowd into a smoothly running community.

ARISTOTLE   384–322 B.C.

Man is by nature a social animal, and an individual who is unsocial naturally and not accidentally is either beneath our notice or more than human. Society is something in nature that precedes the individual. Anyone who either cannot lead the common life or is so self-sufficient as not to need to, and therefore does not partake of society, is either a beast or he is a god.

Life is peculiar, said Jeremy. As compared with what? asked the Spider.

WILLIAM ALLEN WHITE   1868–1944

Let strong men be mean. Let weaklings be lazy and envious. Let the mediocre man be complacently befuddled. So it has always been. Put them to work side by side —

the grasping, the do-less, the bewildered. A hidden grace in each of them — perhaps tolerance or a shamefaced nobility or maybe an innate sense of fairness — amalgamates their baser qualities. A pattern of social conduct emerges, strange and full of friendly purpose. They who seem to be pulling and hauling, jostling and clamoring, have done a day's work that is somehow good. But they only are as competent and wise as they are free. So the wisdom of kindness — let us call it the love of man — comes to bless the labor.

JOHN MILTON   1608–1674

And as for you, citizens, it is of no small concern, what manner of men ye are, whether to acquire, or to keep possession of your liberty. Unless your liberty be of that kind which can neither be gotten nor taken away by arms (and that alone is such which, springing from piety, justice, temperance, in fine from real virtue, shall take deep and intimate root in your minds), you may be assured that there will not be wanting one who, even without arms, will speedily deprive you of what it is your boast to have gained by force of arms. For know (that you may not feel resentment, or be able to blame anybody but yourselves) that as to be free is precisely the same thing as to be pious, wise, just, and temperate, careful of one's own, abstinent from what is another's, and thence, in fine, magnanimous and brave — so to be the opposite of these is the same thing as to be a slave; and by the wonted judgment and as it were by the just retribution of God, it comes to pass that the nation, which has been incapable of governing and ordering itself, and has delivered itself up to the slavery of its own lusts, is itself delivered over against its will to other masters — and whether it will or no is compelled to serve.

What Is Liberty?

WOODROW WILSON   1856–1924

I have long had an image in my mind of what constitutes liberty. Suppose that I were building a great piece of powerful machinery, and suppose that I should so awkwardly and unskilfully assemble the parts of it that every time one part tried to move it would be interfered with by the others, and the whole thing would buckle up and be checked. Liberty for the several parts would consist in the best possible assembling and adjustment of them all, would it not? If you want the great piston of the engine to run with absolute freedom, give it absolutely perfect alignment and adjustment with the other parts of the machine, so that it is free not because it is let alone or isolated, but because it has been associated most skilfully and carefully with the other parts of the great structure.

What is liberty? You say of the locomotive that it runs free. What do you mean? You mean that its parts are so assembled and adjusted that friction is reduced to a minimum, and that it has perfect adjustment. We say of a boat skimming the water with light foot, "How free she runs," when we mean, how perfectly she is adjusted to the force of the wind, how perfectly she obeys the great breath out of the heavens that fills her sails. Throw her head up into the wind and see how she will halt and stagger, how every sheet will shiver and her whole frame be shaken, how instantly she is "in irons," in the expressive phrase of the sea. She is free only when you have let her fall off again and have recovered once more her nice adjustment to the forces she must obey and cannot defy.

Human freedom consists in perfect adjustments of human interests and human activities and human energies.

Honey Bees

SHAKESPEARE 1564–1616

> *So work the honey bees,*
> *Creatures that by a rule in nature teach*
> *The act of order to a peopled kingdom.*
> *They have a king and officers of sorts;*
> *Where some, like magistrates, correct at home;*
> *Others, like merchants, venture trade abroad;*

> *Others, like soldiers, armed in their stings,*
> *Make boot upon the summer's velvet buds.*
> *Which pillage they with merry march bring home*
> *To the tent royal of their emperor*
> *Who, busied in his majesty, surveys*
> *The singing masons building roofs of gold,*
> *The civil citizens kneading up the honey,*
> *The poor mechanic porters crowding in*
> *Their heavy burdens at his narrow gate,*
> *The sad-ey'd justice, with his surly hum,*
> *Delivering o'er to executors pale*
> *The lazy yawning drone.*

The Communist Manifesto

KARL MARX AND FRIEDRICH ENGELS 1818–1883, 1820–1895

The bourgeoisie has been the first to show what man's activity can bring about. It has accomplished wonders far surpassing Egyptian pyramids, Roman aqueducts, and Gothic cathedrals; it has conducted expeditions that put in the shade all former Exoduses of nations and crusades.

The bourgeoisie has through its exploitation of the world-market given a cosmopolitan character to production and consumption in every country. To the great chagrin of reactionists, it has drawn from under the feet of industry the national ground on which it stood. All old-established national industries have been destroyed or are daily being destroyed. They are dislodged by new industries, whose introduction becomes a life-and-death question for all civilized nations, by industries that no longer work up indigenous raw material, but raw material drawn from the remotest zones; industries whose products are consumed, not only at home, but in every quarter of the globe. In place of the old wants, satisfied by the productions of the country, we find new wants, requiring for their satisfaction the products of distant lands and climes. In place of the old local and national seclusion and self-sufficiency, we have intercourse in every direction, universal interdependence of nations. And as in material, so also in intellectual production. The intellectual creations of individual nations become common property. National one-sidedness and narrow-mindedness become more and more impossible, and from the numerous national and local literatures there arises a world-literature.

The bourgeoisie, by the rapid improvement of all instruments of production, by the immensely facilitated means of communication, draws all, even the most barbarian, nations into civilization. The cheap prices of its commodities are the heavy artillery with which it batters down all Chinese walls, with which it forces the barbarians' intensely obstinate hatred of foreigners to capitulate. It compels all nations, on pain of extinction, to adopt the bourgeois mode of production; it compels them to introduce what it calls civilization into their midst, i.e., to become bourgeois themselves. In a word, it creates a world after its own image.

The bourgeoisie keeps more and more doing away with the scattered state of the population, of the means of production, and of property. It has agglomerated population, centralized means of production, and has concentrated property in a few hands. The necessary consequence of this was political centralization. Independent, or but loosely connected provinces, with separate interests, laws, governments, and systems of taxation, become lumped together in one nation, with one government, one code of laws, one national class-interest, one frontier and one customs-tariff.

The bourgeoisie, during its rule of scarce one hundred years, has created more massive and more colossal productive forces than have all preceding generations together. Subjection of Nature's forces to man, machinery, application of chemistry to industry and agriculture, steam navigation, railways, electric telegraphs, clearing of whole continents for cultivation, canalization of rivers, whole populations conjured out of the ground — what earlier century had even a presentiment that such productive forces slumbered in the lap of social labor?

Modern bourgeois society with its relations of production, of exchange and of property, a society that has conjured up such gigantic means of production and of exchange, is like the sorcerer, who is no longer able to control the powers of the nether world whom he has called up by his spells. For many a decade past the history of industry and commerce is but the history of the revolt of modern productive forces against modern conditions of production, against the property relations that are the conditions for the existence of the bourgeoisie and of its rule. It is enough to mention the commercial crises that by their periodical return put on its trial, each time more threateningly, the existence of the entire bourgeois society. In these crises a great part not only of the existing products, but also of the previously created productive forces, are periodically destroyed. In these crises there breaks out an epidemic that, in all earlier epochs, would have seemed an absurdity — the epidemic of over-production. Society suddenly finds itself put back into a state of momentary barbarism; it appears as if a famine, a universal war of devastation, had cut off the supply of every means of subsistence; industry and commerce seem to be destroyed; and why? Because there is too much civilization, too much means of subsistence, too much industry, too much commerce. The productive forces at the disposal of society no longer tend to further the development of the conditions of bourgeois property; on the contrary, they have become too powerful for these conditions, by which they are fettered, and so soon as they overcome these fetters, they bring disorder into the whole of bourgeois society, endanger the existence of bourgeois property. The conditions of bourgeois society are too narrow to comprise the wealth created by them. And how does the bourgeoisie get over these crises? On the one hand by enforced destruction of a mass of productive forces; on the other, by the conquest of new markets, and by the more thorough exploitation of the old ones. That is to say, by paving the way for more extensive and more destructive crises, and by diminishing the means whereby crises are prevented.

The weapons with which the bourgeoisie felled feu-

dalism to the ground are now turned against the bourgeoisie itself.

But not only has the bourgeoisie forged the weapons
that bring death to itself; it has also called into existence
the men who are to wield those weapons — the modern
working-class — the proletarians.

In proportion as the bourgeoisie, i.e., capital, is developed, in the same proportion is the proletariat, the modern working-class, developed, a class of laborers, who live
only so long as they find work, and who find work only
so long as their labor increases capital. These laborers,
who must sell themselves piecemeal, are a commodity,
like every other article of commerce, and are consequently exposed to all the vicissitudes of competition, to
all fluctuations of the market.

The lower strata of the middle class — the small trades-
people, shopkeepers, and retired tradesmen generally,
the handicraftsmen and peasants — all these sink gradually into the proletariat, partly because their diminutive
capital does not suffice for the scale on which modern
industry is carried on, and is swamped in the competition
with the large capitalists, partly because their specialized
skill is rendered worthless by new methods of production. Thus the proletariat is recruited from all classes of
the population.

With the development of industry the proletariat not
only increases in number, it becomes concentrated in
greater masses, its strength grows, and it feels that
strength more. The various interests and conditions of
life within the ranks of the proletariat are more and
more equalized, in proportion as machinery obliterates
all distinctions of labor, and nearly everywhere reduces
wages to the same low level. The growing competition
among the bourgeois, and the resulting commercial crises,
make the wages of the workers ever more fluctuating.
The unceasing improvement of machinery, ever more
rapidly developing, makes their livelihood more and
more precarious; the collisions between individual workmen and individual bourgeois take more and more the
character of collisions between two classes. Thereupon

the workers begin to form combinations against the bourgeois; they club together in order to keep up the rate of wages; they found permanent associations in order to make provision beforehand for these occasional revolts. Here and there the contest breaks out into riots.

Now and then the workers are victorious, but only for a time. The real fruit of their battles lies, not in the immediate result, but in the ever-expanding union of the workers. This union is helped on by the improved means of communication that are created by modern industry, and that place the workers of different localities in contact with one another. It was just this contact that was needed to centralize the numerous local struggles, all of the same character, into one national struggle between classes. But every class struggle is a political struggle. And that union, to attain which the burghers of the Middle Ages, with their miserable highways, required centuries, the modern proletarians, thanks to railways, achieve in a few years.

This organization of the proletarians into a class, and consequently into a political party, is continually being upset again by the competition between the workers themselves. But it ever rises up again, stronger, firmer, mightier. It compels legislative recognition of particular interests of the workers, by taking advantage of the divisions among the bourgeoisie itself.

Finally, in times when the class-struggle nears the decisive hour, the process of dissolution going on within the ruling class, in fact, within the whole range of old society, assumes such a violent, glaring character, that a small section of the ruling class cuts itself adrift, and joins the revolutionary class, the class that holds the future in its hands. Just as, therefore, at an earlier period, a section of the nobility went over to the bourgeoisie, so now a portion of the bourgeoisie goes over to the proletariat, and in particular, a portion of the bourgeois ideologists, who have raised themselves to the level of comprehending theoretically the historical movements as a whole.

Of all the classes that stand face to face with the bourgeoisie today, the proletariat alone is a really revolutionary class. The other classes decay and finally disappear in the face of modern industry; the proletariat is its special and essential product.

The proletarian is without property; his relation to his wife and children has no longer anything in common with the bourgeois family relations; modern industrial labor, modern subjection to capital, the same in England as in France, in America as in Germany, has stripped him of every trace of national character. Law, morality, religion, are to him so many bourgeois prejudices, behind which lurk in ambush just as many bourgeois interests.

All the preceding classes that got the upper hand sought to fortify their already acquired status by subjecting society at large to their conditions of appropriation. The proletarians cannot become masters of the productive forces of society, except by abolishing their own previous mode of appropriation, and thereby also every other previous mode of appropriation. They have nothing of their own to secure and to fortify; their mission is to destroy all previous securities for, and insurances of, individual property.

All previous historical movements were movements of minorities, or in the interest of minorities. The proletarian movement is the self-conscious, independent movement of the immense majority, in the interest of the immense majority. The proletariat, the lowest stratum of our present society, cannot stir, cannot raise itself up, without the whole superincumbent strata of official society being sprung into the air.

Hitherto, every form of society has been based, as we have already seen, on the antagonism of oppressing and oppressed classes. But in order to oppress a class, certain conditions must be assured to it under which it can, at least, continue its slavish existence. The serf, in the period of serfdom, raised himself to membership in the commune, just as the petty bourgeois, under the yoke of feudal absolutism, managed to develop into a bourgeois. The modern laborer, on the contrary, instead of rising with the progress of industry, sinks deeper and deeper below the conditions of existence of his own class. He becomes a pauper, and pauperism develops more rapidly than population and wealth. And here it becomes evident that the bourgeoisie is unfit any longer to be the ruling class in society, and to impose its conditions of existence upon society as an overriding law. It is unfit to rule, because it is incompetent to assure an existence to its slave within his slavery, because it cannot help letting him sink into such a state that it has to feed him, instead of being fed by him. Society can no longer live under this bourgeoisie; in other words, its existence is no longer compatible with society.

The essential condition for the existence and for the sway of the bourgeois class is the formation and augmentation of capital; the condition for capital is wage-labor. Wage-labor rests exclusively on competition between the laborers. The advance of industry, whose involuntary promoter is the bourgeoisie, replaces the isolation of the laborers, due to competition, by their involuntary combination, due to association. The development of modern industry, therefore, cuts from under its feet the very foundation on which the bourgeoisie produces and appropriates products. What the bourgeoisie therefore produces, above all, are its own grave-diggers. Its fall and the victory of the proletariat are equally inevitable.

The distinguishing feature of Communism is not the abolition of property generally, but the abolition of bourgeois property. But modern bourgeois private property is the final and most complete expression of the system of producing and appropriating products, that is based on class-antagonism, on the exploitation of the many by the few.

In this sense, the theory of the Communists may be summed up in the single sentence: Abolition of private property.

We Communists have been reproached with the desire of abolishing the right of personally acquiring property as the fruit of a man's own labor, which property is alleged to be the groundwork of all personal freedom, activity, and independence.

Hard-won, self-acquired, self-earned property! Do you mean the property of the petty artisan and of the small peasant, a form of property that preceded the bourgeois form? There is no need to abolish that; the development of industry has to a great extent already destroyed it, and is still destroying it daily.

Or do you mean modern bourgeois private property?

But does wage-labor create any property for the laborer? Not a bit. It creates capital, i.e., that kind of property which exploits wage-labor, and which cannot increase except upon condition of getting a new supply of wage-labor for fresh exploitation. Property, in its present form, is based on the antagonism of capital and wage-labor. Let us examine both sides of this antagonism.

To be a capitalist is to have not only a purely personal, but a social, status in production. Capital is a collective product, and only by the united action of many members, nay, in the last resort, only by the united action of all members of society, can it be set in motion.

Capital is therefore not a personal, it is a social power.

When, therefore, capital is converted into common property, into the property of all members of society, personal property is not thereby transformed into social property. It is only the social character of the property that is changed. It loses its class-character.

Let us now take wage-labor.

The average price of wage-labor is the minimum wage, i.e., that quantum of the means of subsistence which is absolutely requisite to keep the laborer in bare existence as a laborer. What, therefore, the wage-laborer appropriates by means of his labor merely suffices to prolong and reproduce a bare existence. We by no means intend to abolish this personal appropriation of the products of labor, an appropriation that is made for the maintenance and reproduction of human life, and that leaves no surplus wherewith to command the labor of others. All that we want to do away with is the miserable character of this appropriation, under which the laborer lives merely to increase capital, and is allowed to live only in so far as the interest of the ruling class requires it.

In bourgeois society, living labor is but a means to increase accumulated labor. In Communist society, accumulated labor is but a means to widen, to enrich, to promote the existence of the laborer.

In bourgeois society, therefore, the past dominates the present; in Communist society, the present dominates the past. In bourgeois society, capital is independent and has individuality, while the living person is dependent and has no individuality.

And the abolition of this state of things is called, by the bourgeois, abolition of individuality and freedom! And rightly so. The abolition of bourgeois individuality, bourgeois independence, and bourgeois freedom is undoubtedly aimed at.

By freedom is meant, under the present bourgeois conditions of production, free trade, free selling and buying.

But if selling and buying disappear, free selling and buying disappear also. This talk about free selling and buying, and all the other "brave words" of our bourgeoisie about freedom in general, have a meaning, if any, only in contrast with restricted selling and buying, with the fettered traders of the Middle Ages, but have no meaning when opposed to the Communistic abolition of buying and selling, of the bourgeois conditions of production, and of the bourgeoisie itself.

You are horrified at our intending to do away with private property. But in your existing society, private property is already done away with for nine-tenths of the population; its existence for the few is solely due to its non-existence in the hands of those nine-tenths. You reproach us, therefore, with intending to do away with a form of property, the necessary condition for whose existence is the non-existence of any property for the immense majority of society.

In one word, you reproach us with intending to do

away with your property. Precisely so; that is just what we intend.

The Communists disdain to conceal their views and aims. They openly declare that their ends can be attained only by the forcible overthrow of all existing social conditions. Let the ruling classes tremble at a Communistic revolution. The proletarians have nothing to lose but their chains. They have a world to win.

Working men of all countries, unite!

Private Property, Foundation of Liberty

WALTER LIPPMANN   1889–

It has been the fashion to speak of the conflict between human rights and property rights, and from this it has come to be widely believed that the cause of private property is tainted with evil and should not be espoused by rational and civilized men. In so far as these ideas refer to plutocratic property, to great impersonal corporate properties, they make sense. These are not in reality private properties. They are public properties privately controlled, and they have either to be reduced to genuinely private properties or to be publicly controlled. But the issue between the giant corporation and the public should not be allowed to obscure the truth that the only dependable foundation of personal liberty is the personal economic security of private property.

The teaching of history is very certain on this point. It was in the mediaeval doctrine that to kings belong authority, but to private persons, property, that the way was discovered to limit the authority of the king and to promote the liberties of the subject. Private property was the original source of freedom. It is still its main bulwark. Recent experience confirms this truth. Where men have yielded without serious resistance to the tyranny of new dictators, it is because they have lacked property. They dare not resist because resistance meant destitution. The lack of a strong middle class in Russia, the impoverishment of the middle class in Italy, the ruin of the middle class in Germany, are the real reasons, much more than the ruthlessness of the Black Shirts, the Brown Shirts, and the Red Army, why the state has become absolute and individual liberty is suppressed. What maintains liberty in France, in Scandinavia, and in the English-speaking countries is more than any other thing the great mass of people who are independent because they have, as Aristotle said, "a moderate and sufficient property." They resist the absolute state. An official, a teacher, a scholar, a minister, a journalist, all those whose business it is to make articulate and to lead opinion, will act the part of free men if they can resign or be discharged without subjecting their wives, their children, and themselves to misery and squalor.

For we must not expect to find in ordinary men the stuff of martyrs, and we must, therefore, secure their freedom by their normal motives. There is no surer way to give men the courage to be free than to insure them a competence upon which they can rely. Men cannot be made free by laws unless they are in fact free because no man can buy and no man can coerce them. That is why the Englishman's belief that his home is his castle and that the king cannot enter it, like the American's conviction that he must be able to look any man in the eye and tell him to go to hell, are the very essence of the free man's way of life.

Monkeying Around

LEARNED HAND   1872–1961

A society in which each is willing to surrender only that for which he can see a personal equivalent is not a society at all; it is a group already in process of dissolution, and no one need concern himself to stay its inevitable end; it would be a hard choice between it and a totalitarian society. No Utopia, nothing but Bedlam, will automatically emerge from a régime of unbridled individualism, be it ever so rugged.

What, then, you will ask, am I really talking about? If it be true that any orthodoxy can be implanted in us, provided we are caught and schooled while young, or provided even in our later years that we are subjected to the everlasting iteration of sacred rubrics, in school, in press, in moving picture, and by radio; and if, when we have been so "conditioned," we feel authority to be no restraint, but rather a means toward the realization of our deeper self; and if something of the sort is essential to survival in a robbers' world, where the strong are sure to win; if all these things be true, why should we boggle about any other liberty; what more do we need? That other societies so organized have been predatory does not mean that we need be predacious; our communal self can become the chalice for a more exquisite liquor of civilization than the troubled world has yet seen. In our Father's house are many mansions; we will occupy one where life shall be seemly and noble and forbearing and happy and gay; yet strong enough withal to resist any aggression.

Some day such a vision may come true; the future may have in store aeons of beatitude in which men shall find utter self-realization and utter self-expression in the utter self-surrender of the hive; I do not forget the words of the collect: "Whose service is perfect freedom." Be that as it may, it is not on the score of its impracticability that I do not welcome that prospect; but because I believe that its realization would suppress the most precious part of our nature. To put it very baldly, and perhaps a little contentiously, it is man's inherent willfulness that I would preserve, and in which I wish to set the stronghold of that liberty I prize; that stone which social reformers have always rejected, I would make the head of the corner.

I cannot tell why to me personally such a society seems stifling; I only know that, although with Epictetus I can say, "If I were an ant, I should play the part of an ant," in fact I am not an ant, and if I try to play the part of an ant I know that I shall end in the care of a psychoanalyst. I will own that when on occasion I visit my simian cousins in captivity, the spectacle does not refresh me. Not only have they a distressing lack of reserve, but their restlessness affects me with a homeopathic uneasiness. Kipling seems right, and I wince that we have so many family traits in common. My kinship with them becomes even more distasteful when I pass to the cages of the great cats, who lie there serenely with their steady yellow eyes, calm, self-secure, fearing nothing. Why must my cousins and I be so agitated; why this ceaseless, errant curiosity; pausing only for an instant, and then off to something new? It is all very trying; and yet here will I pitch my tent.

James Harvey Robinson used to say that we rose from the ape because like him we kept "monkeying around," always meddling with everything about us. True, there is a difference, because, although the ape meddles, he forgets, and we have learned, first to meddle and remember, and then to meddle and record. But without the meddling nothing would have happened of all that glorious array of achievement: battleships, aeroplanes, relativity, the proton, neutron, and electron, T.N.T., poison gas, sulfathiazole, the *Fifth Symphony, The Iliad, The Divine Comedy, Hamlet, Faust, The Critique of Pure Reason, Das Kapital,* the Constitution of the United States, the Congress of Industrial Organizations, Huey Long, and the New Deal. All these from just "monkeying around!"

My thesis is that any organization of society which depresses free and spontaneous meddling is on the decline, however showy its immediate spoils; I maintain that in such a society Liberty is gone, little as its members may know it; that the Nirvana of the individual is too high a price for a collective Paradise.

How Athens?

WILLIAM S. FERGUSON   1875–1954

The golden age of Greece is, properly speaking, a golden age of Athens, and to its birth many things contributed; but decisive among them, in addition to the intensity of national life already alluded to, was an unrivaled facility for great leaders to get into effective contact with the masses under conditions in which there was the fullest opportunity for men in general to use their natural powers to the utmost. This happy combination of creative genius and receptive multitude arose in the main from the democratic institutions of Athens; but, for the public and private wealth without which Athenian democracy proved unworkable, and for the imaginative stimulus which enterprises of great pitch and moment alone give, the possession of empire was, perhaps, essential.

Pericles' Funeral Oration

THUCYDIDES   471–400 B.C.

And when this power of the city shall seem great to you, consider then, that the same was purchased by valiant men, and by men that knew their duty, and by men that were sensible of dishonour when they were in flight; and by such men, as though they failed of their attempt, yet would not be wanting to the city with their virtue, but made unto it a most honorable contribution. For having every one given his body to the commonwealth, they receive in place thereof an undecaying commendation and a most remarkable sepulchre; not wherein they are buried so much, as wherein their glory is laid up, upon all occasions both of speech and action to be remembered for ever. For to famous men all the earth is a sepulchre: and their virtues shall be testified, not only by the inscription in stone at home, but by an unwritten record of the mind, which more than of any monument will remain with every one for ever. In imitation therefore of these men, and placing happiness in liberty, and liberty in valor, be forward to encounter the dangers of war.

LOUIS D. BRANDEIS   1856–1941

Those who won our independence believed that the final end of the State was to make men free to develop their faculties; and that in its government the deliberative forces should prevail over the arbitrary. They valued liberty both as an end and as a means. *They believed liberty to be the secret of happiness and courage to be the secret of liberty.* They believed that freedom to think as you will and to speak as you think are means indispensable to the discovery and spread of political truth; that without free speech and assembly discussion would be futile; that with them, discussion affords ordinarily adequate protection against the dissemination of noxious doctrine; that the greatest menace to freedom is an inert people; that public discussion is a political duty; and that this should be a fundamental principle of the American government.

In Praise of Controversy and Heresy

WILLIAM H. AUDEN   1907–

In a civilized society, that is, one in which a common faith is combined with a skepticism about its finality, and which agrees with Pascal that "Nier, croire, et douter bien sont à l'homme ce que le courir est au cheval," orthodoxy can only be secured by a co-operation of which free controversy is an essential part.

For what at the time appears to be a heresy never arises without a cause. Either it is a real advance on the old orthodoxy (for example, the Copernican cosmogony was an advance on the Ptolemaic) or it is an unsatisfactory reaction to a real abuse (for example, Manicheeism was an intellectual heresy caused by the moral corruption of the relatively orthodox church). Persecution is futile in either case: in the first because the persecutor is wrong, and in the second because he is only suppressing a symptom while leaving the cause of disease untouched.

Free Trade in Ideas

O. W. HOLMES, JR.   1841–1935

In this case sentences of twenty years imprisonment have been imposed for the publishing of two leaflets that I believe the defendants had as much right to publish as the Government has to publish the Constitution of the United States now vainly invoked by them. Even if I am technically wrong and enough can be squeezed from

these poor and puny anonymities to turn the color of
legal litmus paper; I will add, even if what I think the
necessary intent were shown; the most nominal punishment seems to me all that possibly could be inflicted, unless the defendants are to be made to suffer, not for what
the indictment alleges, but for the creed that they avow
— a creed that I believe to be the creed of ignorance
and immaturity when honestly held, as I see no reason
to doubt that it was held here, but which, although made
the subject of examination at the trial, no one has a right
even to consider in dealing with the charges before the
Court.

Persecution for the expression of opinions seems to
me perfectly logical. If you have no doubt of your premises
or your power and want a certain result with all your
heart, you naturally express your wishes in law and sweep
away all opposition. To allow opposition by speech seems
to indicate that you think the speech impotent, as when
a man says that he has squared the circle, or that you do
not care wholeheartedly for the result, or that you doubt
either your power or your premises. But when men have
realized that time has upset many fighting faiths, they
may come to believe even more than they believe the
very foundations of their own conduct that the ultimate good desired is better reached by free trade in ideas
— that the best test of truth is the power of the thought
to get itself accepted in the competition of the market,
and that truth is the only ground upon which their wishes
safely can be carried out. That at any rate is the theory
of our Constitution. It is an experiment, as all life is an
experiment. Every year if not every day we have to wager
our salvation upon some prophecy based upon imperfect
knowledge. While that experiment is part of our system,
I think that we should be eternally vigilant against attempts to check the expression of opinions that we loathe
and believe to be fraught with death, unless they so im-
minently threaten immediate interference with the lawful and pressing purposes of the law that an immediate
check is required to save the country. . . . I regret that
I cannot put into more impressive words my belief that

in their conviction upon this indictment the defendants were deprived of their rights under the Constitution of the United States.

This is from Holmes's opinion in the Abrams case in 1919. It was about one of the Espionage Act cases that Holmes wrote Pollock:

I hope we have heard the last, or nearly the last, of the Espionage Act cases. Some of our subordinate Judges seem to me to have been hysterical during the war. It is one of the ironies that I, who probably take the extremest view in favor of free speech (in which, in the abstract, I have no very enthusiastic belief, though I hope I would die for it), that I should have been selected for blowing up.

ARCHIBALD MACLEISH   1892–

Criticism in a free man's country is made on certain assumptions, one of which is the assumption that the government belongs to the people and is at all times subject to the people's correction and criticism — correction and criticism such as a man gives, and should give, those who represent him and undertake to act on his behalf. Criticism of the government made upon that basis is proper criticism, no matter how abusive. But abuse of a representative government made, not upon that assumption, but upon the assumption that the government is one thing and the people another — that the President is one thing and the people who elected the President another — that the Congress is one thing and the people who elected the Congress another — that the executive departments are one thing and the people whom the departments serve another — abuse of a representative government made with the implication that the government is something outside the people, or opposed to the people, something the people should fear and hate — abuse of that kind is not "criticism" and no amount of editorial self-justification can make it sound as though it were.

Liberty and Religion

PERRY MILLER   1954

The universities and churches of Germany, we know, have been put to a hard school to learn the lesson of freedom. I like to think that in the darkest of their days some of them might have remembered the University of Jena on November 7, 1825. That was the day on which Duke Karl-August of Saxe-Weimar held a civic celebration of the fiftieth anniversary of Goethe's coming to court. No doubt the University was disposed to please its patron, but its performance on this grandiose occasion was not obsequious. The Faculties of Philosophy and Medicine bestowed honorary degrees of Doctor; the Faculty of Law would have voted Goethe one did he not already have a Doctorate from Strasbourg — this being a naïve time it was thought that one degree of each kind, even honorary, was enough! But the Faculty of Theology was in a bit of a quandary: somehow a Doctorate of Theology did not seem quite appropriate for Goethe. So they resolved to give him instead an inscribed diploma, which Goethe prized above all the gifts he received on that bountiful day. They said:

> *Your Excellency has not only often elevated our peculiar branch of knowledge, and the principles on which it rests, by profound, enlightened, and awakening remarks, but, as creator of a new spirit in science and in life, and as lord of the domain of free and vigorous thought, has powerfully promoted the true interests of the church and of evangelical theology.*

The vexed problem of religion and freedom of the mind might be immensely clarified if and when it can be stoutly declared in this country that the Faculty's statement is profoundly religious.

We Live by Symbols

Mr. Justice FRANKFURTER *delivered the opinion of the Court:*   1940

A grave responsibility confronts this Court whenever in course of litigation it must reconcile the conflicting claims of liberty and authority. But when the liberty invoked is liberty of conscience, and the authority is authority to safeguard the nation's fellowship, judicial conscience is put to its severest test. Of such a nature is the present controversy.

Lillian Gobitis, aged twelve, and her brother William, aged ten, were expelled from the public schools of Minersville, Pennsylvania, for refusing to salute the national flag as part of a daily school exercise. The local Board of Education required both teachers and pupils to participate in this ceremony. The ceremony is a familiar one. The right hand is placed on the breast and the following pledge recited in unison: "I pledge allegiance to my flag, and to the Republic for which it stands; one nation indivisible, with liberty and justice for all." While the words are spoken, teachers and pupils extend their right hands in salute to the flag. The Gobitis family are affiliated with "Jehovah's Witnesses," for whom the Bible as the Word of God is the supreme authority. The children had been brought up conscientiously to believe that such a gesture of respect for the flag was forbidden by command of scripture. Reliance is especially placed on the following verses from Chapter 20 of Exodus: "3. Thou shalt have no other gods before me. 4. Thou shalt not make unto thee any graven image, or any likeness of anything that is in heaven above, or that is in the earth beneath, or that is in the water under the earth: 5. Thou shalt not bow down thyself to them, nor serve them."

We must decide whether the requirement of participation in such a ceremony, exacted from a child who refuses upon sincere religious grounds, infringes without due process of law the liberty guaranteed by the Fourteenth Amendment.

Certainly the affirmative pursuit of one's convictions about the ultimate mystery of the universe and man's relation to it is placed beyond the reach of law. Government may not interfere with organized or individual expression of belief or disbelief. Propagation of belief — or even of disbelief in the supernatural — is protected, whether in church or chapel, mosque or synagogue, tabernacle or meetinghouse.

But the manifold character of man's relations may bring his conception of religious duty into conflict with the secular interests of his fellow-men. When does the constitutional guarantee compel exemption from doing what society thinks necessary for the promotion of some great common end, or from a penalty for conduct which appears dangerous to the general good? To state the problem is to recall the truth that no single principle can answer all of life's complexities. The right to freedom of religious belief, however dissident and however obnoxious to the cherished beliefs of others — even of a majority — is itself the denial of an absolute. But to affirm that the freedom to follow conscience has itself no limits in the life of a society would deny that very plurality of principles which, as a matter of history, underlies protection of religious toleration.

Situations like the present are phases of the profoundest problem confronting a democracy — the problem which Lincoln cast in memorable dilemma: "Must a government of necessity be too *strong* for the liberties of its people, or too *weak* to maintain its own existence?" No mere textual reading or logical talisman can solve the dilemma.

The case before us is not concerned with an exertion of legislative power for the promotion of some specific need or interest of secular society — the protection of the family, the promotion of health, the common defense, the raising of public revenues to defray the cost of government. But all these specific activities of government presuppose the existence of an organized political society. The ultimate foundation of a free society is the binding tie of cohesive sentiment. Such a sentiment is fostered by all those agencies of the mind and spirit which may serve to gather up the traditions of a people, transmit them from generation to generation, and thereby create that continuity of a treasured common life which constitutes a civilization. "We live by symbols." The flag is the symbol of our national unity, transcending all internal differences, however large, within the framework of the Constitution.

Except where the transgression of constitutional liberty is too plain for argument, personal freedom is best maintained — so long as the remedial channels of the democratic process remain open and unobstructed — when it is ingrained in a people's habits and not enforced against popular policy by the coercion of adjudicated law.

The preciousness of the family relation, the authority and independence which give dignity to parenthood, indeed the enjoyment of all freedom, presuppose the kind of ordered society which is summarized by our flag. A society which is dedicated to the preservation of these ultimate values of civilization may in self-protection utilize the educational process for inculcating those almost unconscious feelings which bind men together in a comprehending loyalty, whatever may be their lesser differences and difficulties. That is to say, the process may be utilized so long as men's rights to believe as they please, to win others to their way of belief, and their right to assemble in their chosen places of worship for the devotional ceremonies of their faith, are all fully respected.

Judicial review, itself a limitation on popular government, is a fundamental part of our constitutional scheme. But to the legislature no less than to courts is committed the guardianship of deeply cherished liberties. Where all the effective means of inducing political changes are left free from interference, education in the abandonment of foolish legislation is itself a training in liberty. To fight out the wise use of legislative authority in the forum of public opinion and before legislative assemblies rather than to transfer such a contest to the judicial arena, serves to vindicate the self-confidence of a free people.

Reversed.

Three years later, the Gobitis decision was overruled in the Barnette case, and the Court had this to say, by Mr. Justice JACKSON, *in reply to Frankfurter:* 1943

Government of limited power need not be anemic government. Assurance that rights are secure tends to diminish fear and jealousy of strong government, and by making us feel safe to live under it makes for its better support. Without promise of a limiting Bill of Rights it is doubtful if our Constitution could have mustered enough strength to enable its ratification. To enforce those rights is not to choose weak government over strong government. It is only to adhere as a means of strength to individual freedom of mind in preference to officially disciplined uniformity for which history indicates a disappointing and disastrous end.

The subject now before us exemplifies this principle. Free public education, if faithful to the ideal of secular instruction and political neutrality, will not be partisan or enemy of any class, creed, party, or faction. If it is to impose any ideological discipline, however, each party or denomination must seek to control, or failing that, to weaken the influence of the educational system. Observance of the limitations of the Constitution will not weaken government in the field appropriate for its exercise.

The very purpose of a Bill of Rights was to withdraw certain subjects from the vicissitudes of political controversy, to place them beyond the reach of majorities and officials and to establish them as legal principles to be applied by the courts. One's right to life, liberty, and property, to free speech, a free press, freedom of worship and assembly, and other fundamental rights may not be submitted to vote; they depend on the outcome of no elections.

The task of translating the majestic generalities of the Bill of Rights, conceived as part of the pattern of liberal government in the eighteenth century, into concrete restraints on officials dealing with the problems of the twentieth century, is one to disturb self-confidence.

These principles grew in soil which also produced a philosophy that the individual was the center of society, that his liberty was attainable through mere absence of governmental restraints, and that government should be entrusted with few controls and only the mildest supervision over men's affairs. We must transplant these rights to a soil in which the *laissez-faire* concept or principle of non-interference has withered at least as to economic affairs, and social advancements are increasingly sought through closer integration of society and through expanded and strengthened governmental controls. These changed conditions often deprive precedents of reliability and cast us more than we would choose upon our own judgment. But we act in these matters, not by authority of our competence, but by force of our commissions. We cannot, because of modest estimates of our competence in such specialties as public education, withhold the judgment that history authenticates as the function of this Court when liberty is infringed.

Lastly, and this is the very heart of the Gobitis opinion, it reasons that "national unity is the basis of national security," that the authorities have "the right to select appropriate means for its attainment," and hence reaches the conclusion that such compulsory measures toward "national unity" are constitutional. Upon the verity of this assumption depends our answer in this case.

National unity as an end which officials may foster by persuasion and example is not in question. The problem is whether under our Constitution compulsion as here employed is a permissible means for its achievement.

Struggles to coerce uniformity of sentiment in support of some end thought essential to their time and country have been waged by many good as well as by evil men. Nationalism is a relatively recent phenomenon, but at other times and places the ends have been racial or territorial security, support of a dynasty or régime, and particular plans for saving souls. As first and moderate methods to attain unity have failed, those bent on its accomplishment must resort to an ever-increasing severity. As governmental pressure toward unity becomes greater, so strife becomes more bitter as to whose unity it shall be. Probably no deeper division of our people could proceed from any provocation than from finding it necessary to choose what doctrine and whose program public educational officials shall compel youth to unite in embracing. Ultimate futility of such attempts to compel coherence is the lesson of every such effort from the Roman drive to stamp out Christianity as a disturber of its pagan unity, the Inquisition as a means to religious and dynastic unity, the Siberian exiles as a means to Russian unity, down to the fast-failing efforts of our present totalitarian enemies. Those who begin coercive elimination of dissent soon find themselves exterminating dissenters. Compulsory unification of opinion achieves only the unanimity of the graveyard.

The case is made difficult, not because the principles of its decision are obscure, but because the flag involved is our own. Nevertheless, we apply the limitations of the Constitution with no fear that freedom to be intellectually and spiritually diverse or even contrary will disintegrate the social organization. To believe that patriotism will not flourish if patriotic ceremonies are voluntary and spontaneous instead of a compulsory routine is to make an unflattering estimate of the appeal of our institutions to free minds. We can have intellectual individualism and the rich cultural diversities that we owe to exceptional minds only at the price of occasional eccentricity and abnormal attitudes. When they are so harmless to others or to the State as those we deal with here, the price is not too great. But freedom to differ is not limited to things that do not matter much. That would be a mere shadow of freedom. The test of its substance is the right to differ as to things that touch the heart of the existing order.

If there is any fixed star in our constitutional constellation, it is that no official, high or petty, can prescribe what shall be orthodox in politics, nationalism, religion, or other matters of opinion, or force citizens to confess by word or act their faith therein. If there are any circumstances which permit an exception, they do not now occur to us.

We think the action of the local authorities in compelling the flag salute and pledge transcends constitutional limitations on their power and invades the sphere of intellect and spirit which it is the purpose of the First Amendment to our Constitution to reserve from all official control.

Faith in a Free Society

FRANKFURTER *replies:*   1943

One who belongs to the most vilified and persecuted minority in history is not likely to be insensible to the freedoms guaranteed by our Constitution. Were my purely personal attitude relevant, I should whole-heartedly associate myself with the general libertarian views in the Court's opinion, representing as they do the thought and action of a lifetime. But as judges we are neither Jew nor Gentile, neither Catholic nor agnostic. We owe equal attachment to the Constitution and are equally bound by our judicial obligations, whether we derive our citizenship from the earliest or the latest immigrants to these shores. As a member of this Court I am not justified in writing my private notions of policy into the Constitution, no matter how deeply I may cherish them or how mischievous I may deem their disregard. The duty of a judge who must decide which of two claims before the Court shall prevail, that of a State to enact and enforce laws within its general competence or that of an individual to refuse obedience because of the demands of his conscience, is not that of the ordinary person. It can never be emphasized too much that one's own opinion about the wisdom or evil of a law should be excluded altogether when one is doing one's duty on the bench. The only opinion of our own even looking in that direction that is material is our opinion whether legislators could in reason have enacted such a law. In the light of all the circumstances, including the history of this question in this Court, it would require more daring than I possess to deny that reasonable legislators could have taken the action which is before us for review. Most unwillingly, therefore, I must differ from my brethren with regard to legislation like this. I cannot bring my mind to believe that the "liberty" secured by the Due Process Clause gives this Court authority to deny to the State of West Virginia the attainment of that which we all recognize as a legitimate legislative end, namely, the promotion of good citizenship, by employment of the means here chosen.

When Mr. Justice Holmes, speaking for this Court, wrote that "it must be remembered that legislatures are ultimate guardians of the liberties and welfare of the people in quite as great a degree as the courts," he went to the very essence of our constitutional system and the democratic conception of our society. He did not mean that for only some phases of civil government this Court was not to supplant legislatures and sit in judgment upon the right or wrong of a challenged measure. He was stating the comprehensive judicial duty and rôle of this Court in our constitutional scheme whenever legislation is sought to be nullified on any ground, namely, that responsibility for legislation lies with legislatures, answerable as they are directly to the people, and this Court's only and very narrow function is to determine whether within the broad grant of authority vested in legislatures they have exercised a judgment for which reasonable justification can be offered.

Conscientious scruples, all would admit, cannot stand against every legislative compulsion to do positive acts in conflict with such scruples. We have been told that such compulsions override religious scruples only as to major concerns of the state. But the determination of what is major and what is minor itself raises questions of policy. For the way in which men equally guided by reason appraise importance goes to the very heart of policy. Judges should be very diffident in setting their judgment against that of a state in determining what is and what is not a major concern, what means are appropriate to proper ends, and what is the total social cost in striking the balance of imponderables.

What one can say with assurance is that the history out of which grew constitutional provisions for religious equality and the writings of the great exponents of religious freedom — Jefferson, Madison, John Adams, Benjamin Franklin — are totally wanting in justification for a claim by dissidents of exceptional immunity from civic measures of general applicability, measures not in fact disguised assaults upon such dissident views. The great leaders of the American Revolution were determined to remove political support from every religious establishment. They put on an equality the different religious sects — Episcopalians, Presbyterians, Catholics, Baptists, Methodists, Quakers, Huguenots — which, as dissenters, had been under the heel of the various orthodoxies that prevailed in different colonies. So far as the state was concerned, there was to be neither orthodoxy nor heterodoxy. And so Jefferson and those who followed him wrote guaranties of religious freedom into our constitutions. Religious minorities as well as religious majorities were to be equal in the eyes of the political state. But Jefferson and the others also knew that minorities may disrupt society. It never would have occurred to them to write into the Constitution the subordination of the general civil authority of the state to sectarian scruples.

The uncontrollable power wielded by this Court brings it very close to the most sensitive areas of public affairs. As appeal from legislation to adjudication becomes more frequent, and its consequences more far-reaching, judicial self-restraint becomes more and not less important, lest we unwarrantably enter social and political domains wholly outside our concern. I think I appreciate fully the objections to the law before us. But to deny that it presents a question upon which men might reasonably differ appears to me to be intolerance. And since men may so reasonably differ, I deem it beyond my constitutional power to assert my view of the wisdom of this law against the view of the State of West Virginia.

The whole Court is conscious that this case reaches ultimate questions of judicial power and its relation to our scheme of government. It is appropriate, therefore, to recall an utterance as wise as any that I know in analyzing what is really involved when the theory of this Court's function is put to the test of practice. The analysis is that of James Bradley Thayer (1831–1902):

". . . there has developed a vast and growing increase of judicial interference with legislation. This is a very different state of things from what our fathers contemplated, a century and more ago, in framing the new system. Seldom, indeed, as they imagined, under our system, would this great, novel, tremendous power of the courts be exerted — would this sacred ark of the covenant be taken from within the veil. Marshall himself expressed truly one aspect of the matter, when he said in one of the later years of his life: 'No questions can be brought before a judicial tribunal of greater delicacy than those which involve the constitutionality of legislative acts. If they become indispensably necessary to the case, the court must meet and decide them; but if the case may be determined on other grounds, a just respect for the legislature requires that the obligation of its laws should not be unnecessarily and wantonly assailed.' And again, a little earlier than this, he laid down the one true rule of duty for the courts. When he went to Philadelphia at the end of September, in 1831, on that painful errand of which I have spoken, in answering a cordial tribute from the bar of that city he remarked that if he might be permitted to claim for himself and his associates any part of the kind things they had said, it would be this, that they had 'never sought to enlarge the judicial power beyond its proper bounds, nor feared to carry it to the fullest extent that duty required.'

"That is the safe twofold rule; nor is the first part of it any whit less important than the second; nay, more; today it is the part which most requires to be emphasized. For just here comes in a consideration of very great weight. Great and, indeed, inestimable as are the advantages in a popular government of this conservative influence — the power of the judiciary to disregard unconstitutional legislation — it should be remembered that the exercise of it, even when unavoidable, is always attended with a serious evil, namely, that the correction of legislative mistakes comes from the outside, and the people thus lose the political experience, and the moral education and stimulus that come from fighting the question out in the ordinary way, and correcting their own errors. If the decision in Munn *v.* Illinois and the 'Granger Cases,' twenty-five years ago, and in the 'Legal Tender Cases,' nearly thirty years ago, had been different; and the legislation there in question, thought by many to be unconstitutional and by many more to be ill-advised, had been set aside, we should have been saved some trouble and some harm. But I venture to think that the good which came to the country and its people from the vigorous thinking that had to be done in the political debates that followed, from the infiltration through every part of the population of sound ideas and sentiments, from the rousing into activity of opposite elements, the enlargement of ideas, the strengthening of moral fibre, and the growth of political experience that came out of it all — that all this far more than outweighed any evil which ever flowed from the refusal of the court to interfere with the work of the legislature.

"The tendency of a common and easy resort to this great function, now lamentably too common, is to dwarf the political capacity of the people, and to deaden its sense of moral responsibility. It is no light thing to do that.

"What can be done? It is the courts that can do most to cure the evil; and the opportunity is a very great one. Let them consider how narrow is the function which the constitutions have conferred on them — the office merely of deciding litigated cases; how large, therefore, is the duty intrusted to others, and above all to the legislature. It is that body which is charged, primarily, with the duty of judging of the constitutionality of its work. The constitutions generally give them no authority to call upon a court for advice; they must decide for themselves, and the courts may never be able to say a word. Such a body, charged, in every state, with almost all the legislative power of the people, is entitled to the most entire and real respect; is entitled, as among all rationally permissible opinions as to what the constitution allows, to its own choice. Courts, as has often been said, are not to think of the legislators, but of the legislature — the great, continuous body itself, abstracted from all the transitory individuals who may happen to hold its power. It is this majestic representative of the people whose action is in question, a co-ordinate department of the government, charged with the greatest functions, and invested, in contemplation of law, with whatsoever wisdom, virtue, and knowledge the exercise of such functions requires.

"To set aside the acts of such a body, representing in its own field, which is the very highest of all, the ultimate sovereign, should be a solemn, unusual, and painful act. Something is wrong when it can ever be other than that. And if it be true that the holders of legislative power are careless or evil, yet the constitutional duty of the court remains untouched; it cannot rightly attempt to protect the people, by undertaking a function not its own. On the other hand, by adhering rigidly to its own duty, the court will help, as nothing else can, to fix the spot where responsibility lies, and to bring down on that precise locality the thunderbolt of popular condemnation. The judiciary, today, in dealing with the acts of their co-ordinate legislators, owe to the country no greater or clearer duty than that of keeping their hands off these acts wherever it is possible to do it. For that course — the true course of judicial duty always — will powerfully help to bring the people and their representatives to a sense of their own responsibility. There will still remain to the judiciary an ample field for the determination of this remarkable jurisdiction, of which our American law has so much reason to be proud; a jurisdiction which has had some of its chief illustrations and its greatest triumphs, as in Marshall's time, so in ours, while the courts were refusing to exercise it."[1]

Of course patriotism cannot be enforced by the flag salute. But neither can the liberal spirit be enforced by judicial invalidation of illiberal legislation. Our constant preoccupation with the constitutionality of legislation rather than with its wisdom tends to preoccupation of the American mind with a false value. The tendency of focussing attention on constitutionality is to make constitutionality synonymous with wisdom, to regard a law as all right if it is constitutional. Such an attitude is a great enemy of liberalism. Particularly in legislation affecting freedom of thought and freedom of speech, much which should offend a free-spirited society is constitutional. Reliance for the most precious interests of civilization, therefore, must be found outside of their vindication in courts of law. Only a persistent positive translation of the faith of a free society into the convictions and habits and actions of a community is the ultimate reliance against unabated temptations to fetter the human spirit.

EMILY BRONTË   1818–1848

> *I'll walk, but not in old heroic traces,*
> *And not in paths of high morality,*
> *And not among the half-distinguished faces,*
> *The clouded forms of long-past history.*
>
> *I'll walk where my own nature would be leading:*
> *It vexes me to choose another guide:*
> *Where the grey flocks in ferny glens are feeding;*
> *Where the wild wind blows on the mountain-side.*

The Duty of Civil Disobedience

THOREAU   1817–1862

Unjust laws exist: shall we be content to obey them, or shall we endeavor to amend them, and obey them until we have succeeded, or shall we transgress them at once?

[1] J. B. Thayer, *John Marshall* [1901], 104–110.

Men generally, under such a government as this, think that they ought to wait until they have persuaded the majority to alter them. They think that, if they should resist, the remedy would be worse than the evil. But it is the fault of the government itself that the remedy *is* worse than the evil. *It* makes it worse. Why is it not more apt to anticipate and provide for reform? Why does it not cherish its wise minority? Why does it cry and resist before it is hurt? Why does it not encourage its citizens to be on the alert to point out its faults, and *do* better than it would have them? Why does it always crucify Christ, and excommunicate Copernicus and Luther, and pronounce Washington and Franklin rebels?

If the injustice is part of the necessary friction of the machine of government, let it go, let it go: perchance it will wear smooth — certainly the machine will wear out. If the injustice has a spring, or a pulley, or a rope, or a crank, exclusively for itself, then perhaps you may consider whether the remedy will not be worse than the evil; but if it is of such a nature that it requires you to be the agent of injustice to another, then, I say, break the law. Let your life be a counter-friction to stop the machine. What I have to do is to see, at any rate, that I do not lend myself to the wrong which I condemn.

As for adopting the ways which the state has provided for remedying the evil, I know not of such ways. They take too much time, and a man's life will be gone. I have other affairs to attend to. I came into this world, not chiefly to make this a good place to live in, but to live in it, be it good or bad. A man has not everything to do, but something; and because he cannot do *everything*, it is not necessary that he should do *something* wrong. It is not my business to be petitioning the Governor or the Legislature any more than it is theirs to petition me; and if they should not hear my petition, what should I do then? But in this case the State has provided no way: its very Constitution is the evil. This may seem to be harsh and stubborn and unconciliatory; but it is to treat with the utmost kindness and consideration the only spirit that can appreciate or deserves it. So is all change for the better, like birth and death, which convulse the body.

I have paid no poll-tax for six years. I was put into a jail once on this account, for one night; and, as I stood considering the walls of solid stone, two or three feet thick, the door of wood and iron, a foot thick, and the iron grating which strained the light, I could not help being struck with the foolishness of that institution which treated me as if I were mere flesh and blood and bones, to be locked up. I wondered that it should have concluded at length that this was the best use it could put me to, and had never thought to avail itself on my services in some way. I saw that, if there was a wall of stone between me and my townsmen, there was a still more difficult one to climb or break through before they could get to be as free as I was. I did not for a moment feel confined, and the walls seemed a great waste of stone and mortar. I felt as if I alone of all my townsmen had paid my tax. They plainly did not know how to treat me, but behaved like persons who are underbred. In every threat and in every compliment there was a blunder; for they thought that my chief desire was to stand the other side of that stone wall. I could not but smile to see how industriously they locked the door on my meditations, which followed them out again without let or hindrance, and *they* were really all that was dangerous. As they could not reach me, they had resolved to punish my body; just as boys, if they cannot come at some person against whom they have a spite, will abuse his dog. I saw that the State was halfwitted, that it was timid as a lone woman with her silver spoons, and that it did not know its friends from its foes, and I lost all my remaining respect for it, and pitied it.

Thus the State never intentionally confronts a man's sense, intellectual or moral, but only his body, his senses. It is not armed with superior wit or honesty, but with superior physical strength. I was not born to be forced. I will breathe after my own fashion. Let us see who is the strongest. What force has a multitude? They only can force me who obey a higher law than I. They force me to become like themselves. I do not hear of *men* being *forced* to live this way or that by masses of men. What sort of life were that to live? When I meet a government which says to me, "Your money or your life," why should I be in haste to give it my money? It may be in a great strait, and not know what to do: I cannot help that. It must help itself; do as I do. It is not worth the while to snivel about it. I am not responsible for the successful working of the machinery of society. I am not the son of the engineer. I perceive that, when an acorn and a chestnut fall side by side, the one does not remain inert to make way for the other, but both obey their own laws, and spring and grow and flourish as best they can, till one, perchance, overshadows and destroys the other. If a plant cannot live according to its nature, it dies; and so a man.

I have never declined paying the highway tax, because I am as desirous of being a good neighbor as I am of being a bad subject; and as for supporting schools, I am doing my part to educate my fellow-countrymen now. It is for no particular item in the tax-bill that I refuse to pay it. I simply wish to refuse allegiance to the State, to withdraw and stand aloof from it effectually. I do not care to trace the course of my dollar, if I could, till it buys a man or a musket to shoot one with — the dollar is innocent — but I am concerned to trace the effects of my allegiance. In fact, I quietly declare war with the State, after my fashion, though I will still make what use and get what advantage of her I can, as is usual in such cases.

If others pay the tax which is demanded of me, from a sympathy with the State, they do but what they have already done in their own case, or rather they abet injustice to a greater extent than the State requires. If they pay the tax from a mistaken interest in the individual taxed, to save his property, or prevent his going to jail, it is because they have not considered wisely how far they let their private feelings interfere with the public good.

This, then, is my position at present. But one cannot

be too much on his guard in such a case, lest his action be biased by obstinacy or an undue regard for the opinions of men. Let him see that he does only what belongs to himself and to the hour.

I do not wish to quarrel with any man or nation. I do not wish to split hairs, to make fine distinctions, or set myself up as better than my neighbors. I seek rather, I may say, even an excuse for conforming to the laws of the land. I am but too ready to conform to them. Indeed, I have reason to suspect myself on this head; and each year, as the tax-gatherer comes round, I find myself disposed to review the acts and position of the general and State governments, and the spirit of the people, to discover a pretext for conformity.

> *We must affect our country as our parents,*
> *And if at any time we alienate*
> *Our love or industry from doing it honor,*
> *We must respect effects and teach the soul*
> *Matter of conscience and religion,*
> *And not desire of rule or benefit.*

I believe that the State will soon be able to take all my work of this sort out of my hands, and then I shall be no better a patriot than my fellow-countrymen. Seen from a lower point of view, the Constitution, with all its faults, is very good; the law and the courts are very respectable; even this State and this American government are, in many respects, very admirable, and rare things, to be thankful for, such as a great many have described them; but seen from a point of view a little higher, they are what I have described them; seen from higher still, and the highest, who shall say what they are, or that they are worth looking at or thinking of at all?

They who know of no purer sources of truth, who have traced up its stream no higher, stand, and wisely stand, by the Bible and the Constitution, and drink at it there with reverence and humility; but they who behold where it comes trickling into this lake or that pool, gird up their loins once more, and continue their pilgrimage toward its fountain-head.

The authority of government, even such as I am will-ing to submit to — for I will cheerfully obey those who know and can do better than I, and in many things even those who neither know nor can do so well — is still an impure one: to be strictly just, it must have the sanc-tion and consent of the governed. It can have no pure right over my person and property but what I concede to it. The progress from an absolute to a limited monarchy, from a limited monarchy to a democracy, is a progress toward a true respect for the individual. Even the Chi-nese philosopher was wise enough to regard the indi-vidual as the basis of the empire. Is a democracy, such as we know it, the last improvement possible in govern-ment? Is it not possible to take a step further towards recognizing and organizing the rights of man? There will never be a really free and enlightened State until the State comes to recognize the individual as a higher and independent power, from which all its own power and authority are derived, and treats him accordingly. I please myself with imagining a State at last which can afford to be just to all men, and to treat the individual with respect as a neighbor; which even would not think it inconsistent with its own repose if a few were to live aloof from it, not meddling with it, nor embraced by it, who fulfilled all the duties of neighbors and fellow-men. A State which bore this kind of fruit, and suffered it to drop off as fast as it ripened, would prepare the way for a still more perfect and glorious State, which also I have imagined, but not yet anywhere seen.

Thoreau wrote this in defense of his refusal to pay his poll-tax, because it would go to pay for the Mexican War. And he spent a night in the Concord jail for his failure to pay it. What he wrote was heard as far round the world as the shots fired there a couple of generations before. Gandhi wrote one of the editors that this essay on "The Duty of Civil Disobe-dience" was his bedside book.

P A R T

V I I

THEY BETTER THEIR CONDITION

Thou little thinkest what a little fool-
erye governs the whole world.
SELDEN'S TABLE TALK

As a cousin of mine once said about
money, money is always there but the
pockets change; it is not in the same
pockets after a change, and that is all
there is to say about money.
GERTRUDE STEIN

Now, as I said, the way to the Celes-
tial City lies just through this Town,
where this lusty Fair is kept; and he
that will go to the City, and yet not
go through this Town, must needs go
out of the World.
BUNYAN

Free Enterprise

RICHARD H. TAWNEY   1880–

Few tricks of the unsophisticated intellect are more curious than the naive psychology of the business man, who ascribes his achievements to his own unaided efforts, in bland unconsciousness of a social order without whose continuous support and vigilant protection he would be as a lamb bleating in the desert. That individualist complex owes part of its self-assurance to the suggestion of Puritan moralists, that practical success is at once the sign and the reward of ethical superiority.

Capitalism, in the sense of great individual undertakings, involving the control of large financial resources, and yielding riches to their masters as a result of speculation, money-lending, commercial enterprise, buccaneering, and war, is as old as history. Capitalism, as an economic system, resting on the organization of legally free wage-earners, for the purpose of pecuniary profit, by the owner of capital or his agents, and setting its stamp on every aspect of society, is a modern phenomenon.

All revolutions are declared to be natural and inevitable, once they are successful, and capitalism, as the type of economic system prevailing in Western Europe and America, is clothed today with the unquestioned respectability of the triumphant fact. But in its youth it was a pretender, and it was only after centuries of struggle that its title was established. For it involved a code of economic conduct and a system of human relations which were sharply at variance with venerable conventions, with the accepted scheme of social ethics, and with the law, both of the Church and of most European states. So questionable an innovation demanded of the pioneers who first experimented with it as much originality, self-confidence, and tenacity of purpose as it required today of those who would break from the net that it has woven. What influence nerved them to defy tradition? From what source did they derive the principles to replace it?

The tonic that braced them for the conflict was a new conception of religion, which taught them to regard the pursuit of wealth as, not merely an advantage, but a duty. This conception welded into a disciplined force the still feeble bourgeoisie, heightened its energies, and cast a halo of sanctification round its convenient vices. What is significant, in short, is not the strength of the motive of economic self-interest, which is the commonplace of all ages and demands no explanation. It is the change of moral standards which converted a natural frailty into an ornament of the spirit, and canonized as the economic virtues habits which in earlier ages had been denounced as vices. The force which produced it was the creed associated with the name of Calvin. Capitalism was the social counterpart of Calvinist theology.

The central idea is expressed in the characteristic phrase "a calling." For Luther, as for most mediaeval theologians, it had normally meant the state of life in which the individual had been set by Heaven, and against which it was impious to rebel. To the Calvinist, the calling is not a condition in which the individual is born, but a strenuous and exacting enterprise to be chosen by himself, and to be pursued with a sense of religious responsibility. Baptized in the bracing, if icy, waters of Calvinist theology, the life of business, once regarded as perilous to the soul — *summe periculosa est emptionist et venditionis negotiatio* — acquires a new sanctity. Labour is not merely an economic means: it is a spiritual end. Covetousness, if a danger to the soul, is a less formidable menace than sloth. So far from poverty being meritorious, it is a duty to choose the more profitable occupation. So far from there being an inevitable conflict between money-making and piety, they are natural allies, for the virtues incumbent on the elect — diligence, thrift, sobriety, prudence — are the most reliable passport to commercial prosperity. Thus the pursuit of riches, which once had been feared as the enemy of religion, was now welcomed as its ally.

And yet ——

It would be misleading to dwell on the limitations of Puritan ethics without emphasizing the enormous contribution of Puritanism to political freedom and social progress. The foundation of democracy is the sense of spiritual independence which nerves the individual to stand alone against the powers of this world, and in England, where squire and parson, lifting arrogant eyebrows at the insolence of the lower orders, combined to crush popular agitation, as a menace at once to society and to the Church, it is probable that democracy owes more to Nonconformity than to any other single movement. The virtues of enterprise, diligence, and thrift are the indispensable foundation of any complex and vigorous civilization. It was Puritanism which, by investing them with a supernatural sanction, turned them from an unsocial eccentricity into a habit, and a religion.

The Power of Ideas

J. M. KEYNES   1883–1946

The ideas of economists and political philosophers, both when they are right and when they are wrong, are more powerful than is commonly understood. Indeed, the world is ruled by little else. Practical men, who believe themselves to be quite exempt from any intellectual influences, are usually the slaves of some defunct economist. Madmen in authority, who hear voices in the air, are distilling their frenzy from some academic scribbler of a few years back. I am sure that the power of vested interests is vastly exaggerated compared with the gradual encroachment of ideas. Not, indeed, immediately, but after a certain interval; for in the field of economic and political philosophy there are not many who are influenced by new theories after they are twenty-five or thirty years of age, so that the ideas which civil servants and politicians and even agitators apply to current events are not likely to be the newest. But, soon or late, it is ideas, not vested interests, which are dangerous for good or evil.

Down the Drain

EDWARD H. CARR   1951

Once upon a time I had an uncle who beguiled his declining years by explaining to all who would listen that the world was going rapidly from bad to worse. But, being by nature a cheerful soul, he always ended his lament with the same aphorism: Well, if we *are* all going down the drain, let us go down the drain with our top hats on.

This country today is full of old gentlemen — some of them not so old, and some of them in important places — who are far less worried by the prospect of going down the drain than by the prospect that the gale may blow off their top hats.

Watchman, What of the Night?

WALTER LIPPMANN   1889–

Measured by the creeds that have the greatest vogue, the reaction against freedom is almost everywhere triumphant. Yet, though the reaction is popular, and the masses applaud it, the reactionaries have been winning the battles and losing the war. The people have been promised abundance, security, peace, if they would surrender the heritage of liberty and their dignity as men. But the promises are not being kept. In the ascendancy of collectivism during the past seventy years, mankind has gone deeper and deeper into disorder and disunion and the frustration of its hopes. Because it is entirely incompatible with the economy by which men earn their living, collectivism does not work. Because it dismisses the lessons of long experience in regulating the diversity of human interest by law, it is incapable of regulating the modern social economy. Because it resurrects a primitive form of human polity, it revives the ancient parochial animosities of mankind. Because it affronts the essential manhood of men, it is everywhere challenged and resisted. Though collectivist theory is the fashionable mode in contemporary thought and guides the practice of contemporary politicians, its triumph is in fact a disaster in human affairs.

For human beings, however low and abject, are potentially persons. They are made in a different image. And though, as Jan Smuts has said, "personality is still a growing factor in the universe and is merely in its infancy," it asserts itself and will command respect. Its essence is an energy, however we choose to describe it, which causes men to assert their humanity, and on occasion to die rather than to renounce it. This is the energy the seers discerned when they discovered the soul of man. It is this energy which has moved men to rise above themselves, to feel divine discontent with their condition, to invent, to labor, to reason with one another, to imagine the good life and to desire it. This energy must be mighty. For it has overcome the inertia of the primordial savage.

Against this mighty energy the heresies of an epoch will not prevail. For the will to be free is perpetually renewed in every individual who uses his faculties and affirms his manhood.

There Are Financiers, There Are Engineers—

THORSTEIN VEBLEN   1857–1929

Leaving aside the archaic vocations of war, politics, fashion, and religion, the employments in which men are engaged may be distinguished as pecuniary or business employments on the one hand, and industrial or mechanical employments on the other hand. In earlier times, and indeed until an uncertain point in the nineteenth century, such a distinction between employments would not to

any great extent have coincided with a difference between occupations. But gradually, as time has passed and
production for a market has come to be the rule in industry, there has supervened a differentiation of occupations,
or a division of labour, whereby one class of men has
taken over the work of purchase and sale and of hus-
banding a store of accumulated values. Concomitantly,
of course, the rest, who may, for lack of means or of pecuniary aptitude, have been less well fitted for pecuniary
pursuits, have been relieved of the cares of business, and
have with increasing specialization given their attention
to the mechanical processes involved in this production
for a market. In this way the distinction between pecuniary and industrial activities or employments has come
to coincide more and more nearly with a difference between occupations. Not that the specialization has even
yet gone so far as to exempt any class from all pecuniary
care; for even those whose daily occupation is mechanical work still habitually bargain with their employers for
their wages and with others for their supplies. So that
none of the active classes in modern life is fully exempt
from pecuniary work.

The ultimate ground of validity for the thinking of the
business classes is the natural-rights ground of property
— a conventional, anthropomorphic fact having an institutional validity, rather than a matter-of-fact validity
such as can be formulated in terms of material cause and
effect; while the classes engaged in the machine industry
are habitually occupied with matters of causal sequence,
which do not lend themselves to statement in anthropomorphic terms of natural rights and which afford no guidance in questions of institutional right and wrong, or of
conventional reason and consequence. Arguments which
proceed on material cause and effect cannot be met with
arguments from conventional precedent or dialectically
sufficient reason, and conversely.

The thinking required by the pecuniary occupations
proceeds on grounds of conventionality, whereas that involved in the industrial occupations runs, in the main,
on grounds of mechanical sequence or causation, to the

neglect of conventionality. The institution (habit of thought) of ownership or property is a conventional fact; and the logic of pecuniary thinking — that is to say, of thinking on matters of ownership — is a working-out of the implications of this postulate, this concept of ownership or property. The characteristic habits of thought given by such work are habits of recourse to conventional grounds of finality or validity, to anthropomorphism, to explanations of phenomena in terms of human relation, discretion, authenticity, and choice. The final ground of certainty in inquiries on this natural-rights plane is always a ground of authenticity, of precedent, or accepted decision. The argument is an argument *de jure*, not *de facto*, and the training given lends facility and certainty in the pursuit of *de jure* distinctions and generalizations, rather than in the pursuit or the assimilation of a *de facto* knowledge of impersonal phenomena. The end of such reasoning is the interpretation of new facts in terms of accredited precedents, rather than a revision of the knowledge drawn from past experience in the matter-of-fact light of new phenomena. The endeavour is to make facts conform to law, not to make the law or general rule conform to facts. The bent so given favours the acceptance of the general, abstract, custom-made rule as something real with a reality superior to the reality of impersonal, non-conventional facts. Such training gives reach and subtlety in metaphysical argument and in what is known as the "practical" management of affairs; it gives executive or administrative efficiency, so-called, as distinguished from mechanical work. "Practical" efficiency means the ability to turn facts to account for the purposes of the accepted conventions, to give a large effect to the situation in terms of the pecuniary conventions in force.

The business classes are conservative, on the whole, but such a conservative bent is, of course, not peculiar to them. These occupations are not the only ones whose reasoning prevailingly moves on a conventional plane. Indeed, the intellectual activity of other classes, such as soldiers, politicians, the clergy, and men of fashion, moves on a plane of still older conventions; so that if

the training given by business employments is to be characterized as conservative, that given by these other, more
archaic employments should be called reactionary. Extreme conventionalization means extreme conservatism.
Conservatism means the maintenance of conventions already in force. On this head, therefore, the discipline of
modern business life may be said simply to retain something of the complexion which marks the life of the
higher barbarian culture, at the same time that it has
not retained the disciplinary force of the barbarian culture in so high a state of preservation as some of the
other occupations just named.

One outcome of this persistent and pervasive tardiness
and circumspection on the part of the captains has been
an incredibly and increasingly uneconomical use of material resources, and an incredibly wasteful organization
of equipment and man-power in those great industries
where the technological advance has been most marked.
In good part it was this discreditable pass, to which the
leading industries had been brought by these one-eyed
captains of industry, that brought the régime of the captains to an inglorious close, by shifting the initiative and
discretion in this domain out of their hands into those of
the investment bankers. By custom the investment bankers had occupied a position between or overlapping the
duties of a broker in corporate securities and those of an
underwriter of corporate flotations — such a position, in
effect, as is still assigned them in the standard writings on
corporation finance. The increasingly large scale of corporate enterprise, as well as the growth of a mutual understanding among these business concerns, also had its
share in this new move. But about this time, too, the
"consulting engineers" were coming notably into evidence
in many of those lines of industry in which corporation
finance has habitually been concerned.

So far as concerns the present argument the ordinary
duties of these consulting engineers have been to advise
the investment bankers as to the industrial and commercial soundness, past and prospective, of any enterprise
that is to be underwritten. These duties have comprised a

painstaking and impartial examination of the physical
properties involved in any given case, as well as an equally
impartial auditing of the accounts and appraisal of the
commercial promise of such enterprises, for the guidance
of the bankers or syndicate of bankers interested in the
case as underwriters. On this ground working arrangements and a mutual understanding presently arose between the consulting engineers and those banking-houses
that habitually were concerned in the underwriting of
corporate enterprises.

The effect of this move has been twofold: experience
has brought out the fact that corporation finance, at its
best and soundest, has now become a matter of comprehensive and standardized bureaucratic routine, necessarily comprising the mutual relations between various
corporate concerns, and best to be taken care of by a
clerical staff of trained accountants; and the same experience has put the financial houses in direct touch with the
technological general staff of the industrial system, whose
surveillance has become increasingly imperative to the
conduct of any profitable enterprise in industry. But
also, by the same token, it has appeared that the corporation financier of nineteenth-century tradition is no longer
of the essence of the case in corporation finance of the
larger and more responsible sort. He has, in effect, come
to be no better than an idle wheel in the economic mechanism, serving only to take up some of the lubricant.

Since and so far as this shift out of the nineteenth century into the twentieth has been completed, the corporation financier has ceased to be a captain of industry and
has become a lieutenant of finance; the captaincy having been taken over by the syndicated investment bankers
and administered as a standardized routine of accoun-
tancy, having to do with the flotation of corporation securities and with their fluctuating values, and having also
something to do with regulating the rate and volume of
output in those industrial enterprises which so have
passed under the hand of the investment bankers.

Hitherto, then, the growth and conduct of this industrial system presents this singular outcome. The tech-

nology — the state of the industrial arts — which takes effect in this mechanical industry is in an eminent sense a joint stock of knowledge and experience held in common by the civilized peoples. It requires the use of trained and instructed workmen — born, bred, trained, and instructed at the cost of the people at large. So also it requires, with a continually more exacting insistence, a corps of highly trained and specially gifted experts, of divers and various kinds. These, too, are born, bred, and trained at the cost of the community at large, and they draw their requisite special knowledge from the community's joint stock of accumulated experience. These expert men — technologists, engineers, or whatever name may best suit them — make up the indispensable general staff of the industrial system; and without their immediate and unremitting guidance and correction the industrial system will not work. It is a mechanically organized structure of technical processes designed, installed, and conducted by these production engineers. Without them and their constant attention the industrial equipment, the mechanical appliances of industry, will foot up to just so much junk. The material welfare of the community is unreservedly bound up with the due working of this industrial system, and therefore with its unreserved control by the engineers, who alone are competent to manage it. To do their work as it should be done these men of the industrial general staff must have a free hand, unhampered by commercial considerations and reservations; for the production of the goods and services needed by the community they neither need nor are they in any degree benefited by any supervision or interference from the side of the owners. Yet the absentee owners, now represented, in effect, by the syndicated investment bankers, continue to control the industrial experts and limit their discretion, arbitrarily, for their own commercial gain, regardless of the needs of the community.

Hitherto these men who so make up the general staff of the industrial system have not drawn together into anything like a self-directing working force; nor have they been vested with anything more than an occasional, haphazard, and tentative control of some disjointed sector of the industrial equipment, with no direct or decisive relation to that personnel of productive industry that may be called the officers of the line and the rank and file. It is still the unbroken privilege of the financial management and its financial agents to "hire and fire." The final disposition of all the industrial forces still remains in the hands of the business men, who still continue to dispose of these forces for other than industrial ends. And all the while it is an open secret that with a reasonably free hand the production experts would today readily increase the ordinary output of industry by several fold — variously estimated at some three hundred per cent to twelve hundred per cent of the current output. And what stands in the way of so increasing the ordinary output of goods and services is business-as-usual.

Minds in a Groove

A. N. WHITEHEAD   1861–1947

Another great fact confronting the modern world is the discovery of the method of training professionals, who specialize in particular regions of thought and thereby progressively add to the sum of knowledge within their respective limitations of subject. In consequence of the success of this professionalizing of knowledge, there are two points to be kept in mind, which differentiate our present age from the past. In the first place, the rate of progress is such that an individual human being, of ordinary length of life, will be called upon to face novel situations which find no parallel in his past. The fixed person for the fixed duties, who in older societies was such a godsend, in the future will be a public danger. In the second place, the modern professionalism in knowledge works in the opposite direction so far as the intellectual sphere is concerned. The modern chemist is likely to be weak in zoology, weaker still in his general knowledge of the Elizabethan drama, and completely ignorant of the principles of rhythm in English versification. It is probably safe to ignore his knowledge of ancient history. Of course I am speaking of general tendencies; for chemists are no worse than engineers or mathematicians or classical scholars. Effective knowledge is professionalized knowledge, supported by a restricted acquaintance with useful subjects subservient to it.

This situation has its dangers. It produces minds in a groove. Each profession makes progress, but it is progress in its own groove. Now to be mentally in a groove is to live in contemplating a given set of abstractions. The groove prevents straying across country, and the abstraction abstracts from something to which no further attention is paid. But there is no groove of abstractions which is adequate for the comprehension of human life. Thus in the modern world, the celibacy of the medieval learned class has been replaced by a celibacy of the intellect which is divorced from the concrete contemplation of the complete facts. Of course, no one is merely a mathematician, or merely a lawyer. People have lives outside their professions or their businesses. But the point is the restraint of serious thought within a groove. The remainder of life is treated superficially, with the imperfect categories of thought derived from one profession.

The dangers arising from this aspect of professionalism are great, particularly in our democratic societies. The directive force of reason is weakened. The leading intellects lack balance. They see this set of circumstances, or that set; but not both sets together. The task of co-ordination is left to those who lack either the force or the character to succeed in some definite career. In short, the specialized functions of the community are performed better and more progressively, but the generalized direction lacks vision. The progressiveness in detail only adds to the danger produced by the feebleness of co-ordination.

This criticism of modern life applies throughout, in whatever sense you construe the meaning of a community. It holds if you apply it to a nation, a city, a district, an institution, a family, or even to an individual. There is a development of particular abstractions, and a contraction of concrete appreciation. The whole is lost in one of its aspects. It is not necessary for my point that I should maintain that our directive wisdom, either as individuals or as communities, is less now than in the past. Perhaps it has slightly improved. But the novel pace of progress requires a greater force of direction if disasters are to be avoided. The point is that the discoveries of the nineteenth century were in the direction of professionalism, so that we are left with no expansion of wisdom and with greater need of it.

Skills

T. N. WHITEHEAD, *his son*   1891–

The primitive leader is well exemplified by the highly skilled mechanic. Such a man has by long application acquired an unusual skill in his art. He is also in possession of a traditional set of methods, or sequences of operations, with which he tackles his technical problems. Perhaps the outstanding characteristic of the mechanic-leader is his intense pride in, and unswerving loyalty to, the detailed procedure by which he exercises his skill. Any attempt on the part of his "boss" to modify these by one hair's breadth will evoke the most unmeasured anger. It is as though a brutal assault had been made on his household gods. And that is exactly what it amounts to. The simple leader is above all things loyal to his skill and to its accompanying procedures. Every act of discriminating attention, every guarding and controlled movement has been practised a thousand times and is the basis of a deep sentiment; these *are* his ways of life, and on them his ultimate values are grounded.

But a sympathetic study of a skilled worker over a sufficient period will reveal an apparently erratic streak in his behavior. Sooner or later in his work, our friend will surmount some particular difficulty by an elegant device, and he will explain with pride that "in his young days" they were taught to do such and such, but that he had subsequently "thought of" the procedure just demonstrated. No loyalty is shown towards the discarded traditional procedure, and his common sense would be outraged at the bare suggestion that any value could adhere of the inferior method. In all these respects, he would be followed without question by his group.

The fact is that our mechanic, for once in his life, is thinking for himself and he has temporarily discarded the whole lumber of social sanctions and taboos. Up to that moment he was possessed of an implicit skill in action — a practical wisdom below the level of speech. But in the continual practice of his art, he was learning to notice the connection, the causal relations, between the various operations involved. He began to understand the reasons why, and to be able to give a few logical explanations for some of his actions. He would have once declared that he did such and such because "that was the way to do it" — an appeal to social sanction. Now he can say that too heavy a feed on his lathe will result in "chattering," *because* of lack of rigidity in the construction of the slide. And a designing engineer would, by suitable calculation or experiment, be able to endorse the mechanic's logical deduction, based as it was on discriminating observation of the facts.

We have in outline traced the evolution of explicit logical skill from the implicit skill in action of the superior man, and we have noticed that skills to this day, and specifically in industry, are largely of the more primitive type. But explicit logical skill in itself will result in nothing more than sporadic bursts of change, arising directly from a contemplation of the current procedures. The final step which mankind has so far achieved is deliberately to organize logical thinking in such a way as to lead to a stream of improvements. Broadly speaking, what has been evolved is a direction of the thinking processes towards a continual evolution of better and better technological procedures.

Incentive

GEOFFREY CROWTHER   1907–

Very largely, it is a matter of incentives. Every form of economic activity requires an entrepreneur — someone to hire the labor, to borrow capital, to buy the materials, to take the inherent risks. Private individuals and corporations can undertake entrepreneurial functions only if they see the possibility of a profit, or at least the avoidance of loss. This is the profit incentive, though it could just as well be called the avoidance-of-loss incentive. Governments, because of their control of the machinery of taxation and credit creation, do not need to trouble about the avoidance of loss. Most of their activities, notably defense and education, are in fact run at a loss (and quite rightly so). Governments act by what we may call the social incentive — because they think their action is in the interests of society. With unimportant exceptions there will be no productive activity unless either an individual is motivated by the profit incentive or the government is motivated by the social incentive to initiate it.

What has been happening in recent decades is that the two incentives have been used to blunt and offset each other. The public has not liked the results of leaving the profit motive unchecked and uncontrolled. It has demanded a greater injection of Order into a system that was previously very largely one of Freedom. In so doing it has checked, controlled, licensed, investigated, and taxed the profit motive, with the result that the entrepreneurial opportunities for private individuals have been substantially reduced. But when the government itself has tried to expand the scope of its own economic activities in pursuit of the social motive, it has been assailed by a barrage of sound and unsound argument and by sincere and insincere political opposition. Unemployment has been the result of the conflict and an outstanding example of the danger of mixing motives.

In the political sphere the democratic formula is one of balance, not of mixture. Taxes are wholly compulsory, not partly voluntary. Religion is wholly free, not partly compulsory. So it should be in the economic sphere. There are parts of the economy where the social motive should be paramount; let it not be clogged up by the prejudices of Victorian *laissez-faire*. There are parts of the economy where the government cannot, will not, or should not take the entrepreneur's responsibility; in these cases let the profit motive have its head. In both cases what is needed is the removal of the impeding, prohibitive, negative influences if the rapid march of material progress is to be resumed.

The Communists have their motto: "To each according to his needs, from each according to his means." We have acted as if the second half of the slogan were fulfilled by the payment of graduated income taxes. In remembering how great are the differences between the money possessions of different men, we have forgotten that no man has more, and few have less, than two arms, two legs, one brain, and twenty-four hours a day. The Nazis have revealed, and exploited, the undoubted psychological fact that the average individual does not wish to be on the receiving end only in his relationship to the community. They have grown powerful on the passionate devotion with which a whole people will embrace an opportunity to give service to their community. It is only in wartime that we democrats provide an opportunity for service; and then we are surprised afresh each time by the eagerness with which it is taken.

Is it fantastic to suggest that what is done in war might be done in peace? The scale of operations would be smaller rather than larger. At present something like sixty per cent of the economic activity of the British community is controlled and financed by the government. But the Citizens' Charter, even if every particle of it had to be paid for by the government and paid for at list prices and standard wages, could easily be provided out of one-half of the national income of a community like the British or American, and, for the reasons stated, this is a wild overestimate of the actual cost. There is nothing impossible about the Citizens' Charter. If it is considered as desirable as military victory, it can be more easily attained.

Over approximately half the economy of the nation the social incentive is destined to become dominant, and if private business remains in this sector (as it undoubtedly will), it must expect to conform to the promptings of that incentive. But conversely, in the remaining half or more of the economy, the mainspring of activity will remain the profit motive.

The basic argument of this article is that the incentives of economic action should be, first, distinguished from one another and then liberated from the forces that are now clogging them. "Take off the brakes" must be the slogan for any community that wishes to realize the full fruit of its potentialities. Just as it was argued in the previous section that the brakes should be taken off the social incentive in the sphere that is appropriate to Order, so here the prescription is that the profit motive be liberated from its present handicaps and left free to stimulate the maximum of activity in the sphere of Freedom.

First, as has already been suggested, the so-called "profit" motive could better be called the "avoidance-of-loss" motive. It is not that the capitalist entrepreneur needs a fat yield to tempt his greed before he will move. It is not that employers will close their plants and refuse to play if their profits fall below a satisfactory figure. Indeed, once a plant is built and a firm established, it will continue to do all the business it can, even if the average return is low or an actual loss is being incurred. But the balance and equilibrium of the economic structure depend — and this is one point on which all schools of economists are agreed — on the smoothness and regularity with which the savings of the public are put into *new* capital equipment. The more difficult the earning of profits on existing investments is made, the greater will be the risk of loss on new investments and the smaller will be the part that anybody except the government can play in avoiding unemployment.

Second, the rehabilitation of profits does not mean the rehabilitation of the profiteer. There is no reason why it should not be combined with heavy taxation on rich individuals. This is a point that is almost always misunderstood. There is a most important difference between preventing the emergence of large incomes by throttling profits and taxing them away when they have emerged. The first method increases the risk of loss that faces every entrepreneurial enterprise and therefore diminishes the amount of enterprise that will be shown. The second method neither increases nor diminishes the risk of loss; it merely taxes the reward of success. Both methods diminish the reward of enterprise, but the first also reduces the incentive. It is a perfectly legitimate aim for a democracy to attempt, if it wishes to do so to abolish gross inequality of wealth. Nothing that is said here seriously conflicts with that aim. It is merely pleaded that if the method chosen for reducing inequality is such as to increase the risks of engaging in legitimate business, the community must not be surprised by the emergence of chronic unemployment.

Third, there is the attack on competitive enterprise that comes from monopolies, cartels, trusts, rings, combines, trade associations, and other euphemisms for restraint of trade. It cannot be too strongly emphasized that profits made in this way are not profits with which we are here concerned. The case for private enterprise rests on its efficiency in increasing the total volume of activity. Largely the case is thrown away when there is a restraint of the volume of trade. In this, as in the other respects, the guiding principle must be the removal of restraints, the increase of incentives to activity, the liberation of human ambitions to build and expand. This should be the more easily done when the system of private enterprise runs in double harness with co-operative collectivism, each on its own side of the pole — when Freedom is teamed with Order. For the great urge to the restraint of trade is not greed so much as fear of insecurity. It is the desire to protect existing businesses, existing markets, existing employment that leads one industry after another to try to "stabilize" its own section of the economy. To the extent that security is provided by other means, it will be possible in the sphere of Freedom to insist on a return to the full competitive ruthlessness that is inseparable from rapid progress.

With an economic system, as with an individual, it is only when the basic hungers have been met and the strongest fears removed that the human spirit can develop its full powers. When those conditions are met, there are no limits to the new frontiers that the ingenuity of the free man can conquer.

It is only by some such proposition that democracy can recapture the sense of going forward, that it can leave behind the frustrations of patchwork modifications in which we have been caught for a whole generation, that it can begin once again to forge for itself a positive and dynamic faith. And what a magnificent reply such a policy would be to the specious claims of the despotisms! "What," we could then proclaim, "have the dictators to offer that is even a fraction as attractive? We offer employment without war, security without impoverishment, service without slavery — all this, and freedom too."

A. N. WHITEHEAD   1861–1947

The motive of success is not enough. It produces a short-sighted world which destroys the sources of its own prosperity. The cycles of trade depression which afflict the world warn us that business relations are infected through and through with the disease of short-sighted motives. The robber barons did not conduce to the prosperity of Europe in the Middle Ages, though some of them died prosperously in their beds. Their example is a warning to our civilization.

DRYDEN   1631–1700

> All, all of a piece throughout:
> Thy chase had a beast in view;
> Thy wars brought nothing about;
> Thy lovers were all untrue.
> 'Tis well an old age is out,
> And time to begin a new.

WILLIAM JAMES TO H. G. WELLS   1906

The moral flabbiness born of the exclusive worship of the bitch-goddess Success.

The Love of Money

J. M. KEYNES   1883–1946

At any rate, to me it seems clearer every day that the moral problem of our age is concerned with the love of money, with the habitual appeal to the money motive in nine-tenths of the activities of life, with the universal striving after individual economic security as the prime object of endeavour, with the social approbation of money as the measure of constructive success, and with the social appeal to the hoarding instinct as the foundation of the necessary provision for the family and for the future. The decaying religions around us, which have less and less interest for most people unless it be an agreeable form of magical ceremonial or of social observance, have lost their moral significance just because — unlike some of their earlier versions — they do not touch in the least degree on these essential matters. A revolution in our ways of thinking and feeling about money may become the growing purpose of contemporary embodiments of the ideal. Perhaps, therefore, Russian Communism does represent the first confused stirrings of a great religion.

For my own part, I believe there is social and psychological justification for significant inequalities of incomes and wealth, but not for such large disparities as exist to-day. There are valuable human activities which require the motive of money-making and the environment of private wealth-ownership for their full fruition. More-over, dangerous human proclivities can be canalized into comparatively harmless channels by the existence of opportunities for money-making and private wealth, which, if they cannot be satisfied in this way, may find their outlet in cruelty, the reckless pursuit of personal power and authority, and other forms of self-aggrandizement. It is better that a man should tyrannize over his bank balance than over his fellow-citizens; and whilst the former is sometimes denounced as being but a means to the latter, sometimes at least it is an alternative. But it is not necessary for the stimulation of these activities and the satisfaction of these proclivities that the game should be played for such high stakes as at present. Much lower stakes will serve the purpose equally well, as soon as the players are accustomed to them. The task of transmuting human nature must not be confused with the task of managing it. Though in the ideal commonwealth men may have been taught or inspired or bred to take no interest in the stakes, it may still be wise and prudent statesmanship to allow the game to be played, subject to rules and limitations, so long as the average man, or even a significant section of the community, is in fact strongly addicted to the money-making passion.

Pride of Service

HANS ZINSSER   1878–1940

He also brought back a deep respect for the men of the Regular Army and Navy services, who, with astonishingly few exceptions, rose nobly to immensely expanded responsibilities. Here were groups of expertly trained administrators, artillery officers, engineers, sanitarians, doctors, navigators, applied physicists, and the like, who carried on in the government employ for small pay, while their equals in civil life were selling their services to the highest bidder. It seemed to R. S. that if something of the spirit of the government technical services could be instilled into the politicians, the professions, and even into business, democracy might be cured of some of its ills. It convinced him that the money motive is not essential for high standards of performance. The answer seemed to be professional tradition and pride of service. The medical profession has some of it. It might be developed for other callings. Even bankers and brokers, manufacturers, grocers, and merchants in general might eventually regard their work as necessary specialized functions in a well-ordered world of sane capitalism, and might approach their tasks — as doctors, lawyers, engineers, and men in the learned professions approach their own — not perfectly, of course, and not without exception, but in general with a sense of responsibility and a tradition to restrain the greed of the unadulterated profit motive.

ABOUT AMERICA

I stand here at the window and try to figure out whether American men or women swing their arms more freely. There cannot be much to fear in a country where there are so many right faces going by. I keep asking myself where they all come from, and I keep thinking that maybe God was just making them up new around the next corner.

ROBERT FROST

The American People

BERNARD DEVOTO   1897–1955

And who were the American people? They were the product of the American continent: a new people in a new world. No one understands them who does not understand that the words mean what they say: this is the New World. They were, for instance, the first people in history who had ever had enough to eat. The first people who were able to build a government and a society from the ground up — and on unencumbered ground. The first people whose society had the dynamics of political equality and political freedom, a class system so flexible that it could not stratify into a caste system, and a common wealth so great that it made economic opportunity a birthright. All this makes a difference. It makes so great a difference that the pattern of their neural paths is radically different from any developed in response to the Old World.

They are hopeful and empirical. In their spring morning, those who made the nation did not doubt that it was the hope of the world. Mankind, they thought, must necessarily come to recognize the superiority of American institutions and, insofar as it could, must adopt or imitate them. They were neither visionaries nor utopians. They were realistic, hardheaded men who understood the dynamics of freedom and saw that if they were loosed in an empty continent an augmentation would follow for which nothing in the past could be an adequate gauge.

From then on, not the past but the future has counted in the United States. If it doesn't work, try something else; tomorrow is another day; don't sell America short; the sky is the limit; rags to riches; canal-boat boy to President.

That is what has denied the town dump decisive importance. No one has ever set up Utopia here, our utopian literature has always been clearly understood to be promotional, and the dump is hideous with brutality, exploitation, failure, and human wreckage. The actual line where men meet in society is always a line of blood and struggle. It is perfectly feasible to write American history in terms of blood and struggle, injustice, fraud, desperation. They are on a scale appropriate to the map; they are monstrous. But the difference is that tomorrow is another day. It has always proved to be. No estimate of what the United States could achieve in population, power, comfort, wealth, or living standard has ever proved adequate. When tomorrow came, the expectation proved to have been too moderate, the achievement invariably outran the prophecy.

The Heritage of the Children of Today

LOVELL THOMPSON   1954

We are seldom more than half right in what we tell the next generation; but we do move.

The vision of men is obscured. It is colored with hope and with doubt. The age of peculiar care for youth was a time when youth deeply needed care but scarcely had it. The feminine fifties were a time when the world needed to be feminine in the sense that it needed to be gentler, but it was a time when men were greedy for progress and what they were making was not a gentler world but the gilded age that followed. However, the gilt was false and tarnished before the end of the century, when the world should have been gay and somehow wasn't. All this brings us to the conclusion that the lost generation wanted to be lost and wasn't. It sought for a moment to avoid the complexities that Nicholas Longworth foresaw for it; sought to deceive him but did not. Neither the

Speaker nor the generation that has followed was deceived.

Although delayed by experience, and misled by hope, the miles as well as the years stretch out behind us. In the *Companion*'s century the first truly republican America rose out of its pioneer primitivism, built its great cities and learned to live in them temperately, and even in the end humanely. It learned not to have slaves either on plantations or whaling ships. It learned the responsibilities and limitations of greatness and that free and equal meant two cars and no baby sitter. It learned at last that the responsibility of a brighter day was a world responsibility.

In the first generation of the *Companion* the new republic seemed to grow down, to sink its roots deeply into its new world. In the next it grew out, covering the new land everywhere with the skeleton structure of a new society. In the third it grew in making thick and dense what had been only a living scaffolding. In the last generation it grew up.

But if on the one hand America grew up in these hundred years — with always a wistful backward look at what came to seem a carefree childhood, at what must always seem the only real childhood of America, the childhood of Huck Finn and Tom Sawyer, of the Little Women and the Bad Boy, and of Boy's Town and the youth of the Oregon Trail and the years before the mast — then on the other hand we keep hearing the voices of such men as Washington and Jefferson and Ben Franklin and old John Adams talking over the heads of five generations to an age that is again ready to understand them. They too felt themselves to be participants in an international rather than a national scene, but it was as Englishmen that they reached this point. What happened in between, and what the *Companion* records, is the birth and maturing of a new experience rooted in an unknown hemisphere.

That experience was simply this: hunters and farmers had to teach their great-great-grandchildren to be the scientists and the artists, the spokesmen of the most com-

plex nation in the world. They must create and people
a new nation at the same time out of the savage American
earth. They had to cram a millennium of accomplishment into a century. They must begin by losing their
civilization in order to compete with the stone age of the
Indian. They must forget much of what they had been
learning since the Romans retreated from Britain in order to relearn and reshape the experience of history into
their own pattern of aspiration, which is the heritage of
the children of today. It is their privilege that more was
never given and more was never asked of any other
generation.

Ad Hoc Effort

W. W. ROSTOW   1957

It is, of course, a cliché to assert that America developed,
from at least the 1830's, a cast of mind empirical in
method, pragmatic in solutions. But men have a need
and instinct to generalize their experience, to organize,
somehow, the chaos around them; and, when Americans
busy with limited practical chores reached out for larger
abstractions, they tended to balloon out concepts derived from personal, practical experience. They generalized what they intimately knew.

The American mind came to be one devoted to arduous
practical tasks, but filled also with an arsenal of general
concepts — often legitimate but partial insights — not
rigorously related to each other or to the bodies of fact
they were meant to illuminate. There was little in American life — its content and its values — that encouraged
the care and contemplation required to array the intermediate structure of abstractions, test them for internal
consistency, and to make orderly patterns of thought.

Men successfully operate processes by accumulating experience, feel, judgment, by sensing recurrent patterns
rather than isolating clean-cut logical connections of cause
and effect. This is how good captains of sailing vessels
have worked, good politicians, good businessmen. This
has been the typical American style in operating and de-

veloping the nation's society. Its success, however, is dependent on two conditions which are, to a degree, alternatives: first, that the problems confronted be, in their essence, relatively familiar, capable of solution by only moderately radical innovation, on the basis of existing principles or institutions; second, that time be allowed for the experimental exploration of possible solutions, and the osmotic process of accepting change. The more the time permitted, the greater the workability of a technique of problem-solving by empirical experiment and the institutional change-inertia.

It is, thus, in the less radical orders of innovation — in science, industry, and politics — that the nation has excelled. Or, put another way, the American style is least effective when it confronts issues which require radical innovation promptly.

It is precisely here that we are in trouble. We live in a world of extremely rapid change, where the survival of our society hinges on prompt innovation, while our intellectual style and our national institutions are accommodated to the slow and carefully balanced modifications of a successful ongoing process.

What is the result? American policy-making consists in a series of reactions to major crises. Having failed to define, to anticipate, and to deal with forces loose in the world, having tried merely to keep the great machine of government ticking over from day to day, at last the problems never recognized or swept under the rug come ticking in over the incoming cable. Then, as a nation of operators, we respect the reality of the matter, and — in the past at least — we have turned to with vigor. We rig up an *ad hoc* effort — often bypassing all the bureaucratic machinery created to deal with our affairs, launch hastily some new courses of action; and these become the working norms of policy until the next crisis comes along.

We are, thus, applying an empirical, pragmatic style, created out of a remarkably continuous national experience, to a world where it is altogether possible that crisis take the form of situations where even the most vigorous

ad hoc effort by the nation would come too late to re-
trieve our abiding interests.

Americans

GUNNAR MYRDAL   1956

It is true that the Americans tried eagerly to convince
themselves at the very inauguration of the Marshall Plan
that they were acting solely with their own national interest in view, but this was only a further example of the
strange suspicion on the part of the American people of
their own generous motives, which I once analyzed as a
slightly perverted element of their Puritan tradition.

Money Is Not Enough

CLAUDE M. FUESS   1958

If what we believe to be our American culture is to be
preserved, it will be through the research, the resource-
fulness, and the influence of a comparatively small group
of talented persons. Subjecting a larger and larger proportion of our youth to elementary mathematical and
scientific instruction will not accomplish what we are after.
It is essential that every American child should learn to
read and write and cipher. But it is even more desirable
at the moment that the best should get the best. For the
moment we should be more concerned with the uncommon than with the average. Selecting the best-qualified,
educating them to the highest level of which they are
capable, and then using them as their genius directs —
this is the policy which might conceivably save us from
destruction. Someone said recently, "A keen mind has
become a resource more valuable than uranium . . . The
crying need of our country today is the trained mind, the
skilled worker, the creative thinker." We shall have to
support such a far-reaching plan not only with taxation
but with uneasing cooperation.

Indeed, our present problem can be solved only in part
by the expenditure of vast sums of money. Deep in the
consciousness of a large percentage of Americans is an

anti-intellectualism almost sinister in its manifestations, an emotional distrust of the human mind whenever it functions above the twelfth-grade level. Our only half-concealed contempt for or indifference to the operations of scholars and teachers has brought them into disrepute. How can we help being dismayed when we learn from a recent survey that six out of every ten Americans hadn't read a book — not a single book — in the preceding year?

The national habit of measuring success by cash income has inevitably affected the popular judgment on educators. Higher salaries will naturally improve a professor's status in the community. But it will certainly take some time for public-school teachers, who in the long run must guide every step towards improvement, to attain the living standards of most members of school committees and Parent-Teacher Associations. Here again money cannot do everything. The values of the American people will have to become more spiritual and intellectual and less material.

All this has to some people always seemed important, but it is now important for everybody. We are in direct rivalry with nations which may not possess our money but which have an amazing constructive vitality. Every American should be familiar with Voltaire's oft-quoted aphorism, "History is only the pattern of silken slippers descending the stairs to the thunder of hobnailed boots climbing upward from below" — which is just as appropriate for nations as it is for classes of society. It is nothing new for a vigorous race, adventurous and imaginative, industrious and stoical, to win a place in the sun and have visions of world domination. The pattern from then on is familiar. When prosperity play and pleasure seem more attractive than hard work, and a drop in morale is inevitable then is precisely the moment when a fresh people, barbarian perhaps but willing to endure hardships and make sacrifices, has so often risen and overthrown the enervated and demoralized older society.

The symptoms of deterioration are all around us in our apprehensions, our frequent hysteria, our willingness to think that all our sins can be redeemed by an increased budget. In education we have been repeatedly warned by specialists who know their stuff. We need new school buildings and better salaries for teachers, but we need even more some comprehension of the way in which education on the highest levels may be utilized to make us safe and strong. Let us spend money where it is needed, but let us go further. Let us through every possible agency determine just where we stand and just what is required to restore the pioneer spirit. Only by drastic measures can we reverse a trend so reminiscent of what has happened to earlier empires.

To Save Our Souls

GUNNAR MYRDAL   1956

What, in the end, are we going to do with our wealth, except to increase it all the time and make it ever more certain that all of us have an equal opportunity to acquire it? I admit that we are not there yet. But to reach it is definitely within our grasp. What then, on the other side of the hills, is our distant goal? What shall we strive for? This is an important issue, for "man doth not live by bread alone."

While the dreamers, planners, and fighters of earlier generations are finally getting almost all they asked for, somehow the "better life" in a moral and spiritual sense, the craving for which was their supreme inspiration, is slow in developing. And there is an uncomfortable and deep uncertainty concerning how we should attain it.

To my mind, there is no doubt that our moral dilemma is related to the fact that the "welfare state," which we have built up, with which we feel deeply identified, which we are not going to give up, and which we are bent upon constantly improving, is nationalistic. Solidarity is rapidly developing but it is increasingly confined within the national boundaries. At the same time, because of revolutionary technological and political changes, nations are inevitably moving towards greater interdependence.

Not merely to save the world, but primarily to save our

own souls, there should again be dreamers, planners, and
fighters, in the midst of our nations, who would take upon
themselves the important social function in democracy
of raising our sights — so far ahead that their proponents
again form a definite minority in their nations and avoid
the unbearable discomfort for reformers of a climate of
substantial agreement.

"Not merely to save the world, but primarily to save our
own souls," as Walt and Elspeth Rostow quoted, and then
added, "There is all the moral intensity of a great Lutheran
bishop in Gunnar Myrdal, . . . and it is the Lutheran bishop
who gives the final word."

The Perfectionists

THORNTON WILDER   1952

To this day many an American is breaking his life on an
excessive demand for the perfect, the absolute, and the
boundless in realms where it is accorded to few — in love
and friendship, for example. The doctrines of moderation
and the golden mean may have flourished in Rome and
in China (overcrowded and overgoverned countries),
but they do not flourish here, save as counsels of despair.
The injunction to be content with your lot and in the
situation where God has placed you is not an expression
of New World thinking. We do not feel ourselves to
be subject to lot and we do not cast God in the role of a
civil administrator or of a feudal baron.

PART
VIII

THEY MUST HAVE PEACE, SECURITY, AND LIBERTY

Republics have a longer life and en-joy better fortune than principalities, because they can profit by their greater internal diversity. They are the better able to meet emergencies.
MACHIAVELLI

Democracy

JULIEN BENDA   1867–1956

Bring all these attacks upon democracy together.
Whether they are led by people thirsting for conquest,
or by a class jealous of government, or by another class
eager to exercise force, or by artists frustrated in their
need to express their feelings, they all spring from a single desire, the desire for sensation. They all verify what
Socrates said two thousand years ago to the sophist Callicles. He is their true patron when, in the name of personal interest, they attack the commands of conscience.
"The basis of your philosophy," Socrates said, "is the
need for sensation." The true enemy of democratic principles is the *libido sentiendi,* of which the *libido domi-
nandi* is only one phase. And that is natural enough, for
the essence of democracy is asceticism.

Callicles was one of Socrates' antagonists in the *Gorgias.*
Where does Santayana say that to make a democracy successful
its citizens must have something of the saint and something too
of the hero?

CARL L. BECKER   1873–1945

The case for democracy is that it accepts the rational and
humane values as ends, and proposes as the means of
realizing them the minimum of coercion and the maximum of voluntary assent. We may well abandon the cos-
mological temple in which the democratic ideology originally enshrined these values without renouncing the

faith it was designed to celebrate. The essence of that faith is belief in the capacity of man, as a rational and humane creature, to achieve the good life by rational and humane means. Apart from this faith, there is no alternative for the modern man except cynicism or despair — or the resort to naked force, which is itself but masked despair or cynicism disguised. For even more obvious now than in the seventeenth century is the truth of Pascal's famous dictum: "Thought makes the whole dignity of man; therefore, endeavor to think well, that is the only morality." The chief virtue of democracy, and the sole reason for cherishing it, is that with all its faults it still provides the most favorable conditions for the maintenance of that dignity and the practice of that morality.

Fascism

BARTOLOMEO VANZETTI
April 14, 1923
Charlestown Prison

Dear Comrade Blackwell:

The really and great damage that the fascism has done, or has revealed, is the moral lowness in which we have fallen after the war and the revolutionary over-excitation of the last few years.

It is incredible the insult made to the liberty, to the life, to the dignity of the human beings, by other human beings. And it is humiliating, for he who feels the common humanity that ties together all the men, good and bad, to think that all the committed infamies have not produced in the crowd an adequate sense of rebellion, of horrors, of disgust. It is humiliating to human beings, the possibility of such ferocity, of such cowardness. It is humiliating that men, who have reached the power only because, deprived of any moral or intellectual scrupols, they had known how to pluck the good moment to blackmail the *borgesia,* may find the approbation, no matter if by a momentary abberration, of a number of persons sufficient to impose upon all countries their tyranny.

Therefore, the rescue expected and invocated by us must be before all a moral rescue; the re-valuation of the human liberty and dignity. It must be the condamnation of the Fascismo not only as a political and economic fact, but also and over all, as a criminal phenomenon, as the exploitation of a purulent growth which had been going, forming and ripening itself in the sick body of the social organism.

There are some, also among the so-called subversives, who are saying that the Fascisti have taught to us how we must do, and they, these subversives, are intentioned to imitate and to exacerbate the fascisti methods.

This is the great danger, the danger of the tomorrow; the danger, I mean, that, after the Fascismo, declined from internal dissolution or by external attack, may have to follow a period of insensate violences, of sterile vendettes, which would exhaust in little episodes of blood that energy which should be employed for a radical transformation of the social arrangements such to render impossible the repetition of the present horrors.

The Fascisti's methods may be good for who inspires to become a tyrant. They are certainly bad for he who will make "opera" of a liberator, for he who will collaborate to rise all humanity to a dignity of free and conscient men.

We remain as always we were, the partisans of the liberty, of all the liberty.

I hope you will agree my bad translation of Malatesta's words. They are words of one of the most learned, serene, courageous, and powerful mind, among the minds of the sons of women through the whole history, and of a magnanimous heart.

Politicians — A Dilemma

F. S. OLIVER   1864–1934

Few men are placed in such fortunate circumstances as to be able to gain office, or to keep it for any length of time, without misleading or bamboozling the people. A classic instance of the difficulty of plain dealing is, that though men can often be induced, when their faculties are on the alert, to make an admirable resolution, they are not easily kept at the sticking point. Their decision is rarely fixed so firmly or so permanently in their minds that when the bills fall due, which by implication they have accepted, they will honor them without protest. It is often harder to induce them to do the things by which alone their resolution can be carried into effect than it was at the beginning to lead them to it. This arises not from perfidy, but from forgetfulness or confusion of mind, or because some new interest has driven out the old. Sometimes, as with children, their attention must be occupied with an entertaining toy while the politician stealthily makes the matter secure; sometimes, like horses, they have to be blindfolded in order to get them out of a burning stable.

In dealing with foreign nations the politician who wishes to act uprightly is even harder put to it; for there the difficulty is not popular ignorance and simplicity, but the expert knowledge of able officials who, as part of their professional training, have had to make themselves conversant with the blunders, deceptions, and disappointments of the past, and who are filled with suspicions that are none the less justified because they happen to be centuries old.

If the conscience of an honest man lays down stern rules, so also does the art of politics. At a juncture where no accommodation is possible between the two, the politician may be faced by these alternatives: "Shall I break the rules of my art in order to save my private honor? or shall I break the rules of my conscience in order to fulfill my public trust?"

How a politician will use idols and ideals for helping him to gain power and keep it:

No politician can hope to prosper unless he has a weather-sense that warns him in good time what to expect from each of these forces. Though neither the one nor the other is in any way concerned with the principles of his art, though both are merely external phenomena that at one time he will have cause to curse, at another to bless, it is an important part of his business to keep them under constant observation. An ideal which appears to be attracting an unusual degree of popular sympathy, or an idol whose worshippers have taken alarm, may threaten him with disaster or, on the other hand, they may provide him with an opportunity for overwhelming his opponents and raising himself to power on a wave of enthusiasm, prejudice, or panic. In much the same way it was an important part of the business of the master of one of the old sailing-ships to watch the sky and the sea, and to use both winds and currents for bringing him safe into harbor, or, if the elements were wholly adverse, for enabling him at least to escape shipwreck.

The politician will almost certainly fail who devotes his energies either to the discovery of ideals or to the installation of idols. These are matters for prophets in the one case and for high-priests in the other. But if the politician feels strongly or sees clearly that professions of devotion to a certain ideal or idol are likely to serve his purpose, he will not be acting contrary to the principles of his art in echoing the prophetic phrases or in prostrating himself devoutly in the temple.

It is, however, a moot question how far it is advantageous for him to be a true believer. The answer will not be the same in every case. Broadly speaking, his action is more likely to be effective if he has an unshaken faith in the idol he is defending than if he is a sceptic. But it is very dangerous for him to believe whole-heartedly in any ideal. He may profess as strong a sympathy as he pleases for its declared objective or ultimate goal; but this is as far as he can safely go. He is no true politician if he allows his judgment to be subjugated by the creeds and dogmas of fanatics who, when they gain power, are ready to assassinate with a puerile and remorseless logic, first their opponents, and afterwards the ideal itself which they have undertaken to serve. Moreover, idealism cannot support itself without enthusiasm, which is a force no less destructive and incalculable than logic; for, like wine, it puts the judgment in a heat. The politician who desires to advance his own fortunes through the success of the cause he has espoused, should keep his head cool.

The brief period of idealistic exhilaration, when old idols are thrown crashing from their pedestals, is followed surely by a reaction, during which disappointment works strongly and suspicions are rife. The early leaders are liable to lose their prestige in a tumult of reproaches. There is confusion, doubt, discontent, and often the whole movement lies breathless and exhausted at the mercy of any able and audacious reactionary. The politician will act wisely if, at the beginning, he gladly suffers his own importance to be eclipsed by the brilliancy of ephemeral iconoclasts. For these men soon begin to blunder, to distrust one another, and to be distrusted by their followers. When they have fallen into discredit, the politician will find his opportunity in rallying the mutinous and broken ranks, in reviving their courage with common sense, in staving off defeat, and possibly in securing and consolidating some considerable portion of the previous gains.

In praise of politicians:

The notion that politics is all a cheat and that politicians are no better than welshers has subsisted ever since the beginning. Raleigh's early malediction is not lacking in vigor:

> *Tell men of high condition*
> *That manage the Estate,*
> *Their purpose is ambition,*
> *Their practice only hate:*
> *And if they once reply,*
> *Then give them all the lie.*

Raleigh was himself a politician — a politician whose career when he wrote was ending in calamity.

Nearly two hundred years later, Adam Smith wrote less violently, but even more contemptuously, of "that insidious and crafty animal, vulgarly called a statesman or politician, whose councils are directed by the momentary fluctuations of affairs." Adam Smith was no politician, but one of the serenest and most kindly spirits that ever practised philosophy and took delight in the society of their fellow-men. Moreover, he enjoyed the confidence of Mr. Pitt and the friendship of Mr. Burke. It would be hard to find any character in literature who was more immune from the gnawings of envy and a sense of personal grievance.

Many of us, carried away at one time and another by hero-worship or partisanship, have attempted to discriminate between politicians and statesmen; that is, between the "insidious and crafty animal" and the disinterested public servant. But Adam Smith, being an accurate observer, refused to draw this false distinction. Any representative list of the most illustrious British statesmen would surely include the names of Bolingbroke, Walpole, Chatham, William Pitt the younger, Charles James Fox, Castlereagh, Peel, Disraeli, Gladstone. And the same names would figure for certain in any representative list of our most artful and indefatigable politicians. Adam Smith was in error, not in confounding the one with the other, but only in his too wholesale condemnation of both. Even the serenest philosopher may be forgiven an occasional outburst of vivacity.

Moralists, idealists, and humanitarians are equally severe. They hold converse with the politician from necessity, but rarely from choice. Their attitude is one of cold suspicion. They are shocked by his unveracity, by the deadness of his soul to all the higher emotions. Obviously he cares for nothing in the world except the grinding of his own axe. He is never more than a lip-servant of sacred causes, and then only when they happen to be in fashion.

The antipathy that soldiers, sailors, and country gentlemen show for the politician is rooted in their conviction that no one who talks so much, and obviously knows so little, about the conduct of war and the management of land can possibly understand any department whatsoever of public affairs.

The great army of company directors and others of a certain age, whom newspapers describe as "captains of industry," condemn him for his lack of practical ability, initiative, push-and-go; they suspect him of being a lazy fellow who likes to draw a salary for doing next to nothing.

Jingos denounce him as a traitor if he is not forever plucking foreign nations by the beard. Pacifists, on the other hand, consider him to be the chief cause of war by reason, sometimes of his timid opportunism, at others of his truculence; the compromises he agrees to in order to curry favor with public opinion are fatal to peace; he is the puppet of military cliques, and shares all the passions and panics that degrade the mob.

The magnates of the popular press, secure behind their private telephone entanglements, sneer at his want of courage; and the man-of-the-world — most ingenuous of dotterels — takes up the same tale from his club armchair.

What humbug it is, for the most part! And what a welter should we be in, if the politicians, taking these lectures to heart, were to hand over the management of public affairs to their critics!

It must be placed to the politician's credit that he takes our contumelious treatment of him in such good part, with so little whining and loss of temper. He has a good case against us, if he cared to press it, inasmuch as we insist upon regarding him as part of a public show got up for our entertainment, and look on — hissing or applauding — while he is baited in the House of Commons, on the platform, and in the press.

This sport has been so long customary that we are callous to its cruelty. The contemporaries of a politician are apt to value him less for the useful services he does them than for the skill and sturdiness of his fighting. He rarely gets a just appraisement until historians come to deal with him long after he is dead. In order to keep his popularity he must stand torture as stoically as a Red Indian or a Chinaman; if he is seen to flinch, it is all up with him. And he has even worse things to bear than these personal assaults and batteries. For the average politician, though he thinks a great deal about his own career, is by nature a constructive animal. He has a craving — often an insatiable craving — to be making something. No sooner is he in office than he becomes engrossed in shaping policies, in legislation, and in administrative acts. It is through this passion that he is most vulnerable. For it takes a man of singular fortitude to watch with composure, on his outgoing from office, the foundations that he has dug with so much pain and labor left to silt up; or worse still, his all-but-finished building let go to rack and ruin for want of the little effort, the few slates and timbers, that would have made it weather-proof and habitable.

We shall do the politician an injustice if we take too seriously the heroics and pathetics with which he is so apt to decorate and conclude his speeches. These for the most part are only common form, tags which everybody uses, because the audience is supposed to relish them. It would be harsh to judge him a hypocrite on sentiments so undeliberate. The true temperature of his benevolence cannot be deduced from his rhetoric, which is for the most part meaningless and empty; but it may be gauged with some approach to accuracy from his acts, and by noting the things he does or tries to do, prevents or tries to prevent.

By nature he is probably no poorer and no richer than the rest of us in kindly warmth and desire to alleviate suffering; but the conditions of his calling place him at a manifest advantage. For the soil of politics is peculiarly congenial to the growth and burgeoning of an understanding sympathy with one's fellow-creatures. By force of circumstances the politician mixes, fights, and fraternizes with all sorts and conditions of men. He cannot listen day after day to his opponents without shaking off much of his original narrow-mindedness. On his first arrival at Westminster he may be shocked and astounded to hear men asseverating doctrines that strike at the very roots of his philosophy. And he is also taken aback because it is evident that the House of Commons does not regard such speakers as either lunatics or criminals. But it is not long before he begins to realize that even the most outrageous of them are often sincere and sometimes right. If you would know whether a man is true or false, it is a great help to be placed where you can watch his eyes and listen to the tones of his voice. The politician has the good fortune to meet people face to face whose opinions he abhors, to be buffeted by them, to give as good as he gets and note how they take it. This method draws a great deal of the venom out of controversy.

The fact that we are so much bewildered and bedevilled at the present time, instead of moving us to sympathy for the politician, makes us all the angrier with him. If we saw our way clearly, we should probably be less censorious. We resent his being less flurried, less puzzled, than we are; and we therefore conclude that he must be a shallow creature, without sense enough to be aware of danger. For many of us have convinced ourselves that the old world is coming to an end; and while some appear to think that civilization will be quenched utterly in the darkness of barbarism, others are hopeful that, from the fuliginous bonfire of antique systems, a new and more radiant order will arise.

These high-wrought fancies leave the average politician untouched. He would agree that the light is bad; but he cannot understand why this should set us wondering whether we are watching a sunset or waiting for the dawn. He sees no mysterious glimmerings in any part of the horizon. He is a commonplace fellow who goes by his watch, and his watch tells him it is broad day. The darkness is nothing more than an overhead autumnal fog, which will clear away when the wind rises. The obscurity interferes to some extent with his work; but he does not make it an excuse for idling or despondency. When people talk to him about an impending doom, he is uninterested and incredulous. It is perhaps one of his defects to place too much confidence in familiar custom. Left entirely to himself, he has been known to carry on his business as usual, until the falling skies caught him unawares and crushed him. He is little troubled with nightmares. His eyes are not fixed on the millennium nor yet precisely on the end of his own nose, but somewhere between the two. He deals with things as they occur, and prides himself on not thinking of them too far ahead. We abuse him: he expects this, and does not complain. Indeed, like a donkey that is accustomed to being beaten behind, he might stand stock-still from sheer astonishment were the abuse suddenly to cease.

If we eventually escape from our present perplexities, it will not be because theorists have discovered some fine new principle of salvation; or because newspapers have scolded and pointed angry fingers at this one or that; or because we, their readers, have become excited and have demanded that "something must be done." It will be because these decent, hard-working, cheerful, valiant, knock-about politicians, whose mysterious business it is to manage our affairs by breaking one another's heads, shall have carried on with their work as if nothing extraordinary was happening — just as Walpole did even in the worst of times — and shall have "jumbled something" out of their contentions that will be of advantage to their country. The notion that we can save ourselves without their help is an illusion; for politics is not one of those crafts that can be learned by the light of nature without an apprenticeship.

The Smile of the World

JOHN MORLEY   1838–1923

And what is this smile of the world, to win which we are bidden to sacrifice our moral manhood; this frown of the world, whose terrors are more awful than the withering up of truth and the slow going out of light within the souls of us? Consider the triviality of life and conversation and purpose, in the bulk of those whose approval is held out for our prize and the mark of our high calling. Measure, if you can, the empire over them of prejudice unadulterated by a single element of rationality, and weigh, if you can, the huge burden of custom, unrelieved by a single leavening particle of fresh thought. Ponder the share which selfishness and love of ease have in the vitality and the maintenance of the opinions that we are forbidden to dispute. Then how pitiful a thing seems the approval or disapproval of these creatures of the conventions of the hour, as one figures the merciless vastness of the universe of matter sweeping us headlong through viewless space; as one hears the wail of misery that is forever ascending to the deaf gods; as one counts the little tale of the years that separate us from eternal silence. In the light of these things, a man should surely dare to live his small span of life with little heed of the common speech upon him or his life, only caring that his days may be full of reality, and his conversation of truth-speaking and wholeness.

Politics and Philosophy

PLUTARCH   46–120

They are wrong who think that politics is like an ocean voyage or a military campaign, something to be done with some particular end in view, something which leaves off as soon as that end is reached. It is not a public chore, to be got over with. It is a way of life. It is the life of a domesticated political and social creature who is born with a love for public life, with a desire for honor, with a feeling for his fellows; and it lasts as long as need be.

It is not simply office-holding, not just keeping your place, not just raising your voice from the floor, not just ranting on the rostrum with speeches and motions; which is what many people think politics is; just as they think of course you are a philosopher if you sit in a chair and lecture, or if you are able to carry through a dispute over a book. The even and consistent, day in day out, work and practice of both politics and philosophy escape them.

Politics and philosophy are alike. Socrates neither set out benches for his students, nor sat on a platform, nor set hours for his lectures. He was philosophizing all the time — while he was joking, while he was drinking, while he was soldiering, whenever he met you on the street, and at the end when he was in prison and drinking the poison. He was the first to show that all your life, all the time, in everything you do, whatever you are doing, is the time for philosophy. And so also it is of politics.

Philosophers and Statesmen

SPINOZA, *in the opening chapter of his "Tractatus Politicus"*   1632–1677

Philosophers regard the emotions by which we are torn as vices into which men fall by their own fault; they therefore laugh at them, weep over them, sneer at them, or (if they wish to appear more pious than others) denounce them. So they think they are doing something wonderful and pre-eminently scientific when they praise a human nature which exists nowhere and attack human nature as it really is. They conceive men, not as they are, but as they would wish them to be. The result is that they write satires instead of ethics, and that they have never produced a political theory which is of any use, but something which could be regarded as a Chimera, or put in practice in Utopia or in the Golden Age the poets talk about, where, to be sure, it was not needed. The result is that theory is held to be discrepant from practice in all the studies intended to be of use, but above all in the study of politics, and no men are thought less fitted to govern a state than theorists or philosophers.

Statesmen, on the other hand, are supposed to plot against men rather than to look after them, and to be clever rather than wise. Experience forsooth has taught them that there will be vices so long as there are men. They study to be beforehand with human depravity. Because they do this by those arts which long experience has taught and which are practised by men more moved by fear than by reason, they seem to be hostile to religion and especially to theologians. These think that the authorities ought to carry on public business by the rules of piety which are binding on individuals. But there is no doubt that the statesmen have written much better about politics than the philosophers. Experience was their teacher, and they learnt nothing which could not be used.

HORACE WHITE *said about Lincoln:* 1834–1916

The popular conception of Mr. Lincoln as one not seeking public honors, but not avoiding public duties, is a *post-bellum* growth, very wide of the mark. He was entirely human in this regard, but his desire for political preferment was hedged about by a sense of obligation to the truth which nothing could shake. This fidelity to truth was ingrained and unchangeable. In all the speeches I ever heard him make — and they were many — he never even insinuated an untruth, nor did he ever fail when stating his opponent's positions to state them fully and fairly. He often stated his opponent's position better than his opponent did or could. To say what was false, or even to leave his hearers under a wrong impression, was impossible to him. Within this high inclosure he was as ambitious of earthly honors as any man of his time. Furthermore, he was an adept at log-rolling or any political game that did not involve falsity. I was Secretary of the Republican State Committee of Illinois during some years when he was in active campaign work. He was often present at meetings of the committee, although not a member, and took part in the committee work. His judgment was very much deferred to in such matters. He was one of the shrewdest politicians of the State. Nobody had had more experience in that way, nobody knew better than he what was passing in the minds of the people. Nobody knew better how to turn things to advantage politically, and nobody was readier to take such advantage, provided it did not involve dishonorable means. He could not cheat people out of their votes any more than out of their money. The Abraham Lincoln that some people have pictured to themselves, sitting in his dingy law office, working over his cases till the voice of duty roused him, never existed. If this had been his type, he never would have been called at all. It was precisely because he was up and stirring, and in hot, incessant competition with his fellows for earthly honors, that the public eye became fixed upon him and the public ear attuned to his words. Fortunate was it for all of us that he was no shrinking patriot, that he was moved as other men are moved, so that his fellows might take heed of him and know him as one of themselves, and as fit to be their leader in a crisis.

Politics Is an Art

FELIX FRANKFURTER   1882–

Government is itself an art, one of the subtlest of the arts. It is neither business, nor technology, nor applied science. It is the art of making men live together in peace and with reasonable happiness. Among the instruments for governing are organization, technological skill, and scientific methods. But they are all instruments, not ends. And that is why the art of governing has been achieved best by men to whom governing is itself a profession. One of the shallowest disdains is the sneer against the professional politician. The invidious implication of the phrase is, of course, against those who pursue self-interest through politics. But too prevalently the baby is thrown out with the bath. We forget that the most successful statesmen have been professionals. Walpole, Pitt, Gladstone, Disraeli, and Asquith were professional politicians. Beveridge's *Life of Abraham Lincoln* serves as a reminder that Lincoln was a professional politician. Politics was Roosevelt's profession; Wilson was all his life, at least preoccupied with politics; and Calvin Coolidge, though nominally a lawyer, has had no profession except politics. Canada emphasizes the professionalism of politics by making the leader of the Opposition a paid officer of state.

"The duties of all public officers" (Jackson wrote in his first message to Congress) "are, or at least admit of being made, so plain and simple that men of intelligence may readily qualify themselves for their performance; and I cannot but believe that more is lost by the long continuance of men in office than is generally to be gained by their experience. I submit, therefore, to your consideration whether the efficiency of the Government would not be promoted and official industry and integrity better secured by a general extension of the law which limits appointments to four years."

There is this much to be said for Jackson's rustic view. Government then was operating within a relatively limited scope. In large measure, it was forbidding conduct; it was not itself an extensive participant in devising complicated arrangements of society and composing the conflict of its manifold interests. But Harding, nearly a hundred years after Jackson, had not even Jackson's excuse. The growing complexity of social organization had compelled a steady extension of legal control over economic and social interests. At first this intervention was largely through specific legislative directions, depending for enforcement generally upon the cumbersome and ineffective machinery of the criminal law. By the pressure of experience, legislative regulation of economic and social activities turned to administrative instruments. The extent and range of governmental participation in affairs, the complexity of its administrative devices, and the intricacy of the technical problems with which they were dealing had never been greater than when Harding came to the Presidency. There never was a more pathetic misapprehension of responsibility than Harding's touching statement that "Government after all is a very simple thing."

I recall the sentence and it deserves to be remembered, because Harding expressed the traditional American conception of government still deeply inured in American opinion. It is an assertion of faith in simplicity that serves as an escape from the painful problems due to the complexity of government. Until these notions of deluding simplicity are completely rooted out, we shall never truly face our problems of government.

ELIHU ROOT   1845–1937

The real difficulty appears to be that the new conditions incident to the extraordinary industrial development of the last half-century are continuously and progressively demanding the readjustment of the relations between great bodies of men and the establishment of new legal rights and obligations not contemplated when existing laws were passed or existing limitations upon the powers of government were prescribed in our Constitution. In place of the old individual independence of life in which every intelligent and healthy citizen was competent to take care of himself and his family, we have come to a high degree of interdependence in which the greater part of our people have to rely for all the necessities of life upon the systematized co-operation of a vast number of other men working through complicated industrial and commercial machinery. Instead of the completeness of individual effort working out its own results in obtaining food and clothing and shelter, we have specialization and division of labor which leaves each individual unable to apply his industry and intelligence except in co-operation with a great number of others whose activity conjoined to his is necessary to produce any useful result. Instead of the give-and-take of free individual contract, the tremendous power of organization has combined great aggregations of capital in enormous industrial establishments working through vast agencies of commerce and employing great masses of men in movements of production and transportation and trade, so great in the mass that each individual concerned in them is quite helpless by himself. The relations between the employer and the employed, between the owners of aggregated capital and the units of organized labor, between the small producer, the small trader, the consumer, and the great transporting and manufacturing and distributing agencies, all present new questions for the solution of which the old reliance upon the free action of individual wills appears quite inadequate. And in many directions the intervention of that organized control which we call government seems necessary to produce the same result of justice and right conduct which obtained through the attrition of individuals before the new conditions arose.

Democracy and Administration

DAVID E. LILIENTHAL   1899–

I find it impossible to comprehend how democracy can be a living reality if people are remote from their government and in their daily lives are not made a part of it, or if the control and direction of making a living — industry, farming, the distribution of goods — is far removed from the stream of life and from the local community.

"Centralization" is no mere technical matter of "management," of "bigness versus smallness." We are dealing here with those deep urgencies of the human spirit which are embodied in the faith we call "democracy."

It was ironic that centralized businesses should become, as they did, eloquent advocates of the merits of decentralization in government. From their central headquarters they began to issue statements and brochures. And a wondrous state of confusion arose in the minds of men: they ate food bought at a store that had its replica in almost every town from coast to coast; they took their ease in standard chairs; they wore suits of identical weave and pattern and shoes identical with those worn all over the country. In the midst of this uniformity they all listened on the radio to the same program at the same time, a program that bewailed the evils of "regimentation," or they read an indignant editorial in their local evening papers (identical with an editorial that same day in a dozen other newspapers of the same chain) urging them to vote for a candidate who said he would bring an end to centralization in government.

I am not one who is attracted by that appealing combination of big business and little government. I believe that the federal government must have large grants of power progressively to deal with problems that are national in their consequences and remedy, problems too broad to be handled by local political units. I am convinced, as surely most realistic men must be, that in the future further responsibilities will have to be assumed by the central government to deal with national issues which centralized business inevitably creates. The war has advanced this trend.

The people have a right to demand that their federal government provide them an opportunity to share in the benefits of advances in science and research, the right to demand protection from economic abuses beyond the power of their local political units to control. But they have the further right to insist that the methods of administration used to carry out the very laws enacted for their individual welfare will not atrophy the human resources of their democracy.

It is folly to forget that the same dangers and the same temptations exist whether the centralization is in government or in mammoth business enterprise. In both cases the problem is to capture the advantages that come with such centralized authority as we find we must have, and at the same time to avoid the hazards of overcentralized administration of those central powers.

The distinction between authority and its administration is a vital one. For a long time all of us — administrators, citizens, and politicians — have been confused on this point. We have acted on the assumption that because there was an increasing need for centralized authority, the centralized execution of that authority was likewise inevitable. We have assumed that, as new powers were granted to the government with its seat at Washington, these powers therefore must also be administered from Washington. Out of lethargy and confusion we have taken it for granted that the price of federal action was a topheavy, cumbersome administration. Clearly this is nonsense. The problem is to divorce the two ideas of authority and administration of authority.

Centralization at the national capital or within a business undertaking always glorifies the importance of pieces of paper. This dims the sense of reality. As men and organizations acquire a preoccupation with papers, they become less understanding, less perceptive of the reality of those matters with which they should be dealing: particular human problems, particular human beings, actual things in a real America — highways, wheat, barges, drought, floods, back yards, blast furnaces. The reason why there is and always has been so much bureaucratic spirit, such organizational intrigue, so much pathological personal ambition, so many burning jealousies and vendettas in a capital city (any capital city, not only Washington), is no mystery. The facts with which a highly centralized institution deals tend to be the men and women of that institution itself, and their ideas and ambitions. To maintain perspective and human understanding in the atmosphere of centralization is a task that many able and conscientious people have found wellnigh impossible.

Making decisions from papers has a dehumanizing effect. Much of man's inhumanity to man is explained by it. Almost all great observers of mankind have noted it. In *War and Peace* Tolstoy makes it particularly clear. Pierre Bezukhov is standing a captive before one of Napoleon's generals, Marshal Davout. "At the first glance, when Davout had only raised his head from the papers where human affairs and lives were indicated by numbers, Pierre was merely a circumstance, and Davout could have shot him without burdening his conscience with an evil deed, but now he saw in him a human being . . ." To see each citizen thus as a "human being" is easy at the grass roots. That is where more of the functions of our federal government should be exercised.

The permanence of democracy indeed demands this. For the cumulative effect of overcentralization of administration in a national capital is greatly to reduce the effectiveness of government. It is serious enough in itself when, because of remoteness and ignorance of local conditions or the slowness of their operation, laws and programs fail of their purposes. We are threatened, however, with an even more disastrous sequence, the loss of the people's confidence, the very foundation of democratic government. Confidence does not flourish in a "government continually at a distance and out of sight," to use the language of Alexander Hamilton, himself a constant advocate of strong central authority. On the other hand, said Hamilton, "the more the operations of the national authority are intermingled in the ordinary exercise of government, the more the citizens are accustomed to meet with it in the common occurrences of their political life, the more it is familiarized to their sight and to their feelings, the further it enters into those objects which touch the most sensible chords and put into motion the most active springs of the human heart, the greater will be the probability that it will conciliate the respect and attachment of the community."

When "the respect and attachment of the community" give place to uneasiness, fears develop that the granting of further powers may be abused. Ridicule of the capriciousness of some goverrment officials takes the place of pride. Democracy cannot thrive long in an atmosphere of scorn or fear. One of two things ultimately happens: either distrustful citizens, their fears often capitalized upon by selfish men, refuse to yield to the national government the powers which it should have in the common interest; or an arrogant central government imposes its will by force. In either case the substance of democracy has perished.

Eastman on Administration

JOSEPH B. EASTMAN   1882–1944

With the country as big and complex as it is, administrative tribunals like the Interstate Commerce Commission are necessities. Probably we shall have more rather than less. To be successful they must be masters of their own souls, and known to be such. It is the duty of the President to determine their personnel through the power of appointment, and it is the duty of Congress to determine by statute the policies which they are to administer; but in the administration of those policies these tribunals must not be under the domination or influence of either the President or Congress or of anything else than their own independent judgment of the facts and the law. They must also be in position and ready to give free and untrammeled advice to both the President and Congress at any time upon request. Political domination will ruin such a tribunal. I have seen this happen many times, particularly in the states.

The courts were at one time much too prone to substitute their own judgment on the facts for the judgment of administrative tribunals. They are now in danger of going too far in the other direction.

An administrative tribunal has a broader responsibility than a court. It is more than a tribunal for the settlement of controversies. The word "administrative" means something. The policies of the law must be carried out. If in any proceedings the pertinent facts are not fully presented by the parties, it is the duty of the tribunal to see to it, as best it can, that they are developed of record. A complainant without resources to command adequate professional help should be given such protection. The tribunal should also be ready to institute proceedings on its own motion, whenever constructive enforcement of the law so requires.

It is not necessary for the members of the tribunal to be technical experts on the subject matter of their administration. As a matter of fact, you could not find a man who is a technical expert on any large part of the matters upon which the Interstate Commerce Commission finds it necessary to pass. The important qualifications are ability to grasp and comprehend facts quickly and to consider them in their relation to the law logically and with an open mind.

Moral courage is, of course, a prime qualification, but there are often misapprehensions as to when it is shown. The thing that takes courage is to make a decision or take a position which may react seriously in some way upon the one who makes or takes it. It requires no courage to incur disapproval, unless those who disapprove have the desire and power to cause such a result. Power is not a permanent but a shifting thing. I can well remember the time when it was a dangerous thing to incur the displeasure of bankers, but there has been no danger in this since 1932. It became a greater danger to incur the displeasure of farm or labor organizations. There is nothing more important than to curb abuse of power, wherever it may reside, and power is always subject to abuse.

Selection of the members of an administrative tribunal from different parts of the country has its advantages, but they turn to disadvantages if the members regard themselves as special pleaders for their respective sections.

Sitting in dignity and looking down on the suppliants from the elevation of a judicial bench has its dangers. A reversal of the position now and then is good for the soul. It has for many years been my good fortune to appear rather frequently before legislative or congressional committees. They are a better safeguard against inflation than the OPA.

One of the great dangers in public regulation by administrative tribunals of business concerns is the resulting division of responsibility, as between the managements and the regulators, for the successful functioning of these concerns. For example, there was a tendency at one time, and it may still exist, on the part of those financially interested in the railroads to think of the financial success of those properties solely in terms of rates and wages and the treatment of rates and wages by public authorities. Sight was lost of the essentiality of constant, unremitting enterprise and initiative in management. The importance of sound public regulation cannot be minimized, but it must not be magnified to the exclusion of those factors in financial success upon which ordinary private business must rely.

The Insolence of Office

GRAHAM WALLAS   1858–1932

Historians tell us that the great periods of intellectual activity are apt to follow the coincidence of the discovery of important new facts with the wide extension of a sense of personal liberty. It has been asked what has social or political liberty to do with the success or failure of the unconscious process of individual thought? Most men can provide an answer from their own personal experience. There are some emotional states in which creative thought is impossible, and the chief of these is the sense of helpless humiliation and anger which is produced in a sensitive nature by conscious inability to oppose or avoid the "insolence of office." Let any man who doubts it sit down for a day's work at the British Museum after being grossly insulted by someone whom he is not in a position to resist.

Mr. M'Kenna's training has been that of a barrister and not that of a thinker or writer. His parliamentary treatment of the Court Censorship of Plays as Home Secretary in 1911 would probably have been different if he had realized that the question was not whether the Censor was likely to cut out this or that percentage of the words in any play submitted to him, but whether, when a serious dramatist knows that what he writs will be submitted to the blue pencil of the author, say, of "Dear Old Charlie," the spontaneous presentation of creative thought may not refuse to take place in his mind. Tolstoy once wrote: "You would not believe how, from the very commencement of my activity, that horrible Censor question has tormented me! I wanted to write what I felt; but at the same time it occurred to me that what I wrote would not be permitted, and involuntarily I had to abandon the work. I abandoned, and went on abandoning, and meanwhile the years passed away."

A man, again, who is dominated by the common-sense intellectualism of ordinary speech may fail to see any "reason" why an elementary-school teacher or a second-division clerk cannot do his work properly after he has been "put in his place" by some official who happens to combine personal callousness with social superiority. But no statesman who did so could create an effective educational or clerical service.

This is one of the considerations which trouble some Englishmen who hope that, on the whole, our empire in India makes for good. The thousand members of the covenanted Civil Service obviously cannot do all the thinking required by a population of three hundred millions living under rapidly changing social and industrial conditions. If India is to fight successfully against the plague which ships and railways spread, if she is to revive the arts and industries which have been killed by Manchester and Birmingham, above all, if she is to contribute her fair share to the world's literature and science, a much larger number of creative thinkers must appear among her native inhabitants. But Anglo-Indian officials do not, one fears, often produce or perhaps often desire to produce an emotional condition favorable to the growth of creative thought in the natives with whom they are brought into contact. Athens during the last quarter of the fifth century B.C. was not well governed; and if the British Empire had then existed, and if Athens had been brought within it, the administration of the city would undoubtedly have been improved in some important respects. But one does not like to imagine the effect on the intellectual output of the fifth century B.C. if even the best of Mr. Rudyard Kipling's public-school subalterns had stalked daily through the agora, snubbing, as he passed, that intolerable bounder Euripides, or clearing out of his way the probably seditious group that were gathered round Socrates.

Change

JOHN MORLEY   1838–1923

We are thus brought to the position — to which indeed, bare observation of actual occurrences might well bring us, if it were not for the clouding disturbances of selfishness, or of a true philosophy of society wrongly applied — that a society can only pursue its normal course by means of a certain progression of changes, and that these changes can only be initiated by individuals or very small groups of individuals. The progressive tendency can only be a tendency; it can only work its way through the inevitable obstructions around it, by means of persons who are possessed by the special progressive idea. Such ideas do not spring up uncaused and unconditioned in vacant space. They have had a definite origin and ordered antecedents. They are in direct relation with the past. They present themselves to one person or little group of persons rather than to another, because circumstances, or the accident of a superior faculty of penetration, have placed the person or group in the way of such ideas. In matters of social improvement the most common reason why one hits upon a point of progress and not another is that the one happens to be more directly touched than the other by the unimproved practice. Or he is one of those rare intelligences, active, alert, inventive, which by constitution or training find their chief happiness in thinking in a disciplined and serious manner how things can be better done. In all cases the possession of a new idea, whether practical or speculative, only raises into definite speech what others have needed without being able to make their need articulate. This is the principle on which experience shows us that fame and popularity are distributed. A man does not become celebrated in proportion to his general capacity, but because he does or says something which happened to need doing or saying at the moment.

THOMAS JEFFERSON   1743–1826

I am certainly not an advocate for frequent and untried changes in laws and constitutions. I think moderate imperfections had better be borne with; because, when once known, we accommodate ourselves to them, and find practical means of correcting their ill effects. But I know also, that laws and institutions must go hand in hand with the progress of the human mind. As that becomes more developed, more enlightened, as new discoveries are made, new truths disclosed, and manners and opinions change with the change of circumstances, institutions must advance also, and keep pace with the times.

LINCOLN'S FIRST INAUGURAL   1861

This country with its institutions belongs to the people who inhabit it. Whenever they shall grow weary of the existing government, they can exercise their constitutional right of amending it, or their revolutionary right to dismember or overthrow it.

EMERSON   1803–1882

The two parties which divide the state, the party of conservatives and that of innovators, are very old, and have disputed the possession of the world ever since it was made. This quarrel is the subject of civil history.

T. B. MACAULAY

And those behind cried "Forward!"
And those in front cried "Back!"

A. LAWRENCE LOWELL   1856–1943

A tale is told of a man in Paris during the upheaval in 1848, who saw a friend marching after a crowd toward the barricades. Warning him that these could not be held against the troops, that he had better keep away, and asking why he followed those people, he received the reply, "I must follow them. I am their leader."

The Business of Today

CLEMENCEAU   1841–1929

Cleon, in Thucydides, speaking against the people of Mitylene to the Athenians, said to them, "You are spectators and listeners." We are now Athenians in our turn. Conquerors or conquered, we are always fighting, always talking, writing, disputing, always intent on enlarging the field of human thought, on extending the horizons of art in quest of the sovereign beauty, living a life that is more intense and more complete than men of other countries, abandoning the conduct of affairs to routine, to the chance of events, or to unforeseen fancies, and we find ourselves suddenly launched, without knowing just how, into the worst adventures.

"You are seeking," Cleon added, "for what is not of the world you live in, and you do not know how to judge soundly of what is under your eyes." This reproach is that which our reactionaries are accustomed to address to reformers. It can as well be turned against this bourgeois government, that their chimerical fears of the morrow divert them from the business of today.

Instability

A. N. WHITEHEAD   1861–1947

The prosperous middle classes, who ruled the nineteenth century, placed an excessive value upon placidity of existence. They refused to face the necessities for social reform imposed by the new industrial system, and they are now refusing to face the necessities for intellectual reform imposed by the new knowledge. The middle-class pessimism over the future of the world comes from a confusion between civilization and security. In the immediate future there will be less security than in the immediate past, less stability. It must be admitted that there is a degree of instability which is inconsistent with civilisation. But, on the whole, the great ages have been unstable ages.

Aristocracy

THOMAS JEFFERSON TO JOHN ADAMS   1813

There is also an artificial aristocracy, founded on wealth and birth, without either virtue or talents; for with these it would belong to the first class. The natural aristocracy I consider as the most precious gift of nature, for the instruction, the trusts, and government of society. And indeed, it would have been inconsistent in creation to have formed man for the social state, and not to have provided virtue and wisdom enough to manage the concerns of the society. May we not even say, that that form of government is the best, which provides the most effectually for a pure selection of these natural aristoi into the offices of government?

The artificial aristocracy is a mischievous ingredient in government, and provision should be made to prevent its ascendency. On the question, what is the best provision, you and I differ; but we differ as rational friends, using the free exercise of our own reason, and mutually indulging its errors. You think it best to put the pseudo-aristoi into a separate chamber of legislation, where they may be hindered from doing mischief by

their co-ordinate branches, and where, also, they may be
a protection to wealth against the agrarian and plunder-
ing enterprises of the majority of the people. I think that
to give them power in order to prevent them from doing
mischief, is arming them for it, and increasing instead of
remedying the evil. For if the co-ordinate branches can
arrest their action, so may they that of the co-ordinates.
Mischief may be done negatively as well as positively.
Of this, a cabal in the Senate of the United States has
furnished many proofs. Nor do I believe them necessary to protect the wealthy; because enough of these will
find their way into every branch of the legislation, to protect themselves. From fifteen to twenty legislatures of
our own, in action for thirty years past, have proved that
no fears of an equalization of property are to be apprehended from them. I think the best remedy is exactly
that provided by all our constitutions, to leave to the
citizens the free election and separation of the aristoi
from the pseudo-aristoi, of the wheat from the chaff. In
general they will elect the really good and wise. In some
instances, wealth may corrupt, and birth blind them;
but not in sufficient degree to endanger the society.

It is probable that our difference of opinion may, in
some measure, be produced by a difference of character
in those among whom we live. From what I have seen of
Massachusetts and Connecticut myself, and still more
from what I have heard, and the character given of the
former by yourself, who know them so much better, there
seems to be in those two states a traditionary reverence
for certain families, which has rendered the offices of the
government nearly hereditary in those families. I pre-
sume that from an early period of your history, members
of those families happening to possess virtue and talents,
have honestly exercised them for the good of the people,
and by their services have endeared their names to them.
In coupling Connecticut with you, I mean it politically
only, not morally. For having made the Bible the common law of their land, they seemed to have modeled
their morality on the story of Jacob and Laban. But although this hereditary succession to office with you, may,

in some degree, be founded in real family merit, yet in a much higher degree, it has proceeded from your strict alliance of Church and State. These families are canonized in the eyes of the people on common principles, "you tickle me, and I will tickle you." In Virginia we have nothing of this. Our clergy, before the Revolution, having been secured against rivalship by fixed salaries, did not give themselves the trouble of acquiring influence over the people. Of wealth, there were great accumulations in particular families, handed down from generation to generation, under the English law of entails. But the only object of ambition for the wealthy was a seat in the King's Council. All their court then was paid to the crown and its creatures; and they Philipized in all collisions between the King and the people. Hence they were unpopular; and that unpopularity continues attached to their names. A Randolph, a Carter, or a Burwell must have great personal superiority over a common competitor to be elected by the people even at this day.

At the first session of our legislature after the Declaration of Independence, we passed a law abolishing entails. And this was followed by one abolishing the privilege of primo-geniture, and dividing the lands of intestates equally among all their children, or other representatives. These laws, drawn by myself, laid the axe to the foot of pseudo-aristocracy. And had another which I prepared been adopted by the legislature, our work would have been complete. It was a bill for the more general diffusion of learning. This proposed to divide every county into wards of five or six miles square, like your townships; to establish in each ward a free school for reading, writing, and common arithmetic; to provide for the annual selection of the best subjects from these schools, who might receive, at the public expense, a higher degree of education at a district school; and from these district schools to select a certain number of the most promising subjects, to be completed at an University, where all the most useful sciences should be taught. Worth and genius would thus have been sought out from every condition of life, and completely prepared by education for defeating the competition of wealth and birth for public trusts. My proposition had, for a further object, to impart to these wards those portions of self-government for which they are best qualified, by confiding to them the care of their poor, their roads, police, elections, the nomination of jurors, administration of justice in small cases, elementary exercises of militia; in short, to have made them little republics, with a warden at the head of each, for all those concerns which, being under their eye, they would better manage than the larger republics of the county or state. A general call of ward meetings by their wardens on the same day through the state, would at any time produce the genuine sense of the people on any required point, and would enable the state to act in mass, as your people have so often done, and with so much effect by their town meetings. The law for religious freedom, which made a part of this system, having put down the aristocracy of the clergy, and restored to the citizen the freedom of the mind, and those of entails and descents nurturing an equality of condition among them, this on education would have raised the mass of the people to the high ground of moral respectability necessary to their own safety, and to orderly government; and would have completed the great object of qualifying them to select the veritable aristoi, for the trusts of government, to the exclusion of the pseudalists.

I have thus stated my opinion on a point on which we differ, not with a view to controversy, for we are both too old to change opinions which are the result of a long life of inquiry and reflection; but on the suggestions of a former letter of yours, that we ought not to die before we have explained ourselves to each other. We acted in perfect harmony, through a long and perilous contest for our liberty and independence. A constitution has been acquired, which, though neither of us thinks perfect, yet both consider as competent to render our fellow citizens the happiest and the securest on whom the sun has ever shone. If we do not think exactly alike as to its imperfections, it matters little to our country, which, after devoting to it long lives of disinterested labor, we have delivered over to our successors in life, who will be able to take care of it and of themselves.

LINCOLN   1862

The dogmas of the quiet past are inadequate to the stormy present. The occasion is piled high with difficulty, and we must rise with the occasion. As our case is new, so we must think anew and act anew. We must disenthrall ourselves.

Pooling Minds

A. LAWRENCE LOWELL   1856–1943

In Washington's first cabinet, of only four members, where Hamilton was striving to evolve a strong central government and Jefferson a weak one, there could be no common opinion, and Washington, who had to decide, was not a leader but an arbiter. But assuming that the members of a group are in general accord in their objects, how large a number can throw their minds into the common stock — to use Gladstone's expression — so that the result is the combined opinion of all, in which no one had yielded or merely acquiesced, and to which each has contributed? One test is how rarely is dissent finally expressed or felt. That depends, of course, largely upon the members, their similarity of experience and traditions, their personal flexibility, and above all on their habit of working frequently together. Granted a body drawn from a community fairly homogeneous, and familiar with the nature of their work, experience has shown that seven can do so, and under very favorable circumstances more. In such a body there may be very little conscious compromise in order to agree. There is much more mutual give-and-take, changing of minds by discussion, and real ultimate unanimity.

The seven Lowell has in mind is the Harvard Corporation.

The Birth of the Constitution

BENJAMIN FRANKLIN   1706–1790

Monday Sepr. 17, 1787. In Convention

The engrossed Constitution being read,

Docr. Franklin rose with a speech in his hand, which he had reduced to writing for his own conveniency, and which Mr. Wilson read in the words following:

Mr. President

I confess that there are several parts of this constitution which I do not at present approve, but I am not sure I shall never approve them: For having lived long, I have experienced many instances of being obliged by better information or fuller consideration, to change opinions even on important subjects, which I once thought right, but found to be otherwise. It is therefore that the older I grow, the more apt I am to doubt my own judgment, and to pay more respect to the judgment of others. Most men indeed as well as most sects in Religion, think themselves in possession of all truth, and that wherever others differ from them it is so far error. Steele, a Protestant in a Dedication tells the Pope, that the only difference between our Churches in their opinions of the certainty of their doctrines is, the Church of Rome is infallible and the Church of England is never in the wrong. But though many private persons think almost as highly of their own infallibility as of that of their sect, few express it so naturally as a certain French lady, who in a dispute with her sister, said, "I don't know how it happens, Sister, but I meet with no body but myself, that's always in the right" — "Il n'y a que moi qui a toujours raison."

In these sentiments, Sir, I agree to this Constitution with all its faults, if they are such; because I think a general Government necessary for us, and there is no form of Government but what may be a blessing to the people if well administered, and believe farther that this is likely to be well administered for a course of years, and can only end in Despotism, as other forms have done before it, when the people shall become so corrupted as to need despotic Government, being incapable of any other. I doubt too whether any other Convention we can obtain may be able to make a better Constitution. For when you assemble a number of men to have the advantage of their joint wisdom, you inevitably assemble with those men, all their prejudices, their passions, their errors of opinion, their local interests, and their selfish views. From such an Assembly can a perfect production be expected? It therefore astonishes me, Sir, to find this system approaching so near to perfection as it does; and I think it will astonish our enemies, who are waiting with confidence to hear that our councils are confounded like those of the Builders of Babel; and that our States are on the point of separation, only to meet hereafter for the purpose of cutting one another's throats. Thus I consent, Sir, to this Constitution because I expect no better, and because I am not sure, that it is not the best. The opinions I have had of its errors, I sacrifice to the public good — I have never whispered a syllable of them abroad — Within these walls they were born, and here they shall die — If every one of us in returning to our Constituents were to report the objections he has had to it, and endeavor to gain partizans in support of them, we might prevent its being generally received, and thereby lose all the salutary effects and great advantages resulting naturally in our favor among foreign Nations as well as among ourselves, from our real or apparent unanimity. Much of the strength and efficiency of any Government in procuring and securing happiness to the people, depends, on opinion, on the general opinion of the goodness of the Government, as well as of the wisdom and integrity of its Governors. I hope therefore that for our own sakes as a part of the people and for the sake of our posterity, we shall act heartily and unanimously in recommending this Constitution (if approved by Congress and confirmed by the Conventions) wherever our influence may extend, and turn our future thoughts and endeavors to the means of having it well administered.

On the whole, Sir, I cannot help expressing a wish that every member of the Convention who may still have objections to it, would with me, on this occasion doubt a little of his own infallibility — and to make manifest our unanimity, put his name to this instrument.

He then moved that the Constitution be signed.

When the last members were signing it, Doctor Franklin looking towards the President's Chair, at the back of which a rising sun happened to be painted, observed to a few members near him, that Painters had found it difficult to distinguish in their art a rising from a setting sun. I have, said he, often and often in the course of the Session, and the vicissitudes of my hopes and fears as to its issue, looked at that behind the President without being able to tell whether it was rising or setting: But now at length I have the happiness to know that it is a rising and not a setting Sun.

The Open Mind

LEARNED HAND   1872–1961

I dare hope that it may now begin to be clearer why I am arguing that an education which includes the "humanities" is essential to political wisdom. By "humanities" I especially mean history; but close beside history and of almost, if not quite, equal importance are letters, poetry, philosophy, the plastic arts, and music. Most of the issues that mankind sets out to settle, it never does settle. They are not solved, because, they are incapable of solution properly speaking, being concerned with incommensurables. At any rate, even if that be not always true, the opposing parties seldom do agree upon a solution; and the dispute fades into the past unsolved, though perhaps it may be renewed as history, and fought over again. It disappears because it is replaced by some compromise that, although not wholly acceptable to either side, offers a tolerable substitute for victory; and he who would find the substitute needs an endowment as rich as possible in experience, an experience which makes the heart generous and provides his mind with an understanding of the hearts of others.

Out of such a temper alone can come any political success which will not leave behind rancor and vindictiveness that are likely so deeply to infect its benefits as to make victory not worth while; and it is a temper best bred in those who have at least what I like to call a bowing acquaintance with the "humanities." For these are fitted to admonish us how tentative and provisional are our attainments, intellectual and moral; and how often the deepest convictions of one generation are the rejects of the next. That does not indeed deny the possibility that, as time goes on, we shall accumulate some body of valid conclusions; but it does mean that these we can achieve only by accumulation; that wisdom is to be gained only as we stand upon the shoulders of those who have gone before.

I cannot but think that we of this generation are politically in especial need of such education. Our nation is embarked upon a venture as yet unproved; we have set our hopes upon a community in which men shall be given unchecked control of their own lives. That community is in peril; it is invaded from within, it is threatened from without; it faces a test which it may fail to pass. The choice is ours whether, if we hear the pipes of Pan, we shall stampede like a frightened flock, forgetting all those professions on which we have claimed to rest our polity. God knows, there is risk in refusing to act till the facts are all in; but is there not greater risk in abandoning the conditions of all rational inquiry? Risk for risk, for myself I had rather take my chance that some traitors will escape detection than spread abroad a spirit of general suspicion and distrust, which accepts rumor and gossip in place of undismayed and unintimidated inquiry. I believe that that community is already in process of dissolution where each man begins to eye his neighbor as a possible enemy, where non-conformity with the accepted creed, political as well as religious, is a mark of disaffection, where denunciation, without specification or backing, takes the place of evidence; where orthodoxy chokes freedom of dissent; where faith in the eventual supremacy of reason has become so timid that we dare not enter our convictions in the open lists, to win or lose. Such fears as these are a solvent which can eat out the cement that binds the stones together; they may in the end subject us to a despotism as evil as any that we dread; and they can be allayed only in so far as we refuse to proceed on suspicion, and trust one another until we have tangible ground for misgiving. The mutual confidence on which all else depends can be maintained only by an open mind and a brave reliance upon free discussion. I do not say that these will suffice; who knows but we may be on a slope which leads down to aboriginal savagery. But of this I am sure: if we are to escape, we must not yield a foot upon demanding a fair field and an honest race to all ideas.

The House of Commons

WINSTON CHURCHILL   1943

The Prime Minister: I beg to move, "That a Select Committee be appointed to consider and report upon plans for the rebuilding of the House of Commons and upon such alterations as may be considered desirable while preserving all its essential features."

On the night of 10th May, 1941, with one of the last bombs of the last serious raid, our House of Commons was destroyed by the violence of the enemy, and we have now to consider whether we should build it up again, and how, and when. We shape our buildings and afterwards our buildings shape us. Having dwelt and served for more than forty years in the late Chamber, and having derived very great pleasure and advantage therefrom, I, naturally, would like to see it restored in all essentials to its old form, convenience, and dignity. I believe that will be the opinion of the great majority of its Members. It is certainly the opinion of His Majesty's

Government and we propose to support this resolution to the best of our ability.

There are two main characteristics of the House of Commons which will command the approval and the support of reflective and experienced Members. They will, I have no doubt, sound odd to foreign ears. The first is that its shape should be oblong and not semi-circular. Here is a very potent factor in our political life. The semi-circular assembly, which appeals to political theorists, enables every individual of every group to move round the centre, adopting various shades of pink according as the weather changes. I am a convinced supporter of the party system in preference to the group system. I have seen many earnest and ardent Parliaments destroyed by the group system. The party system is much favored by the oblong form of Chamber. It is easy for an individual to move through those insensible gradations from Left to Right, but the act of crossing the Floor is one which requires serious consideration. I am well informed on this matter, for I have accomplished that difficult procedure not only once but twice. Logic is a poor guide compared with custom. Logic, which has created in so many countries semi-circular assemblies which have buildings which give to every Member, not only a seat to sit in but often a desk to write at, with a lid to bang, has proved fatal to Parliamentary Government as we know it here in its home and in the land of its birth.

The second characteristic of a Chamber formed on the lines of the House of Commons is that it should not be big enough to contain all its Members at once without overcrowding and that there should be no question of every Member having a separate seat reserved for him. The reason for this has long been a puzzle to uninstructed outsiders and has frequently excited the curiosity and even the criticism of new Members. Yet it is not so difficult to understand if you look at it from a practical point of view. If the House is big enough to contain all its Members, nine-tenths of its Debates will be conducted in the depressing atmosphere of an almost empty or half-empty Chamber. The essence of good House of Commons speaking is the conversational style, the facility for quick informal interruptions and interchanges. Harangues from a rostrum would be a bad substitute for the conversational style in which so much of our business is done. But the conversational style requires a fairly small space, and there should be on great occasions a sense of crowd and urgency. There should be a sense of the importance of much that is said and a sense that great matters are being decided, there and then, by the House.

We attach immense importance to the survival of Parliamentary democracy. In this country this is one of our war aims. We wish to see our Parliament a strong, easy, flexible instrument of free Debate. For this purpose a small Chamber and a sense of intimacy are indispensable. It is notable that the Parliaments of the British Commonwealth have to a very large extent reproduced our Parliamentary institutions in their form as well as in their spirit, even to the Chair in which the Speakers of the different Assemblies sit. We do not seek to impose our ideas on others; we make no invidious criticisms of other nations. All the same we hold, none the less, tenaciously to them ourselves. The vitality and the authority of the House of Commons and its hold upon an electorate, based upon universal suffrage, depends to no small extent upon its episodes and great moments, even upon its scenes and rows, which, as everyone will agree, are better conducted at close quarters. Destroy that hold which Parliament has upon the public mind and has preserved through all these changing, turbulent times and the living organism of the House of Commons would be greatly inpaired. You may have a machine, but the House of Commons is much more than a machine; it has earned and captured and held through long generations the imagination and respect of the British nation. It is not free from shortcomings; they mark all human institutions. Nevertheless, I submit, to what is probably not an unfriendly audience on that subject, that our House has proved itself capable of adapting itself to every change which the swift pace of modern life has brought upon us. It has a collective personality which enjoys the regard of the public and which imposes itself upon the conduct not only of individual Members but of parties. It has a code of its own which everyone knows, and it has means of its own of enforcing those manners and habits which have grown up and have been found to be an essential part of our Parliamentary life.

The House of Commons has lifted our affairs above the mechanical sphere into the human sphere. It thrives on criticism, it is perfectly impervious to newspaper abuse or taunts from any quarter, and it is capable of digesting almost anything or any body of gentlemen, whatever be the views with which they arrive. There is no situation to which it cannot address itself with vigor and ingenuity. It is the citadel of British liberty; it is the foundation of our laws; its traditions and its privileges are as lively today as when it broke the arbitrary power of the Crown and substituted that Constitutional Monarchy under which we have enjoyed so many blessings. In this war the House of Commons has proved itself to be a rock upon which an Administration, without losing the confidence of the House, has been able to confront the most terrible emergencies. The House has shown itself able to face the possibility of national destruction with classical composure. It can change Governments, and has changed them by heat of passion. It can sustain Governments in long, adverse, disappointing struggles through many dark, grey months and even years until the sun comes out again. I do not know how else this country can be governed other than by the House of Commons playing its part in all its broad freedom in British public life. We have learned — with these so recently confirmed facts around us and before us — not to alter improvidently the physical structures which have enabled so remarkable an organism to carry on its work of banning dictatorships within this island and pursuing and beating into ruin all dictators who have molested us from outside.

FRANCIS BACON   1561–1626

A long table and a square table, or seats about the walls,
seem things of form, but are things of substance; for at
a long table a few at the upper end sway all the business;
but in the other form there is more use of the counsel-
lors' opinions that sit lower.

PLATO   427–347 B.C.

At last I perceived that the constitution of all existing
states is bad and their institutions all but past remedy
without a combination of radical measures and fortunate
circumstance; and I was driven to affirm, in praise of true
philosophy, that only from the standpoint of such philosophy was it possible to take a correct view of public and
private right, and that accordingly the human race
would never see the end of trouble until true lovers of
wisdom should come to hold political power, or the holders of political power should, by some divine appointment, become true lovers of wisdom.

MONTAIGNE   1533–1592

On the most exalted throne in the world, we are still
seated on nothing but our arse.

Liberty

DON MARQUIS' *cockroach, archy*

> *you can stuff your bellies*
> *with oysters and shrimp*
> *you may have your ribbon and bell*
> *for bill and me it is liberty*
> *o wotthehell bill wotthehell*

Liberty for Everybody

EDWARD H. CARR   1951

The concept towards which the modern historian needs
most of all to define his attitude is freedom. It is per-

haps difficult today to realize the immense impact of the French revolution in the contemporary world. Let us recall the remark of Goethe, that most sober and balanced of men of genius, at Valmy: "Here and now begins a new epoch of world history, and you can say that you were there." Under the same inspiration Hegel described history as "nothing else than the progress of the consciousness of freedom." And a hundred years after the great event the cautious Acton was to write: "Never till then had men sought liberty knowing what they sought." There may be some hyperbole about this claim. But, though some anticipations can be found in primitive Christianity and some perhaps in the English Puritan revolution, it is on the whole fair to attribute to the French revolution the conception of universal liberty as the goal of human endeavour. Hitherto freedom had meant freedom for some people to do certain things. Henceforth the demand was freedom in general, freedom as a matter of principle, freedom for all. The makers of the French revolution did not know what this meant; indeed, we have been trying to find out ever since.

It is now apparent that the consequence of the French revolution was to change the conception of freedom in two ways. By universalizing freedom, it linked it with equality; if all were to be free, then all must be equal. Secondly, it gave freedom a material content; for, once freedom was extended from the limited class which could take economic well-being for granted to the common man who was concerned first and foremost with his daily bread, freedom from the economic constraint of want was clearly just as important as freedom from the political constraint of kings and tyrants.

Civil Rights

CHRISTIAN A. HERTER   1955

You and I, your neighbors and my neighbors, we share with each other our liberties and the civil rights that we celebrate during "Civil Rights Week." They are ours.

They belong to all of us, not just to each of us. Liberty is not any one man's possession. When a man asks freedom for himself alone, both he and his neighbor lose what he thinks he has gained.

The spirit of liberty is more than jealousy for your own rights. It is a decent respect for the rights and the opinions of others. We are free, not because we have freedom, but because we serve freedom. The love of liberty cannot be separated from loving your neighbor as yourself.

I ask you to be grateful, and to take thought. The more we know about our civil rights, the more we shall cherish them. The love of liberty talks with better knowledge, and knowledge with dearer love.

I ask you also to be eager, as well as grateful, remembering that we cannot simply preserve our liberties. They can be preserved only by being enjoyed. We may well take a proper pride in the past and have good hope for the future, but liberty keeps fresh and felicitous only in the sanctity of the present.

Is This All the Freedom
We Are Going to Get?

ARNOLD J. TOYNBEE   1956

Security against War, against accidents, and against want was an objective that could not be pursued effectively without restricting freedom in the spheres of political, economic, and perhaps eventually even domestic life. In A.D. 1956 the surviving parochial governments were already embarked on that course; and there was no reason for expecting that this tendency in public policy would change if and when these parochial governments were superseded, or, short of that, were subordinated, through the establishment of an oecumenical régime. In these circumstances it might be forecast that, in the next chapter of the World's history, Mankind would seek compensation for the loss of much of its political, economic, and perhaps even domestic freedom, and that the public authorities would tolerate this inclination among their subjects in an age in which Religion had come to seem as harmless as Technology had seemed 300 years back.

When world-government does come, the need for it will have become so desperate that Mankind will not only be ready to accept it even at the most exorbitantly high price in terms of loss of liberty, but will deify it and its human embodiments, as an excruciated Graeco-Roman World once deified Rome and Augustus. The virtual worship that has already been paid to Napoleon, Mussolini, Stalin, Hitler, and Mao indicates the degree of the idolization that would be the reward of an American or a Russian Caesar who did succeed in giving the World a stable peace at any price; and in this baleful light it looks as if the oecumenical welfare state may be the next idol that will be erected in a still discarded Christianity's place.

Inner Restraints

REINHOLD NIEBUHR   1954

When considering the problem of freeing the mind, we are too prone to think first of the various political and social restraints upon the free play of man's rational faculty. It would be more helpful to consider first the inner restraints which the self places upon its mind; for the mind is not a simple sovereign of the self, but the servant. It is one of the illusions of a rationalistic age that the mind would control the self, if only irrelevant political restraints were not intervening. The fact is that the processes of the mind are very much colored either by the self's own interests or by its commitments and loyalties. These commitments may redeem the self from itself, but they do not necessarily emancipate its mind, for the self's commitments may be as restrictive upon the mind as its interests. In other words, if we define religion as the self's commitment to some system of meaning, or its loyalty to some scheme of values, we must accept the fact that there is a basic contradiction between religion and the freedom of the mind. This contradiction is not due to the baneful effects of what modern men term religious "dogma." It operates just as effectively within the lives of very modern "emancipated" people who have disavowed every kind of "explicit dogma," but are nevertheless governed by "implicit dogmas." In the case of communism, the dogma is of course very explicit, but pretends to be implicit in the sense that the communist faith pretends to be the conclusion arrived at by a "scientific" inquiry into the facts of history.

Modern culture exhibits all the characteristics of the Biblical parable of the "house swept and garnished," of the man, free of one devil into whose empty life there entered "seven devils more evil than the first," and "the last estate of that man was worse than the first." In other words, political commitments of religious dimensions have entered the emptiness of uncommitted lives. Man is the kind of creature who cannot be whole except he be committed, because he cannot find himself without finding a center beyond himself. In short the emancipation of the self requires commitment.

A Neurotic Sense of Tidiness

GEORGE F. KENNAN   1953

I suspect that a neurotic sense of tidiness in political arrangements can be a great danger to any society. Too great an urge for symmetry and order, too strong an insistence on uniformity and conformity, too little tolerance for the atypical and minority phenomenon: these are all things that can grease the path by which nations slide into totalitarianism. Lucky, in this respect, are countries like Great Britain, with its bizarre pattern of nationalities and dialects, its far-flung bonds of blood and interest, and its picturesque ceremonies and traditions; lucky is Switzerland, with its mountain barriers, its unique historical path, and its multilingual balance. Lucky, even, we Americans have been up to this time, with our sectional diversities, our checks and balances, and our deference to the vital interests of competing minorities. Woe to any of us, if these things begin to yield to the leveling influences of the perfectionist, to utopian dreams of progress and equality, to the glorification of conformity in tongue or outlook that have been embraced in the concept of romantic nationalism and have gone before the disasters of totalitarian triumph. Diversity, in all the glorious disorder of nature, is the best defense of healthy societies.

In short, I suspect totalitarianism to be the retribution that befalls all peoples who give free rein to extremists and extremisms, who forget the golden rule of political life, which is that ideas are never good except in moderation, and that anything carried to its logical conclusion becomes a menacing caricature of itself. For this reason one must not be too morbid about incipient totalitarian tendencies, which are only a part of life — so long as they remain incipient and counterbalanced. All totalitarianism is only a matter of degree; but it is precisely in this fact that its mortal danger lies. Who says differences of degree are not vital differences? Remember Shakespeare's words:

> *Take but degree away, untune that string,*
> *And, hark! What discord follows . . .*
> *Then every thing includes itself in power,*
> *Power into will, will into appetite;*
> *And appetite, a universal wolf . . .*
> *Must make perforce a universal prey,*
> *And last eat up himself . . .*

I would like to suggest to you that these words of Shakespeare are no less important in their relation to liberty than in relation to authority. There is, of course, no such thing as freedom in the abstract. There is only a freedom *from* something, and a freedom *to* something. It is therefore not just "freedom," but the kind of freedom that is important as an antidote and an alternative to totalitarianism. And here I would only like to say that it is by no means the maximum absence of restraint that is demanded. On the contrary, I sometimes think that totalitarianism finds it hardest to enter where the framework of individual obligation is firmest, and where certain forms of restraint are most highly developed.

Those forms of restraint are of course the voluntarily accepted ones — the ones that deal most gently and considerately with the real needs of men — and not just those needs that lend themselves to idealization, but the absurd needs, the pathetic ones, the anarchic ones. These are the forms of restraint that give recognition to charity and to humor and to sadness — the ones that take man as he is, not as other people would like to make him. They are ones that make it possible for him to arrive at acceptable compromises with himself and his fellows to live life without destroying its meaning, or disgracing the Image in which he was created.

Such a system of restraints — in reality, the highest form of freedom — must be sought in the wisdom of the ages, and in the ethical codes that the great religions of civilization have developed. Never, but really never, will it be found in utopian visions and undertakings that set out to change the nature of man and the order of human affairs within our time. If we Americans wish, then, to hold aloft at this time a standard of freedom that will truly serve to rally and inspire the forces of resistance to modern totalitarianism, we will have to reject many of our favored predilections, outstandingly our belief in human perfectibility and the miracle of progress. We will have to see to it that our visions of the human future, unlike those of totalitarianism, are tuned to the deepest needs of man, that they show a certain tenderness to his weakness, and a forbearance for all the childishness and helplessness of his nature.

The Attitude of Man

GEORGE C. HOMANS   1956

The doctrine that man is infinitely tough and resourceful and not easily cheated of his freedom to sin.

Privacy

LOUIS D. BRANDEIS   1928

The makers of our Constitution conferred, as against the Government, the right to be let alone — the most comprehensive of rights and the right most valued by civilized men.

This is his dissenting opinion to the decision of the Supreme Court that evidence of a telephone conversation obtained by wire tapping was not inadmissible.

CHESTER I. BARNARD   1951

I think we left out one of the really important elements contributing to the dynamism of society, and that is the right to privacy. I mean something more than the right to shave in private. I mean the right to join what I want to join, to do what I want to do, or *not* to do what I might do without giving anyone a reason, either in advance or afterwards. That does not mean that I am seeking for irresponsibility socially.

THOREAU *in Walden*   1817–1862

We live thick and are in each other's way, and stumble over one another, and I think that we thus lose some respect for one another.

And in the Journal   1841

I make my own time. I make my own terms. I cannot see how God or Nature can ever get the start of me.

PART IX

AND JUSTICE

I told him it was law logic — an artificial system of reasoning, exclusively used in courts of justice, but good for nothing anywhere else.

JOHN QUINCY ADAMS TO JOHN MARSHALL(?)

Sub Deo et lege, said Coke to the King

EDWARD COKE   1552–1634

A controversy of land between parties was heard by the King, and sentence given, which was repealed for this, that it did belong to the common law: then the King said, that he thought the law was founded upon reason, and that he and others had reason, as well as the Judges: to which it was answered by me, that true it was, that God had endowed His Majesty with excellent science, and great endowments of nature; but His Majesty was not learned in the laws of his realm of England, and causes which concern the life, or inheritance, or goods, or fortunes of his subjects, are not to be decided by natural reason but by the artificial reason and judgment of law, which law is an act which requires long study and experience, before that a man can attain to the cognizance of it: and that the law was the golden met-wand and measure to try the causes of the subjects; and which protected His Majesty in safety and peace: with which the King was greatly offended, and said, that then he should be under the law, which was treason to affirm, as he said; to which I said, that Bracton saith, *quod Rex non debet esse sub homine, sed sub Deo et lege.*

The Critical Age of Our Common Law

EDWARD COKE   1552–1634

Let us now peruse our ancient authors, for out of the old fields must come the new corn.

FREDERICK POLLOCK AND F. W. MAITLAND
1845–1937, 1850–1906

The law of the age that lies between 1154 and 1272 deserves patient study. It was the critical moment in English legal history and therefore in the innermost history of our land and our race. It was the moment when old custom was brought into contact with new science. Much in our national life and character depended on the result of that contact. It was a perilous moment. There was the danger of an unintelligent "reception" of misunderstood and alien institutions. There was the danger of a premature and formless equity. On the other hand, there was the danger of a stubborn *Nolumus,* a refusal to learn from foreigners and from the classical past. If that had not been avoided, the crash would have come in the sixteenth century and Englishmen would have been forced to receive without criticism what they once despised. Again, we have stood at the parting of the ways of the two most vigorous systems of law that the modern world has seen, the French and the English. Not about what may seem the weightier matters of jurisprudence do these sisters quarrel, but about "mere matters of procedure," as some would call them, the one adopting the canonical inquest of witnesses, the other retaining, developing, transmuting the old *enquête du pays.* But the fate of two national laws lies here. Which country made the wiser choice no Frenchman and no Englishman can impartially say: no one should be judge in his own cause. But of this there can be no doubt, that it was for the good of the whole world that one race stood apart from its neighbors, turned away its eyes at an early time from the fascinating pages of the *Corpus Iuris,* and, more Roman than the Romanists, made the grand experiment of a new formulary system. Nor can we part with this age without thinking once more of the permanence of its work. Those few men who were gathered at Westminster round Pateshull and Raleigh and Bracton were penning writs that would run in the name of kingless commonwealths on the other shore of the Atlantic

Ocean; they were making right and wrong for us and for our children.

This is the Pollock who was Holmes's friend.

O. W. HOLMES, JR. 1841–1935

At present, in very many cases, if we want to know why a rule of law has taken its particular shape, and more or less if we want to know why it exists at all, we go to tradition. We follow it into the Year Books, and perhaps beyond them to the customs of the Salian Franks, and somewhere in the past, in the German forests, in the needs of Norman kings, in the assumptions of a dominant class, in the absence of generalized ideas, we find out the practical motive for what now best is justified by the mere fact of its acceptance and that men are accustomed to it. The rational study of law is still to a large extent the study of history. History must be a part of the study, because without it we cannot know the precise scope of rules which it is our business to know. It is a part of the rational study because it is the first step toward an enlightened scepticism, that is, toward a deliberate reconsideration of the worth of those rules. When you get the dragon out of his cave onto the plain and in the daylight, you can count his teeth and claws, and see just what is his strength. But to get him out is only the first step. The next is either to kill him, or to tame him and make him a useful animal. For the rational study of the law the black-letter man may be the man of the present, but the man of the future is the man of statistics and the master of economics. It is revolting to have no better reason for a rule of law than that so it was laid down in the time of Henry IV. It is still more revolting if the grounds upon which it was laid down have vanished long since, and the rule simply persists from blind imitation of the past.

O. W. HOLMES, JR. 1841–1935

Continuity with the past is a necessity, not a duty.

The End of Law

WILLIAM JAMES   1842–1910

There is an inevitable tendency to slip into an assumption which ordinary men follow when they are disputing with one another about questions of good and bad. They imagine an abstract moral order in which the objective truth resides; and each tries to prove that this pre-existing order is more accurately reflected in his own ideas than in those of his adversary. It is because one disputant is backed by this overarching abstract order that we think the other should submit. Even so, when it is a question no longer of two finite thinkers, but of God and ourselves — we follow our usual habit, and imagine a sort of *de jure* relation, which antedates and over-arches the mere facts, and would make it right that we should conform our thoughts to God's thoughts, even though he made no claim to that effect, and though we preferred *de facto* to go on thinking for ourselves.

But the moment we take a steady look at the question, we see not only that without a claim actually made by some concrete person there can be no obligation, but that there is some obligation wherever there is a claim. Claim and obligation are, in fact, coextensive terms; they cover each other exactly. Our ordinary attitude of regarding ourselves as subject to an overarching system of moral relations, true "in themselves," is therefore either an out-and-out superstition, or else it must be treated as a merely provisional abstraction from that real Thinker in whose actual demand upon us to think as he does our obligation must be ultimately based. In a theistic-ethical philosophy that Thinker in question is, of course, the Deity to whom the existence of the universe is due.

I know well how hard it is for those who are accustomed to what I have called the superstitious view to realize that every *de facto* claim creates in so far forth an obligation. We inveterately think that something which we call the "validity" of the claim is what gives to it its obligatory character, and that this validity is something outside of the claim's mere existence as a matter of fact. It rains down upon the claim, we think, from some sublime dimension of being, which the moral law inhabits, much as upon the steel of the compass needle the influence of the Pole rains down from out of the starry heavens. But again, how can such an inorganic abstract character of imperativeness, additional to the imperativeness which is in the concrete claim itself, exist? Take any demand, however slight, which any creature, however weak, may make. Ought it not, for its own sole sake, to be satisfied? If not, prove why not. The only possible kind of proof you could adduce would be the exhibition of another creature who should make a demand that ran the other way. The only possible reason there can be why any phenomenon ought to exist is that such a phenomenon actually is desired. Any desire is imperative to the extent of its amount; it makes itself valid by the fact that it exists at all. Some desires, truly enough, are small desires; they are put forward by insignificant persons, and we customarily make light of the obligations which they bring. But the fact that such personal demands as these impose small obligations does not keep the largest obligations from being personal demands.

Liberty as the End of Law

JAMES C. CARTER   1827–1905

There is a guide which, when kept clearly and constantly in view, sufficiently informs us what we should aim to do by legislation and what should be left to other agencies. This is what I have so often insisted upon as the sole function both of law and legislation, namely, to secure to each individual the utmost liberty which he can enjoy consistently with the preservation of the like liberty to all others. Liberty, the first of blessings, the aspiration of every human soul, is the supreme object. Every abridgment of it demands an excuse, and the only good excuse is the necessity of preserving it. Whatever tends to preserve this is right, all else is wrong. To leave each man to work out in freedom his own happiness or mis-

ery, to stand or fall by the consequences of his own conduct, is the true method of human discipline.

Justice Holmes

FELIX FRANKFURTER   1882–

The ultimate accomplishment of a thinker is found not
in his books nor in his opinions, but in the minds of men.
The Common Law, the *Collected Legal Papers,* the
thousand opinions in the Massachusetts Reports and the
six hundred in the United States Reports have been most
powerful generators of fresh thinking in the necessary
adaptations of the legal tradition to new demands upon
it. By his own example, enhanced by his great judicial
prestige, Mr. Justice Holmes made legal scholarship at
once exciting and respectable. The labors of Langdell
and Gray, of Ames and Thayer, of Maitland and Holds-
worth, stirred his admiration and encouragement. When
most needed, he gave a strong impetus to the academic
study of law. Though he occupied a chair at the Harvard Law School for only a very brief period, indirectly
he remained for the next fifty years probably the most
influential law teacher in the land.

For decades throughout the English-speaking world
major legal issues have been discussed at the universities
and at the bar, and with increasing frequency decided
by the courts, in the perspective of Holmes's formulation.
The considerations of preference and policy, usually inarticulate and too often unconscious, especially in constitutional controversies, were by him given explicitness
and thereby an outlook of tolerance essential to the
maintenance of our constitutional system. And both
analysis and insight he expressed in language at once
phosphorescent and permanent.

Extracts from "The Common Law" and the "Collected Legal Papers"

O. W. HOLMES, JR.   1841–1935

On the nature of law:

The primary rights and duties with which jurisprudence busies itself again are nothing but prophecies. One of the many evil effects of the confusion between legal and moral ideas, about which I shall have something to say in a moment, is that theory is apt to get the cart before the horse, and to consider the right or the duty as something existing apart from and independent of the consequences of its breach, to which certain sanctions are added afterward. But, as I shall try to show, a legal duty so called is nothing but a prediction that if a man does or omits certain things he will be made to suffer in this or that way by judgment of the court; and so of a legal right.

The right approach is that of the bad man:

If you want to know the law and nothing else, you must look at it as a bad man, who cares only for the material consequences which such knowledge enables him to predict, not as a good one, who finds his reasons for conduct, whether inside the law or outside of it, in the vaguer sanctions of conscience. The theoretical importance of the distinction is no less, if you would reason on your subject aright. The law is full of phraseology drawn from morals, and by the mere force of language continually invites us to pass from one domain to the other without perceiving it, as we are sure to do unless we have the boundary constantly before our minds. The law talks about rights, and duties, and malice, and intent, and negligence, and so forth, and nothing is easier, or, I may say, more common in legal reasoning, than to take these words in their moral sense, at some stage of the argument, and so to drop into fallacy.

Take the fundamental question, What constitutes the law? You will find some text writers telling you that it is something different from what is decided by the courts of Massachusetts or England, that it is a system of reason, that it is a deduction from principles of ethics or admitted axioms or what-not, which may or may not coincide with the decisions. But if we take the view of our friend the bad man, we shall find that he does not care two straws for the axioms or deductions, but that he does want to know what the Massachusetts or English courts are likely to do in fact. I am much of his mind. The prophecies of what the courts will do in fact, and nothing more pretentious, are what I mean by the law.

Take again a notion which as popularly understood is the widest conception which the law contains — the notion of legal duty, to which already I have referred. We fill the word with all the content which we draw from morals. But what does it mean to a bad man? Mainly, and in the first place, a prophecy that if he does certain things he will be subjected to disagreeable consequences by way of imprisonment or compulsory payment of money. But from his point of view, what is the difference between being fined and being taxed a certain sum for doing a certain thing? That his point of view is the test of legal principles is shown by the many discussions which have arisen in the courts on the very question whether a given statutory liability is a penalty or a tax. On the answer to this question depends the decision whether conduct is legally wrong or right, and also whether a man is under compulsion or free.

Cynical acid:

You see how the vague circumference of the notion of duty shrinks and at the same time grows more precise when we wash it with cynical acid and expel everything except the object of our study, the operations of the law.

Contracts:

Nowhere is the confusion between legal and moral ideas more manifest than in the law of contract. Among other things, here again the so-called primary rights and duties are invested with a mystic significance beyond what can be assigned and explained. The duty to keep a contract

at common law means a prediction that you must pay
damages if you do not keep it — and nothing else. If you
commit a tort, you are liable to pay a compensatory sum.
If you commit a contract, you are liable to pay a compensatory sum unless the promised event comes to pass,
and that is all the difference. But such a mode of looking at the matter stinks in the nostrils of those who think
it advantageous to get as much ethics into the law as they
can.

Torts:

The law of torts abounds in moral phraseology. It has
much to say of wrongs, of malice, fraud, intent, and negligence. Hence it may naturally be supposed that the
risk of a man's conduct is thrown upon him as the result
of some moral shortcoming. But while this notion has
been entertained, the extreme opposite will be found to
have been a far more popular opinion; — I mean the
notion that a man is answerable for all the consequences
of his acts, or, in other words, that he acts at his peril always, and wholly irrespective of the state of his consciousness upon the matter.

The standards of the law are standards of general application. The law takes no account of the infinite varieties of temperament, intellect, and education which
make the internal character of a given act so different in
different men. It does not attempt to see men as God
sees them, for more than one sufficient reason. In the
first place, the impossibility of nicely measuring a man's
powers and limitations is far clearer than that of ascer-
taining his knowledge of law, which has been thought
to account for what is called the presumption that every
man knows the law. But a more satisfactory explanation
is, that, when men live in society, a certain average of
conduct, a sacrifice of individual peculiarities going beyond a certain point, is necessary to the general welfare.
If, for instance, a man is born hasty and awkward, is always having accidents and hurting himself or his neighbors, no doubt his congenital defects will be allowed for
in the courts of Heaven, but his slips are no less trouble-

some to his neighbors than if they sprang from guilty neglect. His neighbors accordingly require him, at his proper peril, to come up to their standard, and the courts which they establish decline to take his personal equation into account.

It must be borne in mind that law only works within the sphere of the senses. If the external phenomena, the manifest acts and omissions, are such as it requires, it is wholly indifferent to the internal phenomena of conscience. A man may have as bad a heart as he chooses, if his conduct is within the rules. In other words, the standards of the law are external standards, and, however much it may take moral considerations into account, it does so only for the purpose of drawing a line between such bodily motions and rests as it permits, and such as it does not. What the law really forbids, and the only thing it forbids, is the act on the wrong side of the line, be that act blameworthy or otherwise.

Again, any legal standard must, in theory, be one which would apply to all men, not specially excepted, under the same circumstances. It is not intended that the public force should fall upon an individual accidentally, or at the whim of any body of men. The standard, that is, must be fixed. In practice, no doubt, one man may have to pay and another may escape, according to the different feelings of different juries. But this merely shows that the law does not perfectly accomplish its ends. The theory or intention of the law is not that the feeling of approbation or blame which a particular twelve may entertain should be the criterion. They are supposed to leave their idiosyncrasies on one side, and to represent the feeling of the community. The ideal average prudent man, whose equivalent the jury is taken to be in many cases, and whose culpability or innocence is the supposed test, is a constant, and his conduct under given circumstances is theoretically always the same.

The life of the law:

You may assume, with Hobbes and Bentham and Austin, that all law emanates from the sovereign, even when the first human beings to enunciate it are the judges, or you may think that law is the voice of the Zeitgeist, or what you like. It is all one to my present purpose. Even if every decision required the sanction of an emperor with despotic power and a whimsical turn of mind, we should be interested none the less, still with a view to prediction, in discovering some order, some rational explanation, and some principle of growth for the rules which he laid down. In every system there are such explanations and principles to be found. It is with regard to them that a fallacy comes in, which I think it important to expose.

The fallacy to which I refer is the notion that the only force at work in the development of the law is logic. In the broadest sense, indeed, that notion would be true. The postulate on which we think about the universe is that there is a fixed quantitative relation between every phenomenon and its antecedents and consequents. If there is such a thing as a phenomenon without these fixed quantitative relations, it is a miracle. It is outside the law of cause and effect, and as such transcends our power of thought, or at least is something to or from which we cannot reason. The condition of our thinking about the universe is that it is capable of being thought about rationally, or, in other words, that every part of it is effect and cause in the same sense in which those parts are with which we are most familiar. So in the broadest sense it is true that the law is a logical development, like everything else. The danger of which I speak is not the admission that the principles governing other phenomena also govern the law, but the notion that a given system, ours, for instance, can be worked out like a mathematics from some general axioms of conduct. This is a natural error of the schools, but it is not confined to them. I once heard a very eminent judge say that he never let a decision go until he was absolutely sure that it was right. So judicial dissent often is blamed, as if it meant simply that one side or the other were not doing their sums right, and, if they would take more trouble, agreement inevitably would come.

Not logic, but experience:

The life of the law has not been logic: it has been experience. The felt necessities of the time, the prevalent moral and political theories, intuitions of public policy, avowed or unconscious, even the prejudices which judges share with their fellow-men, have had a good deal more to do than the syllogism in determining the rules by which men should be governed. The law embodies the story of a nation's development through many centuries, and it cannot be dealt with as if it contained only the axioms and corollaries of a book of mathematics. In order to know what it is, we must know what it has been, and what it tends to become. We must alternately consult history and existing theories of legislation. But the most difficult labor will be to understand the combination of the two into new products at every stage. The substance of the law at any given time pretty nearly corresponds, so far as it goes, with what is then understood to be convenient; but its form and machinery, and the degree to which it is able to work out desired results, depend very much upon its past.

And social advantages:

A very common phenomenon, and one very familiar to the student of history, is this. The customs, beliefs, or needs of a primitive time establish a rule or a formula. In the course of centuries the custom, belief, or necessity disappears, but the rule remains. The reason which gave rise to the rule has been forgotten, and ingenious minds set themselves to inquire how it is to be accounted for. Some ground of policy is thought of, which seems to explain it and to reconcile it with the present state of things; and then the rule adapts itself to the new reasons which have been found for it, and enters on a new career. The old form receives a new content, and in time even the form modifies itself to fit the meaning which it has received.

The very considerations which judges most rarely mention, and always with an apology, are the secret root from which the law draws all the juices of life. I mean, of course, considerations of what is expedient for the community concerned. Every important principle which is developed by litigation is in fact and at bottom the result of more or less definitely understood views of public policy; most generally, to be sure, under our practice and traditions, the unconscious result of instinctive preferences and inarticulate convictions, but none the less traceable to views of public policy in the last analysis. And as the law is administered by able and experienced men, who know too much to sacrifice good sense to a syllogism, it will be found that, when ancient rules maintain themselves in the way that has been and will be shown in this book, new reasons more fitted to the time have been found for them, and that they gradually receive a new content, and at last a new form, from the grounds to which they have been transplanted.

I think that the judges themselves have failed adequately to recognize their duty of weighing considerations of social advantage. The duty is inevitable, and the result of the often proclaimed judicial aversion to deal with such considerations is simply to leave the very ground and foundation of judgments inarticulate, and often unconscious, as I have said. When socialism first began to be talked about, the comfortable classes of the community were a good deal frightened. I suspect that this fear has influenced judicial action both here and in England, yet it is certain that it is not a conscious factor in the decisions to which I refer. I think that something similar has led people who no longer hope to control the legislatures to look to the courts as expounders of the constitutions, and that in some courts new principles have been discovered outside the bodies of those instruments, which may be generalized into acceptance of the economic doctrines which prevailed about fifty years ago, and a wholesale prohibition of what a tribunal of lawyers does not think about right. I cannot but believe that if the training of lawyers led them habitually to consider more definitely and explicitly the social advantage on which the rule they lay down must be justified, they sometimes would hesitate where now they are confident, and see that really they were taking sides upon debatable and often burning questions.

Legislation

JOHN C. GRAY   1839–1915

After all, it is only words that the legislature utters; it is for the courts to say what those words mean; that is, it is for them to interpret legislative acts; undoubtedly there are limits upon their power of interpretation, but these limits are almost as undefined as those which govern them in their dealing with the other sources.

And this is the reason why legislative acts, statutes, are to be dealt with as sources of law, and not as part of the law itself; why they are to be co-ordinated with the other sources which I have mentioned. It has been sometimes said that the law is composed of two parts — legislative law and judge-made law — but, in truth, all the law is judge-made law. The shape in which a statute is imposed on the community as a guide for conduct is that statute as interpreted by the courts. The courts put life into the dead words of the statute. To quote again from Bishop Hoadly, a sentence which I have before given: "Nay, whoever hath an absolute authority to interpret any written or spoken laws, it is he who is truly the Lawgiver to all intents and purposes, and not the person who first wrote or spoke them." [1] I will return to this later.

A fundamental misconception prevails, and pervades all the books as to the dealing of the courts with statutes. Interpretation is generally spoken of as if its chief function was to discover what the meaning of the legislature really was. But when a legislature has had a real intention, one way or another, on a point, it is not once in a hundred times that any doubt arises as to what its intention was. If that were all that a judge had to do with a statute, interpretation of statutes, instead of being one of the most difficult of a judge's duties, would be ex-

[1] Benjamin Hoadly, Bishop of Bangor. Sermon preached before the King, 1717, p. 12.

tremely easy. The fact is that the difficulties of so-called interpretation arise when the legislature has had no meaning at all; when the question which is raised on the statute never occurred to it; when what the judges have to do is, not to determine what the legislature did mean on a point which was present to its mind, but to guess what it would have intended on a point not present to its mind, if the point had been present. If there are any lawyers among those who honor me with their attention, let them consider any dozen cases of the interpretation of statutes, as they have occurred consecutively in their reading or practice, and they will, I venture to say, find that in almost all of them it is probably, and that in most of them it is perfectly evident, that the makers of the statutes had no real intention, one way or another, on the point in question; that if they had, they would have made their meaning clear; and that when the judges are professing to declare what the legislature meant, they are in truth, themselves legislating to fill up *casus omissi*.[1]

A. LAWRENCE LOWELL   1856–1943

An example both of the defects of statutes and of the embarrassment courts may have in interpreting them was furnished a few years ago when a Chinese woman who had a permit to come to this country landed at San Francisco with a child born on the voyage. The immigration officer asked the authorities in Washington whether

[1] "The intent of the legislature is sometimes little more than a useful legal fiction, save as it describes in a general way certain outstanding purposes which no one disputes, but which are frequently of little aid in dealing with the precise points presented in litigation. Moreover, legislative ambiguity may at times not be wholly unintentional. It is not to be forgotten that important legislation sometimes shows the effect of compromises which have been induced by exigencies in its progress, and phrases with a convenient vagueness are referred to the courts for appropriate definition, each group interested in the measure claiming that the language adopted embodies its views." Mr. Justice Hughes, in 1 *Mass. Law Quart.* (No. 2), pp. 13, 15. On the point that the legislature sometimes deliberately leaves its intention doubtful, see Sir Courtenay Ilbert, *Mechanics of Law-Making*, pp. 19–23.

the child, having no permit to land, must be sent back to China. In view of the statute refusing immigration without a permit the legal question might have presented difficulties, and the answer was appropriate: "Don't be a damned fool." Now suppose the question had come before a court. Obviously Congress had no such case in mind, and yet the statute was in terms explicit. If the court, relying on the language of the act, had decided that the child must be sent back, who would have been the "damned fool?"

LORD HALSBURY   1823–1921
My Lords, I have more than once had occasion to say that in construing a statute I believe the worst person to construe it is the person who is responsible for its draft.

The Lawyers

JUDGE BERNARD L. SHIENTAG   1887–
We are told that on the Bench, "Lord Lyndhurst's lips would often be seen to move, but no sound proceeding from them would be heard by the Bar. The registrar writing beneath him could tell another tale. He could hear his Lordship mutter in the course of an argument, 'What a fool that man is!' Then, after an interval, 'Eh, not such a fool as I thought'; then after another interval, 'Egad, it is I that was the fool.'"

BOSWELL AND JOHNSON   1768
I asked him whether, as a moralist, he did not think that the practice of the law, in some degree, hurt the nice feeling of honesty. JOHNSON. "Why no, Sir, if you act properly. You are not to deceive your clients with false representations of your opinion: you are not to tell lies to a judge." BOSWELL. "But what do you think of supporting a cause which you know to be bad?" JOHNSON. "Sir, you do not know it to be good or bad till the Judge determines it. I have said that you are to state facts fairly; so that your thinking, or what you call knowing, a cause

to be bad, must be from reasoning, must be from your supposing your arguments to be weak and inconclusive. But, Sir, that is not enough. An argument which does not convince yourself, may convince the Judge to whom you urge it; and if it does convince him, why, then, Sir, you are wrong, and he is right. It is his business to judge; and you are not to be confident in your own opinion that a cause is bad, but to say all you can for your client, and then hear the Judge's opinion." BOSWELL. "But, Sir, does not affecting a warmth when you have no warmth, and appearing to be clearly of one opinion when you are in reality of another opinion, does not such dissimulation impair one's honesty? Is there not some danger that a lawyer may put on the same mask in common life, in the intercourse with his friends?" JOHNSON. "Why, no, sir. Every body knows you are paid for affecting warmth for your client; and it is, therefore, properly no dissimulation: the moment you come from the bar you resume your usual behavior. Sir, a man will no more carry the artifice of the bar into the common intercourse of society, than a man who is paid for tumbling upon his hands will continue to tumble upon his hands when he should walk on his feet."

MONTAIGNE   1533–1592

You state your case to a lawyer, simply. He answers you doubtfully, hesitatingly. You feel that it's quite indifferent to him which side he would take. But once you have retained him and paid him to bite into it, he begins to be interested and his will becomes warmed up to it. His reasoning and his learning warm up more and more. A manifest and indubitable truth presents itself. He discovers a wholly new light, and he honestly believes it. He is convinced. Indeed, I do not know if the zeal that is born of despite and obstinacy in an encounter with the violence of a magistrate and with danger, or a concern for reputation, has not driven a man to be burned at the stake for an opinion for which among his friends and at ease he would not have been willing to singe the tip of his finger.

JUSTICE FELIX FRANKFURTER   1942

Future lawyers should be more aware that law is not a system of abstract logic, but the web of arrangements, rooted in history but also in hopes, for promoting to a maximum the full use of a nation's resources and talents.

JUSTICE ROBERT H. JACKSON   1892–

The county-seat lawyer, counsellor to railroads and to Negroes, to bankers and to poor whites, who always gave to each the best there was in him — and was willing to admit that his best was good. That lawyer has been an American institution — about the same in South and North and East and West. Such a man understands the structure of society and how its groups interlock and interact, because he lives in a community so small that he can keep it all in view. Lawyers in large cities do not know their cities; they know their circles, and urban circles are apt to be made up of those with a kindred outlook on life; but the circle of the man from the small city or town is the whole community and embraces persons of every outlook. He sees how this society lives and works under the law and adjusts its conflicts by its procedures. He knows how disordered and hopelessly unstable it would be without law. He knows that in this country the administration of justice is based on law practice. Paper "rights" are worth, when they are threatened, just what some lawyer makes them worth. Civil liberties are those which some lawyer, respected by his neighbors, will stand up to defend. Any legal doctrine which fails to enlist the support of well-regarded lawyers will have no real sway in this country.

It has been well said that "The life of the law has not been logic: it has been experience." The experience that gave life to our judge-made and statutory law, at least until the last few years, was this type of country life. From such homes came the lawyers, the judges, and the legislators of the nineteenth century. Their way of living generated independence and amazing energy, and these country boys went to the cities and dominated the professions and business as well. They controlled the county court houses and the state houses and the nation's capital as well, and they weighed legal doctrines, political theories, and social policies in the light of the life they knew. If we would understand the product of those court houses and state houses, we must understand that life and the impression it made on the minds of men. Much of the changing trend of law and of political and social policy is due to the declining number of men who have shared this experience. More men now come to the profession from the cities, fewer from farms. There isn't a whiff of the stable in a carload of college freshmen. More and more those who in court and classroom and legislative body restate our legal principles are men who have not experienced the country life of which our law was so largely the expression.

The county-seat lawyer and the small-town advocate are pretty much gone, and the small-city lawyer has a struggle to keep his head above water. Control of business has been concentrated in larger cities, and the good law business went to the city with it. The lawsuit has declined in public interest before the tough competition of movie and radio. Most rural controversies are no longer worth their cost to litigate. Much controversy has now shifted to the administrative tribunal, and the country lawyer hates it and all its works.

But this vanishing country lawyer left his mark on his times, and he was worth knowing. He "read law" in the *Commentaries* of Blackstone and Kent and not by the case system. He resolved problems by what he called "first principles." He did not specialize, nor did he pick and choose clients. He rarely declined service to worthy ones because of inability to pay. Once enlisted for a client, he took his obligation seriously. He insisted on complete control of the litigation — he was no mere hired hand. But he gave every power and resource to the cause. He identified himself with the client's cause fully, sometimes too fully. He would fight the adverse party and fight his counsel, fight every hostile witness, and fight the court, fight public sentiment, fight any obstacle to his client's success. He never quit. He could think of motions for every purpose under the sun, and he made them all. He moved for new trials, he appealed; and if he lost out in the end, he joined the client at the tavern in damning the judge — which is the last rite in closing an unsuccessful case, and I have officiated at many. But he loved his profession, he had a real sense of dedication to the administration of justice, he held his head high as a lawyer, he rendered and exacted courtesy, honor, and straightforwardness at the Bar. He respected the judicial office deeply, demanded the highest standards of competence and disinterestedness and dignity, despised all political use of or trifling with judicial power, and had an affectionate regard for every man who filled his exacting prescription of the just judge. The law to him was like a religion, and its practice was more than a means of support; it was a mission. He was not always popular in his community, but he was respected. Unpopular minorities and individuals often found in him their only mediator and advocate. He was too independent to court the populace — he thought of himself as a leader and lawgiver, not as a mouthpiece. He "lived well, worked hard, and died poor." Often his name was in a generation or two, forgotten. It was from this brotherhood that America has drawn its statesmen and its judges. A free and self-governing Republic stands as a monument for the little known and unremembered as well as for the famous men of our profession.

Judges

JUDGE BERNARD L. SHIENTAG   1887–

Chief Justice Jervis, in giving judgment for the plaintiff, expressed himself in terms of violent indignation at the disgraceful and dishonest conduct he had resorted to in deceiving the defendant, and deeply lamented that, as the law stood, the court had no power to deal with him as he deserved. When Mr. Justice Maule's turn came to give his opinion, he said: "I entirely agree with the decision my lord has come to; the only difference between us is that, in arriving at it, I cannot bring myself to exhibit the emotion he has displayed. I, too, am sorry we are obliged to give judgment for the plaintiff, but I don't see why I should put myself out about the matter. There are so many anomalies in the law, and so many fraudulent people in the world, that a newly discovered specimen of either gives me no uneasiness, nor does it produce in me the least excitement. But my lord is younger than I am. When he has reached my age he will cease to give way to that virtuous indignation — perhaps I ought rather to say that generous enthusiasm — by which he seems oppressed."

SELDEN   1584–1654

We see the judges look like lions, but we do not see who moves them.

RABELAIS   1494–1553

The next day, at the appointed hour, Pantagruel arrived in Mirelingues. The president, senators, and councillors invited him to be with them at the hearing of the causes and reasons which Judge Bridlegoose was to give for having sentenced a tax assessor, named Touchafee, the which had not seemed at all equitable to the Court.

Pantagruel willingly accepted their invitation. When he went into the courtroom, he found Bridlegoose sitting in the middle of the bar inclosure. Immediately upon Pantagruel's coming, accompanied by the members of the Court, he rose, went to the bar, heard the charge against him read and for all his reasons, defense, and excuse, answered nothing but that he had grown old and that his sight had been failing and dimmer than it had been; and he recited the many miseries and calamities that come with old age. For this reason, he said, he had not been able to read the points on the dice as he had in the past. So, just as Isaac, when he was old and half blind, had mistaken Jacob for Esau, he had taken a four for a five, particularly, he said, because he was using his little dice. And the law provides that the imperfections of Nature should not be accounted a crime. For whoever did otherwise would be accusing not the men but Nature.

"What dice," asked Trinquamelle, the presiding justice, "do you mean, my friend?"

"The dice of judgment," Bridlegoose answered, "the hazards of justice, the same dice that all your honors ordinarily use in this honorable court, as all other judges do in the decision of a case, according to the precedents and authorities, who all observe that chance and hazard is exceedingly sound, honest, useful, and necessary in the disposition of cases and controversies at law."

"And how," Trinquamelle asked, "do you do it, my friend?"

Bridlegoose briefly replied, "According to the provisions of the statutes made and provided, I do as your honors, and pursuant to judicial usage, to which our law commends us always to defer. Having carefully viewed, reviewed, read, reread, shuffled and leafed through the writ, summons, declaration, answer, replication, appearances, interrogatories, depositions, exhibits, transcript, briefs, and all such other confections and delicatessens from one end to the other, as every good judge ought to do, then I put on one side of my desk all the respondent's papers and I give him the first throw, just as your honors do. For it is the law that the burden of proof is on the complainant. Having done that, I place the papers of the complainant, just as your honors do, on the other side, and then likewise, I give him the same chance."

"But," asked Trinquamelle, "how do you come to an understanding of the difficult and perhaps obscure law points which have been raised by the opposing parties?"

"Just as your honors do," replied Bridlegoose. "That is to say, by the number of papers and documents on each side. And in such case I use my small dice, just as your honors do, pursuant to the statute and the verified law of the land, in cases of doubt, incline to the lesser. I have other larger dice, very just and harmonious, which I use, as your honors do, when the case is clearer, that is, when there are fewer papers in the case."

"That done," said Trinquamelle, "how do you announce your decision?"

"Just as your honors do," he said. "I give the decision to him who wins the throw of the judicial dice."

Here one of the editors has taken liberties with Rabelais. It's a translation, but it's been cut and it's been modernized.

JUSTICE SAMUEL F. MILLER   1816–1890

I must say that in my experience in the conference room of the Supreme Court of the United States, which consists of nine judges, I have been surprised to find how readily those judges come to an agreement on questions of law and how often they disagree in regard to questions of fact which apparently are as clear as the law.

Justice Miller has not been properly appreciated by laymen. He was one of the great members of the United States Supreme Court. Read Fairman's life. Miller began as a country doctor before he turned to the law. When his friends came to urge his appointment, Lincoln listened, then untwined his legs from underneath his chair, and said, "Oh, this is important. I thought at first you wanted me to appoint him a brigadier general."

JUDGE BERNARD L. SHIENTAG   1887–

In his "Essay on Intellect" Emerson says: "You cannot, with your best deliberation and heed, come so close to any question as your spontaneous glance shall bring you while you rise from your bed or walk abroad in the morning after meditating the matter before sleep on the previous night." Emerson may be right if he has in mind those intuitions which penetrate to the very core of human existence. But what he says is open to grave question so far as it related to judicial decision.

CHIEF JUSTICE JOHN MARSHALL   1755–1835

The power, and the restriction on it, though quite distinguishable when they do not approach each other, may yet, like the intervening colors between white and black, approach so nearly as to perplex the understanding, as colors perplex the vision in marking the distinction between them. Yet the distinction exists, and must be marked as the cases arise. Till they do arise, it might be premature to state any rule as being universal in its application.

The Spirit of Moderation

JUDGE LEARNED HAND   1872–1961

And so to sum up, I believe that for by far the greater part of their work it is a condition upon the success of our system that the judges should be independent; and I do not believe that their independence should be impaired because of their constitutional function. But the price of this immunity, I insist, is that they should not have the last word in those basic conflicts of "right and wrong — between whose endless jar justice resides." You may ask what then will become of the fundamental principles of equity and fair play which our constitutions enshrine; and whether I seriously believe that unsupported they will serve merely as counsels of moderation. I do not think that anyone can say.

What will be left of those principles? I do not know whether they will serve only as counsels; but this much I think I do know — that a society so riven that the spirit of moderation is gone, no court *can* save; that a society where that spirit flourishes, no court *need* save; that in a society which evades its responsibility by thrusting upon courts the nurture of that spirit, that spirit in the end will perish. What is the spirit of moderation? It is the temper which does not press a partisan advantage to its bitter end, which can understand and will respect the other side, which feels a unity between all citizens — real and not the factitious product of propaganda — which recognizes their common fate and their common aspirations — in a word, which has faith in the sacredness of the individual. If you ask me how such a temper and such a faith are bred and fostered, I cannot answer. They are the last flowers of civilization, delicate and easily overrun by the weeds of our sinful human nature; we may even now be witnessing their uprooting and disappearance until in the progress of the ages their seeds can once more find some friendly soil. But I am satisfied that they must have the vigor within themselves to withstand the winds and weather of an indifferent and ruthless world; and that it is idle to seek shelter for them in a courtroom. Men must take that temper and that faith with them into the field, into the market-place, into the factory, into the council-room, into their homes; they cannot be imposed; they must be lived.

THUCYDIDES   471–400 B.C.
Of all manifestations of power, restraint impresses men most.

This is as quoted by Walter Lippmann. The editors, even with the aid of the best scholars, cannot find it in Thucydides.

PART X

HE SEEKS SOLACE AND BEAUTY

There are two kinds of taste, the taste for emotions of surprise and the taste for emotions of recognition.

HENRY JAMES

Pedants and Passions

JOHN JAY CHAPMAN   1862–1933

The pedant is as old as history, but no age has ever taken
him so seriously as we do. Ever since Winckelmann began the examination of Greek statuary with the notion
of translating Hellenic art into the German language,
learned critics who have never had a chisel in their hands
have been writing up art, each in the cant psychology of
his own decade, and all believing that they had laid hands
on the subject. Men who had no religion, no sympathy
with dogma, and no experience with the government of
men, have been writing tomes about the Middle Ages.
Egyptologists and anthropologists are today endeavoring
to get an insight into the most subtle mysteries of the antique or prehistoric consciousness, mysteries which, if
they should really be understood, could only be recorded
in the vehicles of the imagination, as for instance, by
poetry, by ritual or gesture, yet which the learned dash
down in the lingo of their classroom, to be read by the
spectacled world and regarded as very profound. The
talk is all of Music and the Muses; but where are the
instruments? If some one of these investigators should
really hear a strain that once issued from Saint Cecilia's
pipes or a tune sung by Orpheus, what organ would he
play it on? He would reproduce it with perfect self-assurance on his typewriter. The arrogance with which
we sit down to sum up the Past, and advise our young
Ph.D.'s — who have never written a couplet — to write

essays about the influence of Shenstone on Wordsworth, is perhaps a sign that the epoch is drawing to a close. The absurdity of it is revealed in its dissolution.

I say that the great illusion of the period which is now passing has been that anything whatever, no matter how recondite, could be discovered through hard intellectual work and mental concentration. Would it not then be natural if, when once honestly baffled in our search for truth through concentration, we should be unexpectedly invaded by truth in the relaxation that followed on our acknowledgment of failure? Surely the world will give a great sigh of relief when it discovers that a tremendous intellectual power has been misapplied. We have been endeavoring to express the fluid universe of man's emotions in terms and symbols drawn from the study of physical science; and in the meantime we have all but forgotten the languages of Art, Poetry, and Religion which alone can express the passion for truth with which we burn.

Genius

GOETHE TO ECKERMANN   1749–1832

"Productiveness of the highest order," said Goethe, "significant *aperçus,* remarkable discoveries, great thoughts that bear fruit and have results, do not lie within anyone's power. They are exalted above earthly control. Man must consider such as unexpected gifts from above, as pure children of God, which he must welcome and honor with thanks and joy. They are kin to the daemonic, which overcomes him and does with him what it pleases, and to which he unconsciously yields himself, believing he is acting on his own initiative. In such cases, we must often consider a man as an instrument of a higher world order — a vessel found worthy to receive a divine influence.

"At the same time," he continued, "there is a productiveness of another kind, one more subjected to earthly influences, one that man has more within his power — though here also he finds cause to bow himself before something of the divine. Here I place all that concerns the execution of a plan, all the links of a chain of thought, the ends of which already light the way. Here I place also all that makes the visible body of a work of art.

"Thus it was that the first thought of his *Hamlet* came to Shakespeare. The spirit of the whole presented and impressed itself unexpectedly on his mind, and he surveyed the several situations, characters, and conclusion, in an exaltation, as a pure gift from above in which he had no immediate influence, although the possibility of such an *aperçu* must always presuppose a spirit like his. But the individual scenes and the dialogue of the characters, he had completely in his power, so that he was able to produce them daily and hourly, and work them out for weeks, just as he chose."

Eckermann reports this conversation with Goethe, on the night of March 11, 1828; and he adds, "Goethe was particularly wonderful this evening. The tone of his voice and the fire in his eyes made him seem to glow, as if the best days of his youth were flaming up in him." The old man was nearly eighty.

JONATHAN SWIFT   1667–1745

When a true genius appears in the world, you may know him by this sign, that the dunces are all in confederacy against him.

Imagination Creatrix

JOHN LIVINGSTON LOWES   1867–1945

Every great imaginative conception is a vortex into which everything under the sun may be swept. "All other men's worlds," wrote Coleridge once, "are the poet's chaos." In that regard *The Ancient Mariner* is one with the noble army of imaginative masterpieces of all time. Oral traditions — homely, fantastic, barbaric, disconnected — which had ebbed and flowed across the planet in its unlettered days, were gathered up into that marvel of constructive genius, the plot of the *Odyssey,* and out of "a tissue of old *märchen*" was fashioned a unity palpable as flesh and blood and universal as the sea itself. Well-nigh all the encyclopedic erudition of the Middle Ages was forged and welded, in the white heat of an indomitable will, into the steel-knit structure of the *Divine Comedy*. There are not in the world, I suppose, more appalling masses of raw fact than would stare us in the face could we once, through some supersubtle chemistry, resolve that superb, organic unity into its primal elements. It so happens that for the last twenty-odd years I have been more or less occupied with Chaucer. I have tracked him, as I have trailed Coleridge, into almost every section of eight floors of a great library. It is a perpetual adventure among uncharted Ophirs and Golcondas to read after him — or Coleridge. And every conceivable sort of thing which Chaucer knew went into his alembic. It went in x — a waif of travel-lore from the mysterious Orient, a curious bit of primitive psychiatry, a racy morsel from Jerome against Jovinian, alchemy, astrology, medicine, geomancy, physiognomy, Heaven only knows what not, all vivid with the relish of the reading — it went in stark fact, "nude and crude," and it came out pure Chaucer. The results are as different from *The Ancient Mariner* as an English post-road from spectre-haunted seas. But the basic operations which produced them (and on this point I may venture to speak from first-hand knowledge) are essentially the same.

As for the years of "industrious and select reading, steady observation, insight into all seemly and generous arts and affairs" which were distilled into the magnificent romance of the thunder-scarred yet dauntless Rebel, voyaging through Chaos and old Night to shatter Cosmos, pendent from the battlements of living sapphire like a star — as for those serried hosts of facts caught up into the cosmic sweep of Milton's grandly poised design, it were bootless to attempt to sum up in a sentence here the opulence which countless tomes of learned comment have been unable to exhaust. And what (in apostolic phrase) shall I more say? For the time would fail me to tell of the *Aeneid,* and the *Orlando Furioso,* and the

Faërie Queene, and *Don Juan,* and even *Endymion,*
let alone the cloud of other witnesses. The notion that
the creative imagination, especially in its highest exercise, has little or nothing to do with facts is one of the
pseudodoxia epidemica which die hard.

For the imagination never operates in a vacuum. Its
stuff is always fact of some order, somehow experienced;
its product is that fact transmuted. I am not forgetting
that facts may swamp imagination, and remain unassimi-
lated and untransformed. And I know, too, that this
sometimes happens even with the masters. For some of
the greatest poets, partly by virtue of their very greatness,
have had, like Faust, two natures struggling within them.
They have possessed at once the instincts of the scholar
and the instincts of the artist, and it is precisely with regard to facts that these instincts perilously clash. Even
Dante and Milton and Goethe sometimes clog their powerful streams with the accumulations of the scholar who
shared bed and board with the poet in their mortal
frames. "The Professor still lurks in your anatomy" —
"Dir steckt der Doktor noch im Leib" — says Mephis-
topheles to Faust. But when, as in *The Ancient Mariner,*
the stuff that Professors and Doctors are made on has
been distilled into quintessential poetry, then the passing
miracle of creation has been performed.

But "creation," like "creative," is one of those hypnotic
words which are prone to cast a spell upon the understanding and dissolve our thinking into haze. And out
of this nebulous state of the intellect springs a strange
but widely prevalent idea. The shaping spirit of Imagination sits aloof, like God as He is commonly conceived,
creating in some thaumaturgic fashion out of nothing its
visionary world. That and that only is deemed to be "originality" — that, and not the imperial moulding of old
matter into imperishably new forms. The ways of creation are wrapt in mystery; we may only marvel, and bow
the head.

Now it is true beyond possible gainsaying that the operations which we call creative leave us in the end confronting mystery. But that is the fated terminus of all

our quests. And it is chiefly through a deep-rooted reluctance to retrace, so far as they are legible, the footsteps
of the creative faculty that the power is often thought of
as abnormal, or at best a splendid aberration. I know
full well that this reluctance springs, with most of us,
from the staunch conviction that to follow the evolution
of a thing of beauty is to shatter its integrity and irre-
trievably to mar its charm. But there are those of us who
cherish the invincible belief that the glory of poetry
will gain, not lose, through a recognition of the fact that
the imagination works its wonders through the exercise,
in the main, of normal and intelligible powers. To establish that, without blinking the ultimate mystery of
genius, is to bring the workings of the shaping spirit in
the sphere of art within the circle of the great moulding
forces through which, in science and affairs and poetry
alike, there emerges from chaotic multiplicity a unified
and ordered world.

For the operations which we have been tracing are, in
essentials, the stuff of general experience. We live, every
one of us — the mutest and most inglorious with the rest
— at the centre of a world of images. And they behave with us, and you and I behave with them, in such
fashion that, were only the ineffable increment of genius
present, *Ancient Mariners* might hang on every bush. No
one could with more unchallenged fitness represent the
mute majority than I, and here, fresh-picked, is a commonplace case in point. I received an hour ago (as I now
write) a letter from an English friend. I had last seen
him at an international conference of scholars, and instantly, as I read the letter, pictures connected with that
gathering began to rise and stream. And before I knew
it, as I sat for a moment thinking (if what was going on
may properly be labeled "thought"), associated images
from far and near were crowding on each other's heels.
They flashed, by way of a distinguished mediaevalist who,
as one of a hundred services, had edited *The Pearl*, to
the river and cliff at Durham, which I long had thought
of as oddly suggestive of the etherealized landscape of
that baffling poem. And with what seemed utter incon-

sequence I instantly saw, sharp as if etched, a dark alley debouching on a river, and a policeman holding with one hand (his pistol in the other) a kicking, struggling ruffian, while a pair of sinister figures intent on rescue manoeuvred for position in the background. Yet that, like the cliff at Durham, crowned with its mighty pile, was paradoxically called up by that most other-worldly of performances, *The Pearl*. For the scene was an incident of the last midnight walk I had taken with a friend (now dead) who years ago had speculated brilliantly about the problem of the poem — and had been answered by the writer of my letter! Then (although in reality the strands of recollection were simultaneously interweaving like a nest of startled snakes), with another leap of association I was on an island in the Thames, where, of a Sunday afternoon, there used to recline against a tree, like a glorious old British river-god with white and curling beard, the Chaucerian whom Chaucer would have most dearly loved. And in a twinkling the island in its turn dissolved, and the river-god became the *genius loci* of the teashop in New Oxford Street, where, in a flowing tie of unforgettable flamboyancy, he still lives in a thousand memories. And at once there slipped into the picture, displacing that glorified establishment, a dingy A. B. C. eating-house in Aldgate Street, where thirty years ago delectable little lambpies were to be had. And off in every direction all the while were shooting other associations, recalling and linking other fleeting glimpses of yesterday, and long ago, and far away. And then the telephone incontinently cut the panorama off.

There is an instance, normal enough, of "the streamy nature of association." And two or three perfectly obvious facts are pertinent enough to call to mind. I am not, for example, perpetually haunted by the pictures of this morning's casual raree-show. At the moment when I tore my letter open, they had, for the "I" of that moment, absolutely no existence. Collectively and severally they were not. Where, indeed, at any given instant, *are* all the countless facts we know, and all the million scenes we have experienced? Wherever that shadowy limbo may be, these were. The Well is only a convenient symbol for a mystery. And there they had lain, "absorbed by some unknown gulf into some unknown abyss," to all intents and purposes in utter non-existence — asleep, some for weeks, some for months, and some for a period of years. Then, all at once, they awoke.

And they awoke at the summons of a definite suggestion. Had that particular letter not arrived, they might have slept on for yet more months and years, or even never have waked at all. But once called, they came pell-mell, as if the fountains of the deep were broken up. Moreover, to my certain knowledge, most of them had never come into conjunction in the field of consciousness before. *The Pearl* in the course of five hundred years had never consorted with quite this queer gallimaufry. Dr. Furnivall on his beloved island in the Thames and a policeman with a pistol on the banks of the Cantabrigian Charles achieved propinquity, I can affirm with confidence, for the first time. Yet there they were — like the marine fauna of Spitzbergen and the phosphorescence of tropical seas. A definite impetus had struck down into the Well and set the sleeping images in motion. And when they emerged, they were linked in new and sometimes astonishing combinations. Nor, be it noted, am I now discussing the inception of a poem.

But there is more. The panorama was set in motion and unrolled without my will. For the moment I simply allowed the images to stream. Then I deliberately assumed control. For when, an hour later, I came back to write, I saw that here, like manna from heaven, was grist for my mill. The sentence about the world of images at the center of which we live stood already on the page, and the skeleton of a plan was in my head. And with the play of free associations fresh in mind, a new agency was interposed. For I have now consciously selected and rejected among the crowding elements of the phantasmagoria, and the elements accepted have been fitted into my design. The streamy nature of association has been curbed and ruddered — and the result is as innocent of poetry as a paradigm.

Now all that, trivial though it be, is a perfectly normal and typical proceeding. The thronged yet sleeping subliminal chambers; the summons which unlocks their secret doors; the pouring-up of images linked in new conjunctions provocative of unexpected *aperçus;* the conscious seizing and directing to an end of suggestions which the unconscious operations have supplied — not one stage of the process, nor even the transaction as a whole, is the monopoly of poetry. It is the stuff of which life weaves patterns on its loom; and poetry, which is life enhanced and glorified, employs it too in fashioning more rarely beautiful designs. Intensified and sublimated and controlled though they be, the ways of the creative faculty are the universal ways of that streaming yet consciously directed something which we know (or think we know) as life.

Creative genius, in plainer terms, works through processes which are common to our kind, but these processes are superlatively enhanced. The subliminal agencies are endowed with an extraordinary potency; the faculty which conceives and executes operates with sovereign power; and the two blend in untrammelled interplay. There is always in genius, I imagine, the element which Goethe, who knew whereof he spoke, was wont to designate as "the Daemonic." But in genius of the highest order that sudden, incalculable, and puissant energy which pours up from the hidden depths is controlled by a will which serves a vision — the vision which sees in chaos the potentiality of Form.

Out of the vast, diffused, and amorphous nebula, then, with which we started, and through which we have slowly forged our way, there emerged, framed of its substance, a structure of exquisitely balanced and co-ordinated unity — a work of pure imaginative vision. "The imagination," said Coleridge once, recalling a noble phrase from Jeremy Taylor's *Via Pacis,* ". . . *sees all things in one.*" It sees the Free Life — the endless flux of the unfathomed sea of facts and images — but it sees also the controlling Form. And when it acts on what it sees, through the long patience of the will the flux itself is transformed and fixed in the clarity of a realized design. For there enter into imaginative creation three factors which reciprocally interplay: the Well, and the Vision, and the Will. Without the Vision, the chaos of elements remains a chaos, and the Form sleeps forever in the vast chambers of unborn designs. Yet in *that* chaos only could creative Vision ever see *this* Form. Nor without the co-operant Will, obedient to the Vision, may the pattern perceived in the huddle attain obtective reality. Yet manifold though the ways of the creative faculty may be, the upshot is one: from the empire of chaos a new tract of cosmos has been retrieved; a nebula has been compacted — it may be! — into a star.

Yet no more than the lesser are these larger factors of the creative process — the storing of the Well, the Vision, and the concurrent operation of the Will — the monopoly of poetry. Through their conjunction the imagination in the field of science, for example, is slowly drawing the immense confusion of phenomena within the unfolding conception of an ordered universe. And its operations are essentially the same. For years, through intense and unremitting observation, Darwin had been accumulating masses of facts which pointed to a momentous conclusion. But they pointed through a maze of baffling inconsistencies. Then all at once the flash of vision came. "I can remember," he tells us in that precious fragment of an autobiography — "I can remember the very spot in the road, whilst in my carriage, when to my joy the solution occurred to me." And then, and only then, with the infinite toil of exposition, was slowly framed from the obdurate facts the great statement of the theory of evolution. The leap of the imagination, in a garden at Woolsthorpe on a day in 1665, from the fall of an apple to an architectonic conception cosmic in its scope and grandeur is one of the dramatic moments in the history of human thought. But in that pregnant moment there flashed together the profound and daring observations and conjectures of a long period of years; and upon the instant of illumination followed other years of rigorous and protracted labour, before the *Prin-*

cipia appeared. Once more there was the long, slow storing of the Well; once more the flash of amazing vision through a fortuitous suggestion; once more the exacting task of translating the vision into actuality. And those are essentially the stages which Poincaré observed and graphically recorded in his *Mathematical Discovery*. And that chapter reads, as we saw long ago, like an exposition of the creative processes through which *The Ancient Mariner* came to be. With the inevitable and obvious differences we are not here concerned. But it is of the utmost moment to more than poetry that, instead of regarding the imagination as a bright but ineffectual faculty with which in some esoteric fashion poets and their kind are specially endowed, we recognize the essential oneness of its function and its ways with all the creative endeavours through which human brains, with dogged persistence, strive to discover and realize order in a chaotic world.

For the Road to Xanadu, as we have traced it, is the road of the human spirit, and the imagination voyaging through chaos and reducing it to clarity and order is the symbol of all the quests which lend glory to our dust. And the goal of the shaping spirit which hovers in the *poet's* brain is the clarity and order of pure beauty. Nothing is alien to its transforming touch. "Far or forgot to [it] is near; Shadow and sunlight are the same." Things fantastic as the dicing of spectres on skeleton-barks, and ugly as the slimy spawn of rotting seas, and strange as a star astray within the moon's bright tip, blend in its vision into patterns of new-created beauty, "herrlich, wie am ersten Tag." Yet the pieces that compose the pattern are not new. In the world of the shaping spirit, save for its patterns, there is nothing new that was not old. For the work of the creators is the mastery and transmutation and reordering into shapes of beauty of the given universe within us and without us. The shapes thus wrought are not that universe; they are "carved with figure strange and sweet, All made out of the carver's brain." Yet in that brain the elements and shattered fragments of the figures already lie, and what the carver-creator sees, implicit in the fragments, is the unique and lovely Form.

THOREAU   1817–1862

The poet is he that hath fat enough, like bears and marmots, to suck his claws all winter. He hibernates in this world, and feeds on his own marrow. Alas, the poet too is, in one sense, a sort of dormouse gone into winter quarters of deep and serene thoughts, insensible to surrounding circumstances; his words are the relation of his oldest and finest memory, a wisdom drawn from the remotest experience. Other men lead a starved existence, meanwhile, like hawks that would fain keep on the wing and trust to pick up a sparrow now and then.

The Devil's Advocate Takes a First View

OSWALD SPENGLER   1880–1936

In the beginning there is the timid, despondent, naked expression of a newly awakened soul which is still seeking for a relation between itself and the world that, though its proper creation, yet is presented as alien and unfriendly. There is the child's fearfulness in Bishop Bernward's building at Hildesheim, in the Early-Christian catacomb-painting, and in the pillar-halls of the Egyptian Fourth Dynasty. A February of art, a deep presentiment of a coming wealth of forms, an immense suppressed tension, lies over the landscape that, still wholly rustic, is adorning itself with the first strongholds and townlets. Then follows the joyous mounting into the high Gothic, into the Constantinian age with its pillared basilicas and its domical churches, into the relief-ornament of the Fifth-Dynasty temple. *Being* is understood, a sacred form-language has been completely mastered and radiates its glory, and the style ripens into a majestic symbolism of directional depth and of Destiny. But fervent youth comes to an end, and contradictions arise within the soul itself. The Renaissance, the Dionysiac-musical hostility to Apollinian Doric, the Byzantine of 450 that looks to Alexandria and away from the overjoyed art of Antioch, indicate a moment of resistance, of effective or ineffective impulse to destroy what has been acquired. It is very difficult to elucidate this moment, and an attempt to do so would be out of place here.

And now it is the manhood of the style-history that comes on. The Culture is changing into the intellectuality of the great cities that will now dominate the countryside, and *pari passu* the style is becoming intellectualized also. The grand symbolism withers; the riot of superhuman forms dies down; milder and more worldly arts drive out the great art of developed stone. Even in Egypt sculpture and fresco are emboldened to lighter movement. The *artist* appears, and "plans" what formerly grew out of the soil. Once more existence becomes self-conscious, and now, detached from the land and the dream and the mystery, stands questioning, and wrestles for an expression of its new duty — as at the beginning of Baroque when Michelangelo, in wild discontent and kicking against the limitations of his art, piles up the dome of Saint Peter's — in the age of Justinian I which built Hagia Sophia and the mosaic-decked domed basilicas of Ravenna — at the beginning of that Twelfth Dynasty in Egypt which the Greeks condensed under the name of Sesostris — and at the decisive epoch in Hellas (*c.* 600) whose architecture probably, nay certainly, expressed that which is echoed for us in its grandchild Aeschylus.

Then comes the gleaming autumn of the Style. Once more the soul depicts its happiness, this time conscious of self-completion. The "return to Nature," which already thinkers and poets — Rousseau, Gorgias, and their "contemporaries" in the other Cultures — begin to feel and to proclaim, reveals itself in the form-world of the arts as a sensitive longing and presentiment of the end. A perfectly clear intellect, joyous urbanity, the sorrow of a parting — these are the colours of these last Culture-decades of which Talleyrand was to remark later: "Qui n'a pas vécu avant 1789 ne connaît pas la douceur de vivre." So it was, too, with the free, sunny, and superfine art of Egypt under Sesostris III (*c.* 1850 B.C.) and the brief moments of satiated happiness that produced the varied splendour of Pericles' Acropolis and the works of Zeuxis and Phidias. A thousand years later again, in the age of the Ommaiyads, we meet it in the glad fairyland of Moorish architecture with its fragile columns and horseshoe arches that seem to melt into air in an iridescence of arabesques and stalactites. A thousand years more, and we see it in the music of Haydn and Mozart, in Dresden shepherdesses, in the pictures of Watteau and Guardi, and the works of German master-builders at Dresden, Potsdam, Würzburg, and Vienna.

Then the style fades out. The form-language of the Erechtheum and the Dresden Zwinger, honeycombed with intellect, fragile, ready for self-destruction, is followed by the flat and senile Classicism that we find in the Hellenistic megalopolis, the Byzantium of 900, and the "Empire" modes of the North. The end is a sunset reflected in forms revived for a moment by pedant or by eclectic — semi-earnestness and doubtful genuineness dominate the world of the arts. We today are in this condition — playing a tedious game with dead forms to keep up the illusion of a living art.

Again, the translation approved by the author, not by the Editors.

O. W. HOLMES, JR., TO POLLOCK   1932

We are reading Spengler, *The Decline of the West,* a learned original book, written with incredible German arrogance, and not in all believed by me, but wonderfully suggestive — an odious animal who must be read. He has as swelled a head as man can have and live, but the beast has ideas, many of which I don't know enough to criticize. I wish he was dead.

MUSSORGSKY   1835–1881

Art is not an end in itself, but a means of addressing humanity.

JOHN DEWEY   1859–1952

Language exists only when it is listened to as well as spoken. The hearer is an indispensable partner. The

work of art is complete only as it works in the experience
of others than the one who created it. Thus, language
involves what logicians call a triadic relation. There is
the speaker, the thing said, and the one spoken to. The
external object, the product of art, is the connecting link
between artist and audience. Even when the artist works
in solitude, all three terms are present. The work is there
in progress, and the artist has to become vicariously the
receiving audience. He can speak only as his work appeals to him as one spoken to through what he perceives.
He observes and understands as a third person might
note and interpret. Matisse is reported to have said:
"When a painting is finished, it is like a new-born child.
The artist himself must have time for understanding it."
It must be lived with as a child is lived with, if we are to
grasp the meaning of his being.

GOETHE   1749–1832

Whatever you cannot understand, you cannot possess.

JAMES JOYCE   1882–1941

The artist, like the God of the creation, remains within
or behind or beyond or above his handiwork, invisible,
refined out of existence, indifferent, paring his finger-
nails.

Vox Pop

STRAWINSKI   1882–

I am convinced that the spontaneous judgment of the
public is always more authentic than the opinion of those
who set themselves up to be judges of works of art. You
may take that from a man who has had occasion in the
course of his career to come into contact with the most
varied publics. I can myself state, in my double capacity
of composer and performer, that the less the public is prej-
udiced for or against a piece of music, the sounder, and
the more favorable for music in general, are its reactions.

A playwright of some wit suggested, after his last play
had failed, that the public was becoming less and less

talented. It strikes me, on the contrary, that it is the authors who sometimes lack talent; and that the public has always, perhaps not talent, which is difficult to attribute to any collectivity, but at any rate, at least when it is left to itself, a freshness of judgment that gives high value to its reactions. But the public must not be infected with snobbery.

Artists have often told me, "Why do you complain about snobs? They are most usefully menial to new movements. If not from conviction, at any rate from their character as snobs. They are your best clients." And I always reply that they are bad clients, false clients, because they are as menial to the false as they are to truth. By serving every cause, they hurt the best, because they confuse it with the worst.

All in all, I prefer candid abuse, from an honest audience that has not understood anything, to false praise. For that is as useless to those who receive it as it is to those who offer it.

Like every kind of evil, snobbery tends to generate another evil, which is its contrary. I call it *pompiérisme*. Perhaps there is no English word for it, but there is for a *pompier* of the advance guard and that is Bunthornism.

These Bunthornes talk music as they talk Freud or Marx. They invoke on every occasion the complexes of psychoanalysis, and today they go so far, in spite of themselves — but *snobbesse oblige* — to let themselves be taken over by the great Saint Thomas Aquinas. All in all, I prefer the simple Pompiers who talk melody, who appeal, with their hands on their hearts, to the inalienable right of sentiment, who defend the privacy of emotion, who affirm their preoccupation with things that are noble, and who get caught now and then in an adventure with something orientally picturesque. They go so far as to pay homage to my Fire Bird. That, you will understand, is not why I prefer them to the others. I simply find them less dangerous.

The Bunthornes would do wrong to look down too

emphatically on their less advanced colleagues. Though both will never get over it, the more revolutionary pass out of fashion much sooner than the others. Time is more of a menace to them.

The true enthusiast for music, like the true patron of music, escapes these categories; but both are rare, as all genuine things are rare. The false patron is commonly recruited from the ranks of the snobs, just as the simple Pompiers come from the bourgeois.

For the same reasons that I have already given, the bourgeois irritates me much less than the snob. Not that I am defending the bourgeois, but he is really too easy to attack. Let us leave such attacks to the great specialists of that, the communists. From the point of view of humanity and of spiritual development, the bourgeois is of course an obstacle and a danger. But the danger is too obvious to give us as much cause for concern as snobbery, which is not so often denounced for what it is.

I cannot, in closing, not say a few words on the patron, who has played such a fundamental part in the development of the arts. The pressure of the times and an increasing demagoguery are turning the state into an anonymous patron, and one that is stupidly equalitarian. We cannot help regretting the Elector of Brandenburg who gave aid to John Sebastian Bach, or Prince Esterhazy who took care of Haydn, or Louis II of Bavaria who protected Wagner. Now that such patrons are failing us, let us pay our respects to those who remain to the artist, to the poor patron who thinks he has done what he could when he offers them a cup of tea in exchange for the courtesy of their presence, and to the rich man who remains anonymous and, having delegated the duty of distributing his liberality to a secretariat of munificence, is nevertheless a patron of the arts without really being quite aware of it.

Translated by the editors, with acknowledgments for the happy rendering, "Bunthornism," which is not Strawinski, but surely what he would have said. Why is it that musicians as a rule seem to write so much better than other artists?

CHARLES LAMB   1775–1834

I allow no hotbeds in the gardens of Parnassus.

Greenery-Yallery

G. K. CHESTERTON   1874–1936

Any man with a vital knowledge of the human psychology ought to have the most profound suspicion of anybody who claims to be an artist, and talks a great deal about art. Art is a right and human thing, like walking or saying one's prayers; but the moment it begins to be talked about very solemnly, a man may be fairly certain that the thing has come into a congestion and a kind of difficulty.

The artistic temperament is a disease that afflicts amateurs. It is a disease which arises from men not having sufficient power of expression to utter and get rid of the element of art in their being. It is healthful to every sane man to utter the art within him; it is essential to every sane man to get rid of the art within him at all costs. Artists of a large and wholesome vitality get rid of their art easily, as they breathe easily, or perspire easily. But in artists of less force, the thing becomes a pressure, and produces a definite pain, which is called the artistic temperament. Thus, very great artists are able to be ordinary men — men like Shakespeare or Browning. There are many real tragedies of the artistic temperament, tragedies of vanity or violence or fear. But the great tragedy of the artistic temperament is that it cannot produce any art.

EMERSON   1803–1882

Perpetual modernness is the measure of merit in every work of art.

What versus How

JOHN DEWEY   1859–1952

A work of art no matter how old and classic is actually, not just potentially, a work of art only when it lives in some individualized experience. As a piece of parchment, of marble, of canvas, it remains (subject to the ravages of time) self-identical throughout the ages. But as a work of art, it is re-created every time it is esthetically experienced. No one doubts this fact in the rendering of a musical score; no one supposes that the lines and dots on paper are more than the recorded means of evoking the work of art. But what is true of it is equally true of the Parthenon as a building. It is absurd to ask what an artist "really" meant by his product; he himself would find different meanings in it at different days and hours and in different stages of his own development. If he could be articulate, he would say, "I meant just *that,* and *that* means whatever you or anyone can honestly, that is, in virtue of your own vital experience, get out of it." Any other idea makes the boasted "universality" of the work of art a synonym for monotonous identity. The Parthenon, or whatever, is universal because it can continuously inspire new personal realizations in experience.

It is simply an impossibility that anyone today should experience the Parthenon as the devout Athenian contemporary citizen experienced it, any more than the religious statuary of the twelfth century can mean, esthetically, even to a good Catholic today, just what it meant to the worshipers of the old period. The "works" that fail to become *new* are not those which are universal, but those which are "dated." The enduring art-product may have been, and probably was, called forth by something occasional, something having its own date and place. But *what* was evoked is a substance so formed that it can enter into the experiences of others and enable them to have more intense and more fully rounded-out experiences of their own.

This is what it is to have form. It marks a way of envisaging, of feeling, and of presenting experienced matter so that it most readily and effectively becomes material for the construction of adequate experience on the part of those less gifted than the original creator. Hence there can be no distinction drawn, save in reflection, between form and substance. The work itself *is* matter formed into esthetic substance. The critic, the theorist, as a reflective student of the art-product, however, not only may but must draw a distinction between them. Any skilled observer of a pugilist or a golf-player will, I suppose, institute distinctions between *what* is done and *how* it is done — between the knockout and the manner of the delivery of a blow; between the ball driven so many yards to such and such a line and the way the drive was executed. The artist, the one engaged in doing, will effect a similar distinction when he is interested in correcting an habitual error, or learning how better to secure a given effect. Yet the act itself is exactly *what* it is because of *how* it is done. In the act there is no distinction, but perfect integration of manner and content, form and substance.

The Abyss of Liberty

STRAWINSKI   1882–

As for myself, I experience a sort of terror if I sit down to work and find an infinity of possibilities open to me. If all are open, the best and the worst, there is no resistance. No effort is conceivable. I stand on nothing. Endeavor is futile.

Need I throw myself into an abyss of liberty? What can I grasp to avoid the dizziness that comes over me when I face these infinite possibilities? I will not succumb to it. I can conquer my terror. I can reassure myself with the knowledge that I have within my grasp the seven notes of the scale, and the chromatic intervals, and the tempos fast and slow. For then I have hold of something solid and concrete. These things offer me a field of experience, quite as vast as the fearful and giddy infinity which so frightened me, and in that field I can root myself. I know that the twelve notes in each octave and the varieties of rhythm offer me opportunities that all of human genius will never exhaust.

I am saved from the anguish into which I was plunged by unconditional liberty by the faculty of addressing and confining myself to these concrete things. My liberty is only theoretical. Give me the finite and the definite. Give me matter that will serve my purpose within the scope of my powers. Let it come to me with its limitations. Then it will be for me to impose my own on it. Together, like it or not, we enter into the realm of necessity.

Yet who has ever heard talk of art except as the realm of liberty? That is the common heresy, because people imagine art to be something outside of common activity. But in art as in everything else you can build only upon a firm resisting foundation, and anything that resists you must likewise restrict your freedom of motion. So my liberty consists in moving inside the narrow bounds within which I set myself for each thing I undertake.

More than that, my liberty will be the greater and the more profound, the more strictly I limit my field of action and the more obstacles I place in my way. Each tie that is loosened deprives me of a strength. The more constraints, the more I am liberated from the chains that bind my spirit.

So to the voice that commands me to create, I reply with fear, and I am reassured only when I take up the things which must participate in my act of creation; they are external to it, and their constraint is arbitrary. But only with them can I make my execution rigorous.

From all this I infer the need of dogma if I would achieve my purpose. If what I say disturbs you, if my words seem hard, let us not say them. Nevertheless, they contain the secret of success. As Baudelaire wrote, "Plainly, rhetoric and prosody are not arbitrarily invented tyrannies. They are the rules required by the very organization of the spirit; and never have prosodies or rhetorics prevented originality from making itself distinct. The contrary would be far nearer the truth, that it is they which have brought originality from the bud to the flower."

Shaper of Earth

DIEGO RIVERA   1886–1958

The subject is to the painter what the rails are to the locomotive. He cannot do without it. In fact, when he refuses to seek or accept a subject, his own plastic methods and his own esthetic theories become his subject instead. And even if he escapes them, he himself becomes the subject of his work. He becomes nothing but an illustrator of his own state of mind, and in trying to liberate himself he falls into the worst sort of slavery. That is the cause of all the boredom which emanates from so many of the large expositions of modern art, a fact testified to again and again by the most different temperaments.

Does It Not Counterwork the Artifice of Nature?

W. B. YEATS   1865–1939

SAILING TO BYZANTIUM

I

That is no country for old men. The young
In one another's arms, birds in the trees
— Those dying generations — at their song,
The salmon-falls, the mackerel-crowded seas,
Fish, flesh, or fowl, commend all summer long
Whatever is begotten, born, and dies.
Caught in that sensual music all neglect
Monuments of unageing intellect.

II

An aged man is but a paltry thing,
A tattered coat upon a stick, unless
Soul clap its hand and sing, and louder sing
For every tatter in its mortal dress,
Nor is there singing school but studying
Monuments of its own magnificence;
And therefore I have sailed the seas and come
To the holy city of Byzantium.

III

O sages standing in God's holy fire
As in the gold mosaic of a wall,
Come from the holy fire, perne in a gyre,

And be the singing-masters of my soul.
Consume my heart away; sick with desire
And fastened to a dying animal
It knows not what it is; and gather me
Into the artifice of eternity.

IV

Once out of nature I shall never take
My bodily form from any natural thing
But such a form as Grecian goldsmiths make
Of hammered gold and gold enamelling
To keep a drowsy Emperor awake;
Or set upon a golden bough to sing
To lords and ladies of Byzantium
Of what is past, or passing, or to come.

Yeats published the first of these two poems in 1927. Three years before, in "A Vision," he had written: "I think if I could be given a month of Antiquity and leave to spend it where I chose, I would spend it in Byzantium a little before Justinian opened Saint Sophia and closed the Academy of Plato. I think I could find in some little wine shop some philosophical worker in mosaic who could answer all my questions, the supernatural descending nearer to him than to Plotinus even, for the pride of his delicate skill would make what was an instrument of power to princes and clerics, a murderous madness in the mob, show as a lovely flexible presence like that of a perfect human body."

"Perne in a gyre" is simply a buzzard in a spiral turn.

Byzantium

The unpurged images of day recede;
The Emperor's drunken soldiery are abed;
Night resonance recedes, night-walkers' song
After great cathedral gong;
A starlit or a moonlit dome disdains
　　All that man is,
　　All mere complexities,
The fury and the mire of human veins.

Before me floats an image, man or shade,
Shade more than man, more image than a shade;
For Hades' bobbin bound in mummy-cloth

May unwind the winding path;
A mouth that has no moisture and no breath
    Breathless mouths may summon;
    I hail the superhuman;
I call it death-in-life and life-in-death.

Miracle, bird or golden handiwork,
More miracle than bird or handiwork,
Planted on the star-lit golden bough,
Can like the cocks of Hades crow,
Or, by the moon embittered, scorn aloud
    In glory of changless metal
    Common bird or petal
And all complexities of mire or blood.

At midnight on the Emperor's pavement flit
Flames that no faggot feeds, not steel has lit,
Nor storm disturbs, flames begotten of flame,
Where blood-begotten spirits come
And all complexities of fury leave,
    Dying into a dance,
    An agony of trance,
An agony of flame that cannot singe a sleeve.

Astraddle on the dolphin's mire and blood,
Spirit after spirit! The smithies break the flood,
The golden smithies of the Emperor!
Marbles of the dancing floor
Break bitter furies of complexity,
    Those images that yet
    Fresh images beget,
That dolphin-torn, that gong-tormented sea.

Art IS Nature

SHAKESPEARE   1564–1616

    Perdita.   For I have heard it said
There is an art which in their piedness shares
With great creating Nature.
    Polixenes.   Say there be;
Yet Nature is made better by no mean

But Nature makes that mean: so, over that art,
Which you say adds to Nature, is an art
That Nature makes. You see, sweet maid, we marry
A gentler scion to the wildest stock,
And make conceive a bark of baser kind
By bud of nobler race: this is an art
Which does mend Nature, change it rather, but
The art itself is Nature.

    Perdita.   *So it is.*

    Polixenes. *Then make your garden rich in gillivors,*
And do not call them bastards.

Style

THOREAU   1817–1862

As for style of writing, if one has anything to say, it drops from him simply and directly, as a stone falls to the ground. There are no two ways about it, but down it comes, and he may stick in the points and stops wherever he can get a chance.

A sentence should read as if its author, had he held a plough instead of a pen, could have drawn a furrow deep and straight to the end.

A man's whole life is taxed for the least thing well done. It is its net result. The word which is best said came nearest to not being spoken at all, for it is cousin to a deed which the speaker could have better done. Nay, almost it must have taken the place of a deed by some urgent necessity, even by some misfortune, so that the truest writer will be some captive knight, after all.

Classic and Romantic

GOETHE   1829

"From this," Eckermann said, "we came to speak of the latest French poets and the meaning of classic and romantic."

"To me," Goethe said, "it comes as a new expression

which describes the relation not at all badly. I call the Classic the healthy, and the Romantic the sick. And so the *Nibelungenlied* is as classic as Homer, since both are healthy and strong. The most of the moderns are not romantic because they are new, but because they are weak, sickish, and sick, nor the ancients classic because they are old, but because they are strong, fresh, happy, and healthy. If we distinguish the Classic and Romantic after these qualitites, we shall soon be in the clear."

STENDHAL   1783–1842

Romanticism is the art of presenting to people those literary works which, in the present state of their habits and beliefs, are susceptible of giving them the greatest possible pleasure. Classicism, on the contrary, offers them a literature which gave the greatest possible pleasure to their great-grandfathers.

WILLIAM BLAKE   1757–1827

The road of excess leads to the palace of wisdom.

Consistency

HENRY ADAMS   1838–1918

Adams, too, was Bostonian, and the Bostonian's uncertainty of attitude was as natural to him as to Lodge. Only Bostonians can understand Bostonians and thoroughly sympathize with the inconsequences of the Boston mind. His theory and practice were also at variance. He professed in theory equal distrust of English thought, and called it a huge rag-bag of bric-à-brac, sometimes precious but never sure. For him, only the Greek, the Italian, or the French standards had claims to respect, and the barbarism of Shakespeare was as flagrant as to Voltaire; but his theory never affected his practice. He knew that his artistic standard was the illusion of his own mind; that English disorder approached nearer to truth, if truth existed, than French measure or Italian line, or German logic; he read his Shakespeare as the Evangel of conservative Christian anarchy, neither very conservative nor very Christian, but stupendously anarchistic. He loved the atrocities of English art and society, as he loved Charles Dickens and Miss Austen, not because of their example, but because of their humor. He made no scruple of defying sequence and denying consistency — but he was not a Senator.

PAINTING

We might adapt for the artist the joke about there being nothing more dangerous than instruments of war in the hands of generals. In the same way, there is nothing more dangerous than justice in the hands of judges, and a paint brush in the hands of a painter! Just think of the danger to society! But today we haven't the heart to expel the painters and poets because we no longer admit to ourselves that there is any danger in keeping them in our midst.

PABLO PICASSO

Eyes to See

JOSHUA REYNOLDS   1723–1792

Though a man cannot at all times and in all places paint or draw, yet the mind can prepare itself by laying in proper materials at all times and in all places. Both Livy and Plutarch, in describing Philopoemen, one of the ablest generals of antiquity, have given us a striking picture of a mind always intent on its profession, and by assiduity obtaining those excellences which some all their lives vainly expect from nature. I shall quote the passage in Livy at length, as it runs parallel with the practice I would recommend to the painter, sculptor, and architect:

"Philopoemen was a man eminent for his sagacity and experience in choosing ground, and in leading armies; to which he formed his mind by perpetual meditation, in times of peace as well as war. When in any occasional journey he came to a strait, difficult passage, if he was alone he considered with himself, and if he was in company he asked his friends what it would be best to do if in this place they had found an enemy, either in the front or in the rear, on the one side or on the other. 'It might happen,' says he, 'that the enemy to be opposed might come on drawn up in regular lines, or in a tumultuous body formed only by the nature of the place.' He then considered a little what ground he should take; what number of soldiers he should use, and what arms he should give them; where he should lodge his carriages, his baggage, and the defenseless followers of his camp; how many guards, and of what kind he should send to defend them; and whether it would be better to press forward along the pass, or recover by retreat his former station. He would consider likewise where his camp could most commodiously be formed; how much ground he should enclose within his trenches; where he should have the convenience of water, and where he might find plenty of food and forage; and when he should break up his camp on the following day through what road he could most safely pass, and in what form he should dispose his troops. With such thoughts and disquisitions he had from his early years so exercised his mind that on these occasions nothing could happen which he had not been already accustomed to consider."

I cannot help imagining that I see a promising young painter equally vigilant, whether at home or abroad in the streets or in the fields. Every object that presents itself is to him a lesson. He regards all Nature with a view to his profession, and combines her beauties or corrects her defects. He examines the countenances of men under the influence of passion, and often catches the most pleasing hints from subjects of turbulence or deformity. Even bad pictures themselves supply him with useful documents; and, as Leonardo da Vinci has observed, he improves upon the fanciful images that are sometimes seen in the fire, or are accidentally sketched upon a discolored wall.

A. N. WHITEHEAD   1861–1947

We look up and see a colored shape in front of us, and we say — there is a chair. But what we have seen is the mere colored shape. Perhaps an artist might not have jumped to the notion of a chair. He might have stopped at the mere contemplation of a beautiful color and a beautiful shape. But those of us who are not artists are very prone, especially if we are tired, to pass straight from the perception of the colored shape to the enjoyment of the chair, in some way of use, or of emotion, or of thought. We can easily explain this passage by reference to a train of difficult logical inference, whereby, having regard to our previous experiences of various shapes and various colors, we draw the probable conclusion that we are in the presence of a chair. I am very sceptical as to the high-grade character of the mentality required to get from the colored shape to the chair. One reason for this scepticism is that my friend the artist, who kept himself to the contemplation of color, shape, and position, was a very highly trained man, and had acquired this facility of ignoring the chair at the cost of great labor. We do not require elaborate training merely in order to refrain from embarking upon intricate trains of inference. Such abstinence is only too easy.

Leonardo Speaks

LEONARDO DA VINCI   1452–1519

How painting surpasses all human works by reason of the subtle possibilities which it contains:

The eye, which is called the window of the soul, is the chief means whereby the understanding may most fully and abundantly appreciate the infinite works of Nature; and the ear is the second, inasmuch as it acquires its importance from the fact that it hears the things which the eye has seen. If you historians, or poets, or mathematicians had never seen things with your eyes, you would be ill able to describe them in your writings. And if you, O poet, represent a story by depicting it with your pen, the painter with his brush will so render it as to be more easily satisfying and less tedious to understand. If you call painting "dumb poetry," then the painter may say of the poet that his art is "blind painting." Consider then which is the more grievous affliction, to be blind or to be dumb! Although the poet has as wide a choice of subjects as the painter, his creations fail to afford as much satisfaction to mankind as do paintings, for while poetry attempts to represent forms, actions, and scenes with words, the painter employs the exact images of these forms in order to reproduce them. Consider, then, which is more fundamental to man, the name of man or his image? The name changes with change of country; the form is unchanged except by death.

And if the poet serves the understanding by way of the ear, the painter does so by the eye, which is the nobler sense.

I will only cite as an instance of this how, if a good painter represents the fury of a battle and a poet also describes one, and the two descriptions are shown together to the public, you will soon see which will draw most of the spectators, and where there will be most discussion, to which most praise will be given and which will satisfy the more. There is no doubt that the painting, which is by far the more useful and beautiful, will give the greater pleasure. Inscribe in any place the name of God and set opposite to it His image, you will see which will be held in greater reverence!

Since painting embraces within itself all the forms of Nature, you have omitted nothing except the names, and these are not universal like the forms. If you have the results of her processes we have the processes of her results.

Take the case of a poet describing the beauties of a lady to her lover and that of a painter who makes a portrait of her; you will see whither nature will the more incline the enamoured judge. Surely the proof of the matter ought to rest upon the verdict of experience!

In Art we may be said to be grandsons unto God. If poetry treats of moral philosophy, painting has to do with natural philosophy; if the one describes the workings of the mind, the other considers what the mind effects by movements of the body; if the one dismays folk by hellish fictions, the other does the like by showing the same things in action. Suppose the poet sets himself to represent some image of beauty or terror, something vile and foul, or some monstrous thing, in contest with the painter, and suppose in his own way he makes a change of forms at his pleasure, will not the painter still satisfy the more? Have we not seen pictures which bear so close a resemblance to the actual thing that they have deceived both men and beasts?

If you know how to describe and write down the appearance of the forms, the painter can make them so that they appear enlivened with lights and shadows which create the very expression of the faces; herein you cannot attain with the pen where he attains with the brush.

That sculpture is less intellectual than painting, and lacks many of its natural parts:

As practising myself the art of sculpture no less than that of painting, and doing both the one and the other in the same degree, it seems to me that without suspicion of unfairness I may venture to give an opinion as to which of the two is the more intellectual, and of the greater difficulty and perfection.

In the first place, sculpture is dependent on certain lights, namely, those from above, while a picture carries everywhere with it its own light and shade; light and shade, therefore, are essential to sculpture. In this respect, the sculptor is aided by the nature of the relief, which produces these of its own accord, but the painter artificially creates them by his art in places where Nature would normally do the like. The sculptor cannot render the difference in the varying natures of the colors of objects; painting does not fail to do so in any particular. The lines of perspective of sculptors do not seem in any way true; those of painters may appear to extend a hundred miles beyond the work itself. The effects of aerial perspective are outside the scope of sculptors' work; they can neither represent transparent bodies nor luminous bodies nor angles of reflection nor shining bodies, such as mirrors and like things of glittering surface, nor mists, nor dull weather, nor an infinite number of things which I forbear to mention lest they should prove wearisome.

The one advantage which sculpture has is that of offering greater resistance to time; yet painting offers a like resistance if it is done upon thick copper covered with white enamel and then painted upon with enamel colors and placed in a fire and fused. In degree of permanence it then surpasses even sculpture.

And tells how he did it:

Show first the smoke of the artillery mingled in the air with the dust stirred up by the movement of the horses and of the combatants. This process you should express as follows: the dust, since it is made up of earth and has weight, although by reason of its fineness it may easily rise and mingle with the air, will nevertheless readily fall down again, and the greatest height will be attained by such part of it as is the finest, and this will in consequence be the least visible and will seem almost the color of the air itself.

The smoke which is mingled with the dust-laden air will as it rises to a certain height have more and more the appearance of a dark cloud, at the summit of which the smoke will be more distinctly visible than the dust. The smoke will assume a bluish tinge, and the dust will keep its natural color. From the side whence the light comes this mixture of air and smoke and dust will seem far brighter than on the opposite side.

As for the combatants, the more they are in the midst of this turmoil, the less they will be visible, and the less will be the contrast between their lights and shadows.

You should give a ruddy glow to the faces and the figures and the air around them, and to the gunners and those near to them, and this glow should grow fainter as it is farther away from its cause. The figures which are between you and the light, if far away, will appear dark against a light background, and the nearer their limbs are to the ground, the less will they be visible, for there the dust is greater and thicker. And if you make horses galloping away from the throng, make little clouds of dust as far distant one from another as is the space between the strides made by the horse, and that cloud which is farthest away from the horse should be the least visible, for it should be high and spread out and thin, while that which is nearest should be most conspicuous and smallest and most compact.

Let the air be full of arrows going in various directions, some mounting upwards, others falling, others flying horizontally; and let the balls shot from the guns have a train of smoke following their course. Show the figures in the foreground covered with dust on their hair and eyebrows and such other level parts as afford the dust a space to lodge.

Make the conquerors running, with their hair and other light things streaming in the wind, and with brows bent down; and they should be thrusting forward opposite limbs; that is, if a man advances the right foot, the left arm should also come forward. If you represent anyone fallen, you should show the mark where he has been dragged through the dust which has become changed to blood-stained mire, and roundabout in the half-liquid earth you should show the marks of the trampling of men and horses who have passed over it.

Make a horse dragging the dead body of his master, and leaving behind him in the dust and mud the track of where the body was dragged along.

Make the beaten and conquered pallid, with brows raised and knit together, and let the skin above the brows be all full of lines of pain; at the sides of the nose show the furrows going in an arch from the nostrils and ending where the eye begins, and show the dilatation of the nostrils which is the cause of these lines; and let the lips be arched displaying the upper row of teeth, and let the teeth be parted after the manner of such as cry in lamentation. Show someone using his hand as a shield for his terrified eyes, turning the palm of it towards the enemy, and having the other resting on the ground to support the weight of his body; let others be crying out with their mouths wide open, and fleeing away. Put all sorts of armor lying between the feet of the combatants, such as broken shields, lances, swords, and other things like these. Make the dead, some half-buried in dust, others with the dust all mingled with the oozing blood and changing into crimson mud; and let the line of the blood be discerned by its color, flowing in a sinuous stream from the corpse to the dust. Show others in the death agony grinding their teeth and rolling their eyes, with clenched fists grinding against their bodies and with legs distorted. Then you might show one, disarmed and struck down by the enemy, turning on him with teeth and nails to take fierce and inhuman vengeance; and let a riderless horse be seen galloping with mane streaming in the wind, charging among the enemy and doing them great mischief with his hoofs.

You may see there one of the combatants, maimed and fallen on the ground, protecting himself with his shield, and the enemy bending down over him and striving to give him the fatal stroke; there might also be seen many men fallen in a heap on top of a dead horse; and you should show some of the victors leaving the combat and retiring apart from the crowd, and with both hands wiping away from eyes and cheeks the thick layer of mud caused by the smarting of their eyes from the dust.

And the squadrons of the reserves should be seen standing full of hope but cautious, with eyebrows raised, and shading their eyes with their hands, peering into the thick, heavy mist in readiness for the commands of their captain; and so, too, the captain with his staff raised, hurrying to the reserves and pointing out to them the quarter of the field where they are needed; and you should show a river, within which horses are galloping, stirring the water all around with a heaving mass of waves and foam and broken water, leaping high into the air and over the legs and bodies of the horses; but see that you make no level spot of ground that is not trampled over with blood.

Communication and Picasso

FRANCIS HENRY TAYLOR   1957

If we accept the definition of art as the rendering of truth in sensible form, and truth as the interpretation of human experience, it is obvious that *a work of art is essentially communicative. It must mean something to someone other than the person who created it — in fact, and more important still, it can mean the same thing or several different things to a number of persons. But meaning it must have.* Not until the second quarter of the twentieth century was the essential communicability of art ever denied. Communication has been common to all the great racial traditions and, once established, can take any variety of expressions. It is unlimited in content or subject matter, free to adopt any style or technique. The one and only quality denied a work of art throughout the ages is privacy. Unless participation is allowed the spectator, it becomes a hopeless riddle and ceases to be a work of art at all.

If the artist is obligated to communicate his meaning, the public in return should bear in mind that they are no less obligated to make an effort to understand what the artist is attempting to say to them. The message of art is not necessarily a simple message or an easy one; and it is quite legitimate that a painting or a statue be meaningless to persons at one level of education and yet be clear and explicit to those at another level, who are particularly trained to understand it. The same layman who takes offense at an abstract picture in an exhibition, into which the artist has put years of self-discipline in logical and orderly arrangement of abstract or theoretical ideas, will accept without question the right of a university or a research foundation to publish abstruse mathematical conclusions and equations which, as an untrained person, he can never hope to comprehend. In the sciences, in the social sciences, and in the humanities there is a general acceptance of the fact that certain studies are reserved for the higher intellect. Unfortunately this is not true in the arts.

It is, however, this very appeal to the higher intellect in the early works of such masters as Picasso, Braque, Matisse, and Paul Klee which has had such influence on the present generation. For the art of the past fifty years has been more an art of cerebration than one of reflective and constructive thought. Absorption is technical experiment and the influence of psychiatric and physical investigation have engrossed the larger and more experimental minds. Picasso's startling quality of revelation, actually a revaluation of the art of seeing, has come through excessive introspection and cynicism to do a terrible disservice to those younger artists who lack his extraordinary talents and mercurial virtuosity. Whether or not one likes the message these larger talents are communicating, whether one thinks them good or evil, or prophetic of destruction or nihilistic in their purpose, one must nevertheless admit that they do at least communicate a message of importance to the present day.

That this message is more often than not a message of propaganda for some popular and current ideology is, of course, one of the fundamental dangers inherent in the modern movement. But Picasso, even when he is most socially destructive, is free from the charge of producing something meaningless or utterly private in its concept. As the storm center of the contemporary movement, he has become the symbol in the public mind of what is good or bad in modern art. Yet few of the visitors to an exhibition who are not trained in the history of design realize the fundamental significance of his contribution to the thought of our time.

PABLO PICASSO   1881–

I paint a window just as I look out of a window. If a window looks wrong in a picture open, I draw the curtain and shut it, just as I would in my own room. One must act in painting as in life, directly.

E. B. WHITE   1899–

I Paint What I See

A Ballad of Artistic Integrity, on the Occasion of the Removal of Some Rather Expensive Murals from the RCA Building

> *"What do you paint, when you paint on a wall?"*
> *Said John D.'s grandson Nelson.*
> *"Do you paint just anything there at all?*
> *Will there be any doves, or a tree in fall?*
> *Or a hunting scene, like an English hall?"*

> "I paint what I see," said Rivera.

> *"What are the colors you see when you paint?"*
> *Said John D.'s grandson Nelson.*

"Do you use any red in the beard of a saint?
If you do, is it terribly red, or faint?
Do you use any blue? Is it Prussian?"

"I paint what I paint," said Rivera.

"Whose is that head that I see on my wall?"
Said John D.'s grandson Nelson.
"Is it anyone's head whom we know, at all?
A Rensselaer, or a Saltonstall?
Is it Franklin D.? Is it Mordaunt Hall?
Or is it the head of a Russian?"

"I paint what I think," said Rivera.

"I paint what I paint, I paint what I see,
    I paint what I think," said Rivera,
"And the thing that is dearest in life to me
In a bourgeois hall is Integrity;
    However . . .
I'll take out a couple of people drinkin'
And put in a picture of Abraham Lincoln;
I could even give you McCormick's reaper
And still not make my art much cheaper.
But the head of Lenin has got to stay
Or my friends will give me the bird today,
    The bird, the bird, forever."

"It's not good taste in a man like me,"
    Said John D.'s grandson Nelson,
"To question an artist's integrity
Or mention a practical thing like a fee,
But I know what I like, to a large degree,
    Though art I hate to hamper;
For twenty-one thousand conservative bucks
You painted a radical. I say shucks,
    I never could rent the offices —
    The capitalistic offices.
For this, as you know, is a public hall
And people want doves, or a tree in fall,
And though your art I dislike to hamper,
I owe a little to God and Gramper,

> *And after all,*
> *It's my wall . . ."*

"We'll see if it is," said Rivera.

Nelson Rockefeller did take Lenin out of Rivera's mural.

The Archaic Smile

FRANCIS HENRY TAYLOR   1957

A smile appears on the faces of most archaic figures, a happiness of expression seeming to transcend that of human beings. The almond shaping of the eyes, widespread upon the forehead, thick ribbon lids, and shelving brows give an impersonal dignity to their regard. The eyes are superb and proud, not vacant. There is a complete indifference to portraiture, a tranquility and resignation which is sometimes observed on the faces of dead persons. Not only in the treatment of the eyes are eliminations apparent but in the nostrils as well; placed above coarse cubic lips, they bring the flattened surfaces of the cheeks together between definite nose and chin. The jawbone continues the boundaries of a compact head set upon massive shoulders which are gradually welded into an organic trunk, immobile and majestic. The figure is built up step by step from the base on which it stands and of which it is a part.

Certainly the Greek of the sixth century B.C. did not observe such heroic individuals in his daily life. Yet one cannot dismiss these images as the product of inferior execution. The fact that the artist did not attempt the actual portraiture of those about him must be laid more to a sense of consecration within himself than to technical deficiency. His figures were conceived in immortality, and, since he had not inquired too closely into the character of his gods, he created ideal representations of them, generalizations of supermen, bearing none of the arresting peculiarities of actual persons. This was, of course, not destined to continue in the later and more classical periods of Hellenism.

The archaic concept is, however, too often overlooked

simply because archaic art has always appeared to be a product of the past. Yet the fact that its simple qualities are so appealing to the individualists of the twentieth century is worthy of consideration. It suggests perhaps that in the present day we are starved for universals — for ideas and ideals that transcend our all too finite lives and habits of thought. In contemporary art the emphasis is nearly always placed upon the particular rather than the general; the great community of belief in which all men shared and shared alike has fallen prey to the privy experience and the momentary incident.

The problem today, then, is not so much that of a lack of a single conviction but the multiplicity of convictions with which the creative artist is confronted. For two thousand years western civilization has been concerned primarily with a monotheism in which the various levels of the hierarchy have been not only established but accepted by people in all walks of life. The iconography of the Judeo-Christian world has thus been for many centuries clear to both the artist and the spectator; and it has been taken by each of them as a matter of course. So, too, was it with the classical heritage of the Greco-Roman pantheism. Bacchus was as identifiable as St. John, and Moses could be distinguished from Hercules by the most lowly member of society.

All of this is changed today. In the rapidly expanding, secularized world in which we live, where neither the Bible nor Bulfinch's *Age of Fable* seems to play any useful role and where one person's gods appear to be as good as the next person's, it becomes imperative that there be a return, if not to the gods of our fathers themselves, to some unifying principle in which the twentieth century man of many faiths can find the comfort of authority. For the artist has ever required authority as a framework — a point of departure — for his own experience. The most telling lesson of the history of art, indeed, is that there is nothing new under the sun; a new movement at most is a return to a simpler expression of an already accepted fact.

MUSIC

*When I hear music I fear no danger,
I am invulnerable, I see no foe. I am
related to the earliest times, and to
the latest.*

THOREAU

*Music is a higher revelation than phi-
losophy.*

BEETHOVEN

*On Beethoven's writing-table he kept
framed and under glass always before
him some sentences copied in his own
hand. He had found them in an essay
by Schiller having to do with the religion of ancient Egypt. They read as
follows: "I am that which is. I am
all, what is, what was, what will be;
no mortal man has lifted my veil. He
is only and solely of himself, and to
this only one all things owe their
existence." That singular desk-com-
panion was not there to work magic.
He was not one to rely on incanta-
tion. It was there as a reminder to
himself of where he found the ultimate source of his creative power; that
it had spoken to him and through
him time and again; and that it would
continue to speak.*

LUCIEN PRICE

E-flat Major

RICHARD WAGNER   1813–1883

After a night spent in fever and sleeplessness, I forced myself to take a long tramp the next day through the hilly country, which was covered with pine woods. It all looked dreary and desolate, and I could not think what I should do there. Returning in the afternoon, I stretched myself, dead tired, on a hard couch, awaiting the long-desired hour of sleep. It did not come; but I fell into a kind of somnolent state, in which I suddenly felt as though I were sinking in swiftly flowing water. The rushing sound formed itself in my brain into a musical sound, the chord of E-flat major, which continually re-echoed in broken forms; these broken chords seemed to be melodic passages of increasing motion, yet the pure triad of E-flat major never changed, but seemed by its continuance to impart infinite significance to the element in which I was sinking. I awoke in sudden terror from my doze, feeling as though the waves were rushing high above my head. I at once recognized that the orchestral overture to the *Rheingold*, which must long have lain latent within me, though it had been unable to find definite form, had at last been revealed to me. I then quickly realized my own nature; the stream of life was not to flow to me from without, but from within. I decided to return to Zurich immediately, and begin the composition of my great poem. I telegraphed to my wife to let her know my decision, and to have my study in readiness.

Music — Good, Bad, and Infinite

DONALD FRANCIS TOVEY   1875–1940

Let us descend to a few crass illustrations of the difference between good and bad. The subject is relevant,
because bad music, whatever else it can be, cannot be
infinite; unless it is infinitely boring, and this it seldom
is. If the truth must be faced, it is often amusing, sometimes intentionally and sometimes unintentionally. A
matter perhaps more suitable for discussion over walnuts and port than in a serious lecture is the question
whether bad good music is better than good bad music.
Do not ask me to define without the aid of port, if not of
walnuts, what these terms mean, but let us take it for
granted that good bad music is infinitely preferable to
bad good music. I refuse to yield to my natural impulse
to abuse bad good music, by which I mean the vast bulk
of honest well-schooled work without which the soil
would never have become manured for any crop of great
music; but good bad music is fair game. It is never infinite except in the most distressing negative sense, but
it is often inventive, and it can demonstrate with almost
sublime simplicity and perfection what music ought not
to be. Wagner, Meyerbeer's worst enemy, was quite generous in his praise of the really emotional duet at the
end of the fourth act of *Les Huguenots;* and my own
feeling towards Meyerbeer is sometimes a little wistful,
like that of the daughter whose mother, having seen the
folly of all such things as balls, would not let her see the
folly of just one. For me this wistfulness might have
survived through a whole Meyerbeer opera, had I as
yet had the good luck to hear a first-rate performance.
Nothing less will carry a sensitive musician through four
hours, or one hour, of Meyerbeer's appalling style. And
so I must content myself with enjoying its naughtiness in
furtive glances at his scores. All art, says Aristotle, is
imitation; and in all imitation there is an element of
illusion which is more accurately called "suggestion."
The term "suggestion" distinguishes what we may paradoxically call "true" illusion from false. True artistic

illusion does not deceive. False illusion deceives the unwary and exasperates everyone when it is found out.

Now you cannot accept a suggestion which you know to be false. Doctor Johnson, dealing with the grounds alleged for unity of place and other dramatic conventions, played skittles with volumes of pretentious nonsense by roundly asserting that the spectator of a drama is in his senses all the time, and is quite aware that he is in the theatre in London and not in Athens or on the seacoast of Bohemia. Children resent a violation of their make-believe, not because it upsets their faith, but because they, being as much in their senses as Johnson's spectator, wish to play the game.

The artist must not suggest what is self-contradictory. If resources are manifestly present and implied by the circumstances, it is folly to behave as if their absence must be supplied by suggestion. Many would-be schol-arly players make nonsense of Bach when they translate his harpsichord music on to the pianoforte. In the slow movement of the Italian concerto, and many other harpsichord cantabiles, Bach writes for the harpsichord in a style that powerfully suggests the cantabile re-sources of a violin. The harpsichord can produce such a cantabile in a fascinatingly plaintive quality of tone with more actual sustaining power than you might expect. These elements, taken in connexion with the style of the music, will suggest many varieties of light and shade which the harpsichord is in reality not capable of giving. The pianoforte cannot give the harpsichord's quality of tone, but it can give the light and shade. The player who then argues that he must imitate the flat uniformity of the harpsichord is obviously misinterpreting, or fail-ing to see, the suggestiveness of Bach's music.

One of the aspects of infinity in music is precisely this element of suggestion. There is no end to it, it is omni-present, and any identifiable specimens will be a sample of the whole. Now let us use the inexhaustible, but crassly finite, Meyerbeer as our ideal awful example. In *Les Huguenots* we have soldiers and military bands ga-lore in real presence. One of the famous choruses is the

"Rataplan," in which an unaccompanied chorus imitates in those inspiriting syllables the sound of side-drums and other military incitements to a breach of the peace. I ask whether it is possible to conceive a more impotent misuse of the device of suggestion, and I do not pause for a reply.

Do not expect a connected argument on the modes of infinity in music. I borrow from Andrew Bradley's lectures on Shakespeare an illustration of another category in which we may find infinity. Bradley ends his lecture upon that painful incident in Shakespeare, the rejection of Falstaff, by saying that Shakespeare has denied to Prince Hal and King Henry V the infinity which he gave to Falstaff. Manifestly, this kind of infinity is no less, if not more, clearly an aspect of perfection than any measurable arithmetical or geometrical matters of proportion. It means that the character is consistent from all points of view. We need not worry how this consistency has been attained. The shortest account of the matter is to say that the artist is inspired. This, as we have already seen, is inadequate, because there is a strong probability that inspiration is a state of mental athletic form which in itself gives no security whatever that the results may be artistically valuable. Modern Shakespearian criticism and research has removed many occasions for awestruck admiration by showing that Shakespeare was often using the most convenient means ready to hand without the slightest regard for the consistency of character which we are at such pains to vindicate by subtle analysis. This does not always affect the question, for the infinities of artistic perfection are not bounded by the artist's own calculations. A good action does not become less good because it is expedient, and only a vainglorious and self-righteous man will be unwilling to plead expediency as the ground or excuse for his noblest actions.

The character of Falstaff gives an excellent occasion for studying examples of perfection and infinity in music, because it forms the subject of two very great works and one faded semi-classic. The faded semi-classic is Nicolai's opera, *The Merry Wives of Windsor,* in which the straw-stuffed dummy of Shakespeare's perfunctory farce plays its part in an efficiently constructed and tolerably musical adaptation of that farce diluted in the cabbage-water of a German libretto. It is impossible to write an opera upon the real Falstaff, because, though the real Falstaff provides the quality of infinity to three plays in which the title-rôle is that of a man who must satisfy himself and us merely with the divine right of kings, it is round this royal person that the only coherent story is formed. But it is possible to do as Boito did: to put into the framework of *The Merry Wives* most of the speeches of the great Falstaff, reduce the farcical escapades by half, and let an element of lyric beauty into the intrigue of Anne Page and Fenton. The rest is Verdi's business, and the result is of a quality which I believe is still disputed in some quarters, but of which I have seen no adverse criticism that does not betray itself by inattention.

Perfect works of art have this quality of infinity, that they cannot be compared. You cannot even say that an infinity of three dimensions is larger than one of two, though you may be allowed to say that it is of a higher order. You cannot say that the art of Beethoven is greater than that of Bach, or even than that of Mozart. You can only say that it has more dimensions; and so I dare not say that Elgar's symphonic poem — or, as he wisely calls it, symphonic study — *Falstaff* is greater than Verdi's opera; but I can confidently say that it is inexhaustible, and that both in relation to its programme and in its pure musical form it is a perfect example of music in full integrity.

DAUDET   1840–1897
Music is another planet.

WALTER SAVAGE LANDOR   1775–1864
I sometimes think that the most plaintive ditty has brought a fuller joy and of longer duration to its composer than the conquest of Persia to the Macedonian.

The Musical Temperament

HECTOR BERLIOZ   1803–1869

I found life in town perfectly intolerable, and spent all the time I could in the mountains. I often went as far as Subiaco, a big village some miles from Tivoli, inside the Papal States, a part of the country which is usually only visited by landscape painters.

This was a favorite remedy for one of my attacks of "spleen," and it always seemed to give me new life. I started off, in an old grey shirt, with half a dozen piastres in my pocket, and my gun or guitar in my hand, strolling along, shouting or singing, careless as to where I should sleep, knowing that, if other shelter failed me, I could always turn into one of the countless shrines by the wayside. Sometimes I went along at racing pace, or I might stop to examine an old tomb; or, standing on the summit of one of the dreary hillocks which dot the Roman plain, listen meditatively to the far-off chime of the bells of Saint Peter's, whose golden cross shone on the horizon; or, halting in pursuit of a lapwing, note down an idea for a symphony which had just entered my brain; always, however, drinking in, in deep draughts, the ceaseless delights of utter liberty.

Sometimes, when I had my guitar with me instead of my gun, a passage from the *Aeneid,* which had lain dormant in my mind from childhood, would suddenly rise to my recollection, aroused by some aspect of the surrounding scenery; then, improvising a strange recitative to a still stranger harmony, I would sing the death of Pallas, the despair of the good Evander, of his horse Ethon, unharnessed and with flowing mane and falling tears, following the young warrior's corpse to its last resting-place; of the terror of good King Latinus; the siege of Latium, which had stood on the ground beneath my feet; Amata's sad end, and the cruel death of Lavinia's noble lover. This combination of the past — the poetry and the music — used to work me into the most wonderful state of excitement, and this intensified condition of mental intoxication generally culminated in torrents of tears. The funniest part of it all was that my grief was so real. I mourned for poor Turnus, whom the hypocrite Aeneas had robbed of his state, his mistress, and his life; I wept for the beautiful and pathetic Lavinia, forced to wed the stranger-brigand bathed in her lover's blood. I longed for the good old days when the heroes, sons of the gods, walked the earth, clad in shining armor, hurling slender javelins at targets framed in burnished gold. Then, quitting the past, I wept for my personal sorrows, my dim future, my spoiled career; and at length, overwhelmed by this chaos of poetry, would suddenly fall asleep with scraps of Shakespeare or Dante on my lips: *Nessun maggior doler . . . che recordarsi . . . O poor Ophelia! . . . Good night, sweet ladies . . . vitaque cum gemitu . . . fugit indignata sub umbras . . .*

What folly! many will exclaim. Possibly; but also, what joy! *Sensible* people have no conception of the delight which the mere consciousness of living intensely can give: one's heart swells, one's imagination soars into space, life is inexpressibly quickened, and one loses all consciousness of one's bodily limitations. I did things then which would kill me now.

Absolute Music

DONALD FRANCIS TOVEY   1875–1940

The absoluteness of music is forced upon musicians by every unauthorized attempt to fit music to the purpose of other arts. Brahms's *Fourth Symphony,* for instance, has been used for a ballet. The third and fourth movements of the symphony might seem to invite such a proceeding, inasmuch as Brahms confessed that the third movement was first inspired by the sight of a famous frieze representing a procession of Bacchanals, and the finale is in the tempo and form of a *passacaglia,* which is originally a dance-form; but even in these movements the emotional and dramatic contents are such as cannot but be weakened by association with the most sublime of ballets. And the rest of the symphony is about as amenable to expression in ballet as the whole drama of *Hamlet* or *King Lear*. The failure to appreciate the enormous concentration and intensity of absolute music is not surprising when we consider that the historic origins of absolute music arise from dance and from the singing of words. Moreover, the teaching of composition is incomparably more practical if it takes account of these origins than if it ignores them or tries to exclude them. From the middle of the nineteenth century onwards academic musicians made the fatal mistake of confusing between the accomplished absoluteness of music and the means of attaining it. The editors of the first standard editions of the complete works of Mozart and Beethoven descended to the imbecility of publishing full scores of operas without the spoken dialogue. This faulty abstraction of the music from its surroundings extended, and in some places still extends, to the practice of opera houses, in which the conductor of the orchestra was completely out of touch with the stage manager, and the stage manager might almost have been selected for his ignorance of music. Wagner rendered that state of things obsolete, but musicians proceeded to retard matters by dividing themselves into absolute musicians and Wagnerians. Mozart is now recognized as the unique miracle of a composer who was supreme both in opera and in instrumental music; but for practical purposes he is like the giraffe: there ain't no such animal.

Perhaps the work that has done most to preserve music from drying up on one side into false abstraction and spreading into a dismal swamp of omnium gatherum on the other side is Beethoven's glorious failure in opera. Any child can see that *Fidelio* is all wrong, but, as a recent critic has well remarked, it nevertheless makes most other operas seem shabby. Sir Henry Hadow put his finger on the spot that is nearly fatal to *Fidelio* as an opera, but he drew the wrong inference from it. There are defects in the libretto, and in the handling of the necessary conventions of its operatic forms, which make the work unconvincing as a drama, though its story is thrilling enough in as far as we can understand it. Hence *Fidelio*

contains many passages which its defenders will describe
as unmistakably dramatic. "Yes," said Sir Henry Hadow,
"but only as the D-minor Sonata is dramatic." It is surprising that a critic not only so eminent as a writer, but
so excellent as a musician, should allow himself to imply
that a sonata is less dramatic than an opera. The dramatic events of a sonata move ten times as fast as any
stage drama; and no stage music could support five minutes of music at the normal emotional concentration of
the sonata style. The stage is the region of art in which
a very little goes a long way. The most elaborate stage
machinery produces its greatest effects with colors
splashed by the pailful onto wooden boards. Staginess
seen by daylight in the open air is not more glaring nor
more gorgeous than a framed easel picture. It is flimsy,
dingy, and rough. One of my most amusing experiences
was that of being haunted by the memory of a mighty
climax which I could not place in any Wagner opera,
though I could conceive of no drama less emotional than
Tristan which it could fit. The difficulty in finding a
place for it in Wagner was that I knew that it subsided
into a delightful kind of moonlit coolness far less tropical than any Wagnerian climate, even in *Die Meister-
singer.* I eventually ran it to earth, or rather to heaven,
in the coda of a movement by Brahms which most people would describe as of statuesque dignity. There is no
drama and no epic that can achieve the intensity of absolute music.

POETRY

When I was young,
I had not given a penny for a song
Did not the poet sing it with such airs
That one believed he had a sword
upstairs.

W. B. YEATS

What shall I say about poetry? What
shall I say about those clouds, or
about the sky? Look; look at them;
look at it! And nothing more. Don't
you understand that a poet can't say
anything about poetry? Leave that to
the critics and the professors. For
neither you, nor I, nor any poet knows
what poetry is.

LORCA

Poetry and Music

LUDWIG WITTGENSTEIN   1945

Uttering a word is like striking a note on the keyboard of the imagination.

Poetry Is Like Horses

HANS ZINSSER   1878–1940

"Poetry," he said, "has been to me much like horses. Though I was often cheated in consequence, I never enjoyed critically appraising a horse, walking around it, feeling its hocks, looking at its teeth, and then seeing other people ride it. A horse meant little to me until I could feel it under me, between my thighs, swing with the rhythm of its gaits, rise over fences with it, and lean over its neck in the exhilaration of its galloping vigor.

"And so a poem means nothing to me unless it can carry me away with the gentle or passionate pace of its emotion, over obstacles of reality into meadows and coverts of illusion. Nor is it the material that matters — whether it be the old stirrings of nature and love, or war, or whether it deals with the tragedies and complexities of human fate. The sole criterion for me is whether it can sweep me with it into emotion or illusion of beauty, terror, tranquillity, or even (Herder to the contrary) disgust — as in Baudelaire — so long as it arouses fundamental feelings or reflections which, encountered without the poet, might have passed half-realized, like a tongue of flame or a flying leaf. For the poet arrests emotions at their points of greatest supportable heat, just short of the melting point as it were, and can hold in that perfect state, permanent in his words and meters, those feelings and comprehensions which pass too quickly through the minds of ordinary men. The poet imprisons them in words or color or marble, so that we lesser men can contemplate them and recognize in them our own hearts and minds."

This was the last serious conversation I had with R. S.

KEATS   1795–1821
Poetry should please by a fine excess and not by singularity. It should strike the reader as a wording of his own highest thoughts, and appear almost as a remembrance.

ROBERT FROST   1875–
Like a piece of ice on a hot stove the poem must ride on its own melting.

Tom o' Bedlam's Song

ANON.

> With a host of furious fancies,
> Whereof I am commander:
> With a burning spear
> And a horse of air,
> To the wilderness I wander.
>
> By a knight of ghosts and shadows,
> I summoned am to Tourney:
> Ten leagues beyond
> The wild world's end;
> Methinks it is no journey.

EMERSON   1845
Poetry must be as new as foam, and as old as the rock.

A Passion of Awe

W. H. AUDEN   1957

In his book *Witchcraft,* Mr. Charles Williams has described it thus:

> One is aware that a phenomenon, being wholly itself,
> is laden with universal meaning. A hand lighting a ciga-
> rette is the explanation of everything; a foot stepping
> from the train is the rock of all existence . . . Two light
> dancing steps by a girl appear to be what all the School-
> men were trying to express . . . but two quiet steps by
> an old man seem like the very speech of hell. Or the
> other way round.

The response of the imagination to such a presence or significance is a passion of awe. This awe may vary greatly in intensity and range in tone from joyous wonder to panic dread. A sacred being may be attractive or repulsive — a swan or an octopus — beautiful or ugly — a toothless hag or a fair young child — good or evil — a Beatrice or a Belle Dame sans Merci — historical fact or fiction — a person met on the road or an image encountered in a story or a dream — it may be noble or something unmentionable in a drawing-room, it may be anything it likes on condition, but this condition is absolute, that it arouse awe.

The Great Bartender

PETER VIERECK   1948

Being absurd as well as beautiful,
Magic — like art — is hoax redeemed by awe.
(Not priest but clown, the shuddering sorcerer
Is more astounded than his rapt applauders:
"Then all those props and Easters of my stage
Came true? But I was joking all the time!")
Art, being bartender, is never drunk;
And magic that believes itself, must die.
My star was rocket of my unbelief,
Launched heavenward as all doubt's longings are;

It burst when, drunk with self-belief,
I tried to be its priest and shouted upward:
"Answers at last! If you'll but hint the answers
For which earth aches, that famous Whence and Whither;
Assuage our howling Why with final fact."

WILLIAM VAUGHN MOODY   1869–1910

> *I stood within the heart of God;*
> *It seemed a place that I had known:*
> *(I was blood sister to the clod,*
> *Blood brother to the stone.)*
>
> *I found my love and labor there,*
> *My house, my raiment, meat and wine,*
> *My ancient rage, my old despair, —*
> *Yea, all things that were mine.*

WALT WHITMAN   1819–1892

Agonies are one of my changes of garments.

MARIANNE MOORE   1887–

> *You do not seem to realize that beauty is*
> *a liability rather than*
>
> *An asset —*
> *Your thorns are the best part of you.*

ROBERT PAUL SMITH   1957–

People who don't have nightmares don't have dreams.

Suitable for the Young

REBECCA WEST   1958

It might have been thought that Hood's "The Bridge of Sighs" was not a poem suitable for the young, since it deals with the suicide by drowning of a street–walker. But fifty years ago many children knew it by heart and loved it. Its jingling meter had something to do with its popularity, but not everything. Subtler and rebellious instincts were at work. The poem contains a couplet which children used to recite with special glee. "Look at her garments, Clinging like cerements." It was the false rhyme which delighted. A child who realizes that a poem is bad has caught a grown-up doing wrong and breaking its own rules. This is funny in the primal way, like seeing somebody very dignified walking across a frozen pond and suddenly becoming undignified by slipping and sitting down on the ice. But it is also part of growing up. These adults are not invulnerable, as they pretend. For long they towered above one; but day by day they lose that advantage, and there must come a time when it cannot be denied that soon child and adult will stand on a level and will be demonstrably of the same kind. "I am supposed to be a silly little thing that can be ordered about because I cannot do the things grown-ups do, such as writing good poetry," the child's heart says, "But here is a poem written by a grown-up, and grown-ups seem to think it is good, but I know it's bad, and I am right and they are wrong." The pleasing thing was that it obviously did not matter too much. This was a rebellion of child against adult which was being fought not in deeds but over words, which hurt far less.

At the same time a lesson in English was being given by negative example. Someone had died who had been very unhappy. But no one could feel sad about it, because Thomas Hood's statement of the case did not sound right, "Still for all slips of hers One of Eve's family, Wipe those poor lips of hers, Oozing so clammily"; the lines went, if one sang them, to a gay tune, the sort of tune that butchers' boys sang as they rode their bicycles; and this was even more comically discreditable to the grown-up who had written the poem, and the grown-ups who had preserved it, than the bad rhyme of 'garments" and "cerements." There was instilled a sense that matter dictated manner, and that style involved a sympathetic regard for substance.

The Craft of Verse

W. B. YEATS   1865–1939

All things can tempt me from this craft of verse:
One time it was a woman's face, or worse —

The seeming needs of my fool-driven land;
Now nothing but comes readier to the hand
Than this accustomed toil.

I Dislike It

MARIANNE MOORE   1887–

I, too, dislike it: there are things that are important beyond
        all this fiddle.
    Reading it, however, with a perfect contempt for it, one
        discovers in
    it after all, a place for the genuine.
        Hand that can grasp, eyes
        that can dilate, hair that can rise
            if it must, these things are important not because a

high-sounding interpretation can be put upon them but because
        they are
    useful. When they become so derivative as to become
        unintelligible,
    the same thing may be said for all of us, that we
        do not admire what
        we cannot understand: the bat
            holding on upside down or in quest of something to

eat, elephants pushing, a wild horse taking a roll, a tireless wolf
        under
    a tree, the immovable critic twitching his skin like a horse
        that feels a flea, the base-
    ball fan, the statistician —
        nor is it valid
        to discriminate against "business documents and

school-books"; all these phenomena are important. One must
        make a distinction
    however: when dragged into prominence by half poets, the
        result is not poetry,
    nor till the poets among us can be
        "literalists of
        the imagination" — above
            insolence and triviality and can present

for inspection, "imaginary gardens with real toads in them,"
   shall we have

   it. In the meantime, if you demand on the one hand,
   the raw material of poetry in
      all its rawness and
      that which is on the other hand
         genuine, you are interested in poetry.

W. H. AUDEN   1957

Speaking for myself, the questions which interest me
most when reading a poem are two. The first is technical: "Here is a verbal contraption. How does it work?"
The second is, in the broadest sense, moral. "What kind
of a guy inhabits this poem? What is his notion of the
good life or the good place? His notion of the Evil One?
What does he conceal from the reader? What does he
conceal even from himself?"

And you must not be surprised if he should have nothing but platitudes to say; firstly because he will always
find it hard to believe that a poem needs expounding,
and secondly because he doesn't consider poetry quite
that important: any poet, I believe, will echo Miss Marianne Moore's words: *"I, too, dislike it."*

Unzip the Veil

E. B. WHITE   1899–

"I wish poets could be clearer!" shouted my wife angrily
from the next room.

Hers is a universal longing. We would all like it if the
bards would make themselves plain, or we think we
would. The poets, however, are not easily diverted from
their high mysterious ways. A poet dares be just so clear
and no clearer; he approaches lucid ground warily, like
a mariner who is determined not to scrape his bottom
on anything solid. A poet's pleasure is to withhold a little of his meaning, to intensify by mystification. He un-
zips the veil from beauty, but does not remove it. A poet
utterly clear is a trifle glaring.

The subject is a fascinating one. I think poetry is the

greatest of the arts. It combines music and painting and story-telling and prophecy and the dance. It is religious in tone, scientific in attitude. A true poem contains the seed of wonder; but a bad poem, egg-fashion, stinks. I think there is no such thing as a long poem. If it is long, it isn't a poem; it is something else. A book like *John Brown's Body,* for instance, is not a poem — it is a series of poems tied together with cord. Poetry is intensity and nothing is intense for long.

Some poets are naturally clearer than others. To achieve great popularity or great fame, it is of some advantage to be either extremely clear (like Edgar Guest) or thoroughly opaque (like Gertrude Stein). The first poet in the land — if I may use the word loosely — is Edgar Guest. He is the singer who, more than any other, gives to Americans the enjoyment of rhyme and meter. Whether he gives also to any of his satisfied readers that blinding, aching emotion which I get from reading certain verses by other writers is a question which interests me very much. Being democratic, I am content to have the majority rule in everything, it would seem, but literature.

There are many types of poetical obscurity. There is the obscurity which results from the poet's being mad. This is rare. Madness in poets is as uncommon as madness in dogs. A discouraging number of reputable poets are sane beyond recall. There is also the obscurity which is the result of the poet's wishing to appear mad, even if only a little mad. This is rather common and rather dreadful. I know of nothing more distasteful than the work of a poet who has taken leave of his reason deliberately, as a commuter might of his wife.

Then there is the unintentional obscurity, or muddiness, which comes from the inability of some writers to express even a simple idea without stirring up the bottom. And there is the obscurity which results when a fairly large thought is crammed into a three- or four-foot line. The function of poetry is to concentrate; but sometimes over-concentration occurs, and there is no more comfort in such a poem than there is in the subway at the peak hour.

Sometimes a poet becomes so completely absorbed in the lyrical possibilities of certain combinations of sounds that he forgets what he started out to say, if anything, and here again a nasty tangle results. This type of obscurity is one which I have great sympathy for: I know that quite frequently in the course of delivering himself of a poem, a poet will find himself in possession of a lyric bauble — a line as smooth as velvet to the ear, as pretty as a feather to the eye, yet a line definitely out of plumb with the frame of the poem. What to do with a trinket like this is always troubling to a poet, who is naturally grateful to his Muse for small favors. Usually he just drops the shining object into the body of the poem somewhere and hopes it won't look too giddy. (I sound as though I were contemptuous of poets; the fact is I am jealous of them. I would rather be one than anything.)

My quarrel with poets (who will be surprised to learn that a quarrel is going on) is not that they are unclear, but that they are too diligent. Diligence in a poet is the same as dishonesty in a bookkeeper. There are rafts of bards who are writing too much, too diligently, and too slyly. Few poets are willing to wait out their pregnancy — they prefer to have a premature baby and allow it to incubate after being safely laid in Caslon Old Style.

GOETHE 1749–1832

All lyrical work must, as a whole, be perfectly intelligible, but in some particulars a little unintelligible.

T. S. ELIOT 1956

I do not think of enjoyment and understanding as distinct activities — one emotional and the other intellectual . . . It is certain that we do not fully enjoy a poem unless we understand it; and, on the other hand, it is equally true that we do not fully understand a poem unless we enjoy it.

Aposiopesis

ROBERT OPPENHEIMER   1955

One evening more than twenty years ago Dirac, who was
in Goettingen working on his quantum theory of radiation, took me to task with characteristic gentleness,

"I understand that you are writing poetry as well as
working at physics. I do not see how you can do both.
In science one tries to say something that no one knew
before in a way that everyone can understand. Whereas
in poetry. . . ."

I. A. RICHARDS *comments:*   1955

Let me fill out this superb aposiopesis (I leave that to
you): *In poetry one tries to say something which everyone knew before in a way which no one can understand.*

This I take to be (if suitably regarded) not quite what
Dirac intended, but a saying profoundly and dazzlingly
true: *true* in a breath taking way, but only if and provided that one realizes that — along with the mathematical switch of *no one* with *everyone* — the meanings of
know and of *understand* undergo deep, systematic corresponding changes."

T. S. ELIOT *quotes* EZRA POUND   1935

The repeated reminder of Mr. Pound: that poetry
should be as well written as prose.

En Deux Mots

MARIE-FRANÇOISE CATHERINE DE BEAUVEAU,
MARQUISE DE BOUFFLERS   1711–1786

> *Il faut dire en deux mots*
> *Ce qu'on veut dire;*
> *Les long propos*
> *Sont sots.*
>
> *Il faut savoir lire*
> *Avant que d'écrire,*

Et puis dire en deux mots
     Ce qu'on veut dire.
     Les long propos
       Sont sots.

Il ne faut pas toujour conter,
       Citer,
       Dater,
     Mais écouter.
Il faut éviter l'emploi
     Du moi, du moi,
     Voici pourquoi:

     Il est tyrannique,
     Trop académique;
       L'ennui, l'ennui
       Marche avec lui.
Je me conduis toujours ainsi
       Ici,
       Aussi,
       J'ai réussi.

Il faut dire en deux mots
     Ce qu'on veut dire;
     Les long propos
       Sont sots.

T. S. ELIOT

     The word neither diffident nor ostentatious,
     An easy commerce of the old and new,
     The common word exact without vulgarity,
     The formal word precise but not pedantic,
     The complete consort dancing together.

Don't Think!

DON MARQUIS' *cockroach, archy*

     i never think at all when i write
     nobody can do two things well at the same time
     and do them both well

Zen

SUZUKI

Man is a thinking reed but his great works are done when he is not calculating and thinking. "Childlikeness" has to be restored with long years of training in the art of self-forgetfulness. When this is attained, man thinks yet he does not think. He thinks like the showers coming down from the sky; he thinks like the waves rolling on the ocean; he thinks like the stars illuminating the nightly heavens; he thinks like the green foliage shooting forth in the relaxing spring breeze. Indeed, he is the showers, the ocean, the stars, the foliage.

Exempli Gratia

CANDACE THURBER STEVENSON   1950

"Nectar and ambrosia," said the teacher.
"And what are nectar and ambrosia?" asked the boy.
"Food and drink," said the teacher,
"Food and drink for the gods."
"Was it like bacon in the woods
and soda at the soda fountain?
Was it like turkey in the oven
and hot cookies baking?
Was it like . . . ?"
"It was like every beautiful thing
you ever smelled or tasted.
It was like . . ."
Suddenly the teacher
was in a white-paneled house
with air washed fresh by the sea.
The *Iliad* was in his hand
and himself standing
no higher than the newel post,
while the goddess descended. He could not see her
    dress,
her eyes or hair,
but his nose smelled goddess.
It was neither lemon verbena

nor rose nor lily, lilac or orange-blossom.
It was not clover in a hot meadow
nor new-mown hay, nor wild grape.
It was neither Honey of Hymettus
nor a stirrup-cup held in a knight's hand.
Ladies might smell of perfume
out of phials and bottles; but this was goddess.
He remembered galloping to the barns horsy and
*   doggy,*
the sharp ammoniac of cow-dung, the scent of turned
*   earth.*
"Did you ever taste it?" said the boy.
"Nectar and ambrosia?"
"Yes," he answered.
"Yes, but it was a long while ago.
It was brought to me by some one —
or maybe it was out of the pages of a book.
I do not remember exactly —
Only that it was in a white-paneled house,
with air washed fresh by the sea."

The Poet

J. DOVER WILSON   1957

> *Lord! who would live turmoiled in the court*
> *And may enjoy such quiet walks as these?*
> *This small inheritance my father left me*
> *Contenteth me, and worth a monarchy.*
> *I seek not to wax great by others waning,*
> *Or gather wealth I care not with what envy:*
> *Sufficeth that I have maintains my state,*
> *And sends the poor well pleased from my gate.*

Thus meditates a country gentleman as he paces his
garden in one of the earliest of the plays. Shakespeare
comes very near, I suspect, to revealing his own worldly
ambitions in these lines.

His skill as a dramatic poet, his unrivalled command
of the language, his imaginative sweep, his profound
knowledge of human nature, were amazing, so amazing

as to seem wellnigh superhuman. Yet all agree that he is one of the sanest writers who ever attained greatness. What kept him sane? Surely that this genius was balanced by a nature of simple taste and homely aspirations.

To certain persons, who assume that what he called "the bubble reputation" is the lodestar of life, this is a paradox which seems quite incredible. The plays, they say, must have been written by someone else, some lord at Court — it was always a lord until the other day Marlowe was dragged from his grave — or was it Walsingham's? — to become the hero of another of the *Tales of Hoffmann*. The son of a shopkeeper and provincial mayor, who preferred his little country town to London, could not have been fine enough for fine poetry, and it is absurd to suppose that anyone should count living his own life more interesting than running after success "faster and faster till he sink into his grave."

This was not the opinion of another if minor poetic dramatist, Nicholas Rowe, his first biographer, who wrote: "the latter part of his life was spent, as all men of good sense wish theirs may be, in ease, retirement, and the conversation of his friends." And if we want to see something of Shakespeare's mood as his heart turned back to find its center out, we have only to read *The Tempest,* the play in which he said goodbye to London, King James and his art:

> We are such stuff
> As dreams are made on, and our little life
> Is rounded with a sleep.

That is the gist of it. Would a man who thought of life like this worry over-much about fame or a career? And if it came to a choice between Stratford and London could a poet hesitate, even if he had no ties of affection, no Hermione or Perdita to draw him home? For Stratford, still one of the loveliest of towns, must, in the days before industrialization ruined the world, have been far lovelier, standing with the still unravished forest of Arden behind it, the unpolluted Avon before it, and across the river the open fields and meadows.

In any case, if what kept his high-built intellect upon

an even keel was the very simplicity of his values and of his affections, it is assuredly to this, too, we must look for the secret of his unchallenged and universal popularity. His genius was the gift of Heaven: what made him a dramatist was his intense interest in life, the ordinary life of ordinary men and women. Keats called him "the mighty Poet of the Human Heart." No other poet has expressed in such perfect language, with deeper understanding, with more tender delicacy or such god-like compassion, the joys and sorrows, the good and evil, the whole gamut of moods and emotions that belong to ordinary people, whether they are rich or poor, wise or foolish, white or black, brown or yellow. He has the ear of the world and whispers to it the things about ourselves we know nothing of until he tells us.

And so he has been crowned the greatest of all poets with an empire that spreads to wider and wiser circles of humanity in each generation. In the past the peoples created their own mythologies, a conflux of stories about gods and heroes, in which their views, their national and racial ideals, perplexities and troubles reflected and transfigured. Shakespeare's book supplies a mythology for the whole human race. Agnostic and Christian, Hindu and Mohammedan, Conservative, Liberal and Bolshevik, the unnumbered multitudes of India, China and Japan, Othello's myriad brothers and sisters throughout Africa, he speaks for and to them all. And he has a winning voice, the voice not of a conqueror, a preacher or a propagandist, but of a poet, who is also a friend and brother, until to-day all the world's his stage and his is the one spirit, the plays the only sacred book that the snarling, struggling peoples can unite to revere.

Loneliness

J. ROBERT OPPENHEIMER   1955

In the situation of the artist today there are both analogies to and differences from that of the scientist; but it is the differences which are the most striking and which raise the problems that touch most on the evil of our day.

For the artist it is not enough that he communicate with others who are expert in his own art. Their fellowship, their understanding, and their appreciation may encourage him; but that is not the end of his work, nor its nature. The artist depends on a common sensibility and culture, on a common meaning of symbols, on a community of experience and common ways of describing and interpreting it. He need not write for everyone or paint or play for everyone. But his audience must be man; it must be man, and not a specialized set of experts among his fellows. Today that is very difficult. Often the artist has an aching sense of great loneliness, for the community to which he addresses himself is largely not there; the traditions and the culture, the symbols and the history, the myths and the common experience, which it is his function to illuminate, to harmonize, and to portray, have been dissolved in a changing world.

There is, it is true, an artificial audience maintained to moderate between the artist and the world for which he works: the audience of the professional critics, popularizers, and advertisers of art. But though, as does the popularizer and promoter of science, the critic fulfills a necessary present function and introduces some order and some communication between the artist and the world, he cannot add to the intimacy and the directness and the depth with which the artist addresses his fellow men.

To the artist's loneliness there is a complementary great and terrible barrenness in the lives of men. They are deprived of the illumination, the light and tenderness and insight of an intelligible interpretation, in contemporary terms, of the sorrows and wonders and gaieties and follies of man's life. This may be in part offset, and is, by the great growth of technical means for making the art of the past available. But these provide a record of past intimacies between art and life; even when they are applied to the writing and painting and composing of the day, they do not bridge the gulf between a society, too vast and too disordered, and the artist trying to give meaning and beauty to its parts.

TRANSLATIONS

About translations, Emerson asks somewhere in his Journal, why he should have to swim the Charles River when there was a bridge.

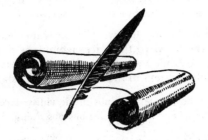

How It Is Done

C. M. BOWRA   1898–

Everyone knows that translators are traitors, and that they show the wrong side of the tapestry. Some, too, may remember that two-horned question recorded by Robert Bridges, "If you really thought the original was like that, what can you have seen in it to make you think it was worth translating?"; or how to Bohn's translations the "signal service" was once attributed "of having finally shown up the Classics." But other arguments, less often heard, were more convincing. No disparagement can obscure the essential value of an art which alone can mediate between past and present, or between living men of different speech. In every school and college it is taught and practised; and if practice must be guided by example, a book of this kind, at least in its intention, has a plausible excuse.

This is from Bowra's introduction to the *Oxford Book of Greek Verse in Translation,* and then he goes on to give an example:

The process of translating a single elegiac couplet will bring together all the problems already discussed and show their issue in practice.

Three hundred Spartans under Leonidas had been ordered to hold Thermopylae at all costs. None survived. Simonides composed the inscription for their tomb, which runs:

'Ω ξεῖν', ἀγγέλλειν Λακεδαιμονίοις ὅτι τῇδε
κείμεθα τοῖς κείνων ῥήμασι πειθόμενοι.

A makeshift "word for word" construe would be: "O stranger, take-news to the Lacedaemonians that here we-are-lying, to their words obedient." Cicero, using a slightly different text in the second line, translated:

Dic, hospes, Spartae nos te hic vidisse iacentis
dum sanctis patriae legibus obsequimur.

The first thing to notice is this — that by a fiction the dead are made to speak, and that their epitaph takes the form of a message from the field. As none survived, someone else must deliver that message. Hence the appeal in the first two words — a form of address found in many another Greek epitaph, but with less excuse.

These first two words are the first difficulty. Cicero rendered them by "hospes," a closer approximation than English allows. No single word in English has the same meanings, inherent and adherent, as the Greek. "Stranger" is too remote, and tends to be American: "friend" is too familiar. The compromise "passer-by" has found, perhaps, most favor.

Next, the word ἀγγέλλειν. Here a problem of adherent meaning is raised, not by the word itself, but by the use of the infinitive to convey an injunction. This idiom was common in Dorian speech, and would therefore be appropriate on the lips of the Spartan dead, while to Greek readers in general, familiar with its use in Hesiod and other old poets, it would also have had a dignified, archaic ring. If that were the whole truth, an archaizing translation, such as "Take tiding(s)," might be defended. But the idiom is also military and not confined to the Dorians. In this dispatch from the field its military use is appropriate; and hence a very different suggestion, namely, that we should translate "*Report* to the Lacedaemonians . . .*"

Modern poetry is wholesomely inclusive in its diction; but even so, *Report* would be out of keeping. For the diction of the epitaph as a whole has a conscious poetic coloring, as the forms ξεῖν' for ξέν' and κείνων for ἐκείνων attest. And after all, the idiom was archaic and poetical as well as military. Once again, then, we must compromise on some neutral expression, such as "Tell them in Lacedaemon . . ."

Two further problems of meaning are set by the last two words. Some have argued that ῥήμασι bears much the same sense as ῥημάτων in the poem written by Simonides on Danae. It would then mean not "orders" or "ordinances," but "words" or "sayings," such as Plutarch collected in his *Sayings of Laconian Women*; e.g., "Come back with your shield — or upon it." One may answer, of course, that the meaning "orders" is better suited to a soldierly dispatch; but why demand one meaning and one only? A poet's economy, especially in epigram, is to say one thing and suggest much more. In English "word" (rather than "words") has some of the requisite associations, and also covers the possible alternatives most completely.

Finally, πειθόμενοι. It is often said that the use of the present participle implies continuity and demands the translation *"still* obeying." But the temporal reference of the participle cannot be stressed; and *"still* obeying" is a sentimental, un-Greek idea, certainly out of place on the lips of Spartans.

And Bowra ends up by translating Simonides himself:

> *"Tell them in Lakedaimon, passer-by,*
> *That here obedient to their word we lie."*

READING

There is a sentence in Dr. Johnson's Life of Gray which might well be written up in all those rooms, too humble to be called libraries, yet full of books, where the pursuit of reading is carried on by private people. ". . . I rejoice to concur with the common reader; for by the common sense of readers, uncorrupted by literary prejudices, after all the refinements of subtility and the dogmatism of learning, must be finally decided all claim to poetical honors."

VIRGINIA WOOLF

Nothing is more painful to me than the disdain with which people treat second-rate authors, as if there were room only for the first-raters.

SAINTE-BEUVE

To put away one's original thoughts in order to take up a book is the sin against the Holy Ghost.

SCHOPENHAUER

Who knows if Shakespear might not have thought less, if he had read more?

EDWARD YOUNG

He ate and drank the precious words,
His spirit grew robust;
He knew no more that he was poor,
Nor that his frame was dust.
He danced along the dingy days,
And this bequest of wings
Was but a book. What liberty
A loosened spirit brings!

EMILY DICKINSON

O. W. HOLMES, JR., TO WU   1925

The ideas of the classics, so far as living, are our com-
monplaces. It is the modern books that give us the latest
and most profound conceptions. It seems to me rather
a lazy makeshift to mumble over the familiar.

FRANCIS BACON   1561–1626

As for antiquity, the opinion touching it which men entertain is quite a negligent one, and scarcely consonant
with the word itself. For the old age of the world is to be
accounted the true antiquity; and this is the attribute of
our own times, not of that earlier age of the world in
which the ancients lived; and which, though in respect of
us it was the elder, yet in respect of the world it was the
younger. From our age, if it but knew its own strength
and chose to essay and exert it, much more might
fairly be expected than from the ancient times, inasmuch
as it is a more advanced age of the world, and stored and
stocked with infinite experiments and observations.

NAPOLEON   1769–1821

People take England on trust, and repeat that Shakespeare is the greatest of all authors. I have read him:
there is nothing that compares with Racine or Corneille:
his plays are unreadable, pitiful.

MONTAIGNE   1533–1592

Will the licence of the times excuse me when I maintain that, in my opinion, even the *Dialogues* of Plato drag? That they are overwritten, and I regret that a man who had many better things to say wasted so much time in long and needless preliminary conversations? At least my ignorance will excuse me, for I do not understand enough Greek to appreciate the beauty of his style.

DAVID HUME   1711–1776

When we run over libraries, persuaded of these principles, what havoc must we make? If we take in our hand any volume; of divinity or school metaphysic, for instance; let us ask, Does it contain any experimental reasoning concerning matter of fact and existence? No. Commit it then to the flames: for it can contain nothing but sophistry and illusion.

PETRARCH   1304–1374

Books never pall on me. They discourse with us, they take counsel with us, and are united to us by a certain living chatty familiarity. And not only does each book inspire the sense that it belongs to its readers, but it also suggests the name of others, and one begets the desire of the other.

MONTAIGNE   1533–1592

In my opinion, the most fruitful and natural play of the mind is conversation. I find it sweeter than any other action in life; and if I were forced to choose, I think I would rather lose my sight than my hearing and voice. The study of books is a drowsy and feeble exercise which does not warm you up.

If I converse with a strong mind and rude jouster, who presses me hard and digs me right and left, his ideas touch off my own. Jealousy, emulation, and contention stimulate and raise me something above myself. Agreement is absolutely boring in conversation. And it can't be said how much we lose and degenerate by continual intercourse with poor and sickly minds. No contagion spreads as that does — I know only too well from experience how much it is worth a yard.

When I am reading a book, whether wise or silly, it seems to me to be alive and talking to me.

Sometimes I read a book with pleasure, and detest the author.

It is easy enough for a man to walk who has a horse at his command. The invalid is not to be pitied who has a cure up his sleeve. And such is the advantage I receive from books.

They relieve me from idleness, rescue me from company I dislike, and blunt the edge of my grief, if it is not too extreme. They are the comfort and solitude of my old age.

When I am attacked by gloomy thoughts, nothing helps me so much as running to my books. They quickly absorb me and banish the clouds from my mind. And they don't rebel because I use them only for lack of pastimes more natural and alive. They always receive me with the same welcome.

EMERSON   1873

Read proudly — put the duty of being read invariably on the author. If he is not read, whose fault is it? I am quite ready to be charmed, but I shall not make-believe I am charmed.

JOHN LOCKE   1632–1704

Those who have read of everything are thought to understand everything too; but it is not always so — reading furnishes the mind only with materials of knowledge; it is thinking that makes what is read ours. We are of the ruminating kind, and it is not enough to cram ourselves with a great load of collections; unless we chew them over again, they will not give us strength and nourishment.

EDWARD GIBBON   1737–1794

Let us read with method, and propose to ourselves an end to what our studies may point. The use of reading is to aid us in thinking.

WALT WHITMAN   1819–1892

Books are to be called for and supplied on the assumption that the process of reading is not a half-sleep, but in the highest sense an exercise, a gymnastic struggle; that the reader is to do something for himself.

The Future of Reading

E. B. WHITE   1954

In schools and colleges, in these audio-visual days, doubt has been raised as to the future of reading — whether the printed word is on its last legs. One college president has remarked that in fifty years "only five per cent of the people will be reading." For this, of course, one must be prepared. But how prepare? To us it would seem that even if only one person out of a hundred and fifty million should continue as a *reader,* he would be the one worth saving, the nucleus around which to found a university. We think this not impossible person, this Last Reader, might very well stand in the same relation to the community as the queen bee to the colony of bees, and that the others would quite properly dedicate themselves wholly to his welfare, serving special food and building special accommodations. From his nuptial, or intellectual, flight would come the new race of men, linked perfectly with the long past by the unbroken chain of the intellect, to carry on the community. But it is more likely that our modern hive of bees, substituting a coaxial cable for spinal fluid, will try to perpetuate the race through audio-visual devices, which ask no discipline of the mind and which are already giving the room the languor of an opium parlor.

Reading is the work of the alert mind, is demanding, and under ideal conditions produces finally a sort of ecstasy. As in the sexual experience, there are never more than two persons present in the act of reading — the writer, who is the impregnator, and the reader, who is the respondent. This gives the experience of reading a sublimity and power unequalled by any other form of communication. It would be just as well, we think, if educators clung to this great phenomenon and did not get sidetracked, for although books and reading may at times have played too large a part in the educational process, that is not what is happening today. Indeed, there is very little true reading, and not nearly as much writing as one would suppose from the towering piles of pulpwood in the dooryards of our paper mills. Readers and writers are scarce, as are publishers and reporters. The reports we get nowadays are those of men who have not gone to the scene of the accident, which is always farther inside one's own head than it is convenient to penetrate without galoshes.

REUEL DENNEY   1957

Some members of the younger generation can move from comic books to science fiction to the *Oresteia* in two jumps.

PART
XI

AND FRIENDSHIP AND LOVE

Doubt that the stars are fire.

Psyche

KEATS 1795–1821

Yes, I will be thy priest, and build a fane
In some untrodden region of my mind,
Where branchèd thoughts, new grown with pleasant pain,
Instead of pines shall murmur in the wind:
Far, far around shall those dark-clustered trees
Fledge the wild-ridged mountains steep by steep;
And these by zephyrs, streams, and birds, and bees,
The moss-lain Dryads shall be lull'd to sleep;
And in the midst of this wide quietness
A rosy sanctuary will I dress
With the wreath'd trellis of a working brain,
With buds, and bells, and stars without a name,
With all the gardener Fancy e'er could feign,
Who breeding flowers will never breed the same:
And there shall be for thee all soft delight
That shadowy thought can win,
A bright torch, and a casement ope at night,
To let the warm Love in!

DR. O. W. HOLMES 1809–1894

Love is the master key that opens the gates of happiness,
of hatred, of jealousy, and, most easily of all, the gate
of fear.

PROUST 1871–1922

There is not a woman in the world the possession of whom is as precious as that of the truth which she reveals to us by causing us to suffer.

Profane and Sacred Love

WALTER LIPPMANN 1889–

There are two arts of love and it makes a considerable difference which one is meant. There is the art of love as Casanova, for example, practiced it. It is the art of seduction, courtship, and sexual gratification: it is an art which culminates in the sexual act. It can be repeated with the same lover and with other lovers, but it exhausts itself in the moment of ecstasy. When that moment is reached, the work of art is done, and the lover as artist "after an interval, perhaps of stupor and vital recuperation," must start all over again, until at last the rhythm is so stale it is a weariness to start at all; or the lover must find new lovers and new resistances to conquer. The aftermath of romantic love — that is, of love that is consummated in sexual ecstasy — is either tedium in middle age or the compulsive adventurousness of the libertine.

CHARLES MONTAGU, LORD HALIFAX 1661–1715

Love is a passion that has friends in the garrison.

DOCTOR JOHNSON 1709–1784

There are few things that we so unwillingly give up, even in advanced age, as the supposition that we have still the power of ingratiating ourselves with the fair sex.

WALTER BAGEHOT 1826–1877

Men who do not make advances to women are apt to become victims to women who make advances to them.

LIPPMANN *goes on to say:*

Now this is not what Mr. Ellis means when he talks about love as an art. "The act of intercourse," he says, "is only an incident, and not an essential in love." Incident to what? His answer is that it is an incident to an "exquisitely and variously and harmoniously blended" activity of "all the finer activities of the organism, physical and psychic." I take this to mean that when a man and woman are successfully in love, their whole activity is energized and victorious. They walk better, their digestion improves, they think more clearly, their secret worries drop away, the world is fresh and interesting, and they can do more than they dreamed that they could do. In love of this kind sexual intimacy is not the dead end of desire as it is in romantic or promiscuous love, but periodic affirmation of the inward delight of desire pervading an active life. Love of this sort can grow: it is not, like youth itself, a moment that comes and is gone and remains only a memory of something which cannot be recovered. It can grow because it has something to grow upon and to grow with; it is not contracted and stale because it has for its object, not the mere relief of physical tension, but all the objects with which the two lovers are concerned. They desire their worlds in each other, and therefore their love is as interesting as their worlds and their worlds are as interesting as their love.

PROUST   1871–1922

It's odd how a person always arouses admiration for his moral qualities among the relatives of another with whom he has sexual relations. Physical love, so unjustifiably decried, makes everyone show, down to the least detail, all he has of goodness and self-sacrifice, so that he shines even in the eyes of those nearest to him.

ANON.

> O Western wind, when wilt thou blow
> That the small rain down can rain?
> Christ, that my love were in my arms
> And I in my bed again!

W. B. YEATS   1865–1939

> What lively lad most pleasured me
> Of all that with me lay?

I answer that I gave my soul
And lived in misery,
But had great pleasure with a lad
That I loved bodily.

Flinging from his arms I laughed
To think his passion such
He fancied that I gave a soul
Did but our bodies touch,
And laughed upon his breast to think
Beast gave beast as much.

I gave what other women gave
That stepped out of their clothes,
But when this soul, its body off,
Naked to naked goes,
He it has found shall find therein
What none other knows.

A shudder in the loins engenders there
The broken wall, the burning roof and tower
And Agamemnon dead.

The Intercourse of Friendship

RANDOLPH S. BOURNE   1886–1918

One comes from much reading with a sense of depression and a vague feeling of something unsatisfied; from friends or music one comes with a high sense of elation and of the brimming adequacy of life.

If one could only retain those moments! What a tragedy it is that our periods of stimulated thinking should be so difficult of reproduction; that there is no intellectual shorthand to take down the keen thoughts, the trains of argument, the pregnant thoughts, which spring so spontaneously to the mind at such times! What a tragedy that one must wait till the fire has died out, till the light has faded away, to transcribe the dull flickering remembrances of those golden hours when thought and feeling seemed to have melted together, and one said and thought what seemed truest and finest and most worthy of one's immortalizing! This is what constitutes the hopeless labor of writing — that one must struggle constantly to warm again the thoughts that are cold or have been utterly consumed. What was thought in the hours of stimulation must be written in the hours of solitude, when the mind is apt to be cold and gray, and when one is fortunate to find on the hearth of the memory even a few scattered embers lying about. The blood runs sluggish as one sits down to write. What worry and striving it takes to get it running freely again! What labor to reproduce even a semblance of what seemed to come so genially and naturally in the contact and intercourse of friendship!

Venus and the Virgin

HENRY ADAMS   1838–1918

When Adams was a boy in Boston, the best chemist in the place had probably never heard of Venus except by way of scandal, or of the Virgin except as idolatry; neither had he heard of dynamos or automobiles or radium; yet his mind was ready to feel the force of all, though the rays were unborn and the women were dead.

Here opened another totally new education, which promised to be by far the most hazardous of all. The knife-edge along which he must crawl, like Sir Lancelot in the twelfth century, divided two kingdoms of force which had nothing in common but attraction. They were as different as a magnet is from gravitation, supposing one knew what a magnet was, or gravitation, or love. The force of the Virgin was still felt at Lourdes, and seemed to be as potent as X-rays; but in America neither Venus nor Virgin ever had value as force — at most as sentiment. No American had ever been truly afraid of either.

This problem in dynamics gravely perplexed an American historian. The Woman had once been supreme; in France she still seemed potent, not merely as a sentiment, but as a force. Why was she unknown in America? For evidently America was ashamed of her, and she was ashamed of herself, otherwise they would not have strewn fig-leaves so profusely all over her. When she was a true force, she was ignorant of fig-leaves, but the monthly-magazine-made American female had not a feature that would have been recognized by Adam. The trait was notorious, and often humorous, but anyone brought up among Puritans knew that sex was sin. In any previous age, sex was strength. Neither art nor beauty was needed. Everyone, even among Puritans, knew that neither Diana of the Ephesians nor any of the Oriental goddesses was worshipped for her beauty. She was goddess because of her force; she was the animated dynamo; she was reproduction — the greatest and most mysterious of all energies; all she needed was to be fecund. Singularly enough, not one of Adams's many schools of education had ever drawn his attention to the opening lines of Lucretius, though they were perhaps the finest in all Latin literature where the poet invoked Venus exactly as Dante invoked the Virgin:

"Quae quoniam rerum naturam *sola* gubernas."

The Great Lovers

RILKE   1875–1926

The following letter, written from Schloss Duino in January, 1912, only two days after he had sent the "First Elegy" to Princess Marie, reveals what Rilke understood by the great lovers:

And then: I have no window on human beings, definitely. They yield themselves to me only in so far as they are able to make themselves heard within myself, and, during these last years, they have been communicating with me almost entirely through two figures, on which I base my conjectures about human beings in general. What speaks to me of humanity, immensely, with a calmness of authority that makes my hearing spacious, is the phenomenon of those who have died young, and, still more unconditionally, purely, inexhaustibly: *the woman who loves*. In these two forms humanity gets mixed into my heart whether I will or no. They make their appear-

ance in me both with the clearness of the marionette
(which is an exterior charged with conviction), and as
finished types, which can no longer be improved upon,
so that the natural history of their souls might be written.

Let us keep to the woman who loves — by whom I
don't so much mean Saint Theresa and such magnificence as has occurred in that direction: she yields herself
to my observation much more unambiguously, purely,
i.e., undilutedly, and (so to speak) *unappliedly* in
the situation of Gaspara Stampa, the Lyonnaise Labé,
certain Venetian courtesans, and, above all, Marianna
Alcoforado, that incomparable creature, in whose eight
heavy letters woman's love is for the first time plotted
from point to point, without display, without exaggeration or mitigation, as by the hand of a sibyl. And there,
my God! there the fact is revealed that, as the result of
the irrepressible logic of the feminine heart, this line was
finished, completed, not to be carried any further in the
terrestrial sphere, and could only be prolonged into infinity, towards the divine. Nay, there, in the example of
this highly irrelevant Chamilly (whose foolish vanity
was used by Nature to preserve the Portuguese's letters),
with the sublime expression of the nun: "My love no
longer depends on the way you treat me" — Man, as a
lover, was done with, finished with, *outloved* — if one
may put it so considerately — outloved, as a glove is
outworn. What a melancholy figure he cuts in the history of love! He has almost no strength there beyond
the superiority which tradition ascribes to him, and even
this he carries with a negligence that would be simply
revolting, were it not that his absent-mindedness and
absent-heartedness have often had great occasions, which
partly justify him. No one, however, will persuade me
out of what becomes apparent in the case of this extremest lover and her ignominious partner: the fact that this
relationship definitely brings to light how very much
on one side, that of woman, everything performed, en-
dured, accomplished contrasts with man's absolute insufficiency in love. She receives, as it were — to put the

matter with banal clarity — the Diploma of Proficiency in Love, while he carries in his pocket an Elementary Grammar of this discipline, from which a few words have scantily passed into him, out of which, as opportunity offers, he forms sentences, beautiful and ravishing as the well-known sentences on the first pages of Language Courses for Beginners. The case of the Portuguese is so wonderfully pure because she does not fling the streams of her feeling on into the imaginary, but, with infinite power, conducts the geniality of this feeling back into herself: enduring it, nothing but that. She grows old in the convent, very old, she becomes no saint, not even a good nun. It is repugnant to her singular tact to apply to God what was not intended for him from the beginning, and what the Comte de Chamilly could disdain. And yet it was almost impossible to check the heroic onrush of this love before the final leap, and not, in the course of such a vibration of one's innermost being, to become a saint. Had she — creature glorious beyond measure! — yielded for one moment, she would have plunged into God like a stone into the sea; and had it pleased God to attempt with her what He continually does with the angels, casting their whole effulgence back into themselves — I am certain that, forthwith, just as she was, in this sad convent, she would have become an angel, within, in the depths of her nature.

HANS ZINSSER   1878–1940
> *How cold your hands are, Death,*
> *Come, warm them at my heart.*

PART XII

AND EVEN SOMETHING MORE

*I swear I will never henceforth have
to do with the faith that tells the
best!
I will have to do only with that faith
that leaves the best untold.*

WALT WHITMAN

*Gertrude Stein, dying, asked, "But
then what is the answer?" She lay
silent for a moment, and said, "But
then, what is the question?"*

*Milton answered, "One demanding,
How God employed Himself before
the world was made? had answer:
that He was making hell for curious
questioners."*

Natural Law

O. W. HOLMES, JR.   1841–1935

It is not enough for the knight of romance that you agree
that his lady is a very nice girl — if you do not admit
that she is the best that God ever made or will make, you
must fight. There is in all men a demand for the superlative, so much so that the poor devil who has no other
way of reaching it attains it by getting drunk. It seems
to me that this demand is at the bottom of the philosopher's effort to prove that truth is absolute and of the
jurist's search for criteria of universal validity which he
collects under the head of natural law.

WILLIAM JAMES   1842–1910

The simplest rudiment of mystical experience would
seem to be that deepened sense of the significance of a
maxim or formula which occasionally sweeps over one.

Providence

LINCOLN   1862

The subject is one upon which I have thought much for
weeks past, and I may even say for months. I am approached with the most opposite opinions and advice,
and that by religious men who are equally certain that
they represent the divine will. I am sure that either the
one or the other class is mistaken in the belief, and perhaps in some respects both. I hope it will not be irrever-

ent for me to say that if it is probable that God would reveal His will to others on a point so connected with my duty, it might be supposed He would reveal it directly to me; for, unless I am more deceived in myself than I often am, it is my earnest desire to know the will of Providence in this matter. And if I can learn what it is, I will do it.

These are not, however, the days of miracles, and I suppose it will be granted that I am not to expect a direct revelation. I must study the plain physical facts of the case, ascertain what is possible, and learn what appears to be wise and right. The subject is difficult, and good men do not agree.

Sandburg gives the occasion for these remarks of Lincoln. They were made to a delegation of clergymen on the subject of the Emancipation Proclamation, which he signed a week later.

Is There a False Religion?

MR. JUSTICE JACKSON, *dissenting*   1944

I should say the defendants have done just that for which they are indicted. If I might agree to their conviction without creating a precedent, I cheerfully would do so. I can see in their teachings nothing but humbug, untainted by any trace of truth. But that does not dispose of the constitutional question whether misrepresentation of religious experience or belief is prosecutable; it rather emphasizes the danger of such prosecutions.

The Ballard family claimed miraculous communication with the spirit world and supernatural power to heal the sick. They were brought to trial for mail fraud on an indictment which charged that the representations were false and that they "well knew" they were false. The trial judge, obviously troubled, ruled that the court could not try whether the statements were untrue, but could inquire whether the defendants knew them to be untrue; and, if so, they could be convicted.

I find it difficult to reconcile this conclusion with our traditional religious freedoms.

In the first place, as a matter of either practice or philosophy I do not see how we can separate an issue as to what is believed from considerations as to what is believable. The most convincing proof that one believes his statements is to show that they have been true in his experience. Likewise, that one knowingly falsified is best proved by showing that what he said happened never did happen. How can the Government prove these persons knew something to be false which it cannot prove to be false? If we try religious sincerity severed from religious verity, we isolate the dispute from the very considerations which in common experience provide its most reliable answer.

In the second place, any inquiry into intellectual honesty in religion raises profound psychological problems. William James, who wrote on these matters as a scientist, reminds us that it is not theology and ceremonies which keep religion going. Its vitality is in the religious experiences of many people. "If you ask what these experiences are, they are conversations with the unseen, voices and visions, responses to prayer, changes of heart, deliverances from fear, inflowings of help, assurances of support, whenever certain persons set their own internal attitude in certain appropriate ways." If religious liberty includes, as it must, the right to communicate such experiences to others, it seems to me an impossible task for juries to separate fancied ones from real ones, dreams from happenings, and hallucinations from true clairvoyance. Such experiences, like some tones and colors, have existence for one, but none at all for another. They cannot be verified to the minds of those whose field of consciousness does not include religious insight. When one comes to trial which turns on any aspect of religious belief or representation, unbelievers among his judges are likely not to understand and are almost certain not to believe him.

And then I do not know what degree of skepticism or disbelief in a religious representation amounts to actionable fraud. James points out that "Faith means belief in something concerning which doubt is theoretically possible." Belief in what one may demonstrate to the senses is not faith. All schools of religious thought make enormous assumptions, generally on the basis of revelations authenticated by some sign or miracle. The appeal in such matters is to a very different plane of credulity than is invoked by representations of secular fact in commerce. Some who profess belief in the Bible read literally what others read as allegory or metaphor, as they read Aesop's fables. Religious symbolism is even used by some with the same mental reservations one has in teaching of Santa Claus or Uncle Sam or Easter bunnies or dispassionate judges. It is hard in matters so mystical to say how literally one is bound to believe the doctrine he teaches and even more difficult to say how far it is reliance upon a teacher's literal belief which induces followers to give him the money.

There appear to be persons — let us hope not many — who find refreshment and courage in the teachings of the "I Am" cult. If the members of the sect get comfort from the celestial guidance of their "Saint Germain," however doubtful it seems to me, it is hard to say that they do not get what they pay for. Scores of sects flourish in this country by teaching what to me are queer notions. It is plain that there is wide variety in American religious taste. The Ballards are not alone in catering to it with a pretty dubious product.

The chief wrong which false prophets do to their following is not financial. The collections aggregate a tempting total, but individual payments are not ruinous. I doubt if the vigilance of the law is equal to making money stick by overcredulous people. But the real harm is on the mental and spiritual plane. There are those who hunger and thirst after higher values which they feel wanting in their humdrum lives. They live in mental confusion or moral anarchy and seek vaguely for truth and beauty and moral support. When they are deluded and then disillusioned, cynicism and confusion follow. The wrong of these things, as I see it, is not in the money the victims part with half so much as in the mental and spiritual poison they get. But that is precisely the thing the Constitution put beyond the reach of the prosecutor, for the price of freedom of religion or of speech or of the press is that we must put up with, and even pay for, a good deal of rubbish.

Prosecutions of this character easily could degenerate into religious persecution. I do not doubt that religious leaders may be convicted of fraud for making false representations on matters other than faith or experience, as for example if one represents that funds are being used to construct a church when in fact they are being used for personal purposes. But that is not this case, which reaches into wholly dangerous ground. When does less than full belief in a professed credo become actionable fraud if one is soliciting gifts or legacies? Such inquiries may discomfort orthodox as well as unconventional religious teachers, for even the most regular of them are sometimes accused of taking their orthodoxy with a grain of salt.

I would dismiss the indictment and have done with this business of judicially examining other people's faiths.

CARDINAL NEWMAN   1801–1890

Egotism is true modesty. In religious enquiry each of us can speak only for himself.

The Biological Value of Theology

JANE ELLEN HARRISON   1850–1928

We recognize nowadays two types of thinking. The first which Jung calls "directed thinking" is what we normally mean by thinking. It "imitates reality and seeks to direct it." It is exhausting and is the sort of thinking employed in all scientific reaearch; it looks for adaptations and creates innovations. With that type of thought, which is comparatively late in development, though in embryo it may have existed from the outset, we have little to do in religion.

The second kind of thought is what is called "dream or phantasy-thinking." It turns away from reality and sets free subjective wishes. In regard to adaptation, because of its neglect of reality, it is wholly unproductive.

Giving free rein to impulse as it does, it is not exhausting. Freud calls this sort of mind-functioning the "pleasure and pain principle," it is ontogenetically older than directed thinking, it is typified by the mental operations of children and savages and by those of adults in their dreams, reveries, and mental disorders.

In like manner arises the myth. The myth is not an attempted explanation of either facts or rites. Its origin is not in "directed thinking," it is not rationalization. The myth is a fragment of the soul-life, the dream-thinking of the people, as the dream is the myth of the individual. As Freud says, "it is probable that myths correspond to the distorted residue of the wish-phantasies of whole nations, the secularized dreams of young humanity." Mythical tradition it would seem does not set forth any actual account of old events — that is the function of legend — but rather myth acts in such a way that it always reveals a wish-thought common to humanity and constantly rejuvenated.

What, then, is the biological function of theology and myth?

We hear much nowadays of the danger of "suppressed complexes." It is indeed in the discovery of the danger of these complexes and the methods of their cure that the main originality of the Freudian school consists. Man finds himself in inevitable conflict with some and often many elements of his environment; he shirks the conflict. Just because it is harassing and depressing, he forcibly drives it out of his conscious life. But his unconscious life is beyond his control. Into that unconscious stratum the conflict sinks and lives there an uninterrupted life. Now the function of religion is to prevent, to render needless, just this suppression of conflict. Man has made for himself representations of beings stronger and more splendid than himself; he has lost all sense that they are really projections of his own desire, and to these beings he hands over his conflict; he no longer needs to banish the conflict into the unconscious, but gods will see to it and fight on his side: "God is our refuge and strength," "Cast all your care upon Him, for He careth for you." The function of theology is to keep the conflict that would be submerged in the sphere of the conscious and prevent its development into a mischievous subliminal complex. Theology thus is seen to have high biological value. Probably but for its aid man, long before he developed sufficient reason to adapt himself to his environment, must have gone under.

JOHN SELDEN   1584–1654

We look after religion as the butcher did after his knife, when he had it in his mouth.

POLYBIUS   204?–125? B.C.

The point in which the Roman constitution excels others most conspicuously is to be found, in my opinion, in its handling of religion. In my opinion the Romans have managed to forge the main bond of their social order out of something which the rest of the world execrates. I mean, out of superstitition. In dramatizing their superstition theatrically and introducing it into private as well as into public life, the Romans have gone to the most extreme lengths conceivable; and to many observers this will appear extraordinary. In my opinion, however, the Romans have done it with an eye to the masses. If it were possible to have an electorate that was composed exclusively of sages, this chicanery might perhaps be unnecessary; but, as a matter of fact, the masses are always unstable and always full of lawless passions, irrational temper, and violent rage; so there is nothing for it but to control them by "the fear of the unknown" and play-acting of that sort. I fancy that this was the reason why our forefathers introduced among the masses those theological beliefs and those notions about Hell which have now become traditional: and I also fancy that, in doing this, our ancestors were not working at random but knew just what they were about. It might be more pertinent to charge our contemporaries with lack of sense and lapse from responsibility for trying to eradicate religion, as we actually see them doing.

Theology as a Game

ALDOUS HUXLEY   1894–

Or if we must play the theological game, let us never forget that it is a game. Religion, it seems to me, can survive only as a consciously accepted system of make-believe. People will accept certain theological statements about life and the world, will elect to perform certain rites and to follow certain rules of conduct, not because they imagine the statements to be divinely dictated, but simply because they have discovered experimentally that to live in a certain ritual rhythm, under certain ethical restraints, and as if certain metaphysical doctrines were true, is to live nobly, with style. Every art has its conventions which every artist must accept. The greatest, the most important of the arts is living.

TOLSTOY   1828–1910

It is terrible to watch a man who has the incomprehensible in his grasp, does not know what to do with it, and sits playing with a toy called God.

ROBERTA T. SWARTZ   1903–

> At first I shouted, "God!" I cried,
> "My valuable dream has died!"
> He did not even look aside.
> So I went nearer. "God," I said,
> "I suppose you know my dream is dead."

Agnosticism

HANS ZINSSER   1878–1940

I recall having read that the ancient Greeks, with all their reverence for philosophy, at times applied the word σπουδο-γελοῖος, or "serio-comic," to some of their philosophers. This gives me courage to proceed, if only with the purpose of tracing the course by which one modern individual of average intelligence tossed for a long lifetime between headlands where the sweet voices of sirens lured him to comforting mysticism and the cold, open seas to stark reason; and, nearing the end of his voyage, he was still unable to find harbor in either direction, but was content — with agnostic modesty and reverence — to let the currents of forces he could not comprehend carry him to his destined anchorage.

Pasteur's feeling that "we can only kneel" in the face of the incomprehensible is actually nothing less than a reverently expressed confession of agnosticism. His Catholicism was the adherence to an ethical system of morals and submission to the eternal order which probably he would not have undertaken to define anthropomorphically. This surely is the case with two of my most intimate professional friends, both of them among the great bacteriologists of all time; one of whom became a Catholic at thirty, the other about a year before he died, at sixty-nine. In both cases I am convinced from frequent conversations that their adherence to a church represented an urge for some form of symbolic expression of the conviction of an orderly purpose in the harmonious operation of eternal laws. A subconscious streak of mysticism may also have played a part. In both cases naked reason left them unsatisfied.

Darwin, in his letters, frankly declared himself an agnostic, for a reason that appears to me the strongest that can be advanced: "But there arises the doubt: Can the mind of man which has, as I fully believe, been developed from a mind as low as that possessed by the lowest animals, be trusted when it draws such grand conclusions? I cannot pretend to throw light on such abstruse problems. The mystery at the beginnings of all things is insoluble by us; and I, for one, must be content to remain an agnostic."

A similar point of view comes from Clerk-Maxwell, speaking of the supposed Regulator of causes and effects: "If He is the Deity, I object to any argument founded on a supposed acquaintance with the conditions of divine foreknowledge."

Subsequent experiences have often made me wonder why theological schools do not include a rigid discipline in the fundamental sciences. To be sure, it might modify religion in some of its most tradition-cherished minor superstitions. To offset this, it would almost certainly strengthen the inevitable conviction of the unalterable harmony of the natural laws which govern the universe and all that moves and lives within it. And on this, the revelation of the marvelous orderliness, is based, after all, the final refutation of chance and purposelessness.

The questions of immortality of the soul and freedom of the will, though they have called forth libraries of controversial literature, continue to appear not only utterly beyond any possibility of satisfactory proof but, indeed, trivial in being so definitely personal, once the principle of an all-pervading and ordering force is accepted. And the conception of a God so constituted that we are, as individuals, of direct concern to Him appears both presumptuous — considering our individual insignificance in the scheme as a whole — and unnecessary for that feeling of helpless reverence in face of the universal order which is the essence of religious experience. Moreover, palaeontologically considered, one would have to assume that such a "personal" God existed long before the evolution of man. "Why did He wait so long to create man?" asked Diderot. Yet reward, punishment, immortality of the soul in the theological sense, could have no meaning whatever until there had developed creatures possessing a nervous organization capable of abstract thinking and of spiritual suffering. One cannot imagine such a God occupied through millions of years, up to the Pleistocene, with personal supervision, reward and punishment, of amoebae, clams, fish, dinosaurs, and sabre-toothed tigers; then, suddenly, adjusting His own systems and purposes to the capacities of the man-ape He had allowed to develop.

O. W. HOLMES, JR., TO E. A. C.   1903

One great impression I have had from Saint-Gaudens' statue over Clover Adams' unnamed grave. It is apart by a high thick hedge of evergreen and a tree holds its arm over the spot. A figure that is no more despair than hope, hardly more woman than man, defying epithets as the universe defied them — it is silence and the end. As we went away there was a soldier's funeral taking place and the bugler blew taps. Let us return to the world.

HENRY ADAMS   1905

Of all the elaborate symbolism which has been suggested for the Gothic cathedral, the most vital and most perfect may be that the slender nervure, the springing motion of the broken arch, the leap downwards of the flying buttress — the visible effort to throw off a visible strain — never let us forget that Faith alone supports it, and that, if Faith fails, Heaven is lost. The equilibrium is visibly delicate beyond the line of safety; danger lurks in every stone. The peril of the heavy tower, of the restless vault, of the vagrant buttress; the uncertainty of logic, the inequalities of the syllogism, the irregularities of the mental mirror — all these haunting nightmares of the Church are expressed as strongly by the Gothic cathedral as though it had been the cry of human suffering, and as no emotion had ever been expressed before or is likely to find expression again. The delight of its aspirations is flung up to the sky. The pathos of its self-distrust and anguish of doubt is buried in the earth as its last secret. You can read out of it whatever else pleases your youth and confidence; to me, this is all.

HEINE   1797–1856

Be entirely tolerant or not at all; follow the good path or the evil one. To stand at the crossroads requires more strength than you possess.

BUNYAN   1628–1688

When the time was come for them to depart, they went to the Brink of the River. The last words of Mr. Despondency were, Farewell Night, welcome Day. His daughter went through the River singing, but none could understand what she said.

EMILY DICKINSON   1830–1886

> *I asked no other thing,*
> *No other was denied.*
> *I offered Being for it;*
> *The mighty merchant smiled.*
>
> *Brazil? He twirled a button.*
> *Without a glance my way:*
> *"But, madam, is there nothing else*
> *That we can show today?"*

Miracles

HERBERT DINGLE   1890–

The quite irrational idea that the ability to perform a miracle was a guarantee of authority in matters of conduct and belief, and that somehow the credentials of Jesus were the authenticity of his miracles. This idea is not active today, and we will not dwell on it except to note that, although it has left the religious sphere, its spirit still walks abroad in public life. When we find our newspapers inviting men who have knocked a golf-ball into a series of holes in the smallest number of attempts to express their views on the problem of survival after death, and when prominent geometricians or novelists are expected to have something of value to say about the philosophy of democracy, we have no difficulty in recognizing the type of mind which regarded the miraculous draft of fishes as an argument for the Sermon on the Mount.

The Last Judgment

CARL L. BECKER   1873–1945

The extraordinary sway which the Christian story exercized over the minds of men is easily understood. No interpretation of the life of mankind ever more exactly reflected the experience, or more effectively responded to the hopes of average men. To be aware of present trials and misfortunes, to look back with fond memories to the happier times (imagined so at least) of youth, to look forward with hope to a more serene and secure old age — what could more adequately sum up the experience of the great majority? And what was the Christian story if not an application of this familiar individual experience to the life of mankind? Mankind had its youth, its happier time in the Garden of Eden, to look back upon, its present middle period of misfortunes to endure, its future security to hope for. The average man needed no theology to understand universal experience when presented in terms so familiar; and it consoled him — it no doubt added something to his sense of personal significance — to realize that his own life, however barren and limited it might be, was but a concrete exemplification of the experience which God had decreed for all the generations of men. But better than all that — best of all — he could understand that there should sometimes be an end made, a judgment pronounced upon the world of men and things, a day of reckoning in which evil men would be punished and good men rewarded: he could believe that with all his heart, with a conviction fortified by the stored-up memories of the injustices he had witnessed, the unmerited injuries he had suffered. The average man could believe all that; and in the measure that he could believe it he could hope, he could so easily convince himself, that in that last day he would be found among those judged good, among those to be admitted into that other world in which things would be forever right.

Jehovah Explains to Job

ROBERT FROST   1945

> Yes, by and by. But first a larger matter.
> I've had you on my mind a thousand years
> To thank you some day for the way you helped me
> Establish once for all the principle
> There's no connection man can reason out
> Between his just deserts and what he gets.
> Virtue may fail and wickedness succeed.

'Twas a great demonstration we put on.
I should have spoken sooner had I found
The word I wanted. You would have supposed
One who in the beginning was the Word
Would be in a position to command it.
I have to wait for words like anyone.
Too long I've owed you this apology
For the apparently unmeaning sorrow
You were afflicted with in those old days.
But it was of the essence of the trial
You shouldn't understand it at the time.
It had to seem unmeaning to have meaning.
And it came out all right. I have no doubt
You realize by now the part you played
To stultify the Deuteronomist
And change the tenor of religious thought.
My thanks are to you for releasing me
From moral bondage to the human race.
The only free will there at first was man's,
Who could do good or evil as he chose.
I had no choice but I must follow him
With forfeits and rewards he understood —
Unless I liked to suffer loss of worship.
I had to prosper good and punish evil.
You changed all that. You set me free to reign.
You are the Emancipator of your God,
And as such I promote you to a saint.

SONG OF THE I.W.W.

> *Work and pray,*
> *Live on hay!*
> *You'll get pie,*
> *In the sky,*
> *When you die —*
> *It's a lie.*

Immortality

EMERSON   1855

The blazing evidence of immortality is our dissatisfaction with any other solution.

GOETHE 1823

Reinhard's gift of the Tibullus led to a very earnest discussion on the belief in personal survival. Goethe expressed himself definitely. It would be thoroughly impossible for a thinking being to think of a cessation of
thought and life. Everyone carries the proof of immortality within himself, and quite involuntarily. But just
as soon as a man tries to step outside of himself and become objective, just as soon as a man wants to prove or
wants to understand personal survival dogmatically, and
in a narrow way make that inner perception clear to himself, then he loses himself in contradictions.

Mankind, however, is always unconsciously driven to
want to achieve the impossible. Almost all laws are syn-
theses of the impossible; for example, the institution of
marriage. It is a good thing that it is so. The possible
will be attempted only because we have postulated the
impossible.

Goethe was far more himself and at ease with the Chancellor von Müller, who is our reporter here, than he was with
Eckermann, and not talking so much for the record.

KIRSOPP LAKE 1872–1946

After all, Faith is not belief in spite of evidence, but life
in scorn of consequence — a courageous trust in the great
purpose of all things and pressing forward to finish the
work which is in sight, whatever the price may be. Who
knows whether the "personality" of which men talk so
much and know so little may not prove to be the temporary limitation rather than the necessary expression of
Life?

There was once an archipelago of islands off a moun-
tainous coast separated from each other and from the
mainland by the sea. But in course of time the sea dried
up, the islands were joined to the great mountain behind
them, and it became clear that they had always been
united by solid ground under a very shallow sea. If those
islands could have thought and spoken, what would they
have said? Before the event they would have protested
against losing their insularity, but would they have done

so afterwards, when the water which divided them from each other was gone, and they knew that they were part of the great mountain which before they had only dimly seen, obscured by the mists rising from the sea?

GRAHAM WALLAS   1858–1932

What will be their prevailing conception of the universe and what will be the effect of that conception on their social judgment? They may drop the Palestinian mythology as easily as a worn-out garment, but what will happen, for instance, to that belief in personal immortality with which so many of our ethical traditions are entwined? Plato, in his best years, thought and felt as freely about the universe as ever man did, and Plato was convinced of the immortality of the individual soul. Modern knowledge, however, forces us to recognize in a new way the continuity of existence.

If a modern man believes that the particular combination of "genes" from his maternal and paternal ancestry which constitutes the personality with which he is born is immortal, he can hardly prevent himself from believing in the personal immortality of the anthropoid apes. If an ape is personally immortal, how can we deny that a dog or a jellyfish or a bacillus is also immortal? Or if each of us is immortal, would we not have been immortal if we had died in our mother's womb? If the generative cells which combined at the moment of our conception had perished like countless millions of millions of others before they were combined, would each of them have been immortal? If we answer that that which is personally immortal is only temporarily connected with the visible organism and will continue to exist after the visible organism has decayed, must not that also be true of the personally immortal element in the ape or the jellyfish or of the uncombined spermatozoon?

We may never know whether the consciousness of an adult human being and the lesser consciousness or potential consciousness of the infant and the ape and the bacillus may be related to some larger principle which gives meaning, and even something which we may call purpose, to the universe. But such a relation is not what Plato and the Church meant by the immortality of the soul, and cannot be made, as Plato and the fathers of the Church made it, the foundation of a doctrine of personal rewards and punishments.

PASCAL   1623–1662

We are so unfortunate that we can only take pleasure in a thing on condition of being annoyed if it turn out ill, as a thousand things can do, and do every hour. He who found the secret of rejoicing in the good without troubling himself with its contrary evil would have hit the mark.

And T. S. ELIOT *wrote in his "Ash Wednesday":*

> *Teach us to care and not to care:*
> *Teach us to sit still*
> *Even among these rocks,*
> *Our peace in His will.*

When Huxley's young son died, Charles Kingsley wrote him. HUXLEY *replied:*

My Dear Kingsley — I cannot sufficiently thank you, both on my wife's account and my own, for your long and frank letter, and for all the hearty sympathy which it exhibits — and Mrs. Kingsley will, I hope, believe that we are no less sensible of her kind thought of us. To myself your letter was especially valuable, as it touched upon what I thought even more than upon what I said in my letter to you. My convictions, positive and negative, on all the matters of which you speak, are of long and slow growth and are firmly rooted. But the great blow which fell upon me seemed to stir them to their foundation, and had I lived a couple of centuries earlier I could have fancied a devil scoffing at me and them — and asking me what profit it was to have stripped myself of the hopes and consolations of the mass of mankind? To which my only reply was and is — Oh devil! Truth is better than much profit. I have searched over the grounds of my belief, and if wife and child and name and fame were all to be lost to me one after the other as the penalty, still I will not lie.

And now I feel that it is due to you to speak as frankly as you have done to me. An old and worthy friend of mine tried some three or four years ago to bring us together — because, as he said, you were the only man who would do me any good. Your letter leads me to think he was right, though not perhaps in the sense he attached to his own words.

To begin with the great doctrine you discuss. I neither deny nor affirm the immortality of man. I see no reason for believing in it, but, on the other hand, I have no means of disproving it.

Pray understand that I have no *a priori* objections to the doctrine. No man who has to deal daily and hourly with Nature can trouble himself about *a priori* difficulties. Give me such evidence as would justify me in believing anything else, and I will believe that. Why should I not? It is not half so wonderful as the conservation of force, or the indestructibility of matter. Whoso clearly appreciates all that is implied in the falling of a stone can have no difficulty about any doctrine simply on account of its marvellousness. But the longer I live, the more obvious it is to me that the most sacred act of a man's life is to say and to feel, "I believe such and such to be true." All the greatest rewards and all the heaviest penalties of existence cling about that act. The universe is one and the same throughout; and if the condition of my success in unravelling some little difficulty of anatomy or physiology is that I shall rigorously refuse to put faith in that which does not rest on sufficient evidence, I cannot believe that the great mysteries of existence will be laid open to me on other terms. It is no use to talk to me of analogies and probabilities. I know what I mean when I say I believe in the law of the inverse squares, and I will not rest my life and my hopes upon weaker convictions. I dare not if I would.

Measured by this standard, what becomes of the doctrine of immortality?

You rest in your strong conviction of your personal

existence, and in the instinct of the persistence of that existence which is so strong in you as in most men.

To me this is as nothing. That my personality is the surest thing I know — may be true. But the attempt to conceive what it is leads me into mere verbal subtleties. I have champed up all that chaff about the ego and the nonego, about noumena and phenomena, and all the rest of it, too often not to know that in attempting even to think of these questions, the human intellect flounders at once out of its depth.

It must be twenty years since, a boy, I read Hamilton's essay on the unconditioned, and from that time to this, ontological speculation has been a folly to me. When Mansel took up Hamilton's argument on the side of orthodoxy (!) I said he reminded me of nothing so much as the man who is sawing off the sign on which he is sitting, in Hogarth's picture. But this by the way.

I cannot conceive of my personality as a thing apart from the phenomena of my life. When I try to form such a conception I discover that, as Coleridge would have said, I only hypostatise a word, and it alters nothing if, with Fichte, I suppose the universe to be nothing but a manifestation of my personality. I am neither more nor less eternal than I was before.

Nor does the infinite difference between myself and the animals alter the case. I do not know whether the animals persist after they disappear or not. I do not even know whether the infinite difference between us and them may not be compensated by *their* persistence and *my* cessation after apparent death, just as the humble bulb of an annual lives, while the glorious flowers it has put forth die away.

Surely it must be plain that an ingenious man could speculate without end on both sides, and find analogies for all his dreams. Nor does it help me to tell me that the aspirations of mankind — that my own highest aspirations even — lead me towards the doctrine of immortality. I doubt the fact, to begin with, but if it be so even, what is this but in grand words asking me to believe a thing because I like it?

Science has taught to me the opposite lesson. She warns me to be careful how I adopt a view which jumps with my preconceptions, and to require stronger evidence for such belief than for one to which I was previously hostile.

My business is to teach my aspirations to conform themselves to fact, not to try and make facts harmonise with my aspirations.

Science seems to me to teach in the highest and strongest manner the great truth which is embodied in the Christian conception of entire surrender to the will of God. Sit down before fact as a little child, be prepared to give up every preconceived notion, follow humbly wherever and to whatever abysses Nature leads, or you shall learn nothing. I have only begun to learn content and peace of mind since I have resolved at all risks to do this.

There are, however, other arguments commonly brought forward in favor of the immortality of man, which are to my mind not only delusive but mischievous. The one is the notion that the moral government of the world is imperfect without a system of future rewards and punishments. The other is: that such a system is indispensable to practical morality. I believe that both these dogmas are very mischievous lies.

With respect to the first, I am no optimist, but I have the firmest belief that the Divine Government (if we may use such a phrase to express the sum of the "customs of matter") is wholly just. The more I know intimately of the lives of other men (to say nothing of my own), the more obvious it is to me that the wicked does *not* flourish nor is the righteous punished. But for this to be clear we must bear in mind what almost all forget, that the rewards of life are contingent upon obedience to the *whole* law — physical as well as moral — and that moral obedience will not atone for physical sin, or *vice versa*.

The ledger of the Almighty is strictly kept, and every one of us has the balance of his operations paid over to him at the end of every minute of his existence.

Life cannot exist without a certain conformity to the surrounding universe — that conformity involves a certain amount of happiness in excess of pain. In short, as we live we are paid for living.

And it is to be recollected, in view of the apparent discrepancy between men's acts and their rewards, that Nature is juster than we. She takes into account what a man brings with him into the world, which human justice cannot do. If I, born a bloodthirsty and savage brute, inheriting these qualities from others, kill you, my fellowmen will very justly hang me, but I shall not be visited with the horrible remorse which would be my real punishment if, my nature being higher, I had done the same thing.

The absolute justice of the system of things is as clear to me as any scientific fact. The gravitation of sin to sorrow is as certain as that of the earth to the sun, and more so — for experimental proof of the facts is within reach of us all — nay, is before us all in our own lives, if we had but the eyes to see it.

Not only, then, do I disbelieve in the need for compensation, but I believe that the seeking for rewards and punishments out of this life leads men to a ruinous ignorance of the fact that their inevitable rewards and punishments are here.

If the expectation of hell hereafter can keep me from evildoing, surely *a fortiori the* certainty of hell now will do so? If a man could be firmly impressed with the belief that stealing damaged him as much as swallowing arsenic would do (and it does), would not the dissuasive force of that belief be greater than that of any based on mere future expectations?

And this leads me to my other point.

As I stood behind the coffin of my little son the other day, with my mind bent on anything but disputation, the officiating minister read, as a part of his duty, the words, "If the dead rise not again, let us eat and drink, for tomorrow we die." I cannot tell you how inexpressibly they shocked me. Paul had neither wife nor child, or he must have known that his alternative involved a blasphemy against all that was best and noblest in human nature. I could have laughed with scorn. What! because

I am face to face with irreparable loss, because I have given back to the source from whence it came, the cause of a great happiness, still retaining through all my life the blessings which have sprung and will spring from that cause, I am to renounce my manhood, and, howling, grovel in bestiality? Why, the very apes know better, and if you shoot their young, the poor brutes grieve their grief out and do not immediately seek distraction in a gorge.

Kicked into the world, a boy without guide or training, or with worse than none, I confess to my shame that few men have drunk deeper of all kinds of sin than I. Happily, my course was arrested in time — before I had earned absolute destruction — and for long years I have been slowly and painfully climbing, with many a fall, towards better things. And when I look back, what do I find to have been the agents of my redemption? The hope of immortality or of future reward? I can honestly say that for these fourteen years such a consideration has not entered my head. No, I can tell you exactly what has been at work. *Sartor Resartus* led me to know that a deep sense of religion was compatible with the entire absence of theology. Secondly, Science and her methods gave me a resting-place independent of authority and tradition. Thirdly, love opened up to me a view of the sanctity of human nature, and impressed me with a deep sense of responsibility.

If at this moment I am not a worn-out, debauched, useless carcass of a man, if it has been or will be my fate to advance the cause of science, if I feel that I have a shadow of a claim on the love of those about me, if in the supreme moment when I looked down into my boy's grave my sorrow was full of submission and without bitterness, it is because these agencies have worked upon me, and not because I have ever cared whether my poor personality shall remain distinct forever from the All from whence it came and whither it goes.

And thus, my dear Kingsley, you will understand what my position is. I may be quite wrong, and in that case I know I shall have to pay the penalty for being wrong.

But I can only say with Luther, "Gott helfe mir, Ich kann nichts anders."

I know right well that ninety out of a hundred of my fellows would call me atheist, infidel, and all the other usual hard names. As our laws stand, if the lowest thief steals my coat, my evidence (my opinions being known) would not be received against him.

But I cannot help it. One thing people shall not call me with justice and that is — a liar. As you say of yourself, I too feel that I lack courage; but if ever the occasion arises when I am bound to speak, I will not shame my boy.

I have spoken more openly and distinctly to you than I ever have to any human being except my wife.

If you can show me that I err in premises or conclusion, I am ready to give up these as I would any other theories. But at any rate you will do me the justice to believe that I have not reached my conclusions without the care befitting the momentous nature of the problems involved.

And I write this the more readily to you, because it is clear to me that if that great and powerful instrument for good or evil, the Church of England, is to be saved from being shivered into fragments by the advancing tide of science — an event I should be very sorry to witness, but which will infallibly occur if men like Samuel of Oxford are to have the guidance of her destinies — it must be by the efforts of men who, like yourself, see your way to the combination of the practice of the Church with the spirit of science. Understand that all the younger men of science whom I know intimately are *essentially* of my way of thinking. (I know not a scoffer or an irreligious or an immoral man among them, but they all regard orthodoxy as you do Brahmanism.) Understand that this new school of the prophets is the only one that can work miracles, the only one that can constantly appeal to Nature for evidence that it is right, and you will comprehend that it is of no use to try to barricade us with shovel hats and aprons, or to talk about our doctrines being "shocking."

I don't profess to understand the logic of yourself, Maurice, and the rest of your school, but I have always said I would swear by your truthfulness and sincerity, and that good must come of your efforts. The more plain this was to me, however, the more obvious the necessity to let you see where the men of science are driving, and it has often been in my mind to write to you before.

If I have spoken too plainly anywhere, or too abruptly, pardon me, and do the like to me.

My wife thanks you very much for your volume of sermons.

Ever yours very faithfully,

T. H. Huxley

O. W. HOLMES, JR., TO WILLIAM JAMES   1907

The great act of faith is when man decides that he is not God.

DON MARQUIS' *cockroach, archy*

> *if all the bugs*
> *in all the worlds*
> *twixt earth and betelgoose*
> *should sharpen up*
> *their little stings*
> *and turn their feelings loose*
> *they soon would show*
> *all human beans*
> *in saturn*
> *earth*
> *or mars*
> *their relative significance*
> *among the spinning stars*

E. B. WHITE   1946

Well, archys boss is dead, God rest his untransmigrated soul, but archy himself is probably good for another hundred million years. There will be enough gold lettering from pulverized books to keep him going, and, his nitrogen needs are small. Because he had the soul of a poet and saw things from the under side, archys writings are pertinent today, as the cosmos slithers drunkenly into its Bikini Lagoon phase. One of archys acquaintances, you will recall, was a toad named warty bliggens, who was convinced that toadstools had been especially created for him, planned for his personal shelter:

> *a little more*
> *conversation revealed*
> *that warty bliggens*
> *considers himself to be*
> *the center of the said*
> *universe*
> *the earth exists*
> *to grow toadstools for him*
> *to sit under*
> *the sun to give him light*
> *by day and the moon*
> *and wheeling constellations*
> *to make beautiful*
> *the night for the sake of*
> *warty bliggens*

archy asked him what he had ever done to deserve such favors from the Creator of the universe.

> *ask rather*
> *said warty bliggens*
> *what the universe*
> *has done to deserve me*

Dionysos versus Orpheus

JANE ELLEN HARRISON   1850–1928

There are some to whom by natural temperament the religion of Bromios, son of Semele, is and must always be a dead letter, if not a stumbling-block. Food is to such a troublesome necessity, wine a danger or a disgust. They dread all stimulus that comes from without; they would fain break the ties that link them with animals and plants. They do not feel in themselves and are at a loss to imagine for others the sacramental mystery of life and nutrition that is accomplished in us day by day; how in the faintness of fasting the whole nature of man, spirit as well as body, dies down, he cannot think, he cannot work, he cannot love; how in the breaking of bread, and still more in the drinking of wine, life spiritual as well as physical is renewed, thought is reborn, his equanimity, his magnanimity are restored, reason and morality rule again. But to this sacramentalism of life most of us bear constant, if partly unconscious, witness. We will not eat with the man we hate; it is felt a sacrilege leaving a sickness in body and soul. The first breaking of bread and drinking of wine together is the seal of a new friendship; the last eaten in silence at parting is more than many words. The sacramental feast of bread and wine is spread for the newly married, for the newly dead.

Those to whom wine brings no inspiration, no moments of sudden illumination, of wider and deeper insight, of larger human charity and understanding, find it hard to realize what to others of other temperament is so natural, so elemental, so beautiful — the constant shift from physical to spiritual that is of the essence of the religion of Dionysos. But there are those also, and they are saintly souls, who know it all to the full, know the exhilaration of wine, know what it is to be drunken with the physical beauty of a flower or a sunset, with the sensuous imagery of words, with the strong wine of a new idea, with the magic of another's personality, yet having known, turn away with steadfast eyes, disallowing the madness not only of Bromios but of the Muses and of Aphrodite. Such have their inward ecstasy of the ascetic, but they revel with another Lord, and he is Orpheus.

JOHN SELDEN   1584–1654

Men say they are of the same religion, for quietness' sake; but if the matter were well examined, you would scarce find three anywhere of the same religion on all points.

Happiness

CASANOVA   1725–1798

Yes, death is the last line of the book. It's the end of all, since with death man ceases to feel. But I am far from pretending that the spirit follows the fate of matter. A man should affirm no more than he positively knows. Doubt begins only at the last frontiers of what is possible.

Yes, you moralists morose and imprudent, there is happiness on earth, there is a lot of it, and each has his own. It's not permanent, no. It passes, it comes back, and passes you again, by that law which is inherent in the nature of all created things, the movement, the eternal rotation of man and thing. And it may be that the sum total of ill, consequence of our imperfection, our physical and intellectual imperfection, surpasses the sum total of each individual's happiness. All that is possible, but it does not follow that there is no happiness, and a great deal of happiness. If there were not happiness on earth, the creation would be a monstrosity, and Voltaire would have been right when he called our planet the latrines of the universe. An evil pleasantry, which is no more than an absurdity, or rather meaningless, if not a jet of poetic bile.

Yes, there is happiness, and much of it. I repeat that today I know it only by remembrance. Those who admit candidly what they feel are worthy of having it. Those who are not worthy of it are those who have it and yet deny it, and those who are able to get it, yet neglect it. I have no reproach to make to myself on either score.

Know Yourself

PASCAL   1623–1662

If man would begin by studying himself, he would see how incapable he is of knowing anything beyond himself. How can a part know the whole? Man is related to everything that he knows. And everything is both cause and effect, working and worked upon, mediate and immediate, all things mutually dependent. A bond that is

both natural and imperceptible binds together things
the most distant and things the most different. I hold it,
therefore, impossible to know the parts without knowing
the whole, any more than we can know the whole without knowing each particular part.

But what completes our incapacity to understand
things is the fact that they are simple and that we are
composed of two different natures which are opposed to
each other, the soul and the body. For that part of us
which reasons is spiritual; and if we pretend that we are
simply corporeal, that alone excludes us from any knowledge of things, since nothing is more inconceivable than
that matter can know itself. If we are simply matter,
we can know nothing. If we are both matter and spirit,
we cannot know perfectly either things that are simply
spiritual or things that are simply material.

Philosophers, confusing ideas with things, speak of
material things in terms of the spirit and things of the
spirit in terms of matter. They say boldly that bodies
fall because they seek a center, they speak of things trying to avoid their own destruction, of fearing a vacuum,
of their sympathies, and their antipathies, which are all
terms belonging to the spirit. And in speaking of spiritual
things they consider them in a place, and attribute movement to them from one place to another, which are terms
that belong only to matter. Instead of conceiving things
in their purity, we color them with our own qualities
and stamp them with our own composite nature.

Man considering himself is the great prodigy of nature.
For he cannot conceive what his body is, even less what
his spirit is, and least of all how body can be united with
spirit. That is the peak of his difficulty, and yet it is his
very being. The way in which the spirit is united to the
body is incomprehensible to man, and yet that is man,
said Saint Augustine.

W. B. YEATS   1865–1939

> *Sickness brought me this*
> *Thought, in that scale of his:*
> *Why should I be dismayed*

Though flame had burned the whole
World, as it were a coal,
Now I have seen it weighed
Against a soul?

"God"

EDMUND WILSON 1956

The word *God* is now archaic, and it ought to be
dropped by those who do not need it for moral support.
This word has the disadvantage of having meant already far too many things in too many ages of history
and to too many kinds of people, along with the disadvantage that the one thing these various meanings have
all had more or less in common is an anthropomorphic
picture. In the case of the conceptions of the metaphy-
sician — such as Whitehead's "principle of concretion"
in the universe — in which the anthropomorphic image
tends to disappear, this term seems farfetched and un-
called-for; and in the case of the ordinary man, it is lazy
to use it to designate the impetus which rouses him up
from bed in the morning, sends him about his business
and makes him believe that that business is important,
as well as to provide a "first cause" for the force that sets
the ions of physics revolving around their nuclei and
the planets around their suns. There is no classical conception of God that can really be made to fit what we
know today, in the middle of the twentieth century, of
the behavior of what we call "energy" and the behavior
of human beings, and of the relation of these to one another. Yet we still use the word in this indolent sense
to cover up our inability to account, in a "rational" way,
for the fact that we exist, that the universe exists, and
that everything is as it is. At some point in the distant
past, human beings became aware that their bodies had
been developed in an intricate and remarkably effective
way, and since they could not remember having planned
this or worked it out themselves, they came to the conclusion, as Paley did — thinking in mechanical terms —
that where one found what one took for a clock, there

must previously have been a clockmaker. Today such conceptions are obsolete. Though we still make mechanical models of the movements of the planets and the fission of the atom, we do not see the world as an immense machine. We do not speak of unvarying scientific laws; we speak of "statistical averages." We have been forced to recognize the "organic," to admit that what we used to call "reason" may land us in a cul-de-sac. Yet we keep on performing experiments which we observe from the rational point of view of the cause that produces the effect, and we know that we can find out certain things in this way: techniques for procuring results. What is behind the processes involved? What is involved in our wish to control them? We do not know. The best we can say is that the universe is not a machine, set going by a machine-maker, God, but an organism that is always developing, in which we, interrelated with everything else, have our life-cycles as unified groups of impermanently clustering particles. But to say that all this was created by "God" or to identify it somehow with "God" is to supplement our human ignorance with a gratuitous fairy story. As we come to understand more and more about the processes of "life" and "matter," we discover that it is less and less easy to differentiate clearly between them. As we probe into the happenings in the universe — electrical and cerebral phenomena, the transit of light waves and sound waves, the multiplication of cells in organisms, the inherited combinations of genes — we find them, to be sure, less amenable to the "laws" of the old-fashioned scientist who thought in mechanical terms. But we do not find a God.

The "Existence" of God

PAUL TILLICH   1954

Both the theological and the scientific critics of the belief that religion is an aspect of the human spirit define religion as man's relation to divine beings, whose existence the theological critics assert and the scientific critics deny. But it is just this idea of religion which makes

any understanding of religion impossible. If you start
with the question whether God does or does not exist,
you can never reach Him; and if you assert that He does
exist, you can reach Him even less than if you assert that
He does not exist. A God about whose existence or
non-existence you can argue is a thing beside others
within the universe of existing things. And the question is quite justified whether such a thing does exist,
and the answer is equally justified that it does not exist.
It is regrettable that scientists believe that they have refuted religion when they rightly have shown that there
is no evidence whatsoever for the assumption that such a
being exists. Actually, they have not only not refuted
religion, but they have done it a considerable service.
They have forced it to reconsider and to restate the meaning of the tremendous word *God*. Unfortunately, many
theologians make the same mistake. They begin their
message with the assertion that there is a highest being
called God, whose authoritative revelations they have
received. They are more dangerous for religion than
the so-called atheistic scientists. They take the first step
on the road which inescapably leads to what is called
atheism. Theologians who make of God a highest being
who has given some people information about Himself,
provoke inescapably the resistance of those who are told
they must subject themselves to the authority of this
information.

THOREAU   1817–1862

It is not when I am going to meet him, but when I am
just turning away and leaving him alone, that I discover
that God is. I say, God. I am not sure that that is the
name. You will know what I mean.

Lavinia and the Captain

GEORGE BERNARD SHAW   1856–1950

Roman Captain: What you are facing is certain death.
You have nothing left now but your faith in this craze
of yours: this Christianity. Are your Christian fairy

stories any truer than our stories about Jupiter and Diana? ——

Lavinia: Captain, all that seems nothing to me now. I'll not say that death is a terrible thing; but I will say that it is so real a thing that when it comes close, all the imaginary things — all the stories, as you call them — fade into mere dreams beside that inexorable reality. I know now that I am not dying for stories or dreams. ——

The Captain: Are you then going to die for nothing?

Lavinia: Yes: that is the wonderful thing. It is since all the stories and dreams have gone that I have now no doubt at all that I must die for something greater than dreams or stories.

The Captain: But for what?

Lavinia: I don't know. If it were for anything small enough to know, it would be too small to die for. I think I'm going to die for God. Nothing else is real enough to die for.

The Captain: What is God?

Lavinia: When we know that, Captain, we shall be gods ourselves.

A Thinking Reed

PASCAL   1623–1662

Man is a reed, a bit of straw, the feeblest thing in nature. But he thinks. He is a thinking reed. When the universe chooses to crush him, the universe need not take arms against him. A whiff of vapor, a drop of water; either will kill him.

When the universe decides to crush a man, he is nobler than what killed him. For as he dies, he recognizes the greater power that the universe has over him. And the universe does not, and knows not.

Man's dignity, our dignity, lives in our thoughts. Thereby we rise. Only thereby. Not through space; and not through time. Never can we fill either. So we take pains, such pains as we can, to think well. For therein lie all morals and all principles.

A thinking reed. Not in space am I to seek my dignity. But in my thinking. Possessions give me no more than I have already. The universe comprehends me. It encompasses me. In its space, I am but a geometrical point. But in thought, in my thought, I comprehend the universe.

PAUL VALÉRY

"L'Homme pense; donc je suis," dit l'Univers.

Noises

THORNTON WILDER   1952

Paul Valéry — playing — once inserted four minus signs into Pascal's most famous sentence.

Pascal had said that the eternal silence of infinite space filled him with fright (*le silence éternal des espaces infinies m'effraie*). Valéry restated it by saying that the intermittent racket of our little neighborhood reassures us (*le vacarme des petits coins ou nous vivons nous rassure*).

The Cosmic Wiggle

JOHN DEWEY   1859–1952

By an indirect path we are brought to a consideration of the most far-reaching question of all criticism: the relationship between existence and value, or, as the problem is often put, between the real and ideal.

Philosophies have usually insisted upon a wholesale relationship. Either the goods which we most prize and which are therefore termed ideal are identified completely and thoroughly with real Being; or the realms of existence and of the ideal are wholly severed from each other. In the European tradition in its orthodox form the former alternative has prevailed. *Ens* and *verum, bonum* are the same. Being, in the full sense, is perfection of power to be; the measure of degrees of perfection and of degrees of reality is extent of power. Evil and error are impotences; futile gestures against omnipotence — against Being. Spinoza restated to this effect medieval theology in terms of the new outlook of science. Modern professed idealisms have taught the same doctrine. After magnifying thoughts and the objects of thought, after magnifying the ideals of human aspiration, they have then sought to prove that after all these things are not ideal but are real — real not *as* meanings and ideals, but as existential being. Thus the assertion of faith in the ideal belies itself in the making; these "idealists" cannot trust their ideal till they have converted it into existence — that is, into the physical or the psychical, which, since it lacks the properties of the empirically physical and psycho-physical, becomes a peculiar kind of existence, called metaphysical.

There are also philosophies, rarer in occurrence, which allege that the ideal is too sacredly ideal to have any point of contact whatever with existence; they think that contact is contagion and contagion infection. At first sight such a view seems to display a certain nobility of faith and fineness of abnegation. But an ideal realm that has no roots in existence has no efficacy nor relevancy. It is a light which is darkness, for shining in the void it illumines nothing and cannot reveal even itself. It gives no instruction, for it cannot be translated into the meaning and import of what actually happens, and hence it is barren; it cannot mitigate the bleakness of existence nor modify its brutalities. It thus abnegates itself in abjuring footing in natural events, and ceases to be ideal, to become whimsical fantasy or linguistic sophistication.

These remarks are made not so much by way of hostile animadversion as by way of indicating the sterility of wholesale conceptions of the relation of existence and value. By negative implication, they reveal the only kind of doctrine that can be effectively critical, taking effect in discriminations which emancipate, extend, and clarify. Such a theory will realize that the meanings which are termed ideal as truly as those which are termed sensuous are generated by existences; that as far as they continue in being they are sustained by events; that they are indications of the possibilities of existences, and are, therefore, to be used as well as enjoyed; used to inspire action to procure and buttress their casual conditions. Such a doctrine criticizes particular occurrences by the particular meanings to which they give rise; it criticizes also particular meanings and goods as their conditions are found to be sparse, accidental, incapable of conservation, or frequent, pliant, congruous, enduring; and as their consequences are found to afford enlightenment and direction in conduct, or to darken counsel, narrow the horizon of vision, befog judgment and distort perspective. A good is a good anyhow, but to reflection those goods approve themselves, whether labeled beauty or truth or righteousness, which steady, vitalize, and expand judgments in creation of new goods and conservation of old goods. To common sense this statement is a truism. If to philosophy it is a stumbling-block, it is because tradition in philosophy has set itself in stiff-necked fashion against discriminations within the realm of existences, on account of the pluralistic implications of discrimination. It insists upon having all or none; it cannot choose in favor of some existences and against others because of prior commitment to a dogma of perfect unity. Such distinctions as it makes are therefore always hierarchical; degrees of greater and less, superior and inferior, in one homogeneous order.

I gladly borrow the glowing words of one of our greatest American philosophers; with their poetry they may succeed in conveying where dry prose fails. Justice Holmes has written: "The mode in which the inevitable comes to pass is through effort. Consciously or unconsciously we all strive to make the kind of world that we like. And although with Spinoza we may regard criticism of the past as futile, there is every reason for doing all that we can to make a future such as we desire." He then goes on to say, "There is every reason also for trying to make our desires intelligent. The trouble is that our ideals for the most part are inarticulate, and that even if we have made them definite, we have very little experimental knowledge of the way to bring them about." And this effort to make our desires, our strivings and our ideals (which are as natural to man as his aches and his clothes) articulate, to define them (not in themselves, which is impossible) in terms of inquiry into conditions and consequences, is what I have called criticism; and when carried on in the grand manner, philosophy. In a further essay, Justice Holmes touches upon the relation of philosophy (thus conceived) to our scientific and metaphysical insight into the kind of world in which we live.

"When we come to our attitude toward the universe I do not see any rational ground for demanding the superlative — for being dissatisfied unless we are assured that our truth is cosmic truth, if there is such a thing. . . . If a man sees no reason for believing that significance, consciousness, and ideals are more than marks of the human, that does not justify what has been familiar in French sceptics; getting upon a pedestal and professing to look with haughty scorn upon a world in ruins. The real conclusion is that the part cannot swallow the whole. . . . If we believe that we came out of the universe, not it out of us, we must admit that we do not know what we are talking about when we speak of brute matter. We do know that a certain complex of energies can wag its tail and another can make syllogisms. These are among the powers of the unknown, and if, as may be, it has still greater powers that we cannot understand . . . why should we not be content? Why should we employ the energy that is furnished to us by the cosmos to defy it and to shake our fist at the sky? It seems to me silly.

"That the universe has in it more than we understand, that the private soldiers have not been told the plan of campaign, or even that there is one . . . has no bearing on our conduct. We still shall fight — all of us because we want to live, some, at least, because we want to realize our spontaneity and prove our powers, for the joy of it, and we may leave to the unknown the supposed final valuation of that which in any event has value to us. It is enough for us that the universe has produced us and has within it, as less than it, all that we believe and love. If we think of our existence not as that of a little god outside, but as that of a ganglion within, we have the infinite behind us. It gives us our only but our adequate significance. If our imagination is strong enough to accept the vision of ourselves as parts inseparable from the rest, and to extend our final interest beyond the boundary of our skins, it justifies even the sacrifice of our lives for ends outside of ourselves. The motive, to be sure, is the common wants and ideals that we find in man. Philosophy does not furnish motives, but it shows men that they are not fools for doing what they already want to do. It opens to the forlorn hopes on which we throw ourselves away, the vista of the farthest stretch of human thought, the chord of a harmony that breathes from the unknown."

Men move between extremes. They conceive of themselves as gods, or feign a powerful and cunning god as an ally who bends the world to do their bidding and meet their wishes. Disillusioned, they disown the world that disappoints them; and hugging ideals to themselves as their own possession, stand in haughty aloofness apart from the hard course of events that pays so little heed to our hopes and aspirations. But a mind that has opened itself to experience and that has ripened through its discipline knows its own littleness and impotencies; it knows that its wishes and acknowledgments are not final measures of the universe whether in knowledge or in conduct, and hence are, in the end, transient. But it also knows that its juvenile assumption of power and achievement is not a dream to be wholly forgotten. It implies a unity with the universe that is to be preserved. The belief and the effort of thought and struggle which it inspires are also the doing of the universe, and they in some way, however slight, carry the universe forward. A chastened sense of our importance, apprehension that it is not a yardstick by which to measure the whole, is consistent with the belief that we and our endeavors are significant not only for themselves but in the whole.

O. W. HOLMES, JR., TO POLLOCK   1931

But although Dewey's book [*Experience and Nature*] is
incredibly ill written, it seemed to me after several re-
readings to have a feeling of intimacy with the inside
of the cosmos that I found unequalled. So methought
God would have spoken had He been inarticulate but
keenly desirous to tell you how it was.

Holmes wrote in the copy of Dewey's *Experience and Nature* belonging to one of the editors that of any book he
knew, it came nearest to expressing "the cosmic wiggle."

Existentialism

JEAN-PAUL SARTRE   1946

Existence comes before essence — or, if you will, we must
begin from the subjective. What exactly do we mean by
that?

If one considers an article of manufacture — as, for
example, a book or a paper-knife — one sees that it has
been made by an artisan who had a conception of it;
and he has paid attention, equally, to the conception of
a paper-knife and to the pre-existent technique of production which is a part of that conception and is, at
bottom, a formula. Thus the paper-knife is at the same
time an article producible in a certain manner and one
which, on the other hand, serves a definite purpose, for
one cannot suppose that a man would produce a paper-
knife without knowing what it was for. Let us say, then,
of the paper-knife that its essence — that is to say the
sum of the formulae and the qualities which made its
production and its definition possible — precedes its
existence. The presence of such-and-such a paper-knife
or book is thus determined before my eyes. Here, then,
we are viewing the world from a technical standpoint,
and we can say that production precedes existence.

When we think of God as the creator, we are thinking
of him, most of the time, as a supernal artisan. Whatever doctrine we may be considering, whether it be a
doctrine like that of Descartes, or of Leibniz himself, we

always imply that the will follows, more or less, from the understanding or at least accompanies it, so that when God creates he knows precisely what he is creating. Thus, the conception of man in the mind of God is comparable to that of the paper-knife in the mind of the artisan: God makes man according to a procedure and a conception, exactly as the artisan manufactures a paper-knife, following a definition and a formula. Thus each individual man is the realization of a certain conception which dwells in the divine understanding. In the philosophic atheism of the eighteenth century, the notion of God is suppressed, but not, for all that, the idea that essence is prior to existence; something of that idea we still find everywhere, in Diderot, in Voltaire and even in Kant. Man possesses a human nature; that "human nature," which is the conception of human being, is found in every man; which means that each man is a particular example of a universal conception, the conception of Man. In Kant, this universality goes so far that the wild man of the woods, man in the state of nature and the bourgeois are all contained in the same definition and have the same fundamental qualities. Here again, the essence of man precedes that historic existence which we confront in experience.

Atheistic existentialism, of which I am a representative, declares with greater consistency that if God does not exist there is at least one being whose existence comes before its essence, a being which exists before it can be defined by any conception of it. That being is man or, as Heidegger has it, the human reality. What do we mean by saying that existence precedes essence? We mean that man first of all exists, encounters himself, surges up in the world — and defines himself afterwards. If man as the existentialist sees him is not definable, it is because to begin with he is nothing. He will not be anything until later, and then he will be what he makes of himself. Thus, there is no human nature, because there is no God to have a conception of it. Man simply is. Not that he is simply what he conceives himself to be, but he is what he wills, and as he conceives himself after already existing — as he wills to be after that leap toward existence.

Man is nothing else but that which he makes of himself. That is the first principle of existentialism. And this is what people call its "subjectivity," using the word as a reproach against us. But what do we mean to say by this, but that man is of a greater dignity than a stone or a table? For we mean to say that man primarily exists — that man is, before all else, something which propels itself towards a future and is aware that it is doing so. Man is, indeed, a project which possesses a subjective life, instead of being a kind of moss, or a fungus or a cauliflower. Before that projection of the self nothing exists; not even in the heaven of intelligence: man will only attain existence when he is what he purposes to be. Not, however, what he may wish to be. For what we usually understand by wishing or willing is a conscious decision taken — much more often than not — after we have made ourselves what we are. I may wish to join a party, to write a book or to marry — but in such a case what is usually called my will is probably a manifestation of a prior and more spontaneous decision. If, however, it is true that existence is prior to essence, man is responsible for what he is. Thus, the first effect of existentialism is that it puts every man in possession of himself as he is, and places the entire responsibility for his existence squarely upon his own shoulders.

And, when we say that man is responsible for himself, we do not mean that he is responsible only for his own individuality, but that he is responsible for all men. The word "subjectivism" is to be understood in two senses, and our adversaries play upon only one of them. Subjectivism means, on the one hand, the freedom of the individual subject and, on the other, that man cannot pass beyond human subjectivity. It is the latter which is the deeper meaning of existentialism. When we say that man chooses himself, we do mean that every one of us must choose himself; but by that we also mean that in choosing for himself he chooses for all men. For in effect, of all the actions a man may take in order to create himself as he wills to be, there is not one which is not creative, at the same time, of an image of man such as he believes he ought to be. To choose between this or that is at the same time to affirm the value of that which is chosen; for we are unable ever to choose the worse. What we choose is always the better; and nothing can be better for us unless it is better for all. If, moreover, existence precedes essence and we will to exist at the same time as we fashion our image, that image is valid for all and for the entire epoch in which we find ourselves. Our responsibility is thus much greater than we had supposed, for it concerns mankind as a whole.

Ultimate Concern

PAUL TILLICH   **1950**

Reality has changed and the interpretation of reality has changed with it. History has become the scene of a continuous chain of catastrophes, and thought has become an interpretation of the human predicament as manifest in these catastrophes, partly before they actually happened. In the beginning of the twentieth century the European intelligentsia included a vanguard of prophetic minds, in art as well as in philosophy, who anticipated what was to come. And when it came and their visions were confirmed by revolutions and reactions they became the leaders of the new generation, first in Europe and since the great crisis also in America. This development is not a "failure of nerve" but it is the courage to see what a favorable historical constellation had covered for almost a century what could not be hidden any longer, the dark underground of the personal and social life. The picture of man as the master not only of nature but also of his personality and his society and therefore of his individual and historical destiny, this shining picture took on darker and darker colors. Destiny proved to be the master of man, not as a strange power but as power in the depth of man himself. The view was in no way influenced by theological pessimism. People like Nietzsche and Freud, Van Gogh and Strindberg, Heidegger and Unamuno, Sartre and O'Neill have no direct contact with the doctrine of man in classical theology. Nevertheless they all helped preparing the turn toward religion in large groups of the Western intelligentsia. If the human predicament is as they have seen it, only two honest ways are open, the way of accepting and the way of transcending this predicament. The first way can be called negative-religious, the second positive-religious. On one of these ways we find all those intellectuals whose belief in the mastery of rational man over his destiny has broken down and who reject a compromise between their former belief and their new insight, who are not satisfied by a restricted and moderate optimism about the potentialities of man and history. The negative-religious way is the way of despair and heroism. Its heroism is the acceptance of its despair. But since nobody can live in an absolute despair about meaning and being, one consolation is accepted by those who have chosen this way: As intellectuals they can express the despair of existence artistically or philosophically, and can create a meaning of the meaningless. The heroism of despair transcends despair through the power of the intellectual in expressing it, not in outcries, but in creative forms. By this expression of despair the intellectual is saved from the radicalism of the despair he expresses. For two reasons one can call this attitude negative-religious. Despair is *negative*-religious insofar as within it all finite securities break down and lose their power of preventing the question of the infinite, of the ultimate meaning of existence. The expression of despair is negative-*religious* insofar as it tries to transcend the situation of absolute despair by expressing it although confirming it, at the same time. These inner contradictions of the negative-religious attitude drive the intellectual towards the other, the positive-religious way. Not all of them take this way, but all of them have experienced the negative preparation for it. The positive religious way transcends the human predicament radically by transforming it into a question to which religion gives the answer. On this way the despaired character of man's predicament is acknowledged. But man is not considered to be the last word about man. Within the symbols of historical religion an answer is seen which accepts and transcends the human situation, its despair and its self-destruction.

But the modern intellectual could not honestly accept religion, in spite of all that drives him to it if religion were what it was supposed to be in the atheistic criticism of previous generations. Religion — at least in some of its recent interpreters — is a whole of symbols in which our relation to the ground and meaning of existence is expressed. Being religious is being ultimately concerned — and this the intellectual of our days is, even if he expresses his ultimate concern in negative terms. Religion is *not* a collection of theoretical statements of a questionable or absurd or superstitious character. Such a religion could not be accepted by any intellectual who is not willing to sacrifice his intellectual honesty. Some of them make this sacrifice and surrender their intellectual autonomy to Ecclesiastical or Biblical authorities. But their turn to religion is still an expression of their despair, not a victory over it. Others are waiting for a religious answer which does not destroy reason but points to the depth of reason; which does not teach the supernatural, but points to the mystery in the ground of the natural, which denies that God is a being and speaks of Him as the ground and depth of being and meaning, which knows about the significance of symbols in myth and cult, but resists the distortion of symbols into statements of knowledge which necessarily conflict with scientific knowledge. A theology which takes this position, which preserves the intellectual honesty of the intellectual and expresses, at the same time, the answers to the questions implied in man's existence and existence generally — such a theology is acceptable to the intelligentsia (and to many non-intellectuals as well). It prevents the turn of the intellectuals toward religion from becoming a matter of romantic concessions or of self-surrender to authority.

Mr. Valiant-for-Truth Is Summoned

BUNYAN 1628–1688

When he understood it, he called for his friends, and told them of it. Then said he, I am going to my Father's; and though with great difficulty I have got hither, yet now I do not regret me of all the trouble I have been at to arrive where I am. My sword I give to him that shall succeed me in my pilgrimage, and my courage and skill to him that can get it. My marks and scars I carry with me, to be a witness for me that I have fought His battle who will now be my rewarder. When the day that he must go hence was come, many accompanied him to the river-side, into which as he went, he said, "Death, where is thy sting?" And as he went down deeper, he said, "Grave, where is thy victory?" So he passed over, and all the trumpets sounded for him on the other side.

LAST WORDS OF STONEWALL JACKSON 1863

"Let us cross over the River, and rest under the shade of the Trees."

PART
XIII

HE TAKES BETTER AIM

The target lies over the hill; and the longer the range, the higher the sights are raised. And the bullet leaves the muzzle at a tangent to the line of flight.

The End of Time

LUCRETIUS   96–55 B.C.

No single thing abides, but all things flow.
Fragment to fragment clings; the things thus grow
   Until we know and name them. By degrees
They melt, and are no more the things we know.

Globed from the atoms, falling slow or swift
I see the suns, I see the systems lift
   Their forms; and even the systems and their suns
Shall go back slowly to the eternal drift.

Thou too, O Earth — thine empires, lands and seas —
Least, with thy stars, of all the galaxies,
   Globed from the drift like these, like these thou too
Shalt go. Thou art going, hour by hour, like these.

Nothing abides. Thy seas in delicate haze
Go off; those mooned sands forsake their place;
   And where they are shall other seas in turn
Mow with their scythes of whiteness other bays.

ROBERT FROST   1875–

   Some say the world will end in fire,
   Some say in ice.
   From what I've tasted of desire
   I hold with those who favor fire.
   But if it had to perish twice,
   I think I know enough of hate

To say that for destruction ice
Is also great
And would suffice.

ARTHUR JAMES BALFOUR   1848–1930

Man, so far as natural science by itself is able to teach us, is no longer the final cause of the universe, the Heaven-descended heir of all the ages. His very existence is an accident, his story a brief and transitory episode in the life of one of the meanest of the planets. Of the combination of causes which first converted a dead organic compound into the living progenitors of humanity, science, indeed, as yet knows nothing. It is enough that from such beginnings famine, disease, and mutual slaughter, fit nurses of the future lords of creation, have gradually evolved, after infinite travail, a race with conscience enough to feel that it is vile, and intelligence enough to know that it is insignificant. We survey the past, and see that its history is of blood and tears, of helpless blundering, of wild revolt, of stupid acquiescence, of empty aspirations. We sound the future, and learn that after a period, long compared with the individual life, but short indeed compared with the divisions of time open to our investigation, the energies of our system will decay, the glory of the sun will be dimmed, and the earth, tideless and inert, will no longer tolerate the race which has for a moment disturbed its solitude. Man will go down into the pit, and all his thoughts will perish. The uneasy consciousness, which in this obscure corner has for a long space broken the contented silence of the universe, will be at rest. Matter will know itself no longer. "Imperishable monuments" and "immortal deeds," death itself, and love stronger than death, will be as though they had never been. Nor will anything that *is* be better or be worse for all that the labor, genius, devotion, and suffering of men have striven through countless generations to effect.

Time hath, my lord, a wallet at his back
Wherein he puts alms for oblivion.

SHAKESPEARE   1564–1616

Hotspur. *But thought's the slave of life, and life time's fool;*
And time, that takes survey of all the world,
Must have a stop. O I could prophesy,
But that the earth, and the cold hand of death,
Lies on my tongue. No, Percy thou art dust
And food for—
Prince Harry. *For worms, brave Percy. Fare thee well, great*
  heart!

THOMAS BROWNE   1605–1682

But the iniquity of oblivion scattereth her poppy, and
deals with the memory of men without distinction to
merit of perpetuity. Who can but pity the founder of
the pyramids? Erostratus lives that burnt the Temple
of Diana; he is almost lost that built it. Time hath
spared the epitaph of Adrian's horse, confounded that
of himself. In vain we compute our felicities by the advantage of our good names, since bad have equal dura-
tions; and Thersites is like to live as long as Agamemnon. Who knows whether the best of men be known, or
whether there be not more remarkable persons forgot
than any that stand remembered in the known account
of time? Without the favor of the everlasting register,
the first man had been as unknown as the last, and
Methuselah's long life had been his only chronicle.

Oblivion is not to be hired. The greater part must be
content to be as though they had not been, to be found
in the register of God, not in the record of man.
Twenty-seven names make up the first century. The
number of the dead long exceedeth all that shall live.
The night of time far surpasseth the day; and who knows
when was the equinox? Every hour adds unto that current arithmetic, which scarce stands one moment.

Osler made a note on the margin of his copy of *Urn Burial*
opposite this passage, "Wonderful page — always impressed
me as one of the great ones in B. 6 xii 19 W. O." That was
on his deathbed, shortly before he died.

W. B. YEATS   1865–1939

> From man's blood-sodden heart are sprung
> Those branches of the night and day
> Where the gaudy moon is hung.
> What's the meaning of all song?
> "Let all things pass away."

LEONARDO DA VINCI   1452–1519

O time, thou that consumest all things! O envious age, thou destroyest all things and devourest all things with the hard teeth of the years, little by little, in slow death! Helen, when she looked in the mirror and saw the withered wrinkles which old age had made in her face, wept, and wondered to herself why ever she had been twice carried away.

E. E. CUMMINGS   1894–1962

> being to timelessness as it's to time,
> love did no more begin than love will end;
> where nothing is to breathe to stroll to swim
> love is the air the ocean and the land
>
> (do lovers suffer? all divinities
> proudly descending put on deathful flesh:
> are lovers glad? only their smallest joy's
> a universe emerging from a wish)
>
> love is the voice under all silences,
> the hope which has no opposite in fear;
> the strength so strong mere force seems feebleness:
> the truth more first than sun more last than star
>
> —do lovers love? why then to heaven with hell.
> Whatever sages say and fools, all's well

YEATS   1938

> Draw rein, draw breath,
> Cast a cold eye
> On life, on death.
> Horseman, pass by!

HARLOW SHAPLEY   1885–

I may be obsessed, or suffering from anthropocentric illusions, but I cannot escape the feeling that the human mind and human curiosity are significant in this world —even perhaps in the cosmos of geological time and intergalactic space. With this impression (or illusion) that the mind is the best of us, and the best of biological evolution, I cannot escape (and neither can you!) the feeling of a responsibility to glorify the human mind, take it seriously, even dream about its ultimate flowering into something far beyond the primitive muscle-guider and sensation-recorder with which we started.

The Man Who Worried about Heaven

LIEHTSE   5TH OR 4TH CENTURY B.C.

There was a man of the country of Ch'i who was worrying that the sky might one day fall down, and he would not know where to hide himself. This so much troubled him that he could not eat or sleep. There was another who was worried about this man's worry, and he went to explain it to him, saying, "The sky is only formed of accumulated air. There is no place where there is no air. Whenever you move or breathe, you are living right in this sky. Why do you need ever to worry that the sky will fall down?" The other man said, "If the sky were really nothing but air, would not the sun and moon and the stars fall down?" And the man who was explaining said, "But the sun, the moon, and the stars are also nothing but accumulated air (gases) which has become bright. Even if they should fall down, they would not hurt anybody." "But what if the earth should be destroyed?" And the other replied, "The earth is also only formed of accumulated solids, which fill all space. There is no place where there are no solids. As you walk and stamp on the ground, you are moving the whole day on this earth. Why do you ever need to worry that it may be destroyed?" Then that man seemed to understand and was greatly pleased, and the one who was explaining it to him also felt he understood and was greatly pleased.

When Ch'anglutse heard about it, he laughed and said, "The rainbow, the clouds and mists, the winds and rains and the four seasons — are all these not formed of accumulated air and the sky? The mountains and high peaks, the rivers and seas, metal and stone, water and fire — are these not formed of accumulated solids on the earth? Since we know they are formed of accumulated air and accumulated solids, how can we say then that they are indestructible? The infinitely great and the infinitesimally small cannot be exhaustively known or explored, or conjectured about — that is a matter taken for granted. Those who worry about the destruction of the universe are, of course, thinking too far ahead, but those who say they cannot be destroyed are also mistaken. Since the heaven and earth must be destroyed, they will end finally in destruction. And when they are destroyed, why shouldn't one worry about it?"

Liehtse heard about what Ch'anglutse had said, and laughed and said, "Those who say that heaven and earth are destructible are wrong, and those who say they are indestructible are also wrong. Destruction and indestructibility are not things we know anything about. However, they are both the same. Therefore, one lives and does not know about death; one dies and does not know about life; one comes and does not know about going away; and one goes away and does not know about coming. Why should the question of destruction or nondestruction ever bother our minds?"

And Yet, Meanwhile

EMERSON   1845

Here is the world, sound as a nut, perfect, not the smallest piece of chaos left, never a stitch nor an end, not a mark of haste, or botching, or second thought; but the theory of the world is a thing of shreds and patches.

CARL L. BECKER   1873–1945

There are always some eccentric individuals, and on occasion certain groups who find the present temporal world of men and things intolerable. So they withdraw from it, living in spiritual exile, or else they endeavor to transform it. In either case they are likely to lose the approval of the community, and losing the approval of the community they seek the approval of some power above or beyond it, of some authority more universally valid than that of the present world of men and things: they seek the approval of God, or the law of nature, or the inevitable class conflict, or the force outside themselves that makes for righteousness. The isolated ones, like Archimedes, find that without a fulcrum upon which to rest their lever they cannot move the inert and resistant world of men and things as they are. The eighteenth-century revolutionists, whether in thought or in deed, responded to this need. Finding themselves out of harmony with the temporary world of men and things, they endeavored to put themselves in tune with the finite powers: over against the ephemeral customs and mores, they set the universal law of nature and of nature's God; from the immediate judgments of men, they appealed to the universal judgment of humanity. Humanity was an abstraction, no doubt; but through the beneficent law of progress the wisdom of the ages would be accumulated, transmitted, and placed at the disposal of posterity. Every age would be the posterity of all preceding ages.

DIDEROT   1713–1784

Posterity is for the Philosopher what the other world is for the religious.

Which Is Better?

WALTER T. MARVIN   1872–

If science wins, the world will prove to be one in which man is thrown entirely on his own resources, skill, and self-control, his courage and his strength, perhaps on his ability to be happy in adjusting himself to pitiless fact. If science fails, there is room for childlike hopes that unseen powers may come to the aid of human weakness. If science wins, the world is the necessary consequence of logically related facts, and man's enterprise the playing of a game of chess against an opponent who never errs and never overlooks our errors. If science fails, the world resembles fairyland, and man's enterprise no longer a test of skill and knowledge, but conditioned by the goodness of his will or the possibility of luck.

E. E. CUMMINGS   1894–

> *A world of made*
> *is not a world of born — pity poor flesh*
> *and trees, poor stars and stones, but never this*
> *fine specimen of hypermagical*
> *ultraomnipotence. We doctors know*
> *a hopeless case if — listen: there's a hell*
> *of a good universe next door; let's go.*

What Are the Necessary Virtues?

JOHN VON NEUMANN   1955

The problems created by the combination of the presently possible forms of nuclear warfare and the rather unusually unstable international situation are formidable and not to be solved easily. Those of the next decades are likely to be similarly vexing, "only more so." The U.S.–U.S.S.R. tension is bad, but when other nations begin to make felt their full offensive potential weight, things will not become simpler.

Present awful possibilities of nuclear warfare may give way to others even more awful. After global climate control becomes possible, perhaps all our present involvements will seem simple. We should not deceive ourselves: once such possibilities become actual, they will be exploited. It will, therefore, be necessary to develop new political forms and procedures. All experience shows that even smaller technological changes than those now in the cards profoundly transform political and social relationships. Experience also shows that these transformations are not *a priori* predictable and that most contemporary "first guesses" concerning them are wrong. For all these reasons, one should take neither present difficulties nor presently proposed reforms too seriously.

The one solid fact is that the difficulties are due to an evolution that, while useful and constructive, is also dangerous. Can we produce the required adjustments with the necessary speed? The most hopeful answer is that the human species has been subjected to similar tests before and seems to have a congenital ability to come through, after varying amounts of trouble. To ask in advance for a complete recipe would be unreasonable. We can specify only the human qualities required: patience, flexibility, intelligence.

GOETHE

> *The shudder of awe is humanity's*
> *highest faculty,*
> *Even though this world is forever*
> *altering its values.*

THORNTON WILDER'S *Gloss:*

Out of man's recognition in fear and awe that there is an Unknowable comes all that is best in the explorations of his mind, — even though that recognition is often misled in superstition, enslavement, and overconfidence.

DON MARQUIS' *cockroach, archy*

> *i suppose the human race*
> *is doing the best it can*
> *but hells bells thats*
> *only an explanation*
> *its not an excuse*

WALT WHITMAN   1819–1892

It is provided in the essence of things that from any fruition of success, no matter what, shall come forth something to make a greater struggle necessary.

WILLIAM MORRIS

I pondered how men fight and lose the battle, and the thing that they fought for comes about in spite of their defeat, and when it comes turns out to be not what they meant, and other men have to fight for what they meant under another name.

Neighborly Affection

LEARNED HAND   1872–1961

Brandeis believed that there could be no true community save that built upon the personal acquaintance of each with each; by that alone could character and ability be rightly gauged; without that "neighborly affection" which would result, no "faith" could be nourished, "charitable" or other. Only so could the latent richness which lurks in all of us come to flower. As the social group grows too large for mutual contact and appraisal, life quickly begins to lose its flavor and its significance. Among multitudes relations must become standardized; to standardize is to generalize, and to generalize is to ignore all those authentic features which mark, and which indeed alone create, an individual. Not only is there no compensation for our losses, but most of our positive ills have directly resulted from great size. With it has indeed come the magic of modern communication and quick transport; but out of these has come the sinister apparatus of mass suggestion and mass production. Such devices, always tending more and more to reduce us to a common model, subject us — our hard-won immunity now gone — to epidemics of hallowed catchword and formula. The herd is regaining its ancient and evil primacy; civilization is being reversed, for it has consisted of exactly the opposite process of individualization — witness the history of law and morals. These many inventions are a step backward; they lull men into the belief that because they are severally less subject to violence, they are more safe; because they are more steadily fed and clothed, they are more secure from want; because their bodies are cleaner, their hearts are purer. It is an illusion; our security has actually diminished as our demands have become more exacting; our comforts we purchase at the cost of a softer fibre, a feebler will, and an infantile suggestibility.

I am well aware of the reply to all this; it is on every tongue. "Do not talk to us," you say, "of the tiny city utopias of Plato or Aristotle; or of Jefferson with his dream of a society of hardy, self-sufficient freeholders, living in proud, honorable isolation, however circumscribed. Those days are gone forever, and they are well lost. The vast command over nature which the last century gave to mankind and which is but a fragmentary earnest of the future, mankind will not forego. The conquest of disease, the elimination of drudgery, the freedom from famine, the enjoyment of comfort; yes, even that most doubtful gift, the not too distant possession of a leisure we have not yet learned to use — on these, having once tasted them, mankind will continue to insist. And, at least so far as we have gone, they appear to be conditioned upon the co-operation and organization of great numbers. Perhaps we may be able to keep and to increase our gains without working on so vast a scale; we do not know; show us and we may try; but for the present we prefer to keep along the road which has led us so far, and we will not lend an auspicious ear to jeremiads that we should retrace the steps which have brought us in sight of so glorious a consummation."

It is hard to see any answer to all this; the day has clearly gone forever of societies small enough for their members to have personal acquaintance with one another, and to find their station through the appraisal of those who have any first-hand knowledge of them. Publicity is an evil substitute, and the art of publicity is a black art; but it has come to stay, every year adds to its potency and to the finality of its judgments. The hand that rules the press, the radio, the screen, and the far-spread magazine rules the country; whether we like it or not, we must learn to accept it. And yet it is the power of reiterated suggestion and consecrated platitude that at this moment has brought our entire civilization to imminent peril of destruction. The individual is as helpless against it as the child is helpless against the formulas with which he is indoctrinated. Not only is it possible by these means to shape his tastes, his feelings, his desires, and his hopes; but it is possible to convert him into a fanatical zealot, ready to torture and destroy and to suffer mutilation and death for an obscene faith, baseless in fact, and morally monstrous. This, the vastest conflict with which mankind has ever been faced, whose outcome still remains undecided, in the end turns upon whether the individual can survive; upon whether the ultimate value shall be this wistful, cloudy, errant You or I, or that Great Beast, Leviathan, that phantom conjured up as an *ignis fatuus* in our darkness and a scapegoat for our futility.

Common Interest

SUMNER H. SLICHTER   1892–1959

What then is to be the design of the economic world of tomorrow? Will it be a world in which national life is dominated by highly organized groups which use the government in a struggle for group advantage; in which national policies are not really national; a world of parochialism and restrictions? Or will it be a world in which economic life is pretty much dominated by bureaucrats through the control of expenditures, sources of information, and power to grant or withhold favors to industries, enterprises, localities, and groups; in which the government is jealous of private enterprise, careful not to encourage it lest it challenge the power of the bureaucrats; careful to maintain tax laws that penalize initiative and daring? Or is it to be a world in which each individual thinks of himself first of all as a member of the commonwealth, highly conscious of the interests which he has in common with all other members of the commonwealth; in which individuals regard public officials of all ranks as their servants and hold them all, from President down, to strict accountability for actions and failure to act; in which public policy undertakes, not only to provide some minimum of security against the vicissitudes of economic life, but also to stimulate more vigorously than ever a wide dispersion of initiative, a vigorous spirit of enterprise, and a large amount of innovation?

Doubtless the world will be a mixture of all three. Doubtless the struggle to mould it in different directions will continue indefinitely. I like to think that victory will gradually go to those who are striving to get common interests, concern for the well-being of the other fellow, placed higher and higher in the scales of value of more and more people and who believe that the encouragement of the innovator, the experimenter, and the enterpriser is one of the most important interests which all members of the community have in common. In fact, it is difficult for me to believe that the outcome of the struggle can be otherwise. At any rate, we can feel fortunate that we live when we do; that we have an opportunity to help mould events when things are in such a state of flux; when decisions so momentous are being made. When I was a small boy, I used to think that I had missed the boat; that the men who lived at the time of the Revolution were the lucky ones. Now I know that isn't so. Of all generations we are the most fortunate. We live in an epic age. We play in by far the greatest drama the human race has ever staged; and we determine whether the outcome is tragedy.

Prologue or Epilogue

BERTRAND RUSSELL   1955

Sometimes, in moments of horror, I have been tempted to doubt whether there is any reason to wish that such a creature as man should continue to exist. It is easy to see man as dark and cruel, as an embodiment of diabolic power, and as a blot upon the fair face of the universe. But this is not the whole truth, and is not the last word of wisdom.

Man, as the Orphics said, is also the child of the starry heaven. Man, though his body is insignificant and powerless in comparison with the great bodies of the astronomer's world, is yet able to mirror that world, is able to travel in imagination and scientific knowledge through enormous abysses of space and time. What he knows already of the world in which he lives would be unbelievable to his ancestors of a thousand years ago; and in view of the speed with which he is acquiring knowledge there is every reason to think that, if he continues on his present course, what he will know a thousand years from now will be equally beyond what *we* can imagine. But it is not only, or even principally, in knowledge that man at his best deserves admiration. Men have created beauty; they have had strange visions that seemed like the first glimpse of a land of wonder, they have been capable of love, of sympathy for the whole human race, of vast hopes for mankind as a whole. These achievements, it is true, have been those of exceptional men, and have very frequently met with hostility from the herd. But there is no reason why, in the ages to come, the sort of man who is now exceptional should not become usual, and if that were to happen, the exceptional man in that new world would rise as far above Shakespeare as Shakespeare now rises above the common man. So much evil use has been made of knowledge that our imagination does not readily rise to the thought of the good uses that are possible in the raising of the level of excellence in the population at large to that which is now only achieved by men of genius. When I allow myself to hope that the world will emerge from its present troubles, and that it will someday learn to give the direction of its affairs, not to cruel mountebanks, but to men possessed of wisdom and courage, I see before me a shining vision: a world where none are hungry, where few are ill, where work is pleasant and not excessive, where kindly feeling is common, and where minds released from fear create delight for eye and ear and heart. Do not say this is impossible. It is not impossible. I do not say it can be done tomorrow, but I do say that it could be done within a thousand years, if men would bend their minds to the achievement of the kind of happiness that should be distinctive of man. I say the kind of happiness distinctive of man, because the happiness of pigs, which the enemies of Epicurus accused him of seeking, is not possible for men. If you try to make yourself content with the happiness of the pig, your suppressed potentialities will make you miserable. True happiness for human beings is possible only to those who develop their godlike potentialities to the utmost. For such men, in the world of the present day, happiness must be mixed with much pain, since they cannot escape sympathetic suffering in the spectacle of the sufferings of others. But in a society where this source of pain no longer existed, there could be a human happiness more complete, more infused with imagination and knowledge and sympathy, than anything that is possible to those condemned to live in our present gloomy epoch.

LEARNED HAND   1952

Suppose then that in the end the chance we take — the chance which we deliberately make implicit in our creed — suppose that that chance goes against us; suppose that in democracies the conflicts between the constituent groups turn out so often to submerge the common weal, that societies so organized cannot "hang together and . . . fight," as Holmes wondered. What then? Shall we have failed? I will venture to say no, not even then. For consider. Win or lose, the day will come when "the great globe itself, yea, all which it inherit, shall dissolve and . . . leave not a rack behind"; and on that day it can be said of each of us: "Thou thy worldly task hast done, home art gone, and ta'en thy wages." That is the nature of all things; though, little as we may like to acknowledge it, it is irrelevant to their value and their significance; for permanence as such has neither value nor significance. All that will then matter will be all that matters now; and what matters now is what are the wages we do take home. Those are what we choose to make them; we can fix our pay; the splendor and the tragedy of life lie just in that. Values are ultimate, they admit of no reduction below themselves; you may prefer Dante to Shakespeare, or claret to champagne; but that ends it. Nevertheless, I believe you will agree to put among the most precious and dependable of our satisfactions the joy of craftsmanship. In that I include all efforts to impose upon the outside world an invention of our own: to embody an idea in what I shall ask your leave to call an artifact. It is not important what form that may take; it may be in clay, in bronze, in paint or pencil, in a musical score or in words; it may even be in a sport; it may be in the mastery or exercise of a profession; it may be in a well-balanced nature, like Aristotle's "Great-Souled" man; or it may be in redeeming the world. It is enough that we set out to mold the motley stuff of life into some form of our own choosing; when we do, the performance is itself the wage. "The play's the thing." Never mind that we are bound to fail, for the artifact will never quite embody the image; and besides, the image changes as the work goes on. A friend recently sent me this quotation from Lord Acton: "There is no error so monstrous that it fails to find defenders among the ablest men. Imagine a congress of eminent celebrities such as More, Bacon, Pascal, Cromwell, Bossuet, Montesquieu, Jefferson, Napoleon. . . . The result would be an encyclopedia of error." Therefore let us not fear failure: " 'Tis not in mortals to command success but we'll do more, Sempronius, — we'll deserve it." And deserve it we can; not necessarily in our harvest, but in the resolution with which we till the soil. In the work, moreover, we shall find our reward, and reward enough — on the whole the best of rewards — let performance fall as far behind conception as it may.

W. B. YEATS   1865–1939

> *Everything that man esteems*
> *Endures a moment or a day.*
> *Love's pleasure drives his love away,*
> *The painter's brush consumes his dreams;*
> *The herald's cry, the soldier's tread*
> *Exhaust his glory and his might:*
> *Whatever flames upon the night*
> *Man's own resinous heart has fed.*

The Freedoms and the Goal

SUMNER WELLES   1892–1961

As the months pass, two extreme schools of thought will become more and more vocal — the first, stemming from the leaders of the group which preached extreme isolation, will once more proclaim that war in the rest of the world every twenty years or so is inevitable; that we can stay out if we so desire, and that any assumption by this country of any form of responsibility for what goes on in the world means our unnecessary involvement in war; the other, of which very often men of the highest idealism and sincerity are the spokesmen, will maintain that the United States must assume the burdens of the entire globe; must see to it that the standards in which we ourselves believe must immediately be adopted by all of the peoples of the earth, and must undertake to inculcate in all parts of the world our own policies of social and political reform, whether the other peoples involved so desire or not. While under a different guise, this school of thought is in no way dissimilar in theory from the strange doctrine of incipient "bear-the-white-man's-burden" imperialism which flared in this country in the first years of this century.

The people of the United States today realize that the adoption of either one of these two philosophies would prove equally dangerous to the future well-being of our nation.

Our free world must be founded on the four freedoms — freedom of speech and of religion — and freedom from want and from fear.

I do not believe that the two first freedoms — of speech and of religion — can ever be assured to mankind, so long as want and war are permitted to ravage the earth. Freedom of speech and of religion need only protection; they require only relief from obstruction.

Freedom from fear — the assurance of peace; and freedom from want — the assurance of individual personal security, require all of the implementation which the genius of man can devise through effective forms of international co-operation.

Peace — freedom from fear — cannot be assured until the nations of the world, particularly the great powers, and that includes the United States, recognize that the threat of war anywhere throughout the globe threatens their own security — and until they are jointly willing to exercise the police powers necessary to prevent such threats from materializing into armed hostilities.

And since policemen might be tyrants if they had no political superiors, freedom from fear also demands some form of organized international political co-operation, to make the rules of international living and to change them as the years go by, and some sort of international court to adjudicate disputes. With effective institutions of that character to insure equity and justice, and the continued will to make them work, the peoples of the world should at length be able to live out their lives in peace.

Freedom from want requires these things:

People who want to work must be able to find useful jobs, not sometimes, not in good years only, but continuously.

These jobs must be at things which they do well, and which can be done well in the places where they work.

They must be able to exchange the things which they produce, on fair terms, for other things which other people, often in other places, can make better than they.

Efficient and continuous production, and fair exchange, are both necessary to the abundance which we seek, and they depend upon each other. In the past we have succeeded better with production than exchange. Production is called into existence by the prospects for exchange, prospects which have constantly been thwarted by all kinds of inequalities, imperfections, and restrictions. The problem of removing obstacles to fair exchange — the problem of distribution of goods and purchasing power — is far more difficult than the problem of production.

It will take much wisdom, much co-operative effort,

and much surrender of private, short-sighted, and sectional self-interest to make these things all come true, but the goal is freedom from want — individual security and national prosperity — and is everlastingly worth striving for.

As mankind progresses on the path towards the goal of freedom from want and from fear, freedom of religion and of speech will more and more become a living reality.

Never before have peace and individual security been classed as freedom. Never before have they been placed alongside of religious liberty and free speech as human freedoms which should be inalienable.

Upon these four freedoms must rest the structure of the future free world.

Gentlemen, we won't get a free world any other way.

A Wise New World

LLOYD GARRISON   1897–

Once, not so long ago, we were pioneers. Pioneers were the original rugged individualists, and from them we have inherited many of our ideals. But today when we point to the virtues of rugged individualism we are apt to forget that the typical pioneer was in fact a member of a community. He was building, not just a home for himself, but a village, a town. He was founding communities; and this sense of working for something larger than himself, of giving the best of himself to a joint undertaking, lent meaning to his life. In addition, he was something of an artist, a creator; he made gardens out of a wilderness, he built houses and furniture and wagons, he fashioned tools, and his wife spun wool. This creativeness also lent meaning to his life.

In our times the disappearance of the frontier, the minute subdivision of labor, the proliferation of great cities in which men are mere atoms, and the multiplication of white-collar jobs of every description, have done two things to us. They have robbed life of its creativeness, and they have thrown people in upon themselves instead of outward into community undertakings. The result has been a shrivelling of the spirit and a moral emptiness and uncertainty which have made people increasingly sick at heart. I do not say that this is true of all of us. There are skilled craftsmen, artists, inventors, executives, organizers, engineers, intellectuals, who know the satisfaction of creating things by hand or brain. There are farmers who share the same satisfaction. But the majority of people lead lives of routine repetition and, particularly in the larger cities, they are cut off from participation in community undertakings, which are mainly in the hands of subdivided and routinized civil servants. And I say that these are the chief causes of the spiritual uneasiness which has gripped western civilization.

No one would turn the clock back if he could. The wilderness and the pioneer are gone, and we have said farewell to them. We must take life as we find it and improve it as we can. We can improve it only if we have a vision of things worth working for. Here is such a vision.

Peace has returned to earth. America is part of an association of nations with a joint pool of forces ready to prevent the breaking of a new international code of order. Through international agencies of which America is a part, staffed with an international civil service in which young men and women like yourselves, drawn from many lands, are serving, a great work of rehabilitation and reconstruction is going forward. Waste areas throughout the world are being reclaimed by irrigation. New power projects are harnessing untapped sources of power, to be utilized by new industries, including synthetics of all sorts. The nations are becoming more self-sufficient and less likely as a consequence to be tempted into wars. Colonial possessions have been put under international management by the international civil service. Capital has been pooled for the further deveolpment of these possessions, particularly to make them more habitable for people from temperate climates, in order to facilitate immigration and reduce population pressures in particular areas.

This world-wide effort to raise the standard of living of mankind is accompanied by educational and public health programs designed to bring into the stream of the world's culture the hidden and undeveloped talents of hundreds of millions of so-called backward people of all races and colors.

While all of this co-operative and creative activity has been going forward abroad, and the first outlines of a true world community have been laid at home many changes have been taking place. Everywhere great housing developments have been undertaken; most of the city workers have been moved into rural neighborhoods, whence they are transported to work by busses over superhighways. Slums have disappeared from the cities and parks have taken their places. Crime has been reduced to the vanishing point. Health is at a new peak.

Because of vastly increased productivity, hours of labor per shift have been greatly reduced so that people have time to be with their children, to work in their gardens or about their houses, to make things, to play games and music, to read, to live as men and women were meant to live. Everywhere parks, concert-halls, tennis courts, skating rinks, swimming pools, picnic grounds, and other civic improvements have been built or are being built, largely by volunteer community labor under skilled direction. Further plans for community undertakings of this sort are constantly being discussed, in the schools, in the homes, in meetings. Everyone is invited to do something according to his talents — painter, sculptor, landscape architect, musician, athlete, woodcarver, metal-worker — old and young, men and women, all alike participate voluntarily in one or another undertaking. Some give one day a week, some two, some several hours a day.

New skills are taught in the schools to aid in these projects. The latest developments in moving pictures are revolutionizing education. Through their visual magic the horizons of the mind are being constantly expanded, and the high schools and colleges are becoming centers of adult education and of community discussion on a scale hitherto undreamed of. The career of teaching has taken on a new significance and dignity, and the work of the classroom has been revivified and stimulated by the newly aroused adult interest in education.

By international agreement, universal military training has been abolished, but the principle of universal service has been retained. Each young man on finishing high school serves the country for a year. He spends a summer in a camp in some part of the country which is new to him. There he receives physical training, and he helps in various public projects — reforestation, road-building, soil conservation, and the like. After that he is put to work back home in some municipal, county, or state department of government. He is paid a subsistence wage. He learns in school to prepare himself for his governmental assignment, which has been made in advance for this purpose. During his governmental period of service he is taught as much as possible about the work of his department and of other departments. He learns his civics by doing. He becomes a citizen by participation in government. He is a member of a democratic community, and he knows it.

Each young man on leaving college is similarly mustered into the government service for a year, this time in more advanced positions, normally in some federal department or agency. For this task he similarly prepares himself in college. There is the closest co-operation between educational authorities and government. Many of the best men are recruited into permanent positions. The quality of government personnel has gone up as a result. Graft and petty partisanship have declined; politics has taken on a new tone.

Whatever I have said about men applies equally to women. They too are recruited for service, with the same objectives.

The citizens, having thus participated directly in government, no longer look upon it as something alien or to be feared. It is theirs, for their service. They have helped to make it. They know all about it. They understand what it is up to. Their advice and criticisms are informed and helpful. They have brought about many changes, have simplified much, have decentralized much. They do not hesitate to use government freely, in whatever connections it can be most useful. They know its limitations also.

This would be a democracy worth striving for. It would give to its citizens a new pride, a new knowledge, a new sense of belonging and contributing to a going community, and a better chance to put their talents to creative uses.

This is what Garrison said at Lawrence College, Wisconsin, in 1942.

Solidarity

CLEMENCEAU   1841–1929

If Jay Gould found himself shipwrecked on a desert island with a beggar, the two of them, finding themselves more and more comrades, would work for each other like brothers, and soon probably they would love each other. But now, because the island is very large and instead of there being only two of them there are millions, the beggar starves at Gould's door, and he pays no heed and takes credit for paying some clergyman of I know not what church to tell him that the poor hate the rich and the rich fear the poor.

That is anarchy, no less.

Jay Gould, my good friend and brother, and you, poor wretch, I tell you, you are two shipwrecked sailors for a day, on a great floating island drawn by unknown currents through an ocean without horizons. The law of solidarity which you felt so deeply when you were confined on a narrow ledge of rock and soil beaten by the waves does not depend on the quantity of earth on which you live. On the great continent of this planet, that same law holds you and will not let you go. The evil you do, on a day unknown but sure to come, will be fatally re-

paid to you. It would be wise to help each other here as
you did there. When this feeling of solidarity truly becomes yours, when it descends from your lips into your
heart, when it has penetrated your life, new duties will
become plain to you that are now sleeping obscurely in
your soul. A man dying of hunger beside a man who is
piling up more than he can enjoy, an accumulation of
wealth that he makes out of others' privation, will become a spectacle as intolerable as slavery would be for
us today, which was yet an institution that was accepted
by souls as high as Washington and Jefferson a hundred
years ago.

EMERSON					1844

I have just been conversing with one man, to whom no
weight of adverse experience will make it for a moment
appear impossible that thousands of human beings
might exercise towards each other the grandest and simplest sentiments, as well as a knot of friends, or a pair of
lovers.

Political Love

HENRY DEMAREST LLOYD					1847–1903

Love is the ideal, and the real is the progressive compromises it makes with its other half — self-interest. The
reconciliation of individual love and social love with
each other, of individual self-interest and social self-
interest, of both kinds of love with both kinds of self-
interest — that is the life of all for all. Every act of life,
like every act of the plants or the planets, is a compromise. If we don't like the word compromise, we can say
composition. To go anywhere, to do anything, we have
to balance. We cannot by any smoothness of phrase nor
cunning of panacea save ourselves the trouble of making
a new decision at every crisis, and every act is a crisis.
The political economist thinks he has made the social
world simple by throwing away sympathy. But he has
only made it impossible. The transcendentalist thinks
we have but to deny self-interest and we will find in love

the universal solvent. But the solvent has nothing to solve. Self-interest, the competition of self-interest, are as right as love and its self-surrenders. Love makes for the centre, the people. Self-interest for the circumstance, the individual. Love unites, self-interest separates.

Private property being individualism, and its abolition being socialism, the two are correlative and must yield to each other just as rapidly as experience and necessity dictate. Civilization is a growth both ways — an intensification of private property in certain ways, an abolition of it in others. The home property is likely to become more and more individual or familistic as against the community, but those forms of property in which the welfare of others is more concerned than that of the owner will be modified or abolished. The wonderful development of the modern individual out of the rudimentary monotony of the tribe or animal life has gone on with an equally wonderful development of the socialization of the postoffice, the administration of justice, wagon roads, schools, currency, police, and war, all of which used to be entirely or partially individual. The higher the individualism, the higher must be the socialism. The resultant of these opposing forces of socialism and individualism must be determined by each age for itself, but history shows plainly how the lines advance on each other.

In the coming crash, which must follow the insane wars of troops and tariffs and all the insensate suppression of wealth involved in property become monopoly and opportunity become privilege, those countries will have the best chance of survival which have the least wealth and the most commonwealth. What oak there is left in the timbers of England is co-operative. That co-operative one-sixth of the population will be the saving remnant that will save the rest. The wealth created by a thousand men under the motive power of the self-interest of the capitalist is not, and cannot be, equal to the wealth that will be created by the same men under the motive power of co-operation or democracy. The system which comes nearest to calling out all the self-interests and using all the faculties and sharing all the benefits will outcompete any system that strikes a lower level of motive faculty and profit. The capitalists are the co-operators that were; the people are the co-operators that will be.

The Master Motive

HENRY GEORGE   1839–1897

Give labor a free field and its full earnings; take for the benefit of the whole community that fund which the growth of the community creates, and want and the fear of want would be gone. The springs of production would be set free, and the enormous increase of wealth would give the poorest ample comfort. Men would no more worry about finding employment than they worry about finding air to breathe; they need have no more care about physical necessities than do the lilies of the field. The progress of science, the march of invention, the diffusion of knowledge, would bring their benefits to all.

With this abolition of want and the fear of want, the admiration of riches would decay, and men would seek the respect and approbation of their fellows in other modes than by the acquisition and display of wealth. In this way there would be brought to the management of public affairs, and the administration of common funds, the skill, the attention, the fidelity, and integrity that can now be secured only for private interests, and a railroad or gas works might be operated on public account, not only more economically and efficiently than as at present, under joint-stock management, but as economically and efficiently as would be possible under a single ownership. The prize of the Olympian games, that called forth the most strenuous exertions of all Greece, was but a wreath of wild olive; for a bit of ribbon men have over and over again performed services no money could have bought.

Shortsighted is the philosophy which counts on selfishness as the master motive of human action. It is blind to facts of which the world is full. It sees not the present, and reads not the past aright. If you would move men to action, to what shall you appeal? Not to their pockets, but to their patriotism; not to selfishness, but to sympathy. Self-interest is, as it were, a mechanical force — potent, it is true; capable of large and wide results. But there is in human nature what may be likened to a chemical force; which melts and fuses and overwhelms; to which nothing seems impossible. "All that a man hath will he give for his life" — that is self-interest. But in loyalty to higher impulses men will give even life.

And this force of forces — that now goes to waste or assumes perverted forms — we may use for the strengthening, and building up, and ennobling of society, if we but will, just as we now use physical forces that once seemed but powers of destruction. All we have to do is but to give it freedom and scope. The wrong that produces inequality; the wrong that in the midst of abundance tortures men with want or harries them with the fear of want; that stunts them physically, degrades them intellectually, and distorts them morally, is what alone prevents harmonious social development. For "all that is from the gods is full of providence. We are made for co-operation — like feet, like hands, like eyelids, like the rows of the upper and lower teeth."

There are people into whose heads it never enters to conceive of any better state of society than that which now exists — who imagine that the idea that there could be a state of society in which greed would be banished, prisons stand empty, individual interests be subordinated to general interests, and no one seek to rob or to oppress his neighbor, is but the dream of impracticable dreamers, for whom these practical level-headed men, who pride themselves on recognizing facts as they are, have a hearty contempt. But such men — though some of them write books, and some of them occupy the chairs of universities, and some of them stand in pulpits — do not think.

The fact is that the work which improves the condition of mankind, the work which extends knowledge and increases power, and enriches literature, and elevates thought, is not done to secure a living. It is not the work of slaves, driven to their task either by the lash of a master or by animal necessities. It is the work of men who perform it for its own sake, and not that they may get more to eat or drink, or wear, or display. In a state of society where want was abolished, work of this sort would be enormously increased.

To remove want and the fear of want, to give to all classes leisure, and comfort, and independence, the decencies and refinements of life, the opportunities of mental and moral development, would be like turning water into a desert. The sterile waste would clothe itself with verdure, and the barren places where life seemed banned would ere long be dappled with the shade of trees and musical with the song of birds. Talents now hidden, virtues unsuspected, would come forth to make human life richer, fuller, happier, nobler. For in these round men who are stuck into three-cornered holes, and three-cornered men who are jammed into round holes; in these men who are wasting their energies in the scramble to be rich; in these who in factories are turned into machines, or are chained by necessity to bench or plow; in these children who are growing up in squalor, and vice, and ignorance, are powers of the highest order, talents the most splendid. They need but the opportunity to bring them out.

Consider the possibilities of a state of society that gave that opportunity to all. Let imagination fill out the picture; its colors grow too bright for words to paint. Consider the moral elevation, the intellectual activity, the social life. Consider how by a thousand actions and interactions the members of every community are linked together, and how in the present condition of things even the fortunate few who stand upon the apex of the social pyramid must suffer, though they know it not, from the want, ignorance, and degradation that are underneath. Consider these things and then say whether the change I propose would not be for the benefit of everyone — even the greatest landholder? Would he not be safer of the future of his children in leaving them

penniless in such a state of society than in leaving them
the largest fortune in this? Did such a state of society
exist, would he not buy entrance to it cheaply by giving
up all his possessions?

EMERSON   1845

Our impatience of miles, when we are in a hurry; but it
is still best that a mile should have seventeen hundred
and sixty yards.

The Task of Morals

GEORGE SANTAYANA   1863–1952

For the Greek as for the Jew the task of morals is the
same: to subdue nature as far as possible to the uses of
the soul, by whatever agencies material or spiritual may
be at hand; and when a limit is reached in that direction,
to harden and cauterize the heart in the face of inevitable evils, opening it wide at the same time to every
sweet influence that may descend to it from heaven.
Never for a moment was positive religion entangled in
a sophistical optimism. Never did it conceive that the
most complete final deliverance and triumph would *justify* the evils which they abolished. As William James
put it, in his picturesque manner, if at the last day all
creation was shouting hallelujah and there remained
one cockroach with an unrequited love, *that* would spoil
the universal harmony; it would spoil it, he meant, in
truth and for the tender philosopher, but probably not
for those excited saints. James was thinking chiefly of
the present and future, but the same scrupulous charity
has its application to the past. To remove an evil is not
to remove the fact that it has existed. The tears that
have been shed were shed in bitterness, even if a remorse-
ful hand afterwards wipes them away. To be patted on
the back and given a sugar plum does not reconcile even
a child to a past injustice. And the case is much worse if
we are expected to make our heaven out of the foolish
and cruel pleasures of contrast, or out of the pathetic
obfuscation produced by a great relief. Such a heaven

would be a lie, like the sardonic heavens of Calvin and Hegel. The existence of any evil anywhere at any time absolutely ruins a total optimism.

Vision Is Virtue

A. N. WHITEHEAD   1861–1947

Mankind is now in one of its rare moods of shifting its outlook. The mere compulsion of tradition has lost its force. It is the business of philosophers, students, and practical men to re-create and re-enact a vision of the world, conservative and radical, including those elements of reverence and order without which society lapses into riot, a vision penetrated through and through with unflinching rationality. Such a vision is the knowledge which Plato identified with virtue.

Epochs for which, within the limits of their development, this vision has been widespread, are the epochs unfading in the memory of mankind. There is now no choice before us: either we must succeed in providing a rational co-ordination of impulses and thoughts, or for centuries civilization will sink into a mere welter of minor excitements. We must produce a great age, or see the collapse of the upward striving of our race.

The next piece is from the *Republic.* It has been very freely done into English by one of the editors. The analogy of the movie instead of Plato's complicated apparatus of shadows in a cave cast by images carried by men hidden by a wall, etc., is not his own. Francis M. Cornford refers to it in a footnote to his recent and excellent translation, but he keeps it out of his text. We understand that it was Frank C. Babbitt's.

About the *Republic,* many say simply that it is the best book of all. But not everybody. Jefferson wrote to John Adams:

> I amused myself with reading seriously Plato's *Republic.* I am wrong, however, in calling it amusement, for it was the heaviest task-work I ever went through. I had occasionally before taken up some of his other works, but scarcely ever had patience to go through a whole dialogue. While wading through the whimsies, the puerilities, and unintelligible jargon of this work, I laid it down often to ask myself how it could have been, that the world should have so long consented to give reputation to such nonsense as this?

Anyhow, don't forget what Pascal said:

> We can only think of Plato and Aristotle in grand academic robes. They were good fellows, like anyone, laughing with their friends, and when they enjoyed themselves with writing their Laws and their Politics, they did it for amusement. That was the least philosophic and the least serious part of their life. The most philosophic was living simply and tranquilly. If they wrote politics, it was like making rules for a lunatic asylum, and if they have seemed to speak of it in the grand manner, it was because they knew that the lunatics for whom they were speaking thought of themselves as kings and emperors.

The Cave

PLATO   427–347 B.C.

Let me offer you an analogy. Suppose a race of men who were born and brought up all their lives in a movie, who have never taken their eyes off the screen. All they have ever seen are the pictures, and all they have ever heard, except each other, is the sound track. That, and only that, is their world.

I am not concerned with what sort of picture they see. My point is that all they see, all they have ever seen, are pictures on a screen; and that those pictures are all the reality they know.

Now suppose that one of them is taken out; forcibly, because he is being taken away from everything he has been used to, from everything he regards as his world and his life. He is taken out into the sunlight, and the sunlight blinds him. The glitter and dazzle hurt him, and he cannot see any of the things he is shown, the things we now tell him are real.

He would have to get slowly used to these real things, perhaps by looking sideways at them at first, or at their shadows, or by looking at the stars or at the moon, before he could look at things by the light of the sun, let alone the sun itself.

What would he think, when he was finally able to look at these real things? He would know at last that it is the sun that relates the seasons and the courses of time, and

that the sun is the reason behind all that he and his comrades used to see on the screen. He would remember his
old companions and their opinions. And would he not
be happy over what had happened to him and sorry for
them, even a little contemptuous?

Now suppose he went back into the movie, suddenly
out of the sunshine and into the dark. Wouldn't his old
friends laugh at him? For he would not be able to see
the shadows on the screen. He would take a long time
to get used again to the darkness. And they would laugh
at anyone who had been out and come back with his
sight nearly gone; and as for the person who had taken
him up and might force another of them up, and set
others free of their darkness, would they not want to kill
him?

Yes, they would.

This is the analogy I wanted to make. Our visible
world is the inside of the movie house, and the light of
the projector corresponds to the sun. Coming out of the
movie into the sunlight is the soul's ascent into regions
of intelligence. God knows if that is a true simile. But
so it seems to me. In the visible world, where only things
can be known and scarcely understood, this idea of the
Good which we are seeking is the last thing to be understood, and that darkly. But once it is seen and understood, it is obvious to all that it is the very cause of all
that is right and all that is beautiful. To the eye, it is
the sun giving light and the lord of light, at once the
seeing and the seen. To the mind and intelligence, it is
the lord and very truth itself, both the understanding
and the understood. And for anyone to act with wisdom,
whether in private or in public affairs, he must have seen
it and understood it, this idea of the Good.

No wonder that those who have seen and understood
want nothing to do with the affairs of men. Naturally
enough, their souls strike upwards toward that other
world. I think this, too, lies in our analogy. And no
wonder, too, that our man coming down among the miseries of mankind again feels out of place and clumsy, and
appears rather ridiculous. Let him, still blind, not yet

used to the dark, have to appear in a court or some such place and have to wrangle over the shadows of justice with men who have never seen justice itself as he has seen it.

A man who understands would not laugh when he saw our man clumsy and confused. He would know that our man had just come out of the light into darkness, and not out of the darkness into light. He would know which way the man's soul had been turned.

For, as such a man would know, our eyes can be turned to the light as well as toward the dark. If our whole soul is turned away from this visible world toward the bright regions, then our eyes can become able to understand the Good.

There must be some way, some technique of doing this. Do you not believe that it is a turning round of the soul into the right direction so that the eyes may see? For we all have eyes, though we do not know where to look. Untaught we cannot look in the right direction. There are mean men with keen eyes, small men, but smart, bad men, who are quick to discern what concerns them. They see only the things in the way they are looking. If their souls were turned round and pointed in the other direction, then that same keen vision would be as quick to see the Good as our man whom we have forced out into the sunlight and forced to turn his soul toward the Good.

Thus, I think, we draw toward a conclusion, and I believe it is this. Men whose souls have never been turned and who have never had sight of the Good and thereby experience of the truth cannot govern us. They lack that single illuminated purpose toward which all they do must be directed. And I conclude likewise that the others cannot be allowed to go on to the end they seek. Such men must be made to turn back, though it brings them back from the Isles of the Blessed, where they think they are already abiding.

Yes, I said, we are the founders of this state and we must compel the best of our citizens to reach what we think is the greatest understanding, to see the Good, and to climb the heights. But then, as soon as they have seen enough, we must refuse to let them linger there. They must go back again and share the labors and the honors of those who are the darkness inside.

We must do them this wrong. We must lay the worse life upon them, though they are capable of the best. For we are not concerned to make any one class in our state happy. We are trying to make our commonwealth happy as one whole, uniting them all in a harmony which we shall secure partly by compulsion, partly by persuasion. We shall require each to contribute what each can, and if we force a man into the sun and teach him to see the Good, we may not allow him to go his own way. We must likewise force him down and make him bind the state together in the common good and to a common end.

LEONARDO DA VINCI   1452–1519

In rivers the water that you touch is the last of what has passed and the first of that which comes: so with time present.

Reference to Sources

THIS LIST is not complete. Many of the sources already appear in the course of the book. Many are obvious. For some, picked up in secondary sources, the editors had no specific reference, but that seemed no good reason not to use what was worthy to be received for its own sake. Who wrote it is much less important than what was written.

This is no apparatus for scholars. It is by way of a general answer to a good many inquiries and a response to more than a few protests that references were not given in the first place.

PAGE

1   Emerson, "The American Scholar," Phi Beta Kappa Address, 1837.

3   Holmes said, in a speech to the Middlesex (Massachusetts) Bar Association on December 3, 1902, "Goethe said that two wise men could tell each other all they knew in a couple of days." The editors got their improved version from a man who painted Holmes's portrait years later.

     Adams wrote this to Jefferson on June 28, 1812, in the course of the correspondence between them when they were both old and retired and at last friends. See *Life and Works of John Adams,* edited by C. F. Adams, page 19.

4   The Thoreau is from his *Journal* for March 15, 1842. You will find it in the extracts edited by H. G. O. Blake called *Early Spring in Massachusetts,* page 139.

     The Holmes letter to Pollock was written on November 22, 1920. It is in the second volume of the *Holmes-Pollock Letters,* page 59.

     Unamuno, in the translation by Flitch, on page 34.

5   Robinson, *The Mind in the Making,* pages 33, 37–38, 40–42.

PAGE

7   *Pascal's Pensées,* No. 276, in Brunschwicq's edition.
    Keats's letter to Reynolds on February 19, 1818.

8   Freud. This is from *A General Selection from Freud,*
    edited by John Rickman, Hogarth Press, 1937, pages 45–
    51.

13 Wallas's *The Great Society,* page 214.

14 For the Heraclitus, Burnet's *Early Greek Philosophy.*

20 Whitehead's *Science and the Modern World,* chapter 6.

31 The piece from Peirce is too much cut. If you can't
    find the old files of the *Popular Science Monthly,* look
    in the *Collected Papers* edited by Hartshorne and Weiss,
    published by the Harvard University Press, volume V,
    or in Buchler's selections published by Harcourt Brace
    in 1940.

39 The first paragraph of the James comes from *Some Prob-
    lems of Philosophy,* the rest from the preface to *The
    Meaning of Truth,* which you will find in Charles M.
    Bakewell's selections in the Everyman volume on page
    164.

41 Bacon's *De Augmentis,* book I. Plato somewhere com-
    pares his dialectic, with its question and answer coming
    closer and closer to a definition, to sexual intercourse,
    mind working on mind.
    Holmes's *Collected Legal Papers,* pages 310–11.

42 Freud's *Civilization and Its Discontents.*
    The Whitehead is in chapter 1 of *Science and the
    Modern World.*
    The Henry Adams is from *The Education of Henry
    Adams,* pages 231–32.

43 Holmes's *Collected Legal Papers,* pages 311–12.

44 Freud's "Reflections on War and Death."
    Whitehead's *Science and the Modern World* again, chap-
    ter 3.
    Bridgman's *The Intelligent Individual and Society.*

47 But the book of Bridgman's to read is *The Logic of
    Modern Physics,* at least the early chapters.

PAGE

49   Dickinson, the Centenary Edition, page 22, and the poem on the next page, page 160.

Eliot's little book on Dante, pages 58–59.

50   Dingle's *Science and Human Experience,* pages 96–97. There is more, just as good and better in this short book.

52   The Peirce is in Buchler's selections, page 156, and in Peirce's *Collected Papers,* volume VI, section 477. Hence, as Whitehead says, to be distrusted. However, to go on, see Goethe's short essay on nature, or almost anything he wrote about nature.

55   Philip Shen writes us that David Yu told him that these five words of Whitehead come from his *Concept of Nature,* page 163.

The Poincaré comes from "La Science et L'Hypothèse," and it is quoted in *The Education,* on page 454.

The Whitehead comes from chapter 3 of *Science and the Modern World.*

58   Henderson's lecture "The Study of Man," published by the University of Pennsylvania in 1941.

Pareto's *General Sociology,* section 540.

59   James's *Principles of Psychology,* volume 2, a footnote on page 674.

60   Dewey's *The Quest for Certainty,* chapter 6.

61   Whitehead's *Symbolism.*

65   Emerson's *Journal* for October, 1872.

Wendell's *English Composition,* 1891.

Wallas's *The Art of Thought,* chapter 4. This is the Wallas to read, this and *The Great Society.*

73   Whitehead's *Science and the Modern World,* chapter 12.

Sumner's *Folkways,* section 1.

75   Chapman's *Emerson Sixty Years Later*; and his letter to Henry James in *John Jay Chapman and His Letters,* edited by M. A. DeWolfe Howe, page 418.

76   The Holmes, from *Lochner v. New York,* 198 U.S. at 74. The great dissent, in 1905, when a New York statute

fixing maximum hours for bakers was held unconstitutional as an interference with liberty of contract. So great that it is now a classic commonplace.

The Peirce can be found in his *Collected Papers,* volume I, sections 619–21 and section 672.

78   Chesterton's *Heretics.*

Huxley in a letter to Tyndall.

81   *Holmes-Pollock Letters,* volume II, page 178.

Huxley's *Lay Sermons.*

83   Thoreau's *Letters,* edited by R. W. Emerson.

85   Montaigne's *Autobiography* which Marvin Lowenthal made up from the *Essays.*

This letter from Machiavelli of December 10, 1513, appears in Toynbee's *Study of History,* volume III. See Somervell's one-volume abridgment, page 229, for what use Toynbee makes of it.

88   The Vinci from his notebooks.

The Jane Austen comes, of course, from *Emma.*

Bagehot's *Physics and Politics,* pages 186–87. There's not enough Bagehot in this book.

89   Selden's *Table Talk.*

Thomas Love Peacock in *The Misfortunes of Elphin.*

The Duchess of Argyle — we wish we knew.

Lowes Dickinson's *Letters from a Chinese Official,* pages 49–50.

90   Huxley's *Proper Studies,* the chapter on the Essence of Religion.

The bits from Confucius were culled from Lin Yutang's *The Wisdom of China and India.*

94   Chesterfield's letter to his son is easy to find. Bacon somewhere refers to "the culture and manurance of minds in youth."

95   For the Newton letter, look in Sir David Brewster's *Memoirs of Newton,* volume I, page 387.

98   The Pavlov appeared in *Sciences* on April 17 (1935), page 369.

PAGE

99   The James letter to T. W. Ward, *Letters of William James,* volume I, page 133.

Osler, to his students at McGill, in 1899, in his *Aequanimitas,* page 213.

100   Goethe, from *Xenien.*

Ruskin is quoted by Irving Babbitt in "On Being Creative."

The Emerson is in his essay on Plato.

The next Osler is from his *Life* by Harvey Cushing, volume II, page 304.

101   The Hobbes is from chapter 6 of the *Leviathan.*

The James is from *Principles of Psychology,* page 187 of the "Briefer Course."

103   Chesterton's "Alarms and Discussions."

Léon Blum's book on Marriage.

107   *Holmes-Pollock Letters,* volume I, page 161.

Huckleberry Finn.

109   Again from Peirce's *Collected Papers,* volume I, sections 666, 667, and 669.

110   Learned Hand said this at the Bryn Mawr Commencement on June 2, 1927. Read anything of him you can put your hand on.

112   Emerson's *Journal* for June, 1863, and the other on October 25, 1867.

Pavlov, *Lectures on Conditioned Reflexes.*

113   The Holmes is from a letter he wrote to Charles Bunn, who had been selected to be his secretary but went to war instead.

Lowell wrote this in *What a University President Has Learned,* 1938.

Emerson, also from the *Journal,* April 11, 1834.

Holmes, again the *Collected Legal Papers,* page 273.

114   Henderson, this from his preface to a translation of Claude Bernard's *Experimental Medicine.*

Bertrand Russell, from a Haldeman-Julius pamphlet, *How to Become a Mathematician,* 1942.

PAGE

Pascal's *Pensées,* no. 18, Brunschwicq's edition.

The Maitland is from his "Memoir on Mary Bateson," in his *Papers,* volume III, page 541.

115   This is the last paragraph of Cozzen's *The Just and the Unjust,* which well may be the best novel for the young lawyer to read.

Holmes spoke on Memorial Day, this first one on May 30, 1884, the other on May 30, 1895. Read with these his letters home from the Civil War, *Touched with Fire,* edited by Mark Howe, 1947, and you will know better what he meant on Memorial Day.

116   The last paragraph from *The Last Adam,* which is as much a novel for young doctors as the other is for young lawyers.

119   James's essay "The Energies of Men" is in the Everyman volume.

122   So is his essay "On a Certain Blindness in Human Beings."

123   This is from *Walden.* More on page 221 below.

124   This is more from "On a Certain Blindness. . . ."

131   Trevelyan, from *The Present Position of History.*

132   Oppenheimer's *The Open Mind,* pages 123–24.

Lanfrey's *History of Napoleon,* volume 3, page 2 (1870).

133   Barraclough, in his inaugural lecture as Toynbee's successor in the Chair of International History at Chatham House, reprinted in *International Affairs,* January, 1958.

Nash, *The University and the Modern World.*

134   Ferguson's *Greek Imperialism,* pages 108–9 (1913).

Basil Willey in *The Seventeenth Century Background,* pages 12–14. A Doubleday Anchor book.

136   This address is reprinted in Henry Adams' *The Degradation of Democratic Dogma.*

141   Brooks Adams' *The Law of Civilization and Decay.* There is a new edition edited by Charles Beard.

143   Maitland's *Collected Papers,* volume III, page 439.

Acton's *The Study of History*. The paragraphs, as Judge Charles E. Wyzanski, Jr., spotted, are out of order: pages 61–68, 73–74, and 53–56.

147   This is reported by Goethe's friend, Chancellor von Mueller, on November 4, 1823. There is another on page 510. See the note there.

Lord Acton's cryptic remark comes from *The Study of History,* a lecture given on June 11, 1895.

148   Beard is thus quoted in the *Reader's Digest* for February, 1941.

This is from Buchan's Rede Lecture in 1929.

151   Pascal's *Pensées,* no. 176, again from Brunschwicq's edition.

From *Jefferson Himself,* edited by Bernard Mayo, pages 339–40.

152   Fisher's *A History of Europe,* preface.

Isaiah Berlin, in *Historical Inevitability,* pages 3, 13–15.

155   This is all from volume I of the *Study,* and a most inadequate presentation of Toynbee.

164   Barraclough's *History in a Changing World,* pages 235–38.

171   Trevelyan's *History of England,* pages 351–52.

172   Elizabeth to a committee of Parliament. You will find it in Chamberlain's *Sayings of Queen Elizabeth.*

Maitland's *Collected Papers,* volume 3, pages 157–60. Is the misprint in the third line on page 173 corrected in your copy? It should be *wears,* not *gears.*

175   Clarendon's *History of the Civil Wars in England,* volume III. Here is history in the grand manner.

183   Buchan's *Oliver Cromwell.*

The other two pieces are in the *Dictionary of National Biography,* volume XIII, in C. H. Firth's article on Cromwell.

Parkman's *The Jesuits in North America,* much too much cut.

192   From DeVoto's *Minority Report*. American history as she ought to be writ. Read *The Year of Decision* and *Across the Wide Missouri*.

195   Dos Passos' *U.S.A.*

205   From John Adams' "Diary for 1775," in his *Works*, edited by C. F. Adams.

208   Montaigne, book II, chapter 10.
       From *Cobb of "The World"* by John L. Heaton.

213   The Dickinson is on page 235 of the Centenary Edition.

215   From *Storm*, pages 7–8. Read about this storm. Her name was Maria.

216   Emerson's *Journal* again, for May 25, 1843.
       Guy Murchie, from *Song of the Sky*.

218   From The Corsican, pages 471–2, which R. M. Johnston edited. It is Napoleon speaking for himself.
       Francis Darwin edited his father's *Life and Letters* and added some reminiscences to his father's *Autobiography*, a slice of which is on page 258 below.

219   Chuangtse, from Lin Yutang's collection of *The Wisdom of China and India*.
       This is one of the Uncle Dudley editorials which are daily in the *Boston Globe*. Lucien Price writes some. James H. Powers wrote this one.

221   More of *Walden*. Only a little of one of the best of books.

226   Another small piece from Thoreau's diary.
       Wheeler was a zoologist and one of the most erudite and exciting of men. This is from his presidential address to the Boston Society of Natural History in April, 1931.

229   Keats wrote Bailey on November 22, 1817.
       From Emerson's essay on Nature. Contrast Holmes on page 113 above. Both are right.

230   Dewey's great book, *Experience and Nature*, chapter 7.

233   Reprinted in *A Keepsake in Honor of Vannevar Bush*,

PAGE

a bibliography of his work published by the Massachusetts Institute of Technology, 1959.

235   *Science and the Modern World* again, chapter 1.

236   Chesterton's "Heretics."

237   Bernard's *Experimental Medicine,* for which Lawrence Henderson wrote a preface. See page 114 above.

Galton's *Memories of My Life,* pages 257–8. This and *Inquiries into Human Faculty,* which is in Everyman's.

238   Francis Darwin — see page 218 above.

Weiner's *The* Human *Use of Human Beings: Cybernetics and Society.*

241   Sarton's book *The History of Science and the New Humanism,* pages 46–48. See page 243 below.

242   *As I Remember Him,* pages 331–2. It is not Zinsser's autobiography. Hans Zinsser writes as he chooses about R. S. There is no forgetting the third movement of Brahms's *First Symphony* after finding Hans Zinsser playing it to himself alone at an early breakfast, after a hunt and before he went to the medical school.

Hobbes's *Leviathan,* chapter 6.

243   Sarton's *History of Science and the New Humanism,* pages 66–67, 70–72, 74–78, 80–82, 83, 84–85, 87–89, 92–95, and 97–102.

253   Another piece of Whitehead's *Science and the Modern World.*

254   Dingle's "The Sources of Eddington's Philosophy," the Eighth Arthur Stanley Eddington Memorial Lecture, published by Cambridge University Press.

257   The Keynes in "Newton, the Man," from *Essays in Biography,* Horizon Press.

258   Wordsworth's line is on Newton's statue in Cambridge.

Heraclitus had already said much the same thing as Newton — "We are children amusing ourselves playing checkers."

Darwin, more from his *Autobiography.*

262   Dewey's *Experience and Nature.*

PAGE

263   Pareto's *General Sociology*, sections 2022 and 2092.

264   The Goethe is one of his Maxims.

        The Pearson is from *The Grammar of Science*, in Everyman's, pages 74–75.

266   Don Marquis' cockroach, archy, is too well known for comment.

        Needham's *Time: the Refreshing River*.

267   From Needham's *The Skeptical Biologist*, pages 123–4 and 126–8.

268   Hans Zinsser also wrote *Rats, Lice and History*, from which this is taken, and a book of verse, *Spring, Summer and Autumn*. See page 562 below.

269   Paget's *Confessio Medici*.

272   The Clerk-Maxwell is in his life by Lewis Campbell. It is also in Lawrence Henderson's *The Order of Nature*.

275   Henry Adams wrote a book on Mont-Saint-Michel as well as a nine-volume history of the United States in the times of Jefferson and Madison (which Herbert Agar has appropriately abridged for us as *The Formative Years*) and *The Education*.

        This is from pages 377–8 of the *Mont-Saint-Michel*.

276   The Bridgman from *Daedalus*, the Proceedings of the American Academy of Arts and Sciences, Winter, 1958.

281   Chesterton's *Heretics*.

        Castiglioni's *A History of Medicine*.

283   Nicarchus is in *The Greek Anthology*.

284   Lawrence Henderson was a physician. He was also a learned man. He was also a great teacher. He gave Sociology 23 at Harvard and this is from his introductory lectures.

290   Montaigne, book III, chapter 13.

        Peabody died too young. This is from a lecture which was published, *The Care of the Patient*.

293   Dickinson, Centenary Edition, page 12.

        Henderson, in *Transactions of the Association of American Physicians for 1936*, volume LI.

PAGE

295   Montaigne, book II, chapter 37.

      Hamilton, his dissent in *Medical Care for the American People,* which was published by the Chicago University Press in 1932.

301   More from *As I Remember Him,* page 218. See page 242 above.

305   *A Study of History,* volume III, page 89.

306   *Symbolism.*

309   Aristotle's *Politics,* 1253 A.

      The Librarian of the Fountain Valley School, Colorado Springs, has searched all six of Walpole's Jeremy books and it is not there.

      The White is from *The Changing West,* page 143.

310   Woodrow Wilson's campaign speeches, *The New Freedom,* pages 281–3.

311   *Henry V,* Act I, Scene 2.

312   From the translation by Samuel Moore, in a pamphlet by Harold J. Laski. No good Marxist will have anything but contempt for this abridgment.

321   Lippmann's *The Method of Freedom,* pages 100–2.

322   Learned Hand said this before the Elizabethan Club in New Haven at its thirtieth anniversary on May 10, 1941.

324   Ferguson's *Greek Imperialism,* pages 41–42.

325   Hobbes's translation. Try the one in Zimmern's *The Greek Commonwealth,* a book which Brandeis, according to tradition, read once a year.

      Brandeis in *Whitney v. California,* 274 U.S. at 375.

326   Auden in *The New Republic,* February 1, 1941.

      Holmes, dissenting, Brandeis with him, in *Abrams v. United States,* 250 U.S. at 629.

328   *Holmes-Pollock Letters,* October 26, 1919, volume II, page 28.

      MacLeish, *A Time to Act,* page 134.

329   Miller's "The Location of American Religious Freedom" in *Religion and Freedom of Thought,* page 22.

Frankfurter in the Gobitis case, for the Court, 310 U.S. 586.

333   Jackson in the Barnette case, for the Court, 319 U.S. 624.

336   Frankfurter dissenting in the Barnette case, at page 646.

341   Thayer's *Life of John Marshall* is very short, very hard to buy, and very well worth buying as well as reading.

349   The Stein is in *Wars I Have Known.*

351   Tawney's *Religion and the Rise of Capitalism*, page 221 for the first paragraph and page 225 for the last, that is, in the Penguin edition. The four middle paragraphs come from Tawney's foreword to Talcott Parson's translation of Max Weber's *The Protestant Ethic.*

353   Keynes's *The General Theory of Employment, Interest, and Money*, chapter 24. Skip, as we did, what is too hard to understand. There is more to it.

354   From a series of lectures by Carr on the B.B.C. in 1951. Lippmann's *The Good Society*, pages 387–9.

355   From "The Theory of Business Enterprise" in Wesley C. Mitchell's *What Veblen Taught*, pages 313–20.

361   More from Whitehead's *Science and the Modern World*, chapter 13.

363   *Leadership in a Free Society*, pages 70, 71, 75.

364   From an article Crowther ran in *Fortune* for October, 1941.

369   The Whitehead is from *Adventures of Ideas*, page 124. Dryden's *Secular Masque.*

James to H. G. Wells on September 11, 1906, in the *Letters of William James*, volume II, page 260.

370   The first paragraph of the Keynes is in his *Laissez Faire and Communism*, pages 134–5. It is quoted in Frankfurter's *The Public and its Government*, pages 138–9. The second paragraph is from Keynes's *The General Theory*, etc., chapter 24.

371   Hans Zinsser's *As I Remember Him*, page 242.

373   Frost, quoted by James Reston in the *New York Times*, October 27, 1957.

PAGE

375 DeVoto's *The Easy Chair,* pages 24–25.

376 From Lovell Thompson's "Afterword" in *Youth's Companion Anthology.*

378 From an address by Rostow, "The Fallacy of the Fertile Gondolas," reprinted in the *Harvard Alumni Bulletin,* May 25, 1957.

380 Gunnar Myrdal in *An International Economy,* page 122. Fuess in "Money Is Not Enough," the *Saturday Review,* February 1, 1958.

382 More from Myrdal's *An International Economy,* page 322.

383 The Rostows in the *Reporter,* July 12, 1956.
From Wilder's "The American Loneliness," a Charles Eliot Norton Lecture at Harvard, published in the *Atlantic Monthly,* August, 1952.

385 Machiavelli's *Discourses on Livy.*

387 Benda's *La Grande Épreuve des Democraties.*
Becker's article in the *Yale Review* for 1940, "Generalities that Still Glitter."

388 *The Letters of Sacco and Vanzetti,* edited by Marion Frankfurter, pages 91–93.

389 Oliver's *The Endless Adventure,* pages 35–36, 48–50, 92–111. Read it.

397 Morley, *On Compromise.*

398 Plutarch, "Old Men in Public Affairs," 791*c,* 796*c, d,* and *e.*

400 In the introduction to Herndon and Weik's life of Lincoln.

401 Frankfurter's *The Public and its Government,* pages 160–1 and 148–9.

402 Root's Addresses on Government and Citizenship. This too is quoted by Frankfurter, in *The Public and its Government,* pages 32–33.

404 Lilienthal's *T.V.A. — Democracy on the March.*

PAGE

407   Eastman said this in an article in the *Railway Age* for March 25, 1944.

409   Wallas's *The Great Society*, pages 196–8.

411   More from Morley's *On Compromise*.

412   Ford's edition of *The Writings of Thomas Jefferson*, volume X, page 42.

413   Macaulay's *Lays of Ancient Rome*. We beg you not to look at our first printing.

     Lowell's *Conflicts of Principle*, page 138.

     L'Esprit de Clemenceau, Paris, 1925, page 119.

414   Whitehead's *Science and the Modern World*, chapter 13.

     Ford's *The Writings of Thomas Jefferson*, volume IX, pages 425–9. The letter was written on October 28, 1813.

418   Lincoln in a message to Congress on December 1, 1862. It is quoted by Norman Rockwell in the *Saturday Evening Post* for February 10, 1945.

     Lowell's *Conflicts of Principle*, pages 142–3.

419   Farrand's "Records of the Federal Convention" is the best place for this, volume II, pages 641–3 and 648.

421   Learned Hand, *The Spirit of Liberty*, pages 281–4, with cuts.

423   Churchill to the Commons on October 28, 1943. See Hansard for the whole.

427   From Bacon's essay "Of Counsel." Anyone who seats a dinner party knows as much.

     Plato's Seventh Epistle.

     Montaigne, book III, chapter 13.

     Carr's *The New Society*, page 107 in the Beacon Press paperback edition.

428   From a Proclamation of Civil Rights Week, December, 1955, by the Governor of the Commonwealth of Massachusetts.

429   Toynbee in *An Historian's Approach to Religion*, pages 246, 219.

430   Niebuhr's "The Commitment of the Self and the Free-

dom of the Mind," in *Religion and Freedom of Thought,* Doubleday, pages 55–56.

431 Kennan's "Totalitarianism," pages 29–31 in the *Proceedings of a Conference Held at the American Academy of Arts and Sciences,* published by Harvard University Press, 1954.

433 Homans on the B.B.C., published in the *Listener,* August 16, 1956.

Brandeis, *Olmstead v. United States,* 277 U.S. 438 at 478.

434 Barnard in "Basic Elements of a Free Dynamic Society," *Harvard Business Review.*

Thoreau's *Journal* of 1841 is quoted in Henry Seidel Canby's biography, page 186.

435 We cannot find this. We have tried.

437 Coke's Reports, volume XII, pages 64–65. By all means read also Holdworth's *History of English Law,* volume 5, page 430, where, it seems, at least from a letter which one Sir Roger Boswell wrote to one Doctor Milborne, "his Majestie fell into that high indignation as the like was never knowne in him, looking and speaking fiercely with bended fist, offering to strike him, etc., which the lo. Cooke perceaving fell flat on all fower." From which we know that Coke is pronounced Cook and that the Lord Chief Justice, though he may have fallen flat on all fours, nevertheless maintained the dignity of the law.

The sentence from Coke is from his *Fourth Institute* on page 109.

438 Pollock and Maitland wrote a *History of English Law.* This is from volume II, pages 669–70.

439 Holmes's *Collected Legal Papers,* pages 186–7.

440 James's *The Will to Believe,* pages 194–5.

441 Carter's *Law: Its Origin, Growth, and Function.*

442 Frankfurter, from the *Harvard Law Review,* volume XLVIII, page 1279.

450 Gray's *The Nature and Sources of the Law,* pages 124–5. One of the two or three best books on the law which this country has done.

PAGE

451 Again from Lowell's *Conflicts of Principles,* pages 82–83.

452 Halsbury in 1902 Appeal Cases at 477. Go to a law library.

Judge Shientag's good small book *The Personality of the Judge.*

Boswell's Johnson.

453 Montaigne, book II, chapter 12.

454 Frankfurter's address to the College of the City of New York on September 30, 1942.

Jackson's review in the *American Bar Association Journal* for March, 1944, of A. G. Powell's book, *I Can Go Home Again.*

456 More from Judge Shientag's *The Personality of the Judge.*

457 Selden's *Table Talk.*

Rabelais, book III, chapter 39.

459 Justice Miller in *American Law Review,* volume 21, page 863 (1887).

Judge Shientag's book again, *The Personality of the Judge.*

Marshall in *Brown v. Maryland,* 12 Wheaton at 441.

460 This of Hand's was published by the Massachusetts Bar Association in 1942.

461 In Lippmann's column in 1944. It's in the preface to the *Thucydides* in the Loeb edition, but without a reference to the text.

463 Henry James's *Partial Portraits,* on Trollope.

465 Chapman's *Dante.*

467 Swift's *Thoughts on Various Subjects.*

Lowes's *The Road to Xanadu,* pages 426–34.

476 Thoreau's *A Week on the Concord,* Sunday.

Spengler, *The Decline of the West,* volume 1, page 265, in the original.

478 Holmes to Pollock on April 21 and May 15, 1932; volume II, pages 307 and 309.

Dewey's *Art as Experience*, page 106.

479 Joyce, *A Portrait of the Artist*, Modern Library Edition.

Strawinski, or Stravinski if you prefer, in his *Poétique Musicale*.

485 The Rivera is quoted by Lippmann in his *Preface to Morals*, page 334.

486 Yeats' *Collected Poems*, page 191. Marcus A. Goldman says a pern is a spool, and refers to a note in the *Collected Poems* on page 243, but a pern is a buzzard in the Oxford Dictionary, and in the poem "Demon and Beast" on page 184 a gull is described as "gyring down and perning." The poet himself in the same poem "had long perned in the gyre, Between my hatred and desire," on page 183. If perne with a final "e" is not a noun meaning a buzzard, it is a verb describing the motion of a bird.

488 *Winter's Tale*, Act 4, Scene 3.

489 The first is from Thoreau's *Letters*, edited by Emerson, page 158; the other two come from "Sunday" in *A Week on the Concord*.

The Goethe is to Eckermann on April 2, 1829.

490 *The Education of Henry Adams*, page 420.

493 Picasso, from *The Painter's Object*, by Gerald Howe.

495 Reynold's *Discourses*, the "Second Discourse."

496 Whitehead's *Symbolism*.

497 Leonardo, *The Notebooks*, edited by McCurdy.

502 The Taylor from "The Archaic Smile" in *Daedalus*, the Proceedings of the American Academy of Arts and Sciences, Autumn, 1957.

504 The Picasso, we do not know.

The White, from *The Fox of Peapack*.

506 The beginning of Taylor's "The Archaic Smile," see above.

509 Lucien Price's *The Will to Create*, page 14.

511 Price quotes this from Wagner in his *The Will to Create*.

PAGE

512 *The Integrity of Music,* pages 147–52.

516 Berlioz's *Autobiography,* translated by Rachel and Eleanor Holmes.

517 "Musical Textures," *A Musician Talks,* pages 77–99.

521 Yeats, *Collected Poems,* page 96.

Lorca quoted by Jacques Prévert in his "Spectacle," page 178, *Nouvelle Revue Française,* 1951.

523 Wittgenstein in *Philosophical Investigations,* page 4.

Hans Zinsser, *As I Remember Him.*

524 The Keats, in his letters, we think.

Frost, from his preface to his *Collected Verse.*

Anon., to be found in Walter de la Mare's *Come Hither.* Who wrote it? When did he write it? How did he come to write it?

The Emerson is from his *Journal* for March, 1845.

525 The Auden in *Making, Knowing and Judging,* page 27–28.

Peter Viereck in *Terror and Decorum,* page 53.

526 Moody's "The Fire-Bringer," *Selected Poems* edited by Lovett, page 161.

Robert Paul Smith, *Where Did You Go? Out. What Did You Do? Nothing.,* page 124.

West in *The Times Literary Supplement,* August 15, 1958.

527 Yeats's *Collected Poems,* page 95. Most of the rest of this poem is on page 521.

528 "Poetry," from Marianne Moore's *Collected Poems,* page 40.

529 Also from Auden's *Making, Knowing and Judging,* page 23.

The White is from *One Man's Meat,* pages 143–6.

531 Goethe's *Maxims and Reflections.*

T. S. Eliot speaking at the University of Minnesota, 1956; quoted by John Hall Wheelock in *The American Scholar,* Summer, 1957, page 348.

PAGE

532 The Oppenheimer from *Scientific American,* September, 1950.

I. A. Richards' *Speculative Instruments,* page 110.

T. S. Eliot in his introduction to Marianne Moore's *Selected Poems,* page 7.

Madame de Boufflers is quoted in a note in *Like a Bulwark* by Marianne Moore, pages 26–27.

533 Eliot's "Little Gidding," last of the *Four Quartets.*

More from Don Marquis.

534 From the introduction to *Zen in the Art of Archery* by Eugen Herrigel.

Stevenson in *First the Blade.*

535 Wilson in "The Shakespeare Paradox: Universal Stage of the Man from Stratford," pages 9–10 in *The Times* (London), September 2, 1957.

537 Oppenheimer in *The Open Mind,* pages 139–40.

541 Bowra's preface to the *Oxford Book of Greek Verse.*

545 The opening sentence of Virginia Woolf's *The Common Reader.*

The Sainte-Beuve is quoted by Hans Zinsser in *As I Remember Him,* page 8.

Wallas quotes the Schopenhauer in the piece on page 65 above.

546 Young's *Night Thoughts.*

Dickinson's *Collected Poems,* page 13.

547 Holmes wrote Wu on March 26, 1925. The letters are in *Book Notices, Uncollected Papers, etc.,* edited by Harry C. Shriver.

Bacon's *Novum Organum,* book 1, aphorism 84.

The Corsican, edited by R. M. Johnston.

548 The Montaigne is from the autobiography which Marvin Lowenthal made up from the Essays, page 140.

Hume, "Concerning Human Understanding," the last paragraph.

Petrarch's *Letters.*

The Montaigne again from the Lowenthal.

549   Emerson's address on the dedication of the library in Concord, in May, 1873.

550   The E. B. White is from *The Second Tree from the Corner*, pages 160–1.

551   Denney in *The Astonished Muse*, page 35.

553   *Hamlet.*

555   The last stanza in the "Ode to Psyche."
Doctor Holmes's *A Mortal Antipathy.*

556   Lippmann's *A Preface to Morals*, as also on page 556.

557   Where is this piece of Proust?
Oxford Book of English Verse, no. 27.
Yeats's *Collected Poems*, page 270.

558   Yeats's *Collected Poems*, page 212.
The Bourne, from his *Youth and Life*, page 139.

559   Henry Adams' *Education*, page 383.

560   Rilke's *Duino Elegies*, in the appendix.

562   Hans Zinsser's poems, *Spring, Summer and Autumn.*

563   Walt Whitman also said, "It is provided in the essence of things that from any fruition of success, no matter what, shall come forth something to make a greater struggle necessary." And William Morris said, "I pondered how men fight and lose the battle, and the thing that they fought for comes about in spite of their defeat, and when it comes turns out to be not what they meant, and other men have to fight for what they meant under another name."

565   Holmes's *Collected Legal Papers*, page 310.
James's *Varieties of Religious Experience.*
Lincoln, on September 13, 1862.

566   Jackson, for the Court, in *United States v. Ballard*, 322 U.S. 78.

569   Aldous Huxley quotes this from Newman in *Proper Studies.*

Harrison, in her *Epilegomena to the Study of Greek Religion*, pages 31–33. This is a pamphlet. Read the *Prolegomena*, a great book.

571   Selden's *Table Talk.*

The most famous remarks on this subject are what Polybius said in his *History.* Toynbee's translation, page 483 of the single-volume edition.

572   Aldous Huxley's *Texts and Pretexts.*

The Tolstoy is a chapter heading in Huneker's *Ivory, Apes, and Peacocks.*

Roberta Swartz's book of poems, *Lord Juggler.*

Hans Zinsser's *As I Remember Him.*

574   A private letter to Mrs. Charles P. Curtis.

575   Henry Adams' *Mont-Saint-Michel.*

Hans Zinsser quotes this from Heine in *As I Remember Him,* page 40.

Pilgrim's Progress.

576   Dickinson, Centennial Edition, page 8.

Dingle's *Science and Human Experience,* page 125.

Becker's *The Heavenly City of the Eighteenth Century Philosophers,* pages 126–7.

577   The Frost is "God's Speech to Job" from "A Masque of Reason."

578   The "Song of the I.W.W." is ascribed to Joe Hill in Sandburg's *American Songbag.*

Emerson's *Journal,* July, 1855.

579   Goethe to Chancellor von Mueller, October 19, 1823.

Lake's *Landmarks in the History of Early Christianity,* page 96.

580   Wallas's *Social Judgment,* page 162.

581   Pascal's *Pensées,* no. 181, in Brunschwicq's edition.

Life and Letters of Huxley, by Leonard Huxley, volume I, page 233.

We have tried and we have failed to find Kingsley's reply, and we hope he did not make any.

588   Holmes to William James, March 24, 1907.

Don Marquis again.

E. B. White in *The Wild Flag;* editorials from the *New*

PAGE

Yorker on Federal World Government and Other Matters, pages 163–4.

589   Harrison, this from the *Prolegomena to the Study of Greek Religion*, page 452. Ruskin said that a Greek never entered a wood without expecting to meet a god in it.

590   Selden's *Table Talk.*

591   Casanova's *Memoirs*, volume VI, page 135, in the Garnier edition. All of it is well worth reading.

       Pascal's *Pensées*, no. 72, in Brunschwicq's edition.

592   Yeats's *Collected Poems*, page 95.

593   Wilson's *A Piece of My Mind*, pages 6–8.

594   From Tillich's "Religion," in *Man's Right to Knowledge*, 2d series, Columbia University Press, pages 79–80.

595   From a letter of Thoreau, quoted in H. G. O. Blake's volume of selections, *Thoreau's Thoughts*, page 49.

       Shaw, *Androcles and the Lion.*

596   Pascal's *Pensées*, Nos. 347–8.

597   From another of Wilder's Charles Eliot Norton lectures at Harvard, "Toward an American Language," published in the *Atlantic Monthly*, July, 1952.

       Dewey's *Experience and Nature.*

602   *Holmes-Pollock Letters*, May 15, 1931, volume II, page 287.

       From Sartre's famous lecture of 1946, in the translation of Philip Mairet; reprinted in Morton White's *The Age of Analysis*, pages 122 ff.

605   Tillich's "Religion and the Intellectuals," *Partisan Review*, 1950, pages 137–9.

608   *Pilgrim's Progress*, Part 2.

611   This is W. H. Mallock's verse translation.

       Frost's *Collected Poems*, page 268.

612   Balfour's *Foundations of Belief*, page 30.

       Troilus and Cressida.

613   *Henry IV* Part 1; Act V Scene IV.

PAGE

Browne's "Urn Burial."

Harvey Cushing's *Life of Osler,* Volume 1, page 680.

Yeats's "Vacillation," from *Collected Poems,* page 247.

614   This Yeats in a letter to Lady Gerald Wellesley, August 15, 1938; in Joseph Howes's *W. B. Yeats,* page 507. It's a little different in *Last Poems.*

Shapley's Phi Beta Kappa address on September 13, 1944, printed in the *American Scholar,* winter, 1944.

615   Liehtse, from Lin Yutang's *The Wisdom of China and India.*

616   Emerson's essay on Plato.

617   The Marvin is quoted in Joseph Needham's *Time — the Refreshing River.*

618   Cummings' XLI.

Von Neumann's "Can We Survive Technology?" in *Fortune,* June, 1955.

619   The Goethe is in *Faust,* Part Two.

The Wilder, on the frontispiece of *The Ides of March.* Don Marquis.

620   Hand's memorial address on Brandeis before the Supreme Court, in 317 U.S. Reports.

622   Slichter, in "The Word of Tomorrow," Radcliffe College.

623   Russell's *Human Society in Ethics and Politics,* pages 224–6.

625   Hand's *The Spirit of Liberty* again, pages 260–2.

626   The Yeats from the second of "Two Songs from a Play," *Collected Poems,* page 211.

627   Welles, from a speech in New York before the Herald-Tribune Forum, on November 17, 1942; printed in Welles's *The Four Freedoms.* Read *The Time for Decision* and *Where Are We Heading?*

629   Garrison, unpublished as yet.

633   *L'Esprit de Clemenceau,* Paris, 1925.

634   Emerson's essay on Politics.

PAGE

Lloyd's *The Social Creator,* published after his death and edited by Jane Addams, pages 228, 252, 255.

636   George's *Progress and Poverty,* Modern Library edition, pages 461 through 470 (cut).

639   Santayana's *Character and Opinion in the United States.*

640   Whitehead's preface to Wallace B. Donham's *Business Adrift,* and reprinted, not quite like this, in Whitehead's *Adventures of Ideas,* pages 125–6.

Jefferson to Adams on July 5, 1814; Ford, volume 9, p. 462.

641   Pascal's *Pensées,* no. 331, in Brunschwicq's edition.

Plato, *The Republic,* book 7, pages 514–20.

Index

Index

"A little madness in the Spring," 213

"A Rosy Sanctuary will I dress," 7

"A world of made is not a world of born," 618

Abstraction, Whitehead on, 55–58, 61
William James on the necessity for, 59–60

Action, habits of, as function of thought, 34–35
as the source of thought, 73, 75
versus quiet thinking, 88–89

Acton, Lord, on lessons to be learned from history, 143–47
quoted by Learned Hand, 626

Ad hoc effort, 378–80

Adams, Brooks, theory of history, 141–43

Adams, Henry, on freedom of will, 275–76
on his inconsistency, 490–91
on psychology, 42–43
on the symbolism of the Gothic cathedral, 575
theory of history, 136–41
on Woman, 559–60

Adams, John, on choosing Washington as commander-in-chief, 205–8
on his faith in work and the workman, 3

Adams, John Quincy, on law logic, 435

Adams, Samuel, John Adams on his talk with, 206

Administration, 407–9
democracy and, 404–7

Agnosticism, 572–74

Alcmaeon of Croton, mentioned by Henderson, 287, 288

Alcoforado, Marianna, Rilke on, 561–62

"All, all of a piece throughout," 369

"All things can tempt me from this craft of verse," 527

"Also fragen wir beständig," 141

America, growth of, 377–78

American Historical Association, 141

Americans, 373, 375–76, 380

Ancient Mariner, Lowes on, 467, 469

"And those behind cried 'Forward!' " 413

Anderson, Maxwell, on Frank Cobb and Woodrow Wilson, 208–11

Ant-heaps and Utopias, 305–6

Anti-intellectualism, 381

Antiquity, Bacon on, 547

Apes and men, 323–24

Aposiopesis, 532

Approval, desire for, 397–98

Arab civilization and culture, 247–50

archy the cockroach. *See* Marquis, Don

Aristocracy, artificial and natural, 414–18

Aristotle, on art, quoted by Tovey, 512
on independent people, quoted by Lippmann, 322
on man as social animal, 309
Pascal on, 641n.
on poetry and history, 132
on politicians, mentioned by Henderson, 289
syllogistic scheme of, 13

Art, archaic, 506–7
communicative nature of, 502–4
and esthetic experience, 482–84
form and style in, 476–78
Leonardo on, 497–502
measuring merit in, 482
Mussorgsky on, 478
is nature, 488–89